LOGIC AND LOGICAL THINKING
A Modular Approach

AND LOGICAL THINKING

A MODULAR APPROACH

Peter A. Facione/Donald Scherer

Bowling Green State University

OX BOW PRESS
Woodbridge, Connecticut 06525
1984

LOGIC AND LOGICAL THINKING: A Modular Approach

First Published, 1978

1984 Reprint published by
Ox Bow Press
P.O. Box 4045
Woodbridge, Connecticut 06525

Library of Congress Cataloging in Publication Data

Facione, Peter A
   Logic and logical thinking.

   Includes index.
   1. Logic. I. Scherer, Donald, joint author.
II. Title.
BC108.F32   160   77-24173

ISBN 0-918024-33-1

CONTENTS

PART TWO

USING SYMBOLS IN LOGIC

PART THREE

ILLOGICAL THINKING

PART FOUR

LOGICAL THINKING

PREFACE

As the main weapons against the ever-present threats to existence and to the quality of that existence, humans were given the abilities to reason, to acquire and transmit knowledge, to anticipate and plan for the future, and, in general, to think, reflect upon experience, and communicate with others. If we develop these abilities, we can use them to secure food, shelter, cures for disease, harmonious social structures, recreation, indeed almost anything. But if we fail to develop them, we guarantee our own more or less swift end.

This book has two main purposes, which go hand in hand: It aims to help you improve your powers of logic and it introduces logic as a field of study. These purposes, considered jointly, motivate the selection of material, the choice of examples, and the tone of the presentation. In this way the book develops practical skills in logical thinking and also provides the theoretical framework that explains why the skills can be successfully applied.

Almost every aspect of our collective and individual lives involves thinking or reasoning. All things being equal, the more logically you think, the better you can use the opportunities open to you. This book is an aid. It will alert you to the deceptiveness of fallacious arguments and help you to see the logical correctness of other arguments and the reasonableness of often-used proof strategies. Through examples and exercises it reinforces and sharpens your natural logical abilities. Use it to improve your critical thinking skills and, thereby, your chances of making good use of your opportunities.

As you study logic, you will learn what an argument is, what validity amounts to, what a fallacy is, and what indirect proofs and conditional proofs are. Most importantly, you will learn when an argument is worthy of acceptance. One of the most efficient and powerful tools that has been developed by twentieth-century logicians is the systematic use of symbolization. By uncovering the logical structure of arguments and representing these structures symbolically, logicians have devised reliable ways to test arguments for validity. Logic, like physics or medicine, is an ongoing study. Since Aristotle's time an ever larger class of arguments has become amenable to analysis through application of logic. We will look at both traditional logic and modern symbolic logic. We will study techniques and learn to apply them.

We wish to offer a special thanks to the thousands of students at Bowling Green State University who had a part in motivating this book, selecting its contents, and working through its exercises and its earlier editions. We also are most grateful to the many colleagues and graduate teaching assistants who did so much to help with the selecting and testing of examples, checking of exercises, and organizing of materials over the years. We are especially grateful to Michael Bradie, James Stuart, and Paul Lastas for their helpful ideas and comments. We also thank all those many people who spent so many hours in the careful typing, reviewing, and proofreading of our manuscript, most especially S. Jack Odell and Pat Bressler. We dedicate this book to Charlotte and Noreen with love.

Peter A. Facione
Donald Scherer

INTRODUCTION
How to Use This Book

We designed this book for anyone who wishes to learn about logic and logical thinking. It aims at being self-contained so that it can be used in any type of classroom setting, traditional or innovative. You can study it totally on your own or with the guidance of an instructor. We try to present material in an intuitive and lucid way, using a generous number of examples, exercises, and explicitly stated decision procedures to aid you in both understanding and applying what you learn.

There are four major parts in this text. Part One explores the relationship between logic and language. We will explain what logic is all about, how logic relates to our everyday language and use of words, why it makes a difference how we define our terms, and what the strengths and weaknesses of various types of definitions are. We will also develop careful, systematic definitions for many of the central concepts of logic. Part Two develops skills normally associated with the study of formal logic. We will learn how to render English arguments into symbolic notation in order to show their logical structure more clearly. These skills pay off as we develop the ability to use mechanical decision procedures to examine arguments of propositional logic for validity. We will also learn techniques for testing syllogistic arguments and other arguments of predicate logic for validity.

Part Three explains illogical thinking in terms of mistakes in structure or content of arguments. These mistaken arguments, called fallacies, result from common human errors like those cataloged and explained in Part Three. Part Three tells us what makes illogical arguments illogical, and Part Four explains what makes logical arguments logical. In Part Four we discuss various kinds of direct and indirect proof strategies which can be used to build reasonable proofs. We will apply our discussion of proof strategies to expand both the deductive techniques of symbolic logic and the inductive techniques of modern research design. All four major parts end with comprehensive self-quizzes which you can use to measure your understanding of each.

In each section of the book you will find lists of instructional objectives. An instructional objective is, as you may know, a complex statement of a particular educational goal. These statements usually have three parts: (1) a specification of some goal activity, (2) a specification of the conditions under which the goal activity is to be achieved, and (3) a specification of the minimum level of achievement that will be accepted as a demonstration of mastery. The four parts of this text are divided into chapters on specific topics. Chapters, in turn, are broken into brief learning units called modules. Each section of the text (module, chapter, or part) is organized around its own specific instructional objectives. The larger the section, the broader and more abstract are its educational goals; the smaller the section, the more specific are its objectives. The goals and objectives of each portion are explicitly stated. Use these statements as guides to what you should learn in that part, chapter, or module. Each module of the text begins with a precise statement of its objectives. Within each module the text, examples, and exercises are organized to develop and test precisely those objectives. You can use the exercises at the end of a module either to better learn the skills of that module through practice or to measure how well you have acquired those skills.

Exercises are the key to learning logic and logical thinking. Used texts that have exercises and answer spaces marked up are no bargain. What you may save in initial cost is not worth what you lose by not doing the exercises from scratch yourself. You should strive to meet the objectives of any given module after having read the module, studied its examples, worked its exercises, checked your answers against the ones provided, and done any review work suggested by the comments that appear by the exercise answers. Complete one module at a time, and meet its objectives before going on to later modules in the same chapter.

Although within a chapter the modules are to be studied in order, there are a large number of different ways to sequence the chapters. They can be organized to suit many different goals, abilities, interests, and time-frames. For example, if your interest is formal logic, you might wish to study Chapters 1, 3, 4, 11, 12, 13, 5, and 6 in that order. If you are more interested in developing your critical thinking skills in the area of informal logic, study Chapters 1, 2, 3, 7, 9, 10, 11, 12, and 14 in that order. If you prefer a more integrated study of both logic and logical thinking, work through the chapters in the order they are presented.*

Just as each section of the text has its own instructional goal, there is an overall objective for the text itself. Let's assume you already have some initial intuitive ability to distinguish between acceptable arguments and unacceptable arguments. All of us make judgments of this kind every day. Some people are more *accurate* in doing so, which means they make the right evaluation more often than others do. Some people are more *efficient*, which means they can tell acceptable arguments from unacceptable arguments relatively quickly, that is, with less hesitation, doubt, and guesswork. After having worked through this text, you should be able to discriminate between acceptable and unacceptable arguments with at least 50 percent greater efficiency and at least 30 percent greater accuracy.† To help you achieve this goal the text provides discussions of all the relevant evaluative concepts of logic, schema for classifying acceptable arguments and unacceptable arguments, and explicit decision procedures that allow you to apply efficiently and accurately the evaluative concepts and theoretical explanations. The text is supplemented by examples all along the way, as well as a large number of exercises.

Please share with us any suggestions you might have for improving this text. We wish you well in your study.

---

* Several alternative sequences are suggested in the Instructor's Manual.
† Pretests and posttests on logical thinking bear out these predictions. See Donald Scherer and Peter A. Facione, "A Pre/Post Test for Introductory Logic," *Metaphilosophy*, Summer 1977.

ONE

LOGIC AND LANGUAGE

Part One lays the foundation for the integrated study of logic and logical thinking. It clarifies what logic is and defines its main concern as the study of arguments. All the basic ideas necessary to develop your critical thinking skills through the study of logic are carefully presented here. Part One starts with common and familiar ideas about the issues: what is logic, what are arguments, how do you recognize an argument, how do you begin to evaluate arguments, and what is logical correctness? It then refines these ideas, using examples first and then presenting careful definitions, adding the technical precision and sophistication needed so that in later parts of the book practical skills can be both learned and understood. Not only does Part One present systematic and useful definitions for basic terms like 'statement,' 'argument,' 'induction,' 'deduction,' 'valid,' 'justified,' 'logically correct argument,' and 'sound argument,' but it also explains what definitions are and how they are used, and presents some virtues and vices of a variety of types of definitions.

1

WHAT LOGIC IS
ALL ABOUT

Bertrand Russell is supposed to have said "People would rather die than think—
and most do." We are not sure whether his generalizations are true, but we agree
with the cautionary note implicit in his remark. Each of us uses logic daily, sometimes in trivial and sometimes in momentous matters. We ask ourselves whether
or not a particular set of views or beliefs warrants our concluding that certain other
positions or ideas ought to be accepted as true. We might be concerned about nothing
more important than the chances of our winning a hand of poker with two pairs. But
we might be concerned about whether or not we can afford to buy a car or a house
given our present financial condition.

Logicians concern themselves with much the same kind of thing but in more
theoretical ways. They ask what *would be* true *if* we were to assume a certain set of
facts or beliefs. They ask what *follows* from a given set of views or beliefs. Whereas
we ask these things about the particular facts and beliefs that are the circumstances
of our own lives, they ask these questions more abstractly. Their aim is to determine
the *procedures* to use to tell what follows from any given set of premises, to tell what
the *logical consequences* of premises are. Once they develop these procedures, they
can be passed on to others. These procedures are tools we can use in judging the
logical correctness of the particular inferences we deal with daily.

The educational goal of Chapter 1 is to learn what it means to say that logic is
concerned with procedures for evaluating arguments. In Modules 1 and 2 we examine a variety of ideas that are more or less closely related to logic in order to clarify
by examples the differences between these ideas and logic. Then we refine our ideas
of logic by focusing on its chief concern, the process of evaluating arguments. In
Modules 3 and 4 we begin again with common examples, trying to distinguish the
logician's technical meaning of 'argument.' We then learn how to identify the
premises and conclusions of arguments, a skill which is a prerequisite for the evaluation of an argument as worthy or unworthy of acceptance.

As we learn what logic is all about, the relevance of logic to the concerns of
our own lives will grow clearer. It will become more and more obvious that the ability to think logically and to analyze arguments logically is of tremendous practical
importance.

MODULE 1

BEING LOGICAL

If you were to teach someone to play golf, you would begin by giving them an easy golf club to use, teaching them the proper grip and swing, and allowing them to master the skill of hitting a golf ball with reasonable ease, distance, accuracy, and loft. As the person acquired that skill and others, like putting and hitting woods off tees and fairways, you would begin to concentrate more of your teaching on the rules of the game, the strategies of club selection and ball placement, and definitions of key terms. Of course you would also teach more advanced skills like how to punch a ball low under branches, chip out of a sand trap, or deliberately hit a slice or hook to avoid natural hazards like large trees or roughs. Learning logic and logical thinking is a lot like learning golf. There are basic skills to master; there are strategies of proof, rules for the proper use of techniques, and definitions of key terms. There are also more advanced skills, which should be easy to learn later if the fundamental skills are mastered properly. At the outset of our study you are like the beginning golfer, concerned with what golf clubs and a golf ball look like and how they are held and used. We are concerned with what being logical is. Our initial strategy for finding out will be to distinguish instances of logical thinking from examples of related but different things like being sharp, persuasive, emotional, or reasonable. If we can manage even a rough understanding of what being logical is from the examples in Module 1, we can then go on in Module 2 to formulate an idea about what logic is.

● After reading Module 1 you should be able to:

1. Distinguish a concern for trying to be logical from similar yet different human concerns like trying to be reasonable, sharp, emotional, or persuasive, given a brief passage expressing one of these concerns

1:1* Key words What is it like to be a really logical person? Is that different from being a reasonable person? How about being sharp? How do all these differ from being an emotional person or, again, from being persuasive?

There *are* answers to these questions. They may not be hard and fast, definite answers, but they are good answers. There are answers because each of the key terms 'logical,' 'reasonable,' 'sharp,' 'smart,' etc., has a slightly different meaning in our language. If you know how to speak English, you know that saying "*Star Trek*'s Mr. Spock and Agatha Christie's fictional detective Hercule Poirot are logical" is different from saying "they are reasonable" or "they are persuasive."

Often when trying to get a clear idea about an abstract term, it is useful to begin by contrasting that term's conventional use with the ordinary uses of terms with similar meanings. If we wanted to clarify our idea of what 'knowledge' means, we would begin by reflecting on and contrasting the meanings of statements like "I know that the bread should be baked at 194°C," "It's my opinion that we should bake the bread at 194°C," "I think that bread is to be baked at 194°," and "I've heard

---

* Throughout the text we number each section so that you can find specific discussions on various topics easily. Our coding is to list the module number first and then the section number, separating the two by a colon. So 8:4 would mean Module 8, section 4; 8:5.1 would mean Module 8, section 5, sub-section 1.

that . . .." We may not end up with a precise definition of knowledge this way, but we will come to understand better what it does mean because we will have a better idea of how the concept of knowledge contrasts with similar ideas—like 'belief,' for instance. Of course, much more can be said about 'knowing' and 'believing,' but more advanced philosophical treatments usually are not undertaken unless our original purposes call for highly technical and refined definitions. Since our purposes involve learning logic and how to think logically, we do need to be able to contrast the ability of being logical from similar but different abilities. We do not, at least for now, require a highly refined definition.

1:2 Two puzzles To help clarify the differences between being reasonable, being sharp, being logical, being emotional, and being persuasive we will look at two puzzles. After stating the puzzle we will shift our attention first to the skills (being logical, reasonable, or sharp) required for solving the puzzles and second to the qualities (being logical, persuasive, emotional) exhibited by some of the characters in the puzzles. As we describe these skills and characteristics, you should reflect on and contrast the meanings of words like 'logical,' 'reasonable,' 'sharp,' 'persuasive' in our descriptive statements. If you want to enjoy the puzzles for their own sakes, you can cover up our discussions of the solutions and have some fun solving them for yourself.

Puzzle 1:
The football coach at Whatsamatta U. has a problem. He has a twelve-member coed football squad. When they are dressed for a game in pads and uniforms, they all look exactly alike in both size and weight. The only way he can tell one from another is by the numbers on the back of each player's uniform. The coach knows that eleven of the players really are identical in weight but one happens to be different. The coach wants to know two things: which one is different and whether this odd one is lighter or heavier than the others. Not only would it be viewed as rude if he should just come out and ask their respective weights, but also he is afraid they might lie. After all, they know that he plans to bench the odd person if the odd person turns out to be lighter and use the odd person if he or she turns out to be heavier. This coach is reasonable and knows that there is more than one way to weigh a football player. He is also rather resourceful and has borrowed the bronze seesaw that the Psychology Department owns. He takes his team over to the seesaw on the pretense of doing a new exercise to build up their ability to balance while in motion. To further hide his scheme he tells them that none of them is allowed to ride the seesaw more than three times altogether. Now that he has the team ready and his real intentions hidden, can you figure out how he should place his players on the seesaw to solve his problems: Who is the odd one, and is he or she lighter or heavier?

The reasonable thing to do is to first realize that there are two ways to find a solution: (1) puzzle it out or (2) read the next few paragraphs. If you decide to puzzle it out, the next reasonable thing is to note that you need a strategy. Recall that in a puzzle there is often more information given than at first seems evident, so the first step in your strategy is to reread the puzzle. If you are not sharp, though, you may have to give up trying to figure it out. To be able to figure it out means being able to hit on the right strategy and also to execute the strategy once it is discovered. But finding the winning strategy for puzzle solving (as for any game or sport) is usually more a matter of insight, coaching, practice, and experience with puzzles than simply a matter of natural mental ability.

Solution 1:

A sharp person might have hypothesized that the key problem could be solved if the coach could find a standard-weight player. Using a standard-weight player on one side of the seesaw, the coach could put each of the other players on the other side one at a time. In this way the coach could compare each player to the original standard weight player.

A logical person could take it from here and draw out the consequences of this hypothesis, testing it to see whether it solves the coach's problems without violating any of the restrictions imposed by the puzzle.

Solution 1 continued:

The logical person would begin to test the hypothesis by figuring out what could happen with a standard-weight person on one side and a person of unknown weight on the other. If the seesaw remains level, the new person is also a standard-weight person. If it tilts, then the new person is the odd one. If the odd one's side went up, then the person is lighter than the others; if it went down, heavier. The logical consequence, then, is that the proposed solution does solve the coach's problem. Unfortunately there are two further difficulties. The first remaining difficulty is how to get the process started, i.e., how to find the original standard-weight person.

The second difficulty arises if we recall that each player is restricted to no more than three weighings on the seesaw. The logical consequence of this is that if our odd player does not show up early in the process, we will have to find a substitute for our original standard-weight player.

A reasonable person would see a number of ways of handling the first problem. Perhaps the most obvious one is simply to start by picking any two players at random and sitting them one on each side of the seesaw. Logically, if it remains level they are both standard-weight people and so either could serve as the original standard-weight person to get the process of comparison going. The other person, as well as anyone who turns out to be equal in weight to the original, can serve as a substitute if more than three turns seem to be needed. So if the seesaw remains level, logic has solved both remaining problems. If the seesaw moves, on the other hand, both problems are still solved. If it moves, one of the people on it is odd. This means that the other ten are all standard weight. Any one of them could be selected to start the comparison procedure, the remaining nine standing in reserve as substitutes if needed.

Can we infer anything else from the fact that the seesaw moved? Yes. We can infer that the following two statements are true: (1) If the odd person is the one on the side that went up, the odd person is lighter than the others; (2) if the odd person is the one on the side that went down, the odd person is heavier than the others. From these facts a sharp person might hypothesize that in this case only one more use of the seesaw is really needed. Test that idea out using your powers of logic. Put one of the other ten players on the seesaw in place of the person on the down side. If the seesaw returns to level, then the person who just came off the down side is heavier than the other eleven players. If the seesaw does not move but remains tilted, the person still up in the air is lighter.

We can generalize what we have observed so far. Reasonableness *shows us our choices or options* and perhaps leads us to rule out obviously wrong or silly possibilities. Sharpness *discovers or suggests the hypotheses, the ideas, we should test* as possible solutions to our problem. Logicalness tests them: *it draws out their consequences*, good or bad.

Let's apply these ideas to a more realistic problem. Suppose our problem is that the wooden floors of our house become painfully cold in the winter. Being reasonable shows us that we have three options for dealing with the problem: (1) try to find the cause for the cold floors and remove that cause; (2) try to treat the symptoms, rather than the cause, by finding ways that will make the floors warmer or make the cold more tolerable; and (3) try to work around the problem by living with it or moving to a new house. Reasonableness also indicates that (3) is a good option only if (1) and (2) fail because (3) is either going to be very expensive, if we move, or very painful, if we stay. Being sharp gives us ideas about how we might implement either option 1 or 2. For example, if we want to try option 2, we might hit on ideas like turning the heat way up, carpeting the whole house, putting in extra baseboard heating units, and wearing thermal socks, or heavy shoes. If we try option 1, being sharp might yield ideas like checking the basement or crawl space for open vents or windows which could then be closed and insulated, or checking under the floor for ways of insulating the floor so that heat from the living area is not lost and so that cold from the basement or crawl space does not penetrate up. We can test out the consequences of these ideas and infer, using logic, that each would work to achieve one or another of the three options.

Suppose now that someone said that every cold-floor problem could be solved by just one of the ideas we mentioned, say, turning up the heat in the house. Using logic we can also test this kind of more general claim. If we find any house where the floors are cold even if the heat is on full, this finding will constitute a counterexample to the general idea and, logically, we can reject the idea once such a counterexample is discovered. A little imagination suggests that a house with uninsulated wooden floors over a crawl space with open vents will have cold floors in cold weather no matter how effective its standard home heating unit is. This case is, then, a counterexample leading us logically to reject the general idea that cold floors can always be made warm enough by turning up the heat.

Now for another puzzle.

Puzzle 2:
You and two others find yourselves competing for the one place at the banquet table. To settle your fight you decide to have a three-sided duel with crossbows. You stand like the three corners of a triangle; each of you has a crossbow and an unlimited supply of arrows. You are granted the first shot because you hit your mark only one in three times. B gets the second shot because he hits twice out of three, and A, who never misses, gets her turn to shoot last. Whom should you shoot at?

Solution 2:
A reasonable person would never have gotten into this mess, but here you are in the duel. You see your two obvious choices, shoot at A or shoot at B. If you hit either one, the one that is left will hit you or have at least a 67 percent chance of hitting you. That is the logical consequence of selecting to shoot at either A or B. If you miss, though, it is reasonable to expect that B would shoot at A, his bigger threat. If B does not hit A, A will probably shoot at, and hit B. Then you can shoot at A. If B does hit A, it will be your turn next and you can shoot at B. The reasonable person sees these options, and, if logical, infers what will happen. If you are sharp, you will see that you're better off missing everyone on your first shot and taking your chances shooting at B or A, whoever survives, on your next shot. If you are sharp, you will figure out that one way to ensure that you miss is to shoot at the ground, deliberately not trying for either A or B.

Now B observantly watches you standing around, looking at the ground, and he begins to speculate about what's going on in your head. He approaches you and says, "We're sure in a tough fix, buddy. That A never misses. When she gets her turn, she's sure going to hurt us." B gulps hard, looks you straight in the eye, and continues, "We could both wind up dead! I don't want to die." Then after a short pause, he continues, "I suppose you don't either. We've got to gang up on her. If we both shoot at her, one of us is very likely to hit her. What we really need is to rid ourselves of this terrible menace. Buddy, it's you and me together. We need each other!"

Reflection 2:
When B leaves, you take a moment to reflect. Your situation is scary, but B has done more than say so. He has tried to actually scare you. He has used many emotional terms to stir your emotions and to move you to action. It all amounts to an emotional appeal. And it is persuasive! The stakes are very high and A is a crack shot. It is easy to believe that B is "on the right track" and accordingly should be heeded. Both B's emotionality and his inclusion of some truths and partial truths contribute to his persuasiveness. But should he be believed? Has he ever indicated that the earlier starting points of your thought were false? No. Has he shown how your earlier conclusions fail to follow? No. He has suggested no contrary kind of case where your reasoning would be proved faulty. He hasn't addressed himself to the logic of your thought. No flaw in your reasoning has been uncovered. B is using *emotionality* to contribute to his *persuasiveness* without challenging the correctness of your thought. He simply hopes you will be moved to abandon your own correct thought.

Can you provide an example of a conclusion that one could logically draw even though it would not be reasonable? Can you give an example of a plea that is emotional but neither persuasive nor logical? How about one that is logical but not very persuasive? What about a plea that is persuasive and logical but not emotional? How can someone become sharp? How can we recognize an appeal that is persuasive but illogical? How can someone become logical? Obviously, there are a lot of questions here; and there are probably more that could be asked too. We believe that if you think them all through in the light of our explanations of the puzzles, you will see more clearly what being logical, as distinct from being sharp, reasonable, emotional, or persuasive, is all about.

The life insurance salesperson knows that it is logical for a young person not to buy life insurance because statistically chances are that a client will not die until after age sixty-five. But the salesperson also knows that it is not always reasonable to risk playing those odds because if the client should die at an unexpectedly early age, it could be a great financial disaster for the client's family. The fact that it is reasonable for certain people to buy life insurance does not, however, necessarily persuade them actually to buy the insurance. Knowing this, the salesperson often appeals to more emotional motivations by describing in detail the financially desperate condition the client's loved ones would face if the client died uninsured. Of course, if the client is sharp, he or she might find another way of taking care of the family's financial security in the event of the client's death. The client might, for example, invest money in real estate or mutual funds or see to it that his or her spouse is prepared to undertake a self-supporting career.

1:3 The differences Being logical focuses on following out the consequences of an idea. It is logical to ask: If we accept your assumption, what would then be true? When we want to test a hypothesis, we must first be logical enough to see what the hypothesis implies. A logical person recognizes which ideas contradict certain others, which are consistent with others, and which guarantee the implication that the others are true.

Being sharp relates to being discerning, discovering solutions, creating strategies to accomplish goals. This skill will be worked on in Part Four, when we talk about proof strategies and when we actually build some proofs. Being reasonable relates to knowledge and preliminary assessment of the overall wisdom of certain beliefs or courses of action. Being reasonable also relates to knowing one's options and being able to tell the absurd ones from the more or less plausible ones. This skill comes into play in our discussion of fallacies in Part Three as well as in certain sections of Part Four dealing with things like proofs with questionable or doubtful premises. Being emotional relates to using one's own emotions or eliciting the emotions of other people in order to accomplish goals. Being emotional also relates to responding to situations, especially stressful ones, with emotion. Being persuasive is being able to get others to believe you. Emotion and logic are both tools used by persuasive people.

Being logical can be contrasted with each of the characteristics we have been discussing. Being logical means being able to infer the consequences of various views, beliefs, ideas, and assumptions. A logical person is one who uses his or her intellectual powers to think through situations, to try to predict the likely outcome of various alternative courses of action, to anticipate the necessary and probable consequences of believing certain things or acting certain ways. A person can have any of the characteristics we discussed, or a person can fail to have any one of them. Since they are all different, a person can also have any combination of them. So, for example, one person can be logical, sharp, and emotional while another is persuasive and reasonable and still another is logical, unemotional, and unreasonable.

There are many things that could be said to further distinguish each of these characteristics from each other and also to give an even more refined definition of each. Our needs at this point require only that we be able to distinguish being logical from all the others. The exercises below should help in further clarifying your idea of what being logical is. In the next module we will focus on what logic is and how its main concern of evaluating arguments relates to our common goal of improving our logical skills.

EXERCISES FOR MODULE 1
BEING LOGICAL

Ex. 1 There are thirteen questions below. In the space to the left of each question identify the concern or issue raised by that question. Select your answer from:

A. The concern is with being logical.
B. The concern is with being reasonable or sharp.
C. The concern is with persuasion through appeals to emotions.
D. The concern is none of the above.

_____ 1. Yes, Senator, but I ask you, what do you take to be the consequence of this mass of evidence?

_____ 2. Doctor, please tell me what would you do in my situation?

_____ 3. The puzzled professor turned to the class and asked, "Can any of you help me figure out how to start this machine?"

_____ 4. I'm very sorry but I just haven't finished the job. As considerate as you are, I'm sure you'll give me an extension.

_____ 5. Now that we have assembled the facts, let me ask, "Do they lead where we thought they would lead or not?"

_____ 6. Jones, what do you make out of this? How could that steel buttress have collapsed?

_____ 7. Surely you're not the kind of coward who would sneak away from danger without even telling your comrades!

_____ 8. Now, I recognize that the facts are overwhelming; but I ask, should we vote this policy into law given the uncertainty of the marketplace?

_____ 9. It's not clear to me what we should do about this situation; what do you suggest?

_____ 10. The murderer has killed five people whose names have one, two, three, four, and five letters in them respectively; I see the pattern but can anybody see the motive?

_____ 11. If statement A is true and A implies statement B, then what must we say about B?

_____ 12. When do we eat?

_____ 13. If you had to choose between one year in jail, two years in jail, or death, which would you choose?

Ex. 2 There are ten situations described below. In the space to the left of each identify the concern of the person or people involved or the characteristic illustrated by the speaker. Select your answers from:

A. The passage illustrates or is concerned with being logical.
B. The passage illustrates or is concerned with being reasonable or being sharp.
C. The passage illustrates or is concerned with being persuasive.
D. The passage illustrates or is concerned with none of the above.

_____ 1. You're playing cards. Each person has one card from a standard deck of fifty-two. Ace is high. You hold a jack. High card will win, and you do not know what the other three players are holding. Should you bet on your jack or not?

_____ 2. The situation is the same as that as described in item 1. With four queens, four kings, and four aces out against you there are twelve cards that can beat your jack, three that can tie it, and thirty-six that would lose to it. These facts seem to be implied by the way the game is to be played and by the way that the cards were dealt so far as we know.

_____ 3. The child approached the teacher quietly, obviously on the verge of tears. The teacher asked what had happened, and the child replied that he had been unable to master riding a bicycle that had been left in the school yard. The teacher comforted him.

_____ 4. I want you to know that we have three choices. We can try to produce more products, we can lower our overhead, or we can raise our prices. If we produce more, we will have to make capital improvements. If we lower our overhead, we will have to cut back on staff. If we raise our prices, we may price ourselves right out of the market. That's our problem, and I have no idea what to do about it. Do any of you smart young college people have a solution to offer?

_____ 5. Watson, you say that there were no signs of violence when you examined the body? None whatsoever? . . . Aha! I see there was a drop of blood on the victim's neck. So, . . . just as I expected the victim must have been poisoned. Why the conclusion is as elementary as could be. I believe Watson that if you examine the wound, you will find that it was made with a hairpin, undoubtably dipped in deadly poison first.

_____ 6. The three boys stole quietly through the dark hallway toward the mess hall door. Once inside the mess hall they felt their way past tables and chairs toward the kitchen where the food locker and the fresh strawberries lay. Just then the lights flashed on, and the headmaster appeared, larger than life, standing in the entrance to the mess hall. The boys froze —caught in the act; but Bill, the quickest of them, said, "Oh, thank God it's you Mr. Fudgebutter. We were hiding because some older boys were running about catching kids and throwing them into the showers."

_____ 7. Tell me, class, what follows from "all cars are not alike"? Is it "no car is like any other car" or "not all cars are alike"?

_____ 8. After you have waited 5 weeks for a reply, it seems fair to send the bank a letter. You can at least find out whether they received your deposit.

_____ 9. What do you think we can infer from the fact that the house is empty, totally without furniture, and yet the lights are on? Can it mean anything but that some thieves have just made quite a haul?

_____ 10. Suppose we know that everyone in Lavonia always lies whereas everyone in Plymouth always tells the truth. We wake up one morning in one of those cities and ask a resident "Do you live here?" We can infer that if we are in Lavonia the person will say no, but if we are in Plymouth the person will say yes.

ANSWERS TO EXERCISES
FOR MODULE 1

Ex. 1 (Throughout this text, answers are numbered across the page, not down.)

1. A	2. B	3. B	4. C
5. A	6. B	7. C	8. B
9. B	10. B	11. A	12. D
13. B			

If you missed more than four or five overall, or if you missed items 1, 5, or 11, you should reread the module, concentrating especially on 1:3. Our main interest is that you should be able to tell if an issue being raised is an issue of logic as opposed to other kinds of related but different issues.

Ex. 2

1. B (reasonable)
2. A
3. D
4. B (sharp)
5. A
6. B (sharp)
7. A. What follows is "No car is like any other car."

8. B (reasonable)
9. A. The issue is what one should infer from certain facts, and so it is an issue of logic. The inference made in 9 is not the only one to make, nor is it necessarily the best one.
10. A

If you had problems with Ex. 2, review 1:1 to 1:3.

Before we get into Module 2, just for the fun of it, here are two more puzzles.

Puzzle 3:
In Puzzle 1 reduce the restriction on the number of times each player is allowed to be weighed from three times to two times.

Puzzle 4:
(This one is tough.) In Puzzle 1 add the restriction that the coach can use the seesaw only three times. (No restriction on how often each player is weighed, though obviously the limit is three.) The seesaw is big enough to hold all twelve players.

Partial solution 3:
The reasonable thing is to see that not only can you replace one person at a time, as was done in the solution to Puzzle 1, but you can also replace them two at a time. Try weighing two players and then two more and then another pair. Keep this up until you come to the pair that makes the seesaw move.

Partial solution 4:
A reasonable person would see that there are lots of ways to start: six on each side, five on each side, four on each side, etc. Also in this puzzle, you have to maximize the information you get out of each use of the seesaw. For example, if each player is numbered you might learn that player 4 is possibly heavy, player 5 is possibly light, and player 9 is known to be standard. *Hints:* On your first use of the seesaw try four on each side. If you come up with a group of four that are all, say, possibly light, compare three of them with three that are known to be standard. If you have eight, four of which are possibly light and the other four of which are possibly heavy, put three people on each side as follows: leave two possibly heavy ones where they are, switch one possibly heavy with one possibly light, and replace one possibly light with a standard-weight person.

MODULE 2

LOGIC

Having focused briefly on being logical, let's compare that with the field of study called logic in order to get the general idea of what logic, as a discipline or study, is all about.

● After reading Module 2 you should be able to:

1. Pick out and list the chief characteristics of logic as a field of study

2:1.1 Concern with arguments We have already said that logic is the field of study concerned with the procedures for evaluating arguments. Although we will put off the more rigorous definition of 'argument' until Module 3, you can easily grasp the basic idea: an argument is a group of statements that a person presents such that one of the person's statements is intended to be the upshot, or conclusion, of the others. These others, called premises, are presented as if they supported or entailed that conclusion.

Here are some examples of logical arguments. In these examples (P) means that the statement that follows is a premise and (C) means that the statement that follows is a conclusion.

EG. 2.1 (P) Any act performed voluntarily should be subject to either praise or blame. (P) John voluntarily entered into a contract to redecorate the Smith house. (C) So John's act of entering into the contract should be subject to praise or blame.

EG. 2.2 (P) We want to become parents either by becoming biological parents or adoptive parents. (P) We should not adopt a child unless we both really want to do that. (P) We do not both really want to do that at this time in our marriage. (C) So we should try to become biological parents rather than adoptive parents at this time

EG. 2.3 (C) Barbara is an intelligent person. This is so because (P) everyone who goes to St. Mary's is intelligent and (P) Barbara goes to St. Mary's.

Logic is concerned with the relationships that might exist between the premises and the conclusions of arguments. A person has presented us with an argument. In so doing the person has alleged or purported that a certain set of statements entails, or has as its consequence, or can be regarded as the evidence for, another statement so that *if* the premises are true, *then* the conclusion must be considered at least probably, if not necessarily, true as well.

2:1.2 Logic studies relationships Logic, as characterized above, studies the *relationships between* the stated premises and their purported conclusion. It asks: Do these premises in fact entail, imply, strongly warrant, or strongly support this conclusion, or do they not? If they do, we will say that the argument is *logically correct*. But if the premises neither imply, nor entail, nor strongly support, nor strongly warrant the purported conclusion, then we will say that the argument is not logically correct.

The three example arguments given above were all logically correct; here are two examples of arguments that are not logically correct.

EG. 2.4 (P) I took one course in economics and the prof was a real bore. (C) So all economics profs must be terrible teachers.

Here the premise asserts only that *one* economics professor is boring, so you can see that there is little or no basis supplied for the conclusion that *all* are boring.

EG. 2.5 (P) Everyone who goes to St. Mary's is intelligent. (P) Charles does not go to St. Mary's. (C) Therefore Charles cannot be intelligent.

In Eg. 2.5 the first premise asserts the intelligence of all those who do go to St. Mary's. But no premise says anything about the intelligence of those who don't attend. Thus, the fact that Charles doesn't go allows us no conclusion at all about his intelligence.

Logic also has a general, but related, concern. It studies the relationships between the premises and the conclusions of arguments in order to find out why certain *kinds* of arguments are logically correct and other kinds are not. In seeking and securing these explanations, logic makes our practical concern of evaluating individual arguments easier. Through these more theoretical explanations logicians provide the means for recognizing logical correctness and incorrectness in large classes of arguments.

2:1.3 Logical correctness It is very important to note that logic is *not* concerned with the actual truth or falsity of the individual premises or the conclusion of an argument. In this respect logic might be called "cold." Whether or not the individual statements in an argument are true or false, wise or foolish, offensive or polite, fortunate or unfortunate, clumsy or elegant, funny or aggravating is totally irrelevant from the point of view of logic. Logic's concern is with whether or not these premises actually do have as their consequence that particular conclusion. One way to ask the logician's question is: *Would* this conclusion be true *if* these premises were true? In asking the question this way we are not saying that the premises are true, we are inquiring into what *would* be the case *if* they were true.

Having said that logic is concerned with the logical correctness of arguments, not the truth or falsity of the premises or conclusions, we can reinforce this fundamental distinction between logical correctness and truth by considering two examples. Examples 2.6 and 2.7 are both logically correct arguments, but each has at least one false premise; in Eg. 2.7 the conclusion is also false. Let (T) stand for true and (F) for false.

EG. 2.6 (C) Los Angeles is likely to be smoggy (T) because (P) weather tends to move from east to west (F) and (P) if weather moves from east to west, then smog tends to develop west of the mountains (F). (P) Los Angeles is west of the Rockies, you know. (T)

EG. 2.7 (P) Reno is a large industrial city over which air tends to stagnate (F). So (C) probably it's very smoggy in Reno (F).

Are these arguments logically correct even with their false assertions? Indeed they are. The question of logical correctness does not involve whether the premises—or the conclusion—is actually true; it asks only: *What* if? So ask yourself: What if the premises of Eg. 2.6 were true? If they were, would the conclusion be certified as probably true on the basis of the (assumed) truth of the premises? Inspection of the argument should lead you to answer yes. To confirm your ability to distinguish between truth and logical correctness, check to see that Eg. 2.7 is also logically correct by asking the question: Would the conclusion be true if the premise were true, despite the fact that both statements happen to actually be false? You should answer yes.

2:2.1 Logic: a machine Logic is independent of any particular group. It operates like a machine fulfilling its function no matter who is pressing the buttons. If we give it certain input, it will give us a certain conclusion. But if we give it other input, it will give us a quite different conclusion. The variation is not in the machine but in the data.

The logic machine can be thought of as one of two things. It can be thought of as a person's brain which operates on ideas, or it can be thought of as a set of operations embodied in language and operating on sentences. Although both ways of imagining the situation have their problems, each brings out something that we should know. The machine of logic is like a brain; it is able to compute, to see consequences, to perform operations, and to generate inferences. The machine of logic is like a set of linguistic operations; it is public, it can be used and evaluated by several people, and it can be used mistakenly as well as correctly.

2:2.2 Logical elements in language The logical operations that a given language contains may vary widely. In natural spoken languages they are very elaborate. In artificial languages and computer languages they may be very limited. One logical operation is called *negation*. It is the operation of changing one assertion into its exact opposite. If the first assertion is 'All people are silly,' its negation (or contradiction) is 'Not all people are silly.' If the first statement is 'Some dogs are wild,' its contradiction, or exact opposite, is 'No dogs are wild.' No matter which natural language we use to write these sentences, we can express negation or contradiction in that language.[1]

Another logical operation is called *quantification*. By the use of words like 'all' and 'some' we can quantify the things we are talking about. We can say, for example, "all God's children" or "some of God's children," and these signify different things. Other logical words (words that in some of their uses perform logical operations) are: 'and,' 'or,' 'if . . ., then . . .,' 'but,' 'is identical to,' 'neither,' 'every,' and 'any.' These logical words work no matter what one is talking about. For instance, consider this argument structure:

1. *All A*'s are *B*'s.
2. *No B*'s are *C*'s.
3. *So no A*'s are *C*'s.

The logical words are italicized. Notice that this argument structure can be fleshed out in many different ways to yield logically correct arguments. The A's can be cats, B's olive-haired mammals, and C's beings that exist before 1900. Thus the fleshed out argument would be: (1) All cats are olive-haired mammals. (2) No olive-haired mammals are beings that existed before 1900. So (3) no cats are beings that existed before 1900. On the other hand, the group using this argument structure might be less concerned with zoological fiction and more concerned with selling cars. If so, they might flesh out the argument structure something like this: (1) All mechanically defective cars are hard to sell. (2) No hard-to-sell items are good business investments. So (3) no mechanically defective cars are good business investments. The reason both of these arguments are logically correct is that since the linguistic argument structure is a logically correct structure, no matter which three terms you use to fill in the nonlogical elements, the logical words in that structure determine the logical correctness of the argument that results.[2]

The only possible way that arguments built on various logically correct argument structures in language could cease to be logically correct is if the meanings of the logical words changed. For example, if 'not' came to mean the same as 'all' or 'some,' then it would no longer do the logical job of negation. With such changes the argument structure above would lose its validity. But such changes in the meanings of words would indicate radical changes in our language. Such changes could

[1] If two statements are *contradictory*, whenever either one is true the other must be false and whenever either one is false the other must be true.
[2] Remember that an argument can be logically correct even if it contains false statements (see 2:1.3).

even render language dysfunctional and make it impossible to use language to communicate.

EXERCISES FOR MODULE 2
LOGIC

Ex. 1 Below is a list of ten characteristics. If a characteristic in the list is a characteristic of logic write 'yes' in the space to its left; if it is not a characteristic of logic write 'no.'

_____ 1. The concern is with arguments.

_____ 2. The concern is with whether or not premises do support or imply their conclusions.

_____ 3. The concern is with how many people would be persuaded if a certain argument were presented.

_____ 4. The people who study logic study how people's brains work.

_____ 5. People who study logic try to decide what people ought to believe.

_____ 6. Logic helps make certain kinds of value judgments more objective.

_____ 7. Logic is a disciplined study.

_____ 8. Logic is only concerned with whether or not an argument's conclusion is true.

_____ 9. Logic asks: Are these premises true, is this conclusion true?

_____ 10. Logic is the study which examines the relationship between what people say and what they actually do.

Ex. 2 List three or four of the most central characteristics of logic.

SELECTED ANSWERS
TO EXERCISES FOR MODULE 2

Ex. 2

1. Logic is a certain kind of study.
2. It studies certain relationships.
3. The relationships it studies are those that exist between the premises and the conclusions of arguments.
4. Logic is concerned with finding out how to evaluate arguments objectively to see whether they are logically correct.

Problems here can be cleared up by reviewing 2:1.1 and 2:1.2.

MODULE 3
ARGUMENTS

Now that we know that logic is concerned with developing new procedures for evaluating the logical correctness of arguments it is reasonable to ask: What exactly does 'argument' mean as logicians use that term? Module 3 answers this question.

● After reading Module 3 you should be able to:

1. Define the terms 'argument' and 'assertive sentence' as used by logicians
2. Identify assertive sentences, distinguish them from other kinds of sentences, and state how they differ
3. Identify and distinguish arguments from nonarguments

3:1.1 In 2:1.1 we gave three examples of arguments. In each case the passage we presented was a series of sentences. One of the sentences was presented as a conclusion that could be inferred from the others. The others were presented as support for, or premises of, that conclusion. Here are more examples of arguments. As you read these examples notice that the same characteristics just listed apply here as well.

EG. 3.1 (P) All ducks are feathered. (P) My pet, Socrates, is a duck. (C) So Socrates must be feathered.

EG. 3.2 (P) Whenever I play hole number seven, I hit into the pond that's to the right of the green. (C) I'll probably do the same thing today when I go out to play golf.

EG. 3.3 (C) I believe that if the enemy retreats, we will have him licked. (I) He cannot hope to win in his current position. (P) If he pulls back, old General Hotcollar is waiting for him. (P) Hotcollar has never lost a battle.

EG. 3.4 (P) Carpenters and plumbers do equal work. That's why (C) they should get equal pay. (P) Equal work for equal pay. (I) Who could deny an idea like that?

In these examples (P) indicates that the sentence that follows is a premise, (C) that it is a conclusion, and (I) that it is irrelevant to that argument. Check to see that you agree.

3:1.2 'Argument,' a preliminary definition Looking at these examples and the examples of arguments given in earlier modules, we can observe that arguments are made up of sentences—not just any kind of sentence, but sentences which are used to assert things to be true, as opposed to sentences which are used for other activities like asking, thanking, pledging, greeting, nominating, pleading, etc. For now we can call sentences used to assert things *assertive sentences*; we will come back to them in a moment. In examining arguments, we find a second commonality: in each example argument one of the assertive sentences is presented as a conclusion. The other sentences are offered as premises or support for the conclusion. You can imagine the assertive sentences of any argument being grouped together and thought of as a set. In this way we can say that *an argument is a set of assertive sentences one of which is presented as a conclusion, the others as premises.* Let's take this as our preliminary definition of the term 'argument.' So when logicians talk about arguments, they are talking about sets of sentences, all of which sentences are assertive sentences, and moreover sentences which are not randomly members of the set but each of which is *intended to play a role* as either the conclusion or as one of the premises for the conclusion. So any sentence which is not an assertive sentence is not part of an argument. Further, any assertive sentence in a given passage which is not presented as either a premise or a conclusion is not to be considered part of an argument. Thus, for example, the sentence marked (I) in Eg. 3.4 is not part of the argument given in Eg. 3.4; the argument in Eg. 3.4 is the set of sentences {(P), (C), (P)} as marked in that example.

3:2 The meaning of 'Argument' There are other things that people call arguments besides those things for which logicians prefer to reserve the word 'argument.' One of the independent variables upon which a mathematical function depends is called the argument of the function, but that is probably a far less familiar use of the word 'argument' than the common practice of referring to altercations, quarrels, and the like as arguments. Unfortunately when things have degenerated into emotion-charged shouting matches, there is little that is going on that can be called logical. The arguments that logicians are concerned with are not these heated debates but the batch of sentences, written or spoken, that people present, such that one of them, the conclusion, is to be taken to be true on the grounds that others, the premises, are true. Logicians deal with these kinds of things because they are, in a sense, the public product of people's thinking. The assertive sentences, if not already written down, can be written down, and their logical relationships to each other can be examined. Unlike quarrels, questions of logic are not decided on the basis of emotion, pride, prejudice, or noise level.

3:3.1 What are assertive sentences? We promised to clarify the point that arguments are sets of assertive sentences. In order to understand what assertive sentences are we will have to look again at what language is and what people do in and through using language. Assertive sentences turn out to be that class of sentences which people use to make statements, offer descriptions, make reports, state facts, relate information, make predictions, and in general assert things to be true.

An assertive sentence can be either written or spoken. If it is written, we can call it an inscription; if spoken, an utterance. It is true of all assertive sentences (and, for that matter, only assertive sentences) that it makes sense to ask of them: Is this sentence true or false? That it is reasonable to ask this question of them becomes their defining characteristic. We can define *assertive sentences as those sentences about which it makes sense to ask: Is this true or false?* This definition agrees with our common experience of being able to ask concerning any person's statement, report, or prediction: Is what he or she said true or false? Unless it makes sense to ask about a sentence's truth or falsity, it is not assertive.

In most contexts of ordinary usage the following would be examples of assertive sentences:

1. The books on that shelf are all written by Woolf.
2. Egad, this is the last time I will ever ask that one for help!
3. Socrates was a great philosopher and a bit of a troublemaker, too.

All the premises of the examples in this part of the book are also assertive sentences. Likewise all the conclusions of these example arguments are assertive sentences. In each and every case it would make sense to ask: Is this true or false? The point is not that we should always be able to answer this question. Limitations on our knowledge and abilities, or perhaps the vagueness of the language in which the assertion is cast, make it impossible to answer such a question each time it comes up. The point is that it makes sense to raise the question. We can tell that the following inscriptions are not assertive sentences because in most contexts of ordinary usage it would not make sense to ask if they were true or false:

4. When will it be time to eat?
5. Damn it!
6. I strongly recommend that you plead guilty.

7. I apologize for having told you that.
8. Look out!
9. Will you marry me?
10. The an or of mine loves run over up the?

3:3.2 Arguments as sets of assertions It is important to be able to think of arguments as sets of assertive sentences because if they are thought of in that way, we can ascribe a truth-value (i.e., the characteristic of being true or being false) to each sentence in an argument. In other words, as assertive sentences, each sentence in an argument is either true or false. This makes it possible for us to look at an argument and ask: If all of the premises were in fact true, would their truth strongly warrant or entail the conclusion's being true? As you remember from Module 2, this is the question of logical correctness. The question of logical correctness can be put in terms of what would be true if certain other things were true. When we ask: If the premises of an argument were *true*, would its conclusion have to be *true*? we are assuming that each of the premises and the conclusion of every argument can sensibly be assessed as true or false. In other words when we ask whether an argument is logically correct, we presuppose that each premise and the conclusion too are what we have here called assertive sentences. Logic asks: Do these assertions entail or warrant this assertion? In terms of the fact that assertions can be called true or false, logic's concern can be restated as: If all these assertions were true, would this necessitate or make it probable that this other assertion is true?

When logicians set out to examine an argument, they normally assume that the words in the assertions and the assertions as a whole have their ordinary, conventional meanings. The possibility that the argument's author intended that his words have some unusual or esoteric meaning is disregarded unless there is evidence to suggest that the author did intend to speak esoterically. If we know the author intended to make certain assertions not actually made, given the (ordinary) meaning of what he or she did say, we can rewrite the argument to include the intended but unmade assertions. But unless we are presented evidence of the author's esoteric meaning, it is normally quite reasonable to assume that the authors of arguments mean to argue as indicated by the ordinary meaning of what they say. This assumption of ordinary meaning will be our practice throughout this text, as indeed it is in all our daily lives.

The assumption of ordinary or standard meaning removes the subjectivity involved in what the argument's author "might have meant." It removes the subjectivity involved in what purposes its author might have had. The argument, the set of assertions, is objective. The logical issue is objective too: If all of the premises were true, would the conclusion be true?

3:4 Identifying arguments You can tell whether something is an argument or not by applying the following procedure. Start with a group of sentences since it alone can contain an argument. (1) To see whether it does qualify, ask whether there are some assertive sentences among the sentences in that group. If not, stop, because the item is not an argument. If there are assertive sentences, mark them, because they are the only sentences in the group that can be part of an argument. (Non-assertive sentences are often helpful in giving clues to the author's intent, but more of this in Module 4.) Now go on. (2) Ask whether the assertive sentences in the group are presented as if some of them are to be taken as implying, entailing, warranting, or supporting another of them. If not, stop; the group contains no argument. If yes, however, you have an argument: it is precisely the set of those assertive sentences involved in the purported implication or support relationship just discovered.

EXERCISES FOR MODULE 3
ARGUMENTS

Ex. 1 Below is a list of ten sentences. If a sentence is assertive put 'yes,' in the answer space; otherwise put 'no.'

_____ 1. Hear ye, Hear ye!

_____ 2. God bless America.

_____ 3. Now is the time for all good men to come to the aid of their party.

_____ 4. The rain in Spain is wet.

_____ 5. Love your neighbor.

_____ 6. Come here right now.

_____ 7. I wish you all a million happy days.

_____ 8. Nobody in this room knows who the thief really is.

_____ 9. If I were you, I would take the money and run.

_____ 10. Ouch!

Ex. 2 There are ten passages below. If the passage is an argument write 'arg' in the answer space; otherwise write 'no' in the answer space.

_____ 1. Dance, the dreamers dance, and hear the divine din dash doubts against the day's long night. Who can wonder when mind and ear and eye are full of sounds and lights and wine? Or who can know or think or doubt or fear when all the human race has lost its sight and dances in dreams in thoughtless search for one small sign?

_____ 2. Given a group of arguments, you should be able to identify the conclusion and premises of each. You should also be able to determine when a given sentence is irrelevant from the point of view of what the indicated conclusion is and what the indicated premises are. (Note: Later we will learn the circumstances under which even some of the premises can be considered irrelevant, but our concern now is isolating arguments, not testing for fallacies.) You should also be able to convert enthymemes into full-fledged arguments.

_____ 3. Mommy, all the other kids have candy. Why can't I have some, huh?

_____ 4. An argument is logically correct if, and only if, its premises actually do entail or strongly warrant (support) its conclusion. Logic is concerned with finding out which arguments and types of arguments are correct and which are not. It tries to develop procedures for testing arguments for correctness. It catalogs the kinds of arguments that people, in their long history, have found to be correct and reliable. It also catalogs the ones that people have found to be fallacious and unreliable.

_____ 5. I believe for every drop of rain that falls a rose grows red. I believe that when there is no light at night the spookies come out of their beds. I suppose that every rose that grows pricks a spook who should not be walking around in the dark.

_____ 6. John is a letter carrier. Letter carriers deliver the mail. The conclusion should be obvious, then.

_____ 7. There is danger on every hand. Let us arm ourselves now and join the battle before it is too late!

_____ 8. Most dog lovers trust no salespeople. Some salespeople trust no dogs.

_____ 9. When I first saw you you were just a girl. That was 13 years ago, when you were only ten. You must be a woman by now.

_____ 10. Few people realize how difficult it is to govern when all the people disagree with everything one does. Some say it's too little, others say it's too much. Whom can one believe?

Ex. 3 Write out the definitions given in this module for the terms 'assertive sentence' and 'argument.'

Ex. 4 Indicate whether each of the following is true or false.

_____ 1. Assertive sentences are used to ask questions.

_____ 2. 'Argument' as defined by logicians refers to quarrels.

_____ 3. Inscriptions are written sentences, whereas utterances are spoken.

_____ 4. 'Assertive sentence' refers only to written sentences.

_____ 5. Every sentence in an argument can reasonably be thought of as either true or false.

_____ 6. Logic's concern over whether given premises entail a given conclusion is recognizable as a concern over whether a conclusion would have to be considered true if its premises were true.

_____ 7. An argument is any set of assertive sentences.

_____ 8. Every linguistic passage contains at least one argument.

_____ 9. We will always assume that an author is speaking in accord with the ordinary or conventional meanings of words unless there is evidence to the contrary.

_____ 10. Even though the sentence "Who could deny that first moon landing was exciting?" claims that the landing was exciting, the inscription is not assertive because it is grammatically a question.

ANSWERS TO EXERCISES
FOR MODULE 3

Ex. 1

1. No	2. No	3. Yes	4. Yes
5. No	6. No	7. No	8. Yes

9. Yes. This one is a problem because it is out of context. It could be a piece of advice too. If you thought of it as advice then your answer should be 'no.' (The same is true if you took it as a threat.)

10. No

If you missed two or more, besides item 9, review 3:3.1 and 3:3.2

Ex. 2

1. No (a poem)
2. No (a passage of text, or statement of objectives)
3. No (a plea or an effort to bring about action)
4. No (a description)
5. No (a poor joke)
6. Arg
7. No (a warning and a call to action)
8. No (two facts presented side by side)
9. Arg
10. No (a lament)

If you missed four or more of these you should review 3:1.2 and 3:4.

Ex. 3 'Assertive sentence' refers to those sentences about which it makes sense to ask: Is this true or false? (3:3.1). 'Argument' means 'set of assertive sentences one of which is presented as a conclusion, the others as premises' (3:1.2).

Ex. 4

1. F (3:3.1 and 3:1.2)	2. F (3:2)	3. T (3:3.1)
4. F (3:3.1)	5. T (3:3.2)	6. T (3:3.2)
7. F (3:1.2 and 3:4)	8. F (3:4)	9. T (3:3.2)

10. F (3:3.1); grammatical form is not brought into the concept of assertive sentences; rhetorical questions are assertive sentences.

MODULE 4

CONCLUSIONS AND PREMISES

Since logic involves the evaluation of arguments, you must first be able to identify arguments and get them into proper shape for evaluation if you are to apply logic.

● After reading Module 4 you should be able to:

1. Pick out the chief characteristics of arguments
2. Pick out the premises and the conclusion of arguments
3. Isolate and remove any irrelevant sentences that may appear intermingled in the premises and conclusions of arguments
4. Identify assertive sentences that should appear in arguments because they are implicit or obviously part of the argument but which are missing, and include such sentences in restatements of the arguments
5. Distinguish enthymeme arguments from nonenthymeme arguments
6. Pick out the chief characteristics of enthymeme arguments

4:1.1 Finding the conclusion Once we have something that is an argument, we must get it into proper shape before we can begin to evaluate it. We will learn how to evaluate arguments in Parts Two to Four, but now we must focus on the preliminary skills. To get an argument into shape we must first identify its conclusion and its premises. You can accomplish this easily by asking: Which assertive sentence does the author intend to present as the logical product or upshot of the argument? Here you should evaluate the author's intentions as they are revealed implicitly by the context within which the argument appears or, if you are lucky, as revealed explicitly by the author. Ask: What did the author of the argument claim to prove? That statement is the argument's conclusion. *Warning:* Do *not* ask yourself: What does this argument actually prove? That is quite a different question. It will not help you identify the conclusion, but will help you later when you wish to evaluate the argument as logical or illogical.

One way to get a clue to what the author intended as the conclusion is to note words that tip off the presence of the conclusion. Here are some common conclusion indicators.

Thus . . .	This evidence warrants that . . .
Therefore . . .	This supports the view that . . .
So . . .	Let us infer that . . .
We can now infer . . .	As a consequence . . .
Let us conclude . . .	So it seems that . . .
Hence . . .	And so probably . . .
It follows that . . .	We can deduce that . . .
This means that . . .	This supports believing that . . .
This implies that . . .	. . ., then.
These facts indicate . . .	We can justifiably infer that . . .

4:1.2 Finding the premises The procedure for finding the premises of an argument is the same: evaluate the author's intentions. Ask: What assertive sentences has the author supplied as the basis from which the conclusion is supposed to be derived? Or: What assertive sentences are presented as the support or justification for the conclusion? You are asking what the author of the argument presented as the starting point or as the logical basis from which the conclusion can, *in his or her estimation*, be drawn. *Warning:* Do *not* ask: Which statements would make good premises? Again, leave the matter of evaluation for later. The aim now is to get the author's argument in proper shape for its subsequent examination. We can get a clue to which statements the author intended as premises by looking for premise indicators, such tip-off words as:

Since . . .	Suppose . . .
After all . . .	Assume . . .
Given that . . .	Let us take it that . . .
Whereas . . .	Here are the facts: . . .
But . . .	Let us begin with . . .
Although . . .	This is the evidence: . . .
And . . .	We all know that . . .

4:2.1 Deleting irrelevant sentences Part of the business of getting the argument in shape is to trim off unnecessary sentences, either assertive or nonassertive, that might be cluttering up the passage. After we have found what the author's promises and conclusion are, any leftover sentences should be crossed out and disregarded as irrelevant. This means that they are, from the author's point of view, not needed to sustain or support the intended conclusion. Remember the argument we want to evaluate is the one that the author wanted to give us. We are under no obligation to fix it up. So, even if we think that something is relevant, if the author doesn't, put it aside. Similarly, even if we think that some stated premise is irrelevant, if the author thinks it is relevant, keep it in. Sometimes an argument's author may even have drawn the wrong conclusion from the premises. This is not our concern yet; if the author thinks it is the proper conclusion, leave it in. When we come to evaluating arguments in Part Three, we will learn that arguments based on irrelevant premises or which draw wrong conclusions are fallacious and unacceptable. But for now we are not evaluating, only preparing the argument for later evaluation.

4:2.2 Grasping the author's intention We have already noticed that many words function to indicate an assertive sentence as a premise or as a conclusion. Sometimes an author conveys the intended premises and conclusions of the argument by whole sentences.

EG. 4.1 I believe that the best opportunities should go to the most qualified applicants. I have several reasons for believing this. The most qualified applicants will benefit most from the opportunities. They will present a better reflection on us. And they will repay us later with greater contributions.

EG. 4.2 If public services are increased, tax revenues must be increased. Why? The city is already using all the funds available to it. "And how," you ask, "does that prove anything, if the city is spending its present funds unwisely?" The truth is that the city could not spend its present funds more efficiently, more effectively, or for more worthy goals.

In Eg. 4.1, the assertive sentence "I have several reasons for believing this" is neither a premise nor a conclusion. Instead it functions to mark the first sentence as the argument's conclusion and the last three as its premises. Similarly, in Eg. 4.2, the word 'why' functions to mark the sentence following it as the premise supporting the conclusion that an increase in public services will require tax revenues to be increased. The rhetorical question about whether the one premise proves the conclusion is then introduced to clarify that, in the author's view, the argument rests not on one but two premises, the second of which is asserted in the last sentence of the passage. Thus, you will often be able to grasp an author's intention about an argument not only from indicator words, but also from sentences which function to mark others of the author's assertive sentences as premises and conclusions.

4:3 Supplying missing assertions The final step to getting an argument in shape for evaluation is to write in, or supply, its missing assertions. If there are any assertive sentences that are implicit in the presentation of the argument that are not actually spoken or written, they should be counted as part of the argument too. Arguments missing an assertive sentence that is obviously intended to be taken as either a premise or the conclusion are called *enthymeme* arguments. In these arguments the author takes it for granted that the audience will presume certain things or that they believe certain things. Often you can tell from the context of the presentation of the argument, or from knowing who the author is and who the intended audience is, what statements the author would not find it necessary to make. When an argument's author believes that the audience is fully aware of something, he or she will simply omit, for the sake of brevity or convenience, saying again what is assumed to be known. The author may not say everything that is intended to be taken as a premise, or may even leave out the conclusion if it is obvious that an argument is being made and the author believes that the intended conclusion can be immediately and easily inferred. In this way enthymeme arguments result. Before we can evaluate such an argument, we must put it all on the table in shape to examine. When you are a party to conversations involving enthymeme arguments, it is easy to supply the missing parts. When the arguments are encountered in isolation from the contexts in which they originally appeared, it may take a bit longer to figure out what obvious, implicit statements have been omitted. *Warning:* Do *not* convert nonarguments into arguments. A person with an active imagination might turn a nonargument into an argument by supplying all kinds of statements and connections between them that were never implicit in the original passage. So, to avoid this, (1) don't worry about whether or not something is an enthymeme until *after* you have decided it is an argument, and (2) limit yourself to, say, only 5 or 10 seconds of thought when trying to discover the implicit and obvious missing assertion.

4:4 Here are some examples of arguments. Each is presented twice. The second time it appears its premises are identified by (P), its conclusion by (C), and any irrelevant sentences or statements by (I). If the argument is an enthymeme, its missing assertion is supplied and identified as either one of the enthymeme's premises, (E-P), or as the enthymeme's conclusion (E-C). As you read the first presentation, try to determine the proper marking.

EG. 4.3   Whoever loves winter loves snow, cold, and warm sweaters. Blue loves snow, cold, and warm sweaters. Blue must love winter, then.

(P) Whoever loves winter loves snow, cold, and warm sweaters. (P) Blue loves snow, cold, and warm sweaters. (C) Blue must love winter.

EG. 4.4   Since he is a man, Socrates must be mortal.

(P) Socrates is a man. (E-P) All men are mortal. (C) Socrates is mortal.

EG. 4.5   Since so many people believe that our nation is on the side of truth and justice, it is fair to conclude that it is.

(P) Many people believe that our nation is on the side of truth and justice. (E-P) What is very widely believed to be true must be true. (C) Our nation is on the side of truth and justice.

EG. 4.6   If God exists, then there is no evil in the world or no people are free. But people are free. Thus, if God exists, there is no evil in the world.

(P) If God exists, then there is no evil in the world or no people are free. (P) People are free. (C) If God exists, there is no evil in the world.

EG. 4.7   There is evil in the world. So there is no God.

(P) There is evil in the world. (E-P) If there is a God, then there could be no evil in the world. (C) There is no God.

EG. 4.8   "I exist," said God. Thus if there are both free people and evil ways, the first premises of Eg. 4.6 must be false.

(P) God exists. (C) If there are both free people and evil ways, then it is not the case that if God exists there is no evil in the world or no people are free.

EG. 4.9   If everyone believes that something is possible, then we can infer that there is something that everyone believes is possible.

(P) Everyone believes that something is possible. (C) There is something that everyone believes is possible.

EG. 4.10 An argument's conclusion need not be its last sentence. This is so because 'conclusion' means 'logical product' and not 'end.' An argument's conclusion is its logical product, not its end. Sometimes people put the conclusion of their arguments at the beginning. What do you think of that?

(C) An argument's conclusion need not be its last sentence. (P) 'Conclusion' means 'logical product,' not 'end.' (P) An argument's conclusion is its logical product, not its end. (I) Sometimes people put the conclusion of their arguments at the beginning. (I) What do you think of that?

EXERCISES FOR MODULE 4
CONCLUSIONS AND PREMISES

Ex. 1 There are ten characteristics listed below. If a characteristic is true of arguments put 'true' in the answer space. If a characteristic does not accurately describe arguments, put 'false.' Arguments:

_____ 1. Are sets of assertive sentences

_____ 2. Are sets of sentences

_____ 3. Are debates with raised voices

_____ 4. Always have some assertive sentence which is a logical consequence of other assertive sentences

_____ 5. Always have some assertive sentence, either explicit or implicit, which is a logical consequence of others

_____ 6. Always have some assertive sentence, either explicit or implicit, which is a purported logical consequence of others, either explicit or implicit

_____ 7. Contain true premises

_____ 8. Never are missing any assertions

_____ 9. Never contain irrelevant sentences

_____ 10. Seldom are able to be evaluated as logical or illogical

Ex. 2 Five arguments are presented below. In each case circle the conclusion and cross out any irrelevant sentences.

1. Whoever is not the killer would not have come to the cabin. John was the only one who came to the cabin. So John is the killer.
2. Most dog lovers do not trust letter carriers. Marsha is a letter carrier. So Marsha delivers the mail.
3. Most people who have dogs have small children. John has small children. So he must have dogs.
4. When I first saw you, you were just a boy. That was 15 years ago. You were only thirteen then. You must be a man now.
5. Queen Elizabeth was a ruler since she was mortal. And all mortals are rulers.

Ex. 3 Indicate whether each of the following is true or false.

_____ 1. Assertions are all in English.

_____ 2. Assertions are used to issue threats, warnings, and salutations.

_____ 3. It is reasonable to ask whether or not assertions are true or false.

_____ 4. Assertions are the only sentences that can be the premises or the conclusion of an argument.

_____ 5. Assertions are always written in the indicative mood.

_____ 6. Assertions never end in a question mark.

_____ 7. Every sentence that ends in a period is an assertion.

_____ 8. Assertions alone can serve as enthymeme premises.

Ex. 4 There are six passages given below. If the passage is not an argument put 'no' in the answer space. If it is, put 'arg' in the answer space, circle its conclusion, and cross out any irrelevant sentences.

_____ 1. Any act performed involuntarily should not be punished. Some criminal acts are performed involuntarily. So some criminal acts should not be punished.

_____ 2. Anyone who argues that the senator is guilty of criminal conspiracy is a weak-minded person interested in destroying our way of life.

_____ 3. Everyone now alive has two parents, each of whom in turn had two parents. It follows that in our grandparents' day there were four times as many people as there are today.

_____ 4. It is best not to marry, for if one marries, one's husband will be either handsome or ugly; if he is handsome, he will excite jealousy, and if he is ugly, disgust.

_____ 5. That my grandmother ever owned the state of Wyoming seems highly improbable. She was never a rich person, and when she died she left just a small estate—Vermont.

_____ 6. This dog is yours. This dog is a father. So, this dog is your father.

Ex. 5 Four enthymeme arguments are given below. After each a list of the possible missing statements is given. Select from that list the statement that is missing from the enthymeme.

_____ 1. Plato is a snob. Because all sky divers are snobs.
   A. All snobs are snobs.
   B. Plato is a snob.
   C. All snobs are sky divers.
   D. Plato is a sky diver.
   E. Plato is Plato.

_____ 2. If anything is a danger to society, it must be dealt with swiftly and reasonably. So crime must be dealt with swiftly and reasonably.
   A. Crime is a danger to society.
   B. All dangers to society are criminal.
   C. Swift and reasonable crime is a societal danger.
   D. If something is a danger to society, it must be dealt with swiftly.
   E. Crime must be dealt with reasonably.

_____ 3. Either the President's secretary is involved, or there is another answer to our problem. But we know that the President's secretary is not involved. So you can see what follows.

A. The President's secretary is involved.
B. We need not look elsewhere to settle the problem.
C. There is no other answer to our problem.
D. Our problem has no answer.
E. There is another answer to our problem.

_____ 4. Only four people could have killed Delaney. John was out of town. Mary was out of gas. Bill was out of his mind and locked up because of it. So Marty killed Delaney.
A. Five people could have killed Delaney.
B. The four were John, Marty, Bill, and Mary.
C. Marty killed Delaney.
D. John did not kill Delaney.
E. Mary loved Bill, and Bill loved John.

Ex. 6 Go back through the arguments given in Ex. 5 and identify the missing assertion as either a missing premise or a missing conclusion. If it is a missing premise put 'prem' in the answer space provided below, otherwise put 'conc.'

_____ 1.   _____ 2.   _____ 3.   _____ 4.

Ex. 7 Indicate whether each of the following is true or false.

_____ 1. Enthymemes are genuine arguments.

_____ 2. Enthymemes have either a missing premise or a missing conclusion.

_____ 3. An enthymeme's missing assertion is one that is obvious or implicit.

_____ 4. The author of an enthymeme is usually absentminded.

_____ 5. Enthymemes are not sets of assertive sentences.

Ex. 8 Supply the missing assertion for each of the following enthymeme arguments.

1. Barbara is an intelligent person. This is so because everyone who went to St. Mary's is intelligent.
2. Reno is a large industrial city over which air tends to stagnate. So Reno is very smoggy.
3. All acrobats are busy these days. Moreover, everyone who is busy these days is coming into great wealth. So it's clear what will happen to acrobats.
4. My pet, Socrates, is a duck, so he's feathered.
5. Carpenters and plumbers do equal work. That's why they should get equal pay.

SELECTED ANSWERS
TO EXERCISES FOR MODULE 4

Ex. 1

1. True (3:1.2)
2. True (3:1.2)
3. False (3:2)
4. False (4:1.1 and Question 6)
5. False (4:1.1 and Question 6)
6. True. (If you missed 4 or 5, compare them with 6.)
7. False; the premises need not be true.
8. False; don't forget enthymeme arguments.
9. False (4:2.1)
10. False; learning how to make this evaluation is what this book is all about.

Ex. 3

1. False; they can be in any language.
2. False; they are used to assert, describe, report, narrate, tell, inform, and state things.
3. True.
4. True; this is how we have defined our terms.
5. False; our language allows for more novelty than that surely! (That was an example.)
6. False; punctuation is not a reliable clue. Rhetorical questions can be used to make statements, and so they are assertive sentences which end in question marks.
7. False; look over Module 3, Ex. 2 to prove this.
8. True; this is a consequence of the definition of all premises as assertive sentences.

If you missed two or more of these, or if you got them right for the wrong reasons, it would be helpful to go back and review 3:3.1.

Ex. 4

2. No
4. Arg. Conclusion: It is best not to marry.
6. Arg. Conclusion: This dog is your father. (Even bad arguments are arguments.)

Ex. 7

1. True   2. True   3. True   4. False   5. False

If you missed one or more of these, review 4:3.

Ex. 8

1. Barbara went to St. Mary's. (Recall Eg. 2.3.)
2. Any large industrial city over which air tends to stagnate is smoggy. (Compare to Eg. 2.7.)
3. Conclusion: acrobats are coming into great wealth. (This argument relies on the structure discussed in 2:2.2.)
4. All ducks are feathered (Eg. 3.1).
5. People who do equal work deserve equal pay (Eg. 3.4).

2

DEFINITIONS AND
THEIR USES

Our perceptions of reality are in part functions of the terms or "categories" we use in describing our experiences. To explore this point try a little thought experiment. Describe a typical college student as if you were the chairperson of the local chamber of commerce. Tell what is wrong with communism as if you were an archbishop. Explain the reasons for not voting for your conservative opponent as if you were an incumbent liberal. Describe the character of black people as if you were a white racist. The point here is not *what* we say but *how* we say it. We are not after variations in beliefs and attitudes but variations in the way different people conceptualize problems and state the issues. For example, dramatic differences in the way people conceive of things were visible in the recent abortion debates. Some people called an abortion the act of "killing a human person"; others called it the medical "removal of tissue." The old saying that a lot depends on how we define our terms is true. What depends? How we define our terms determines what we are going to say the "facts" are, and, in turn, what ethical and personal decisions we will make on the basis of what we perceive the facts to be.

If so much can depend upon how we define our terms, it would be wise to examine definitions. That is the educational goal of this chapter. First we will determine what a definition is. Then we will ask what makes some definitions good and others poor. Finally we will examine a few of the main kinds of definitions; we will look at how they are put together, what they are supposed to accomplish, and what we can expect their virtues and shortcomings to be.

MODULE 5
WHAT IS A DEFINITION?

Module 5 explains the basic job of a definition: to supply us with a term's meaning. Module 5 also explains how some definitions can be descriptive of a term's meaning while others stipulate a meaning.

● After reading Module 5 you should be able to:

1. Distinguish, through proper punctuation, *using* a word from *mentioning* a word
2. Identify purely descriptive definitions

3. Identify purely stipulative definitions
4. Discriminate between purely descriptive definitions and purely stipulative definitions
5. Pick out from a list the characteristics of a definition
6. Identify definitions that are partially descriptive and partially stipulative
7. Discriminate among (a) purely descriptive, (b) purely stipulative, and (c) partially descriptive and partially stipulative definitions
8. List the chief characteristics of stipulative definitions, descriptive definitions, and conceptual systems
9. Construct examples of both stipulative and descriptive definitions

5:1.1 Definitions give meanings First of all, a definition is used to indicate what a word or phrase signifies. A definition tells us that the word or phrase being defined can be replaced by the expression being used to define it without loss of meaning. That is, whenever we wish, we can substitute the one for the other and there will be no change in the meaning of what we have said. A definition, then, is a linguistic rule permitting one word or phrase to be substituted for another word or phrase while the original meaning is preserved. Thus to say that

Silly = $_{df}$ foolish
Although = $_{df}$ yet
Mason = $_{df}$ bricklayer
Automobile = $_{df}$ car
Manacle = $_{df}$ handcuff
Perfidious = $_{df}$ dangerous, treacherous

is to say that whenever we see the words 'silly' or 'mason' in a sentence we can replace them with 'foolish' or 'bricklayer' respectively without seriously changing what the original sentence means.[1]

5:1.2 Connotation To say that we do not seriously change the meaning when we apply a good definition is not to say that nothing changes. What changes is often the tone or feeling (the 'connotation') of what is said. Note the difference in tone in 'hit the ball, Charley' and 'strike the sphere, Charles.' Or note the change in tone when we substitute 'one of the authors of this book is an Italian' for 'one of the authors of this book is a wop.'

Some words seem to engender certain positive or negative feelings or connotations in certain people, for example, 'commie,' 'fag,' 'bureaucrat,' 'industrious,' 'hippy,' or 'overpopulated.' Notice, for example, the difference in the words 'Betsy is a nut' and 'Elizabeth is insane.' A definition is doing well if it provides either a (rough) synonym for a word or another word which applies to the same things. If it does this, it is guaranteeing that the word it defines is being explained in a way that is sufficient to reproduce its conventional use in assertions and, often, other types of sentences. To expect that a definition will also preserve all the different connotations associated with a word is to expect too much. It is too much because

[1] Our concern is not with meaning in the sense of what did a person mean (or intend) to say but with what a particular word generally or conventionally does mean (or signify) in our common language. We sometimes use the word 'signification' in place of the word 'meaning' in order to avoid confusion on this point.

while the basic meaning of a word remains stable in a given language community, its connotations may vary widely. For example, we all know what a political "liberal" is. But is a liberal a good person or a bad person? To whom?

5:1.3 Use versus mention Everyone knows the difference between naming something and describing it. Everyone, that is, except most two-year-olds like Chris. When you tell Chris he's a good boy he answers, "No I'm not; I'm Christopher." Similarly, but more subtly, there is a difference between defining a word and using it in making a statement. If we say "the sofa needs to be reupholstered," we've made a statement about a sofa. But to say " 'sofa' means 'upholstered lounge furniture' " is to define a word. In this definition we have talked about the word 'sofa,' not the piece of furniture. Keeping in mind the difference between talking about words and using words to talk about things will help us to keep from confusing the definition of a word like 'tautology' with what is said in the text about tautologies. Often we find it necessary in logic and philosophy to *mention* a word and talk specifically about it rather than *using* the word to talk about something else. In this paragraph we have used several words and we have talked about, i.e., mentioned, two: 'sofa' and 'tautology.' In order to avoid confusion, logicians have adopted the convention of putting single quotes around a word when it is being mentioned but not used.

There is not a lot to say about particular words. For example, after we have said that 'love' starts with an 'l,' contains two vowels, and is four letters long, what is left? Well, one very important thing is left—giving an adequate definition of 'love.' To do this well is to do a conceptual analysis; it is to begin to explain what love is, or, if you prefer, what 'love' means.

When you are giving a definition, you mention a word, e.g.,

'Monolith'

and then indicate that it is definitionally equivalent to

'Monolith' = $_{df}$

whatever it means

'Monolith' = $_{df}$ a pillar built of one stone

When definitions are set off from the rest of the text, it is not necessary to use single quotes around the word being defined because no confusion would result from just writing

Monolith = $_{df}$ a pillar built of one stone

But when definitions are incorporated into the text, it is useful to employ the convention of single quotes. Generally a device like single quotes, or some other device for distinguishing the use of a word from mention of a word, is very helpful. Suppose, for example, you were a sign painter and we wrote you a note saying: "Put hyphens between bar and and and and and grill." Our directions would be much clearer if we said "Put hyphens between 'bar' and 'and' and 'and' and 'grill.' "

5:2.1 Description versus stipulation Definitions tell us what words mean. Two extremes are possible in indicating the meaning of a word or term. One can give a purely stipulative definition, or one can give a purely descriptive definition. Of course, since these are the extremes, one can also give definitions which are partially stipulative and partially descriptive.

5:2.2 Stipulative definitions One extreme would be a definition that is a purely stipulative definition. Sometimes we will just *stipulate* that from now on, and for our purposes, a given word is to mean such and such. In a stipulative definition we are setting forth ground rules. We are creating a (new) meaning for a term. Stipulative definitions are very useful when the term being defined is novel, vague, ambiguous, or technical. Stipulative definitions are starting points. They need not have any connection with how the term being defined is ordinarily or commonly used, although, for the sake of ease of communication and relevance of application, it is wise to make your stipulative definitions close to common usage. Often by using a *partially* stipulative definition, you can improve on ordinary discourse. Such will be the case with our definitions of 'valid,' 'correct argument,' 'sound argument,' and 'acceptable argument.' When you encounter a stipulative definition or even one that is only partially stipulative, it is wise to remember that a *meaning is being created*. A *linguistic convention is being set up*; that is, a rule for the future use of a term is being set forth. The way to handle such definitions is to let the word defined mean exactly what the author of the definition says it *shall* mean—nothing more, nothing less.

Here are some examples of purely stipulative definitions:

Xerronic = $_{df}$ color of the moon in early evening
Automobile = $_{df}$ a highly skilled craftsman
Duck = $_{df}$ large-hoofed mammal with three eyes
Blunko = $_{df}$ one who writes a book on fishing and bridge
Yes = $_{df}$ to deny or to disagree
Fast = $_{df}$ to lift a light load

These definitions obviously have no connection with how people really talk, but that does not prevent someone from trying to amend our ways of talking by proposing that we adopt these stipulative definitions.

As suggested above, stipulative definitions are useful in setting out clear meanings for technical terms or for amending our ordinary ways of speaking. But stipulative definitions can also be problematic. If we decide to use a familiar word in an unusual way, we risk causing misunderstandings. For example, if a geologist decides to use the word 'atom' to refer to large bodies of water, the statement "atoms are blue" would certainly mislead anyone who had not been advised of the geologist's novel usage. Stipulative definitions can also stymie debate; this often occurs when they are used to brand certain ideologies or ideas. In 1975 the United Nations voted on a definition of 'Zionism' which said that Zionism was a variety of racism. This vote was intended to cut off debate over the political, religious, or nationalistic aspects of the Zionist movement. The debate over whether or not Zionism contains a racist component was cut short by the stipulative definition. Instead of carefully examining and evaluating its merits, those who branded Zionism as racism effectively used that definition to discredit the movement.

Stipulative definitions also can take on a prescriptive use. For example, consider the wide variety of ways that there are to get people to come to believe certain things. These ways range from lies and deceptions, to indoctrination and instruction, all the way to teaching not only facts but also how to verify them. Debates exist over which methods should properly be employed in schools. Should schools, for example, indoctrinate or instruct? But since these terms are vague, those involved in the debate often begin by setting out their stipulative definitions of 'education,' 'teaching,' and the like. On the basis of some of these definitions political or religious education is commendable instruction, on others it is unacceptable indoctrination. The stipulative definitions of these terms are being used to prescribe which methods and even which topics should be taught. These prescriptive purposes of telling someone what and how to teach are in part concealed by the deliberate use of definitions which lend credibility where an explicit prescription like "do this" or "do it this way" would stir discussion and reveal that the issue of what distinguishes instruction from indoctrination has not been rationally decided.

5:2.3 Descriptive definitions At the other extreme from stipulative definitions lie purely *descriptive definitions*. In presenting a descriptive definition one tries to capture *an ordinary usage* of a term or word. The better examples of these kinds of definitions are found in good dictionaries. The *Oxford English Dictionary,* for example, spends over four pages defining the word 'mean' so as to capture all of its many different meanings. Since a large number of words have more than one precise meaning, it often happens that a more complete descriptive definition of a term will specify several of its conventional meanings. Descriptive definitions are to be taken as reports of how people talk, not as suggestions to improve, amend, or reform language. Here are some examples of purely descriptive definitions drawn from *Webster's Third New International Dictionary:*[2]

> Linchpin = $_{df}$ . . . a pin inserted in an axletree outside of the wheel to prevent the latter from slipping off . . .
> Eutocia = $_{df}$ . . . normal parturition . . .
> Citron yellow = $_{df}$ . . . a variable color averaging a moderate greenish yellow that is redder, stronger, and slightly lighter than linden green and redder, lighter, and stronger than Javel green or oil yellow . . .

A dictionary is a catalog or inventory of the words in a given language with each of the ordinary meanings of each word specified in descriptive definitions. Unless the dictionary is the type used in translation from one language to another (like *Cassell's New Latin Dictionary: Latin-English; English-Latin*) it is probably one that specifies the meanings of each term by using other words in the same language. In a sense each natural language is a very extensive, subtle, and yet powerful closed system of interconnected meanings. If you know a language even a little, you can often make good use of a dictionary to increase your vocabulary and facility in the language; but if you don't know it at all, the dictionary is of no help because to learn what any words mean you have to know what others mean.

Descriptive definitions are used chiefly when a greater sophistication with a language is required. In schools great emphasis is placed on accurate descriptive definitions so that children can become better users of language and thus better able to communicate with others, to express their own ideas, and to understand other people. In legal studies the precise meaning of a term can also be crucial. In the courts and legislatures people often rely on descriptive definitions in order to understand the limits of one's responsibilities or liabilities. In such cases, though, purely

---

[2] By permission, from *Webster's Third New International Dictionary* © 1971 by G. & C. Merriam Co., Publishers of the Merriam-Webster Dictionaries.

descriptive definitions are treated only as the starting points. Often there is need to refine the meanings of terms through laws and precedent-setting court decisions. Thus certain key words like 'property,' 'remedy,' 'dependent,' 'depreciation,' etc., acquire definitions in a given legal system that are partially descriptive and yet partially stipulative. The same occurs with words like 'stress,' 'organ,' 'digestion,' 'hypertension,' 'elimination,' etc., in medicine. In fields like law and medicine the need for greater linguistic precision has led to stipulative refinements in the meanings of words. These, in turn, become the conventional meanings of those terms in those fields. Thus, a legal or medical dictionary will give descriptive definitions of legal or medical terms which describe the legal or medical uses of those terms. These definitions include stipulative refinements which add precision to the meanings of these terms. Thus the same word may have a more precise technical meaning in law or medicine than it has in its more ordinary use by the public at large.

5:3 Conceptual systems Our purpose in this text is to set up a definitional system in which to carry on an intellectual study, logic. Our conceptual system, like those created for the legal or medical establishments, will require us to refine some of the ordinary meanings of terms. Purely descriptive definitions in ordinary use will be ill-advised, except as starting points, because we require greater precision. Although purely descriptive definitions make it easier for someone outside the field to understand what we are saying, they introduce vagueness and ambiguity into the system. On the other hand, stipulative definitions, which can lend the needed prècision, tend to be jargon; they can become too narrow or too arbitrary. Our definitions, like those in law or medicine, will have to combine descriptive accuracy with stipulated refinements. We will have to introduce definitions that are partially descriptive and partially stipulative.

When setting up a definitional system we are, in effect, creating a special, more technical language suited to a particular purpose. We take certain basic concepts central to that purpose and offer redefinitions of their meanings. We are creating a conceptual system, an integrated set of ideas. This systematic set of redefinitions must have certain theoretical qualities. First of all, our conceptual system must be *consistent*; i.e., definitions in one part of the system must not contradict definitions in another part. For example, it cannot be the case that in one definition a given argument is called logically correct while in another the same argument is said to be logically incorrect. Second, the conceptual system should be *complete* in the sense that all the basic concepts of logic are given definitions in the system. We cannot, for example, fail to specify a definition for important terms such as 'fallacy' or 'proof,' although we may defer giving the definitions for a while. Third, our conceptual system must be *applicable* in the sense that there must be ways of applying the definitions and actually diagnosing certain logical flaws or recognizing logical virtues in arguments. For example, our definition of 'valid' must be able to be used, perhaps with some supplementary definitions, assumptions, and techniques, so that we can actually decide whether a given argument is valid or not. In dictionaries of natural languages we do not necessarily look for consistency, completeness, or applicability. Many words in ordinary use are vague or ambiguous, and descriptive definitions of them will reflect these characteristics. In this sense a dictionary is merely a list of definitions as opposed to a system of definitions. Our aim is systematicity. We will have to adjust and fine-tune our definitions so that we achieve consistency, completeness, and applicability. We will have to try to rule out vagueness because it tends to work against our goal of applicability; we will have to stipulate away ambiguities because they introduce potential inconsistency.

We are setting up a network of definitions which will relate terms like 'argument,' 'fallacy,' 'deductive,' and 'valid,' one to another. Our system will reflect common usage to a fair extent, so that our definitions can be understood. Yet our system will stipulate certain limitations on the use of particular words so that certain confusions rooted in the ambiguities of ordinary usage can be prevented from infecting our system. By following this definitional procedure, we will be able to show how logicians approach, understand, and use these terms. To illustrate our procedure, reconsider the definition of an argument we have offered:

> Argument = $_{df}$ a set of assertive sentences one of which is purported to be implied, entailed, strongly supported, or strongly warranted by the others

This definition described one of the ordinary meanings of 'argument,' but it stipulated refinements in that meaning, and it stipulated exclusions too. From now on, for instance, quarrels are not to be counted in what we shall mean by 'argument.' This definition is a partially stipulative and partially descriptive definition.

In this book we hope to set forth the key concepts of the field of logic because, quite obviously, that is important in an introduction to logic. But we also hope that the way these concepts are set forth will exemplify something else—a logical and reasonable approach to setting up a conceptual system that is precise and yet not esoteric or too far from normal usage. To do this we will provide definitions which are partially stipulative and partially descriptive.

5:4 In order to tell purely descriptive definitions and purely stipulative definitions apart from each other and from definitions that are partially stipulative and partially descriptive, use these rules of thumb. If a definition designates the standard meanings of a term, it is descriptive. If it incorporates at least one element into a term's meaning that is not part of its standard meaning, it is stipulative. This can be done either by (1) narrowing or restricting the standard meaning. (2) expanding or augmenting a standard meaning, or (3) designating a meaning totally different from any of a term's standard meanings. A definition which both designates at least one of the standard meanings of a term and amends that meaning in some way is a definition that is partially stipulative and partially descriptive.

EXERCISES FOR MODULE 5
WHAT IS A DEFINITION?

Ex. 1 There are six sentences below. If any word in a sentence is merely mentioned, not used, put 'M' in the answer space; otherwise put 'no.'

_____ 1. 'Great' is a five-letter word.

_____ 2. 'Short' is longer than 'long' but shorter than 'longer.'

_____ 3. "Stop! Stop!," I say. "Stop, sir!"

_____ 4. When can we see the *results*? I'm tired of hearing you babble on about your *expectations*.

_____ 5. Let me suggest that this is not what you *are* doing. It is what you *might* be doing.

_____ 6. "Long, Long Ago" is a song that was written long, long ago.

Ex. 2 In each of the six sentences below, a word or words are intended to be mentioned, not used. Place single quotes around these words.

1. The words on the sign are Bob's and and and Judy's.
2. If is the shortest word I know.
3. The definition of monk is a man who leaves the world to join a religious community.
4. When will we ever see a word like reased again?
5. The minimum number of members of a committee who can legally transact that committee's business is called a quorum.
6. Whiskey and soda is composed of whiskey and and and soda, unlike whiskey and soda, which is a drink.

Ex. 3 Here are four passages. If a passage contains a purely descriptive definition put 'desc' in the answer space; otherwise put 'no.' If you are unsure of a term's conventional meaning, consult a good dictionary.

_____ 1. Everyone who loves people knows that people can disappoint you every once in a while.

_____ 2. Every definition is either stipulative, descriptive, or some combination that makes it partially both.

_____ 3. Every once in a while I have to remind myself that 'esoteric' means private.

_____ 4. Everything which is esoteric is private.

Ex. 4 Here are four passages. If a passage contains a purely stipulative definition put 'stip' in the answer space; otherwise put 'no.'

_____ 1. Everything that is private is esoteric.

_____ 2. The professor announced today that the exam day would be Friday.

_____ 3. The professor announced today that when he said 'quiz' he meant a four-hour essay-type exam.

_____ 4. 'Conclusion' means that part of the upper nose used to support one's glasses.

Ex. 5 Here are six definitions. If a definition is (rather) purely descriptive, put 'desc' in the answer space; if it is (rather) purely stipulative, put 'stip' in the answer space; if it is a mixture of both, put 'mix.'

_____ 1. 'Rabbi' means a man who is a Jewish teacher or interpreter of the law.

_____ 2. 'Quintuplet' means a set of five items.

_____ 3. 'Triangle' means a four-sided closed plain figure.

_____ 4. 'Triangle' means a small animal commonly called a bed bug.

_____ 5. 'Triangle' means a three-sided closed rectilinear plain figure.

_____ 6. 'Quicksand' means an item used in soup to add beef flavor.

Ex. 6 In a few sentences answer each of these questions.

1. What are stipulative definitions? How are they used? What are some of the potential problems their use causes?
2. What are descriptive definitions? How are they used? What are some of the problems their use causes?

3. What is a conceptual system? What three goals are sought in setting up a good conceptual definition? What alteration to purely description or purely stipulation definitions will it use? Why?

Ex. 7 Write out purely descriptive and purely stipulative definitions of each of the following words:

1. Pine   2. Area   3. Condition   4. Death   5. Reasonable

SELECTED ANSWERS
TO EXERCISES FOR MODULE 5

Ex. 1

1. M, 'great'   2. M, 'short,' 'long,' 'longer'   3. No   4. No   5. No
6. No, the song title is being *used* to talk about the song itself.
If you missed more than one, review 5:1.3.

Ex. 2

1. The words on the sign are 'Bob's' and 'and' and 'Judy's.'
2. 'If' is the shortest word I know.
3. The definition of 'monk' is a person who leaves the world to join a religious community.
4. When will we ever see a word like 'reased' again?
5. The minimum number of members of a committee who can legally transact that committee's business is called a 'quorum.'
6. 'Whiskey and soda' is composed of 'whiskey' and 'and' and 'soda,' unlike whiskey and soda, which is a drink.
If you missed more than one, review 5:1.3

Ex. 3

1. No
2. No; there is no definition given here; this is merely a statement.
3. Desc
4. No

Ex. 4

1. No   2. No   3. Stip   4. Stip
If you missed any in Ex. 3, review 5:2.3; if you missed any in Ex. 4, review 5:2.2.

Ex. 6

1. Check 5:2.2 for details. Among other things, you should have mentioned that stipulative definitions create meanings for terms. They are used to remove vagueness and ambiguity and to achieve technical precision. They can become problematic if they are used to cut off debate or conceal prescriptive purposes. Also they may lead to misunderstanding if familiar terms are given highly unusual or novel meanings.
2. Check 5:2.3 for details. You should at least have said that a descriptive definition is one that attempts to capture the ordinary meaning or conventional use of a word. They are used in dictionaries. They are used to help others learn more

about a given language, to increase vocabulary, to aid in improving one's ability to communicate. They can be problematic because they capture the vagueness and ambiguities of natural language, which, in turn, can lead to lack of precision.

3. Check 5:3 for details. You should have said at least that conceptual systems are networks of definitions, partially descriptive and partially stipulative; that they attempt to organize a set of ideas which are central to a given purpose like law, medicine, or logic. They strive for consistency, completeness, and applicability. They stipulate meanings necessary to achieve precision; they use descriptive definitions to preserve initial understanding.

Ex. 7 Check your descriptive definitions against a good dictionary. The closer yours are to the dictionary definitions, the more descriptively accurate they are. Your stipulative definitions, on the other hand, should be quite different from the dictionary definitions of those terms.

MODULE 6

VIRTUES AND VICES OF DEFINITIONS

Sometimes the ways people use words hinder effective communication. Definitions can be used to improve communication. There are many kinds of definition, each designed to expedite some aspect of communication.

● After reading Module 6 you should be able to:

1. Identify and distinguish those characteristics of a word, phrase, or passage (vagueness and ambiguity) which hinder effective communication
2. Identify the characteristics of (a) narrow definitions, (b) arbitrary definitions, and (c) loaded definitions
3. Identify those characteristics of definitions which help rectify ambiguity
4. Identify those characteristics of definitions which help rectify vagueness
5. Identify and list the reasons why narrow, loaded, or arbitrary definitions are problematic
6. Identify the virtues and vices of both descriptive and stipulative definitions
7. Distinguish among narrow, arbitrary, and loaded definitions
8. Construct examples of narrow definitions, arbitrary definitions, and loaded definitions along with explanations of how the examples are narrow, arbitrary, or loaded

6:1.1 Conceptual flaws In 5:3 we suggested that one virtue of a descriptive definition is that it facilitates communication because it links us to the way people actually use their words. But we also said that incorporating descriptive definitions into a conceptual system can cause trouble because ordinary usage is often vague or ambiguous. Obviously definitions that are vague or ambiguous can create a good deal of confusion in any conceptual system that proposes to be a consistent, tightly worked network of closely related but different ideas.

6:1.2 Ambiguity Here is the definition of 'ambiguous': a word is ambiguous if, and only if, it has more than one specific meaning. The words 'duck' and 'love' are ambiguous, for example. 'Duck' can be used to refer to a kind of bird, or it can be a verb which means to quickly assume a bent down or lower posture. 'Love' can be used to refer to a certain emotion, or it can refer to the score in a tennis game or match.

Almost every word in our language is, according to the above definition, ambiguous. But the situation is really quite tolerable because we seldom examine the meaning of a word independent of a particular use of the word. People use words at particular times in particular places with specifiable intentions and discoverable purposes. Further, words are not usually spoken in isolation but are incorporated into sentences, which in turn are parts of texts or conversations. Therefore there are a host of clues and conventions available to language users which generally make it clear which of the possibly many meanings of a word is being relied upon on any given occasion of the use of that word. We can say, then, that the words of our language are *tolerably ambiguous* as long as any ambiguity is resolved by its use in a given context. When at a tennis game someone says "It's love fifteen," everyone familiar with the ambiguities of the word 'love' and the rules of tennis realizes that the speaker is not talking about an emotion of affection, a new European porno movie, or anything but the score of the game. But even if it were not clear what 'love' meant on that particular occasion, one could always ask what it meant. Thus, the ambiguity is tolerable.

However, there are occasions when all the clues and conventions fail us. In these circumstances it is possible for a *particular use* of a term to be *viciously ambiguous*. A particular use of a term is viciously ambiguous if, and only if, it could have more than one standard meaning in that use. For example, consider the term 'duck' in "I saw her duck" or the term 'wrong' in "That's wrong." Here, does 'wrong' mean illegal, immoral, ill-advised, or just mistaken? We cannot tell. So that particular occasion of its use is viciously ambiguous. Similarly, when the President's press secretary says "We find that action would be contrary to the interests of the government." it is often viciously ambiguous whether 'government' means 'administration' or 'country,' and whether the interests are ones of decorum, security, or image. If someone says "I do not understand her meaning in that remark she made," 'meaning' is viciously ambiguous because we cannot tell whether 'meaning' refers to the ordinary meaning of the words she used or her intention (meaning) in using them.

Vicious ambiguity also infects arguments, a theme we develop in Module 29. It is often quite easy to tell which of the several meanings of an ambiguous term is the relevant one when the term is actually being used. However, at times the ambiguities of a term are very subtle. In such cases it takes "a good ear," a bit of practice, knowledge of how language is used and the conventions that govern particular linguistic practices, and some philosophical ability to draw out the distinctions and make the ambiguity known. Here are some more examples of (tolerably) ambiguous terms.

Jar, meaning "bottle" or "bump"
Line, meaning "to cover the inside of something" or "narrow strip"
Fast, meaning "quickly" or "religious diet"
Desirable, meaning "actually is desired" or "is worthy of desire"

6:1.3 Vagueness We know a word is *vague* if its meaning is not clear. But let's try to refine this idea of vagueness. Certain words, like nouns, verbs, and adjectives (but not articles, prepositions, or adverbs), can be called *class terms*. They are used to refer to a class of individuals. For example 'duck' can be used to refer to all ducks as in "A duck is a small bird." Or yellow can be used to refer to a group of things as in "Find me all the bowls that are yellow." Verbs too can be used to point to a class of objects as in "Ducks fly" meaning "All things that are ducks are things that fly." The class of objects that words like these can be said to *refer* to is called the *reference class* of the word. Logicians also call a word's reference class its *extension*. There are many ways to designate a reference class. We normally specify extension by using certain phrases. Suppose we wanted to name the extension of the novel word 'blonk.' If 'blonk' were a noun, we could say:

> Blonks
> All the blonks
> The class blonks
> The class of blonks
> Things that are blonks

If 'blonk' were a verb, we could say

> Anything that blonks
> Blonkers
> Things that blonk
> Blonking things

If 'blonk' were an adjective, we could say

> Anything which has the property blonk
> Anything with blonkness
> Whatever 'blonk' applies to
> Things that are blonk

Sometimes when a word is defined or used on a particular occasion, its extension remains unclear in the sense that it is not always obvious whether or not something belongs in that extension. Suppose, for example, we define 'people' as "all human beings." We understand, now, what 'people' means, but we still may not be sure whether a human infant is a person or if a human fetus is a person or if a human embryo is a person. You may say "You have to draw the line someplace," and what that means is that we have to indicate more precisely the limits of the extension of the term in question.

Now we can define 'vague.' Let us say that a term is vague if its extension is imprecisely defined or delimited. In other words, a term is vague when the boundaries or limits of its reference class are not set forth clearly. This is often true of general terms like:

justice	easy	wealth
love	abstract	pain
openness	lofty	involve
happiness	heavy	slim
evil	dark	speedy
value	pleasant	participate
bright	dirty	wise

A person can know what they signify but still have some trouble identifying hard borderline cases. These terms are vague terms, even though they may not be ambiguous. At times a certain amount of vagueness can not only be tolerated, it can even be an asset. It would not really be very well advised for us to try to define perfectly 'art' or 'music.' But on many occasions a vague term can cause problems. In discussions about organ transplants the vagueness of terms like 'life,' 'death,' and 'human being' has caused considerable trouble. When exactly, for example, is a person observably *dead?*

6:1.4 Words are not the only things that can be called ambiguous or vague. Sentences and particular uses of a given sentence too can suffer from one or both maladies. Sentences that have *more than one* literal meaning are *ambiguous.* Sometimes it is tolerable, even funny; at other times it is vicious and potentially very confusing. Sentences which do *not* have a *clear* or *carefully delineated* meaning are *vague.* Usually vagueness in a sentence results from the use of vague words or phrases; similarly, ambiguity in a sentence can result from the ambiguous uses of words or phrases. Sometimes ambiguity can result from taking things out of context or from misplaced modifiers. Here are some examples of ambiguous sentences.

> The secretary delivered the speech.
> Our mothers bore us.
> He saw her duck.
> She saw her son on the television set.
> John is walking to the bank.
> Mary is going to see her father.
> The headmaster stood quietly on the porch and watched fireworks go off in his pajamas.
> She loved her dusty red car.

Here are some vague sentences, sentences which make you want to ask: What precisely does that mean?

> Everyone is a philosopher.
> High crimes and misdemeanors are impeachable offenses.
> John is quite tall but not so slim as he would like to be.
> Brenda is industrious for her age.
> That's immoral and inhuman.
> Nothing can truly know itself better than any subject can comprehend Being.

6:2.1 Using stipulative definitions We suggested in 5:2.2 that stipulative definitions were useful in removing vagueness and ambiguity. If the term being defined is ambiguous, a person can stipulate which meaning is of interest. If a term is vague, a person can stipulate more carefully the precise limits of its reference class. But stipulative definitions also have drawbacks. They can be too narrow or too arbitrary. If a stipulative definition circumscribes a term's reference class so as to exclude things that are clearly part of that reference class, it has drawn its limits too narrowly. If a definition stipulates a meaning for a term which has nothing to do with any of the term's ordinary meanings, it is an arbitrary definition. Let us examine each drawback more closely.

6:2.2 Narrow definitions Consider all the things that are games. There are card games, ball games, games of chance, sports, games to play alone, games to play with others, kids' games, adult games, party games, etc. If we chose to limit the extension of 'game' to card games, we would be stipulating a definition that is too narrow. We can define a narrow definition as follows: a *narrow definition* is one that specifies a part, but not all, of the term's reference class. From all the different kinds of games mentioned it is clear that the idea of a game is vague. But in an effort to rectify vagueness we would have erred in the other direction. A narrow definition may actually mislead someone because it fails to give the full range of a term's reference class. Here are more examples of narrow stipulative definitions:

Bird = $_{df}$ turkey
Color = $_{df}$ red, yellow, and orange
Automobile = $_{df}$ car produced by the Ford Motor Company
Congressperson = $_{df}$ member of the United States Senate

6:2.3 Loaded definitions Sometimes people deliberately present narrow definitions. Often they are useful to help focus attention. On the other hand, they are often used less honorably. If a person presents a deliberately narrow definition in order to fore-close debate on an issue, the person can be accused of the dishonorable practice of using "loaded" definitions. For example, in order to avoid discussing whether there is any continuing impact to the energy crisis, a person might say:

EG. 6.1 Obviously the energy crisis is over. 'Energy crisis' means standing in line for gas.

Similarly, in order to avoid the professional embarrassment of recognizing that someone who does not have a Ph.D. in philosophy might still be a significant philosopher, one could say,

EG. 6.2 Well, to be a philosopher means to work in a college or university and to hold an earned Ph.D. degree in philosophy from an accredited university.

Loaded definitions are unfair because they deliberately prejudice factual and ethical issues. In the two examples above factual issues were prejudiced. Here is an example in which an ethical question is undercut.

EG. 6.3 Suppose we say that the definition of 'war' is "the unjust state of armed belligerence between communities, states, or nations."

Given such a definition, an ethical question like: "Is there such a thing as a just war?" must always be answered no. The problem is not that the question is silly but that the definition of 'war' is loaded and unfair; it prevents the question from being asked.

The temptation exists to dismiss these issues as "merely semantic" problems. Such a move is mistaken, however. It is a failure to see the significance of how persons define crucial terms. It is a failure to see what conclusions (both factual and ethical) follow from our definitions. The issues are semantic in the sense that they are about how we shall talk. But how we decide to talk can have serious ramifications, as 5:2.2 and Egs. 6.1 and 6.3 suggest.

6:2.4 Arbitrary definitions A stipulative definition that selects as the meaning of a term something that is totally different from any of its conventional or ordinary meanings is an arbitrary definition. Thus we can define an *arbitrary* definition as follows: a definition is arbitrary if it specifies none of the correct or common meanings of a word. Here are some ambiguous words

Chair, meaning "thing used to sit on" or "to direct a committee"

Table, meaning "thing used to work on" or "to suspend debate on a motion"

These can be defined descriptively, but their ambiguity would remain. We could stipulate that we wished to use them to mean "thing used to sit on" and "thing used to work on," and all would be well. And very probably on most occasions their ambiguity is no problem at all. But if we arbitrarily stipulated meanings like "thing used to apply paint" and "thing which covers a building," we would stand accusable of being unsuitably arbitrary or capricious. An arbitrary definition does not yield any part of a term's correct reference class because it misses the term's whole meaning. Thus, an arbitrary definition differs from a narrow definition; narrow definitions do not totally miss a term's meaning, but focus on too small a part of that meaning.

When people give arbitrary definitions, they seriously undermine language in two ways: (1) they create more ambiguity and confusion with regard to the original words, and (2) they lose the subtlety and variety that could be maintained if the *correct* words were used instead of the arbitrarily defined words. Thus we should use 'brush' and 'roof' instead of 'chair' and 'table' when we mean "thing used to apply paint" and "thing which covers a building." People who speak loosely or use arbitrarily defined words run the serious risk of failing to communicate with the rest of us who have not been let in on their jargon.

Even when you are interested in finding a word to fit a new idea, you can avoid using arbitrary definitions. It is always possible to make up a word like 'lunkook' or 'plufoger' to use as the word which will signify your new idea. This is usually wiser too than taking an existing word and amplifying its ambiguity by arbitrarily defining it a new way.

6:3 All definitions fall somewhere on the *continuum between purely stipulative and purely descriptive* definitions. The virtues of stipulative definitions are that they correct ambiguity and vagueness, which are vices of descriptive definitions. The virtues of descriptive definitions are that they guard against the narrowness and arbitrariness that can infest stipulative definitions. The ideal is somewhere in the middle. If you are building a conceptual system, you would like to be able to devise definitions that are neither narrow nor vague, neither ambiguous nor arbitrary. To do this, they will have to be partly descriptive and partly stipulative.

EXERCISES FOR MODULE 6
VIRTUES AND VICES OF DEFINITIONS

Ex. 1 Five terms are given below. After each some alternative definitions are provided. Rank these in order of narrowness, least narrow first and most narrow last.

1. Instrument = $_{df}$ _____ _____ _____
   A. Any item used as a tool to achieve some end
   B. A device used to produce music
   C. Either a drum or a piano or a horn

2. Furniture $-$ $_{df}$ _____ _____ _____ _____ _____
   A. Chairs and sofas
   B. Domestic items used to sit on, sleep on, store goods in
   C. Items used to sit on, sleep on, store goods in, or work on

D. Domestic items used to sit on or store goods in
E. Chairs

3. Transportation = $_{df}$ _____ _____ _____ _____ _____
   A. Bicycles
   B. Cars and bicycles
   C. Any item used to move people or goods over land
   D. Any item used to move people or goods over land or through air
   E. Any item used to move people or goods

4. Human beings = $_{df}$ _____ _____ _____ _____
   A. Boys and girls
   B. Adult males and children
   C. Adult males, adult females, and children
   D. All human persons

5. Aggression = $_{df}$ _____ _____ _____ _____
   A. One person's unprovoked attack on another person
   B. A person or group's unprovoked attack on another person or group
   C. A person or group's unprovoked attack on another person
   D. Any unprovoked attack upon a person or group or nation

Ex. 2 Below are five descriptive definitions. Each is problematic because either it makes ambiguities explicit without resolving them or it is vague. If a definition is ambiguous, put 'amb' in the answer space. If vague, put 'vag' in the answer space. If both, put 'both' in the answer space.

_____ 1. Love = $_{df}$ a strong emotional attachment

_____ 2. Logic = $_{df}$ the study of the relationship of the premises and the conclusions of arguments; a set of beliefs, attitudes, prejudices, centrally important issues, and terminology common to a specific group of people

_____ 3. Mean = $_{df}$ to intend, to refer

_____ 4. Class = $_{df}$ any collection or set of individuals, a scheduled school session at which an instructor lectures to students

_____ 5. Abstract = $_{df}$ difficult to comprehend, lacking concreteness, general or theoretical in nature

Ex. 3 Below are five stipulative definitions. Each is problematic in that it is narrow or arbitrary. If it is only narrow, put 'nar' in the answer space. If it is arbitrary, put 'arb' in the answer space.

_____ 1. Blues = $_{df}$ a set of feelings associated with sadness or melancholy

_____ 2. Freedom = $_{df}$ that characteristic of machines whereby they are said to be charged with positive electrical force

_____ 3. Happiness = $_{df}$ that feeling which can be achieved only by the possession of a friendly young canine

_____ 4. Beaver = $_{df}$ the study of the relationships between the premises and conclusions of arguments

_____ 5. Logic = $_{df}$ the study of logically correct arguments

Ex. 4 Below are five words. Under each a pair of possible definitions are offered. In each case identify the *better* of the two definitions after having examined both for vagueness, narrowness, ambiguity, and arbitrariness. State the reason why the other number is rejected.

Answer	Reason for rejection	
_____	_____	1. Frontage A = $_{df}$ that part of a piece of real estate that borders on a lake or street B = $_{df}$ a boundary of a piece of real estate
_____	_____	2. Label A = $_{df}$ a slip of paper or cloth attached to something for purposes of identification; to label or mark for identification, to designate B = $_{df}$ a slip of paper or cloth attached to something for purposes of identification
_____	_____	3. Landlubber A = $_{df}$ one who paints landings B = $_{df}$ one who is not a sailor
_____	_____	4. Pinch A = $_{df}$ to squeeze B = $_{df}$ to squeeze; to arrest
_____	_____	5. Picnic A = $_{df}$ trip or outing at which previously prepared food is served; a vacation; a junket; a tour; to travel B = $_{df}$ trip or outing to a lake at which previously prepared food is served

Ex. 5 Here is a list of statements. If one is true, mark "T" in the answer space; otherwise, mark 'F.'

_____ 1. All definitions are descriptive or stipulative or some mixture of both.

_____ 2. The problems with stipulative definitions are narrowness and vagueness.

_____ 3. Arbitrary definitions are necessarily narrow as well.

_____ 4. Ambiguity can be overcome by stipulative definitions.

_____ 5. Descriptive definitions are infected with the dangers of vagueness and ambiguity.

_____ 6. Loaded definitions are kinds of arbitrary definitions.

_____ 7. A word is ambiguous if and only if it has more than one specific meaning.

_____ 8. A word is vague if and only if its reference class is not clearly delineated.

_____ 9. A word's extension is the class of objects to which it refers.

_____ 10. A word is defined narrowly if the definition captures part but not all of its reference class.

Ex. 6 Briefly answer the following questions.

1. Why are narrow definitions problematic?
2. Why are loaded definitions problematic?
3. Why are arbitrary definitions problematic?

Ex. 7 Supply example definitions and explanations as indicated.

1. Give narrow definitions of the following terms: 'medical personnel,' 'wise person,' and 'racist.' Explain why each of your example definitions is narrow.
2. Give loaded definitions of each of the following: 'death,' 'professional ethics,' and 'democracy.' Explain why each of your example definitions is loaded.
3. Give arbitrary definitions of each of the following: 'radio,' 'game,' and 'slim.' Explain why each of your example definitions is arbitrary.

SELECTED ANSWERS
TO EXERCISES FOR MODULE 6

Ex. 2

1. Vag   2. Both (second meaning vague)   3. Amb
4. Amb   5. Both

If you missed more than one, review 6:12 and 6:13.

Ex. 3

1. Nar   2. Arb   3. Nar   4. Arb   5. Nar

If you missed more than one, review 6:2.2 and 6:2.4.

Ex. 6

1. See 6:2.2. Narrow definitions may mislead because they do not supply a full picture of the extension of a term.
2. See 6:2.3. Loaded definitions close off crucial ethical or factual questions before they can be examined.
3. See 6:2.4. Arbitrary definitions may increase ambiguity, confuse an audience, and greatly hinder effective communication.

Ex. 7

1. By appeal to a dictionary definitions you should be able to show which part of a term's reference class your definitions fail to cover (see 6:2.2).
2. You should be able to state a factual or ethical question that, given your definition, cannot be raised (see 6:2.3).
3. By appeal to a dictionary definition you should be able to demonstrate that no part of the conventional extension of a term is given in your arbitrary definition (see 6:2.4).

MODULE 7
SOME MAIN KINDS OF DEFINITIONS

Definitions range between stipulative and descriptive, depending upon the aims of their authors. Covering this range are a number of other possible kinds of definitions, each more or less suited to specific intellectual aims. We can distinguish among some of the commoner kinds of definitions and supply background for the kinds of definitions we use in this book by distinguishing among those intellectual aims.

● After reading Module 7 you should be able to:

1. Identify extensional definitions
2. Identify intensional definitions
3. Discriminate between extensional and intensional definitions
4. Identify recursive definitions and operational functions
5. Distinguish between recursive and operational definitions
6. Pick out from a given list of characteristics those which are characteristic of (a) recursive definitions, (b) operational definitions, (c) extensional definitions, and (d) intensional definitions
7. State the chief purposes of both extensional and intensional definitions
8. Give examples of recursive, operational, intensional, and extensional definitions

7:1.1 Extension and intension When supplying the definition of a word, we often have the choice of providing words with (roughly) synonymous meanings or speci-fying the word's extension (its reference class). The latter process derives its name from the fact that such definitions are specifications of a word's extension, and so are called extensional definitions. The word that logicians use to talk about the *sense*, basic idea, or concept which is essential or central to the meaning of a word is 'intension.' Thus we can define two kinds of definitions: An *extensional definition* is one that aims primarily at specifying a word's reference class or extension. An *intensional definition* is one that aims at specifying the sense, central idea, or intension essential to the meaning of a word. Here are examples of intensional definitions:

EG. 7.1 Person = $_{df}$ being capable of self-conscious thought, choice, and communal life-style

EG. 7.2 Good student = $_{df}$ student who studies hard and masters objectives

EG. 7.3 Cheerful color = $_{df}$ color that is culturally associated with joy or happiness

In contrast, here are examples of extensional definitions of the same terms:

EG. 7.4 Person = $_{df}$ that class of two-legged animals which inhabit earth and have no feathers

EG. 7.5 Good student = $_{df}$ student with a B+ or better average grade

EG. 7.6 Cheerful color = $_{df}$ the colors white, yellow, orange, and red

7:1.2 Intensional definitions Intensional definitions are the most useful kinds of definitions for coming to understand what a word means. Since they aim at giving the essential idea or basic sense of a word, they are used to deal with matters in a more theoretical and abstract way. As a by-product they will also allow you to deter-mine the extension of a word. Why? Because once you know what a word means, you can often find out the kinds of specific things that it refers or applies to. Because extensions can be derived from intensions, when there are debates over the precise extension of a word, it is the intensional definition that people appeal to for clarifi-cation. Thus, if we are not sure whether or not a particular thing is part of the reference class of 'art,' we will ask ourselves what 'art' means (what its intensional definition is) in order to make a first step toward a solution. Examples 7.4 to 7.6 illustrate this point; the items named in the extensions of 'person,' 'good student,' and 'cheerful color' have been selected because of intensional definitions of each of the three terms as given in Egs. 7.1 to 7.3. In this way we can say that for nouns, verbs, and adjectives "intension determines extension." What is central to the meaning of a word determines what a word will apply or refer to. Nevertheless, intensional definitions are usually abstract, theoretical, and somewhat vague because their primary concern is with setting out ideas, not with delineating reference classes. When people wish to give descriptive definitions, they generally use intensional definitions because for most nontheoretical purposes intensional definitions present the sense, or meaning, of a word.

7:1.3 Family resemblance One way of stating some traditional philosophical concerns is to ask questions like: What is the nature of man? What is the good? What is truth? This way of posing questions suggests that there is something, "the nature of man," which is essential to being a member of the human race. The questions suggest that there is something called goodness and something called truth that can be discovered by patient, careful searching and analysis. Recent philosophical developments have shifted attention away from a search for "essences" and "natures." Philosophers now are more concerned with examining concepts, meanings, and ideas. The traditional problems have been recast by many philosophers as questions about words: What does 'person,' 'good,' or 'true' mean?

One assumption crucial to the traditional search for essences or natures is that there is some single characteristic or set of properties by virtue of which things are called human, good, or true. But when this assumption has been examined, it has turned out to be false in many cases. There is no particular characteristic that seems to be the core, essential, or crucially defining characteristic of things called games or those called useful or those called interesting (except perhaps that they are classified in those ways). There seem to be many nouns, verbs, and adjectives that have meanings and reference classes, but there is no consensus concerning their essential properties. Recall our discussion concerning the definition of 'game' in 6:2.2. Our problem, at least in part, was that it is very hard, if not impossible, to find those characteristics of games that are (1) common to all games, (2) peculiar only to games, and (3) important enough to call essential to the idea of a game. Yet we know that there are plenty of similarities among types of games. Philosophers of language call this trait of games *family resemblance*. Like the members of a family, games are both similar and different. People who note this family resemblance between the members of a term's reference class are immediately aware of the vagueness of the term. The vagueness is often quite tolerable. This is fortunate because there would be great difficulty in achieving a descriptively accurate intensional definition that tried to overcome this built-in vagueness. To attempt such a definition a large variety of typical games would have to be gathered. The characteristics of all these typical example games would have to be listed. Only after this would it emerge that there are several important properties of games, not all of which are possessed by all games but most of which, in various combinations, are possessed by most games. This cross matching of properties and similarities then becomes the cluster of characteristics which defines this family of objects.

7:1.4 Open texture Not only can present situations, like the number, variety, and complexity of examples, make it hard to come by accurate intensional definitions, but so can future possible situations. Consider terms like 'art,' 'music,' 'death,' 'technological possibility,' 'economic fairness,' and 'discrimination.' As human experience and civilization develop, new events, new social awareness, and new discoveries and inventions can challenge our traditional definitions of these concepts. A new way of producing sound may be regarded as music or it may be thought of as noise, depending not only on how strong its family resemblances are to older more familiar forms of music (or noise) but also on how people are willing to stretch, adapt, or alter the concept of music, to reinterpret its meaning, to extend its boundaries. Words that are subject to these kinds of evolutions in meaning are called *open-textured*.

Modern medical technology has challenged traditional definitions of 'death' by offering reasons why the traditional signs of death are unreliable indicators. Breathing can stop, or it can be sustained by a respirator, or it can merely be assisted by various inhalation devices. There are cases of individuals who have stopped breathing but later have started breathing again. There are simple cases, as when someone is revived using mouth-to-mouth resuscitation, and there are complex cases involving surgical procedures and the use of various machines. Heartbeat, one of the traditional signs of life, is equally problematic. Measurable brain activity is now being presented as the criterion of life. The basic idea that death is the end of life has not changed, but the practical applications of that idea have been drastically altered, significantly changing the membership in the reference class of 'dead persons.' This particular example is especially interesting because there are precise medical and legal definitions of 'death' besides the one understood by the public at large. Thus medical advances make it necessary to rethink the medical definition, and at the same time new legal decisions are influencing the legal definition. Then, too, philosophical discussions of ethics, justice, and religion all operate to alter the public's ideas about death. The differences in meaning, contrary definitions, diversity of opinion, ethical views, and legal responsibilities all pull in potentially different directions as our society tries to resolve the problem: What is death?

At times a certain amount of open texture is desirable. In art or music it allows for novelty, freshness, creativity, and variety. Similarly, as with a term like 'personal foul' in sports, open texture is needed to provide for unusual cases, even though past decisions by referees and rule makers have gone quite far in settling a large variety of typical cases. Contrarily, in other areas, like law, medicine, and ethics, too much open texture can create confusion, serious errors of judgment, possible malpractice, criminal negligence, and great moral and/or legal wrong. As we said before, a lot depends on how you define your terms.

7:2.1 Extensional definitions An "extensional definition" is one that tries to specify the extension of a term, i.e., one that *aims at stating what a term refers to*. An extensional definition does *not try to tell us why* the term refers to that particular object or class of objects. It does not aim to explain what it is about those objects that makes it essential that they be in the extension of a term. Doing that is the job of an intensional definition. An extensional definition just tells us what is inside the extension of a given term. It may tell us this by giving us a list of things, it may tell us how to construct that reference class, or it may merely tell us how to recognize things that happen to be members of that reference class. Extensional definitions are concerned with the group, collection, set, or class of things to which a word applies or refers.[3]

Although intensions determine extensions, we cannot say that extension determines intension. A list of the members of a reference class does not necessarily give

---

[3] The words 'set,' 'class,' 'collection,' and 'group' are all being used synonymously here. Saying that something is a class or set of objects is simply saying that it is a group or collection of those objects.

a clear indication of the idea or sense of the term the reference of which they constitute. For example, motion pictures of many sunsets could be used to show the extension of the term 'sunset.' Yet the intension of 'sunset' would remain ambiguous. Intensionally, a sunset involves a visual experience of the sun sinking below the horizon. The motion pictures leave open the possibility that 'sunset' only means the rotation of the earth so that sunlight cannot reach a part of the earth's surface.

7:2.2 Virtues of extensional and intensional definitions compared A commonly discussed extensional definition of 'learning' is "any change in behavior." Using this definition, teachers and psychologists can recognize when someone has learned something by examining whether or not they act differently. After having learned mathematics, they will solve equations. After having learned to ride a bicycle, they will ride a bicycle. Such a definition can be very useful for purposes of testing and recognizing learning; but it also creates conceptual problems. It suggests that a person who never performs a given skill has not learned it. If a lifeguard never rescued a drowning person, then, on this definition of 'learning,' the lifeguard never learned how to rescue. Obviously such a definition is not conceptually or theoretically adequate. It does not give us a full and generally adequate concept of learning. But, by the same token, an intensional definition, like

Learning = $_\text{df}$ the acquisition of new knowledge

has serious practical drawbacks. How, for example, shall we tell whether knowledge has really been acquired? How shall we tell if it is new? In an example like this you can see the divergent purposes served by extensional and intensional definitions.

7:2.3 One kind of extensional definition that is of special importance to logicians and mathematicians is the recursive definition. A *recursive definition* can be defined as one that specifies an extension by indicating how to construct that extension. For example, we know what a positive integer is. Now let us try to specify exactly which numbers these are. One way to do this would be to list all the positive integers. Another way would be to list all the numbers which are not positive integers and say that all the ones not mentioned are the positive integers. But neither of these ways will do. Both are impractical. Another way would be to give a recursive definition of 'positive integer,' indicating the class of positive integers by providing a means for compiling the members of that set. Here is such a recursive definition.

EG. 7.7 1. The following are positive integers: 1, 2, 3, 4, 5, 6, 7, 8, 9.
2. If X is any positive integer whatsoever, then the result of writing X to the left of 0 (where 0 is zero) is also a positive integer, as in $X0$.
3. If X is any positive integer whatsoever and Y is any positive integer whatsoever, then the result of writing X next to Y, as in XY, is also a positive integer.
4. Nothing is a positive integer unless it is constructed solely on the basis of a number of applications of the above.

On the basis of this definition we can tell that each of these are positive integers:

8	By appeal to clause 1.
80	By appeal to clauses 1 and 2.
800	By appeal to clause 2 and the fact that 80 is a positive integer; thus here $X = 80$.

79	By appeal to clauses 1 and 3, where $X = 7$ and $Y = 9$.
779	By appeal to clauses 1 and 3 and the fact that 79 is a positive integer; here $X = 7$ and $Y = 79$.
80,779	By appeal to clause 3 and the fact that 80 and 779 are positive integers; here $X = 80$ and $Y = 779$.

As we can verify by the examples, the four clauses, taken together, define the set of positive integers.

A recursive definition contains three kinds of clauses or sentences. (1) It contains a sentence (or two) which states that a specific set of elements are members of the extension of the term. (2) It contains sentences which tell how to combine these elements to make new members of the extension. (3) It contains a closure sentence which specifies that only the previous directions can be used to generate members of the extension. Review Eg. 7.7 and note that sentence 1 is the first kind of clause. Sentences 2 and 3 are the second type of clause, and sentence 4 is the closure clause.

7:2.4 Another kind of extensional definition which has become very useful in science is the operational definition. An *operational definition* tells us how to recognize something as part of a term's extension. An operational definition can be defined as one that specifies a term's extension by indicating the observable results of following some specified procedure or performing some operation. What we observe may be any identifiable characteristics, essential or not. Often when terms are defined intensionally, their meanings are clear but their applications are problematic. Operational definitions are used to overcome the problem of applying intensionally understood terms. For example, we know what being human is all about. We understand that the essential features of human beings are their abilities to think, choose, speak, etc., as set forth in Eg. 7.1. But suppose we wanted a more mechanical test to recognize human beings. We could use Eg. 7.4 as our operational definition. Or again, the definition 'human being' $=_{df}$ "rational animal" is of little help. It tells what a human being is, or why something is "human" but not how to tell a human being from, say, a porpoise. What we need is an operational definition of 'rational.' For example, something is to be considered rational if it scores above 50 on an IQ test. Giving a person an IQ test is a procedure or *operation*; the operation has an *observable result*; e.g., a score of 124 is attained. An operational definition defines a word in terms of an observable result of an operation. In general, operational definitions are useful to make our abstract terms applicable to concrete practical problems. In science they allow us to move from theory to experiment by giving us an understanding of abstract theoretical ideas in terms of measurable observable procedures.

We can contrast operational and recursive definitions by noting the differences between the following two definitions of 'odd number.'

(R) Odd number $=_{df}$ 1 is an odd number; if N is an odd number, then $N \pm 2$ is an odd number; nothing is an odd number unless it is constructed solely on the basis of the above

(O) Odd number $=_{df}$ the set of numbers such that if any one of them is divided by 2 the remainder is either -0.5 or $+0.5$

(R), the recursive definition, tells us that the extension can be constructed if we start with the number 1, add 2 to get 3, add 2 to get 5, and so on, while also subtracting 2 from 1 to get -1, subtracting 2 again to get -3, and so on. (O), the operational definition, gives us a procedure for recognizing odd numbers. Take any number, say −439, and divide it by 2. If there is a remainder of either +0.5 or −0.5, then 439 is odd; −439 ÷ 2 = −219.5, so −439 is odd.

7:3 Varieties of definitions Definitions can be classified as either intensional or extensional. Two kinds of extensional definitions are recursive definitions and operational definitions. So we have:

Intensional definitions   various species were not covered

Extensional definitions $\begin{cases} \text{recursive extensional definitions} \\ \text{operational extensional definitions} \\ \text{other kinds of extensional definitions not covered} \end{cases}$

We also know that definitions can range from purely stipulative to purely descriptive. Thus we have:

Purely stipulative intensional definitions (PSID):
    Albeit = $_{df}$ whichever
Purely descriptive intensional definitions (PDID):
    Albeit = $_{df}$ even though
Mixed stipulative and descriptive intensional definitions (MSDID):
    Greet = $_{df}$ to bid casual welcome to a party guest

as well as

Purely stipulative extensional definitions (PSED):
    Bulls = $_{df}$ class of objects used to erase pencil marks
Purely descriptive extensional definitions (PDED):
    Bulls = $_{df}$ formal letters issued by the Pope; the class of male bovine animals
Mixed stipulative and descriptive extensional definitions (MSDED):
    Bulls = $_{df}$ formal letters issued by any civil or ecclesiastical authority

any one of which could be recursive or operational. Thus we reach an even longer list of possible ways of combining definitions:

Purely stipulative recursive extensional definitions (PSRED):
    Zen master = $_{df}$ Fr. Wortowski is a Zen master. If any person has studied Christian theology for 6 or more years with Wortowski, then he or she is a Zen master. Nobody else is a Zen master.
Purely stipulative operational extensional definitions (PSOED):
    1,600-kilogram weight = $_{df}$ any object you find in the junk drawer of my desk
Purely descriptive recursive extensional definitions (PDRED):
    See definition (R) above.
Purely descriptive operational extensional definitions (PDOED):
    See definition (O) above.
Mixed stipulative and descriptive operational extensional definitions (MSDOED):
    Balloon = $_{df}$ any light-colored, rubber, inflatable bag that can be found in the toy department of a retail store.

Mixed stipulative and descriptive recursive extensional definitions (MSDRED):
Conjunction = $_{df}$ The words 'and' and 'but' are conjunctions. Any word in any language except German and Russian that can be translated as 'and' or 'but' is a conjunction. No other words are conjunctions.

Definitions, as we learned in 6:3, can also be vague, ambiguous, narrow, or arbitrary, as well as correct, useful, clear, good, etc. Thus the combination of kinds of definitions and qualities of definitions, both positive and negative, is rather large. This range will give us the versatility we need to develop our conceptual system of logic in Chapter 3. It will also give us a clearer view of the possible strengths and weaknesses of our conceptual system, since it will be a network of these different kinds of definitions.

EXERCISES FOR MODULE 7
SOME MAIN KINDS OF DEFINITIONS

Ex. 1 Identify the extensional definitions in the following passages by putting 'ex' in the answer space. If a passage is not an extensional definition, put 'no.'

_____ 1. Scandinavian country = $_{df}$ Sweden, Norway, Denmark, and Iceland

_____ 2. April is the cruelest month.

_____ 3. Primary colors = $_{df}$ red, blue, yellow

_____ 4. Red, blue, and green are the basic colors used in the transmission of color-television pictures.

_____ 5. A small class is one with a low student-teacher ratio.

_____ 6. 'Small class' means a class with fewer than 20 students enrolled.

_____ 7. In tennis, 'outstanding server' means serving aces 20 percent of the time or serving balls returned only so weakly as to be smashed 20 percent of the time, or some combination of those two 33 percent of the time. Otherwise you're not really outstanding as a server.

Ex. 2 Identify the intensional definitions among the following passages by putting 'in' in the answer space; otherwise put 'no.'

_____ 1. Assertive sentences are usually put into the indicative mood.

_____ 2. Assertive sentence = $_{df}$ any sentence about which the question "Is this true or false?" can meaningfully be raised

_____ 3. Hence the word 'dog' means a male rabbit which has had its left hind leg amputated.

_____ 4. Equal pay for equal work is a right!

_____ 5. 'Argument' means a set of assertive sentences one of which is purported to be entailed, implied, strongly supported, or strongly warranted by the others.

_____ 6. Logic is the subject concerned with evaluating arguments.

_____ 7. 'Logic' can be defined as the study of the relationships between the premises and the conclusions of arguments.

Ex. 3 Here are several definitions. If a definition is extensional put 'ex' in the answer space. If it is intensional put 'in' in the answer space.

_____ 1. Intricate = $_{df}$ involved, complicated, tangled

_____ 2. Good = $_{df}$ valuable, desirable, worthy; a term of praise

_____ 3. Odd number = $_{df}$ 1 is an odd number. If X is an odd number, then $X + 2$ is an odd number. Nothing else is an odd number.

_____ 4. Professional team = $_{df}$ a team which engages in sports for the profit of its owner and the players

_____ 5. Team sport = $_{df}$ baseball, basketball, soccer, and rugby

_____ 6. Reindeer = $_{df}$ large deer native to the Arctic

_____ 7. Sport = $_{df}$ recreational activity

Ex. 4 In the answer space to the left of each of the following statements indicate whether the statement is true or false by marking 'T' or 'F.'

_____ 1. Extensional definitions specify a team's reference class.

_____ 2. Extensional definitions tell us why something is to be counted as part of that reference class.

_____ 3. Intensional definitions do not give the sense or meaning of a term.

_____ 4. Given an intensional definition of a word, we can generally figure out the word's extension.

_____ 5. Given an extensional definition of a term, we may not be able to figure out a term's intension.

_____ 6. Descriptive definitions like those found in dictionaries are usually intensional.

_____ 7. Intensional definitions can be stipulative.

_____ 8. Extensional definitions can be narrow.

_____ 9. Extensional definitions can be a list of a term's reference class.

_____ 10. Intensional definitions are looked to as a first step in deciding on the essential meaning of a vague term.

Ex. 5 The following definitions are all extensional. Some are recursive and some are operational. If a definition is recursive put 'rec' in the answer space; if it is operational put 'op.'

_____ 1. Even number = $_{df}$ 2 is an even number; if X is an even number, $X + 2$ is even; nothing else is an even number.

_____ 2. Intelligent = $_{df}$ anything which scores above 110 on a standard IQ test

_____ 3. Box = $_{df}$ anything with four sides

_____ 4. Box = $_{df}$ $\square$ is a box; anything congruent to $\square$ is a box; only such things are boxes.

_____ 5. Short sentence = $_{df}$ any sentence with three words or less in it

_____ 6. Dollar sign = $_{df}$ anything that looks like $

_____ 7. Book = $_{df}$ the thing you are reading is printed in a book. Anything with an equal number of pages is a book. Nothing else is a book.

Ex. 6 Mark the following sentences 'T' if they are true and 'F' if false.

_____ 1. Operational definitions are intensional.

_____ 2. Operational definitions can be intentionally written too narrowly.

_____ 3. Good recursive definitions have closure clauses.

_____ 4. Operational definitions tell how to recognize something as a member of a term's extension.

_____ 5. Recursive definitions can be arbitrary.

_____ 6. Recursive definitions are not too useful in determining how to construct the reference class of a term.

_____ 7. One good use of stipulative operational definitions is to aid in the definitions of the technical terms used in various sciences or disciplined studies.

Ex. 7 State the chief purpose or objective of intensional definitions and of extensional definitions.

Ex. 8 Supply example definitions as indicated.

1. Supply intensional definitions of 'freedom,' 'clean,' 'home.'
2. Supply recursive definitions of 'even number,' 'circle.'
3. Supply operational definitions of 'even number,' 'circle,' 'clean.'
4. Supply extensional definitions of 'teaching,' 'child.'

SELECTED ANSWERS
TO EXERCISES FOR MODULE 7

Ex. 1

1. Ex
2. No (a statement, not a definition at all)
3. Ex
4. No (a statement)
5. No (a statement)
6. Ex
7. Ex

If you missed one or more of the extensional definitions, you should review 7:1.1 and 7:2.1. If you confused statements with definitions, review 5:1.1 and 5:1.3.

Ex. 2

1. No (a statement)
2. In
3. In
4. No (a slogan)
5. In
6. No (a statement)
7. In

If you missed one or more of the intensional definitions, review 7:1.1 and 7:1.2. If you confused the other sentences with the definitions, review 5:1.1 and 5:1.3.

Ex. 3

1. In   2. In   3. Ex   4. In
5. Ex   6. In   7. In

If you missed more than two of these, review 7:1.2, 7:2.1, and 7:2.2.

Ex. 5

1. Rec   2. Op   3. Op   4. Rec
5. Op   6. Op   7. Rec

If you missed more than one, review 7:2.4 to study operational definitions and 7:2.3 to study recursive definitions. Remember that the definition above need not be good to be operational or recursive.

Ex. 7 In both cases the chief purpose is to supply the meaning of a term. Intensional definitions aim at the meaning more directly by trying to specify the sense, idea, or concept central to a term's meaning. Extensional definitions aim at specifying a term's reference class, at indicating the class of objects to which the term refers or applies (see 7:1.1).

Ex. 8 Here are some sample answers.

1. Freedom = $_{df}$ that characteristic of persons whereby they are said to be able to choose alternative courses of action

   Clean = $_{df}$ opposite of dirty; free from pollution

   Home = $_{df}$ dwelling place for a group of people

2. Even number = $_{df}$ the set of numbers constructed solely on the basis of the following rules: 2 is an even number; if N is an even number, then N ± 2 is even. Nothing else is an even number.

   Circle = $_{df}$ the set of plane figures constructed solely on the basis of the following rules: ○ is a circle; if any figure X is a circle, then any figure Y congruent to X is a circle. Nothing else is a circle.

3. Even number = $_{df}$ the set of numbers such that if any of them is divided by 2 the remainder is 0

   Circle = $_{df}$ any plane figure constructed by placing the point of a drafting compass on a piece of paper and revolving the other leg of the compass completely around that fixed point so as to inscribe a closed curved line

   Clean = $_{df}$ anything which has been scrubbed for 10 minutes

4. Teaching = $_{df}$ any activity which brings about a change in another person's behavior

   Child = $_{df}$ all persons between the ages of ten and fifteen years old

3

KEY CONCEPTS OF LOGIC

In Chapter 3 we will develop a large part of our conceptual system. As explained in 5:3, a conceptual system aims at being consistent, complete, and applicable. Not only will our definitions meet these conditions, but they will also have to accord in large measure with common usage among practicing logicians. Moreover, the usefulness of our system, its ultimate payoff, comes in applying it to particular arguments to see whether they are worthy of acceptance or not. But if the system requires us to call several arguments acceptable which our common prior intuitions would lead us to reject, or if it leads us to reject many which our common prior intuitions would lead us to accept, then our system itself is unacceptable. Hence, it will also be required of our conceptual system that the evaluations it makes of specific arguments largely accord with our common intuitions about the acceptability of those arguments.

A conceptual system is like a web of concepts. A person climbs on and follows the web out from the center as it leads to the different areas of the study. In Chapter 3 we will be creating the center of the web by defining basic concepts. In other books you can follow out some of the interesting advanced concepts and topic areas. It should not be surprising that later definitions rely on earlier ones. That is what a systematic conceptual scheme is all about. The definitions are intended to build upon each other as they map out the field.

Our construction work will begin by wiring in the concepts we first presented in Chapter 1, logic, argument, logically correct, etc. Then we will expand our system to include the classification of statements as either analytic or synthetic. From there we will build in definitions of 'deductive argument' and 'inductive argument'. Then we will move to the evaluative terms 'valid', 'justified', and 'sound'. The major work of setting up our definitional system will be done now, but we will save the finishing touches, the definitions of 'fallacy' and 'proof', for the beginnings of Parts Three and Four.

MODULE 8

LOGIC AND ARGUMENTS

To begin our conceptual system we must go back to the very foundations, the basic ideas of what 'logic', 'argument', 'assertive sentence', 'premise', 'conclusion', 'enthymeme', and 'logically correct' mean. Module 8 draws heavily on the material in Chapter 1. Since a number of discussions and examples were given there, the work now can be briefer. You should review sections of Chapter 1 as indicated below.

● After reading Module 8 you should be able to:

1. Identify the central characteristics of logic, arguments, premises, conclusions, enthymemes, assertive sentences, and logically correct arguments
2. State the correct definition of each of the above
3. Identify and distinguish arguments, conclusions, and premises from other statements or linguistic passages
4. Construct original examples of assertive sentences, arguments, and enthymeme arguments

8:1 Primitives In a good conceptual system there are few primitive terms. A *primitive term* is an *undefined* preliminary concept that is relied upon to define other concepts which are then called *defined* terms. There is no way to define everything. Not only would it be too time-consuming, but it would also fail to advance our study significantly. Moreover, it would ultimately prove pointless. Some words must be understood at the outset, or else definitions which rely on them will not allow us to learn further meanings. The conceptual system would be simply a foreign language to us; like a merry-go-round, unless we get on somewhere, we will not be able to participate. We have to start our line of definitions somewhere and to avoid a viciously circular system we will begin by presuming an understanding of the primitive terms. Primitive terms are supposed to be relatively intuitive, very close to familiar common usage. These are the roots of our conceptual system in the shared concepts of our common language. One thing a person can do to help someone get started with a conceptual system is try to make him or her feel at home with the primitive terms by offering clarifications or examples. Once we feel clear about the primitive terms, we should have very little trouble climbing from them to a firm understanding of the defined terms.

8:2 Assertive sentences (Review 3:3.1.) In setting forth logic's basic concepts let us take as our primitive terms: 'sentence,' 'truth,' 'falsity,' and 'making sense' as these are normally understood when people say things like "Whatever I asked her, she gave me a one-sentence reply," "Let us raise here the question of the truth or falsity of what the Senator said," and "It does make sense to ask whether the promise was *sincere* but not to ask if it was *green*." Thus, let us begin with the definition originally set forth in 3:3.1.

> **Def. 1** Assertive sentence = $_{df}$ a sentence such that raising the question of its truth or falsity makes sense

As the examples in 3:3.1 and in Ex. 1 of Module 3 illustrate, assertive sentences are usually, but not always, in the indicative mood. However, not every indicative-mood sentence is an assertive sentence. Grammatical construction, then, is not an infallible key to recognizing assertive sentences.

Logicians more commonly use the word 'statement' than the phrase 'assertive sentence.' Moreover, a commonly accepted working assumption of logicians is that all statements are either true or false. We can include the word 'statement' in our system using

> **Def. 2** Statement = $_{df}$ assertive sentence

Since, by Def. 1, assertive sentences are reasonably considered as being either true or false, Def. 2 allows us to also incorporate the logicians' working assumption just mentioned.

There is a certain ambiguity in the word 'statement.' It is sometimes used to refer to the sentence (written or spoken) that is stated, while at other times it refers to the act of producing such a sentence. Since logic's concern is with objective evaluation, logic is concerned not with the process of stating something but with the product of that process, the statement produced. When a person makes a statement, he or she is engaging in an event that occurs at a certain time and place and in a certain context. The person also has a certain overall goal or purpose in mind. However, once made, the product of that act, i.e., the inscription or utterance, is open to objective examination. When statements are combined to make arguments, these arguments then become open to the objective examination of logic. Thus logicians focus on statements as public, objectively evaluatable products.

8:3 Argument (Review Module 3 and 4:1.1, 4:1.2, and 4:3.) The concern of logic is what would happen on the hypothesis that all the premises of a given argument are true: Would this mean that the conclusion would be true? If arguments are composed only of statements, then they are composed of the kinds of things about which it is reasonable to ask "Is this true or not?", and, if that is so, then it is reasonable to ask the question of logical correctness: If these premises are true, should this conclusion be regarded as true? Recalling the examples and discussions of Modules 3 and 4, we can enter these four definitions into our system:

> **Def. 3** Argument = $_{df}$ a set of statements one of which is purportedly implied, entailed, strongly supported, or strongly warranted by the others

> **Def. 4** Conclusion = $_{df}$ the statement in an argument that is purported to be implied, entailed, strongly supported, or strongly warranted by the other statements in the argument

> **Def. 5** Premises = $_{df}$ those statements which purportedly strongly support, warrant, imply, or entail an argument's conclusion

> **Def. 6** Enthymeme = $_{df}$ an argument such that a statement that is obviously to be taken as one of its premises or its conclusion is omitted

8:4 Logically correct (Review 2:1.1 to 2:1.3.) Now that we have defined 'argument,' we can also give the formal definition of 'logic.'

> **Def. 7** Logic = $_{df}$ the study of the relationships between the premises and the conclusions of arguments

One of the primary concerns of logic is to develop procedures for determining whether or not premises actually do imply, entail, strongly support, or strongly warrant their conclusion. As we said in 2:1.2, when the premises do one of these, an argument can be evaluated as logically correct.

Def. 8 Logically correct argument = $_{df}$ an argument such that its premises entail, imply, strongly support, or strongly warrant its conclusion

In Def. 8 we rely on four primitive terms which may or may not be intuitively clear: 'entail', 'imply', 'warrant', and 'support'. The descriptive definition of 'entail' in standard dictionaries is that 'entail' means "brings as a necessary consequence." Logicians focus on the idea of *necessity* mentioned in such a definition. They want to say that one statement entails another if the truth of the first is an iron-clad guarantee of the truth of the second. For example the truth of "all good people live long lives" entails (or, if you prefer, necessitates) the truth of "if anyone does not live a long life, then he or she is not a good person." On the other hand, the meaning of 'implies' is less fixed in ordinary language. Sometimes it is synonymous with 'entails,' but at other times it is used the way 'suggest' is used. For example, 'by that remark did you mean to imply that I was at fault?' can reasonably be regarded as synonymous with 'by that remark did you mean to suggest that I was at fault?' Logicians resolve this ambiguity by ruling out the synonymy to 'suggest' and by insisting that, for the purposes of basic logic, 'imply' and 'entail' mean the same thing.

A warrant is a reason for doing or believing something. A warrant may not guarantee that what you believe is true, but a strong warrant gives a very good reason for believing it; it makes what is believed highly probable. For example, the fact that all the females in your immediate family have had breast cancer is a warrant for believing that if you are a woman, you will probably contract breast cancer. It is evidence that warrants believing that your risk of breast cancer is higher than average. Of course, it does not entail (or necessitate) that you will contract it. Strong support is to a strong warrant as implication is to entailment. Strong support gives a good reason for believing something without actually necessitating the truth of what is believed.

The above pairings of 'entails' with 'implies' and of 'strong warrant' with 'strong support' are used to bring out that there are really two, not four, key logical relations to be concerned with: (1) premises that guarantee the truth of the conclusion and (2) premises that make the truth of the conclusion very probable. An argument is logically correct if either of these *two* key logical relations is discovered to exist. Parts Two and Four of this text develop means of ascertaining whether or not these relationships do exist.

By Def. 8 an argument can be counted as *logically correct* if *either* of the two relationships exists. Thus, even if the other relationship from the one originally purported to exist turns out to be the one that actually exists, we will be able to say that the argument presented is logically correct. The argument's author may present the conclusion as a *strongly warranted* consequence of the premises. But if it turns out to be *entailed*, the argument, which can now be evaluated independent of the judgments of its author, is logically correct. Its author was simply mistaken about the exact logical relationship that existed between the premises and the conclusion.

8:5 The logical correctness of an argument does not depend upon the actual truth or falsity of the argument's premises or conclusion. It depends on the existence of certain relationships between the premises and the conclusion, relationships of entailment (implication) or strong support (strong warrant). Here are two logically correct arguments. Note that in Eg. 8.1 the premises are both false but the conclusion is implied by them.

EG. 8.1 Paris is in Ohio.
Ohio is in France
So Paris is in France.

In Eg. 8.2 all the statements are false, but the premises still entail the conclusion:

EG. 8.2 I love to eat potato salad.
Whoever loves potato salad loves to eat leather.
I love to eat leather.

In Eg. 8.3 below, the premises are true and the argument is logically correct because the premises warrant or strongly support the conclusion, even though they do not imply or entail it; while in Eg. 8.4 the premises are true, but yet the argument is not logically correct because the premises do not entail or strongly warrant the conclusion.

EG. 8.3 Whenever Jean comes to see Grandma, her little brother, Steve, usually comes too.
Jean is coming to see Grandma today.
So Steve will probably come along.

EG. 8.4 People are human.
People are alive.
So all live things are humans.

EXERCISES FOR MODULE 8
LOGIC AND ARGUMENTS

Ex. 1 If a statement in the following list is true put 'T' in the answer space; otherwise put 'F.'

_____ 1. All assertive sentences are statements.

_____ 2. All statements are assertive sentences.

_____ 3. All sentences are statements.

_____ 4. All the premises and conclusions of arguments are statements.

_____ 5. Every premise and every conclusion is either true or false.

_____ 6. Every argument has at least two statements in it.

_____ 7. Every argument has at least one premise and one conclusion.

_____ 8. An enthymeme argument is an argument with a missing statement.

_____ 9. Logic studies the relationships among people and the language they use.

_____ 10. Logic is the study of the truth or falsity of specific statements.

_____ 11. Logic is concerned with the actual truth or falsity of the conclusion of an argument.

_____ 12. Logic asks: Is the conclusion true?

_____ 13. Logic asks: Do these premises imply or strongly support this conclusion?

_____ 14. If all of the premises of an argument are true, then the argument is logically correct.

_____ 15. If all of the premises of an argument are in fact false, then the argument cannot be logically correct.

_____ 16. The truth of specific statements in an argument is irrelevant from the point of view of logical correctness.

Ex. 2 Select the best answer from the candidates presented indicating your choice by marking the appropriate letter in the answer space.

_____ 1. The definition of argument as "a set of statements one of which is entailed, implied, strongly supported, or strongly warranted by the premises" is wrong because:
   A. It is arbitrary.
   B. It is stipulative.
   C. It leaves out the fact that in an argument these relationships are only "purported" to exist.
   D. It leaves out the fact that the premises all have to be true.

_____ 2. The definition of logic as "the study of logical correctness" is wrong because:
   A. Logical correctness is studied by psychology.
   B. Logical correctness is not the only relationship that may exist between the premises and the conclusions of arguments.
   C. Logic is really interested more in the actual truth or falsity of the statements in an argument.

_____ 3. The definition of an enthymeme as "an argument which is missing its conclusion" is wrong because:
   A. What is missing must be a premise.
   B. What is missing can be a premise.
   C. An enthymeme is not an argument.

_____ 4. A logically correct argument cannot be defined correctly as "one which purports to entail or strongly support its conclusion" because:
   A. That is the definition of an enthymeme.
   B. That is the definition of logic.
   C. That is the definition of a statement.
   D. Correctness means that one of these relationships actually exists, not that one is merely purported to exist.

Ex. 3 Seven passages are given below. If a passage is a statement put 'S' in the answer space. If it is an enthymeme argument put 'EA' and supply its missing statement and circle its conclusion. If it is an argument, but not an enthymeme, put 'A' in the answer space and circle its conclusion. If none of these apply, put 'none' in the answer space.

_____ 1. Hi there! How are you today?
_____ 2. We all know that the judge has been honest.
_____ 3. No informed person can seriously doubt that the earth revolves around the sun.
_____ 4. Philip is from Utah. So he probably has underworld connections.
_____ 5. Here comes the winner of the mile run. The winner of the mile run is a Frenchwoman. So a Frenchwoman is coming.
_____ 6. If you do not take up the defense of the village, I'll have to court-martial you even though I don't want to.
_____ 7. If you do not defend the village, I'll get you court-martialed.

Ex. 4 Write out the precise definition of each of the following terms: logic, argument, statement, assertive sentence, enthymeme, premise, conclusion, and logically correct.

Ex. 5 Supply three original examples (ones not found in this text) of each of the following: statements, arguments, logically correct arguments, and enthymeme arguments.

SELECTED ANSWERS
TO EXERCISES FOR MODULE 8

Ex. 1

No.	Answer	See section	And section
1	T	8:2	3:3.1
2	T	8:2	3:3.1
3	F	8:2	3:3.1
4	T	8:3	3:3.2
5	T	8:3	3:3.2
6	T	8:3	3:4
7	T	8:3	3:4
8	T	8:3	4:3
9	F	8:4	2:1.1
10	F	8:4	2:1.3
11	F	8:4	2:1.3
12	F	8:4	2:1.3
13	T	8:4	2:1.3
14	F	8:5	2:1.2, 2:1.3
15	F	8:5	2:1.2, 2:1.3
16	T	8:5	2:1.3

Review the indicated sections for each one that you missed.

Ex. 3 These notes should help:

1	8:2
2	8:2
3	8:2
4	8:3; supply: "Most people from Utah have underworld connections." Conclusion = Philip has underworld connections.
5	8:3; conclusion: a Frenchwoman is coming.
7	8:2; this is a threat not a statement.

If you have problems recognizing arguments, review 4:1.1 and 3:4. If you could not identify their conclusions, review 4:1.1 and 4:1.2. If you missed item 4 about the enthymemes, review 4:3. If you confused statements with other kinds of sentences, review 3:3.1.

Ex. 4 Your definitions should be the same as Defs. 7, 3, 2, 1, 6, 5, 4, and 8.

Ex. 5 Check your answers against the examples and definitions provided in the text. Also check your examples of enthymeme arguments to ensure that you do have explicit statements which form an argument. Remember: if it's not an argument, it's not an enthymeme.

MODULE 9

TRUTH-VALUES

Since a statement can be evaluated as either true or false, we can speak of its having the value true or the value false. These are called *truth-values*.

● After reading Module 9 you should be able to:

1. Identify and distinguish those statements which derive their truth-values by virtue of the facts in the world from those which derive their truth-values solely from what their words mean
2. Pick out the chief characteristics of analytic and synthetic statements
3. Construct examples of analytic and synthetic statements
4. State precisely the definitions of 'truth value', 'analytically true', 'analytically false', and 'synthetic statement'.

9:1.1 Truth-value Arguments are sets of statements. From the point of view of logic the key fact about statements is that they can be true or false; i.e., they have truth-values. We can give a descriptive extensional definition of truth-value as:

> **Def. 9** Truth-value = $_{df}$ the members of the set {truth, falsehood}

Or we can supply an intensional definition:

> **Def. 10** Truth-value = $_{df}$ that characteristic of a sentence which it is alleged to have when it is described as being true or being false

Logicians have assumed that each relevant sentence in an argument, each premise and conclusion, has a truth-value. This assumption is embodied in Defs. 3, 2, and 1. The assumption is crucial because it permits the transition from questions like "Do these premises entail this conclusion?" to questions put in terms of truth-values like "If all of these premises were true, would the conclusion have to be true as well?"

9:1.2 Analyticity Although logical correctness does not depend on the actual truth-values of an argument's component statements, our interest in *fully* evaluating arguments will ultimately lead to questioning the actual truth or falsity of the premises. Eventually we will want to know not only that an argument is logically correct but that its premises are really true as well. Because of this it is important to note that different statements can derive their truth-values in quite different ways. Some statements are automatically true (or false). Here are two: "all sisters have siblings" and "either you will be on time or you will not be on time." Such statements are called *analytic*. We can define 'analytically true' and 'analytically false' as follows.

> **Def. 11** Analytically true statement = $_{df}$ a statement such that it is possible to decide that it is true simply by understanding what it means and without looking to any extralinguistic facts

Def. 12 Analytically false statement = _{df} a statement such that it is possible to decide that it is false simply by understanding what it means and without looking to any extralinguistic facts

If we combine the class of analytically true statements with the class of analytically false statements, we get an extensional definition of 'analytic statement.'

Def. 13 Analytic statement = _{df} all statements such that they are either analytically true or analytically false

Here are some examples of analytic statements; those which are true are also examples of analytically true statements, and those which are false are also examples of analytically false statements:

> All circles are round.
> Triangles have three angles.
> People are each other's spouses if they are married to each other.
> All men who are married are bachelors.
> Everything that has weight has a measurable characteristic.
> Nothing is a triangle that has three angles.
> No widows were ever married.
> Widowers are male.
> Aviators are not aviators.

9:1.3 The class of analytic statements contains a subclass called the class of *logically true (false) statements*. A statement is logically true (false) just when it is analytic by virtue of the meanings of its logical words. Logical words are words of a language that in some of their uses perform logical operations. Some such words are 'not,' 'and,' 'or,' 'but,' 'all,' 'some,' 'every.' We will explain logical words more fully in Part Two. Here are some examples of logically true and logically false analytic statements:

> Aviators are not aviators.
> If something is an *A*, then it is not an *A*.
> Either a statement is true or a statement is not true.
> If a statement is false, then it is false.
> Business is business.
> War is war.
> What you have to do is what you have to do.

You should note that the last three examples are treacherous sentences. They themselves are analytic; indeed, they are logically true. But these sentences have important connotations beyond what they literally assert. Everyone can easily agree to what they assert. However, not everyone can accept the attitudes these sentences are usually intended to convey. Agreeing with such a statement often requires looking beyond its purely literal meaning to the feelings, attitudes, and beliefs it is derived from.

9:1.4 Peculiarities of analytic statements Analytic statements are an odd breed of statement, indeed. Those which have the virtue of being true seem to have the significant liability of being uninformative. What have you really learned when you hear "all circles are round" or "in an inflationary period prices for goods and services rise"? A beginning student may find these informative. But the facts being learned are facts about language, the quasi-specialized languages of geometry or economics. The student is learning how to use these terms in geometry or economics, but is not making observations of facts.

An equally curious problem affects analytically false statements in that they seem simultaneously to be obviously false and obviously confused. The temptation one has upon hearing someone say something like "all cats are both mammals and nonmammals" is not so much to say "No, that's false" as to say "That's confused!" The confusion is not really about facts (cats, mammals, or what have you) but about language, about how one goes about classifying things without contradicting oneself.

In 2:2.2 we briefly discussed how two statements could be contradictory. Whenever two statements always have opposite truth-values, like "Smokers are risking their health" and "Smokers are not risking their health" they are contradictory. A self-contradictory sentence is one that cannot possibly be true because it both asserts and denies the same thing. Here are examples:

Pentagons have precisely five sides, but they do not have five sides.
She arrived exactly on time, but she was late.

At times the internal self-contradiction is more subtle, as in

Pentagons do not have five sides.
My father and I are twins.

Analytically false statements are self-contradictory statements. They are not quite as paradoxical as the utterances of a person who contradicts his or her words or actions by saying things like "I'm not here" or "whatever I say is false," but they are nearly that odd when they turn up in arguments as perhaps a premise, Eg. 9.1, or a conclusion, Eg. 9.2. Consider:

EG. 9.1 Either Szylka will be elected or she will not.
However, she will be elected if, and only if, she will not be.
So she cannot be elected.

EG. 9.2 All free things really cost money.
Anything which costs money is not really free.
So no free things are free things.

As with certain analytically true statements, there are certain treacherously misleading analytically false statements. For example, if someone says "Smoking is both a risk and not a risk," they have spoken a literally self-contradictory sentence. But their purpose may be simply to get your attention. Similarly, certain theologians recently claimed "God is dead," even though they argued that careful consideration of 'God' shows that nothing could cause God to cease to exist (provided that indeed God exists in the first place). They also wished to startle their audience into listening to what they wanted to say. Once attention is gained, they may go on to qualify their first statement with additional comments like "smoking is a risk for such and such type of person, but not a risk for such and such other type of person," or "God is not really changed, but many contemporary persons have a new kind of life-style in which they find God irrelevant to them." So, analytically false statements may signal confusion, but they may also be used to set the stage for a more careful discussion of a topic.

9:2 Synthetic statements In contrast to analytic sentences there are those statements which require knowing more than the language to tell whether they are true or false. When, besides knowing what a statement means, you have to know something about nonlinguistic things (the world, business, art, history, philosophy, science, or people) to tell whether a statement is true or false, the statement is called *synthetic* or *empirical*. Here are some examples of synthetic statements.

> Carol learned how to ride a bicycle in June.
> Gary is sensitive.
> There are few people who are willing to support recall.
> This is a page in a book.
> There are hardly any poor students in class today.
> The older you get, the wiser you get.

What is crucial in deciding whether or not an analytic statement is true or false is simply what it means. Its truth, if it is logically true, is derived not so much from what it says (its subject matter or empirical content) but from the way it says it (its structure or the meaning of its logical words). On the other hand, when you are dealing with synthetic statements, you have to look at the subject matter itself. You have to look at the claim it makes and check that claim against facts to tell whether that statement is true or false.

We can give an extensional definition of 'synthetic statement' as follows:

Def. 14 Synthetic statement = $_{df}$ the set of all nonanalytic statements

Although Def. 14 designates a class of objects, it does not aim at telling us the basic idea of what a synthetic statement is. Further, Def. 14 might also be construed as loaded since it does short-circuit debates about the relationship of the classes of analytic and synthetic statements, which arise once a more traditional, intensional definition of 'synthetic statement' is given. Definition 15 aims at specifying the intention, or sense, of 'synthetic statement.'

Def. 15 Synthetic statement = $_{df}$ a statement such that knowledge of more than what it means is required to determine whether it is true or false

9:3 Borderline cases In 9:2 we said that Def. 14 might be loaded. The reason is that it presumes that all statements fall nicely on one side or the other of the analytic-synthetic distinction. This however may not be entirely true. There are some interesting borderline cases like:

1. God is not a Being Which can be experienced.
2. Any physical object that has a detectable color also has a measurable length.
3. Every event has a cause.

Given certain theological and philosophical systems, statement 1 is analytically true. It is part of the definition of God that God cannot be experienced in any ordinary sense of that term. However, mystics offer descriptions of their encounters with God, which, if true and accurate, would make 1 factually false. Because there does not seem to be any well-accepted scientific definition which associates color with length, 2 seems to be synthetic. On the other hand, it hardly seems that to verify a statement like 2 one has to actually perform any experiments or make any special series of observations. Moreover, it isn't even clear what a counterexample to 2 would be. Because of these considerations 2 seems analytic. The link between the idea of an event and some cause for that event seems to be conceptual, so that 3 appears analytic. How could a counterexample to 3 be proved genuine? How could we distinguish events without causes from events the causes of which are only unknown? As such, 3 guides science since it guarantees that events are not unexplanably random but have causes which can be searched for. On the other hand, in analyzing the process of decay of radioactive elements, physicists have found that the decay proceeds at predictable rates but one cannot predict which particle of a particular element will decay at any moment in time to become an atom of a different element. The decay, while predictable, seems to be random. Thus the event of any particular atom's change seems entirely uncaused. This, of course, makes 3 appear factually false and therefore synthetic.

Debates over whether or not examples like these are genuinely analytic or synthetic have led some to reject the analytic-synthetic distinction altogether, while others reject a definition like Def. 14 in favor of one like Def. 15. Yet others view these kinds of examples as almost entirely unproblematic, saying that the existence of tough cases indicates that the terms in question are open-textured, alive, and well in our language.

For our purposes we need not pursue the peculiarities of the analytic-synthetic distinction further. The distinction can be accepted as a working distinction between two types of statements. It is a distinction that alerts us to the fact that at least some statements are true or false simply by virtue of what they mean while others can be known to be true or false only after further information has been gathered about the way the world is. We will rely on this knowledge at various points in the subsequent parts of this text.

EXERCISES FOR MODULE 9
TRUTH-VALUES

Ex. 1 There are several sentences listed below. If a sentence is not a statement, put 'no' in the answer space. If it is analytic (either analytically true or analytically false), put 'ana' in the answer space. If it is synthetic, put 'syn' in the answer space.

_____ 1. When will we be in Detroit?

_____ 2. We will be in Detroit at midnight.

_____ 3. When we get there, we get there.

_____ 4. I'm tired.

_____ 5. Relax! Sleep.

_____ 6. I'm hungry.

_____ 7. Well, I'm John.

_____ 8. Cut out the funny business and drive.

_____ 9. It's getting hot in here.

_____ 10. Well, if it's hot, it's hot.

_____ 11. If it's hot, then it's not cold.

Ex. 2 Indicate by putting 'T' or 'F' in the answer space whether each of the following statements is true or false.

_____ 1. Analytic statements are not synthetic.

_____ 2. Arguments can have synthetic statements as premises.

_____ 3. A statement that is analytically true can be synthetic and false.

_____ 4. Synthetic statements are true or false depending on what they mean and on what the facts in the world are.

_____ 5. Analytically false statements are false because of what they mean.

_____ 6. An argument's conclusion can be analytically true.

_____ 7. An argument's premises can be analytically false.

_____ 8. Only synthetic statements have truth-values.

_____ 9. Every sentence has a truth-value.

_____ 10. Every statement has a truth-value.

Ex. 3 Write out example sentences as indicated.
1. Supply five original examples of synthetic statements.
2. Supply three original examples of analytically true statements.
3. Supply three original examples of analytically false statements.

Ex. 4 State precisely the definition of each of the following terms: truth-value, analytically true statement, analytically false statement, analytic statement, and synthetic statement.

ANSWERS TO EXERCISES
FOR MODULE 9

Ex. 1

1. No	2. Syn	3. Ana
4. Syn	5. No	6. Syn
7. Syn	8. No	9. Syn
10. Ana	11. Ana	

If you confused statements with nonstatements, you should review 8:1.2. If you confused analytic with synthetic, review 9:1.2 and 9:2.

Ex. 2

1. T (9:2)
2. T; they can have any kind of statement.
3. F (9:2)
4. T (9:2)
5. T (9:1.2)
6. T; see answer to item 2.
7. T; see answer to item 2.
8. F; all statements have truth-values.
0. F; only statements have truth values.
10. T

Note the facts or review the appropriate sections as indicated for each one you missed.

Ex. 3 Check your examples against the examples and definitions provided in this module.

Ex. 4 Your definitions should be the same as Defs. 10, 11, 12, 13, and 15. Definition 9 can replace Def. 10, but Def. 14 is inferior to Def. 15, for the reason given in 9:2.

MODULE 10
DEDUCTION AND INDUCTION

Logic is the study of certain relationships that purportedly or actually exist between the premises and the conclusion of an argument. Two relationships that logicians concern themselves with are the *deductive relationship* and the *inductive relationship*. In Module 10 we will explore the differences between these two relationships.

● After reading Module 10 you should be able to:

1. Identify and distinguish inductive and deductive arguments
2. Pick out words or phrases indicating that an argument is deductive and those indicating that it is inductive
3. Identify and distinguish the characteristics of inductive arguments and deductive arguments
4. State the difference between inductive and deductive arguments
5. State the definitions of 'inductive' and 'deductive'
6. Construct original examples of both inductive and deductive arguments

10:1.1 Difference between inductive and deductive arguments In the deductive relationship the premises purport to entail or necessitate the conclusion. In the inductive relationship the premises purport to make the conclusion probable. In classifying arguments as either deductive or inductive we are talking about how the premises, not individually but *as a group*, are presented as relating to the conclusion. When an argument is deductive, its premises purportedly require that its conclusion be true. The purport or suggestion of a deductive argument is: if the premises are all true, then the conclusion *must* be true. On the other hand, if we are dealing with an inductive argument, then the premises taken together purportedly make the conclusion very likely. The conclusion is purported to be probably, but not necessarily, true. Unlike deductive arguments, the purport or suggestion of an inductive argument is: if the premises are all true, then the conclusion will *probably* also be true.

10:1.2 Arguments as purporting In Chapter 1 we described an argument as a set of assertive sentences in which some statements *purport* to entail or warrant another. We emphasized that a set of statements is an argument because of the way the statements are *presented*, some as entailing or warranting another. We asked you to focus not on whether the premises actually entail or warrant the conclusion but on whether the author presents the relationship as existing. Notice now that this emphasis on *purport* is carried through in the definitions of deductive and inductive arguments. What makes arguments deductive or inductive is again purport, the way they are presented, in other words. An argument is deductive because its premises *are presented* as entailing its conclusion. An argument is inductive because its premises *are presented* as strongly warranting its conclusion.

10:1.3 Defining deduction and induction Let us suppose we are dealing with an arbitrarily selected argument. Let us number its premises as $P_1, P_2, \ldots, P_n$. [If it has five premises then its last premise is P_5 ($n = 5$).] Let us call its conclusion C. Thus we have:

$$P_1$$
$$P_2$$
$$\cdot$$
$$\cdot$$
$$\cdot$$
$$\frac{P_n}{\therefore C}$$

The symbol $\therefore$ is read "therefore." The conclusion of an argument is the next sentence to the right of the $\therefore$ sign. The line drawn between the premises and the conclusion is also used to indicate that the list of premises is ending and the next statement written is the conclusion of the argument.[1]

    Now let's focus on how the premises of the argument might relate to that conclusion. They can either purport to necessitate it

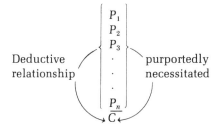

making the argument deductive. Or they can purport to make it probable that the conclusion is true

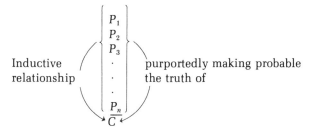

thus yielding an inductive argument.

    We can also say that a deductive argument purports to *entail* or *imply* its conclusion. As we said in 8:4, logicians understand these words as saying that the premises of a deductive argument purport to *necessitate* the argument's conclusion.

---

[1] The dots ($\therefore$) and the line are conventions. This means that they are convenient and helpful devices. Conventions make a systematic study like logic easier. Thus having conventions is justified. There are, however, many ways we might mark a conclusion. We might use four dots :: or a square □. Nothing except current practice makes any of these conventions significantly better than the others.

Inductive arguments purport to *strongly warrant, strongly support,* or *strongly confirm* their conclusions; i.e., they present their conclusions as if they were very likely true. The conclusions of inductive arguments are purported to be very probably true but still remotely possibly false. This is what it means to say that the falsity of the conclusions of inductive arguments is made improbable but not impossible.

Def. 16 Deductive argument = _{df} an argument such that it is purportedly not possible for its conclusion to be false and all its premises true

Def. 17 Inductive argument = _{df} an argument such that it is purportedly im probable, although possible, for its conclusion to be false given that all its premises are true

10:2.1 Here are some examples of deductive arguments. Note that in each case the conclusion is either *implicitly* or *explicitly presented as a necessary* consequence of the premises taken together. As you examine these examples, do not be distracted by the subject matter, content, or the truth-value of any of the statements. Look instead at the purported relationships between the premises and the conclusion.

EG. 10.1   All my children went to the fair. Everyone who went to the fair was surprised at the crowd size. Everyone who was surprised at the crowd size left quickly to return home. So my kids must have left quickly to return home.

EG. 10.2   John will attend the rehearsal if, and only if, his parents are not going to be out of town that night. Since his parents are not going to be out of town that night, John definitely will attend the rehearsal.

EG. 10.3   The fact that everybody believes in something follows necessarily from the fact that there is something that everyone believes in.

EG. 10.4   If every boat has a rudder, then every rudder has a boat. Some rudders, however, do not have boats. Thus we can conclude that not every boat has a rudder.

EG. 10.5   Teresa enjoys barbecues. This is entailed by two facts: she enjoys whatever her family enjoys, and her family enjoys barbecues.

10:2.2 Deduction indicators   The way to recognize or identify deductive arguments is to ask: Is this conclusion *being presented as a necessary consequence* of these premises? If yes, the argument is deductive. Do *not* ask whether the conclusion actually is a necessary consequence; that question is concerned with logical correctness, which is a later issue. For now we are only concerned with how things are made to appear, not how they actually are. As an aid in answering the question "Is this conclusion being presented as a necessary consequence of these premises?" we suggest: (1) looking at the intention of the author as either directly stated or as made known through clues in the context of the argument's presentation and (2) looking for tip-off words leading into the conclusion that suggest purported necessity like:

It follows that . . .
It must be that . . .
It cannot fail to be that . . .

It is definitely true that . . .
It is necessary that . . .
The premises imply that . . .
We cannot escape concluding that . . .
The premises entail that . . .
It follows necessarily that . . .
It is a necessary consequence that . . .
Thus we can conclude that . . .

(3) In the absence of the author's own comments and in the absence of tip-off words, presume that any argument that has an unqualified or absolute conclusion is deductive; i.e., if an argument does not temper its conclusion but just lays it out as a matter-of-fact flat statement, presume that the argument is intended to be taken as a deductive argument. Here are two examples of deductive arguments that lack tip-off words but should be taken as deductive because their conclusions are stated absolutely.

EG. 10.6 All bears love honey.
All animals that love honey live in forests.
Thus all bears live in forests.

EG. 10.7 If Brenda is a senior, she will graduate in June since it's true that all seniors will graduate in June.

10:2.3 The deductive relationship Consider the following examples of deductive arguments. Our purpose here is to give examples of deductive arguments. The fact that some are logically correct and some are not is secondary for now. If the subject matter is extravagant, that does not matter. It is only a device to help you focus on the *deductive relationship*. In each case the conclusion is *purportedly a necessary* consequence of the premises. As it happens, though, in groups *A* and *B* what is purportedly the case turns out to be actually the case; i.e., the examples happen to also be logically correct because the premises *do* entail or imply these conclusions. In group *C* all the examples are logically incorrect arguments; in other words, although those deductive arguments purport to necessitate their conclusions, they actually do not entail or even strongly warrant them.

Group A:
Below are some examples of deductive arguments. They are logically correct. Their logical correctness is by virtue of certain logical relationships that exist between their statement units. These logical relationships are the structures, or the logical form, in virtue of which these example arguments are logically correct. By a *statement unit* we mean the simplest possible subject-predicate statement to which a truth-value can be ascribed. The statement units for each example in this group are indicated below the example. The remaining words in the premises and the conclusions are words that here have a logical force. For our current purposes it is not crucial to understand how to distinguish between statement units and logical words. We will take this up in Part Two.

EG. 10.8 1. If ducks fly, then cows do too.
2. Ducks fly.
3. Therefore, cows fly.
The statement units here are 'ducks fly' and 'cows fly.'

EG. 10.9 1. Either ducks fly or cows fly.
2. Cows do not fly.
3. So ducks fly.
The statement units here are 'cows fly' and 'ducks fly.'

EG. 10.10 1. It is not the case that dogs drink beer.
2. People drink beer.
3. So, either people drink beer or birds fly south for the spring, and dogs do not drink beer.
The statement units here are 'dogs drink beer,' 'people drink beer,' and 'birds fly south for the spring.'

EG. 10.11 1. Either my leader is crazy, or there is a riot outside.
2. If my leader is crazy, then I am in big trouble.
3. If there is a riot outside, then I am in big trouble too.
4. So I'm in big trouble!
The statement units here are 'my leader is crazy,' 'there is a riot outside,' and 'I am in big trouble.'

Group B:

Here are more examples of deductive arguments. These are also logically correct. Group B examples differ from group A examples because their logical correctness is by virtue of logical relationships that exist within as well as between their statement units. We will also discuss these kinds of arguments in Part Two. Here, too, logical correctness is a result of logical form or structure.

EG. 10.12 1. All my children are healthy.
2. Carol is one of my children.
3. So Carol is healthy.

EG. 10.13 1. Jerome is a child, and children are messy.
2. So Jerome is messy.

EG. 10.14 1. All the people love to spend money.
2. Whoever loves to spend money is either foolish or rich or both.
3. Whoever is foolish is wasteful.
4. So all the people are either rich or wasteful or both.

Group C:

Here are more examples of deductive arguments. These are all logically incorrect deductive arguments. In each of the following the conclusion is purportedly entailed or necessitated by the premises, but in fact the conclusions are not entailed, implied, strongly supported, or strongly warranted by the premises as stated.

EG. 10.15 1. Either dogs bark, or birds fly north to feed.
2. But no dogs bark.
3. It follows of necessity then that birds do not fly north to feed.

EG. 10.16 1. All cats are gray.
2. All gray things are alive.
3. So all living things are cats.

EG. 10.17 1. The fact that we do good work here follows from these two premises:
2. We always do good work on Thursdays.
3. Nevertheless, today is not Thursday.

EG. 10.18 1. The Communists wish to subvert our country and throw out the existing administration.
2. The gay liberation people want to throw out the present administration.
3. Most minority groups also want to throw out the present administration too.
4. Therefore, most minority groups and gay liberation people are Communists.

10:3.1 In contrast to the sample deductive arguments just offered, here are some examples of inductive arguments. Note that in each case the conclusion is implicitly or explicitly *presented* so that its *falsity seems improbable* if all the premises together are taken as true. As it happens, each of the examples given here is also logically correct. However, their logical correctness is not derived from their form but from the fact that in each the content of the premises supplies good reason for believing the conclusion. The strong support variety of logical correctness is a matter of the content or subject matter of an argument. If the premises provide strong support or a strong warrant for the conclusion, we have justification for evaluating the argument as logically correct. Of course, new or added information or additional data can unseat a previously justified conclusion, no matter how probable a conclusion may seem in a given inductive argument. If we know independently that it is false, or if we have some counterevidence that leads us to think it's false, the conclusion is or may well be untrue. *Inductive arguments purport probability, not necessity.* Look for this purported relationship in these examples of inductive arguments:

EG. 10.19 My children went to the fair. Most of the folks who went to the fair had a good time. So my children probably had a good time.

EG. 10.20 Everybody pays taxes, but only lucky people win at poker. I'm usually not too lucky, so I'll probably do more tax paying than poker winning.

EG. 10.21 Teresa, as far as I can tell, enjoys barbecues. I say that because she usually enjoys whatever her family enjoys and her family enjoys barbecues.

EG. 10.22 John will attend the rehearsal if, and only if, his folks are not going out of town that night. His folks are probably not going out of town that night. So its a fair bet that he will attend the rehearsal.

You might find it helpful to compare these examples with the earlier examples of deductive arguments given in 10:2.1. Compare Eg. 10.19 with Eg. 10.1, Eg. 10.21 with Eg. 10.5, and Eg. 10.22 with Eg. 10.2.

10:3.2 Inductive indicators The way to recognize inductive arguments is to ask: Is this conclusion being presented as probably but not necessarily true? If yes, the argument is inductive. Do *not* ask whether the premises actually do strongly support or strongly warrant the conclusion. That would be to ask if the argument is logically correct, but for now our concern is with what kind of argument it is, not with how to evaluate its logical correctness. As an aid in answering the question "Is this conclusion being presented as probably but not necessarily true?", we suggest: (1) Ask the author directly or through author clues in the context within which the argument is presented. (2) Look for induction tip-off words leading into the conclusion, such as:

So probably . . .
It seems that . . .
It is likely that . . .
It's a good bet that . . .
It could hardly fail that . . .
We can probably go on its being true that . . .
The facts strongly suggest that . . .
The facts strongly warrant believing that . . .
The evidence strongly indicates that . . .
The facts strongly support concluding that . . .
It seems beyond reasonable doubt that . . .
It is not improbable that . . .

(3) Presume that the argument is deductive unless the conclusion is presented hesitantly, tentatively, cautiously, or as something less than a flat bold assertion. Examples of hesitant, less than completely confident, or less than absolute conclusions were given in Egs. 10.19 to 10.22. (4) Generally count arguments that are generalizations or statistical or mathematical probabilities as inductive arguments unless there is strong reason, e.g., the author's own statement or a clear deductive tip-off word, to the contrary. Some examples of each type are given below (10:3.4). (If you wish, you may check your ability to recognize inductive arguments and distinguish them from deductive arguments by doing Exs. 1 and 2 of Module 10 now.)

10:3.3 An inductive argument does not purport to necessitate its conclusion; it merely purports to warrant it. It is allegedly possible (though not likely) for all the premises of a good inductive argument to be true and yet for the conclusion to be false. It is possible to add a premise to an argument which merely strongly supports or strongly warrants the conclusion such that (1) it contradicts the argument's conclusion but (2) it is compatible with the truth of all of its premises. For example, consider the inductive argument:

EG. 10.23 There are fifteen tennis balls in the covered bushel. I have, without looking, withdrawn ten. Each, so far, has been white. So it is very probable that the remaining five are white also.

This argument would, as it stands, have to be regarded as logically correct in that its premises give strong support to the truth of the conclusion. However, consider another piece of information which is compatible with the premises:

At least three of the fifteen balls are bright green.

This could be true, for we have five balls left in the bushel as yet uninspected. But if we add this information, the conclusion is no longer strongly warranted. In fact, the new information is straightforward counterevidence which falsifies the conclusion. Yet we do not want to say that Eg. 10.23 was not logical. It was. But the strong support for the conclusion showed it to be, at that time, probably but not necessarily true.

When the conclusion of an inductive argument turns out to be false, we cannot infer that one of the premises must be false. A premise may be false, or it may be that there is some relevant information missing. There is no reason to say that any of the premises of Eg. 10.23 was made false when the new data made the conclusion false. New information can lead us to alter the conclusions of even good inductive arguments.[2] On the other hand, if an argument's conclusion is actually entailed by its premises, then no new information can alter the logical force of argument. For example, consider this logically correct deduction.

EG. 10.24 All vegetarians avoid eating meat dishes.
Beefsteak is a meat dish.
So all vegetarians avoid eating beefsteak.

There is no new information that could cause us to say that the conclusion of Eg. 10.24 is false, granting that all its premises are true. Any information that would falsify the conclusion of Eg. 10.24 would also be counterevidence to its premises. Any such information could not be viewed as consistent or compatible with those premises.

These contrasts between logical correctness by entailment and logical correctness by strong support are due to the fact that in the case of entailment logical correctness is a matter of structure but in cases of strong support it is a matter of content.

If you wanted to decide whether or not the inductive arguments given below were logically correct, you would make two judgments. First, you should make a judgment about the relevance of the information given in the premises to that offered as their conclusion, and second, you should apply your own background knowledge of the subject matter of the argument to judge whether or not relevant information not mentioned in the premises would weaken the evidential support given by the stated premises. Again, the fact that these sorts of considerations are useful in judging one variety of logical correctness is because the strength of the support that premises give to their conclusion is a matter of the content or subject matter of the argument.[3]

10:3.4 Here are some examples of the three standard types of inductive arguments: those which deal with mathematical probabilities, those which deal with statistical inferences, and those which are generalizations.

Group D:
Here are inductive arguments that deal with mathematical probabilities. They operate on the "principle of insufficient reason," which says that "in the absence of any evidence to the contrary one should act as if no particular outcome or event, in a given set of possible events, is more likely to occur than any one of the others." For example, a coin is no more likely to come up heads than to come up tails. On the basis of this principle, we apply our knowledge of mathematical probabilities in order to judge the odds of something's happening.

EG. 10.25 1. The chances of drawing to an inside straight are very low.
2. I am holding a five, seven, eight, nine, queen in a game of draw poker.
3. So I probably will not be able to drop the queen, draw the six, and get a straight.

[2] To see another example of this read Eg. 11.1. It appears that the premises supply ample evidence for the conclusion. Now, however, consider the truth or falsity of the conclusion in the light of new evidence: Rufus Washington is black, and no blacks voted Republican in the last election.
[3] A more thorough discussion of logical correctness based on strong support will be presented in Chapter 14.

EG. 10.26 1. High die wins in this game.
 2. My opponent rolled a five.
 3. So he'll probably win.

EG. 10.27 1. We are playing a game in which we flip three coins.
 2. If they all come up heads or all come up tails, I win $1.
 3. Otherwise, I pay you 37 cents.
 4. This game is probably going to cost me money.

Of course, the postulate of insufficient reason could be wrongly applied to any given situation. For example, it was once believed that there was no more reason why a baby should be of one sex than the other. From this belief we could rightly infer that half of all births will be male, half female. But today knowledge derived from statistical surveys and from genetics has led us to reject the application of the principle of insufficient reason to the ratio of male and female births. Whenever the principle of insufficient reason proves suspect (or even false), the conclusion derived using mathematical probabilities may present inaccurate (and hence false) mathematical probabilities. Thus the inference that half of all births will be of each sex is false because sex is not randomly determined and so pure mathematical probabilities do not apply.

Group E:

Inductive arguments that deal with statistical inferences are those which try to work through a multiplicity of possible factors to determine which events or conditions can be viewed as reliable predictors of other events.

EG. 10.28 1. Recently the vice-president has been angry, irritable, and very un-friendly.
 2. This is not like him.
 3. Very often this is caused by stress and personal difficulty.
 4. The vice-president is probably under stress.

EG. 10.29 1. At least three people wanted Kowalski dead.
 2. His wife wanted his money.
 3. His best friend wanted his wife.
 4. And his brother wanted his job.
 5. His wife had little opportunity.
 6. His brother was a coward.
 7. So his best friend probably killed him.

EG. 10.30 8. But his best friend was in Detroit at the time Kowalski died in Chicago.
 9. His butler was a psychotic killer.
 10. The butler was the only person in the house on the night of the killing.
 11. The killing took place in the den.
 12. The wife and the brother were seen together at a motel at about the time of the killing.
 13. So the butler probably did it. You see, Watson, it's simply a matter of induction.

Group F:
Some arguments that are inductive have to do with making generalizations from various samples. For example:

EG. 10.31   1. Of the students who take logic 78 percent get an A or a B in the course.
                     2. The grading curve in logic is typical of other classes.
                     3. So 78 percent of the students in this college get high grades.

EG. 10.32   1. For the last 14 hours Dr. Middlemind has been randomly selecting stones from the barrel.
                     2. All the stones he has selected have been green.
                     3. All the stones in the barrel are probably green.

EG. 10.33   4. So most stones at the collection site are probably green.

EG. 10.34   1. 80 percent of all freshmen become sophomores.
                     2. 90 percent of all sophomores graduate.
                     3. 20 percent of all graduates go on to graduate school.
                     4. 50 percent of all graduate students get an M.A.
                     5. 20 percent of all Ph.D. graduate students finish the doctorate successfully.
                     6. These data were taken from a study of one university.
                     7. So, nationwide only 14 out of 1000 freshmen will earn a Ph.D.

EG. 10.35   1. Most young children with problems learning to read have eye-hand coordination problems.
                     2. Many eye-hand coordination problems can be significantly improved by activities like playing catch.
                     3. So a lot of young children with reading problems could probably improve their reading if they played catch more often.

10:4 Form versus content The distinction between the logician's concern for form and structure and the logician's concern for content and subject matter was latent but operative in 8:4. There we contrasted two kinds of logical correctness, the implies or entails variety with the strongly warrants or strongly supports variety. Logicians assume that entailment is a matter of structure whereas support is a matter of content. This distinction was evident again in 9:2. There we described statements that were logically true or logically false. We contrasted these two subclasses of analytic statements with statements that were synthetic. We can say that in the case of synthetic statements truth-values are a matter of subject matter whereas for logically true (false) statements truth-values are a matter of form. Several times in Module 10 we noted that the logical correctness of certain examples was derived from their structure or form. In other places in Module 10 we noted that the logical correctness of other examples was based on their content. One of the differences between logical correctness by entailment and logical correctness by strong support is what influence additional information compatible with the premises could have on the stated conclusion. When we discussed this in 10:3.3, we attributed the difference to the fact that where entailment exists logical correctness is a matter of form, while where strong support exists, it is a matter of content. The form-content distinction runs throughout our treatment of logic. It yields two varieties of logical correctness, as we have already seen. It dictates that in assessing arguments for entailment or implication we will have to develop ways of isolating and examining logical form; that is what Part Two will be about. It indicates that in evaluating for the strength of the support that premises give to their conclusion we will have to rely on ways of treating various kinds of content; this is what Part Four, in large measure, is about. The distinction also suggests that those flawed arguments which we will come to call fallacies can be flawed in either their content or their form. In Part Three we will learn ways of recognizing both types of flaws. For the moment, however, we should develop definitions that more accurately reflect the differences between logical correctness based on entailment and logical correctness based on strong support. This will be the chief task of Module 11.

EXERCISES FOR MODULE 10
DEDUCTION AND INDUCTION

Ex. 1 Here are some tip-off words. Distinguish those which indicate deductive arguments from those which indicate inductive arguments by putting 'D' or 'I' in the answer spaces.

_____ 1. So it is very likely that . . .

_____ 2. We can thus conclude . . .

_____ 3. Therefore . . .

_____ 4. Therefore probably . . .

_____ 5. The evidence strongly indicates that . . .

_____ 6. It could hardly fail that . . .

_____ 7. These premises entail . . .

_____ 8. It is definitely proper to infer . . .

_____ 9. It follows that . . .

_____ 10. It must be the case that . . .

Ex. 2 Here are several arguments. Distinguish the deductive arguments from the inductive arguments by marking 'D' or 'I' in the answer space.

_____ 1. Bethany is athletic. Athletic people tend to be slim. So Bethany is probably a slim person.

_____ 2. So far all intelligent students have done A work in logic. So it seems that all intelligent students in this class will get an A.

_____ 3. If Karl Marx had been J. D. Rockefeller, then he would have been a capitalist. But Karl Marx was not a capitalist. Therefore Karl Marx was not J. D. Rockefeller.

_____ 4. All artificial satellites are important scientific achievements. Therefore, some important scientific achievements are not American inventions. You see, several artificial satellites are not American inventions.

_____ 5. All frogs are amphibians. So all frog's legs are amphibian's legs.

_____ 6. I bought a pair of socks of this brand and style before, and they lasted a long time. If I buy another pair, they will last a long time, I expect.

_____ 7. Whoever is drunk ought to be arrested. Anyone who is arrested ought to be in jail. So everyone who is drunk ought to be in jail.

_____ 8. All events so far observed have been seen to be caused. So every event has some cause or other.

_____ 9. If capital punishment deterred crime, it would be justified. But capital punishment does not deter crime. So capital punishment is not justified.

_____ 10. Two-thirds of the last 100 tosses of this coin came up heads. So two-thirds of the next 50 tosses will come up heads.

Ex. 3 Indicate whether the following statements are true, 'T,' or false, 'F':

_____ 1. Deductive arguments are those arguments which go from specific to general.

_____ 3. Inductive arguments are the kind of arguments that go from specific to general.

_____ 3. Inductive arguments never occur in detective stories because crime detectives use deduction.

_____ 4. Deductive arguments are always logically correct.

_____ 5. Deductive arguments necessitate their conclusions.

_____ 6. Deductive arguments are never enthymemes.

_____ 7. Inductive arguments purport to make the falsity of their conclusions improbable.

_____ 8. Inductive arguments strongly support their conclusions.

_____ 9. Deductive arguments purport to require or imply their conclusion.

_____ 10. Inductive arguments sometimes deal with statistical inferences.

Ex. 4 State the difference between inductive and deductive arguments.

Ex. 5 State the precise definition of 'deductive argument' and 'inductive argument.'

Ex. 6 Supply original examples of arguments as indicated.

1. Two examples of deductive arguments like those in group A, 10:2.3
2. Two examples of deductive arguments like those in group B, 10:2.3
3. Two examples of logically incorrect deductive arguments like those in group C, 10:2.3
4. Two examples of inductive arguments that deal with mathematical probabilities like the examples given in group D, 10:3.4
5. Two examples of inductive arguments that deal with statistical inferences like those in group E, 10:3.4
6. Two examples of inductive arguments that have to do with making generalizations like those examples in group F, 10:3.4

SELECTED ANSWERS
TO EXERCISES FOR MODULE 10

Ex. 1

1. I   2. D   3. D   4. I
5. I   6. I   7. D   8. D
9. D   10. D
If you missed two or more, review 10:1.1, 10:2.2, and 10:3.2.

Ex. 3

1. F   2. F   5. F; they only *purport* to   7. T   9. T
If you missed one or more of these questions for which you have answers, review 10:1.1, 10:1.3, 10:2.3, 10:3.1, 10:3.3, and 10:3.4.

Ex. 4 The difference is that in a deductive argument the conclusion is presented as if it were a necessary consequence of the premises whereas in an inductive argument the conclusion is presented as if were is a probable but not necessary consequence of the premises.

Ex. 5 Your two definitions should be exactly like Defs. 16 and 17, respectively.

Ex. 6 Check your answers by comparison to the various groups of examples in the text. When constructing items 1 and 2, note that you are sure to succeed, no matter what the content of your examples, as long as your examples parallel the form in the text's examples. Remember that except for your answers to items 1 and 2 of this exercise none of your other examples need to be logically correct arguments. The aim here is to write examples of deductions and inductions, not necessarily of logically correct deductions and inductions.

MODULE 11
LOGICAL CORRECTNESS AND SOUNDNESS

Logic is concerned with the evaluation of arguments. There are three distinct evaluative questions to ask: Is this argument logically correct? Does this argument have premises which are true? and Is this argument fallacious or not? In this module we will develop the conceptual machinery to raise the first two of these questions more precisely; our discussion of fallacies will be deferred to Part Three. As indicated in 10:4, our chief aim now will be to develop definitions of each of the two species of logical correctness, the one that focuses on structure and the one that focuses on content.

● After having read Module 11 you should be able to:

1. Identify and distinguish the chief characteristics of validity and justification
2. Identify and distinguish the chief characteristics of logical correctness and soundness
3. Apply these concepts by identifying and distinguishing sound arguments from rather outrageously unsound arguments
4. State precisely the definitions of 'valid argument', 'justified argument', 'logically correct', and 'sound'
5. Construct original examples of valid arguments, justified arguments, and sound arguments

11:1.1 The principal aim of logic is to develop procedures which can be used to *identify logically correct arguments.* Judging logical correctness amounts to different things for assessing entailment and assessing strong support. The only way to judge the strength of the support the premises of an argument lend to their conclusion is to have some idea about the subject matter of the argument and to weigh what the argument says against your own background information. The discussion in 10:3.3

and examples in 10:3.4 illustrate this point. Logical correctness through entailment, on the other hand, is not a matter of subject matter. It is a matter of the form or structure of the argument. The assumption that guides contemporary logicians is that all the relevant logical structure of any given argument can be exposed and examined in such a way as to make judging for entailment entirely independent of the subject matter of the argument.

11:1.2 Validity and justification We can express the difference cited in 11:1.1 by developing two concepts of logical correctness, one for formal correctness and one for content-based correctness. We will use the word 'valid' for the first and the word 'justified' for the second.

> **Def. 18** Valid argument = $_{df}$ an argument such that its premises entail or imply its conclusion cn the basis of the logical form or structure of the argument

See group A and B examples in 10:2.3, which should now be viewed as exemplifying valid arguments. Examples 10.19 to 10.22 illustrate justified arguments; we can define 'justified argument' as follows:

> **Def. 19** Justified argument = $_{df}$ an argument such that its premises, on the basis of their content, give strong support or a strong warrant to the truth of its conclusion

We defined logical correctness in 8:4 as follows:

> **Def. 8** Logically correct argument = $_{df}$ an argument such that its premises entail, imply, strongly support, or strongly warrant its conclusion

An inspection of Defs. 18 and 19 reveals that we could also derive a second definition of 'logically correct' which highlights its two subspecies.

> **Def. 20** Logically correct argument = $_{df}$ an argument that is either valid or justified

11:1.3 Entailment There is a connection between the idea of a deductive argument (Def. 16) and the idea of a valid argument (Def. 18). *Deductive arguments purport to be valid.* To detect validity we must, according to Def. 18, look to an argument's structure or form. When evaluating an argument from the view point of form, we are trying to discover whether there is anything in the structure of the premises and/or the conclusion which compels us to say that the conclusion must be true should all the premises be true. If we are compelled, it is because assuming the premises to be true necessitates that the conclusion also be true. In such a case entailment or implication, as these terms were discussed in 8:4, exists. We can state more precisely the kind of entailment or implication our examination of structure is aiming to find. Consider:

(E) A group of statements, call it G, entails or implies a given statement, call it S, if, and only if, S must necessarily be true in the event that every member of G is true.

(E) can be thought of as the *principle of entailment*. Note, (E) does *not* say that entailment is a matter of structure, although the definition of 'valid argument' (Def. 18) does explicitly make the connection. Definition 18 embodies a working assumption of logicians that has turned out to be very powerful and successful. The assumption is that all logical entailment and logical implication can be discovered by analyzing the structures of various types of arguments. Part Two begins with this assumption and traces out its consequences in both theoretical and practical ways.

11:1.4 Probability There is also a connection between the idea of an inductive argument (Def. 17) and the idea of a justified argument (Def. 19). *Inductive arguments purport to be justified.* That is, they are presented as if the truth of their premises were ample justification for taking their conclusion to be true as well. When we evaluate an argument to see whether its premises justify our taking its conclusion to be true, we focus our attention on what those premises say. We ask: How strong is the evidence presented here? Are there any other data that would weaken our confidence in the truth of this conclusion? Our focus, then, is on subject matter and content. We are looking at the evidence as given in the premises to see if it justifies believing that the conclusion is probably true. The following *principle of probability* expresses more precisely what it is for a group of premises to make the truth of a conclusion probable.

(P) A group of statements G can be said to make the truth of a given statement S probable if, and only if, should each member of G be true this would, in the absence of any additional, contrary information, give a strong warrant, strong support, or strong justification for taking S to be true.

In Chapter 14 we will amplify this principle by describing in detail how one goes about making the judgment that premises strongly warrant a particular conclusion.

11:1.5 Purported versus actual As Defs. 16 and 17 indicate, the names 'deductive' and 'inductive' arise and are properly applied on the basis of how arguments are *presented*, i.e., how a set of premises *purportedly relates* to a conclusion. However, 'valid' and 'justified' are applied *not* on the basis of how arguments are presented but on the basis of how the premises *actually do* relate to the conclusion. This situation is similar to what happens when we evaluate an action as legal. If a person says that a particular action, say making a right turn on a red light, is legal, the person may or may not be correct, even though the statement has been presented as true. We would look to the traffic ordinances to see whether the action actually is legal. In the same way, a person could present an argument as correct. However, we must still evaluate that argument to see whether the premises actually do justify the conclusion as probably true or entail its being true.

The business of logic is to establish the procedures for applying the definitions 'valid' and 'justified.' We will assume, as all logicians do, that judging validity is best accomplished by using the tool of a *formal system*, one that uses various special notational devices to exhibit or represent the logical structure of arguments. We will also presume that to evaluate justification our formal system will be of little help, since formal systems focus on structure while justification is a matter of content. In such cases we will have to turn to the development of useful procedures and guidelines for making wise and reasonable judgments about the strength or weakness of the support that premises lend to their conclusions.

11:1.6 Evaluating for logical correctness It is our assumption that we can judge logical entailment or validity by isolating the logical form of an argument and examining that form to see if the way the conclusion is constructed requires that it be true when all the premises, constructed in the way they are, are also true. But if an argument does not turn out to be valid, we know only that its conclusion is not entailed by its premises. Such an argument is not necessarily logically incorrect. It may turn out that its premises, on the basis of content, do justify the conclusion. (Then again, it may simply be logically incorrect after all.) Here is an example of an argument that is not valid, but is justified by its stated content.

EG. 11.1
1. All the people who voted Republican in the last election owned two summer homes.
2. All the people who voted Republican in the last election also work as executives in large corporations.
3. All the people who voted Republican in the last election are married and have two teen-aged daughters.
4. All the people who voted Republican in the last election have sold their holdings in small South American oil companies.
5. All the people who voted Republican in the last election have recently received money back from the IRS on their taxes.
6. Rufus Washington owns two summer homes, works as an executive in a large corporation, is married, has two teen-aged daughters, has recently sold his holdings in small South American oil companies, and has just received money back from the IRS on his taxes.
7. Therefore, Rufus voted Republican in the last election.

There are no tip-off words leading into the conclusion of Eg. 11.1. Thus, using the procedures given in 10:3.2 we would probably want to call Eg. 11.1 "deductive." But this only means that the conclusion is *presented as if* it were entailed by the premises. Evaluation of Eg. 11.1 reveals that it is not valid. The conclusion is not entailed. Yet Eg. 11.1 is logically correct because the premises justify the conclusion. We, as evaluators of Eg. 11.1, might also wish to urge the author of Eg. 11.1 to restate the conclusion as: 7′. "Therefore, Rufus Washington *probably* voted Republican in the last election."

Just as deductive arguments can turn out to be invalid but justified, inductive arguments can turn out to be unjustified but valid. This can happen when weak support is offered for a conclusion which does not require any support at all.

EG. 11.2 Every bisexual marriage probably has one man and one woman in it—at least the five I checked on did.

Here the definition of 'bisexual marriage' makes the conclusion analytically true and so guarantees the truth of the conclusion independently of the obviously weak evidence presented in the premise. The same thing happens when a person mentions many facts, some of which entail the conclusion, even though the person presents the argument as inductive. For instance, consider the argument:

EG. 11.3 (1) Fall term starts on Wednesday again this year. (2) Once before when it started on Wednesday it ended on Tuesday. (3) So probably it will end on Tuesday again. All I know for sure is that (4) no vacations or holidays are scheduled during any fall term and (5) there are an equal number of Mondays, Tuesdays, Wednesdays, Thursdays, and Fridays with the first day being Wednesday every year. (6) The Provost thinks that's important.

In this passage the premises given in 1 and 2 describing what happened once before do not justify the conclusion 3. But statements 1 and 5 entail 3, as is indicated more clearly in

EG. 11.3′ (1) The fall term starts on a Wednesday. (5) There are an equal number of Mondays, Tuesdays, Wednesdays, Thursdays, and Fridays in every term. (3) Hence it follows (given the usual ordering of the days in a week) that Tuesday will be the last day of term.

11:2 Soundness When you are going to *fully evaluate* an argument you have to consider much more than logical correctness. You must ask three questions of each argument: (1) Is it a logically correct argument? (2) Are all its premises actually true? (3) Is the argument fallacious? These three questions are independent questions. We can have arguments like

EG. 11.4 Detroit is in Ohio, and Ohio is in the United States. So Detroit is in the United States.

that are logically correct but have a false premise. Similarly we can have arguments like

EG. 11.5 Detroit is an industrial city. So if Detroit is in the state of Michigan, Detroit is in a state.

which are structurally valid and are composed exclusively of true statements but which are still not worthy of acceptance because they contain some flaw (in this case an analytically true conclusion) that renders them fallacious. We will catalog various types of fallacies in Part Three. We will learn that fallacies result from flaws of either structure or content.

A person who thinks logically should be able to make decisions about questions 1 and 3. If this logical person is observant and careful in constructing arguments, a process which we shall examine in Part Four, he or she will also be able to answer 2 reasonably well.

Arguments that are both logically correct and have all true premises are worthy of a special name because of their importance. These arguments are called *sound*.

> **Def. 21** Sound argument = $_{df}$ a logically correct argument such that all its premises are true.

An argument can fail to be sound for either of two reasons. If it has even one false premise, it is unsound. If it fails to be logically correct, it is unsound. Thus, going back to Eg. 11.1, even though that argument is, in the absence of any additional information, justified, it can be called sound only if each premise statement, 1 to 6, is also factually true.

The following diagram maps out our conceptual system as it has, so far, been developed.

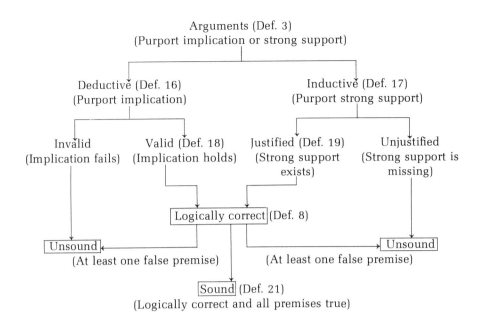

Arguments (Def. 3)
(Purport implication or strong support)

Deductive (Def. 16)
(Purport implication)

Inductive (Def. 17)
(Purport strong support)

Invalid
(Implication fails)

Valid (Def. 18)
(Implication holds)

Justified (Def. 19)
(Strong support exists)

Unjustified
(Strong support is missing)

Logically correct (Def. 8)

Unsound
(At least one false premise)

Unsound
(At least one false premise)

Sound (Def. 21)
(Logically correct and all premises true)

EXERCISES FOR MODULE 11
LOGICAL CORRECTNESS AND SOUNDNESS

Ex. 1 Identify the valid arguments in the passages below. Put 'V' in the answer space if the passage is a valid argument; otherwise put 'no.'

_____ 1. Everyone is mortal. Socrates is a person. So Socrates is mortal.

_____ 2. There is no direct correlation between high grades in high school and college and either personal worth or success after leaving educational institutions.

_____ 3. Every apple I've ever seen was green or red or yellow. So, all apples are green or red or yellow.

_____ 4. There is a good correlation between artistic or musical success in high school and college and success in these fields after graduation.

_____ 5. If there is snow on the ground, then it is cold outside. There is snow on the ground. Thus we can infer that it is cold outside.

Ex. 2 Identify the justified arguments in the following passages. Put 'J' in the answer space if a passage is a justified argument; otherwise put 'no.'

_____ 1. All women are mortal; Madame Curie is a woman. Thus, Madame Curie is mortal.

_____ 2. Of the students at this college 75 percent are healthy, normal people. That fact is the result of analyzing our sample of a cross section of 1,000 people enrolled at this college of 2,000. In our study about 750 were normal and about 250 had some physical or emotional problem.

_____ 3. There is no reason to expect that the present administration will be any better able to handle the economy.

_____ 4. A coin comes up heads 50 percent of the time. If I flip two coins, then the chances of both coming up heads are 1 in 4. In this game I win only if both coins come up heads. I will probably not win.

_____ 5. Either the weather will improve or the corn crop will be ruined. The weather will not improve. This entails that the corn crop will be ruined.

_____ 6. Either the weather will improve or the corn crop will be ruined. It is not very likely that the weather will improve. So probably the corn crop will be ruined.

_____ 7. Children sing loud when they are happy. Jerome is not singing at all. Jerome is probably not happy.

_____ 8. Children sing loud when they are happy.

_____ 9. Children sing loud when they are happy. That is usually the only reason that they sing loud. Christopher is singing loud now. He's probably happy.

_____ 10. Usually the only thing that accounts for a forest fire at this time of year is a careless camper. I see a column of smoke to northnorthwest. It's too big to be a camp fire. It is probably a forest fire caused by some careless camper.

Ex. 3 For each numbered passage below select the characteristic from the list that follows which _best_ describes the passage.

A. Nonargument
B. Valid argument that is sound
C. Justified argument that is sound
D. Unsound argument because not logically correct
E. Unsound argument because contains a false premise

_____ 1. All cats are land mammals. All land mammals have body hair. So all cats have body hair.

_____ 2. The president of Multi-Oil Corp, is a fool. All fools are ignorant of the fact that they are fools. So the president of Multi-Oil Corp. must be ignorant of the fact that he is a fool.

_____ 3. Whenever people say that they have put money in the stock market, it reminds me of the person who played poker for the fun of it and was upset at breaking even.

_____ 4. The chances of selecting a heart from a regular deck of fifty-two playing cards is 1 in 4. The chances of selecting a queen are 1 in 13. So, my chances of selecting the queen of hearts are probably not very good.

_____ 5. The chances of selecting the queen of hearts are 1 in 52. I have ten chances to select the queen of hearts. I'll probably be able to pick it out with all those chances.

Ex. 4 Precisely define the terms valid argument, justified argument, logically correct argument, and sound argument.

Ex. 5 Supply two original examples of each of the following items: valid arguments, justified arguments, and sound arguments.

SELECTED ANSWERS

TO EXERCISES FOR MODULE 11

Ex. 1

1. V
2. No (not an argument)
3. No (but this may be justified)
4. No (nonargument)
5. V

If you confused arguments with nonarguments, go back and review 3:4, 4:1.1, and 8:3. If you recognized that items 1 and 5 were deductive arguments but were not confident that they were valid, you will be happy to find out that Part Two will give you the tools for better judging validity for just these kinds of arguments. If you missed any of these questions, review 11:1.2 and 11:1.3.

Ex. 2

1. No (valid)
2. J
3. No (nonargument)
4. J
5. No (valid)
6. J
7. J
8. No (nonargument)
9. J
10. J

If you missed more than two, review 11:1.2 and 11:1.4. Also review 10:3.2 if you had trouble recognizing the inductive arguments given in this exercise. If you missed items 3 or 8, review 4:1.1 and the definition of argument in 8:3.

Ex. 4 Your definitions of 'valid argument' and 'justified argument' should agree with Defs. 18 and 19 in 11:1.2. Logical correctness is defined in 8:3 (Definition 8). In 11:2 soundness is defined in Def. 21.

Ex. 5 Check your answers by comparing them with the various groups of examples in the text.

SELF-QUIZ FOR PART ONE

LOGIC AND LANGUAGE

Select the best answer from those provided and indicate your choice by circling the appropriate letter (approximate time, 50 minutes).

1. An argument is sound if, and only if, it is:
   A. Valid but not justified
   B. Logically correct
   C. Logically correct and has true premises
   D. Logically correct and has a true conclusion
   E. Justified but not valid

2. The Toyota dealer's definition of 'automobile' is "a car built by Toyota." This definition is *best* called:
   A. Narrow
   B. Descriptive
   C. Stipulative
   D. Loaded
   E. Arbitrary

3. A sentence can be called analytically true if it is:

   A. A synthetic statement
   B. True because of the empirical evidence
   C. True because of what it means
   D. The cause of logical analysis of propositions

4. Extensional definitions:

   A. Are usually recursive
   B. Are usually operational
   C. Do not necessarily specify the term's intension
   D. Do not specify the term's reference class

5. A term is ambiguous if it:

   A. Cannot be defined by a stipulative definition
   B. Cannot be recursively defined
   C. Appears in both the premise and the conclusion of an argument
   D. Has more than one specifiable meaning
   E. Is defined narrowly

6. Logic is:

   A. The study of argumentation and persuasion
   B. The study of mental processes of thinking
   C. The study of validity and justification
   D. The study of the relationships between the premises and conclusions of arguments
   E. The study of the relationships of arguments to issues in philosophy, value theory, and science

7. "Most medications are ineffective in treating viral infections. A cold is a viral infection. So, you know what that means about treating colds." This passage is:

   A. An argument but not an enthymeme
   B. A nonargument
   C. An enthymeme argument

8. The sentence "longer is longer than long but shorter than short" is best punctuated by:

   A. 'Longer' is 'longer' than long but shorter than 'short.'
   B. 'Longer' is longer than 'long' but shorter than short.
   C. Longer is longer than long but shorter than short.
   D. 'Longer' is longer than 'long' but shorter than 'short.'

9. "I apologize for being late" is:

   A. An analytic statement
   B. An assertive sentence
   C. A deductive argument
   D. A sentence that is not assertive

10. "All persons have two shoes, and since he does not have two shoes, he isn't a person" is:

   A. An argument with no stated conclusion
   B. An argument and its conclusion is "all people have two shoes"

C. An enthymeme argument and its missing statement is "all two shoed persons are people"

D. An argument and its conclusion is "he is not a person"

11. "Mom, all the other kids have candy. Why can't I have some too?" is:

A. A nonargument used to motivate someone to act

B. A valid argument

C. An argument with no premises

D. A sequence of assertive sentences, where "I have candy" is purported to be a logical product of the others

12. "Every forest fire has a cause. The cause is human negligence, natural disaster, or human arson. This forest fire was not caused by negligence or arson. So it must have been caused by a disaster." is:

A. Not an argument

B. An inductive argument

C. A sequence of nonassertive sentences

D. A deductive argument

13. "The Browns defeated the Vikings; the Vikings defeated the Cardinals and the Cardinals defeated the Browns. What do you make of that!" is:

A. An argument

B. Not an argument

C. A valid argument

D. A justified argument

14. "If your car has a knocking sound, it means the main bearings need replacement. Your car does make a knocking sound. So you have to replace the bearings." is:

A. An argument without a conclusion

B. An argument; the first sentence is irrelevant

C. An argument; the last sentence is the conclusion

D. An argument; the first sentence is its conclusion

15. "All the children have some candy. So I have candy." is:

A. Not an argument

B. An enthymeme with the statement missing being "Mommy, I want some candy, too"

C. An enthymeme with the missing statement being "all children have candy"

D. An enthymeme with the statement "I am a child" missing

16. "A more complex ecosystem is usually more stable, and stability is desirable in an ecosystem. For this reason, the hardwoods in the forest should not be cut." is:

A. Not an argument

B. An argument with no conclusion

C. An enthymeme argument, the missing statement being "to cut the hardwoods in this forest would make its ecosystem less complex"

D. An enthymeme argument with an analytically true conclusion

17. "People are mortal, and, after all, you are a person; the conclusion is so obvious, need I say more?" is:

A. An enthymeme with a missing premise

B. A factual report, but not an argument

C. An enthymeme with the missing statement being its conclusion "so you are mortal"

D. An argument with no missing statements

18. "There is a greater incidence of heart attack among cigarette smokers. However cigar and pipe smoking has not been positively correlated to heart attack. Quitting cigarette smoking seems to immediately reverse this tendency no matter how long the smoker may have had the habit." This passage is best characterized as:

A. A set of statements that do not here make up an argument

B. An argument that is not an enthymeme

C. An enthymeme that concludes "So, cigarette smoking may trigger a heart attack in a susceptible person."

D. An enthymeme that concludes "So, you should quit smoking at least a week before you would get a heart attack."

E. An enthymeme that concludes "To avoid heart attacks take up cigar and pipe smoking."

19. The definition "eloquence = $_{df}$ articulate persuasiveness" is best called

A. Intensional   B. Extensional

C. Stipulative   D. Recursive

20. In an enthymeme argument the premises and the conclusion

A. Are always explicitly stated   B. Are all statements   C. Are all analytic

D. Imply each other   E. Are true

21. "Billie Jean King won the championship that year" is:

A. A synthetic statement

B. An enthymeme argument, its missing statement being "someone won the championship that year"

C. Analytically false

D. Is an argument but not an enthymeme

22. Consider the passage: "This upper Michigan farmhouse must be cold in the winter. Look, it has no insulation, its windows need to be caulked, it has no storm windows or storm doors, and it does not have forced air heating. And you know it sure gets cold in Upper Michigan." This passage is best characterized as:

A. A set of statements but not an argument

B. An argument but not an enthymeme

C. An enthymeme with the missing premise being "the house is located in a cold climate"

D. An enthymeme with the missing premise being "any structure without insulation, storm windows, and forced air heating, and which needs caulking, is cold in the winter."

E. An enthymeme with the missing conclusion being "the owner of the farmhouse should have it caulked and insulated and should purchase a forced air heating system and storm windows."

23. When a person is being logical he or she is able to:

A. Remember a lot of information

B. See the consequences of various plans, policies, and beliefs

C. Come to decisions that are not obviously wrong

D. Be open-minded about the opinions of others

24. "It is a working assumption of logicians that entailment is a matter of structure, and support a matter of content" is:

A. True

B. False

C. Vague, so has no truth-value

D. Ambiguous, so has no truth-value

25. "Democracy = $_{df}$ a form of government in which those who are governed determine the laws by which they will be governed" is:

A. A recursive definition

B. An operational definition

C. An intensional definition

D. A stipulative definition

E. A restatement of the concept of a people's revolution in terms of geopolitics and economics

26. "The Cleveland Browns defeated the Minnesota Vikings, and the Vikings defeated the St. Louis Cardinals, so it's a fair bet that the Browns will beat the Cardinals when they play" is:

A. Deductive

B. Inductive

C. Not an argument

27. "All grass is equally green. So it can't be greener on the other side of the mountain." is:

A. Deductive

B. Inductive

C. Not an argument

28. Consider the following group of statements:

1. Fish require oxygen to live.
2. Oxygen is a natural substance in our environment.
3. Oxygen is not available in solid form.
4. So fish require something that is natural in our environment.

The argument within this group of statements is made up of

A. 1, 2, and 3   B. 1, 3, and 4   C. 1 and 4

D. 2 and 4   E. 1, 2, and 4

29. "The chances of drawing one card to a full house are remote. But I've been lucky all night. I'll probably get my card." is:

A. Deductive

B. Inductive

C. Not an argument

30 "Either your berflucker is dirty or your kanooten valve is frubby. If your berflucker is dirty, this cleanser will clean it. So if you still have a problem after we apply the cleanser, you have trouble. A frubby kanooten valve is always trouble." is:

A. Deductive
B. Inductive
C. Not an argument

31. Consider the definition: "Your relative = $_{df}$ your son, daughter, sister, brother or parent is your relative; if any person is your relative then all of his or her relatives are your relative; no one else is your relative." This definition is best called:

A. Arbitrary   B. Intensional
C. Recursive   D. Vague

32. A good example of a stipulative definition is:

A. Bird = $_{df}$ an animal
B. Butler = $_{df}$ a servant
C. Son = $_{df}$ a female child
D. Book = $_{df}$ a bound collection of papers

33. Which of the following characteristics is true of operational definitions?

A. They are a subclass of recursive definitions.
B. They remove conceptual problems because they reveal the concept or idea behind a term's definition.
C. They give practical application to intensionally defined terms.
D. They provide rules for building correct intensional definitions.

34. A term is ambiguous if, and only if, it:

A. Is also vague
B. Has more than one connotation
C. Has more than one meaning
D. Cannot be given a stipulative definition

35. A definition that specifies only part of a term's reference class is called:

A. Arbitrary
B. Narrow
C. Vague
D. Loaded

36. Select the phrase which most accurately completes the definition "inductive argument = $_{df}$ an argument that . . ."

A. Goes from specific to general
B. Purports to entail its conclusion
C. Entails or implies its conclusion
D. Purports to strongly support its conclusion

37. Select the phrase which best completes the definition "valid argument = $_{df}$ an argument such that its premises . . ."

A. Entail its conclusion on the basis of structure
B. Purport to support its conclusion
C. And conclusion are true on the basis of fact
D. Strongly support its conclusion on the basis of content

38–40 For each of the following indicate whether it is:

A. An argument
B. A nonargument

38. If we control the toys and candy for both children we can control their behavior. This follows from the fact that should they choose to disobey us we can withhold their treats thus giving negative reinforcement to disobedience. But should they obey we can give positive reinforcements to each.

39. My friends, the income tax structure must be changed. Here's why! The current tax structure allows an examption for each dependent. If a family has seven children, each child counts as a dependent. This tax break encourages larger families. The environmental crisis will become even worse if people have large families. One way to discourage large families is to change the tax rule on exemptions.

40. One medication often used for treating superficial fungal infections is called Griseofulvin. It is quite effective as a treatment. However, certain mutant cells can develop which may be resistant to the action of Griseofulvin. So Griseofulvin is not always totally effective.

ANSWERS TO SELF-QUIZ
FOR PART ONE

Item	Answer	Sec.	Item	Answer	Sec.
1.	C	11:2	21.	A	9:2
2.	D	6:2.3	22.	D	4:3
3.	C	9:1.2	23.	B	1:2
4.	C	7:2.1	24.	A	11:1.3
5.	D	6:1.2	25.	C	7:1.2
6.	D	2:1.2	26.	B	10:3.2
7.	C	4:3	27.	A	10:2.2
8.	D	5:1.3	28.	E	4:2.1
9.	D	3:3.1	29.	B	10:3.2
10.	D	4:1.1	30.	A	10:2.2
11.	A	3:4	31.	C	7:2.3
12.	D	10:2.2	32.	C	5:2.2
13.	B	3:4	33.	C	7:2.4
14.	C	4:1.1	34.	C	6:1.2
15.	D	4:3	35.	B	6:2.2
16.	C	4:3	36.	D	10:1.3
17.	C	4:3	37.	A	11:1.2
18.	A	3:4	38.	A	3:4
19.	A	7:1.2	39.	A	3:4
20.	B	3:1.2	40.	A	3:4

If you missed 10 or less, you can consider yourself to have passed this Self-Quiz. Be sure to recheck the sections clarifying answers to questions you may have missed.

TWO

USING SYMBOLS IN LOGIC

In Part One you learned that the question of logical correctness leads in two very different directions. To test for validity you examine an argument's structure. To test for justification you look to its content. In Part Two our focus is on the first half of this issue, testing arguments for structural validity. We will focus on content in much of Parts Three and Four.

Logicians have developed ways of making clear the logical structure of arguments. They use various notational devices which allow them to present the form of an argument in a way that divorces that form from any particular subject matter or content. This logical structure can then be examined, manipulated, and evaluated for validity, using objective, and in some cases quite mechanical, testing procedures. In Part Two we will learn procedures that are applicable to the first two elementary levels of logic: the logic of statements (propositional logic) and the logic of classes (predicate logic). We will learn how to use the notations or symbols of contemporary symbolic logic to exhibit the logical structure of English arguments. We will learn how to examine those structures for validity. We will use the truth-tabular method to examine arguments of propositional logic; as alternative tests, we will present the diagram method and the syllogistic method for evaluating arguments of predicate logic for validity.

4

PROPOSITIONAL LOGIC

Propositional logic is the study of the logical relationships between statement units, negations of statement units, and statements that are truth-functional compounds. Its aim is to develop a mechanical procedure to test arguments at this level of logic for validity. In Chapter 4 we will learn to use symbols to represent the logical structure of the arguments of propositional logic.[1] Our educational goal is to learn how to take an English-language argument and examine it for validity using the methods set out in this chapter.

MODULE 12

STATEMENT UNITS

We begin our study of propositional logic by coming to grips with the practical implications of the logicians' assumption that validity is a "formal" or structural thing. To do this, in Modules 12 and 13 we will examine some of the logical relationships that can exist between simple statements.

● After reading Module 12 you should be able to:

1. Identify statement units
2. Construct examples of statement units
3. Identify and distinguish truth-functional compounds from temporal and causal compound statements
4. Construct examples of truth-functional compounds, temporal compounds, and causal compounds

12:1.1 First level of structure A statement, being an assertive sentence, is the kind of sentence concerning which it makes sense to ask: Is this true or false? In beginning to clarify the idea of logical structure, we want to identify some relatively small unit or building block as the starting point for discussing structure. The most natural unit to identify seems to be the unit that consists of a simple subject and predicate statement, because this is the smallest unit that we can say is true or false. Truth-values are values of statements, not of classes, nouns, verbs, adjectives, paragraphs, or chapters. Since logic is concerned with what the truth-value of a conclusion would be on the hypothesis that its premises are all true, it is natural to focus, at least at first, on truth-values and the statements which have them.

---

[1] This is called using *Formalization*. Formalization helps us focus on an argument's structure. It helps us overcome our biases by allowing us to disregard the content or subject matter of a given argument as we evaluate it for validity.

We will ultimately find that there is a lot of logical structure submerged *within* each statement unit, but our progression to that knowledge will come only after we have exhausted the logic which deals with the relationships *between* statement units. Logic progresses from less sophisticated to more sophisticated modes of formalization as it searches for that structure which makes a particular kind of argument demonstrably valid or demonstrably invalid. Since the simplest basic unit seems at first to be the statement unit, we must clarify the idea of a statement unit.

12:1.2 Let us *define* a statement unit as the simplest form of assertive sentence to which it is possible to attribute a truth-value. We can begin by adopting a grammatical criterion for recognizing statement units. A statement is a statement unit if it is simple subject-predicate statement, for example:

> Lynn is here.
> I love to eat pie.
> The advertising budget is in bad shape.
> There are forty-seven first-aid books left in stock.
> These secretaries are great typists.
> Roger's car failed to start last night.
> Jerome's pie ended up on his shirt.
> Happiness is a cold beer.
> All political figures who are liberals are Democrats.
> There are many Republican liberals.
> Roger thinks that Emile lived here.[2]

12:2.1 Compounds Statement units can relate to each other in several ways. Those just used as examples are related to each other in that each one except "Lynn is here" is printed below another. Some in the list are longer than others, too. These are relations of position and size. The relations that usually interest us are those that indicate causal connection, temporal connection, or purely logical, what we shall call *truth-functional,* connection. Here are some sentences indicating temporal connection between their component statement units. The English words used to make the connections are set in italics.

> Phyllis is here *now,* but Mary was here *before.*
> *As soon as* the economy is on its feet, I will resign.
> *When* happiness is a cold beer is *after* I play a game of basketball.
> Roger's car failed to start last night; *then* Roger went to the gas station.
> Carol fell in love *and* (then) got married.

Other sentences indicate causal relationships between their component statement units. The causal indicator words are italicized:

[2] For our purposes, statements like "Joan believes that all persons should be treated equally" are going to be considered statement units. For us they raise only one question: Does she or does she not believe it regardless of whether or not it's true? You should notice here that what is talked about is Joan's belief or disbelief, not its truth. The sentence asserts what she believes, not whether her belief is true. In Module 13 we give long lists of words that indicate logical compounds. One rule of thumb for recognizing statement units is to look for any of the words or phrases that indicate one or more of the logical operations discussed in Module 13. If you find none, treat the statement in question as a positive statement unit.

John is here *because* Susan is here.
If you slam the door, the glass will break.
Because his car failed last night, Roger went to the gas station.
Jill fell in love *and* (because of this) got married.

In the above two sets of examples the truth or falsity of the statement compounds depends on whether or not the alleged temporal or causal connections exist. Is it true that Mary was here earlier than Phyllis was? Is it true that John's reason for coming is that Susan is here? To know the truth of these statements it is not enough simply to know the truth of their statement units. Even if it is true that Mary was here and that Phyllis was here, we cannot from those facts know that Mary was here *earlier* than Phyllis was. Just because John came and Susan came does not guarantee that John came *because* Susan did. However in other cases the truth of the statement compound is determined solely by the truth-values of the simple statement units it contains. When the truth-value of a compound statement is a function solely of the truth-values of the component statement units, these compounds are called truth-functional compounds. They can be distinguished from time-functional or cause-functional compounds. Here are some examples of truth-functional compounds. In these examples the words that indicate purely logical connection are italicized.

Carol got married *and* fell in love.
If the economy should get back on its feet, *then* I would resign.
Sue was here *although* Mary was here *too*.
Sherry was here *if* Mary was here.
I will resign *unless* the economy should get back on its feet.
Either Carol got married *or* she fell in love.
I fix my car *only if* I cannot avoid it.
I fix my car *if, and only if,* I cannot avoid it.
I will marry *only if* I get a job.
I will marry *only if* I am fired.

12:2.2 All the examples given in 12:2.1 are examples of *statement compounds*. A statement compound is simply a complex statement built up from statement units. All the ones in 12:2.1 were built up by joining one statement unit to another using some expression indicating that they were temporally, causally, or truth-functionally related. Since statement compounds are still statements, each one still has a specific truth-value. Thus every example in 12:2.1 can reasonably be said to be true or false.

12:2.3 Deriving truth-values There is an important difference between how causal or temporal statement compounds derive their truth-values and how truth-functional compounds derive their truth-values. *Truth-functional compounds are those which derive their truth-values solely from the truth-values of their component statement units.* Thus, for example, the truth-functional statement compound

Sue is here and Billie Jo is here

is true just in the event that

Sue is here

and

Billie Jo is here

are both true statement units. No other factors (like temporal or causal connections) make that compound true, and if either statement unit is false, the compound is false.

On the other hand, the truth-values for temporal, causal, and any other type of statement compound, besides truth-functional compounds, depends on *whether or not the purported* (temporal or causal) *relationship exists as well as the truth-values of the statement units.* Consider, for example, the causal statement compound

We won Saturday because the other team was unprepared.

To judge its truth we look at more than just

We won Saturday

and

The other team was unprepared.

We also, and perhaps chiefly, look at whether the reason we won was their lack of preparation. If we won because of something else, then the causal statement compound is not true, whatever might be the case concerning its two statement units.

At times we assert the truth of statement units by saying things like:

1. Cows fly.
2. The agency is responsive.
3. There is room for one more person here.

However, at other times we assert the falsity of statement units by saying things like:

4. Cows do *not* fly.
5. The agency is un responsive.
6. There is *not* enough room here for anyone else.

When we are asserting that some statement is false, we are making a negative statement, in contrast to the positive statement made in asserting its truth. Example statements 4 to 6 are the negative versions of the positive statement units 1 to 3, respectively.

12:2.4 Ambiguity of connection Recall the example sentence "Carol fell in love and got married." This English sentence is usually used to assert at least that Carol did fall in love and that Carol did get married. This meaning takes the conjunction word 'and' as expressing a truth-functional connection. What is required for the truth of 'Carol fell in love and got married' is simply that each of the conjoined statement units 'Carol fell in love' and 'Carol got married' be true. But you know that the original sentence often means not only this but *more*. It means additionally that she fell in love *first* and that she *subsequently* married *because* she had fallen in love. Thus it ambiguously suggests causal, temporal, and truth-functional connections.

Fortunately, most of the time the validity of an argument does not depend on whatever nonlogical connections might also be expressed. Let us look at a typical example.

EG. 12.1 1. If Carol fell in love, she would treat her husband more kindly.
2. If Carol got married, she would have a better chance to get a job.

3. Carol fell in love and got married.
4. So Carol will treat her husband more kindly and she'll have a better chance to get a job.

This example is valid. Moreover you don't have to worry about the temporal or causal connection between Carol's falling in love and her marrying in order to grasp its validity.

Important convention:
There are some arguments whose logical correctness does depend on whether certain temporal (or time-related) connections exist over and above the logical connections that might exist. Take, for example, 'Carol got married and had a child. So the child was not born out of wedlock.' What allows this argument to be valid is not simply the relation of the two premises to the conclusion. Its validity also requires the temporal relation or ordering implied in presenting the conjunct 'Carol got married' first. Other arguments depend on connections based on cause and effect. The structural relationships involved in arguments depending on temporal and causal connections are very subtle. They take us well beyond the realm of propositional logic, since propositional logic is concerned only with truth-functional connections. Therefore, from now on we will pay attention to the truth-functional connections expressed by words connecting statement units to the exclusion of any temporal or causal connections that may be expressed. For example, "The tree grew well although there are few oaks around" does assert both that the tree grew well *and* that there are few oaks in the area. We *will pay attention only to logical connections* like the connection marked by 'and' in the previous sentence. In the example, however, the word 'although' also suggests some hesitation; perhaps the scarcity of oaks *made* it ecologically improbable that the tree would prosper. That extra suggestion or hesitation is not a suggestion of a truth-functional connection. Why? Because knowing whether the individual statement units are true or false does not allow you to determine the truth or falsity of the suggestion. Accordingly *we will ignore all suggestions about nonlogical connections between statement units.* This convention means that connections between statement units will be *treated as if the only connections expressed were logical.*

Of all the truth-functional connectives those expressing the "if ___, then . . ." connection are the most likely to be used to express temporal and/or causal connections as well. However, our convention allows us to focus exclusively on the truth-functional connections they make.

Our convention will make it easier to determine the logical correctness of many arguments, which is our goal. The convention also means that arguments whose logical correctness depends on the fact that certain temporal or causal relations exist over and above the logical relations will turn out to be arguments too sophisticated to be evaluated by the methods of propositional logic. Logicians work to develop means of testing these more sophisticated arguments, but in this text we will not be able to consider their efforts in these difficult areas.

EXERCISES FOR MODULE 12
STATEMENT UNITS

Ex. 1 Below is a list of 15 sentences. Identify those sentences which are positive statement units. Remembering our convention given at the end of 12:2.4, identify each sentence as either a positive statement unit by marking 'SU' in the answer space) or as a statement compound or negative statement unit (by marking 'no' in the answer space).

_____ 1. All people are mortal.

_____ 2. It is not the case that all people are mortal.

_____ 3. Students detest red tape.

_____ 4. A big university can alienate students.

_____ 5. A big university is well liked by students.

_____ 6. Either students detest red tape or all people are mortal.

_____ 7. Many cities are overpopulated.

_____ 8. If many courses are overenrolled, then students detest red tape.

_____ 9. Few courses are underenrolled.

_____ 10. If I am elected, I will end poverty.

_____ 11. If I am elected, I will end slavery.

_____ 12. Students do not detest red tape.

_____ 13. Students detest red tape only if it frustrates people to be treated impersonally.

_____ 14. It frustrates people to be treated impersonally.

_____ 15. I will be elected if, and only if, people will just go their own way.

Ex. 2 Write ten original examples of statement units.

Ex. 3 Below are ten sentences involving connections between statement units. Put 'TF' beside those sentences which are truth-functional compounds; put 'no' beside those which are temporal or causal compounds. In other words, here are ten sentences. Each is a compound containing at least two statement units. If the units are connected using words suggesting causality or suggesting temporal sequence, put 'no.' If the connection suggested is truth-functional, put 'TF.'

_____ 1. When I was one and twenty, I heard a wise man speak.

_____ 2. Now that I am twenty-two, I know that what he said was true.

_____ 3. George Washington served two terms as president, but John Adams served only one.

_____ 4. Not a word was spoken, nor was there any need for words.

_____ 5. If the police patrol one area more heavily, crime will rise elsewhere as a result.

_____ 6. If your brother marries, you'll have a sister-in-law.

_____ 7. Roberta and Cindy won't come.

_____ 8. I shall become either a farmer or a veterinarian.

_____ 9. Permission is granted only if an emergency exists.

_____ 10. After she got the message, she reconsidered her position.

Ex. 4 Construct eight original examples of truth-functional compounds using each of the following words or phrases at least once: 'or,' 'and,' 'unless,' 'but,' 'only if,' 'if . . .,' then ___,' 'not . . . unless ___,' '. . . if, and only if, ___.' Also construct two examples of causal statement compounds and two examples of temporal statement compounds.

ANSWERS TO EXERCISES
FOR MODULE 12

Ex. 1

1. SU	2. No (a negated statement unit)	3. SU	4. SU
5. SU	6. No	7. SU	8. No
9. SU	10. No	11. No	12. No
13. No	14. SU	15. No	

If you missed two or more, review the whole module from 12:1.2 on.

EX. 2 Compare your answers to the examples in 12:1.2 and also examine your answers in the light of the grammatical criterion given there. Remember that your examples should contain neither negations nor connectives.

Ex. 3

1. No   2. No   3. TF   4. TF
5. No, a causal connection is suggested.
6. TF, but with a certain interpretation it may be that "no" is an acceptable answer.
7. TF   8. TF   9. TF   10. No

If you missed four or more, review the whole module.

EX. 4 Compare your answers to the examples given in 12:2.1 and examine them in the light of the important differences discussed in 12:2.3.

MODULE 13
TRUTH-FUNCTIONAL OPERATORS

Now that you have a preliminary knowledge of how to recognize statement units and truth-functional compounds, it is time to focus on the variety of truth-functional relationships indicated by the variety of logical connectives and operators.

● After reading Module 13 you should be able to:

1. Identify and distinguish some of the logical relationships that can exist between statement units
2. List five types of logical (truth-functional) operators and list words or phrases which indicate each type
3. Write original examples of each type of truth functional statement

13:1.1 Varieties of truth-functional compounds In any natural language there are many words and phrases that can be used to build various types of statement compounds. Those which build up truth-functional compounds are of special interest. The arguments tested for validity in propositional logic are made up of positive and negative statement units and truth-functional statement compounds. Four types of truth-functional compound statements are of special interest:

> conjunctions
> disjunctions
> conditionals
> biconditionals

13:1.2 Here are some words that in many of their standard uses yield *conjunctions*:

> . . . and _____
> Both . . . and _____
> . . . but _____
> . . . yet _____
> . . . although _____
> . . . whereas _____
> However . . ., _____

In each case the . . . and the _____ could be filled in by a statement unit, and a *conjunctive* truth-functional statement compound would result. Let us use 'Karen is smart' and 'Mark is rich' as example statement units. We could *conjoin* them as

> Karen is smart and Mark is rich.
> Both Karen is smart and Mark is rich.
> Karen is smart but Mark is rich.
> Karen is smart yet Mark is rich.
> Karen is smart although Mark is rich.
> Karen is smart whereas Mark is rich.
> However smart Karen is, Mark is rich.

A conjunction is true just in case both component statement units are true.

EXERCISE 1

Here are a group of statements. See if you can identify those which are conjunctions.

1. Some conjuncts are connected by 'and,' and some are connected by 'but.'
2. While some people may not have recognized it, item 1 is a conjunction.
3. Item 2 is also, although 'while' is not one of the more commonly used words for expressing the idea that both statement units are true.
4. Item 3 is a conjunction.
5. But item 4 is not.
6. By now you are probably sure that item 5 is no conjunction although item 6 is.

13:1.3 Here are some words that in many of their standard uses yield *disjunctions*:

> Either . . . or _____
> . . . or _____
> . . . unless _____

Here the ... and _____ are again filled by statement units. Using the same two example statement units we used in 13:1.2, we can generate the following sample disjunctive truth-functional statement compounds.

> Either Karen is smart or Mark is rich.
> Karen is smart or Mark is rich.
> Karen is smart unless Mark is rich.

A disjunction is true if either of its component statement units is true.

There is another, stronger sense of 'or,' the exclusive sense, that should be distinguished from the inclusive sense just noted in the paragraph above. If a restaurant advertises a dinner served with "soup or salad" it means that customers can order either a salad or soup but not both with their meal. Consider another example. If someone says "we can either go to the theater or stay home" it usually means that the two options are mutually exclusive. Logicians focus on the inclusive sense of 'or' as expressed in

> Either ... or _____ (and possibly both)

They do so because the exclusive sense, expressed in

> Either ... or _____ (but not both)

can be derived, if desired, by appealing to a combination of other truth-functional operations as in

> Either ... or _____, and not both ... and _____

EXERCISE 2

Identify the disjunctions among the following.

1. Either Bob will drink pop or he'll prefer cider.
2. Bob will drink pop unless he prefers cider.
3. Maybe he'll drink both.
4. The alternative to Bob's drinking pop is his drinking cider.
5. Who knows what Bob would take if he had other choices?

(Items 1, 2, and 4 are disjunctions. Each says the same thing in different words. Item 3 is interpretable either as a statement unit or as a conjunction: he will drink the one and he will drink the other. Item 5 is a question, not an assertion at all.)

13:1.4 Here are some words and phrases that in many of the standard uses yield "conditionals":

> If ..., then _____
> If ..., _____
> ... only if _____
> _____ on the condition that ...

_____ if . . .
_____, provided that . . .
not . . ., unless _____

Using them, we can build up truth-functional compounds that express that the first statement unit is a logical condition of the second.[3] The . . . (first) part is called the _antecedent_ of the conditional and the _____ (second) part is called the _consequent_ of the conditional. Conditionals are used to assert logical but not necessarily causal or temporal connection between two statement units such that if the first statement unit is true, then the second is true. So a conditional statement compound is true in all cases except when its antecedent is true and its consequent is false.[4] Using these phrases and our two sample statement units, we can construct the following:

> If Karen is smart, then Mark is rich.
> If Karen is smart, Mark is rich.
> Karen is smart only if Mark is rich.
> Mark is rich on the condition that Karen is smart.
> Mark is rich if Karen is smart.
> Mark is rich provided that Karen is smart.
> Karen is not smart unless Mark is rich.

Each of these examples, although worded differently, asserts the same thing, namely: If 'Karen is smart' is true, then 'Mark is rich' is also true.

You will notice that different names (antecedent and consequent) have been given to the statement units of a conditional. This is because their roles are different. Consider the differences between these two statements:

> If it has been raining, the street gets wet.
> If the street gets wet, it has been raining.

The first is probably true; the second can easily be false. In general

> If the antecedent is true, then so is the consequent

does _not_ assure you that

> If the consequent is true, then so is the antecedent.

---

[3] In some of their uses the two phrases:

(1) is a sufficient condition for (2)
(2) is a necessary condition for (1)

can be taken as expressing this logical connection. This is so because one way of reading these phrases is as follows: "If statement unit 1 is true, this is sufficient to make statement unit 2 true" and "The truth of statement unit 2 is a preliminary requirement necessary for the truth of statement unit 1." In both cases we can infer that if statement unit 1 is true, then so is statement unit 2. In such uses the logical connection they express can successfully be treated as truth-functional. However, Eg. 41.5 indicates that this more standard treatment appears to miss a large part of the logical power of these expressions.

[4] We only mention the truth conditions for each of the types of logical connectives here to give a fuller idea of their force. We will give a much more complete explanation of each connective in Module 16.

Hence it is very important to notice in the above that 'Karen is smart' is always the antecedent, and 'Mark is rich' is the consequent. You should review the examples above to assure yourself that each has the same antecedent and the same consequent.

13:1.5 Here are some phrases that in many of their standard uses yield *biconditionals:*

> . . . if, and only if, _____
> . . . when, and only when, _____
> If, and only if, . . ., _____
> . . . just exactly if _____
> The cases where . . . are exactly those where _____

These phrases can give us biconditionals like

> Karen is smart if, and only if, Mark is rich.
> Karen is smart when, and only when, Mark is rich.
> If, and only if, Karen is smart, Mark is rich.
> Karen is smart just exactly if Mark is rich.
> The cases where Karen is smart are exactly those where Mark is rich.

A biconditional statement is true when both of its component statement units have the same truth-value. A biconditional truth-functional compound is used to express a mutual conditional relationship between two statement units. That is, given two statement units, the biconditional of them expresses that the first is a logical condition for the second and the second is a logical condition for the first. A biconditional asserts that both its component statement units have the same truth-value; i.e., either both are true or both are false.

EXERCISE 3

Here are a number of statements. Distinguish the conditionals from the biconditionals.

1. If you can identify conjunctions, then you will manage conditionals.
2. You will manage conditionals provided that you can recognize conjunctions.
3. The price of coal will increase only if gas becomes scarcer.
4. The price will rise if, and only if, gas becomes scarcer.
5. You should feel fairly confident on the condition that you see the difference between items 3 and 4.

(Item 4 is the only biconditional in this exercise.)

13:1.6 Negation In 13:1.1 we said that there were four important types of truth-functional statement compounds. But besides compounding two statement units there are other jobs that can be done by operators. One of these other functions is to negate a single statement unit. Statement units can be *negated,* or asserted *not to be true,* by using words or phrases such as

Not . . .
It is not the case that . . .
It is not true that . . .
There is no way that . . .
. . . is false.
It is false that . . .

Thus we could develop the following negations:

Karen is not smart (from 'not: Karen is smart').
It is not the case that Karen is smart.
It is not true that Karen is smart.
There is no way that Karen is smart.
'Karen is smart' is false.
It is false that Karen is smart.

A negation, which is a statement in its own right, is true exactly when the statement unit it negates is false. In some contexts another verb can perform the function of negation. For example,

Karen did her work but Joe failed to do his.
Joe went to the party but Karen avoided it.

In both these sentences the second statement unit can reasonably be interpreted as asserting a negation: 'Joe did not do his work,' and 'Karen did not go the party.'

EXERCISE 4

Identify the negations among the following:

1. Rebecca is not stupid.
2. There's no fooling her.
3. She is not one to be taken in easily.
4. She avoided becoming involved.
5. She refused to be tricked by my trap.
6. Rebecca really understands the situation.

(Items 1 to 5 are the negations, with the verb doing the work of negation in items 4 and 5.)

13:2.1 The realm of propositional logic is composed of those arguments which are built up by using only truth-functional statement compounds, statement units, and the negations of statement units.[5] Statement units were formerly called *propositions,* so propositional logic is simply the logic that deals with the possible logical relationships among statement units. Reexamine the examples in group A of 10:2.3 to confirm that they meet the requirement just mentioned and qualify as examples of arguments in the realm of propositional logic. Here are two more examples

[5] Bear in mind our convention of 12:2.4.

EG. 13.1 1. We either sell our house or sell our farm only if we obtain enough money to get through college.
2. We cannot sell our house!
3. So we will obtain enough money to get through college if we sell our farm.

EG. 13.2 1. If there have been successful moon landings or our space program is a fraud, then the media are deceiving the public.
2. But there have not been any successful moon landings.
3. So if the space program is a fraud, then the media are deceiving the public.

13:2.2 Identical structures Notice how similar in structure the pair of examples Eg. 13.1 and Eg. 13.2 are. Each one begins with a premise of the form

If . . . or _ _ _, then ____

Each has a second premise of the form

not . . .

and each has a conclusion of the form

If _ _ _, then ____

They differ only in content; they are the same in form, with minor stylistic differences in the way the statement compounds or negated statement units are worded.

We have explicitly accepted the assumption that validity is a matter of form. This assumption is borne out by these examples because Egs. 13.1 and 13.2 are both valid. Their content is not a factor in determining validity.

There are a number of such valid argument forms. We could present much of propositional and even predicate logic in terms of having people learn and memorize a series of valid argument patterns and having them decide validity on the basis of whether or not a given argument matched one of the patterns. But there are many drawbacks to that approach. For one, there are too many valid patterns to learn; for another, in natural contexts many arguments utilize several patterns in tandem to achieve their conclusions. And finally, there are too many chances for error in the process of memorization and comparison which could be avoided if more mechanical procedures were to be discovered and a better theoretical synthesis were achieved. In Modules 14 to 17 we develop reliable mechanical procedures which can be used with confidence to check for validity and invalidity among arguments of propositional logic. We also present enough theory to help you understand why they work.

EXERCISES FOR MODULE 13
TRUTH-FUNCTIONAL OPERATORS

Ex. 5 Identify which of the following statements are negations, conjunctions, disjunctions, conditionals, or biconditionals by writing their numbers in the spaces below.

1. Some people are very wise.
2. It is not the case that all people are mortal.
3. Students detest red tape.
4. A big university can alienate students.
5. A big university is well liked by students.
6. Either grandma came or there were some unhappy youngsters.
7. Many courses are overenrolled.
8. A big university is well liked by students, and many courses are overenrolled.
9. If many courses are overenrolled, then students detest red tape.
10. A big university is well liked by students, but a big university can alienate students.
11. Few courses are underenrolled.
12. If I am elected, I will end poverty.
13. Students do not detest red tape.
14. I will be elected if, and only if, people will just go their own way.

Conjunctions:

Disjunctions:

Conditional:

Biconditional:

Negations:

Ex. 6 Below is a list of fifteen statements. Identify each as a statement unit 'SU,' conjunction 'Cj,' disjunction 'Dj,' conditional 'Cd,' biconditional 'Bc,' or negation 'N.'

_____ 1. John lives here.

_____ 2. John lives here and David lives here.

_____ 3. Either John lives here or David lives here.

_____ 4. Either John or David lives here.

_____ 5. John lives with David.

_____ 6. If John lives here, then David lives here.

_____ 7. John lives here if, and only if, David does.

_____ 8. David lives here provided that John does.

_____ 9. John lives here and yet David lives here.

_____ 10. John lives here only if David lives here.

_____ 11. John does not live here.

_____ 12. David lives here unless John lives here.

_____ 13. John does not live here unless David lives here.

_____ 14. "David lives here" is false.

_____ 15. It is the case that David lives here.

Ex. 7 List the five logical functions discussed in Module 13. Next to each name in your list write at least two words or phrases that indicate that function. Use each phrase in writing original examples of truth-functional statements.

ANSWERS TO EXERCISES
FOR MODULE 13

The answers to Exs. 1 to 4 are given within or below each in the text.

Ex. 5 Conjunctions: 8, 10; disjunctions: 6; conditionals: 9, 12; biconditional: 14; negations: 2, 13. If you missed two or more, review 13:1.1 to 13:1.6.

Ex. 6

1. SU	2. Cj	3. Dj	4. Dj
5. SU	6. Cd	7. Bc	8. Cd
9. Cj	10. Cd	11. N	12. Dj
13. Cd (13:1.4)	14. N	15. SU	

If you missed more than two, review 13:1.2 to 13:1.6, especially the lists, more carefully.

Ex. 7

Conjunction: . . . and _____; both . . . and _____
Disjunction: either . . . or _____; . . . or _____
Conditional: if . . ., then _____; . . . only if _____
Biconditional: . . . if, and only if, _____; . . . when, and only when, _____
Negation: not . . .; it is false that . . .

MODULE 14
THE LANGUAGE OF PROPOSITIONAL LOGIC

In Module 14 we will learn to use the system of symbols that logicians have found most practical in exhibiting the kinds of logical structure we discussed in Module 13, namely the logical structure of the relationships among statement units, negations, and truth-functional compound statements. These statements will be represented in our formalization by *well-formed formulas* of our symbolic language.

● After reading Module 14 you should be able to:

1. Identify well-formed formulas of our language
2. Identify the main characteristics of well-formed formulas and the reasons why some formulas are not well formed
3. Given a formula that is not well formed, rewrite it as a well-formed formula
4. Construct well-formed formulas using specified symbols

14:1.1 Identifying statement units Consider the following four example arguments.

EG. 14.1 1. Peanuts are red.
　　　　　　　2. Either roses are red or peanuts are not red.
　　　　　　　3. So roses are red.

EG. 14.2 1. Peanuts are red if, and only if, roses are red.
2. Roses are not red.
3. So peanuts are not red.

EG. 14.3 1. Both peanuts are red and roses are red.
2. If either peanuts are red or roses are red, then footballs are brown.
3. So footballs are brown.

EG. 14.4 1. If footballs are brown, then roses are red.
2. If roses are red, then peanuts are red.
3. It is not the case that peanuts are red.
4. So it is not the case that footballs are brown.

They are all valid. Our aim is to learn how to prove this using the techniques of formal logic. The first step in this procedure is to exhibit their logical structure using symbolic notation.

These four examples involve the use of only three statement units:

1. Peanuts are red.
2. Roses are red.
3. Footballs are brown.

To isolate the logical form of these kinds of arguments from whatever elements in their content may be distracting, let us employ letters to stand for these statement units. Let p, q, and r be used in place of these statement units. Thus we can rewrite the four examples as follows (for now let 'peanuts are red' = p; 'roses are red' = q; and 'footballs are brown' = r):

EG. 14.1′ 1. p
2. Either q or not p
∴ 3. q

EG. 14.2′ 1. p if, and only if, q
2. Not q
∴ 3. Not p

EG. 14.3′ 1. p and q
2. If either p or q, then r
∴ 3. r

EG. 14.4′ 1. If r, then q
2. If q, then p
3. Not p
∴ 4. Not r

The step we just completed is the first step of the process of "translating" from a natural language, like English, to the artificial formal language of propositional logic. That step is to isolate the statement units and replace each occurrence of each statement unit with a particular letter. Above we replaced each occurrence of 'peanuts are red' with p, each occurrence of 'roses are red' with q, and each occurrence of 'footballs are brown' with r.

14:1.2 Logical relations Our next step is to determine whether any of the statements are negations or truth-functional compounds (conjunctions, disjunctions, conditionals, or biconditionals) as described in 13:1.2 to 13:1.6. If we find any, we will want to express their structure symbolically. The accompanying table indicates the symbol that we will use to express each logical operation.

Logical operation	English wording	Use	Symbol	Name of symbol
Negation	Not ____ (13:1.6)	To deny a statement	~	Tilde
Conjunction	____ and . . . (13:1.2)	To assert the truth of both of two statements	&	Ampersand
Disjunction (alternation)	____ or . . . (13:1.3)	To assert that at least one of two statements is true	∨	Wedge
Conditional	If ____, then . . . (13:1.4)	To assert a conditional relationship between two statements such that the first is a condition for the second	⊃	Horseshoe
Biconditional	____ if, and only if, . . . (13:1.5)	To assert a mutual or biconditional relationship between two statements such that each is a condition for the other	≡	Triple bar

We can now express the logical relationships in our four example arguments using symbols. Of course it will be necessary to preserve the English grouping as indicated by the standard English punctuation marks. We will use parentheses as our grouping indicators. Thus our four examples become:

EG. 14.1″
1. p
2. $(q \vee (\sim p))$
∴ 3. q

EG. 14.2″
1. $(p \equiv q)$
2. $(\sim q)$
∴ 3. $(\sim p)$

EG. 14.3″
1. $(p \,\&\, q)$
2. $((p \vee q) \supset r)$
∴ 3. r

EG. 14.4″
1. $(r \supset q)$
2. $(q \supset p)$
3. $(\sim p)$
∴ 4. $(\sim r)$

14:2.1 Well-formed formulas defined We are now in a position to pull together what we have said about (1) replacing statement units by certain lowercase letters, (2) representing logical structure by the use of our five symbols for structure ~, &, ∨, ⊃, and ≡, and (3) using parentheses for punctuation. All these go into writing well-formed formulas of propositional logic. Here is a recursive definition of 'well-formed formula':

1. p, q, r, s, t, and u standing alone are well-formed formulas.
2. If something, call it A, is a well-formed formula, then $(\sim A)$ is well-formed.

3. If two things, call them A and B for now, are well-formed formulas, then $(A \& B)$, $(A \vee B)$, $(A \supset B)$, and $(A \equiv B)$ are well-formed.
4. Nothing is well-formed unless it is constructed upon the basis of the above rules.

There are several points you should note about well-formed formulas:

1. The letters A and B are not parts of any formula. They are only English letters being used here as variables to stand for any well-formed formula whatsoever. They stand for arbitrary formulas but are not themselves formulas.
2. If there are more than six statement units to consider in any given example, we will have to add to the list of six letters mentioned in part 1 of the definition. We can add p_1, q_1, r_1, s_1, t_1, u_1, p_2, q_2, ...
3. There are always going to be an even number of parentheses (or none at all) in a formula. There will also always be one set of parentheses for each logical operator, $\sim$, &, $\vee$, $\supset$, or $\equiv$, that occurs.
4. The letters p, q, r, s, t, u, p_1, . . . are called *statement letters* because they are used to stand for particular statements units. The symbols $\sim$, &, $\supset$, $\vee$, and $\equiv$ are called *logical operators* because they indicate the various operations of propositional logic, namely the negation of a statement, the conjunction of two statements, the alternation or disjunction of two statements, the conditional of two statements, and the biconditional of two statements. The four logical operators that join two statements are also sometimes called *logical connectives*. The parentheses are often called *grouping indicators*.
5. In order to make groupings easier to read we will use brackets and braces in our well-formed formulas. Consider these devices merely parentheses that are misshapen so that no changes in the definition of a well-formed formula will be needed. In general we use brackets instead of writing a third parenthesis in a row, and we introduce a brace instead of the third bracket in a row. Each bracket or brace must be paired up with another bracket or brace.

14:2.2 Here are some examples of well-formed formulas (also called "wffs," pronounced "wifs"):

p	$(\sim(u \& u))$	$(p_1 \supset (q \supset t))$
$(q \supset p)$	$[\sim(\sim(\sim p))]$	$(q \supset (r \& t))$
$((t \equiv u) \vee p)$	$[(\sim(\sim r)) \equiv (r \equiv s)]$	$\{\sim[[((p \vee r) \& (q \vee s)) \supset r] \vee p]\}$

Notice how each one is built up using *only* those symbols which the recursive definition in 14:2.1 (plus notes 2 and 5) allows and *only* on the basis of the rules for forming wffs that its clauses express.

Here are some items that are *not* wffs and an indication of why they fail to satisfy the definition.

1. $p \vee q$ — Missing outside parentheses.
2. $(\sim p \supset q)$ — Missing parentheses around $\sim p$.
3. $(A \equiv B)$ — A and B are not symbols of the system and so cannot be used to make genuine wffs of our system (see note 1 in 14:2.1).
4. $(p \vee q \supset r)$ — This is ambiguous. It should be $(p \vee (q \supset r))$, or $((p \vee q) \supset r)$. Its ambiguity occurs because it is missing a set of parentheses (see note 3).
5. $p \& (q \& r)$ — Missing outside parentheses.

6.	$\sim(p \supset q)$	Missing outside parentheses.
7.	$((c \lor q) \supset (\sim E))$	Neither c nor E are symbols of our system.
8.	(pq)	Missing a logical connective between p and q. It could be $(p \supset q)$.
9.	$(p \lor (q \equiv))$	Missing a well-formed formula to the right of the $\equiv$. One way to fix it up would be to write $[p \lor (q \equiv (\sim q))]$.
10.	$((\sim(\sim p) \lor q)$	An uneven number of parentheses indicates that one is missing. There should be a) added so as to get $((\sim(\sim p)) \lor q)$.

EXERCISES FOR MODULE 14
THE LANGUAGE OF PROPOSITIONAL LOGIC

Ex. 1 Here is a list of formulas. If a particular item is a wff, mark 'wff' in the answer space; otherwise mark 'no.'

——— 1. p

——— 2. q

——— 3. $(p \lor q)$

——— 4. $(r \equiv s)$

——— 5. $(A \supset B)$

——— 6. $(p \$ r)$

——— 7. $(t \& s)$

——— 8. $(\sim p)$

——— 9. $\sim(\sim q)$

——— 10. $(\sim(\sim q))$

Ex. 2 From the answers provided below, identify each item in the subsequent list of fifteen. Possible answers:

A. This is a wff.
B. This is not a wff because it contains symbols that are not part of our language.
C. This is not a wff because it contains too many parentheses.
D. This is not a wff because it is missing the outside parentheses.
E. This is not well formed because it is missing one or more logical connectives.
F. This is not well formed because it is missing a statement letter.
G. This is not a wff because it is ambiguous and needs clarification by the use of more parentheses.
H. This is not a wff because it is missing one parenthesis.

——— 1. $((p \& q) \quad r)$

——— 2. $(q \supset (p \supset r))$

——— 3. $(p \supset q$

——— 4. $(A \equiv r)$

——— 5. $q \supset p$

——— 6. $\sim(\sim r)$

——— 7. p

——— 8. $p \lor q$

_____ 9. $((p) \lor (q))$

_____ 10. $(\sim(\sim p)$

_____ 11. $((p \supset q) \supset ((p \quad q) \quad r))$

_____ 12. $[[((\sim r) \supset p) \supset p][(\sim r) \quad (\sim q)]]$

_____ 13. $\{[[((\sim r) \supset p) \supset g] \& (r \supset s)] \supset k\}$

_____ 14. $[\sim[(r \equiv) \supset (\sim(\sim q))]]$

_____ 15. $(r \equiv s \supset p)$

Ex. 3 None of the following are well-formed formulas. Correct them so that they become well formed and write the corrected formula to the right of each.

1. $p \lor q$ 2. $((\sim r))$
3. $(p \lor q \& r)$ 4. $(((p \lor r)(p \lor q)) \& p)$
5. (q) 6. $(q \equiv r \lor p)$
7. $\sim(\sim q)$ 8. $(s \lor p) \equiv (q \supset p)$
9. $(\sim(s \equiv r) \lor (p \sim q))$ 10. $[r \supset (\sim p) \lor p)]$

Ex. 4 Construct two wffs for each item using only the symbols indicated in each item.

1. Using only statement letters
2. Using q, r, and parentheses and one $\sim$ in each of your examples
3. Using q, s, parentheses, and one $\equiv$ in each example
4. Using p, q, r, parentheses, and two logical connectives
5. Using p, parentheses, and two logical connectives
6. Using q, r, parentheses, brackets, and any of the logical operators

SELECTED ANSWERS
TO EXERCISE FOR MODULE 14

Ex. 1

1. wff	2. wff	3. wff
4. wff	5. No	6. No
7. wff	8. wff	9. No
10. wff		

If you missed any, review 14:2.1 and 14:2.2

Ex. 2

1. E	2. A	3. H
4. B	5. D	6. D
7. A	8. D	9. C
10. H	11. E	12. E
13. B	14. F	15. G

If you missed two or more, review 14:2.1 and 14:2.2.

Ex. 3

1. $(p \lor q)$
3. $((p \lor q) \& r)$ or $(p \lor (q \& r))$
5. q
7. $(\sim(\sim q))$
9. One way is $((\sim(s \equiv r)) \lor (p \lor q))$;
   another is $[(\sim(s \equiv r)) \lor (p \supset (\sim q))]$

2. $(\sim r)$
4. $[((p \lor r) \& (p \lor q)) \& p]$ or
   $[((p \lor r) \lor (p \lor q)) \& p]$ or
   $[((p \lor r) \supset (p \lor q)) \& p]$ or
   $[((p \lor r) \equiv (p \lor q)) \& p]$
6. $(q \equiv (r \lor p))$ or $((q \equiv r) \lor p)$
8. $((s \lor p) \equiv (q \supset p))$
10. $((r \supset (\sim p)) \lor p)$ or $(r \supset ((\sim p) \lor p))$

If you had any problems, review 14:2.1 and 14:2.2.

Ex. 4 (possible answers)

1. q, r
2. $(\sim q), (\sim r)$
3. $(q \equiv s), (s \equiv q)$
4. $(p \supset (q \& r)), (q \equiv (r \lor p)), ((r \lor p) \supset q)$
5. $((p \lor p) \supset p), ((p \equiv (p \& p)), (p \supset (p \lor p))$
6. $[\sim((r \equiv q) \lor (\sim q))], [q \supset (\sim(\sim r))], [\sim[((q \lor q) \supset (r \equiv r)) \& q]]$

Check your answers against the definition of wff given in 14:2.1.

MODULE 15

TRANSLATION AND PROPOSITIONAL LOGIC

In this module we will learn how to represent the propositional-logic structure of English statements. This process of moving from natural language to formalism is called *translation*.

● After reading Module 15 you should be able to:

1. Translate natural-language statements into symbolic notation as wffs of our language of propositional logic

15:1.1 Translation procedure The process of translating a natural-language statement into logical notation is accomplished by using these rules:

1. Isolate the statement units and designate each statement unit by a separate statement letter. Reword if necessary to fully expand and expose all statement units.
2. Ascertain the truth-functional structure of statement compounds or negations and represent that structure through replacing logical words or phrases by the appropriate symbolic-logic operators. Do the same for any logical substructure that is present. (Use the chart in 14:1.2 as a guide.)
3. Preserve the English grouping and punctuation through the use of parentheses, brackets, and braces. (If the English is ambiguous, the ambiguity must be resolved one way or the other by the use of parentheses, etc.)
4. Check to make sure that the resulting formula is well formed and that all the truth-functional relationships and appropriate groupings have been maintained.

15:1.2 Here are some step-by-step examples of translations.

EG. 15.1 English: Sarah is here and David is here.

    1. Let p = Sarah is here
           q = David is here

      p and q

    2. Logical structure: conjunction
       Appropriate symbol: &

      p & q

    3. Punctuation replaced by parentheses:

      $(p$ & $q)$

    4. Check off: Whether it is a wff, √ whether it has all the original structure, √ whether it preserves grouping. √

EG. 15.2 English: It is not true that Mary loves Joshua.

    1. Let p = Mary loves Joshua

      It is not true that p.

    2. Structure: negation
       Symbol: ~

      ~p

    3. Punctuation replaced:

      $(\sim p)$

    4. Check off: is a wff, preserves structure, and preserves grouping. √√√

EG. 15.3 English: It is not the case either that Joshua loves Mary or that Mary loves Joshua.

    1. Let p = Joshua loves Mary
           q = Mary loves Joshua

      It is not the case that either p or q.

    2. Logical structure: negation
       Symbol: ~

      ~ either p or q

      Further logical substructure: disjunction
       Symbol: $\vee$

      ~$(p \vee q)$

    3. Punctuation replaced:

      $(\sim(p \vee q))$

    4. Check off: is a wff, preserves structure and substructure, and preserves grouping. √√√

EG. 15.4 English: Joshua and Mary love ice cream.

    1. Reword to fully expose all statement units.

Joshua loves ice cream and Mary loves ice cream.

Let p = Joshua loves ice cream

    q = Mary loves ice cream

2. Logical structure: conjunction
Symbol: &

p & q

3. Punctuation replaced:

(p & q)

4. Check off: is a wff, preserves structure, and preserves grouping. √√√

EG. 15.5 English: If it rains today, then it rains today.

1. Let p = it rains today

If p, then p.

2. Structure: conditional
Symbol: ⊃

p, ⊃ p

3. Punctuation replaced:

(p ⊃ p)

4. Check off: is a wff, preserves structure, and preserves grouping. √√√

EG. 15.6 English: If William sells his car, then we will either go to New Jersey or Indiana on our vacation.

1. Reword to expose all statement units.

If William sells his car, then either we will go to New Jersey on our vacation or we will go to Indiana on our vacation.

Let p = William sells his car

    q = we will go to New Jersey on our vacation

    r = we will go to Indiana on our vacation

2. Logical structure: conditional
Symbol: ⊃

Substructure: antecedent of conditional is the statement unit p; consequent of conditional is a disjunction of q with r. Use: ∨.

p ⊃, (q ∨ r).

3. Punctuation replaced:

(p ⊃ (q ∨ r))

4. Check off: is a wff, structures preserved, grouping preserved. √√√

EG. 15.7 English: Either we will win or play hard and we will try our new offense.

1. Let p = we will win

    q = we will play hard

    r = we will try our new offense

2. Logical structure: uncertain because of English ambiguity

3. Punctuation in English is missing; English should be one of the following:

    a. Either p, or q and r.
    b. Either p or q, and r.

    Decide to resolve ambiguity: select form a; go back to step 2. (a is an arbitrary choice unless you know the context.)

4. Logical structure: resolved to be disjunction
    Symbol: $\vee$

    $p, \vee q$ and r

    Substructure: second clause of disjunction is a conjunction. Use: &

    $p, \vee (q \& r)$

5. Punctuation replaced:

    $(p \vee (q \& r))$

6. Check off: is a wff, logical structure preserved after ambiguity resolved, grouping preserved after ambiguity resolved. $\checkmark\checkmark\checkmark$

The individual steps of translation should each be followed out fully until you are comfortable with the procedure. At that time you may choose to move directly from the English to the wffs without actually writing down the intervening steps. But be careful because as you actually write down less, chances for mistakes increase. After practice, though, this kind of translation becomes manageable. Check your understanding of basic translation skills with the following English sentences, which are fairly challenging at this stage. Translate them and compare your translations to the ones provided.

EXERCISE 1

1. Lovers are silly and horses are wild.
2. If I will be late for dinner, then horses are wild.
3. Lovers are silly if and only if it is not the case that lovers are silly.
4. Horses are wild only if either lovers are silly or wild horses love flowers.
5. Either lovers are silly or horses are wild; if, and only if, both wild horses love flowers and I will be late for dinner.
6. If horses are wild, then either lovers are silly or horses are wild; if, and only if, wild horses love flowers.
7. If either lovers are silly or horses are not wild, then lovers are silly only if I will be late for dinner.
8. Lovers are silly if, and only if, either horses are not wild or it is not the case that wild horses love flowers.
9. If horses are wild, then wild horses love flowers, or lovers are not silly.
10. Either lovers are silly or horses are wild.

Use these interpretations:
Let p = lovers are silly
    q = horses are wild
    r = wild horses love flowers
    s = I will be late for dinner

ANSWERS
TO EXERCISE 1

1. $(p \mathbin{\&} q)$
2. $(s \supset q)$
3. $(p \equiv (\sim p))$
4. $(q \supset (p \vee r))$
5. $((p \vee q) \equiv (r \mathbin{\&} s))$
6. $((q \supset (p \vee q)) \equiv r)$
7. $((p \vee (\sim q)) \supset (p \supset s))$
8. $[p \equiv ((\sim q) \vee (\sim r))]$
9. $((q \supset r) \vee (\sim p))$
10. $(p \vee q)$

15:1.3 The business of translating from English into logical notation is complicated by these facts. First, English is not used solely to make logical points, and as a result English statements, even in arguments, are often embellished by the use of words that have slightly different connotations or expressive forces. For example in English we say

> p and q

or
> p, but q!

Both would go into the logical notation as

> $(p \mathbin{\&} q)$

but in so translating some of the expressive force of 'but' rather than the more neutral 'and' would be lost.

At first it may seem that this is a reason not to use symbolic notation. The feeling may be that the symbols are just not able to get the whole point across. Yet after a time this feeling about the expressive force of English or the connotations of particular words or phrases will pass because you will realize that the symbols do capture the *logical* force of the English: they capture everything required for deciding validity.

A second problem for translation is the ambiguity of some English sentences. Example 15.7 showed how to resolve by your decision the ambiguity of any statements you may have to handle. Of course, if the author is available to settle the ambiguity, that's fine; if not, go with your most reasonable judgment about what the English might have been intended to say.

A third problem is caused by stylistic and idiomatic devices. English is made more interesting to listen to and more effective as a device for communication if certain stylistic or idiomatic conventions are followed. Thus people will say

> Judy and Kathy like ice cream

rather than the longer and more repetitive

> Judy likes ice cream and Kathy likes ice cream.

Example 15.4 showed how to deal with this kind of "telescoping" or collapsing of clauses. It can occur in conjunctions like the one in Eg. 15.4 or in disjunctions as exemplified in Eg. 15.7.

People not only telescope the clauses of their conjunctions and disjunctions, they also combine logical operators and create new logical relationships out of these combinations. For example, instead of saying

Not p and not q

people are apt to say

Neither p nor q.

Instead of

Either not p or not q

people will say

Not both p and q.

And instead of

If p, then q

people will say

q, if p

or

p only if q

or

Not p unless q.

Of the many stylistic hurdles to good translations you should notice that verbs may often change tense, mood, and voice while leaving unchanged a basic logical force of an assertion. For example, imagine a conversation:

Jim: Our school's basketball season will be a success unless injury incapacitates Louise.
Marcia: Louise will not be incapacitated.

Jim may now draw the logically correct conclusion that the basketball season will be successful, for despite Marcia's use of the future tense and the passive voice, she is clearly asserting the negation of Jim's alternative that injury may incapacitate Louise.

Especially in a defined context certain words are often exchanged for others having a contextually synonymous meaning. After Jim's assertion, Marcia might have said, "Nothing's going to keep Louise out of those games." Contextually, her assertion again is the negation of Jim's second alternative.

A final way in which context leads to stylistic differences is by telescoping second and subsequent references to a statement. To Marcia's assertion that nothing will stop Louise, Jim might reply, "Well if so [meaning if indeed nothing will stop Louise], our season is bound to be great!" Here "if so" picks up Marcia's statement without explicitly repeating it.

All these factors, plus simply the level of complexity of statements like those found in legal contracts, insurance policies, charters, constitutions, and income tax instruction books, can make the business of translating rather difficult at times. Yet, the four-step procedure outlined in 15:1.1 will work, even for those tough cases, if it is applied carefully and with some feeling for the nuances of various English constructions, idioms, and language usages.

15:1.4 Here are some examples of translations from English to logical notation where the English is problematic in one or more of the ways specified in 15:1.3.

EG. 15.8   English: Neither you nor I will win today.

  1. Rewritten: You will not win today and I will not win today.

     Let p = you will win today
       q = I will win today

  2. Structure: conjunction, each clause being a negation
     Symbols: &, $\sim$

     $\sim p$ & $\sim q$

  3. Complete punctuation and grouping:

     $((\sim p) \, \& \, (\sim q))$

  4. Check off: is a wff, preserves structure, preserves grouping. $\sqrt{}\sqrt{}\sqrt{}$

EG. 15.9   English: Although few people know it, the sky is really falling.

  1. Rewritten: The sky is really falling, although few people know that the sky is really falling.

     Let p = the sky is really falling
       q = few people know that the sky is really falling

  2. Structure: conjunction. Use: &

     p & q

  3. Punctuation replaced:

     $(p \, \& \, q)$

  4. Check off: is a wff, preserves structure, preserves grouping. $\sqrt{}\sqrt{}\sqrt{}$

EG. 15.10 English: If Rome was invaded, the empire collapsed. Attila the Hun invaded Rome, and that meant "Good-bye, empire."

  1. Rewrite the passage dealing with the entire argument.

     Let p = Rome was invaded
       q = the empire collapsed

Contextually we observe that 'Attila the Hun invaded Rome' can be translated here as p and that 'Goodbye, empire' picturesquely asserts 'The empire collapsed' = q.

2. Logical structure: conditional followed by two simple assertions, the last of which is conclusion of argument

$$p, \supset q$$
$$\underline{p \qquad}$$
$$\therefore q$$

3. Punctuation replaced:

$$(q \supset q)$$
$$\underline{p \qquad}$$
$$\therefore q$$

4. Check off: $\checkmark\checkmark\checkmark$

EG. 15.11 English: If marigolds are planted in this soil, they will thrive. Given that development, you will have blossoms all summer. So plant your marigolds, and you'll have flowers 'til fall.

1. Rewording: Again dealing with the entire argument, the first hurdle is to determine how many assertions are involved. Check.

Let p = marigolds are planted in this soil
q = the marigolds thrive
r = you will have blossoms all summer

2. Logical structure: three assertions, two premises, and then the conclusion. The first assertion is clearly conditional. But how should 'given that development' be translated in the second? The development is simply that the marigolds will thrive. So the second sentence asserts "if the marigolds thrive, you will have blossoms," another conditional. *Grammatically* the conclusion is very strange: it is the conjunction of an imperative and an indicative. Grammatically it looks as if there were an assertion only in the second conjunct. But in fact the words 'plant your marigolds' are not used to order marigolds planted. Rather they name a condition, the planting of marigolds; the second clause then says what will be true if the condition is met. In other words the conclusion is also conditional.

$$p, \supset q$$
$$\underline{q, \supset r}$$
$$\therefore p, \supset r$$

3. Punctuation replaced:

$$(p \supset q)$$
$$\underline{(q \supset r)}$$
$$\therefore (p \supset r)$$

4. Check off: $\checkmark\checkmark\checkmark$

EG. 15.12 English: To qualify as the dependent of a taxpayer one has to be a citizen, earn less than $750, have been provided more than one-half of total support for the year, be less than eighteen years old, and be a relative of the taxpayer or a resident in the taxpayer's home.

1. Let p = one qualifies as the dependent of a taxpayer
    q = one is a citizen
    r = one earns less than \$750
    s = one has been provided more than one-half of one's total support
    t = one is less than eighteen years old
    u = one is a relative of the taxpayer
    p_1 = one is a resident in the taxpayer's home

2. Structure: unclear, but given IRS practice such a sentence is regarded as a biconditional: one side is a simple statement unit p.
   Substructure: the other side of the biconditional is the conjunction of five clauses one of which is the disjunction of u with p_1.

   Thus: $(p \equiv$)
   $[p \equiv (\underline{\quad}, \underline{\quad}, \underline{\quad}, \underline{\quad} \& (\underline{\quad} \lor \underline{\quad}))]$
   $[p \equiv (q, \quad r, \quad s, \quad t, \quad \& (u \quad \lor p_1 \quad))]$
   $[p \equiv (q \quad \& r \quad \& s \quad \& t \quad \& (u \quad \lor p_1 \quad))]$

3. Punctuation replaced:

   $[p \equiv (q \& r \& s \& t \& (u \lor p_1))]$

4. More grouping indicators are needed to make this a wff:

   $[p \equiv [((q \& r) \& (s \& t)) \& (u \lor p_1)]]$

   Check off: Logical structure is preserved. $\checkmark$ English grouping is preserved except that the added parentheses on the right side make it seem that a relevant change in logical structure may have been introduced. However upon examination it can be shown that since $((A \& B) \& C)$ has the same logical force as $(A \& (B \& C))$, no crucial structural changes were introduced. $\checkmark$

If you want to check your ability to reword English statements before going further, work Ex. 2.

EXERCISE 2

Below each statement two alternative "rewordings" are presented. One of each pair is a legitimate rewording and the other alters the meaning, or the truth-value, or the logical structure of the original and thus should be rejected. Identify the correct one by putting its letter in the answer space.

_____ 1. There is life on Mars.
    A. It is true that there is life on Mars.
    B. Mars has no life on it.

_____ 2. It is not the case that Socrates is dead.
    A. Socrates is dead.
    B. Socrates is not dead.

_____ 3. If Socrates is dead, philosophy is lost.

A. Socrates is dead if, and only if, philosophy is lost.
B. Socrates is dead only if philosophy is lost.

_____ 4. It is not the case that all people love children.
A. No people love children.
B. Not everyone loves children.

_____ 5. Either it's time for lunch or time for a nap.
A. Either it's time for lunch or it's time for a nap, but not both.
B. It's either time for lunch or for a nap.

_____ 6. If you are rich, you are lucky.
A. You're not rich unless you're lucky.
B. You are rich if you're lucky.

_____ 7. If that doesn't happen, you'll have a fine vacation.
A. Your vacation will be fine in that case.
B. Otherwise, your vacation will be fine.

_____ 8. John will be glad to help you provided you explain what you want.
A. If you make your wants known, John will gladly help you.
B. If John is gladly helping you, your wants must have been known.

_____ 9. Although his action was entirely legal, it was morally questionable.
A. His action was completely legal but morally dubious.
B. His action was fully legal but immoral.

_____ 10. Sue will cooperate, in that case.
A. If so, Sue will cooperate.
B. Otherwise, Sue will cooperate.

ANSWERS
TO EXERCISE 2

1. A	2. B	3. B
4. B	5. B	6. A
7. B	8. A	9. A
10. A		

15:2.1 When *translating arguments* from English into logical notation, the same rules and cautions apply. There is only one additional point to remember, but it is very important: always use the same statement letters for the same statement units each time they appear in a given argument. Thus we would translate:

EG. 15.13 Either Jane is a Republican or she is a liberal.
Jane is not a Republican.
So she is a liberal.

Let p = "Jane is a Republican" and q = "Jane is a liberal" each time; and translate the three statements in this argument as

$(p \lor q)$
$\underline{(\sim p)}$
$\therefore q$

Example 15.13 is valid. (The inference of 'B' from 'either A or B' and 'not A' is valid.) If we translated each statement unit in each premise and the conclusion by its own *separate* letter, the relationships between these premises and the conclusion would disappear, as in:

$(p \vee q)$
$\underline{(\sim r)}$
$\therefore s$

An argument like Eg. 15.13 is valid in part because its premises interact with each other; taken together, they imply the conclusion. Using p for 'Jane is a Republican' in both the premises makes this interaction possible in Eg. 15.13. Thus, just as we translate two occurrences of the same statement unit in a compound statement by the use of the same letter, so we will translate all the occurrences of a given statement unit in a given argument by the same letter.

15:2.2 Here are some examples of translating arguments.

EG. 15.14   If the world is flat, then we can sell our stock in orbiting satellites.
The world is flat.
Thus we can sell our stock.

We can translate Eg. 15.14 as

EG. 15.14' p = the world is flat
q = we can sell our stock in orbiting satellites

$(p \supset q)$
$\underline{p}$
$\therefore q$

EG. 15.15   If milk is nutritious, then protein is tasteless.
However, it is not the case that protein is tasteless.
Moreover, if milk is not nutritious, then fats are unavoidable.
Thus we can conclude that fats must be unavoidable.

We can translate Eg. 15.15 as:

EG. 15.15' $(p \supset q)$ p = milk is nutritious
$(\sim q)$ q = protein is tasteless
$\underline{((\sim p) \supset (\sim r))}$ r = fats are avoidable
$\therefore (\sim r)$

Our four sample arguments, Egs. 14.1 to 14.4, were translated in 14:1.2 as Egs. 14.1'' to 14.4''. These translations also exemplify the principles, guidelines, and provisions for translation set out here in Module 15.

EXERCISES FOR MODULE 15
TRANSLATION AND PROPOSITIONAL LOGIC

Ex. 3 Below each of the following English statements several possible alternative translations are offered. Choose the correct one. For the sake of these exercises, for convenience, and uniformity (but not for any other more theoretical reason), treat the first positive statement unit as p, the second as q, the third as r, and so on.

_____ 1. Either today is a bad day or times are tough all over.

    A. $(p \lor q)$ B. $(p \& q)$ C. $(p \& p)$ D. $(q \supset p)$ E. p

_____ 2. If the men I know are all wise, then times are tough all over.

    A. $(p \supset g)$ B. $(r \equiv p)$ C. $(p \supset q)$ D. $(\sim(p \supset q))$ E. $(q \lor p)$

_____ 3. Today is tough; yet if life is short, then there are some people who are sad.

    A. $((p \& q) \supset r)$ B. $(p \& (r \supset q))$ C. $(p \& (q \supset r))$
    D. $((q \& p) \& r)$ E. $(p \& (p \supset q))$

_____ 4. All the king's horses are fat, and all his men are no help anymore.

    A. $(q \& p)$ B. $(p \& q)$ C. $(p \equiv q)$ D. $(q \supset p)$ E. $(q \lor r)$

_____ 5. Either we will overcome or we won't.

    A. $(p \lor (\sim p))$ B. $(p \lor q)$ C. $(p \supset (\sim p))$ D. $(p \equiv q)$
    E. $((\sim p) \& (\sim q))$

Ex. 4 Translate the following thirty English statements into wffs. In each case treat the first affirmative statement unit as p, the second as q, the third as r, the fourth as s, and so on.

1. If it's not the case that this paper is made of atoms, then this paper is made of atoms.
2. It's not the case that if this paper is made of atoms, then it's made of atoms.
3. If this paper is made of atoms, then this paper is made of atoms.
4. If everything is made of atoms, then this paper is made of atoms.
5. Either this paper is made of atoms or it's not made of atoms.
6. He'll make the team if, and only if, he gives up beer or takes up Flakies; and, moreover, if he doesn't give up beer, football isn't his first love.
7. Jones ate in the cafeteria, and she got very sick.
8. Although Smith arrived on time, Jones and Brown were very late.
9. I went along with Bill to lunch and then to class while you went to class and lunch.
10. If you are wise, hard-working, and lucky, you will do well unless you are favored by the nepotistic benevolent ruler of the kingdom.
11. Those who hate their fellows are killed if these fellows are hateful too; the same happens if there are violent insurrections, provided that the attackers are overcome.
12. If only she would look my way, then I could warn her of the danger.
13. We were all there at the governor's request.
14. I came, saw and conquered; however, so did Caesar the Hun, Attila the Pole, and Samuel the Turk.
15. It is not true that Attila killed Caesar only if either Brutus or Cicero did it.
16. Although from now on neither of us will study, you will fail unless you pass; if, and only if, all this is not the case.
17. Hence, therefore, let us realize that, from all that has gone before, neither 'only if' nor 'provided that' is more difficult to translate than 'if . . . then,' provided that one knows their logical pecularities.
18. To quality as a head of household one must be single and provide more than half the cost of maintaining a dependent father or mother or maintaining a child in one's home.

19. Alimony is tax deductible if, and only if, it is a fixed sum and paid periodically; however, child support is not deductible, nor is it considered taxable income.
20. It's not the case both that God is dead and that God is not dead.
21. If Jones is coming if, and only if, Smith is coming, then either Jones is coming or Smith is coming.
22. If either Jones or Smith is coming, then both Jones and Smith are coming.
23. If both Jones and Smith are coming, then either Jones or Smith is coming.
24. To qualify as a dependent a person must pass relationship, citizenship, support, joint-return, and gross-income tests.
25. If the people are generally wise and the government is honest, then the revolution will be a failure.
26. Either the government is honest or powerful interest groups support the status quo if, and only if, the revolution is a failure.
27. Either people are generally wise and the government is honest, or people are generally wise and the population is easily deceived.
28. One cannot claim a child as an exemption if the child is living with one's divorced spouse unless one contributes at least $600 to the child's support and is granted the exemption in the divorce decree or one contributes over $1,200 in support and one can prove that this constitutes over 50 percent of the total support of that child for the year.
29. You cannot learn enough to best Richard or Edward at swords or cards.
30. If you practice something a lot, then you will become proficient at that activity.

Ex. 5 Translate each of these arguments into the symbolic notation of propositional logic using this dictionary:

p = men are loving
q = people are careful
r = men are sexy
s = women are sexy
t = people love children
u = women are wise

1. If men are loving then men are sexy, only if people are careful. If men are sexy, then people are careful only if women are sexy. Thus, if men are loving, then men are sexy only if women are sexy.
2. Men are loving if and only if people are careful. But either people are careful, or men are loving, or both. Thus, it is not the case that men are not loving.
3. Women are sexy or people love children, only if women are wise. However, if either people are careful or men are loving, then both men and women are sexy. So if women are not wise, then men are not loving.
4. Either women are wise or it is not true that people are careful. But we know that either people are careful or men are sexy. And, we also know that men are not loving. So if men are sexy only if women are, then women are sexy. But, of course, that conclusion follows given the additional premise that men are loving if and only if women are wise.
5. It is not the case that either men are sexy or people are not careful; or, it is true that men are loving. But, either men are sexy or women are sexy. Then, too, if women are not sexy, then it is not the case that people are careful only if men are loving. Therefore we must infer that women are sexy.
6. From the simple premise that women are wise it follows that women are wise.

7. Men are loving. Therefore if people love children and women are wise, then men are loving.
8. Women are wise provided that people are careful. That premise is true if, and only if, it is not the case that both men and women are sexy. But men are sexy and yet people are careful. Therefore women are wise if, and only if, they are not sexy.
9. If it is either not the case that men are loving or not the case that people are careful, then men are sexy. Although either people are careful or men are not sexy. So people are careful.
10. It is neither the case that people love children nor that women are wise. But people do love children if women are sexy. So women are not sexy.

SELECTED ANSWERS
TO EXERCISES FOR MODULE 15

Ex. 3

1. A   2. C   3. C   4. B   5. A

Ex. 4

1. $((\sim p) \supset p)$
2. $(\sim(p \supset p))$
3. $(p \supset p)$
4. $(p \supset q)$
5. $(p \lor (\sim p))$
6. $[(p \equiv (q \lor r)) \& ((\sim q) \supset (\sim s))]$
    r = he takes up Flakies
    s = football is his first love
7. $(p \& q)$
8. $(p \& (q \& r))$
9. $((p \& q) \& (r \& s))$
10. $[((p \& q) \& r) \supset (s \lor t)]$
    q = you are wise
    r = you are hard-working
11. Resolve the ambiguity of "the same happens" so that it is either p or $(q \supset p)$.
12. $(q \supset p)$; if I warned her, then she must have looked my way.
14. $[((p \& q) \& r) \& [[((s \& t) \& u) \& ((p_1 \& q_1) \& r_1)] \& ((s_1 \& t_1) \& u_1)]]$
    p = I came
    s = Caesar the Hun came
    p_1 = Attila the Pole came
16. $\{[((\sim p) \& (\sim q)) \& (r \lor s)] \equiv [\sim[((\sim p) \& (\sim q)) \& (r \lor s)]]\}$
    p = I will study
    r = you will fail
    s = you will pass
18. $[p \supset [q \& (r \lor (s \lor t))]]$
    p = one qualifies as a head of household
    q = one is single
    r = one provides more than one-half the cost of maintaining a dependent father
20. $[\sim(p \& (\sim p))]$

22. $((p \lor q) \supset (p \& q))$
24. $[p \supset [((q \& r) \& (s \& t)) \& u]]$
   r = a person must pass the citizenship test
25. $((p \& q) \supset r)$
26. $((p \lor q) \equiv r)$
27. $((p \& q) \lor (p \& r))$
28. Read q as a condition for either (·p) or the rest. $[q \supset [(\cdot p) \lor ((r \& s) \lor (t \& u))]]$
29. $[((\sim p) \& (\sim q)) \& ((\sim r) \& (\sim s))]$
   p = you can learn enough to best Richard at swords

Ex. 5

1. $((p \supset r) \supset q), (r \supset (q \supset s)), \therefore (p \supset (r \supset s))$
3. $((s \lor t) \supset u), ((q \lor p) \supset (r \& s)), \therefore ((\sim u) \supset (\sim p))$
5. $[(\sim (r \lor (\sim q)) \lor p], (r \lor s), [(\sim s) \supset (\sim (q \supset p))], \therefore s$
7. $p, \therefore ((t \& u) \supset p)$
9. $[((\sim p) \lor (\sim q)) \supset r], (q \lor (\sim r)), \therefore q$

Several of the translations in this set of exercises were quite difficult; it should not be surprising if you were able to manage to translate only about half exactly right on your first try. Carefully go over each one you missed and compare the correct translation to the English to see how the English is structured. Review 15:1.1 to 15:1.4.

MODULE 16

TRUTH-VALUES AND TRUTH-TABLES FOR WFFS

Just as English-language statements have truth-values, so do the wffs of our symbolic language. In this module we will learn how to determine the truth-value of any wff that can be written. We will also learn to construct tables which reveal all the possible truth-values any wff can have. Because the truth-values of truth-functional compounds are built up from the truth-values of their component statement units on the basis of how these are logically related to each other, the process of finding the truth-value of any compound wff is a mechanical and easy procedure once the five logical operations (negation, conjunction, disjunction, conditional, and biconditional) are learned.

● After reading Module 16 you should be able to:

1. Determine the truth-value of any wff after being supplied the truth-values of its component statement letters
2. Construct a truth-table for any given wff which reveals all its possible truth-values given all the various possible combinations of truth-value assignments to its component statement letters

16:1.1 The five logical operations have certain logical powers. In a sense, they are like logic machines that function on truth-values. For example, the tilde is like a machine that turns a truth-value into its opposite.

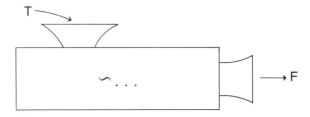

If a 'T' is put into the negation machine, then 'F' comes out. If 'F' goes in, 'T' comes out. ('T' stands for 'true'; 'F' stands for 'false.')

The ampersand works similarly.

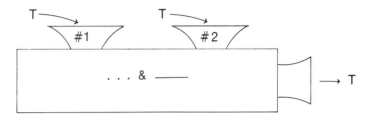

If 'T' goes in both side 1 and side 2, then 'T' comes out. If 'F' goes in either side, then 'F' comes out.

The five logical operations work on the basis of these five rules:

1. A formula (~A) is true if, and only if, A is false; and (~A) is false if, and only if, A is true.
2. A formula (A & B) is true if, and only if, both A and B are true. [This corresponds to the idea that (A and B) is false whenever either A is false or B is false.]
3. A formula (A ∨ B) is true if, and only if, either A is true or B is true (or both A and B are true). [This corresponds to the idea that (A or B) is false just in the case that both A and B are false.]
4. A formula (A ⊃ B) is true if, and only if, either A is false or B is true. [This corresponds to the idea that (if A then B) is false just in the one case that A is true and B is false.]
5. A formula (A ≡ B) is true if, and only if, both A and B have the same truth-value. [This corresponds to the idea that (A, if, and only if, B) is false just when the truth-values of A and B are opposite.]

The rationale for each of these five rules is easy to see when you compare the rules to the chart in 14:1.2. The ~ has the power of 'not,' and it changes a statement's truth-value into its opposite. The & conjoins two statements forming a new compound that asserts that each conjunct is true. The ∨ forms the alternation of two statements into a compound used for asserting that one or the other (or both) of the two is true. The ⊃ joins two statements into a compound used to say that if the first is true then the second will not be false. The ≡ forms a compound of two statements suggesting that each has the same value as the other in that both are true or both are false together.

The only really curious rule in this group is the rule for ⊃ because our first intuitions about 'if . . ., then ____' do not give us clear ideas about what to do when the 'if' part is false. The doubt, however, must be resolved. In propositional logic we do not allow ? as a truth-value; we allow only T or F. One way to address the question is to notice that in English 'if p, then q' is like 'not p unless q,'" as in 'If John wins the pole vault, then the west-side Brones win the league championship' and 'John does not win the pole vault unless the west-side Brones win the league championship.' The translation for the latter is

$$((\sim p) \lor q)$$

Using the rules for $\sim$ and $\lor$ we can generate the rule for the $\supset$.

$$((\sim A) \lor B)$$

will be true if either A is false or B is true, as stated in rule 4 above.

Another way to settle the question of what value to give to $(A \supset B)$ when A is false is to consider an example like this one. Suppose that the Reds and the Yankees are in the World Series again and the Reds win the first two games of that best-of-seven series. Now consider the conditional statement, "If the Yankees win game three, then there will be at least five games in the Series." This statement would be true even if the Yankees lose game three. The only way it can be false is if the Yankees win game three and something happens to prevent the playing of game five (say the commissioner calls off the Series). That is, the only time the conditional statement turns out to be false is when its antecedent is true and its consequent is false; in all other cases it comes out true.

16:1.2 Paradigm tables On the basis of the five rules given above we can construct paradigm tables which define the logical operations performed by the five logical operators. We will use them later when we are constructing truth-tables for individual wffs because the paradigm tables define the logical operators by diagraming how they will function in each possible case.

In reading these tables assume that A and B stand for any two wffs whatsoever, no matter how simple or complex. (As a matter of convention we will save capital letters A and B to stand for wffs.)

The paradigm table for $\sim$ will show that if A is true, then $(\sim A)$ will be false, and if A is false, then $(\sim A)$ will be true. That is what rule 1 in 16:1.1 indicates. Thus, the table for the tilde:

Paradigm table for tilde

	A	$(\sim A)$	
1. If A is	T	F	shall be the value of $(\sim A)$
2. If A is	F	T	shall be the value of $(\sim A)$

There are no more cases to be considered because any wff A that $\sim$ is operating on can have no values other than true and false.

Given two formulas, call them A and B, there are four possible distributions of T's and F's: both true, both false, and either one true with the other false.

	A	B
1.	T	T
2.	T	F
3.	F	T
4.	F	F

Using the four remaining rules we can construct these four paradigm tables:

Paradigm tables for connectives

For ampersand

	A	B	(A & B)	
1. If A and B are	T	T	T	shall be the value of (A & B)
2. If A and B are	T	F	F	shall be the value of (A & B)
3. If A and B are	F	T	F	shall be the value of (A & B)
4. If A and B are	F	F	F	shall be the value of (A & B)

For wedge

	A	B	(A ∨ B)	
1. If A and B are	T	T	T	shall be the value of (A ∨ B)
2. If A and B are	T	F	T	shall be the value of (A ∨ B)
3. If A and B are	F	T	T	shall be the value of (A ∨ B)
4. If A and B are	F	F	F	shall be the value of (A ∨ B)

For horseshoe

	A	B	(A ⊃ B)	
1. If A and B are	T	T	T	shall be the value of (A ⊃ B)
2. If A and B are	T	F	F	shall be the value of (A ⊃ B)
3. If A and B are	F	T	T	shall be the value of (A ⊃ B)
4. If A and B are	F	F	T	shall be the value of (A ⊃ B)

For triple bar

	A	B	(A ≡ B)	
1. If A and B are	T	T	T	shall be the value of (A ≡ B)
2. If A and B are	T	F	F	shall be the value of (A ≡ B)
3. If A and B are	F	T	F	shall be the value of (A ≡ B)
4. If A and B are	F	F	T	shall be the value of (A ≡ B)

16:2.1 Suppose we are given a formula, say $((p \lor q) \supset (\sim q))$. Suppose we are told that p is true and that q is false. On the basis of the paradigm tables we should be able to figure out the *truth-value of the whole formula*.

EG. 16.1   Step 1.   Write the wff down. $((p \lor q) \supset (\sim q))$

Step 2.   Replace p and q by their specified truth-values. $((T \lor F) \supset (\sim F))$

Step 3.   Using line 2 of the tilde table change $(\sim F)$ to T. $((T \lor F) \supset T)$

Step 4.   Using line 2 of the wedge table change $(T \lor F)$ to T. $(\ \ T \ \ \supset T)$

Step 5.   Using line 1 of the horseshoe table change $(T \supset T)$ to T.   T

16:2.2 We can generalize this *procedure for finding truth-values of wffs* into the following set of rules:

1. Write down the wff.
2. Replace each of its statement letters by the given truth-values.
3. Replace (~T) by F, and (~F) by T whenever possible.
4. One at a time, replace each subformula of the structure $(V \otimes V')$ by T or F depending on the value of $(V \otimes V')$ in $\otimes$ paradigm table on the line determined by the values V and V'. ($\otimes$ is not a strange logical connective you forgot. We use it here to represent any of the four truth-functional connectives.)
5. Continue steps 3 and 4 until you end up with either one T or one F, then stop. That T or F is the truth-value of the wff you started with.

For example, consider the formula

$$[(\sim p) \lor (\sim (q \supset q))]$$

Let us assume that p and q are true. Then we get

$$[(\sim T) \lor (\sim (T \supset T))]$$

The whole formula here is a disjunction. On both the left and the right are negations. Rule 3 can be applied immediately to the negation on the left, but not the one on the right. Rule 3 applies on the left because what is negated there is a T or an F—a T in this case. The item negated on the right is no simple T or F but rather a subformula, $(T \supset T)$. Rule 3 can be applied only after a formula or subformula has been reduced to T or to F.

Rule 4 comes into play when you are dealing with one of the four logical connectives. Consider the formula

$$[((p \ \& \ (q \supset r)) \lor s) \equiv (p \ \& \ t)]$$

Let us assume each statement unit is true except p, which is false. Then we get

$$[((F \ \& \ (T \supset T)) \lor T) \equiv (F \ \& \ T)]$$

To apply rule 4 to a complex formula like this one begin with a simple subformula that contains one logical connective between two truth-values surrounded by one set of parentheses. In the above example you can choose either the $(T \supset T)$ or the $(F \ \& \ T)$ to the left of the $\equiv$. Choosing the $(F \ \& \ T)$ we can, by appeal to the third line of the paradigm table for the ampersand, replace it with F.

$$[((F \ \& \ (T \supset T)) \lor T) \equiv F]$$

Now there is only one subformula that rule 4 can be applied to, that is, $(T \supset T)$. By appeal to the first line of the $\supset$ paradigm table we can replace $(T \supset T)$ by T.

$$((F \ \& \quad T) \quad \lor T) \equiv F)$$

That replacement yields a new subformula $(F \ \& \ T)$ to which we can now apply rule 4 to get by appeal to line 3 of the ampersand table

$$((\quad F \quad \quad \lor T) \equiv F)$$

This, in turn, yields another simple subformula (F $\lor$ T). Rule 4 and appeal to line 3 of the paradigm table for $\lor$ yields

$$(\qquad\qquad\quad T \quad \equiv F)$$

which now, by rule 4 and appeal to the second line of the $\equiv$ paradigm table, can be replaced by

$$F$$

Rule 5 tells us that we have now arrived at the truth-value of the original wff, given the original truth-value assignments to its component statement units. The procedure given in this section is easy to manage if you work down the page as we did in Eg. 16.1, and always write the new T or F exactly under the logical operator in the subformula being replaced as follows:

16:2.3 Here are some examples that are fully worked out.

EG. 16.2 $p = T, q = F$ wff $= (\sim((q \supset p) \equiv q))$

Start:

$(\sim((q \supset p) \equiv q))$	Rule 1
$(\sim((F \supset T) \equiv F))$	Rule 2
$(\sim(\quad T \quad \equiv F))$	Rule 4; replace (F $\supset$ T) by T using line 3 of $\supset$ table.
$(\sim \qquad F \quad)$	Rule 4; replace (T $\equiv$ F) by F using line 2 of $\equiv$ table.
$\quad T$	Rule 3

Stop: T is the value of $(\sim((q \supset p) \equiv q))$.

EG. 16.3 $q = F, r = F, p = F$ wff $= [((\sim r) \,\&\, p) \equiv (\sim q)]$

$[((\sim r) \,\&\, p) \equiv (\sim q)]$	Rule 1
$[((\sim F) \,\&\, F) \equiv (\sim F)]$	Rule 2
$((\,T \quad \,\&\, F) \equiv \quad T \quad)$	Two applications of rule 3
$(\qquad F \quad \equiv \quad T \quad)$	Rule 4; replace (T & F) by F on appeal to line 2 of & table.
$\qquad F$	Rule 4; replace (F$\equiv$T) by F on appeal to line 3 of $\equiv$ table.

Result: this wff is false.

EG. 16.4 $p = F$ wff $= [((p \equiv (p \lor p)) \,\&\, (\sim p)) \supset p]$

$[((p \equiv (p \lor p)) \,\&\, (\sim p)) \supset p]$	Rule 1
$[((F \equiv (F \lor F)) \,\&\, (\sim F)) \supset F]$	Rule 2
$[((F \equiv (F \lor F)) \,\&\, \quad T \quad) \supset F]$	Rule 3
$[((F \equiv \quad F \quad) \,\&\, \quad T \quad) \supset F]$	Rule 4; replace (F $\lor$ F) by F on appeal to line 4 of $\lor$ table.
$((\quad T \qquad\quad \,\&\, \quad T \quad) \supset F)$	Rule 4; replace (F $\equiv$ F) by T on appeal to line 4 of $\equiv$ table.
$(\qquad\qquad\quad T \qquad \supset F)$	Rule 4; replace (T & T) by T on appeal to line 1 of & table.
$\qquad\qquad\quad F$	Rule 4; replace (T $\supset$ F) by F on appeal to line 2 of $\supset$ table.

Result: the wff is false.

EG. 16.5 $p = F, q = T$ wff = $[((q \supset p) \equiv (p \vee q)) \& (\sim p)]$

$[((q \supset p) \equiv (p \vee q)) \& (\sim p)]$ Rule 1
$[((T \supset F) \equiv (F \vee T)) \& (\sim F)]$ Rule 2
$[((T \supset F) \equiv (F \vee T)) \&\ T\ ]$ Rule 3
$((\ \ F\ \ \equiv (F \vee T)) \&\ T\ )$ Rule 4
$((\ \ F\ \ \equiv\ \ T\ ) \&\ T\ )$ Rule 4
$(\ \ \ \ \ \ \ F\ \ \ \ \ \ \ \ \&\ T\ )$ Rule 4
$\ \ \ \ \ \ \ \ \ \ \ \ \ \ \ \ F$ Rule 4

Result: the wff is false.

16:3 The main logical operator In using the procedure given in 16:2.2 to find the truth-value of a wff we always move from the simple internal subformulas to the value of the wff as a whole. The final result is written under the *main logical operator* of the compound wff. Thus, if the wff is a complex negation or a complex disjunction, the process we have provided will yield the truth-value of the wff under the $\sim$ and the $\vee$, respectively. To find out what the main logical operator of any wff is, simply (1) write down the wff, (2) associate pairs of left- and right-hand parentheses with each other beginning with any two that form a pair and have no parentheses between them and (3) continue to pair up parentheses which have no unassociated or unpaired parentheses between them. Ultimately you will be left with one last (outermost) pair of parentheses. The logical operator that it contains, but which is contained by no previously associated pair of parentheses, is the main logical operator. Here are some examples of this procedure:

EG. 16.6 wff $((\sim p) \supset (\sim q))$

Step 1. $((\ \sim p\ ) \supset (\ \sim q\ ))$ Write wff.
Step 2. $((\ \overline{\sim p}\ ) \supset (\ \overline{\sim q}\ ))$ Associate pairs of parentheses which have no parentheses between them.
Step 3. $((\ \overline{\sim p}\ ) \supset (\ \overline{\sim q}\ ))$ The $\supset$ is the main operator since it is the logical operator contained between the outermost pair of parentheses which is contained by no previously associated pair.

EG. 16.7 wff = $((\sim((q \supset r) \& p)) \equiv p)$

Step 1. $((\sim((q \supset r) \& p)) \equiv p)$ Write wff.
Step 2a. $((\sim((\overline{q \supset r}) \& p)) \equiv p)$ Innermost pair
      b. $((\sim\overline{((q \supset r) \& p})) \equiv p)$ Next innermost pair
      c. $(\overline{(\sim((q \supset r) \& p}))) \equiv p)$ Next innermost pair
Step 3.   The $\equiv$ is the one left; it is the main operator.

EG. 16.8 wff = $[\sim[((p \equiv q) \vee (\sim q)) \equiv (\sim p)]]$

Step 1. $[\sim[((p \equiv q) \vee (\sim q)) \equiv (\sim p)]]$
Step 2a. $[\sim[((\overline{p \equiv q}) \vee (\overline{\sim q})) \equiv (\overline{\sim p})]]$
      b. $[\sim[\overline{((p \equiv q}) \vee (\overline{\sim q})) \equiv (\overline{\sim p})]]$
      c. $[\sim\overline{[((p \equiv q) \vee (\overline{\sim q})) \equiv (\overline{\sim p}})]]$
Step 3. The main operator is $\sim$, the only one left between outermost parentheses not already captured inside some other pair.

16:4 Compacting the Procedure We can save a lot of room when using the procedures given in 16:2.2 and 16:3 if we collapse all our work into one line. Thus, when finding the main connective in Eg. 16.7 we could have written:

EG. 16.7′ $((\sim((q \supset r) \& p)) \equiv p)$

(arrow pointing up to $\equiv$)

using the arrow to point to the main logical operator after having visually applied the steps of the procedure in turn.

We can do a similar thing when finding the truth-value of a wff if we modify the procedure in two ways. First, let's write the wff down and do the work of writing all the T's and F's underneath it without recopying the parentheses and logical operators. Second, let's adopt the *convention* of crossing out each T or F after we have used it. Thus Eg. 16.3 would be handled this way:

EG. 16.3′ $[((\sim r) \& p) \equiv (\sim q)]$
$$[((\sim F) \& F) \equiv (\sim F)]$$
$$((T\!\!\!/F \ \& \ F) \equiv (T\!\!\!/F)$$
$$(T\!\!\!/ \ F \ \ F \ \ F \ \ \ \ \ \ T\!\!\!/ \ F)$$
$$T\!\!\!/ \ F \ \ F\!\!\!/ \ F \ \ F \ \ T\!\!\!/ \ F$$
(arrow pointing up to the F)

where the only value left is the F under the main logical operator. This means that the wff in Eg. 16.3′ is false.

Here are two more examples. In each, p is given as T and q as F.

$$((\sim p) \supset (\sim q))$$
$$F\!\!\!/ \ T\!\!\!/ \ \ T \ \ \ T\!\!\!/ \ F$$
(arrow up)   value of whole formula is true

$$((p \equiv (\sim q)) \lor p)$$
$$T\!\!\!/ \ T\!\!\!/ \ \ T\!\!\!/ F \ \ \ T \ T\!\!\!/$$
(arrow up)   value of whole formula is true

The preliminary exercise below is to give practice in finding the main logical operator and the truth-value of a wff. Let p be F, q be T, and r be T.

EXERCISE 1
PRACTICE WFFS

1. $(p \supset q)$
3. $(r \supset q)$
3. $((\sim p) \lor (\sim q))$
4. $(q \& r)$
5. $(\sim r)$
6. $((p \supset q) \equiv r)$
7. $((p \equiv q) \lor (\sim r))$
8. $(p \& ((q \supset r) \equiv p))$
9. $[\sim((p \lor r) \supset (\sim q))]$
10. $[\sim[(p \equiv q) \supset (\sim (q \equiv p))]]$

Main connectives	Values
1. ⊃	1. T
2. ⊃	2. T
3. ∨	3. T
4. &	4. T
5. ~	5. F
6. ≡	6. T
7. ∨	7. F
8. &	8. F
9. ~	9. T
10. ~	10. F

16:5.1 Full evaluation of wffs So far we have learned how to write well-formed formulas of our system of propositional logic and how to determine the truth-value of a complex well-formed formula given specific values for all its statement letters (p, q, r, etc.). Now we will learn to evaluate a well-formed formula fully by constructing a truth-table for the formula which represents what its value would be for each of the possible assignments of true or false to each statement letter in the formula.

If we have a formula with two different letters, q and r say, then we can find out what value that formula would have in every possible case. Let us call each different distribution of T and F to the (two) letters a different *interpretation* of the whole formula. There are two ways to interpret a formula which has only one statement letter; four ways to interpret one with two different statement letters; eight ways to interpret one with three different statement letters; and so on. Here are the interpretations:

Pattern for one letter	Pattern for two letters		Pattern for three letters		
Letter	Letter 1	Letter 2	Letter 1	Letter 2	Letter 3
1. T	1. T	T	1. T	T	T
2. F	2. T	F	2. T	T	F
	3. F	T	3. T	F	T
	4. F	F	4. T	F	F
			5. F	T	T
			6. F	T	F
			7. F	F	T
			8. F	F	F

We can construct a table which will tell us the value of a given well-formed formula under every possible interpretation. There are sixteen ways to interpret a wff with four different statement letters and thirty-two ways to interpret a wff with five different statement letters. Generally, given a wff with n different statement letters there are 2^n ways of interpreting it. You can understand the mathematics of this situation through the following reflection. Obviously a wff with one statement letter has two interpretations, T and F.

p	
T	
F	

If a second letter, q, is added, the possibilities *double* because when p is T, q can be T and it can be F.

p	q
T	T
	F

Similarly, if p is F, q can again be T or F.

p	q
F	T
	F

Thus we get

p	q
T	T
T	F
F	T
F	F

When we add a third letter r, the possibilities again double. When p and q are both T, r may be T or F.

p	q	r
T	T	T
		F

Can you generate the eight rows of this table? Could you construct the sixteen-row table for a formula with four letters?

The procedure for constructing the *truth-table* for a wff is given below. Using this procedure each wff will have one, and only one, truth-table. It will list all the possible interpretations of that wff and it will indicate the truth-value of the wff on each interpretation. These values will form a column under the wff's main logical operator. This column is called the *final value column* of the wff. As we state the procedure for constructing truth-tables we will use the wff $(q \supset p)$ as an example of each step.

First List all the statement letters of the wff in alphabetical order (this is a convention which will make our tables alike enough to compare when doing exercises and examples). After the last letter put a double bar, between each letter put a single bar, and draw a line under all of them and out to the right:

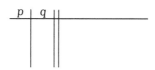

Second Determine how many rows or lines long the table will have to be and fill in the T's and F's under all the statement letters using the patterns given above. (For four letters repeat eight T's and eight F's under the leftmost statement letter; then fill in under the remaining three letters using the pattern for three letters twice, once for rows 1 to 8, then for rows 9 to 16. This process can be used also for a five-letter table, but first start with sixteen T's and sixteen F's.) In our little example, using the pattern for two letters, we would write in

p	q	
T	T	
T	F	
F	T	
F	F	

Third Write the wff to be evaluated or examined in the upper right-hand corner to the right of the double bar and above the line.

p	q	(q ⊃ p)
T	T	
T	F	
F	T	
F	F	

Fourth In columns, under each occurrence of each statement letter in the wff, write the values for that statement letter *on that row* of the table.

p	q	(q ⊃ p)	
T	T	T	T
T	F	F	T
F	T	T	F
F	F	F	F

The values under the p and q in the wff are exactly those specified under the p column and the q column to the left of the double bar.

Fifth Using the procedure given in 16:2.2 as modified in 16:4 fill in the values of the wff for each row of the table, row by row.

p	q	(q ⊃ p)	
T	T	T T T	
T	F	F T T	
F	T	T F F	
F	F	F T F	

The arrow here indicates the final value column of the wff.

16:5.2 Here are some completed truth-tables. They have been constructed using the procedures given in 16:5.1.

EG. 16.9   wff = ((~p) & p)

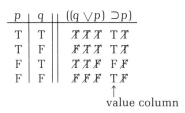

p	((~ p) & p)
T	F̶ T̶ F T̶
F	T̶ F̶ F F̶

value column

EG. 16.10   wff = ((q ∨ p) ⊃ p)

p	q	((q ∨ p) ⊃ p)
T	T	T̶ T̶ T̶ T T̶
T	F	F̶ T̶ T̶ T T̶
F	T	T̶ T̶ F̶ F F̶
F	F	F̶ F̶ F̶ T F̶

value column

EXERCISES FOR MODULE 16
TRUTH-VALUES AND TRUTH-TABLES FOR WFFS

Ex. 2. Construct truth-tables for the wffs given below.

1. (p ∨ r)
2. ((~q) ⊃ p)
3. (p ≡ (~q))
4. ((~p) ∨ q)
5. ((~p) ∨ p)
6. (q ∨ (~q))
7. (p ⊃ (q ⊃ p))
8. (~(p ⊃ p))
9. ((p ⊃ (q ⊃ r)) ∨ (~r))
10. [q ∨ (p & (~p))]

Ex. 3 Write from memory the paradigm tables for negation, conjunction, alternation, the conditional, and the biconditional.

Ex. 4 Determine the main logical operator of each of the following wffs and write it in the answer space.

_____   1. (q ⊃ p)   _____   2. (p ⊃ q)

_____   3. (p ⊃ r)   _____   4. ((p ≡ q) ⊃ r)

_____   5. (p ∨ r)   _____   6. ((q ∨ r) ⊃ p)

_____   7. (p ≡ p)   _____   8. (q ⊃ (p & r))

_____   9. ((q ≡ p) ≡ r)   _____   10. (r & (~p))

_____ 11. $(\sim(p \supset q))$ _____ 12. $[\sim(\sim(q \equiv p))]$

_____ 13. $((p \supset q) \mathbin{\&} (r \supset p))$ _____ 14. $((q \supset p) \equiv (r \supset p))$

_____ 15. $[q \supset [\sim((r \supset p) \lor (p \equiv p))]]$

Ex. 5 Let $p = T, q = T$, and $r = F$. Determine the truth-value of each of the wffs listed in Ex. 4. Mark that value in the answer space.

_____ 1.   _____ 2.   _____ 3.   _____ 4.   _____ 5.   _____ 6.

_____ 7.   _____ 8.   _____ 9.   _____ 10.   _____ 11.   _____ 12.

_____ 13.   _____ 14.   _____ 15.

Ex. 6 Construct the truth-tables for each of the wffs in Ex. 4.

SELECTED ANSWERS
TO EXERCISES FOR MODULE 16

Ex. 2 If your tables are correctly constructed, you could read down the value column and get a sequence of T's and F's. Below are given the sequences of T's and F's that represent the value column of the truth-table for each well-formed formula in the above exercise. [Assume that the tables all begin by listing the sentence letters in alphabetical order (p, q, r, etc.).]

1.	2.	3.	4.	5.	6.	7.	8.	9.	10.
T	T	F	T	T	T	T	F	T	T
T	T	T	F	T	T	T	F	T	F
T	T	T	T			T		T	T
F	F	F	T			T		T	F
								T	
								T	
								T	
								T	

Ex. 3 Consult 16.1.2 for the correct answers.

Ex. 4

1. $\supset$ 2. $\supset$ 3. $\supset$
4. $\supset$ 5. $\lor$ 6. $\supset$
7. $\equiv$ 8. $\supset$ 9. $\equiv$
10. $\mathbin{\&}$

If you missed more than one, review 16:3.

Ex. 5

1. T   2. T   3. F
4. F   5. T   6. T
7. T   8. F   9. F
10. F

If you missed any, review 16:2.1.

Ex. 6 Reading down the final value column your tables should have these values:

1. TTFT
2. TFTT
3. TFTT
4. TFTTTTTF
5. TTTF
6. TTTTFFFT
7. TT
8. TFTTFFTT
9. TFFTFTTF
10. FFTF

If you missed more than two, review 16:5.1 and 16:5.2.

MODULE 17

IMPLICATION, EQUIVALENCE, AND VALIDITY IN PROPOSITIONAL LOGIC

One of the chief purposes of building truth-tables is to test arguments of propositional logic for validity. In Module 17 we will learn how to use truth-tables to test to see if two wffs are logically equivalent or if one wff logically implies another. Then we will learn to test to see if a group of wffs logically implies a single wff. This allows us to determine whether a group of premises logically implies a particular conclusion.

● After reading Module 17 you should be able to:

1. Use complete truth-tables to determine the characteristics or logical properties of individual wffs
2. Use them to test two wffs to see if they are logically equivalent
3. Use them to test to see if one wff or a group of wffs logically implies another wff
4. Use them to test arguments to see if they are valid
5. Use the partial truth-table technique to test for logical implication and validity

17:1 Characteristics of wffs A truth-table for a wff expresses what value that wff would have under every possible combination of value assignments to its various statement letters. If the world were such that all the statement units of a given wff were true, then the first line of the truth-table would show whether that wff were true or false in that world. If the world were such that every statement unit in a wff were false, then the value of that wff on the last line of its truth-table would be the value of that wff in that world. And, for each other possible world (i.e., possible assignment of 'true' or 'false' to the statement units in a wff) there is a row of the truth-table which shows the value of that wff in that world.

Some wffs, like $(p \ \& \ q)$, will come out with T on some lines and F on others because their outcome is contingent upon the values of their statement letters. Others, like $(q \lor (\sim q))$, come out T on every line; while wffs like $(\sim (r \supset r))$ come out F on every line. These kinds of wffs derive their values from their structures independently of the values of the individual statement letters. In this respect they are like the analytically true and analytically false statements discussed in 9:1.2. Those wffs like $(p \ \& \ q)$ which have values that are contingent upon both structure and the individual values of their statement letters are like the synthetic statements discussed in 9:2.

Analytically true wffs are *tautologies*; analytically false wffs are *inconsistent* or *self-contradictory*; synthetic wffs are *contingent*. All wffs can be classified into one and only one of those three groups. All tautologies are analytically true statements and all inconsistent wffs are analytically false statements. However, because our formal symbolic language is not as rich as our natural language, because we cannot say as many things in our symbolic language, and because we cannot express as many subtle relationships, there are more analytically true English statements than there are tautologies. There are also more analytically false statements than there are inconsistent well-formed formulas. We can use the following as operational definitions of these terms:

A tautological wff = $_{df}$ any wff such that when one writes its truth-table there are all and only T's in its final value column

An inconsistent wff = $_{df}$ any wff such that when one writes its truth-table there are all and only F's in its final value column

A contingent wff = $_{df}$ the wff one has when one writes its truth-table and discovers at least one T and at least one F in the final value column

An English statement that can be imagined to be true at least in some remote way is called *consistent* to distinguish it from one that cannot be true under any imaginable or possible circumstances, which is called *inconsistent*. Similarly, a wff that can be true under even one interpretation can be called consistent to distinguish it from inconsistent wffs which are never true.

A consistent wff = $_{df}$ the wff one has when one writes its truth-table and discovers at least one T in its final value column

Thus, tautologies and contingent wffs are the two classes of consistent wffs. We can diagram or map out the extensional relationships developed by these definitions as follows. Let the large rectangle represent the universe of all wffs.

First, the universe can be divided into consistent wffs and inconsistent wffs. Then consistent wffs can be subdivided into tautologous consistent wffs and contingent consistent wffs as follows:

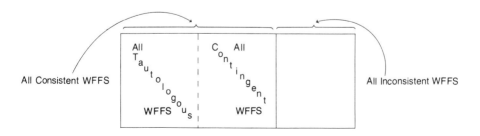

Evaluate the ten wffs that you wrote tables for in Ex. 2 of Module 16 on the basis of our four operational definitions.

ANSWERS TO EXERCISE 1

1. Contingent and consistent
2. Contingent and consistent
3. Contingent and consistent
4. Contingent and consistent
5. Tautology and consistent
6. Tautology and consistent
7. Tautology and consistent
8. Inconsistent
9. Tautology and consistent
10. Contingent and consistent

Tautologies are consistent because they have at least one T in the final value column of their tables. A wff that has at least one T and also has at least one F is contingent. Neither tautological nor inconsistent well-formed formulas can be contingent.

Before going on in Module 17 you may wish to solidify your understanding of these terms by doing Exs. 5 to 9 at the end of the module.

17:2.1 Relationships between wffs By using truth-tables we can also indicate the relationships that one formula has to another formula. Two well-formed formulas are *logically equivalent* if, and only if, they have the *same truth-values under every interpretation*. In terms of truth-tables this amounts to saying that both wffs have identical truth-values on each line of the final value columns of their tables provided that their tables list the same statement letters in the same order on the left. There is an easy way to tell if two wffs are equivalent. One wff, call it A, will be logically equivalent to another wff, call the second one B, if and only if, the new wff $(A \equiv B)$ is a *tautology*. Example 17.1 shows that $(p \supset q)$ is logically equivalent to $((\sim p) \vee q)$.

EG. 17.1 Original wffs $(p \supset q)$ and $((\sim p) \vee q)$

p	q	((p ⊃ q) ≡ ((~p) ∨q))
T	T	T̸ T̸T̸ T F̸T̸ T̸T̸
T	F	T̸ F̸F̸ T F̸T̸ F̸F̸
F	T	F̸ T̸T̸ T T̸F̸ T̸T̸
F	F	F̸ T̸F̸ T T̸F̸ T̸F̸
		↑

We can define 'logical equivalence' operationally as:

A pair of logically equivalent wffs A, B = $_{df}$ any wffs A and B such that when one writes the truth-table for $(A \equiv B)$ it is a tautology

When two wffs are logically equivalent they are interchangeable in that whatever value the one has under any given interpretation, the other will have also.

17:2.2 Sometimes people use the test for logical equivalence as a test to see if two wffs amount, logically speaking, to the same thing. Example 17.1 proves that $(p \supset q)$

and $((\sim p) \lor q)$ are interchangeable because, being equivalent, they have the same logical force.

EG. 17.2 To prove that $((p \lor q) \lor r)$ is interchangeable with $(p \lor (q \lor r))$ we will test for logical equivalence.

p	q	r	$((p \lor q) \lor r) \equiv (p \lor (q \lor r))$
T	T	T	T T T T T **T** T T T T T
T	T	F	T T T T F **T** T T T T F
T	F	T	T T F T T **T** T T F T T
T	F	F	T T F T F **T** T T F F F
F	T	T	F T T T T **T** F T T T T
F	T	F	F T T T F **T** F T T T F
F	F	T	F F F T T **T** F T F T T
F	F	F	F F F F F **T** F F F F F

$\qquad\qquad\qquad\qquad\qquad\qquad\qquad\qquad\uparrow$

You should now be able to prove that $(p \,\&\, (q \,\&\, r))$ and $((p \,\&\, q) \,\&\, r)$ are interchangeable using a truth-table.

Sometimes people wonder whether or not you can "factor" negation signs into or out of conjunctions and disjunctions. In effect they are asking can we move back and forth between something like $(\sim(p \,\&\, q))$ to something like $((\sim p) \,\&\, (\sim q))$. To find out let's test for logical equivalence.

EG. 17.3

p	q	$[((\sim p) \,\&\, (\sim q)) \equiv (\sim (p \,\&\, q))]$
T	T	F T F F T **T** F T T T
T	F	F T F T F **F** T T F F
F	T	T F F F T **F** T F F T
F	F	T F T T F **T** T F F F

$\qquad\qquad\qquad\qquad\qquad\uparrow$

This table shows that the wffs are not logically equivalent; and, so, that they are not interchangeable. One can no more move from $(\sim(p \,\&\, q))$ to $((\sim p) \,\&\, (\sim q))$ than one can move from $-(4 \times 5)$ to (-4×-5).

17:3 One formula *A logically implies* or logically entails another formula *B* if the principle of entailment, (E) in 11:1.3, is satisfied. The principle of entailment requires that it *never* be possible for *A* to be true when *B* is false. In terms of truth-tables, if we did a table for both *A* and *B* and discovered that it never happened that *B* was F when *A* was T, then we could say that *A* logically implied or logically entailed *B*. Thus, we can say that a formula, call it *A*, *logically implies* or *entails* a formula, call it *B*, if the new formula $(A \supset B)$ is a tautology. In such a case it would be impossible for the *B* to be false when *A* was true. Example 17.4 shows that $(p \,\&\, q)$ logically implies *q*. Example 17.5 shows that *p* implies itself.

EG. 17.4

p	q	$((p \,\&\, q) \supset q)$	$(p \,\&\, q)$ implies q.
T	T	T T T **T** T	
T	F	T F F **T** F	
F	T	F F T **T** T	
F	F	F F F **T** F	

$\qquad\qquad\qquad\qquad\uparrow$

EG. 17.5

p	(p ⊃p)
T	T T T
F	F T F

p implies p.

↑

We can also say that a group of wffs logically imply a single wff if, and only if, it is not possible for each member of the group to be true and the single wff to be false. If the three wffs A, B, and C, taken together, logically imply the wff D, the following formula will be a tautology: [((A & B) & C) ⊃D]. Example 17.4 shows that the two wffs p and q, taken together, logically imply the wff q. Here is another example.

EG. 17.6 To show that p and (p ⊃q) taken together logically imply q let us set up the formula structure

((A & B) ⊃C)

Let   p = A
    (p ⊃q) = B
        q = C

Thus let us test ((p & (p ⊃q)) ⊃q) to see if it is a tautology.

p	q	((p & (p ⊃q)) ⊃q)
T	T	T T T T T T T
T	F	T F T F F T F
F	T	F F F T T T T
F	F	F F F T F T F

↑

It is. So p and (p ⊃ q) taken together imply q.

We can define logical implication as follows:

A wff A logically implies a wff B = df the truth-table that one derives for the formula (A ⊃B) reveals that (A ⊃B) is a tautology

We can define what it means for a set of wffs, call them {P₁, P₂, . . ., Pₙ} to *jointly imply* another wff, call it C, as follows:

The wffs P₁, P₂, . . ., Pₙ
jointly imply another wff C = df the truth-table that one derives for
((P₁ & P₂ &, . . ., & Pₙ) ⊃C) is a tautology

Notice that a formula like ((A & B) & C) happens to be logically equivalent to one like this: (A & (B & C)). When we have only ampersands to worry about, parentheses become unimportant because the ambiguities that they resolve do not affect the logical outcome of the whole formula. On the basis of this we can remove the superfluous parentheses from certain formulas so that we can get a closer look at the crucial logical relationships. So, we can say that a group of formulas, P₁, P₂, . . ., Pₙ, logically imply a formula C if, and only if, the formula $((P_1 \& P_2 \& \ldots \& P_n) \supset C)$ is a tautology.

It might be a good idea to do Exercises 10, 12, and 13 now so that you can have a more solid understanding of logical implication and logical equivalence before moving to tests for validity.

17:4 Testing arguments for validity The test for validity amounts to doing a truth-table to see if the premises of an argument (say P_1, P_2, P_3) taken together [i.e., conjoined: $(P_1 \& P_2 \& P_3)$] jointly imply the conclusion, $((P_1 \& P_2 \& P_2) \supset C)$. In other words, to test for validity in propositional logic create a conditional wff (that is, one that uses the horseshoe as its main connective) such that the argument's premises joined by ampersands are the antecedent of that conditional and the argument's conclusion is the consequent of the conditional.[6]

If the argument's premises are P_1, P_2, and P_3, and if its conclusion is C, write the wff:

$$((P_1 \& P_2 \& P_3) \supset C)$$

This wff is called the argument's *corresponding conditional*.

An argument is valid in propositional logic if, and only if, its corresponding conditional is a tautology.

In 14:1.1, we gave four example arguments, Egs. 14.1 to 14.4. In 14:1.2 we translated them into formal symbolic notation as Egs. 14.1'' to 14.4''. To test for validity we will work with their symbolic representations.

EG. 14.1''
$$p$$
$$\underline{(q \lor (\sim p))}$$
$$\therefore q$$

Our testing procedures call for us to form a conditional wff

$$(\quad \supset \quad).$$

with the argument's conclusion q as the consequent

$$(\quad \supset q)$$

and the conjunction of its premises

$$[p \& (q \lor (\sim p))]$$

as the conditional's antecedent

$$[[p \& (q \lor (\sim p))] \supset q]$$

If this conditional is a tautology, then the argument is valid because its being a tautology proves that the premises jointly imply the conclusion.

---

[6] In terms of $((P_1 \& P_2) \supset C)$, the $(P_1 \& P_2)$ is the antecedent and the C is the consequent.

p	*q*	[[p & (q ∨ (~p))] ⊃q]
T	T	T T T T F T T T
T	F	T F F F F T T F
F	T	F F T T T F T T
F	F	F F F T T F T F

↑

The conditional is a tautology, and so the argument Eg. 14.1 is valid.

To test Eg. 14.2 we would take its symbolic representation, Eg. 14.2'', form its corresponding conditional wff,

EG. 14.2''

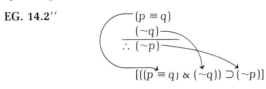

(p ≡ q)
(~q)
∴ (~p)

[((p ≡ q) & (~q)) ⊃ (~p)]

and then test to see if it is a tautology:

p	*q*	((p ≡ q) & (~q)) ⊃ (~p))
T	T	T T T F F T T F T
T	F	T F F F T F T F T
F	T	F F T F F T T T F
F	F	F T F T T F T T F

↑

The truth-table shows that the conditional is a tautology, which, in turn, means that Eg. 14.2 is a valid argument. To find out if Eg. 14.3 is valid we would use

EG. 14.3''   (p & q)
                 ((p ∨ q) ⊃ r)
          ∴ r

to form

[((p & q) & ((p ∨ q) ⊃ r)) ⊃ r]

and check that argument's corresponding conditional to see if it is a tautology.

EG. 14.4''   (r ⊃ q)
                 (q ⊃ p)
                 (~p)
          ∴ (~r)

Example 14.4 will be valid if

[[((r ⊃ q) & (q ⊃ p)) & (~p)] ⊃ (~r)]

is a tautology. Since the grouping (A & (B & C)) is logically equivalent to ((A & B) & C) we could also have written the conditional for Eg. 14.4 as

[[(r ⊃ q) & ((q ⊃ p) & (~p))] ⊃ (~r)]

Exercise 2

Here are some practice arguments in symbolic notation. Write the corresponding conditional necessary to check each for validity and then carry out the check to see if each is valid or not.

A. 1. $(p \supset q)$
    2. $(\sim q)$
    ∴ 3. $(\sim p)$

B. 1. $(p \supset q)$
    2. $((\sim q) \supset (\sim r))$
    3. r
    ∴ 4. p

C. 1. p
    ∴ 2. $(p \lor q)$

D. 1. $(p \& q)$
    ∴ 2. p

E. 1. $(p \supset q)$
    2. $((\sim q) \lor p)$
    3. $(\sim q)$
    ∴ 4. $(\sim p)$

F. 1. $(p \& (\sim r))$
    2. r
    3. $(\sim p)$
    ∴ 4. q

G. 1. $(p \& q)$
    2. $((p \lor q) \supset r)$
    ∴ 3. r

H. 1. $(r \supset q)$
    2. $(q \supset p)$
    3. $(\sim p)$
    ∴ 4. $(\sim r)$

ANSWERS TO EXERCISE 2

	The corresponding conditionals	The result
A.	$[((p \supset q) \& (\sim q)) \supset (\sim p)]$	Valid
B.	$\{[[(p \supset q) \& ((\sim q) \supset (\sim r))] \& r] \supset p\}$	Invalid
C.	$(p \supset (p \lor q))$	Valid
D.	$((p \& q) \supset p)$	Valid
E.	$[[((p \supset q) \& ((\sim q) \lor p)) \& (\sim q)] \supset (\sim p)]$	Valid
F.	$[[((p \& (\sim r)) \& r) \& (\sim p)] \supset q]$	Valid
G.	$[((p \& q) \& ((p \lor q) \supset r)) \supset r]$	Valid
H.	$[[((r \supset q) \& (q \supset p)) \& (\sim p)] \supset (\sim r)]$	Valid

You are now ready to complete Exs. 11, 14, and 15 of this module. Work them through before going on.

17:5.1 The optional shortcut method[7] The decision procedures we just outlined involve using *complete* truth-tables for testing equivalence, implication, and validity. While it is true that using a complete truth-table always works to yield a definite yes or no answer, the procedure is time consuming. Moreover, a person can often see that certain possibilities are not worth considering, while others are crucial for deciding the issue of, say, implication or equivalence.

---

[7] This section is optional, but quite useful. It will be easier for you to follow if you have already worked about half of the problems in Exs. 2, 9, 12, 13, and 14.

For example, suppose you wanted to find out if $(p \lor q)$ logically implied $(\sim(p \ \& \ q))$. The complete truth-table for this is:

EG. 17.7

p	q	$[(p \lor q) \supset (\sim(p \ \& \ q))]$
T	T	T T T F F T T T
T	F	T T F T T T F F
F	T	F T T T T F F T
F	F	F F F T T F F F

↑ Implication fails.

However, if you had seen ahead of time that the consequent $(\sim(p \ \& \ q))$ could be F on only one line, you would have realized that the only line on which the value of $(p \lor q)$ matters is that one on which $(\sim(p \ \& \ q))$ comes out F. If on that one line $(p \lor q)$ is T, then the implication fails; if its value is F, then the implication holds. Thus you could have used a shortened truth-table to examine that specific line as in:

EG. 17.7'

p	q	$[(p \lor q) \supset (\sim(p \ \& \ q))]$
T	T	T T T F F T T T
.	.	. . . .
.	.	. . . .

↑ Implication fails.

We can generalize this procedure as follows. Given any two wffs A and B, if checking $(A \supset B)$ for logical implication, examine B. If there is only one interpretation under which B is false, test $(A \supset B)$ under that interpretation. If under that interpretation $(A \supset B)$ is T, then A logically implies B; otherwise not. For example, does $(q \equiv p)$ logically imply $(p \lor q)$? Examine $(p \lor q)$; it is F only when $p = $ F and $q = $ F. Doing a partial truth-table for $((q \equiv p) \supset (p \lor q))$ we derive the following:

EG. 17.8

p	q	$((q \equiv p) \supset (p \lor q))$
.	.	. . . .
.	.	. . . .
F	F	F T F F F F F

↑ Implication fails.

Similarly, does $(q \lor p)$ logically imply $(p \lor q)$? Examine $(p \lor q)$; it is F only when $p = $ F and $q = $ F. Testing $((q \lor p) \supset (p \lor q))$ under that interpretation we derive

EG. 17.9

p	q	$((q \lor p) \supset (p \lor q))$
.	.	. . . . .
.	.	. . . . .
F	F	F F F T F F F

↑ Implication holds.

We can also work the shortcut method starting with the antecedent. Given any two wffs A and B, if checking $(A \supset B)$ for logical implication examine A. If there is only one interpretation under which A is T, check $(A \supset B)$ under that interpretation. If $(A \supset B)$ is T, then the implication holds; otherwise not. For example, does p logically imply $(p \equiv p)$? The wff p will be T only on one line. So check $(p \supset (p \equiv p))$ on that line:

$$\begin{array}{c|ccccc} p & \multicolumn{5}{c}{(p \supset (p \equiv p))} \\ \hline T & \cancel{T} & T & \cancel{T} & \cancel{T} & \cancel{T} \end{array}$$

↑ Implication holds.

Does $((p \,\&\, q) \,\&\, (\sim r))$ logically imply $((q \equiv r) \vee (\sim p))$? Examine $((p \,\&\, q) \,\&\, (\sim r))$; it is T only when $p = T$, $q = T$, and $r = F$. Check $[((p \,\&\, q) \,\&\, (\sim r)) \supset ((q \equiv r) \vee (\sim p))]$ on that line.

EG. 17.11

$$\begin{array}{ccc|ccccccccccc} p & q & r & \multicolumn{11}{c}{[((p \,\&\, q) \,\&\, (\sim r)) \supset ((q \equiv r) \vee (\sim p))]} \\ \hline T & T & F & \cancel{T} & \cancel{T} & \cancel{T} & \cancel{T} & \cancel{T} & F & F & \cancel{T} & F & F & F & F & \cancel{T} \end{array}$$

↑ Implication fails.

The shortcut method relies for its shortness on there being a minimum of F's in the consequent or of T's in the antecedent. For you to use the method successfully, you should keep in mind which operators will tend to produce T's (in the consequent) and which will tend to produce F's (in the antecedent). The horseshoe and the wedge will produce mostly T's, as will negations of conjunctions. When any of these is the main operator in the consequent, you can effectively use the shortcut method starting with the consequent. The ampersand and the negation of either a conditional or an alternation will tend to produce F's. You should be looking for one of these as the main operators in the antecedent.

EXERCISE 3

Using the shortcut method test the following pairs of wffs to see if the first logically implies the second.

1. p, $(p \vee (\sim p))$
2. $(q \,\&\, (\sim r))$, $((r \equiv q) \vee q)$
3. $(s \equiv (\sim t))$, $(s \vee t)$
4. $(r \,\&\, (\sim p))$, $(p \equiv (\sim r))$
5. $((\sim q) \,\&\, (\sim p))$, $((q \equiv p) \vee (q \vee p))$
6. $((s \vee p) \equiv q)$, $[((\sim p) \,\&\, (\sim s)) \supset q]$

ANSWERS TO EXERCISE 3

1. Yes; check where $p = T$.
2. Yes; check where $q = T$ and $r = F$.
3. Yes; check $s = F$ and $t = F$.
4. Yes; check $p = F$ and $r = T$.
5. Yes; check $p = F$ and $q = F$.
6. No; check $p = F$, $q = F$, and $s = F$.

When using the shortcut method you should take care not to skip accidently any of the crucial interpretations. This risk occurs chiefly when the two subformulas do not contain the same statement letters, for example, in checking to see if $(p \,\&\, (\sim r))$ logically implies $((p \supset (\sim q)) \equiv r)$. Here there is only one way to make $(p \,\&\, (\sim r))$ true, that is, when $p = T$ and $r = F$. But since $((p \supset (\sim q)) \equiv r)$ contains a new statement letter, q, there are two lines to check on the truth-table: where $p = T$, $q = T$, and $r = F$, and where $p = T$, $q = F$, and $r = F$.

EG. 17.12

p	q	r	$[(p \,\&\, (\sim r)) \supset ((p \supset (\sim q)) \equiv r)]$
.	.	.	. . . .
T	T	F	~~T~~ ~~T~~ ~~T~~ F T ~~T~~ ~~F~~ ~~F~~ ~~T~~ ~~T~~ ~~F~~
.	.	.	. . .
.	.	.	. . .
T	F	F	~~T~~ ~~T~~ ~~T~~ F F ~~T~~ ~~T~~ ~~T~~ ~~F~~ ~~F~~ ~~F~~
.	.	.	.

$\qquad\qquad\qquad\qquad\qquad\qquad\uparrow$ Implication fails.

If in this example we had checked only $p = T$, $q = T$, and $r = F$, our shortcut would have led us to the wrong answer.

EXERCISE 4

Check, using the shortcut method, to see if the first wff logically implies the second in each of the following pairs.

1. p, $(p \lor q)$
2. $((\sim r) \,\&\, q)$, $((q \lor p) \supset (\sim r))$
3. $(q \equiv (\sim q))$, $((r \lor (\sim s)) \,\&\, q)$
4. $(\sim(r \supset s))$, $[((p \,\&\, q) \equiv r) \,\&\, (\sim s)]$

ANSWERS TO EXERCISE 4

1. Yes; check $\{p = T, q = T\}$ and $\{p = T, q = F\}$.
2. Yes; check $\{p = T, q = T, r = F\}$ and $\{p = F, q = T, r = F\}$.
3. Yes; an inspection of $(q \equiv (\sim q))$ shows that there is no interpretation of q that makes $(q \equiv (\sim q))$ T, so the wff $[(q \equiv (\sim q)) \supset ((r \lor (\sim s)) \,\&\, q)]$ cannot be F. There are no lines to check once you see that $(q \equiv (\sim q))$ is inconsistent.
4. No; check the four lines where $r = T$ and $s = F$. On those two where p and q have opposite values the whole wff is F.

17:5.2 The shortcut method works because in theory we are really accounting for all the lines of the table even though in practice we write out only some of the lines. When examining a conditional wff $(A \supset B)$ to see if it is a tautology, we have focused either on the B to see where it is F or on the A to see where it is T. In doing so we have ruled out lines where B is T (or where A is F) because on any of those lines $(A \supset B)$ will be T. In other words, whenever $B = T$ (or $A = F$) the value of the wff on the other side of the $\supset$ is no longer a factor since the conditional will be T. Therefore, we need only look at cases where that other side could be a factor; that is, cases when $B = F$ (or $A = T$).

The shortcut method is especially advantageous in speeding up validity checks. For example, consider item B in Ex. 2, 17:4. Its complete truth-table looks like this:

EG. 17.13

p	q	r	{[[(p ⊃ q) & ((~ q) ⊃ (~ r))] & r] ⊃ p}	Line
T	T	T	T T T T F T T F T T T T T	1
T	T	F	T T T T F T T T F F F T T	2
T	F	T	T F F F T F F F T F T T T	3
T	F	F	T F F F T F T T F F F T T	4
F	T	T	F T T T F T T F T T T F F	5
F	T	F	F T T T F T T T F F F T F	6
F	F	T	F T F F T F F F T F T T F	7
F	F	F	F T F T T F T T F F F T F	8

↑

But notice that the time spent constructing lines 1 to 4 of this eight-line table was time you could have saved if you had seen that none of these lines would invalidate the argument. Here is how you could have seen that. Examine the argument's conclusion and note the circumstances under which it can be false; those are the *only* circumstances under which the argument can be invalid. So you could, on the basis of this, confine your work to lines 5 to 8 because only in those cases can this argument's conclusion p be false.

The steps involved in applying the shortened truth-table technique to validity checks are as follows. Begin with the corresponding conditional of the argument to be evaluated. Examine its consequent. If there are clearly only certain ways to make that consequent F, check the whole conditional using those sets of values. Or check the antecedent. If there are only certain ways to make it T, examine the whole conditional using those sets of values. If the corresponding conditional comes out F on any line, the argument is not valid in propositional logic; otherwise it is valid. Rework Exs. 2, 14, and 15 using the shortened truth-table technique.

17:5.3 We can, if we are careful, use the shortcut method in lieu of the full truth-table method in almost any circumstance. For example, to see if $((q \& p) \lor q)$ is a tautology we need examine only those lines where $q = F$, since the whole wff will be T where $q = T$.

p	q	((q & p) ∨ q)
.	.	. . . . . .
T	F	F F T F F
.	.	. . . . . .
F	F	F F F F F

↑
Is not a tautology.

By appeal to the same reasoning and the partial table above we have just demonstrated that $((q \& p) \lor q)$ is contingent. This, in turn, implies that it is not contradictory. Consider another example, the wff $[(r \equiv s) \& ((\sim p) \lor (\sim r))]$. Is this wff contradictory, contingent, or tautological? Let us begin by trying to find some row on a truth-table that will make it come out T. Since it is a conjunction, both sides must come out T for it to be T on any row. $(r \equiv s)$ will be T only if both statement letters have the same value. Thus, we must consider four rows:

p	r	s		[(r ≡ s) & ((~p) ∨ (~r))]
---	---	---		---
T	T	T		T̸ F F̸T̸ F̸ F̸T̸
·	·	·		· · · · · ·
·	·	·		· · · · · ·
T	F	F		T̸ T F̸T̸ T̸ T̸F̸
F	T	T		T̸ T T̸F̸ T̸ F̸T̸
·	·	·		· · · · · ·
·	·	·		· · · · · ·
F	F	F		T̸ T T̸F̸ T̸ T̸F̸

(arrow pointing up under the main column)

This much of the table already reveals that the wff is neither tautological nor contradictory, but contingent. Had it come out with four T's we would have known that the wff was not contradictory; however, we would still have had to try to find a row that made it F. Finding such a row would have meant that the wff was contingent, given that we already had found a row on which it was T. Not finding a row on which it was F would have meant that it was a tautology, presuming, of course, that we had not made a careless mistake.

To use the shortcut method to find the characteristics of a wff begin by trying to find some row on which the wff is T *and* some row on which it is F. If you succeed in finding one of each, then the wff is contingent. If you fail to find a row on which it is F, then the wff is a tautology. If you fail to find a row on which it is T, then the wff is contradictory. If you fail in both quests, you made a mistake somewhere.

EXERCISES FOR MODULE 17

IMPLICATION, EQUIVALENCE, AND VALIDITY IN PROPOSITIONAL LOGIC

Ex. 5 Several wffs and their truth-tables are given below. Identify the wffs that are tautologies by writing 'taut' next to each.

1.

p	q		[(p ∨ q) ≡ [~((~p) & (~q))]]
---	---		---
T	T		T̸T̸T̸ T T̸ F̸T̸ F̸ F̸T̸
T	F		T̸T̸F̸ T T̸ F̸T̸ F̸ T̸F̸
F	T		F̸T̸T̸ T T̸ T̸F̸ F̸ F̸T̸
F	F		F̸F̸F̸ T F̸ T̸F̸ T̸ T̸F̸

(arrow up)

2.

p		(p & (~p))
---		---
T		T̸ F F̸T̸
F		F̸ F T̸F̸

(arrow up)

3.

q	r		(q ⊃ (q ∨ r))
---	---		---
T	T		T̸ T T̸T̸T̸
T	F		T̸ T T̸T̸F̸
F	T		F̸ T F̸T̸T̸
F	F		F̸ T F̸F̸F̸

(arrow up)

4.

s		(s ⊃ (~s))
---		---
T		T̸ F F̸T̸
F		F̸ T T̸F̸

(arrow up)

5.

t		(t ≡ (~t))
---		---
T		T̸ F F̸T̸
F		F̸ F T̸F̸

(arrow up)

6.

r	t		((r ∨ t) ⊃ (r & t))
---	---		---
T	T		T̸T̸T̸ T T̸T̸T̸
T	F		T̸T̸F̸ F T̸F̸F̸
F	T		F̸T̸T̸ F F̸F̸T̸
F	F		F̸F̸F̸ T F̸F̸F̸

(arrow up)

7.

p	r		(p ⊃ (r ≡ r))
---	---		---
T	T		T̸ T T̸T̸T̸
T	F		T̸ T F̸T̸F̸
F	T		F̸ T T̸T̸T̸
F	F		F̸ T F̸T̸F̸

(arrow up)

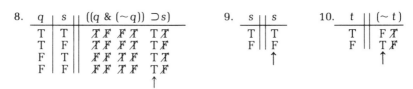

8.

q	s	((q & (~q)) ⊃ s)
T	T	T F F T T T
T	F	T F F T T F
F	T	F F T F T T
F	F	F F T F T F

9.

s	s
T	T
F	F

10.

t	(~t)
T	F T
F	T F

Ex. 6 Identify the contingent wffs in the group given in Ex. 5 by writing 'cont' next to each.

Ex. 7 Identify the inconsistent wffs in the group given in Ex. 5 by writing 'incons' next to each.

Ex. 8 Identify the consistent wffs in the group given in Ex. 5 by writing 'const' next to each.

Ex. 9 Using a truth-table evaluate the following wffs to see if they are contingent, consistent, tautological, or inconsistent.

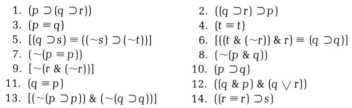

1. $(p \supset (q \supset r))$
2. $((q \supset r) \supset p)$
3. $(p \equiv q)$
4. $(t \equiv t)$
5. $[(q \supset s) \equiv ((\sim s) \supset (\sim t))]$
6. $[((t \& (\sim r)) \& r) \equiv (q \supset q)]$
7. $(\sim (p \equiv p))$
8. $(\sim (p \& q))$
9. $[\sim (r \& (\sim r))]$
10. $(p \supset q)$
11. $(q \equiv p)$
12. $((q \& p) \& (q \lor r))$
13. $[(\sim (p \supset p)) \& (\sim (q \supset q))]$
14. $((r \equiv r) \supset s)$

Ex. 10 Write 'yes' or 'no' in the space provided.

_____ 1. Reading table 1, Ex. 9, does p logically imply $(q \supset r)$?

_____ 2. Reading table 2, Ex. 9, does $(q \supset r)$ logically imply p?

_____ 3. Reading table 3, Ex. 9, is p logically equivalent to q?

_____ 4. Reading table 4, Ex. 9, is a formula t logically equivalent to itself?

_____ 5. Reading table 5, Ex. 9, is $(q \supset s)$ logically equivalent to $((\sim s) \supset (\sim t))$?

_____ 6. Reading table 6, Ex. 9, is an inconsistent formula $((t \& (\sim r)) \& r)$ equivalent to a tautology $(q \supset q)$?

_____ 7. Reading table 7, Ex. 9, is the negation of a tautology itself a tautology?

_____ 8. Reading table 8, Ex. 9, is the negation of a contingent formula itself a contingent formula?

_____ 9. Reading table 9, Ex. 9, is the negation of an inconsistent formula a tautology?

_____ 10. Reading table 10, Ex. 9, does p logically imply q?

_____ 11. Reading table 11, Ex. 9, is q logically equivalent to p?

_____ 12. Reading table 13, Ex. 9, is the conjunction of two inconsistent wffs itself inconsistent?

_____ 13. Would the biconditional of two inconsistent wffs be a tautology?

_____ 14. Reading table 14, Ex. 9, does a tautology $(r \equiv r)$ logically imply any formula s?

_____ 15. Reading table 1, Ex. 5, is $(p \lor q)$ interchangeable or logically equivalent to $[\sim ((\sim p) \& (\sim q))]$?

_____ 16. Reading table 7, Ex. 5, does any wff *p* logically imply a tautology $(r \equiv r)$?

_____ 17. Reading table 8, Ex. 5, does an inconsistent wff logically imply any wff?

Ex. 11 Indicate whether each of the following is true or false by writing 'T' or 'F' in the space provided.

_____ 1. Consistent formulas are never self-contradictory.

_____ 2. Tautologies are not consistent.

_____ 3. Contingent formulas can be negated, thus making them tautological.

_____ 4. The negation of a tautology is an inconsistent formula.

_____ 5. An argument is shown to be valid if the conjunction of its premises logically implies its conclusion.

_____ 6. Any formula logically implies a tautological formula.

_____ 7. Tautologies logically imply only tautologies.

_____ 8. Two formulas that are contingent may not be equivalent.

_____ 9. Two inconsistent formulas conjoined together make a tautology.

_____ 10. The negation of an inconsistent formula is contingent.

_____ 11. All consistent formulas are tautological.

_____ 12. All contingent formulas are consistent.

_____ 13. (p) is a well-formed formula.

_____ 14. The paradigm table for the $\supset$ has an F in its second row only.

_____ 15. A formula like $(A \& B)$ is called a conjunction.

_____ 16. A disjunction and an alternation are the same thing.

_____ 17. The operation of conjunction yields a paradigm table with F in every row of its value column save the first.

_____ 18. A formula that is the negation of a tautology is inconsistent.

_____ 19. A formula that is the negation of a contingent formula is contingent.

_____ 20. $(\sim\sim p)$ is not well-formed.

_____ 21. Tautologies are all analytically true.

_____ 22. A formula A is equivalent to itself.

_____ 23. A formula cannot logically imply itself.

_____ 24. A tautology is logically implied by any formula whatsoever.

_____ 25. An inconsistent formula logically implies any formula whatsoever.

Ex. 12 Test the following pairs of formulas for logical equivalence.

1. p, p 2. p, q 3. $(q \supset r)$, $(p \supset (q \lor r))$
4. $(p \supset q)$, $((\sim q) \supset (\sim p))$ 5. $(p \& q)$, $[\sim((\sim p) \lor (\sim q))]$

Ex. 13 Test the following pairs of formulas to see if the first logically implies the second.

1. p, $(p \lor q)$ 2. $(p \lor q)$, q
3. $(p \& q)$, p 4. p, $(p \& q)$
5. p, $(q \supset p)$ 6. $(p \supset q)$, $((q \supset r) \supset (p \supset p))$

Ex. 14 Determine by using truth-tables whether or not the following arguments are valid.

1. $(\sim q)$ 2. $(p \supset q)$ 3. $(q \equiv p)$ 4. $(p \supset r)$

     $(p \supset q)$ $(q \equiv r)$ $(\sim p)$ $((\sim q) \supset (\sim r))$

    $\therefore (\sim p)$ $\therefore ((\sim r) \supset (\sim p))$ $\therefore ((\sim q) \vee r)$ $\therefore \dfrac{(\sim p)}{q}$

5. $((\sim p) \mathbin{\&} (\sim q))$ 6. $(p \equiv r)$

     $(\sim(\sim q))$ $((\sim p) \equiv r)$

    $\therefore (\sim p)$ $\therefore q$

Ex. 15 Determine whether or not the following arguments are valid.

Translation of 1:

1. Either we all will come or not.
   If not, then you will be alone.
   If so, then you will not be alone.
   So, either you will be alone or you will not be
       alone.   _____

                                   $\therefore$

   p = we all will come
   q = you will be alone

Translation of 2:

2. If either you pass or you don't pass then you
       will graduate.
   But if your graduation happens, then you
       will be out of college.
   If you pass and are out of college, you will be
       in good shape.
   If you do not pass and are out of college, you
       will not be in good shape.
   So you should study logic.   _____

                                   $\therefore$

   p = you will pass
   q = you will graduate, (or, your graduation occurs)
   r = you will be out of college
   s = you will be in good shape
   t = you should study logic

     (Hint: In working out the tables for long arguments with lots of statement letters it is sometimes quicker to work down the table row by row; even though in the case of short tables it is faster to work column by column. The reason is that as soon as one F turns up in the value column you can stop your calculations; the formula will not be a tautology, the argument will not be valid.)

     (The table for item 2 should be thirty-two lines long, but you should not have to work past the first few lines to prove that the argument is invalid.)

Translation of 3:

3. If you deliver the ransom, then you will get
       the children back.
   But if you tell the police about the kidnap-
       ping, then you won't ever see them again.

So if you get the children back, then you de-
livered the ransom and did not tell the
police about the kidnapping.

∴

Translation of 4:

4. You get the children back only if you pay the
ransom.
You get the children back only if you do not
tell the police about the kidnapping.
So if you pay the ransom and do not tell the
police about the kidnapping, you get the
children back.

∴

Translation of 9:

5. If I had the money to buy an electric typewriter, I would write neater papers.
Writing neater papers would get me higher
grades.
But my grades will never improve.
You're right, I'm saying I could never afford
one of those electric jobs.

∴

SELECTED ANSWERS
TO EXERCISES FOR MODULE 17

Ex. 5 (tauts)	$[(p \vee q) \equiv [\sim((\sim p) \ \& \ (\sim q))]]$	Table 1
	$(q \supset (q \vee r))$	Table 3
	$(p \supset (r \equiv r))$	Table 7
	$((q \ \& \ (\sim q)) \supset s)$	Table 8
Ex. 6 (cont)	$(s \supset (\sim s))$	Table 4
	$((r \vee t) \supset (r \ \& \ t))$	Table 6
	s	Table 9
	$(\sim t)$	Table 10
Ex. 7 (inconst)	$(p \ \& \ (\sim p))$	Table 2
	$(t \equiv (\sim t))$	Table 5

Ex. 8 (const)   All, and only, those listed in the answers to Exs. 5 and 6.

If you missed two or more of these identifications (Exs. 5 to 8), review carefully the
definitions and examples in 17:1.

Ex. 9

1. Cont, const	2. Cont, const
3. Cont, const	4. Taut, const
6. Inconst (self-contradictory)	7. Inconst (self-contradictory)
9. Taut, const	10. Cont, const
11. Cont, const	13. Inconst
14. Cont, const	

If you had trouble writing any of the truth-tables, review 16:5.1 and 16:5.2. If you missed any answers, review 17:1.

Ex. 10

1. No	2. No	3. No
4. Yes	5. No	6. No
7. No	8. Yes	9. Yes
10. No	11. No	12. Yes
13. Yes	14. No	15. Yes
16. Yes	17. Yes	

Ex. 11

1. T	2. F	3. F
5. T	6. T	7. T
9. F	10. F	11. F
13. F	14. T	15. T
17. T	18. T	19. T
21. T	22. T	23. F
25. T		

If you missed item 13 or 20, review 14:2.1 and 14:2.2. If you missed item 14, 16, or 17, review 16:1.2. If you missed item 5, review 17:4. Otherwise, if you missed more than two, review 17:1 and the questions and answers for Ex. 10.

Ex. 12

1. Yes; p is equivalent to p.
2. No; p is not equivalent to q (TFFT).
3. No.
4. Yes; $(p \supset q)$ is equivalent to $((\sim q) \supset (\sim p))$.

Ex. 13

1. Yes; p implies $(p \lor q)$.
2. No; $(p \lor q)$ does not imply q (TFTT).
3. Yes; $(p \& q)$ does imply p.
4. No; p does not imply $(p \& q)$ (TFTT).
5. Yes; p does imply $(q \supset p)$.
6. Yes; $(p \supset q)$ does imply $((q \supset r) \supset (p \supset p))$.

If you missed any in Ex. 12, review 17:2.1 and 17:2.2; if you missed any in Ex. 13, review 17:2.2. By now you should have no trouble writing truth-tables and no need to refer back to the paradigm tables. But if you have problems writing tables, review 16:2.1 and 16:2.2. And if you have not already memorized the paradigm tables given in 16:1.2, do so.

Ex. 14

1. $[((\sim q) \& (p \supset q)) \supset (\sim p)]$	Valid
2. $[((p \supset q) \& (q \equiv r)) \supset ((\sim r) \supset (\sim p))]$	Valid
3. $[((q \equiv p) \& (\sim p)) \supset ((\sim q) \lor r))]$	Valid
5. $[[((\sim p) \& (\sim q)) \& (\sim (\sim q))] \supset (\sim p)]$	Valid
6. $[((p \equiv r) \& ((\sim p) \equiv r)) \supset q]$	Valid

Ex. 15

1. $(p \lor (\sim p))$ $[[((p \lor (\sim p)) \& ((\sim p) \supset q)) \& (p \supset (\sim q))] \supset (q \lor (\sim q))]$
     $((\sim p) \supset q)$
     $\underline{(p \supset (\sim q))}$
  $\therefore (q \lor (\sim q))$ Valid

2. $((p \lor (\sim p)) \supset q)$ Invalid by second row of table when
     $(q \supset r)$ $p = T, q = T, r = T, s = T, t = F$
     $((p \& r) \supset s)$
     $\underline{(((\sim p) \& r) \supset (\sim s))}$
  $\therefore t$

    $\{\{[[((p \lor (\sim p)) \supset q) \& (q \supset r)] \& ((p \& r) \supset s)] \& [((\sim p) \& r) \supset (\sim s)]\} \supset t\}$

3. $p =$ you deliver the ransom
   $q =$ you get the children back
   $r =$ you tell the police about the kidnapping

    $(p \supset q)$ $[[(p \supset q) \& (r \supset (\sim q))] \supset [q \supset (p \& (\sim r))]]$
    $\underline{(r \supset (\sim q))}$ Invalid (TTTTTFTT) when $p = F, q = T, r = F$
  $\therefore (q \supset (p \& (\sim r)))$

5. $p =$ I have the money to buy an electric typewriter
   $q =$ I write neater papers
   $r =$ I get higher grades

    $(p \supset q)$ $[[((p \supset q) \& (q \supset r)) \& (\sim r)] \supset (\sim p)]$
    $(q \supset r)$
    $\underline{(\sim r)}$
  $\therefore (\sim p)$ Valid

For more practice in testing arguments for validity using the method of truth-tables, try those arguments given in Ex. 5 of Module 15. Check your translations against the translations supplied in the answers to that exercise. The arguments in that exercise should all turn out valid.

SKETCH
THE MOVE TO PREDICATE LOGIC*

You already understand some of the strength of the logician's assumption that the validity of an argument is a function of its structure. All the valid arguments of propositional logic are valid because of the truth-functional relationships between the statement units mentioned in those arguments. But not all valid arguments can be shown to be valid by focusing on the truth-functional relationships between their statement units.

---

   * From Chapter 4 this transitional sketch leads equally well into either Chapter 5 or Chapter 6. Although it is not a module with objectives and exercises, it does set the stage for further study in Part Two.

Consider the following argument:

EG. 1   If any of the Rojewskis wins the prize, the whole family will celebrate. Stella Rojewski won the prize. Well, then, there will be a family celebration at the Rojewski house!

If you inspect this argument and ask yourself whether the premises could be true and the conclusion simultaneously false, you will probably see quite quickly that the argument is valid.

But suppose you tried to symbolize the argument using the techniques we learned in Chapter 4. You might let $(p \supset q)$ represent the conditional first premise, but then 'Stella Rojewski won a prize' must be represented by r, so that the argument is symbolized

$$(p \supset q)$$
$$\underline{r }$$
$$\therefore q$$

Using the truth-table technique the argument turns out to be invalid in propositional logic.

EG. 1′

p	q	r	$[((p \supset q)$ & $r) \supset q]$
.	.	.	. . .
F	F	T	F̶ T̶ F̶ T̶ T̶ F F̶
.	.	.	. . .
.	.	.	. . .

                                   ↑It is invalid.

Shall we say then, that the argument is invalid? That, we noticed at the outset, would be a mistake. Consequently we can assume that we must not have symbolized the argument adequately to capture the structures on which its validity depends.

Yet if we confine ourselves to the techniques and symbolism we learned in Chapter 4, we have surely translated the argument correctly. We have isolated the statement units correctly and we have correctly identified the relationships between the statement units. Why then have we failed to capture the form of this valid argument? Because this argument, unlike those considered in Chapter 4, depends for its validity on other logical structures than can be exhibited using the translation techniques of propositional logic. In propositional logic, translations can exhibit only the logical structures that can be generated using statement units and the five truth-functional logical operators. But for Eg. 1 the crucial logical structure involves the classes referred to by the subjects and predicates of the statements.

Consider another example:

EG. 2   If Roger enters the race, he will win it.
Roger will enter the race.
So Roger will win.

Compare that argument with the following:

EG. 3   Every person from Delphos who enters the race will be an enthusiastic and tenacious competitor.
Roger, who is from Delphos, is entering.
So Roger will be an enthusiastic and tenacious competitor.

Example 2 is easily symbolized in propositional logic as

EG. 2′ $(p \supset q)$
$$\underline{p}$$
$$\therefore q$$

The validity of Eg. 2 depends, as Eg. 2′ shows, on the fact that the second premise asserts that the condition is met which, according to premise 1, is a condition which if met guarantees the conclusion's being true. But Eg. 3 doesn't work out quite so simply. Using propositional logic we could do no more than to represent Eg. 3 in the way we represented Eg. 1. That form, unlike Eg. 2′ is not valid. But Eg. 3 is valid.

Why is Eg. 3 valid? Typically, the premises of valid arguments interact to guarantee that the conclusion will be true if the premises all are. What then is the interaction between the two premises of Eg. 3? Clearly the antecedent of the first premise talks about *anyone* from Delphos who enters the race, while the second premise says that Roger is *one* such person. In other words, Roger is *included* as a member of the *class* of people mentioned in the antecedent of the first premise. Class containment or inclusion is the centrally important relation to the validity of this argument. Because Roger is included in the class of people who are from Delphos, it follows that whatever is true of all those people is true of Roger.

Consider another example.

EG. 4   Anyone who runs away from this fight is a dirty coward.
The Tornadoes are not dirty cowards.
So they won't run away.

Again we have a valid argument. And again its validity depends on relationships other than the truth-functional relationships between its statement units. The valid-ity of the argument derives from relationships between the classes that are referred to by the subjects and predicates of the statements in the argument. What are these relationships? From our experience with Eg. 3, we now recognize that we want to restate the premise by talking about classes and the relationships between them. The Tornadoes are a group of individuals, a class. What about this class? Well, if someone is a member of this class, what, according to the second premise, will be true of him or her? He or she will not be a dirty coward. In other words, he or she will be ex-cluded from a second class, the class of dirty cowards. The second premise says that any member of the class of Tornadoes is *excluded* from the class of dirty cowards. Like the first premise of Eg. 3, this premise talks about relations between the members of two classes. Unlike that premise, the relation here is *exclusion* rather than *inclusion*. Now we can see how the two premises of this argument interact. The first premise, 'Anyone who runs away from this fight is a dirty coward,' ex-presses a relation of inclusion. Anyone in the class of those who run away from a certain fight is included in the class of dirty cowards. All of the Tornadoes, according to the second premise, are excluded from that same class, the class of dirty cowards. But if it were true that they ran, they would be included in the class of cowards, from which, according to the second premise, they are excluded. So they cannot be in-cluded in the class of those who run away. In other words, they must be excluded from it.

Two classes may relate to each other in a variety of ways. Let us think about some of these relationships. Inclusion may be either *partial* or *total*. For example, some presidents have been over 6 feet tall (partial inclusion). All presidents, even the shortest, 5-feet 4-inch James Madison, have been over 5 feet tall (total inclusion). Exclusion may also be partial or total. Some president has not been married (partial exclusion). (When logicians say 'some' they mean 'at least one,' and Buchanan was a bachelor.) No presidents, however, have been divorced (total exclusion). The class of presidents, thus, bears four relations—partial inclusion, total inclusion, partial exclusion, and total exclusion—to four other classes. *Some* have been over 6 feet, *all* have been over 5 feet, *some* have not been married, and *none* has been divorced.

Relations of *partial* or *total inclusion* or *exclusion* between classes cannot be adequately symbolized in propositional logic. A symbolism for representing classes and the relations of inclusion and exclusion, however, can be devised and applied. Once the new symbolism is developed techniques for demonstrating validity using that symbolism become the chief order of business.

Although it is clear that we have to deal with classes and their members to demonstrate the validity of arguments like those we have just examined, it is not clear that we must use techniques that take us far beyond the realm of propositional logic. Actually, one alternative open to us is to reconstruct the arguments of predicate logic so as to make them ameanable to truth-tabular testing procedures. We might do so by rewriting an argument like the following:

EG. 5 1. No cats are fat things.
2. Some furry things are cats.
3. So some furry things are not fat.

Using the statement units

p = the class of nonfurry, fat cats has members
q = the class of furry, fat cats has members
r = the class of furry, nonfat cats has members
s = the class of furry, nonfat things has members

and the added assumption

If the class of furry, nonfat cats has members, then the class of furry, nonfat things (cats or not) has members

we can reconstruct Eg. 5 as:

EG. 5′ $(\sim p) \mathbin{\&} (\sim q))$ From premise 1
$(r \lor q)$ From premise 2
$\underline{(r \supset s)}$ Assumption
$\therefore s$ Conclusion 3

And Eg. 5′ can be shown valid using truth-tables.

There are, however, a lot of reasons why the approach we just exemplified is undesirable. First of all, it not only requires restating the argument, but also adding an assumption. The assumption may not always be easy to discover. Even when it is, it will, as in the case of Eg. 5′, be an assumption about a relationship between classes. So, in effect, we really have not fully escaped from talk of classes to talk of statement units, even though we have been able to recast the argument as a propositional logic argument. A second liability is that the original argument is no longer the one under direct examination. In recasting it we not only focus our attention on a different argument (a different set of premises and conclusion statements) but we focus on a different truth-functional structure than the original one. Moreover, we risk misinterpretation of the original in the process of transition, and beyond these lie other considerations.

These other considerations relate to the overall goals of our study, one of which is to introduce you to the standard techniques of logicians: (1) the Aristotelian approach, which historically was the first to be developed and achieve virtually worldwide attention; (2) the widely used diagramatic approach, originally introduced by John Venn (an English logician, 1834–1923), which visually depicts the relationships between classes; and (3) the sophisticated notation of contemporary symbolic logic which is powerful enough to handle predicate logic as well as even more structurally complex levels of logic. In Chapter 5 we offer an explanation of the traditional Aristotelian approach. In Chapter 6 we offer the more contemporary diagramatic method. Both are more widely used than the approach we exemplified in Eg. 5'.

Our second goal is to develop skills that are of practical use. Since both the Aristotelian approach and the diagramatic method are easy to learn and apply there seems to be no justification for substituting a nonstandard method for either.

It is always an advantage to be able to perceive the complex logical structure of English statements. The notation of contemporary symbolic logic can be a great tool to you in understanding this structure. Because of this we introduce and teach translation into this notation in Chapter 6. For those who might go further into the study of logic this also becomes a useful foundation for study of contemporary treatments of even more complex and interesting areas of logic like the logic of relations.

We now offer you a choice. You can approach predicate logic using the traditional Aristotelian method explained in Chapter 5, or you can approach predicate logic through a study of contemporary symbolic logic notation and the diagramatic method of testing for validity by using Chapter 6. If your interest is to study logic for its own sake, you can work through both chapters. You will want to be careful if you study both chapters because the two methods depend on different assumptions concerning the treatment of statements about whole classes, like

All children are demanding

and statements that concern individuals, like

Carrie is demanding.

You might anticipate that whenever two methods start from different assumptions they will have different outcomes. This prediction comes true in the case of our two alternative treatments of predicate logic. In the Aristotelian approach the following is a valid argument.

EG. 6   All children are demanding.
            So some children are demanding.

However, Eg. 6 would be invalid using the contemporary approach, since it relies on the assumption

There are children.

This assumption is plausible in cases like Eg. 6, but assumptions of this kind are not plausible in every case. Consider the following:

EG. 7   All moon creatures are green, doglike animals.
            So some moon creatures are green, doglike animals.

we would not find the assumption

There are moon creatures

nearly as plausible as is 'there are children.'

Aside from the type of case described above, however, there is no deviation in the output of the two methodologies. That is, in all other respects they generate the same sets of valid and invalid arguments. The Aristotelian method (Chapter 5) has the advantage of not requiring the use of formal symbolic notation. It is the method that is probably most widely known among philosophers around the world and also outside of the field of philosophy. Our presentation of the diagramatic method (Chapter 6) is made in conjunction with a presentation of translation into contemporary symbolic notation. This makes it useful for any further study of the more powerful techniques of contemporary logic. It is more useful in exhibiting the logical structure of English statements, and more in keeping with what might be called the "thrust" of contemporary Anglo-American philosophical developments.

5

THE SYLLOGISM

This chapter is about syllogisms and how to use traditional methods for determining their validity. Here are two examples of and about syllogisms.

EG. 1   Some arguments are valid syllogisms.
         All syllogisms are arguments that can be shown to be valid using methods originating from Aristotle.
         So some arguments are arguments that can be shown to be valid using methods originating from Aristotle.

EG. 2   Some arguments are invalid syllogisms.
         All invalid syllogisms are arguments that can be proved invalid by methods originating from Aristotle.
         So some arguments are arguments that can be proved to be invalid by methods originating from Aristotle.

These two arguments are both valid syllogisms. As you probably can see, they both follow the same inference pattern, that is, have the same formal structure. In Chapter 5 we will learn that the validity or invalidity of syllogisms depends on structural relationships among classes mentioned in these arguments. The educational goal of Chapter 5 is to apply traditional techniques to syllogistic arguments in order to determine whether particular syllogisms are valid or invalid.

MODULE 18
STATEMENTS IN SYLLOGISTIC ARGUMENTS

Although we must postpone until 18:3.1 a more rigorous definition of a syllogism, we can say for now that syllogisms are arguments purporting to be valid because of the relationships between three classes. These relationships are asserted in a total of three statements, two expressing premises and the third being the conclusion. The overall goal of this module is to understand the statements which make up a syllogism.

● After reading Module 18 you should be able to:

1. Distinguish classes from terms and from statements
2. Rewrite statements into traditional subject-predicate form
3. Distinguish statements about a total class from statements about part of the class
4. Rewrite nonstandard quantifiers into standard syllogistic form
5. Distinguish statements as A-, E-, I-, or O-form statements
6. Construct sample statements of each form
7. Distinguish the major, minor, and middle terms of categorical syllogisms
8. Given a statement of any one of the four forms A, E, I, or O, state and explain what can be validly inferred about the corresponding statement in each of the three other forms
9. Define 'categorical syllogism'
10. Distinguish arguments committing the four-term fallacy
11. Construct examples of categorical syllogisms

18:1 Since syllogisms are arguments whose validity turns on relations between the classes they mention, our first task is to become clear about what classes are. As we noted in 7:2.1, a class is any collection of objects, for example:

dogs	fast runners
leaves	old houses
leaves that have fallen	small elevators
gold bricks	elected officials
things that can fly	lawbreakers
chemicals not soluble in water	persons who act kindly

Classes should be distinguished both from *statements* and from terms. Statements, as you know, can be evaluated as true or false. Collections of objects are neither true nor false. "The leaves have fallen from the tree" can be evaluated as true or false. The leaves that have fallen from the tree are simply a heap of leaves; it makes no sense to ask whether those fallen leaves are true or false.

Classes should also be distinguished from *terms*. The word 'term' is traditionally used in discussing the categorical syllogism. It is used to refer to the *words that name the classes* mentioned in the arguments. We can relate the distinction between classes and terms to our discussion of use and mention in 5:1.3. Terms are words used to talk about classes. When we evaluate syllogisms, we talk about the terms of the argument. As in all cases of talking about words, we shall follow the convention of putting the term into single quotation marks. For example:

'Dogs' refers to a class which has many members.

EXERCISE 1

Distinguish each of the following as a class, a term, or a statement.

1. Leaves that have fallen
2. 'Leaves that have fallen'
3. The leaves have fallen.
4. Siamese kittens
5. 'Tall trees'
6. Tall trees attract lightning.
7. Trees that attract lightning
8. Trees that stay green all year
9. Fir trees stay green all year.
10. 'Trees that stay green all year'

1. Class	2. Term
3. Statement; this is true or false	4. Class
5. Term	6. Statement
7. Class; this is a collection	8. Class
9. Statement	10. Term

18:2.1 Subject-predicate analysis Some statements are obviously about the inclusion or exclusion of one class with respect to a second. 'People who care for children are people who really love children' is such a statement. It says that the *class* of people who care for children is included in the *class* of people who really love children. Many statements, however, are about the inclusion or exclusion of one class with respect to a second, but less obviously so. Think for a moment how our example statement might have been written. We could have written 'any people who care for children really love them' or 'if any person cares for children, then he or she really loves them.' Study these restatements. Notice that the first uses the verb 'love' in such a way as to avoid explicitly mentioning the class of people who love children. Notice that the second restatement is a conditional. Suppose you start with 'Robins migrate.' Can you restate that by completing the following: 'The class of robins is included in the class . . . .'? Suppose you have begun with 'if any advertising sign is in Denver, then it is flat against a building wall'? In what class does it include all the advertising signs in Denver?

Statements like 'the trout is a fish' express a relationship between two classes. In this case the relation is one of inclusion; the class of trout is included in the class of fish. But consider 'the trout is not a reptile.' This assertion expresses a different relation between two classes. Here the class of trout is *excluded* from the class of reptiles. In rewriting a statement so as to make clear the class relations it expresses you can rely on this format:

> The class of so-and-so is included in (is excluded from) the class of such-and-suches.

Can you complete the restatement of each of the following as expressing the exclusion of one class from another?

> No author likes criticism.
> None of the sorority members is attending
> If a person is honest, he or she should not fear scrutiny.
> Goats cannot swim.
> Stubbornness is never respected

> The class of authors excludes the class of persons who . . .
> The class of sorority members excludes the class of . . .
> The class of honest people . . .
> The class of goats . . .
> The class of stubborn persons . . .

18:2.2 Quality of statements By the *quality* of a statement we shall mean whether the statement expresses inclusion (positive quality) or exclusion (negative quality). All statements of inclusion are of *positive* quality; statements expressing exclusion are *negative*.

For each of the statements below mark 'inc' if it expresses a relationship of inclusion, and 'exc' if it expresses a relationship of exclusion. Also, wherever some words are underlined, choose from the given alternatives the one which best defines the class referred to by the underlined words. Item 1 is completed already as an example.

Inc; A   1. Geese lay eggs.
           A. Egg-laying animals   B. Geese   C. Lay eggs

————   2. Geese never lay golden eggs.
           A. Lay eggs   B. Lay golden eggs   C. Layers of golden eggs

————   3. Any decent artist paints a painting every month.
           A. Painters   B. Persons who paint   C. Paint paintings
           D. Person who paints a painting every month

————   4. No decent artist signs a painting.
           A. Signs   B. Paintings   C. Persons who sign paintings

————   5. Colleges are not for imprisoning the young.
           A. Imprisoned young people   B. Imprisonment   C. Prisons
           D. Places designed for imprisoning young people

ANSWERS TO EXERCISE 2

1. Inc; A
2. Exc; C
3. Inc; D
4. Exc; C
5. Exc; D

EXERCISE 3

In the light of the answers to Ex. 2, rewrite its five statements in the form "the class of so-and-so is included in (is excluded from) the class of such-and-suches." Also include the quality of each statement.

ANSWERS TO EXERCISE 3

1. The class of geese in included in the class of egg-laying animals (positive quality).
2. The class of geese is excluded from the class of animals that lay golden eggs. More awkward, but correct, is '. . . the class of golden-egg-laying animals' (negative quality).
3. The class of decent artists is included in the class of persons who paint a painting every month (positive quality).
4. The class of decent artists is excluded from the class of persons who sign paintings (negative quality).
3. The class of colleges is excluded from the class of places designed for imprisoning young people (negative quality).

18:2.3 Universal and particular statements Class inclusion and class exclusion statements each come in two important varieties. Either of these kinds of statements can be about *all* of the members of the subject class or about *at least one* member of the subject class. So far we have looked at examples about all the members of the subject class (*universal statements*).

Example statements
Universal

	All states are sovereign. All snow flakes melt. All literature is pornographic.	No states are sovereign. No snow flakes melt. No literature is pornographic.	

Inclusion	At least one state is
	  sovereign.
	At least one snow flake
	  melts.
	At least one piece of literature
	  is pornographic.
		At least one state is not
		  sovereign.
		At least one snow flake does
		  not melt.
		At least one piece of literature
		  is not pornographic.
			Exclusion

Particular

The statements in the top two rectangles talk about all the members of the class mentioned in the subject of the sentence, while those in the bottom two rectangles talk about at least one member of the subject class. The statements in the two left rectangles talk about the inclusion of all (or part) of the subject class in the class mentioned in the predicate, while those in the two right-hand rectangles talk about the exclusion of all (or part) of the subject class from the predicate class. To assure ourselves of this, let us expand the process of rewriting English statements we began above. So far we have generated statements of this form:

> The class of so-and-so is included in (or excluded from) the class of such-and-suches.

We have so far paid no explicit attention to whether *all* or *some* part of the class of so-and-so is being spoken of. In part the validity of syllogisms depends on the relations of inclusion and exclusion, that is, their quality. But in part their validity also depends on whether it is *all* or *at least one* of the subject class that is included or excluded. Accordingly we shall want to rewrite statements so that they explicitly speak about what we may call the *quantity* of the subject term of our statements.

When rewriting a statement we will permit ourselves to use one of the following two quantifiers: 'all,' meaning "the entire class," and 'some,' meaning "at least one member of the class." Syllogistic logic uses only these two quantifiers. The validity of many arguments depends on which of them is being used. For instance the premises

1. Everyone who sees the movie will enjoy it
2. Some of my friends saw the movie

validly imply the conclusion

Some of my friends enjoyed the movie

but the premises do not imply

All of my friends enjoyed the movie.

18:2.4 Quantity of statements By the *quantity* of a statement we shall mean whether the statement is universal or particular. All statements that use the universal quantifier 'all' are *universal* in quantity. Those that use 'some' are *particular* in quantity. The distinctions between universal and particular (quantity), and between inclusion and exclusion (quality), yield a total of four forms or types of statements. The table below shows each of the four forms. (Here S stands for the subject class and P for the predicate class.)

Universal

All S is included in P.	All S is excluded from P.
Some S is included in P.	Some S is excluded from P.

Inclusion (left)   Exclusion (right)

Particular

Since the validity of categorical syllogisms depends in part on which of these forms its premises and its conclusions take, it is appropriate that these four statement forms be named:

All S is included in P. = A form
All S is excluded from P. = E form
Some S is included in P. = I form
Some S is excluded from P. = O form

By a standard subject-predicate form we shall mean a restatement yielding a statement in one of the four forms A, E, I, or O. Each reads: (quantifier) class (quality expression) class.

EXERCISE 4

Indicate the structure of each of the following statements using the appropriate A, E, I, or O form above and identify that form.

1. Some office managers are Chicano.
2. All holidays are pleasant.
3. Holidays are always pleasant.
4. There is a holiday that is not pleasant.
5. Every mother loves her child.
6. Some mother does not love her child.

7. No ants sting.
8. There are stinging ants.
9. Some plants reproduce through seeds.
10. Some plants do not reproduce through seeds.

ANSWERS TO EXERCISE 4

1. Some S is included in P.	I	
2. All S is included in P.	A	
3. All S is included in P.	A	(just alternative English wording)
4. Some S is excluded from P.	O	
5. All S is included in P.	A	
6. Some S is excluded from P.	O	
7. All S is excluded from P.	E	
8. Some S is included in P.	I	
9. Some S is included in P.	I	
10. Some S is excluded from P.	O	

18:2.5 The square of opposition Exercise 4 hints that certain logical relationships exist between the various four forms of statements (A, E, I, and O). Let us look at some of them.

Consider the relationship between A and O statements:

EG. 18.1 (A) All S are P.   All birds fly.
(O) Some S is not a P.   Some birds don't fly.

Also consider the relationship between E and I statements:

EG. 18.2 (E) No S are P.   No birds fly.
(I) Some S is P.   Some birds fly.

Note in Eg. 18.1 that if A is true, then O must be false. Similarly, in Eg. 18.2 if E is true, then I must be false. So, we can validly infer from a universal statement (A, E), the falsity of the particular statement of the opposite quality (O, I).

EG. 18.3 All S is included in P.
∴ It is not the case that some S is excluded from P.

EG. 18.4 All S is excluded from P.
∴ It is not the case that some S is included in P.

But, by the same token, from a particular statement (I, O), we can validly infer the falsity of the universal of the opposite quality (E, A).

EG. 18.5 Some S is included in P.
∴ It is not true that all S is excluded from P.

EG. 18.6 Some S is excluded from P.
∴ It is not true that all S are included in P.

In other words, A statements contradict O statements and E statements contradict I statements. Recall that two statements are *contradictory* if, and only if, they always have opposite truth-values. So, the A- and O-form statements about two classes have opposite truth-values. Likewise the E- and I-form statements have opposite values. We can also express this relationship in terms of our concepts of quality and quantity. Two statement forms are contradictory if they are the opposite of each other in *both* quantity and quality.

Let us set up a diagram to help us as we explore the relationships between *A*-, *E*-, *I*-, and *O*-form statements. We will put the two universal statements at the top and the two affirmative (positive) statements on the left. Traditionally the diagram we are developing has been called the "square of opposition."

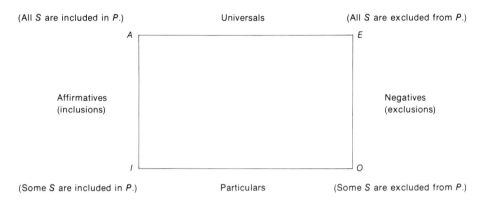

(All *S* are included in *P*.)   Universals   (All *S* are excluded from *P*.)

Affirmatives (inclusions)   Negatives (exclusions)

(Some *S* are included in *P*.)   Particulars   (Some *S* are excluded from *P*.)

The first relationship we have examined is the one that indicates the two sets of contradictions. *A* and *O* forms contradict each other. *E* and *I* forms contradict each other, as is expressed in

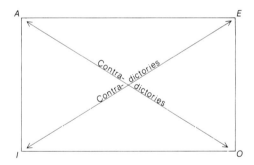

A second relationship emerges if we compare the *A*- and *E*-form statements.

EG. 18.7 (*A*) All S are P.   All politicians are fair-minded.
           (*E*) No S are P.   No politicians are fair-minded.

Note that in Eg. 18.7 both the *A*-form and the *E*-form statement can be false at the same time. The truth about politicians, for example, is somewhere in between. They are neither *all* sinners nor *all* rogues. However, it is not possible for both the *A*-form and the *E*-form statements to be true at the same time. If one is true, its being true rules out the other one's being true. Since these two statement forms do not always have opposite truth-values, we *cannot* call them contradictory. But we do want to express their incompatibility in some way. We will say that they are *contraries*. By contraries we mean two statement forms that can both be false together but cannot both be true together. Filling in our diagram further we have

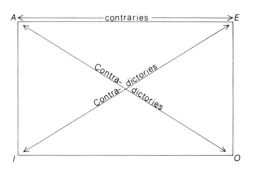

EXERCISE 5

Below are six pairs of statements. If a pair is contradictory, mark 'contr.' Use 'cont' for contraries. If the pair is neither, mark 'neither.'

_____	1. All apples are red.	Some apples are not red.
_____	2. No apples are red.	All apples are red.
_____	3. No apples are red.	Some apples are red.
_____	4. Grapes are always tasty.	No grapes are tasty.
_____	5. Some grapes are tasty.	Some grapes aren't tasty.
_____	6. Some grapes are tasty.	No grapes are tasty.

ANSWERS TO EXERCISE 5

1. Contr (A, O)
2. Cont (E, A)
3. Contr (E, I)
4. Cont (A, E)
5. Neither (I, O); both of them could be true.
6. Contr (I, E)

A third relationship exists between each universal statement and the particular statement of the same quality. Consider

EG. 18.8 (A) All S are included in P.   All birds fly.
(I) Some S are included in P.   Some birds fly.

EG. 18.9 (E) All S are excluded from P.   No birds swim.
(O) Some S are excluded from P.   Some birds don't swim.

The universal statement forms, on the traditional interpretation of things, imply the particular statement forms of the same quality. That is, A implies I; E implies O. These inferences are permitted in the Aristotelian system because the universal statements are not thought of as vacuous. In other words, it is assumed that their subject classes are not empty. 'Children are demanding,' for example, means not only "all of the class of children is included in the class of demanding creatures" but also "there are children." 'No lion is a canine' means "all of the class of lions is excluded from the class of canines" and "there are lions." This assumption, when added to the weaker, conditional meaning of universal statements yields inferences. Consider the following two examples.

EG. 18.10   If anything is S, it is P.
There are S's.
∴ Some S are included in P.

EG. 18.11   If anything is S, it is not P.
There are S's.
∴ Some S are excluded from P.

Notice that both of these inferences are valid, but neither conclusion follows from the first premise alone. On the traditional Aristotelian interpretation, however, a universal also asserts what is contained in the second two premises. Thus, on the traditional interpretation both the above inferences are valid.

Notice that these are *inferences from universal to particular of the same quality*, positive or negative, form A to I and form E to O. (Also notice that a merely conditional interpretation of A or E would not permit these inferences.) The I and O are called the *subalternates* of the *subalternants* A and E, respectively.

(Subalternant of *I*)   (Subalternant of *O*)

(Subalternate of *A*)   (Subalternate of *E*)

It is worth confirming what the subalternates I and O imply about their respective subalternants: nothing! If I (O) is true, we cannot validly infer anything about A (E). Remember that 'some' means "at least one" but it does not imply an upper limit. 'At least one' does not guarantee 'all,' of course, but it does not rule out 'all' either.

When we compare the particulars I and O we immediately see that the truth of one carries no implication about the other. If some apples are green, some still may not be green. But suppose one is false:

EG. 18.12   It is not true that some S is included in P.
(There are S's.)
∴ Some S is excluded from P.

EG. 18.13   It is not true that some S is excluded from P.
(There are S's.)
∴ Some S is included in P.

There two inferences are valid.

In other words what we shall call the *subcontraries* (I and O) can both be true but cannot both be false. (Compare this to the contraries A and E.)

Having noted this relationship we can complete the square of opposition. Study each of the relations to check your understanding.

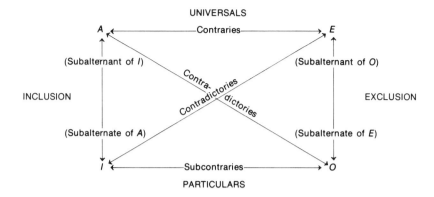

18:3.1 The categorical syllogism You have now learned how to rewrite statements in standard subject-predicate form so as to clearly express total and partial inclusion and exclusion. Since categorical syllogisms (as Aristotle called them), or simply *syllogisms* (as we shall usually call them), are arguments composed of statements capable of being presented in standard subject-predicate form, we are now ready to define what a categorical syllogism is.

> Categorical syllogism = _{df} an argument purporting to mention exactly three classes, composed of two premises and a conclusion, each capable of presentation in standard subject-predicate form

Here are some example syllogisms:

EG. 18.14   No rodents can fly.
All squirrels are rodents.
∴ No squirrels can fly.

EG. 18.15   All iron is magnetic.
No aluminum is magnetic.
∴ No aluminum is iron.

EG. 18.16   Some items of property were people.
All property can be disposed of by its owner.
∴ Some of the things that could be disposed of by their owner were people.

All these examples not only meet the definition, they meet two further standards as well: (1) each actually, not just purportedly, mentions exactly three classes, and (2) each is valid. Of course, eventually we shall be interested in being able to detect syllogisms that fail to meet either of these latter standards. For now, however, you should check to see that each of the examples does meet all the requirements set out in the definition of the syllogism.

18:3.2 Major, minor, and middle terms The purport of a syllogism is to have three terms, one for each of the (purportedly three) classes. Let us assume for now that we are working with syllogisms which have three terms as purported. What can we say about where these terms occur within the argument? Clearly two of them will be in the conclusion, one as its subject and one as its predicate. The conclusion's subject term is called the *minor term*. The conclusion's predicate term is called the *major term*. These leave only one other term, which will occur in both premises. This third term is called the *middle term*. Go back to Egs. 18.14 to 18.16 and pick out the three terms in each of the examples. Using *M* for major, *m* for minor, and 3 for the middle, your results should be as follows.

		Subject class	Predicate class	Terms
EG. 18.14′	Premise	3	M	M = flying things
	Premise	m	3	m = squirrels
	Conclusion	m	M	3 = rodents
EG. 18.15′	Premise	M	3	M = anything made of iron
	Premise	m	3	m = anything made of aluminum
	Conclusion	m	M	3 = anything magnetic
EG. 18.16′	Premise	3	M	M = people
	Premise	3	m	m = anything that can be disposed of by its owner
	Conclusion	m	M	3 = items of property

The predicate term of the conclusion is defined as the syllogism's major term, and we know that the subject term of the conclusion is defined as the syllogism's minor term. Given that each term occurs twice in a proper syllogism, where else do they occur? The major term will be stated in one of the premises and the minor term in the other. The premise mentioning the major term is called the *major premise*, and, by a convention dating from medieval times, it is written first. The premise mentioning the minor term is called the *minor premise*, and it is conventionally written second. The other term, occurring once in each premise, is the middle term.

18:4.1 Four-term fallacy As the definition of the categorical syllogism states, syllogisms apparently or purportedly have three terms. This definition allows the possibility of an (invalid!) four-term argument. (For example, through a vicious ambiguity, a syllogism that seems to have three terms may actually have four terms.) You can see the invalidity of such a syllogism as follows. Consider the two possibilities: the two terms not mentioned in the conclusion are either (1) in the same premise or (2) in separate premises. If they are in the same premise, that premise is clearly irrelevant to the conclusion. But if they are in separate premises, then one of those premises relates the minor term to one of those terms and the other premise relates the major term to the other of those terms. Since the two terms in the conclusion have been related to two different premise terms, no valid conclusion will follow about the relation of the conclusion's terms to each other. Such arguments are always invalid since they have no middle term at all.

18:4.2 Recognition of the fourth term The fourth term is hard to recognize when a word or phrase is used ambiguously. Recognizing the fourth term requires seeing the ambiguity.

EG. 18.17 Bindings hold books together.
Any legal contract is binding.
So legal contracts hold books together.

Rather clearly the ambiguity of 'binding' invalidates this argument. Sometimes the ambiguity is more subtle.

EG. 18.18 You can't call the Arabs anti-Semitic.
After all, no one who is Semitic is anti-Semitic.
And the Arabs are all Semitic.

Reconstructed in standard syllogistic form, we get:

EG. 18.18' All Semitics are excluded from the anti-Semitic.
All Arabs are included in the Semitic.
All Arabs are excluded from the anti-Semitic.

This apparently valid argument fails because of the hidden ambiguity of 'Semitic.' Arabs are, in a genetic or racial sense, Semitic. But those Semitic people excluded from the class of anti-Semitic are, at most, the Jews, who are Semitic in a narrower, social sense. Being Semitic in premise 1 means being Jewish, but in premise 2 it means being a member of a wider racial stock. Here is another example:

EG. 18.19 Every person has a father.
Every father has a child.
So every person has a child.

How does this absurd conclusion seem to follow? Again an ambiguity is involved. It is not enough to notice that 'father' means the same in both of these premises. You must also notice that the first premise talks about the class of those who *have* fathers, while the second is about the class of those who *are* fathers.

EXERCISES FOR MODULE 18
STATEMENTS IN SYLLOGISTIC ARGUMENTS

Ex. 6 Write ten original example statements in each of the following forms: *A*, *E*, *I*, *O*. Use standard subject-predicate form throughout.

Ex. 7 Below are seven categorical syllogisms. Pick out the major (M), minor (m), and middle (3) term in each. (You may wish to rewrite certain items using standard subject-predicate form.)

1. Red flowers shouldn't be planted next to geraniums. So roses shouldn't be planted there because roses are red.
2. Some migrants are wealthy. All migrants travel widely. So clearly some widely traveled persons are wealthy.
3. No tent is properly insulated. Some buildings are properly insulated. Hence, some buildings are not tents.
4. Eskimos are slight in build. But the slight in build are never short. So no short people are Eskimos.
5. Some mollusks regrow lost body parts. No mollusks lay eggs. So some creatures that regrow lost body parts do not lay eggs.
6. Free-standing European sculpture occurs only after 1200. No leprechauns are sculpted after 1200. So, no sculptured leprechauns are free standing.

7. Whatever lights give off great heat are energy inefficient. All mercury lights give off great heat. So mercury lights are all energy inefficient.

Ex. 8 Below a number of subject-predicate forms are listed. Next to each is a list of proposed inferences. Assuming their traditional interpretation, identify all the valid inferences with a 'V.' If an inference cannot be validly drawn, mark 'no.'

1. From 'All S is included in P':
_____ A. Some S is included in P.
_____ B. Some S is excluded from P.
_____ C. It is false that all S is excluded from P.
_____ D. It is false that some S is excluded from P.

2. From 'All S is excluded from P':
_____ A. Some S is included in P.
_____ B. Some S is excluded from P.
_____ C. It is false that all S is included in P.
_____ D. It is false that some S is excluded from P.

3. From 'It is false that all S is excluded from P':
_____ A. Some S is included in P.
_____ B. All S is included in P.
_____ C. Some S is excluded from P.

4. From 'Some S is included in P':
_____ A. Some S is excluded from P.
_____ B. All S is included in P.
_____ C. It is false that all S is excluded from P.
_____ D. It is false that some S is excluded from P.

5. From 'It is false that some S is excluded from P':
_____ A. All S is included in P.
_____ B. Some S is included in P.
_____ C. It is false that all S is excluded from P.
_____ D. All S is excluded from P.

Ex. 9 Define 'categorical syllogism' and construct three original examples of categorical syllogisms. Model your examples on Egs. 18.14 to 18.16 in 18:3.1.

Ex. 10 Mark 'FTF' those of the following syllogisms commiting the four-term fallacy. State the ambiguity in each case of the fallacy you discover.

_____ 1. Whatever is suspended is unfinished.
All bridges over large navigable bodies of water are suspended.
So all bridges over large navigable bodies of water are unfinished.

_____ 2. Any expression of a complete thought is a sentence.
A sentence is what a convict serves.
So a convict serves an expression of a complete thought.

_____ 3. Melodies in minor keys are sometimes happy.
No happy music should be despised.
So some melodies in minor keys should not be despised.

_____ 4. Modern building construction is time-consuming.
Some offices are modern building constructions.
So some offices are time-consuming.

_____ 5. If you are not prejudiced, you are fair.
If you examine each case as it comes without prejudging it, then you are
not prejudiced.
So if you examine each case as it comes without prejudging it, then
you are fair.

ANSWERS TO EXERCISES
FOR MODULE 18

Ex. 6 Check your answers against the examples in 18:2.4. Yours should be structured as follows:

A form: All S is included in P.
E form: All S is excluded from P.
I form: Some S is included in P.
O form: No S is excluded from P.

Ex. 7

1. M = flower that should be planted next to geraniums
   m = roses
   3 = red flowers

2. M = wealthy persons
   m = widely traveled persons
   3 = migrants

3. M = tents
   m = buildings
   3 = properly insulated enclosures

4. M = Eskimos
   m = short people
   3 = persons of slight build

5. M = egg layers
   m = creatures that regrow lost body parts
   3 = mollusks

6. M = free-standing sculptures
   m = sculptured leprechauns
   3 = sculptures sculpted after 1200

7. M = energy inefficient lights
   m = mercury lights
   3 = lights that give off great heat

If you had any problems review 18:3.2.

Ex. 8

	The inferences that
The valid inferences are:	cannot be drawn are:
1. A, C, D	1. B
2. B, C	2. A, D
3. A	3. B, C
4. C	4. A, B, D
5. A, B, C	5. D

If you missed more than four of these, review 18:2.5.

Ex. 9 Check 18:3.1 for the definition of 'categorical syllogism.'

Ex. 10

1. FTF; 'suspended meaning' can mean "held up off or over a surface" or "stopped; interrupted."
2. FTF; 'sentence' can mean "completely expressed (written or spoken) thought" or "punishment for a crime, usually time spent in jail."
3. OK
4. FTF; 'modern building construction' can mean "the process of putting up a building these days" or "the product (building) that has been erected lately."
5. FTF; 'prejudice' can mean "biased, opinionated, without objectivity"; or "making a judgment prior to looking at the evidence."

MODULE 19
VALIDITY BY THE RULES OF SYLLOGISM

Peter of Spain, a thirteenth-century Spanish logician, developed a method to test the validity of any syllogism. He developed a short set of rules that valid syllogisms conform to. These rules are easy to apply once you understand two things: (1) the quality of a statement and (2) whether each of the two terms in a given statement is distributed or undistributed. In Module 18 you developed your ability to recognize and count the terms of purported syllogisms and the ability to distinguish statements of inclusion from statements of exclusion. In order to build from that base, then, you will only have to master the concept of distribution.

● After reading Module 19 you should be able to:

1. Distinguish distributed from undistributed terms
2. Fully analyze any given syllogism for the quality of its statements and the distribution of each of its terms in each occurrence
3. Determine the validity of any given syllogism by appeal to the above analysis and the rules of the syllogism

19:1 Distribution Contrast the following two syllogisms:

EG. 19.1   All M is P.
                 All S is M.
                 ∴ All S is P.

EG 19.2   Some M is P.
              All S is M.
              ∴ All S is P.

Examples 19.1 and 19.2 differ only in that the major premise of Eg. 19.1 is universal, while the major premise of Eg. 19.2 is particular. Since Eg. 19.1 is valid and Eg. 19.2 is invalid, you might rightly suspect that whether all the M's or only part of the M's are mentioned is crucial to the validity of these arguments. This is the kernel of the concept of distribution. In Eg. 19.1 M is said to be *distributed* in the major premise because the *entire* class of M's is talked about. In Eg. 19.2 M is said to be *undistributed* in the major premise because the premise does not consider the entire class of M's, only a part of it. In our definition we shall say that *a use of a term is distributed in a given statement exactly when the entire class mentioned by the term is referred to, or taken into consideration, in that use of the term.*

Since there are exactly four forms of statements which occur in syllogisms, we can easily construct a chart of which subjects and which predicates are distributed in the four forms of statements. We have already noted that in the A statement, the subject term is distributed. In an A-form statement the entire subject class S is considered and asserted to be included in the class of P. We cannot, however, say anything for sure about the entire class of P, given simply 'all S is P.' Even granting 'some P is S,' 'all S is P' does not tell us about the other possible members of P. The upshot of this is that A statements have distributed subjects but undistributed predicates.

In E statements both terms are distributed. 'No crows are pink birds' could plausibly be translated by 'the *entire* class of crows is separated from the *entire* class of pink birds.' Statements in I form are just the reverse. Whereas both terms of E statements are distributed, neither term in an I statement is distributed. 'Some canaries are pink birds' does not talk about all canaries and it does not talk about all pink birds. The class of pink birds is broad enough, after all, to include flamingos as well as some canaries.

What about O statements? Clearly, 'some canaries are not pink birds' speaks only about a part of the class of canaries. But are those canaries excluded from all, or only part, of the class of pink birds? If they were excluded only from a part of the class, they might be elsewhere in the class. But the intent of 'some canaries are not pink birds' is to exclude certain canaries from the *entire* class of pink birds, not from just part of the class. In other words, O statements have a distributed predicate term along with their undistributed subject.

Summing up what we have said about distribution of terms, we get the following table where D = is distributed and U = is not distributed:

		Term 1	Term 2	1	2
A	All S is included in P.			D	U
E	All S is excluded from P.			D	D
I	Some S is included in P.			U	U
O	Some S is excluded from P.			U	D

You should take note that it is possible for any term occurring twice in a syllogism to be distributed once and undistributed the other time. *Each time* a term occurs, its distribution must be determined in accordance with the above table.

EXERCISE 1

Distinguish the distributed from the undistributed terms in the following ten statements by marking 'D' and 'U,' respectively.

_____ 1. Any internal combustion engine eats gas.

_____ 2. Some internal combustion engines do not eat gas.

_____ 3. No V-8 engine is efficient.

_____ 4. Some stick shifts get less than 20 miles per gallon on the highway.

_____ 5. The hummingbird does not hum.

_____ 6. Yellow is a bright color.

_____ 7. Some yellows are saturated.

_____ 8. Some yellows are not pale.

_____ 9. Some door is open.

_____ 10. No door is ajar.

ANSWER TO EXERCISE 1

1. D, U	2. U, D
3. D, D	4. U, U
5. D, D	6. D, U
7. U, U	8. U, D
9. U, U	10. D, D

19:2 Syllogistic analysis Whether a syllogism is valid is a function of whether it follows a short list of rules. These rules turn out to focus on the quality of the statements in a syllogism and the distribution of the terms in those statements. Accordingly your next step is to learn a convenient way to analyze any syllogism for quality and distribution.

We can begin with the symbols we have already developed. We have used M, m, and 3 for the major, minor, and middle terms, respectively. We have used U and D for undistributed and distributed, respectively. Now let us adopt the practice of using $+$ and $-$ to represent the inclusive or exclusive quality of statements, respectively.

We can now analyze Eg. 19.1 and Eg. 19.2 as follows:

EG. 19.1′

D	U		
3	M	$+$	Premise 1
D	U		
m	3	$+$	Premise 2
D	U		
m	M	$+$	Conclusion

EG. 19.2′

U	U		
3	M	$+$	Premise 1
D	U		
m	3	$+$	Premise 2
D	U		
m	M	$+$	Conclusion

EXERCISE 2

Analyze each of the following ten syllogisms for quality and distribution.

1. All friendly towns are old. No small towns are old. So no small towns are friendly.
2. Some friendly towns are not old. No old towns are small. So some small towns are friendly.
3. All friendly towns are old. All friendly towns are small. So some small towns are old.
4. All friendly towns are old. Some friendly towns are small. So some small towns are not old.
5. All old towns are friendly. No friendly towns are small. So no small towns are old.
6. No towns with ghettos are manufacturing towns. All large towns have ghettos. So no large towns are manufacturing towns.
7. No manufacturing towns have ghettos. Some large towns have ghettos. So some large towns are not manufacturing towns.
8. Some towns with ghettos are not manufacturing towns. No towns with ghettos are large. So some large towns are not manufacturing towns.
9. Some manufacturing towns are large. All manufacturing towns have ghettos. Some towns with ghettos are large.
10. Some large towns have ghettos. All large towns are manufacturing towns. So no manufacturing towns have ghettos.

ANSWERS TO EXERCISE 2

1.	D	U		2.	U	D		3.	D	U		4.	D	U	
	M	3	+		M	3	−		3	M	+		3	M	+
	D	D			D	D			D	U			U	U	
	m	3	−		3	m	−		3	m	+		3	m	+
	D	D			U	U			U	U			U	D	
	m	M	−		m	M	+		m	M	+		m	M	−

5.	D	U		6.	D	D		7.	D	D		8.	U	D	
	M	3	+		3	M	−		M	3	−		3	M	−
	D	D			D	U			U	U			D	D	
	3	m	−		m	3	+		m	3	+		3	m	−
	D	D			D	D			U	D			U	D	
	m	M	−		m	M	−		m	M	−		m	M	−

9.	U	U		10.	U	U	
	3	M	+		3	M	+
	D	U			D	U	
	3	m	+		3	m	+
	U	U			D	D	
	m	M	+		m	M	−

19:3 Rules of the syllogism We are now prepared to present six rules such that a syllogism is valid if, and only if, it satisfies these rules. You may use the syllogistic analysis you just learned in order to chart the information needed to apply these rules. You can also apply these rules directly to the English syllogisms. We will state first the only rule which is not derived from the analysis:

Rule 1 A valid syllogism has exactly three terms.

Comment: You will remember that the syllogism has been defined in terms of purport. It is *presented as if* it had three terms. In Module 18 we uncovered and discussed the possibility that because of an ambiguity, a syllogism might have four rather than three terms. We indicated that no such syllogism would be valid. We also provided you practice in detecting ambiguities for yourself. If you are unsure of this rule you should review 18:4.1 and 18:4.2.

Rule 2 If both premises are inclusions, then the conclusion must be an inclusion.

Comment: Rules 2 to 4 all deal with the *quality* of the syllogism's statements. It will be easy for you to determine whether both premises of an analyzed syllogism are inclusions. Notice that this rule directs you if they are both inclusions, but it does not apply when you have one or more exclusion premises.

Rule 3 If both premises are exclusions, no valid conclusion follows.

Comment: The kind of argument to which this rule applies might well have premises like:

EG. 19.3 No M is P.
No M is S.

A syllogistic conclusion from these premises will try to relate S and P, but the fact that both are excluded from M tells us nothing about whether S and P are included or excluded, partially or totally, from each other.

Rule 4 If exactly one premise is an exclusion, then the conclusion must be an exclusion.

Comment: Exactly one rule of the subset 2 to 4 will apply to any given syllogism. Any syllogism, that is, will have two inclusion premises (Rule 2), only one inclusion premise (Rule 4), or no inclusion premise (Rule 3). When checking a syllogism for validity be sure you apply the appropriate rule of quality (2 to 4).

Rule 5 Any term that is distributed in the conclusion must be distributed in the premise.

Comment: This rule is really conditional. It applies exactly in those cases where a conclusion term is distributed. Where no conclusion term is distributed, the rule is safely ignored. Any conclusion term, however, which is distributed must be checked to see that it is distributed in its premise occurrence. If it is not, the syllogism is invalid. If it is, then this distribution test has been passed.

Rule 6 The middle term must be distributed at least once.

Comment: Of all the rules, this one is perhaps the most often broken. Yet the rule is quite necessary and proper. The middle term is supposed to provide some connecting link between the major and minor terms. That link is not provided, however, unless at least one of the premises takes into consideration the whole class to which the middle term refers. If the middle term is never distributed, the possibility remains that the part of that class related to the minor term's class is disconnected from the part related to the major's class. Two especially tempting cases of undistributed middles are worthy of separate exemplifications:

EG. 19.4   Some M is P.
Some M is S.
∴ Some S is P.

EG. 19.5   All P is M.
All S is M.
∴ Some S is P.

Final comment: These six rules define a test for syllogisms. If a syllogism fails any part of this test, it is invalid.

EXERCISE 3

Determine the validity of each of the following syllogisms by appeal to the six rules of the syllogism.

_____ 1. What follows scientific method is correct. Newtonian physics is not correct. So Newtonian physics does not follow scientific method.

_____ 2. All large towns have ghettos. Some manufacturing towns are large. So some manufacturing towns have ghettos.

_____ 3. No large towns have ghettos. All large towns are manufacturing towns. Some manufacturing towns do not have ghettos.

_____ 4. Some large towns have ghettos. Some manufacturing towns have ghettos. So some manufacturing towns are large.

_____ 5. No herbs are mosses. All mosses grow in the tropics. So some plants that grow in the tropics are not herbs.

_____ 6. All mosses grow in the tropics. All herbs grow in the tropics. So all herbs are mosses.

_____ 7. No moss is an herb. All plants growing in the tropics are herbs. So no plant growing in the tropics is a moss.

_____ 8. No moss grows in the tropics. Some herb is a moss. So some herb doesn't grow in the tropics.

_____ 9. No herb is a moss. Some herb grows in the tropics. So some plant that grows in the tropics is not a moss.

_____ 10. All herbs grow in the tropics. Some moss grows in the tropics. So some moss is an herb.

_____ 11. All sulfates are dangerous. All sulfates are pollutants. So some pollutant is dangerous.

_____ 12. Some pollutants are not dangerous. All sulfates are pollutants. So no sulfate is dangerous.

13. No sulfates are pollutants. Some pollutants are dangerous. So some dangerous substances are not sulfates.
14. All pollutants are dangerous. All sulfates are pollutants. So all sulfates are dangerous.
15. All pollutants are dangerous. Whatever is dangerous is a sulfate. So some sulfate is a pollutant.
16. Some birds migrate. No migratory birds lay eggs in tropical climates. So all birds lay eggs in tropical climates.

ANSWERS TO EXERCISE 3

1. Invalid (Rule 1); in the major premise 'correct' means 'correct procedures'; in the minor it means "is (not) correct in its results."
2. Valid
3. Valid
4. Invalid (undistributed middle)
5. Valid
6. Invalid (undistributed middle)
7. Valid
8. Valid
9. Valid
10. Invalid (undistributed middle)
11. Valid
12. Invalid (undistributed middle)
13. Valid
14. Valid
15. Valid
16. Invalid; the conclusion's quality should be negative, and 'birds' is undistributed in the premise but distributed in the conclusion.

6

PREDICATE LOGIC: CONTEMPORARY METHODS

In Chapter 6 we will focus on contemporary treatments of the inclusion and exclusion relationships in predicate logic. We will learn the symbolic notation of modern predicate logic and we will learn how to translate from English into that notation. We will develop a method of testing arguments of predicate logic for validity using diagrams. The educational goal of Chapter 6 is to learn how to translate from English into symbolic notation and how to test arguments of predicate logic for validity using the diagram method.

MODULE 20
INCLUSION AND EXCLUSION

In this module we will focus on six ways of expressing the inclusion and exclusion relations between classes and their members.[1]

● After reading Module 20 you should be able to:

1. Identify classes and distinguish class terms from statement units
2. Identify and distinguish various kinds of statement units on the basis of the relationship of the subject and predicate reference classes
3. Draw a diagram representing each of the six relationships discussed in this module: total, partial, and individual inclusion and total, partial, and individual exclusion

20:1.1 Subject class and predicate class Consider the following statement units:

> Birds are things that fly.
> People are beings that think.
> Free persons love life.
> Horses are beasts of burden.
> Nurses are underpaid.

[1] You might want to review the discussion of reference classes and extensions in 6:1.3.

Children are demanding.
Cows are animals that eat grass.
Students are animals that smoke grass.
The trout is a fish.

Each of these example statements makes reference to two classes:

Birds, flying things
People, thinking beings
Free persons, persons who love life
Horses, beasts of burden
Nurses, underpaid people
etc.

Notice that each of these statement units asserts that all the members of the reference class of the subject term are also members of the reference class of the predicate term. We can use a circle to represent a reference class. An S beside (or in) such a circle means the circle represents the subject term's extension:

The reference class of the predicate term can be diagramed using a circle with P beside it for predicate:

To diagram statements like those in the list above we will need two circles, one for each class. There are a number of ways to draw the two circles. They can be separate from each other, they can overlap, or one can be located entirely inside the other. The most useful way turns out to be

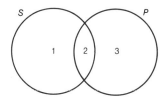

because three regions are clearly indicated: (1) the region in S but not P, (2) the region of the overlap, in both S and P, and (3) the region in P but not S. A fourth region, the region outside both S and P can be created if we locate our two circles inside of a rectangle:

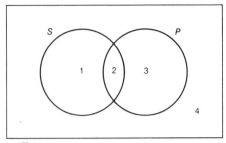

The rectangle can represent the universe within which our two classes can be located.

Statement units like those in the list above assert that the S class is totally included in the P class. We can conveniently diagram this *inclusion* relationship by using a convention of shading empty areas.[2]

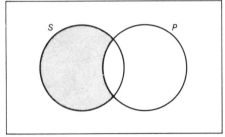

The shadowing means "this area is empty." Thus the area of S outside of P is empty: "All S's are inside the class of P's!"[3]

Other statement units can assert other relationships between these classes, for example:

No S's are P's:

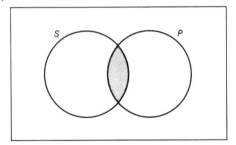

[2] Diagrams like these are called Venn diagrams after John Venn, the English logician who first systematically presented predicate logic relationships using these pictorial devices. We will call them *class region diagrams* because that name is more descriptive. The various regions created by the overlapping circles within the rectangle may either be: (1) known to be empty, (2) known to contain at least one member, or (3) be regions about which nothing is known.

[3] Since 'all S are P' is equivalent to 'no S is non-P,' the region of S outside of P is asserted to be empty. Shading indicates its being empty.

where the shading in the overlap region means "this area is empty." Some S is a P:

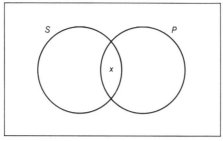

where the little x in a particular area can be read to mean "there is at least one thing here." Some S is not a P:

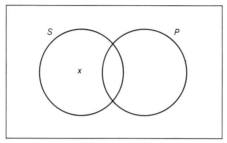

where the little x in the area of S outside of P means that there is at least one S that is not a P.

Now, let us go back over this in more detail.

20:1.2 A *class* is simply a collection or set of objects. It can be a set of anything you wish to designate:

cows	rocks on the moon
people	5-pound baby girls
old men	three-legged hens
microbiologists	fat cats of ancient Rome
flowers	blind airline pilots
roses	deaf telephone operators
roses in your garden	living Civil War heros
lousy lunches	honest monks of the eleventh century
honest presidents	famous unpublished philosophers
sure bets	round squares

Of course, the designation that you use to name the class may guarantee that the class has no members (or is empty) as would be the case with classes like:

round squares
living former presidents from Utah
four-sided triangles
kings of the United States
living Civil War heros

A class is simply a set or collection of objects. A class is not true or false like a statement unit; rather it is either empty or not empty. If a class is not empty, its members may be members of some other classes as well as nonmembers of still other classes. Cows, for example, are members of the class of animals but not members of the class of flowers. The way to find out if a word or phrase designates a class is to ask: Could this term be used to refer to a collection of individuals? If yes, the term is a *class term*. Of course, too, you have to allow for terms that designate classes that have only one member. These classes are often designated or described more definitely than most other classes; thus we would have

> the woman who founded the Grey Panther Movement
> the president of the United States
> the elder senator from Ohio
> the shnook who ate 10,000 hotdogs in one week

and similar designations that purport to designate classes that have only one member in them.

20:1.3 Two basic relationships Predicate logic is the logic which deals with two relationships between classes and their individual members that can yield valid inferences. One of these relationships is

> *Inclusion*

and the other, its opposite, is

> *Exclusion*

Saying 'all S are P' suggests that the predicate class *includes* every member of the subject class. Saying 'no S is P' suggests that the predicate class *excludes* every member of the subject class. There can be partial exclusion and partial inclusion also, as in 'some S is not a P' and 'some S is a P,' respectively. And finally there can be individual inclusion and individual exclusion, as in 'John is a S' or 'John is not a S.' Let us look at those six types of statement units more closely.

20:2.1 The first type of statement unit is the one that expresses *total inclusion* and which can be diagramed as follows.

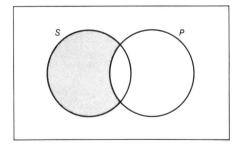

where the shading indicates that no S is outside of the P class, or, in other words, that P contains whatever S's there may be.

Statement units that express total inclusion often take one of the forms

If something's an S, then it's a P.
There are no S's that aren't P's.
All S are P.
If anything is an S, it's a P.
Whatever's an S is a P.
The S is a P.
All the S's are P's.

All the examples in 20:1.1 are examples of total inclusion.

The contemporary treatment of total inclusion statements treats a statement of the form

All S are P

as asserting

Given any member of the universe, if it is a member of S, then it is a member of P.

In contemporary logic this interpretation is explicitly intended to *rule out* the inference to

There is an S that is a P.

For example,

All unicorns have cloven hooves

is interpreted as

If any animal is a unicorn, then it is an animal that has cloven hooves.

This interpretation is intended to rule out the direct inference to

There is a unicorn which is an animal that has cloven hooves.

Shading the region of S outside of P neither affirms nor denies what might be asserted about a statement of the form "some S is P." If there are members of S, then that statement will be true; if not, false. However, since total inclusion statements do not guarantee that there are members of S, it seems an error to do more than indicate where they would not be *if* they did exist. Thus, we use shading to exhibit diagramatically the total inclusion statement; there will not be any members of S that are not also members of P.

20:2.2 Statement units that express *total exclusion* indicate that the relationship between the S class and the P class is that they have no members in common. Or

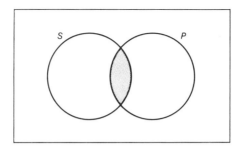

where, again, shading indicates emptiness.

Total exclusion statement units often take one of the following forms:

No S's are P's.
If anything is an S, then it's not a P.
Nothing is both an S and a P.
All S's are not P's
Every S isn't a P.

The following are examples of statements of total exclusion:

No Romans smoke pot.
No students who study hard are students who fail their courses.
No football players went on strike last year.
If anyone hates bridge he or she is not one who would vote for Goren.
No one loves a country and hates its president.
All filters are not for use on this model.
Every fish isn't a mammal.

Statements of total exclusion, like those of total inclusion, are interpreted in contemporary logic as being neutral relative to the existence of members of S. Thus, to say "no S is P" is to say "should there be any members of S, these would not be found in P." To say "no rockets launched in ancient Greece are still orbiting the earth" does not commit the speaker to the existence of rockets launched in ancient Greece. It only asserts that *if* there were any they are not to be found orbiting the earth right now.

20:2.3 The relationship of *partial inclusion* is expressed by statement units of the forms

Some S are P.
At least one S is a P.
There exists an S that is a P.

Here there are two claims made. The first claim is that S actually has at least one member. The second claim is that this member is also a member of P. But the statement is indefinite; it does not say precisely which member of S that might be. Thus, we have the diagram

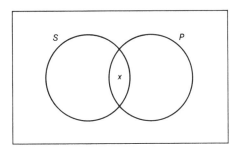

where *x* indicates that unknown or unspecified S that is also a P.

It is also possible that more than one S is a P, of course; but when logicians are concerned with the logic of classes they make the simplifying assumption that all that is being claimed in a statement of partial inclusion is partial, and not total, inclusion. Here are some examples:

Some books are red.
Some cars are economical.
At least one professor knows how to teach.
There exist some reasons that are reasons to acquit the accused.

A statement of partial inclusion asserts that *at least* one member of the subject class S is included in the predicate class P. Of course, if it says two S are P, then at least one is. The relation of partial inclusion holds. Similarly if most S's or many S's are P's, the relationship of partial inclusion holds. Thus all of the following assert partial, but not total, inclusion.

Three alligators are loose in Topeka.
Several metals are magnetic.
Most water mammals have little hair.
Sore throats *often* accompany colds.

Even though these numerical and quasi-numerical statements express more than can be expressed in our diagrams so far, they do express at least that one member of S is P and so can be counted as expressing partial inclusion.

20:2.4 Statement units that express *partial exclusion* are usually written

Some S is not a P.
Some S's are not P's.
At least one S isn't a P.
Not all S's are P's.

The relationship of partial exclusion can be diagramed as

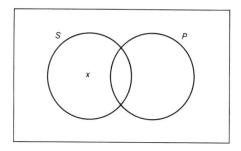

where the x in the area of S outside of P means that there exists at least one S in that region outside of P.

Some examples of statements expressing partial exclusion are:

Some wealthy people are not honest.
Some politicans are not liars.
At least one woman is not a member of congress.
Not every police officer is a communist.

Partial exclusion statements assert that there is *at least one* S which is outside the class P. They do not imply that no S are P, however. To capture an audience's attention advertisers can try almost any trick. One that works is to say something like

All airlines are *not* professional!

when what is really meant is

Not all airlines are professional.

The first claim really means

No airlines are professional.

which is a total exclusion statement separating airlines from professional things. But since the advertisers want eventually to claim that one airline, say Ricket Tee Airways, really is, in contrast to others, professional, what they want to claim is

Some airlines are not professional.

This partial exclusion statement still allows for the logically compatible claim that unlike those others, Ricket Tee is professional. A little logical clarity can help one avoid being misled by this type of advertising sloganism.

20:2.5 Statements that express *individual inclusion* assert that one particular individual, who or which can be uniquely named or described, is a member of P. Because the individual can be named or uniquely described, we can use a special symbol, functioning as a name, to designate it. For example, we could use *a* for Adam, *b* for Brenda, or *c* for Carlene. Statements that express individual inclusion also can designate the individual who is being referred to by a descriptive phase that purports to uniquely or definitely pick that individual out. Such phrases are called definite descriptions and are usually phrased "the so-and-so," as in the examples given at the end of 20:1.2. The following phrases indicate individual inclusion:

> The so-and-so is a P.
> j is a P.

Examples are:

> Socrates is one of those who was put to death.
> The teacher of Plato was put to death.
> The first president lived a long and happy life.
> The man who shot Lincoln was crazy.

The relationship of individual inclusion can be diagramed as

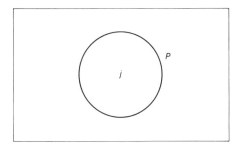

where j names the individual and locates it inside of P.

In the Aristotelian treatment (Chapter 5) the individual named by the subject is thought of as a class that has only one member. That way of interpreting individual statements allows statements of individual inclusion to be treated as special cases of total inclusion. Thus 'Cleopatra ruled Egypt' would, in an Aristotelian approach, be interpreted as 'Anyone who is Cleopatra is a (former) ruler of Egypt.' However, in contemporary logic we treat total inclusion statements as making no claim about there being members in the subject class. Since an individual inclusion statement's subject purports to designate an individual that is an S, it makes a claim of existence that suggests it is inappropriate not to distinguish individual inclusion from total inclusion.

20:2.6 Individual exclusion Individual exclusion is the relationship expressed by statements of the form

> j is not a P.
> The so-and-so is not a P.
> j is no P.

as exemplified by

> John is no friend of mine.
> The elder senator from Ohio does not wish to retire.
> Brenda is not a poor student.

These statements of individual exclusion can be diagramed by

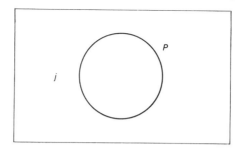

which locates the individual *j* outside of the class *P*.

What we said about the relationship of individual inclusion to total inclusion in 20:2.5 applies to the relationship between individual and total exclusion as well.

20:3 Predicate logic The validity of many arguments depends on the relationships of inclusion and exclusion that the premises set up between the various classes and individuals they refer to. These arguments are the arguments of predicate logic. Here are some examples of such arguments; they are valid because of these inclusion and exclusion relationships.

EG. 20.1 1. All horses are wild.
2. All wild things run around without clothing.
3. So all horses run around without clothing.

EG. 20.2 1. Whatever is a friend of all humanity is easy to get along with.
2. But, if anything is easy to get along with, then it is not wise to bring it home to meet the kids.
3. It follows than that all friends of all humanity are things such that it is not wise to bring them home to meet the kids.

EXERCISES FOR MODULE 20
INCLUSION AND EXCLUSION

Ex. 1 Below is a list of ten passages. If a passage is a statement put 'S' in the answer space; if it only designates a class, put 'C' in the answer space.

_____ 1. The people who live in Ohio.

_____ 2. The people who live in Ohio are among the most prosperous people to have ever lived in North America.

_____ 3. Cars that have dusty hoods and red tops.

_____ 4. Some cars have dusty hoods and red tops.

_____ 5. Not all power tools are alike.

_____ 6. Large land animals that are native to Africa.

_____ 7. Fungus is not a kind of fruit drink!

_____ 8. The finest pianist the world has ever known.

_____ 9. There are some people who do not trust their leaders.

_____ 10. The present administration.

Ex. 2 Here is a list of twenty-eight statements. Identify each as either total inclusion (TI), partial inclusion (PI), individual inclusion (II), total exclusion (TE), partial exclusion (PE), or individual exclusion (IE).

_____ 1. Some people swim.

_____ 2. Some people are easy to get to know.

_____ 3. All my children are children who like candy.

_____ 4. No prisoners are going to be allowed to live.

_____ 5. If anyone likes popcorn, then they will like butter too.

_____ 6. My kids like ice cream.

_____ 7. All of those who live here will have to acquire passports.

_____ 8. Some snowmen are not big.

_____ 9. The whale is a mammal.

_____ 10. The present king of Charlottesville lives in luxury and mortgages.

_____ 11. Plato was not a sailor.

_____ 12. Aristotle was a beggar.

_____ 13. If anything can swim it can't fly.

_____ 14. At least some people remained loyal.

_____ 15. Nobody knows the trouble I've seen.

_____ 16. No wise men are wise women.

_____ 17. Some jets are not safe.

_____ 18. Some packets are empty.

_____ 19. No food was sent to the sub-Sahara.

_____ 20. All the paper was recycled yesterday.

_____ 21. I am not the author of this story.

_____ 22. Some of us feel that you should sign the bill.

_____ 23. All the people I know are people who think that the big problem now is the economy.

_____ 24. Kluto left school at age five.

_____ 25. There are many who love this country.

_____ 26. Some do not love this country.

_____ 27. Some feel little emotion toward the country one way or the other.

_____ 28. You will be the one I pick to do it.

Ex. 3 Draw a diagram representing each of the following:

1. No S are P.
2. Some S is not P.
3. a is not P.
4. All S is P.
5. Some S is P.
6. a is P.

Ex. 1

1. C   2. S   3. C   4. S   5. S
6. C   7. S   8. C   9. S   10. C

If you missed more than one, review 20:1.2, and perhaps 8:2.

Ex. 2

1. PI   2. PI   3. TI   4. TE   5. TI
6. TI   7. TI   8. PE   9. TI   10. II
11. IE   12. II   13. TE   14. PI   15. TE
16. TE   17. PE   18. PI   19. TE   20. TI

Ex. 3

1.

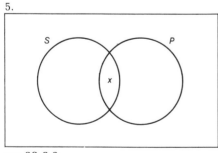

see 20:2.2

2.

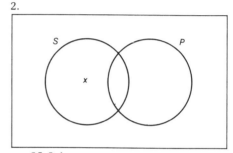

see 20:2.4

3.

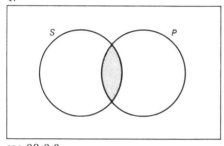

see 20:2.6

4.

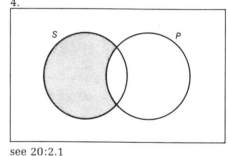

see 20:2.1

5.

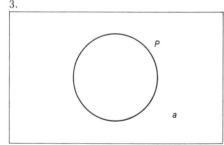

see 20:2.3

6.

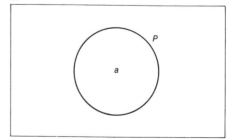

see 20:2.5

Review the appropriate section of Module 20 for each one you missed.

MODULE 21

THE LANGUAGE OF PREDICATE LOGIC

We begin this module by developing the notation which we will use to represent the structure of individual inclusion and individual exclusion statements. From there it is an easy step to expressing the truth-functional relationships that can exist between them using your knowledge of propositional logic notation. We then develop special notation to handle statements that use the English quantifier words 'all' and 'some.' We then draw together the notational techniques into a definition of 'well-formed formula of predicate logic.' In Module 22 we will use this notation to learn to translate a variety of English statements.

● After reading Module 21 you should be able to:

1. Identify predicate expressions
2. Translate statements of individual inclusion and individual exclusion into proper symbolic notation
3. Given a specific interpretation of predicate letters and name letters, determine the truth or falsity of simple statements
4. Translate truth-functional compounds of individual inclusion and individual exclusion statements into proper symbolic notation
5. Identify and distinguish simple examples of open sentences, closed sentences, and quantifier expressions written in both natural language and symbolic notation
6. Identify wffs of predicate logic and distinguish them from formulas that are not well formed
7. Given a list of formulas of predicate logic that are not well formed, state a reason why each is not well formed and rewrite each as a wff of predicate logic
8. Construct sample wffs of predicate logic

21:1.1 Predicate expressions Consider the following individual inclusion and individual exclusion statements.

Harry is merry.
Kim is slim.
Caesar is not dead.
Kogolowski is a New Yorker.
The quarterback is not a good passer.
The champion diver is a woman.
The blue balloon popped.

In each of these assertions, you should notice two basic structural elements:
1. A subject term (that purports to refer to a unique individual), i.e.,

Harry
Kim
Caesar
Kogolowski
The quarterback
The champion diver
The blue balloon

2. A predicate expression that is used to characterize that subject term in some way, i.e.,

> . . . is merry.
> . . . is slim.
> . . . is dead.
> . . . is a New Yorker.
> . . . is a good passer.
> . . . is a woman.
> . . . is popped.

We could replace the . . . in each of these predicate expressions with a subject term and derive a statement unit. Thus, if we used 'Martha' we could derive the statement units:

> Martha is merry
> Martha is slim
> etc.

21:1.2 Predicate expressions can be thought of as referring to characteristics or attributes which can be asserted or denied of specific subjects in the way that

> Martha is a woman

asserts that Martha has the characteristic of "being a woman," and

> Martha is not dead

denies that Martha has the characteristic of "being dead." Predicate expressions can also be thought of as referring to classes. The classes referred to, or designated, by our seven examples are:

> The class of merry people
> The class of slim people
> The class of dead people
> The class of people who are New Yorkers
> The class of good passers
> The class of women
> The class of popped (exploded) things

Thought of as referring to classes, predicate expressions can be used to assert or deny that the subject term is a member of that class, as in

> The class of merry people has Harry as a member.
> The class of slim people has Kim as a member.
> The class of dead people does not have Caesar as a member.
> etc.

21:1.3 Predicate expression defined A predicate expression can be defined as *any phrase or expression which in standard usage can serve to ascribe an attribute, characteristic, or class membership to any object or group of objects.* On the basis of this definition the following expressions are predicate expressions:

. . . is a thief.
. . . is a member of the class of wise people.
. . . is broken.
. . . is a toy.
. . . is a large dog.
. . . are the rulers of the universe.
. . . are things that remind me of home.
. . . are the most interesting books I've ever read.
. . . is one of the finest people we met in Paris.
. . . is a person who knows too much.
. . . are exploited.
. . . are among the most feared animals in this state.

These can be used to ascribe an attribute, characteristic, or class membership to an object or group of objects, as indicated by the following:

Grover Biscomber is a thief.
Grover Biscomber is a member of the class of wise people.
This toy is broken.
This ball is a toy.
Blue is a large dog.
The gods are the rulers of the universe.
These pictures are things that remind me of home.
Books by Ross McDonald are the most interesting books I've ever read.
Emile is one of the finest people we met in Paris.
The prime minister is a person who knows too much.
American workers are exploited.
Rattlesnakes are among the most feared animals in this state.

Notice that when predicate expressions are used in this way they generate positive statement units.

21:1.4 To sum up, predicate expressions are not class terms, although they do designate classes. They are used to ascribe an attribute, characteristic, or class membership. They can apply to either individual objects or groups (classes) of objects. When they are so applied they yield positive statement units. These positive statement units can then enter into other truth-functional settings.

To aid yourself in understanding predicate expressions, try the following exercise.

EXERCISE 1

Identify the predicate expressions in the following list.

1. Joan is a woman.
2. . . . is a woman.
3. The class of women
4. Caesar lived till he died.
5. Those who are alive
6. . . . are among the living.
7. Few people
8. All the king's horses
9. . . . is a horse
10. . . . are members of ethnic minorities
11. Golf, tennis, and bowling
12. The current governor of North Carolina
13. Federal judges
14. . . . are toy kites

1. No; this is a statement unit.
2. Yes
3. No; this is a class term.
4. No; this is a statement unit.
5. No; this is a class term.
6. Yes
7. No; this expression is used to designate a part of a class.
8. No; this is a class term.
9. Yes
10. Yes
11. No; this is a list.
12. No; this is a definite description.
13. No; this is a class term.
14. Yes

21:2.1 Name letters and predicate letters To exhibit the logical structure of statements of individual inclusion and individual exclusion we will need two new kinds of notational devices. We will need a device for designating or naming individuals, and we will need a device to represent predicate expressions. Let us use the lower-case letters from a to o as *name letters* to stand for specific individuals. Let us use the uppercase letters from F to S as *predicate letters* to stand for various predicate expressions.[4] These devices stand for specific names and predicate expressions. Thus, for individuals like Adam, Betty, Carol, and David we can use name letters like a, b, c, and d. And for predicate expressions like

    . . . is a fox.
    . . . is a great person.
    . . . is a humble individual.
    . . . is a good idea.

we can use predicate letters like F, G, H, and I. To generate statement units expressing individual inclusion we will adopt the convention of writing a predicate expression to the immediate left of a name letter, as in these three examples:

    Kj
    Fa
    Sm

If K = ". . . is a kind person," F = ". . . is a tough fighter," and S = ". . . is a gigantic lens"; and if j = Caesar, a = Sylvia, and m = this piece of glass, then we could translate our three examples as

    Caesar is a kind person.
    Sylvia is a tough fighter.
    This piece of glass is a gigantic lens.

21:2.2 To render statements of individual exclusion into symbolic notation we can use the negation devices we developed in Chapter 4. Thus,

---

[4] These are simply conventions adopted for the sake of convenience and in order to avoid overlaps and ambiguities in our use of various upper- and lowercase letters throughout the text. If we need more name letters or predicate letters we can introduce subscripts, for example a_1 or F_1.

$(\sim Ka)$
$(\sim Fj)$
$(\sim Sm)$

can be read as the individual exclusion statements

Sylvia is not a kind person.
Caesar is not a tough fighter.
This piece of glass is not a gigantic lens.

21:2.3 Interpretation By an *interpretation* of a name letter we will understand the assignment of a specific individual or object to the name letter. By an interpretation of a predicate letter we will understand the assignment of a specific predicate expression to the predicate letter. The last paragraph of 21:2.1 exemplifies specific interpretations of the letters K, F, S, j, a, and m. We could, however, have interpreted these letters differently. F could be ". . . is a fancy cookie," G = ". . . is a goose," S = ". . . is slim"; and j could be Joel, a Alice, and m Marva.

21:3 All the truth-functional operations we learned in Chapter 4 can be applied to the statement units we can build using predicate letters and name letters. As we have seen they can be negated. They can also be conjoined, as in

$((\sim Sa) \,\&\, (\sim Sb))$

disjoined, as in

$((\sim Sc) \lor Sd)$

and formed into conditionals and biconditionals, as in

$(Sd \supset (\sim Sd))$
$(Sd \equiv (\sim Sc))$

The following translation exercise is intended to help you master the use of name letters and predicate letters in conjunction with the symbolic notation of propositional logic.

EXERCISE 2

Translate the following using name letters, predicate letters, and propositional logic notation. For each item state the interpretation you give to each of the predicate letters and name letters you use.

1. Mbuti wrote a book about Africa and so did Bourgeiba.
2. Rover is a shepherd but Ruff is not.
3. Archilles was either proud or stubborn.
4. If Karen is an assertive person, Lori will be nasty.
5. George is open-minded.
6. If Nancy is not discouraged, she will succeed.

7. Charlotte cares.
8. Either Ethyl eats too much or Friday was unusual.
9. John will cheat unless Mark acquiesces.
10. It's false that if Ruth reads the book John will be embarrassed.

ANSWERS TO EXERCISE 2

1. (Rm & Rb)   m = Mbuti, b = Bourgeiba, R = ". . . wrote a book about Africa."

2. (Se & (~Sf))   e = Rover, f = Ruff, S = ". . . is a shepherd."

3. (Pa ∨ Sa)   a = Archilles, P = ". . . is proud," S = ". . . is stubborn."

4. (Sk ⊃ Nl)   k = Karen, l = Lori, S = ". . . is an assertive person," N = ". . . is nasty."

5. Og   g = George, O = ". . . is open-minded."

6. ((~Mn) ⊃ Sn)   n = Nancy, M = ". . . is discouraged," S = ". . . is successful."

7. Sc   c = Charlotte, S = ". . . is one who cares."

8. (Fe ∨ Pf)   e = Ethyl, f = Friday, F = ". . . is one who eats too much," P = ". . . is unusual."

9. (Sj ∨ Qm)   j = John, m = Mark, S = ". . . is a cheater," Q = ". . . is one who acquiesces."

10. (~(Rh ⊃ Mj))   h = Ruth, j = John, R = ". . . is one who reads the book," M = ". . . is one who is embarrassed."

21:4.1 Eliminating vagueness We will not allow the vagueness of predicate expressions in English to stand in the way of logical precision. An expression like ". . . is slim" is ordinarily vague. However we will assume that all predicate expressions have been sufficiently sharpened (perhaps by stipulative definition) so that every member of the universe is clearly included or excluded from each class. We rule out, by stipulation, all borderline cases. So, for example, given the universe of men, each is either slim or not slim; there is no third alternative. Let us suppose that there are four men in the universe: Adam, Bill, Charles, and David. Let us further assume that the term 'slim' is so well defined that the predicate expression ". . . is slim" applies only to David. If we use S as the predicate letter for ". . . is slim" and if we use a, b, c, and d to name Adam, Bill, Charles, and David, respectively, then

   Sd

is true, whereas

   Sa
   Sb
   Sc

are all false. However, since by stipulation there are no borderline cases, it also follows that these three negations are true:

   (~Sa)
   (~Sb)
   (~Sc)

21:4.2 The predicate-logic assumption that no members of any given universe are borderline members of any class allows us to operate on the basis of the claim: *Given any class in any given universe of objects every member of that universe either is or is not a member of that class.* So, for example, given two classes, the extensions of, say, the predicate letters G and H, and given a universe of say, three individuals {a, b, c}, it follows that these three conjunctions are true:

$$[(Ga \lor (\sim Ga)) \,\&\, (Ha \lor (\sim Ha))]$$
$$[(Gb \lor (\sim Gb)) \,\&\, (Hb \lor (\sim Hb))]$$
$$[(Gc \lor (\sim Gc)) \,\&\, (Hc \lor (\sim Hc))]$$

An alternative way of determining the *interpretations of predicate letters and name letters* is to *assign a specific member of a given universe to each name letter* and to *assign specific sets of members of that universe as the extension of each predicate letter.* For example, if our universe were Alice, Betsy, and Carol, we could let a = Alice, b = Betsy, and c = Carol. The extension of G could be {a, b}; the extension of H could be {a, c}; and the extension of M could be Λ (that is the empty set—the set with no members).[5] Given these interpretations the following are true:

Ga	Alice is a G.
Gb	Betsy is the extension of G.
(~Gc)	Carol is not a G.
Ha	Alice is in the class H.
(~Hb)	Betsy is not in the extension assigned to H.
Hc	Carol is an H.
(~Ma)	Alice is not an M.
(~Mb)	Betsy is not an M.
(~Mc)	Carol is not an M.

EXERCISE 3

Let the universe be the set of objects {Avery, Bert, Carrie, Dana}. Let a = Avery, b − Bert, c = Carrie, and d = Dana. Let the extension of F = {Avery, Bert} and the extension of H = {Dana}. Indicate whether each of the following is true or false under the above specified interpretation.

1. Fa	2. Fd	3. (~Fb)	4. (~Fc)
5. Hc	6. Hd	7. (~Ha)	8. (~Hb)

ANSWERS TO EXERCISES 3

The only true statement units under this interpretation are Fa, Fb, and Hd. Therefore the answers to this exercise are:

1. T	2. F	3. F	4. T
5. F	6. T	7. T	8. T

[5] Although sometimes the empty set is assigned as an extension of a specific predicate letter, it is always assumed in standard predicate logic that the universe itself is not empty.

21:5.1 Individual variables Suppose we are concerned with a specific universe that has four people as its members. Given a predicate expression like ". . . is a woman" (K) we can assert a number of different things about that universe. We can assert four individual inclusion statements and four individual exclusion statements. But we can also assert things like

> Someone is a woman

and

> Everybody is a woman.

If we were not sure which of the four people, call them a, b, c, and d, were women, we could assert

> $(Ka \vee Kb \vee Kc \vee Kd)$

meaning

> Either a or b or c or d is a woman.

But we would probably prefer to assert

> Someone is a woman

(especially if the universe were of a larger, perhaps indefinite or even infinite, size). Our claim that "someone is a woman" amounts to the following:

EG. 21.1 There is some member of the universe x such that x is a woman.

Notice that the letter x occurs twice in Eg. 21.1. The first time it occurs as a name—not a name that designates a specific known individual but rather a name that can designate *any* member of the universe. The second time x occurs, it is as a reflexive pronoun occurring in the blank space of the predicate expression. We will regard the lowercase letter x as an *individual variable*, that is, a letter which can range over all the individuals in a given universe. (If we need more individual variables we will use v, w, y, z, v_1, w_1, x_1, y_1, z_1, v_2, ...) Individual variables are used not only in statements like "someone is a woman" but also in statements like "everyone is a woman." The latter is understood to say the following.

EG. 21.2 For every member of the universe x it is true that x is a woman.

Going back to our four-member universe we have:

> $(Ka \,\& \, Kb \,\& \, Kc \,\& \, Kd)$

That is, each and every item in our universe, mentioned by name, is a woman.
Individual variables are also used in statements of total inclusion.

EG. 21.3 For every member of the universe, it is true that if x is a woman, then x is industrious.

They are used in statements of partial inclusion.

EG. 21.4 There exists at least one member of the universe x such that x is a woman and x is industrious.

They are used in statements of total exclusion.

EG. 21.5 For every member of the universe x it is true that if x is a woman, then x is not industrious.

And they are used in statements of partial exclusion.

EG. 21.6 There exists at least one member of the universe x such that x is a woman but x is not industrious.

21:5.2 Open sentences In the above English examples a number of predicate expressions with individual variables in them occurred either individually or joined by truth-functional operators. Looking back over the last six examples you will find:

EG. 21.1′ x is a woman

EG. 21.2′ x is a woman

EG. 21.3′ (x is a woman ⊃ x is industrious)

EG. 21.4′ (x is a woman & x is industrious)

EG. 21.5′ (x is a woman ⊃ (~x is industrious))

EG. 21.6′ (x is a woman & (~x is industrious))

Or, using K for ". . . is a woman" and J for ". . . is industrious," these expressions could be symbolically represented as follows.

EG. 21.1″ Kx

EG. 21.2″ Kx

EG. 21.3″ $(Kx \supset Jx)$

EG. 21.4″ $(Kx \,\&\, Jx)$

EG. 21.5″ $(Kx \supset (\sim Jx))$

EG. 21.6″ $(Kx \,\&\, (\sim Jx))$

These expressions, unlike the expressions Ka and $(Kb \supset Kd)$, are incomplete. They do not stand alone as statement units or statement compounds. They leave open the questions: Which one? or Which ones? It is as if a stranger were to walk up to us and, completely out of context, say

>   She is industrious

or

>   If she is industrious then she is wise.

We would probably be quite bewildered and want to know: Who? Which one? Who is the 'she' you're referring to? Predicate expressions with names occurring in the blank spaces form complete statement units. Predicate expressions with individual variables occurring in the blank space yield *open sentences*. A compound sentence will be considered *open* if there is at least one open sentence in it. If a sentence is not *open*, we will call it *closed*.

Identify the open sentences in the following list.

1. x is a woman.
2. x is industrious.
3. Joan is a fine reporter.
4. If Joan comes late, then x will be on time.
5. If Joan comes late, then Bill will be on time.
6. It is not the case that y is a clown.
7. If y is a clown, then y is a circus worker.
8. Casper is a clown only if Casper is a circus worker.

ANSWERS TO EXERCISE 4

1. Open   2. Open
3. Closed   4. Open; only one open sentence is needed for the whole expression to be open.
5. Closed   6. Open; y is a variable.
7. Open   8. Closed

21:5.3 Quantifier expressions *Only closed sentences have truth-values;* open sentences do not. An inspection of the eight items in Ex. 4 shows that the question "Is this true or false?" cannot be asked of items 1, 2, 4, 6, and 7 until we can figure out who these open sentences refer to. Our problem, then, is how we will close open sentences. The clue to an answer comes from a second look at Egs 21.1 to 21.6. Besides the open sentences in each of those examples you can also find another expression:

EG. 21.1′′′ There exists at least one member of the universe x such that . . .

EG. 21.2′′′ For every member of the universe x it is true that . . .

EG. 21.3′′′ For every member of the universe x it is true that . . .

EG. 21.4′′′ There exists at least one member of the universe x such that . . .

EG. 21.5′′′ For every member of the universe x it is true that . . .

EG. 21.6′′′ There exists at least one member of the universe x such that . . .

Observe that these expressions all specify some quantity of the universe, either "every member" or "at least one member." It is convenient, then, to call them *quantifier expressions*. There are only two basic quantifier expressions that we will use. One for 'all' and one for 'some.' The one for 'all' is called the *universal quantifier*, whereas the one for 'some' is called the *existential quantifier*. There are a number of ways to express each of these two quantifiers in English. We will cover these ways more fully in the next module which is on translation. For now there are two paradigm ways to note. The one used for universal quantification occurs in Egs. 21.2′′′, 21.3′′′, and 21.5′′′; the one for existential quantification occurs in Egs. 21.1′′′, 21.4′′′, and 21.6′′′. We can abbreviate the expression for the universal quantifier by

Every x is such that . . .

and we can abbreviate the expression for the existential quantifier by

Some x is such that . . .

21:5.4 The quantifying expressions in Egs. 21.1 to 21.6 answer the question "Which one?" at least enough for us to regard each of these examples as a complete statement. Put in another way, quantifier expressions can be used to close open sentences. Prefixing one quantifying expression on to an open sentence for each of the distinct individual variables in that open sentence will yield a closed sentence. For example, given the open sentences

x is a woman.
y is industrious.
x is wise.

we can generate the following closed sentences using quantifier expressions:

Every x is such that x is a woman.
Some x is such that x is wise.
Every y is such that if y is a woman then y is wise.
Some x is such that if x is a woman then x is wise.
Some x is such that x is wise; and some y is such that y is industrious.

We already have the equipment with which to write open sentences in symbolic notation. To express Egs. 21.1 to 21.6 in notation, all we need, then, is a device for representing quantifying expressions. Let us form universal quantifiers by enclosing an individual variable in parentheses, as

(x)   and   (y)

We can form existential quantifiers the same way but with a *backward* 'E' to the left of the individual variable to remind us of 'existential,' as in

($\exists$x)   and   ($\exists$w)

The choice of which variable to inclose depends on the open sentence to which the quantifier is being prefixed. If that open sentence contains an x, then we will use an x quantifier, either the universal one

(x)

or the existential one

($\exists$x)

So, given the open sentence

Fx

to obtain a closed sentence we could write either

$(x)Fx$ or $(\exists x)Fx$

Or given the open compound sentence

$(Ky \equiv Gw)$

we could get a closed sentence by using a combination of a y quantifier and a w quantifier, as in

$(y)(w)(Ky \equiv Gw)$

We can think of the individual variable in an open sentence like

Kz

as a *free variable*; it is one that can be *captured* or *bound* by the proper quantifier. In this case it takes one of the z quantifiers. So we could capture the free variable z in Kz by writing

$(\exists z)Kz$

Every free variable in an open sentence must be captured by a quantifier in order to generate a closed sentence. Thus given an open sentence like

$((Fx \supset Gx) \lor Kv)$

we need to prefix two quantifiers to generate a closed sentence. We could, for example, write

$(\exists x)(v)((Fx \supset Gx) \lor Kv)$

21:6 We can pull together all the things we have said in this module about quantifiers, predicate letters, name letters, and individual variables to generate a systematic definition of 'well-formed formula of predicate logic.' We will use the following special devices:
1. Individual variables: $\{x, y, z, w, v, x_1, y_1, \ldots\}$
2. Name letters: $\{a, b, c, d, \ldots, o, a_1, b_1, \ldots\}$
3. Predicate letters: $\{F, G, H, \ldots, S, F_1, G_1, \ldots\}$
4. Statement letters: $\{p, q, r, s, t, u, p_1, q_1, \ldots\}$
5. Truth-functional operators: $\{\sim, \lor, \&, \supset, \equiv\}$
6. Quantifiers: (v) and $(\exists v)$, where v is any individual variable
7. Grouping indicators: (and)

Here is our recursive definition:

A. A statement letter standing alone is a wff of predicate logic.
B. If ϕ is a predicate letter and v is a variable or name letter, then ϕv is a wff.
C. If A is a wff, then $(\sim A)$ is a wff.
D. If A is a wff and (Qv) is a quantifier, then $(Qv)A$ is a wff of predicate logic.

E. If A and B are wffs, then (A & B), (A ∨ B), (A ⊃ B), and (A ≡ B) are wffs of predicate logic.

F. Nothing is a wff of predicate logic unless it is built using only the above clauses.[6]

Here are some examples of wffs of predicate logic

p	Sw
(p & q)	(Sw ∨ Gw)
Fc	(~(p ⊃ Sw))
(~Fd)	(w)Fx
((~p) ∨ Ka)	(w)(z)Fx
(∃x)Fx	(y)p
(x)(Fx ⊃ Gx)	((x)Fy ≡ Fz)
(~(x)(~Fx))	(Hw ≡ (y)Gy)

21:7 Here is a list of formulas of predicate logic that are not well formed and a brief
explanation of how each fails to satisfy the definition.

1. x — The only letters that can stand alone and be wffs are statement letters.

2. wF — The predicate letter must occur to the left of an individual variable.

3. Gp — The only letter or symbol that can be written to the right of a predicate letter is an individual variable.

4. Fxy — Although a formula like this might be a wff in a more sophisticated logical system, in predicate logic we can write only one variable to the right of each predicate letter

5. (∃y) — A quantifier alone is not a wff; a quantifier can occur only as a prefix to another wff.

6. (∃x)Fx ∨ Gx — This is ambiguous because it is missing a set of parentheses. It could be either (∃x)(Fx ∨ Gx) or ((∃x)Fx ∨ Gx).

7. (p ∨ qr) — All the requirements for wffs of propositional logic apply to wffs of predicate logic—we cannot juxtapose two statement letters. If you are unsure about wffs of propositional logic review Module 14.

21:8.1 Every wff of propositional logic could be translated into an understandable
English sentence given an interpretation of its statement letters. However, not every
wff of predicate logic can be translated into an understandable English sentence.
For example, wffs that have superfluous quantifiers are not readily translated. Thus
wffs like

(x)(∃x)Fx
(x)(y)Fx
(w)q

cannot be sensibly translated. Also wffs that are not closed sentences cannot be

---

[6] You might wish to work Exs. 9 and 10 at this time.

sensibly translated. Thus we would have trouble making sensible statements out of things like these:

Fx
$(Fy \equiv (\exists x)Fx)$
$(Sw \supset p)$
$((x)Fx \lor Gx)$

21:8.2 Open and closed wffs Now that we have a systematic definition of wff we can generate a more systematic procedure for recognizing open and closed wffs. We can begin by comparing the *scope* or range of a quantifier to the scope or range of the ~. In propositional logic a ~ applies to the first wff to its right. In predicate logic a quantifier's *scope* is the first wff to its right. In the following examples the scope of $(\exists w)$ is underlined.

EG. 21.7 $(\exists w)\underline{Fw}$

EG. 21.8 $((\exists w)\underline{Hw} \supset Gw)$

EG. 21.9 $(\exists w)\underline{(Hw \supset Gw)}$

We can define a *free occurrence of an individual variable* as any one that does not occur in a quantifier and does not occur in the scope of a quantifier of that variable. Thus, in Eg. 21.7 there are two occurrences of w. Both are *bound occurrences* (i.e., not free). The first w is bound because it is part of the quantifier $(\exists w)$; the second w is bound because it occurs in the Fw which is the scope of $(\exists w)$. Now look at Eg. 21.8. There are three occurrences of w here. The first two are bound, but the w in Gw is free because Gw is not in the scope of any w quantifier. However, all three occurrences of w in Eg. 21.9 are bound. We can build on 21:5.4 and say that a *variable is free* in a wff if any of its occurrences in that wff is free. Thus w is a free variable in Eg. 21.8 but not in Egs. 21.7 or 21.9. We can then define a *closed wff* as a wff with no free variables in it. Similarly, an *open wff* is one having at least one free variable in it. In Module 22 we will discuss translation from English into closed wffs of predicate logic.

EXERCISES FOR MODULE 21
THE LANGUAGE OF PREDICATE LOGIC

Ex. 5 Let the universe be composed of $\{\square, 0, ¢, \$\}$. Let $a = \square, b = 0, c = ¢$, and $d = \$$. Let the extension of $N = \{\square, \$\}$; let the extension of $S = \{\square, 0, ¢, \$\}$; and let the extension of $K = \{\square, 0\}$. Using this interpretation determine the truth-value of each of the following wffs.

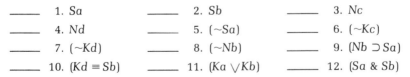

_____ 1. Sa	_____ 2. Sb	_____ 3. Nc
_____ 4. Nd	_____ 5. $(\sim Sa)$	_____ 6. $(\sim Kc)$
_____ 7. $(\sim Kd)$	_____ 8. $(\sim Nb)$	_____ 9. $(Nb \supset Sa)$
_____ 10. $(Kd \equiv Sb)$	_____ 11. $(Ka \lor Kb)$	_____ 12. $(Sa \& Sb)$

Ex. 6 Review the answers to Ex. 5 prior to doing Ex. 6. Given the same interpretation as was specified in Ex. 5 and given the following two equivalences which hold in the four-member universe $\{\square, 0, ¢, \$\}$,

$$((x)Kx \equiv (Ka \ \& \ Kb \ \& \ Kc \ \& \ Kd))$$
$$((\exists x)Kx \equiv (Ka \ \lor Kb \ \lor Kc \ \lor Kd))$$

indicate whether each of the following is true or false.

_____ 1. $(x)Kx$ _____ 2. $(\exists x)Kx$

_____ 3. $(\sim(x)Kx)$ _____ 4. $(\sim(\exists x)Kx)$

_____ 5. $(Sa \supset (x)Kx)$ _____ 6. $((x)Kx \ \lor (\exists x)Kx)$

Ex. 7 Identify the open sentences in the following list by 'OS,' the closed sentences by 'CS,' and the quantifying expressions by 'QE.'

_____ 1. x is a world champion.

_____ 2. There exists at least one member of the universe w such that . . .

_____ 3. Every z is such that . . .

_____ 4. z is too long.

_____ 5. Some y is such that . . .

_____ 6. Some x is such that x is moody.

_____ 7. Every x is such that if x is alive, then x is well.

_____ 8. x was not invited.

Ex. 8 Identify the open sentences among the following using 'OW' (for open wff), the closed sentences using 'CW,' and the quantifiers using 'Q.'

_____ 1. Fw _____ 2. (x)

_____ 3. $(w)Fw$ _____ 4. $(\exists v)$

_____ 5. $(x)(p \supset Fx)$ _____ 6. $(q \ \lor (x)Fx)$

_____ 7. $(Gw \supset Gy)$ _____ 8. $(\exists y)(Gw \supset Gy)$

_____ 9. $(\exists w)(\exists y)(Gw \supset Gy)$ _____ 10. $(q \equiv (\sim p))$

_____ 11. $((\exists y)Fy \ \lor Gy)$ _____ 12. $((\sim(x)Fx) \supset (q \ \& \ (\exists w)Fy))$

Ex. 9 Write 'wff' beside each of the wffs of predicate logic in the following list; otherwise write 'no.'

_____ 1. $(x)Fx$ _____ 2. $(p \supset q)$ _____ 3. $(\sim p)$

_____ 4. Fw _____ 5. $\sim(x)$ _____ 6. $(x)(\sim Kx)$

_____ 7. $(\exists x)(y)Fy$ _____ 8. $(Hw \ \lor Hz) \supset p$ _____ 9. $(x)q$

_____ 10. $(\exists \sim x)Fx$

Ex. 10 Here is a list of formulas that are not well formed. State the reason that each is not well formed and reconstruct each as a wff of predicate logic.

_____ 1. pq _____ 2. $(x)Fx \supset$ _____ 3. $Fz(\exists y)$

_____ 4. Op _____ 5. $Gw \ \& \ Gw$ _____ 6. $(\exists x)Fx \ \lor Hx$

_____ 7. $(\exists w)$ _____ 8. Hxw _____ 9. yH

_____ 10. z

Ex. 11 Construct five sample wffs of predicate logic each of which uses at least one quantifier and one truth-functional operator.

Ex. 5

1. T	2. T	3. F	4. T	5. F	6. T
7. T	8. T	9. T	10. F	11. T	12. T

If you missed two or more, review 21:3 to 21:4.1, Exs. 3 and 4.

Ex. 6

1. F (*Kc* and *Kd* are false).
2. T (*Ka* and *Kb* are true).
3. T [(x)*Kx* is false].
4. F [(∃x)*Kx* is true].
5. F [*Sa* is true and (x)*Kx* is false]; notice that all the rules for the truth-functional operators still apply.
6. T [(∃x)*Kx* is true].

The truth-functional relationships, which should be clear from Chapter 4, and the brief explanations in 21:5.1 should clarify these answers.

Ex. 7

1. OS	2. QE	3. QE	4. OS
5. QE	6. CS	7. CS	8. OS

If you missed any of these, review 21:5.2, 21:5.3, and 21:5.4.

Ex. 8

1. OW	2. Q
3. CW	4. Q
5. CW	6. CW

7. OW; both variables are free.   8. OW; *w* is free.
9. CW; there are no free variables in this wff.
10. CW; there are no free variables in this wff.
11. OW; *y* is a free variable here because the third occurrence of *y* is free in *Gy*, but in (∃y)(*Fy* ∨ *Gy*) the quantifier binds the third *y*, producing a closed wff.
12. OW; *y* is a free variable in this wff.

If you missed two or more of these, review 21:8.2.

Ex. 9

1. wff	2. wff	3. wff	4. wff	5. No
6. wff	7. wff	8. No	9. wff	10. No

If you missed any of these, review 21:6 and 21:7.

Ex. 10

1. This needs a logical operator and parentheses, as in (*p* & *q*). Two statement letters cannot stand side by side.
2. The ⊃ at the end either does not belong there at all, as in (x)*Fx*, or it requires some wff to its right, as in ((x)*Fx* ⊃ *p*).

3. The quantifier must occur to the left of a wff, as in $(\exists y)Fz$.
4. See item 3, 21:7. You might write Gw.
5. This needs outside parentheses: $(Gw \& Gw)$.
6. Either $((\exists x)Fx \lor Hx)$ or $(\exists x)(Fx \lor Hx)$; see item 6, 21:7.
7. $(\exists w)p$; see item 5, 21:7.
8. Hx or Hw; see item 4, 21:7.
9. Hy; see item 2, 21:7.
10. Fz; see item 1, 21:7.

If you had problems with Ex. 10, review 21:7 and 21:6.

Ex. 11 Here are some possible answers:

$(w)(Fx \supset Gx)$
$(\exists x)(Fx \& Gx)$
$(x)(Fx \supset (\sim Gx))$
$(\exists x)(Fx \& (\sim Gx))$
$((\exists x)Fx \supset p)$

Check your answers against the definition of a wff given in 21:6.

MODULE 22
TRANSLATION AND PREDICATE LOGIC

In this module we build on what you learned in Module 21 about translating individual inclusion and individual exclusion, and about writing wffs. Our aim is to learn how to move from English to closed wffs of predicate logic. Along the way we will clarify the ways in which the quantifiers relate to various universes.

● After reading Module 22 you should be able:

1. Given an English passage, to determine its possible universe of discourse
2. Given a universe of small finite size, to
   a. rewrite English statements of partial inclusion as disjunctions
   b. rewrite English statements of partial exclusion as disjunctions
   c. rewrite English statements of total inclusion as conjunctions
   d. rewrite English statements of total exclusion as conjunctions
3. Given a universe of small finite size and simple wffs of predicate logic that contain quantifiers, to rewrite these wffs without the use of quantifiers
4. Given a list of English sentences and a list of translations, to match with each English sentence its proper translation
5. Given a variety of relatively straightforward English statements (statements of individual, partial, or total inclusion; statements of individual, partial, or total exclusion; and statements asserting that a given class has or does not have members) to translate them into closed wffs of predicate logic
6. Given a list of English statements that contain minor complications of style, idiom, or logical structure, to translate them into closed wffs of predicate logic

22:1.1 In considering statements like "Kim is slim" and "Harry is merry" in Module 21 we focused on the classes they refer to and the members of those classes. We noted that the classes were the classes of slim persons and merry persons. In the faithful translation of arguments from English into wffs, it is important to take special note of the kinds of things you are talking about. For instance, it is not just slim things but slim *persons*, not just merry things but merry *persons* who are included in the discussion. Consider the following example.

EG. 22.1 Someone in this room is a little bit merry. John and Brenda haven't had a drop to drink. So it must be Harry.

You can easily understand this bit of conversation as an enthymemetic argument. Add the enthymemetic premises that there are only three persons in the room and only drinking will make them merry. Then, from all of this it certainly does follow that Harry is merry.

EG. 22.2 "But," said Mr. Slippery Sophist, "There was a mouse in the room too. How do you know we're not dealing here with merry Minerva Mouse?!"

What makes the Sophist's objection in Eg. 22.2 a misdirected comment? The presumption in Eg. 22.1 is that the only *individuals under discussion* are the human beings in the room. Given that assumption, the argument is certainly valid and whatever may be true about Minerva Mouse is simply not relevant.

It is important to note carefully that the arguments we construct using predicate logic repeatedly make *a presumption about the kind of individuals who are under discussion*. Example 22.1 presumes that the individuals are human beings in a certain room. Other arguments will make other presumptions. Some presumptions will be much broader, like "all things which have ever or will ever live"; and some narrower, like "only persons who have entered that room within the last 10 seconds."

22:1.2 Universe of discourse Logicians use a technical term to talk about the often very large groups of individuals who are possibly under discussion when members of specific classes are being mentioned. All the individuals who are possibly under discussion in a given argument or group of related arguments in a given passage comprise its *universe of discourse*. As you can probably see, the term universe of discourse is not completely arbitrary or stipulative. The ordinary sense of it is that in the discussion at hand the universe of our discourse is limited to certain groups (as in Eg. 22.2, where only people and not mice are under discussion).

Here are some more examples where context clarifies what the universe of discourse is.

EG. 22.3 Well, let's see Jimmy, you want a small, cuddly dog, your brother wants a dog he can train to hunt rabbits, your mother wants a friendly dog, and I want one that will cost less than $75. What kind do you think we should get?

EG. 22.4 Who can play this role? He's got to be heavy set, and capable of looking surly and walking with a swagger. But later in the film, when he's been crushed by circumstances, the sensitivity he shows has to be credible.

In Eg. 22.3 the final sentence is a question. Grammatically the sentence is indefinite about the kind of object the people should get. The class under discussion, however, is clearly the class of dogs, the idea being that the descriptions of what the family wants will fit some kind of dog. Parakeets and cobras do not count. Similarly, in Eg. 22.4, potential male actors are the universe of discourse.

Sometimes the context of a conversation or an argument will leave the range of the universe of discourse more or less vague. For instance, in Eg. 22.4 it is never clarified whether the race of the actor is important. It might be irrelevant, it might be crucial. The context simply is not sufficiently definite to tell. When this happens, you will be forced to make a decision. Since making the universe of discourse too narrow can have the undesirable result of overly constricting your logical options you should always specify the universe of discourse on the broad side rather than the narrow side. Maybe in Eg. 22.4 the universe of discourse is only Caucasian male actors, but you cannot know this from the context. Therefore, you should specify the universe of a discourse on the broader size as potential male actors. Don't be a victim of tunnel vision in logic.

EXERCISE 1

Below are five passages. For each passage determine the possible universes of discourse. Select your answers from the choices listed below each item.

_____ 1. Well, summertime is coming up again. This year sister says she wants to spend some time at the beach, brother wants to do some hiking, mother wants some leisure time, and father wants to camp. There's exactly two weeks of vacation time available for all this. How are we going to manage?
   A. Chairs   B. Family vacations   C. Small animals   D. Sports events

_____ 2. When you're trying a square knot, it's right over left and then left over right.
   A. Pieces of rope   B. Types of knots   C. Vegetables
   D. Union members

_____ 3. There's something of a tradition in our family. My father is a farmer, his father was a farmer, and his father was a farmer. And you want to know what I'm going to do when I'm an adult!
   A. Occupations   B. Family members   C. Men   D. Steelworkers
   E. Cats

_____ 4. Holmes reviewed the evidence, searching for an answer. Only three had a motive, but two of them had both the opportunity and the ability. No definite conclusion seemed to emerge.
   A. Detectives   B. Suspects   C. Policemen   D. Houses   E. Victims

_____ 5. Because of your illness you're way behind in your work, and here we are near the end of the term. What can I do? I can give you a withdrawal passing, for health reasons; I can help you try to make up the work; I can give you an incomplete and allow you to finish your work within 2 months. Have I missed anything?
   A. Professors   B. Students   C. Grade options   D. Vacations

ANSWERS TO EXERCISE 1

1. B   2. A, B   3. A, B, C   4. B   5. C

22:2.1 Partial inclusion Recall Eg. 22.1: "Someone in this room is a little bit merry." The class of individuals possibly under discussion, the universe of discourse, is the human beings in the room. What exactly does this example statement say about that universe of discourse? It says "There is a member of that universe of discourse (at least one) such that he or she is a little bit merry." The statement does not tell us which member it is. But it does assure us that within the universe of discourse, the class of individuals who are a little bit merry is not empty; the class has at least one member. Each of the following example statements is reworded to clarify the partial inclusion it asserts.

EG. 22.5   Some of the folks who have the ability to do this part are looking for work.

EG. 22.5′   There exists at least one individual within the universe of discourse of potential actors such that the person is in the class of those able to do the part and in the class of employment seekers.

EG. 22.6   Some gorillas are friendly.

EG. 22.6′   There exists at least one individual within the universe of discourse of wild animals such that it is in the classes of gorillas and friendly things.

EG. 22.7   Some spectators stayed until the end of the game.

EG. 22.7′   There exists at least one individual within the universe of discourse of people such that he or she is in the class of spectators and the class of those who stayed till the end of the game.

Observe that each of the three revised assertions (22.5′, 22.6′, and 22.7′) is composed of two distinct parts:

1. A quantifier expression: There exists at least one member of the relevant universe of discourse such that . . .
2. One or more predicate expressions (where there is more than one they are conjoined):

>   *it* is a member of the first class mentioned

and

>   *it* is a member of the second class mentioned.

Review Egs. 22.5′ to 22.7′ to confirm that both the quantifier expression and the open predicate expression(s) are in each.

These facts suggest how we can translate statements of partial inclusion.

1. Assign each predicate expression as the specific interpretation of a predicate letter:

> P = . . . is able to do the part
> L = . . . is an employment seeker

2. Write wffs for the open predicate expressions using the same individual variable in each:

> Px
> Lx

3. Conjoin those wffs:

   (Px & Lx)

4. Prefix an existential quantifier to capture the free occurrences of the individual variable in that conjunction.

EG. 22.5″ (∃x)(Px & Lx)

This wff says exactly what Eg. 22.5′ says.[7] Use this procedure to translate Egs. 22.6′ and 22.7′. Our translations are:

EG. 22.6″ Let F = . . . is a gorilla
            G = . . . is friendly
          (∃x)(Gx & Fx)

EG. 22.7″ Let S = . . . is a spectator
           M = . . . stayed till the end of the game
          (∃x)(Sx & Mx)

Your translations should be exactly like ours except for two possible variations.

1. You might have used different predicate letters to stand for the English predicate expressions.
2. You might have used a different individual variable throughout one or both of the wffs.

You might, for example, have translated Eg. 22.6′ as

EG. 22.6‴ J = . . . is a gorilla
          K = . . . is friendly
          (∃w)(Jw & Kw)

As long as you use the same individual variable throughout your wff, it doesn't make any difference which one you use.[8] The only concern is that the quantifier should capture both free occurrences in its scope formula, as in

(∃y)(Jy & Ky)

captures

---

[7] You do not want to use more than one individual variable in the translation because in an item like Eg. 22.5′ both predicate expressions apply to the *same* individual. If we translate Eg. 22.5′ as

    (∃x)(∃y)(Px & Ly)

we would really be saying:

> There is at least one person x and at least one person y such that x is an actor and y is out of work.

Clearly, though, this allows for x and y to be different people; but Eg. 22.5′ says that they are the same.

[8] The reason it doesn't make any difference is that variables are never given any specific interpretations. Only statement letters, name letters, and predicate letters are associated with specific English expressions (only these are interpreted). Variables, on the other hand, can range over all the members of the universe.

but not like

$(\exists w)(Jx \ \& \ Kx)$

➢ fails to capture anything in its scope formula

and not like

$(\exists x)Jx \ \& \ Kx$

➢ captures only in its scope formula Jx

22:2.2 Partial inclusion and finite universe Statements of partial exclusion are related to statements of individual inclusion. Consider the case of Mr. Worried Homebuilder.

EG. 22.8 Mr. W. Homebuilder saw the truck delivering the doors for the family room of his home. "Four doors," the driver told him. "Good, just as the plans say," he said. "Now, one is a glass door. I want you to be very careful getting it off the truck. I wonder when it will be coming off the truck." "Well," said his wife, somewhat annoyed with her husband's incessant worry, "Either it will come off first, or second, or third, or fourth."

And Ms. Homebuilder is very logical here. The universe of discourse in this case contains just four members, the four doors. Thus 'one of the doors coming off the truck will be the glass door' is logically equivalent to 'either the first one off will be it or the second one or the third one or the fourth one.'

As long as we have a finite universe of say n members, then we can regard a closed existentially quantified wff as a disjunction which ascribes the predicate expression to either one or another member of that n-membered universe. For example, given a universe of n balloons and the closed existentially quantified wff

$(\exists x)Px$

where $P = $ ". . . is purple," '$(\exists x)Px$' means

Either the first balloon is purple, or the second balloon is purple, or the third balloon is purple, . . . , or the nth balloon is purple.

In other words if our universe has five members, $a, \ldots, e$, then

$((\exists x)Px \equiv (Pa \vee Pb \vee Pc \vee Pd \vee Pe))$[9]

Given the truth-functional operation of disjunction, we know that

$(Pa \vee Pb \vee Pc \vee Pd \vee Pe)$

---

[9] We omitted parentheses so as to make the overall logical structure easier to see. The parentheses we omitted are logically superfluous because $(Pa \vee (Pb \vee Pc))$ is equivalent to $((Pa \vee Pb) \vee Pc)$.

is true if any one of its individual inclusion statement units is true.[10] And, if one is true, say Pe, then it is also true that there is at least one purple object in that universe, in other words

$(\exists x)Px$

Statements of partial inclusion are translated as existentially quantified closed wffs, like

$(\exists x)(Fx \& Gx)$

Given a universe of three members (or any finite universe) we can specify exactly what such a wff means for that universe. Suppose our universe were {Avery, Buford, Cleo} and our English was

EG. 22.9 Someone who forgot apologized.

The English is synonymous with the following.

EG. 22.9′ There is at least one member of the universe such that he or she forgot and he or she apologized.

That means:

Either Avery forgot and apologized, or Buford forgot and apologized, or Cleo forgot and apologized.

If we let F = ". . . forgot" and G = ". . . apologized," then Eg. 22.9′ is translated as

EG. 22.9″ $(\exists x)(Fx \& Gx)$

If we let a = Avery, b = Buford, and c = Cleo, then Eg. 22.9″ means

$((Fa \& Ga) \lor (Fb \& Gb) \lor (Fc \& Gc))$

If the universe had four people in it [say David (d) were added], then Eg. 22.9″ would mean

$((Fa \& Ga) \lor (Fb \& Gb) \lor (Fc \& Gc) \lor (Fd \& Gd))$

If Emily (e) were added, then the following equivalence would hold:

$[(\exists x)(Fx \& Gx) \equiv ((Fa \& Ga) \lor (Fb \lor Gb) \lor (Fc \& Gc) \lor (Fd \& Gd) \lor (Fe \& Ge))]$

But if the universe were of indefinite or infinite size, we would not be able to specify the equivalent disjunction.

---

[10] Remember that the truth-functional $\lor$ also allows for more than one of the alternatives to be true.

Translate each of the five English statements below into an existentially quantified wff of predicate logic. A universe and a specific interpretation for various letters are supplied as guides for each.

1. There is at least one black horse.
2. Some children are adopted.
3. Some people drink to excess.
4. Some people abuse children.
5. Jerome painted one of these chairs.

Universe	Predicate letters interpreted
1. Horses	R = . . . is black
2. People	K = . . . is a child
	F = . . . is adopted
3. People	I = . . . is one who drinks to excess
4. Unidentified objects	P = . . . is a person
	H = . . . abuses children
5. Unidentified objects	J = . . . is a chair Jerome painted

ANSWERS TO EXERCISE 2

1. $(\exists x)Rx$
2. $(\exists y)(Ky \mathrel{\&} Fy)$
3. $(\exists z)Iz$
4. $(\exists w)(Pw \mathrel{\&} Hw)$
5. $(\exists x)Jx$

Your answers should be exactly like ours except perhaps for the individual variable you chose to use in each. In cases like item 3 we already know that the one who drinks is a person because of the universe given for item 3. Item 5 is about chairs; it says at least one of them is in a certain class, the class of those Jerome painted.[11]

EXERCISE 3

Rewrite each of the English statements given in Ex. 2 as a disjunction using the finite universe specified below for each.

1. Universe = {Secretariat, Ruffian}
2. Universe = {Carol, Christopher, Jerome, Bethany}
3. Universe = {Roger, Stephen, Anne, Antoinette}
4. Universe = {object 1, object 2, object 3}
5. Universe = {chair 1, chair 2, chair 3}

---

[11] '. . . is a chair Jerome painted' is here a predicate, but it could be recast as a relationship between an object and a painter named Jerome. However to express that *relationship* we would have to go beyond predicate logic into the next level of logic, the logic of relations.

ANSWERS TO EXERCISE 3

1. Either Secretariat is black or Ruffian is black.
2. Either Carol is an adopted child, or Christopher is an adopted child, or Jerome is an adopted child, or Bethany is an adopted child.
3. Either Roger drinks to excess, or Stephen drinks to excess, or Anne drinks to excess, or Antoinette drinks to excess. (You might have written the more idiomatic "Either Roger, Stephen, Anne, or Antoinette drinks to excess.")
4. Either object 1 is a person and he or she abuses children, or object 2 is a person and he or she abuses children, or object 3 is a person and he or she abuses children.
5. Either chair 1 is a chair Jerome painted or chair 2 is a chair Jerome painted or chair 3 is a chair Jerome painted.

EXERCISE 4

Rewrite the wffs in the answers to Ex. 2 as disjunctions using the universes given in Ex. 3. You may omit superfluous parentheses. For the sake of uniformity always name the objects in the universe using our name letters in alphabetical order as needed.

ANSWERS TO EXERCISE 4

1. $(Ra \lor Rb)$
2. $((Ka \& Fa) \lor (Kb \& Fb) \lor (Kc \& Fc) \lor (Kd \& Fd))$
3. $(Ia \lor Ib \lor Ic \lor Id)$
4. $((Pa \& Ha) \lor (Pb \& Hb) \lor (Pc \& Hc))$
5. $(Ja \lor Jb \lor Jc)$

22:2.3 Road map We have just learned how to translate partial inclusion statements into wffs. We will now develop comparable skills for statements of partial exclusion, total inclusion, and total exclusion. When we finish treating these other types of statements, we will be able to specify more generalized translation procedures.

22:3.1 Partial exclusion 'Some gorillas are friendly' asserts that within the universe of discourse, say of wild animals, there is at least one gorilla (and maybe more) who is friendly. The partial exclusion statement in the following example is parallel.

EG. 22.10 Some gorillas are not friendly.

We can start by rewriting Eg. 22.10 as "Within the universe of discourse, say of wild animals, there is at least one gorilla . . . ." This is exactly what we said in translating the partial inclusion. The only difference between the two statements is what is said about that gorilla. Rather clearly the partial exclusion statement says it is *not* friendly, whereas the partial inclusion statement says it is friendly. Thus the partial inclusion statement can be rewritten as follows:

EG. 22.6′ There exists at least one individual within the universe of discourse of wild animals such that it is a gorilla and it is friendly.

The partial exclusion statement is rewritten as follows.

EG. 22.10' There exists at least one individual within the universe of discourse of wild animals such that it is a gorilla and it is not the case that it is friendly.

The translation into symbolism is accomplished using the procedure given in 22:2.1. Let

    G = . . . is a gorilla
    F = . . . is friendly

We will translate the open predicate expression

    It is false that it is friendly

as

    $(\sim Fx)$

Thus the translation of the partial exclusion of Eg. 22.10' is as follows.

EG. 22.10″ $(\exists x)(Gx\ \&\ (\sim Fx))$

Our translation of the partial inclusion statement Eg. 22.6 was

EG. 22.6″ $(\exists x)(Gx\ \&\ Fx)$

The only difference is that in the exclusion statement the second internal wff Fx is negated.

EXERCISE 5

Translate the following into wffs of predicate logic. Indicate your interpretations of the predicate letters you use. Indicate the universe of discourse you use.

1. Some children are not adopted.
2. Some people do not drink to excess.
3. Some of the actors who have the ability to do the part are not seeking work.
4. Some messengers cannot be trusted.
5. There are untrustworthy messengers.
6. Some who are not farmers are not impressed.

ANSWERS TO EXERCISE 5

1. Universe = people
    K = . . . is a child
    F = . . . is adopted
    $(\exists x)(Kx\ \&\ (\sim Fx))$

2. Universe = people
    I = . . . drinks to excess
    $(\exists x)(\sim Ix)$

Or:

Universe = unidentified objects
P = . . . is a person
I = . . . drinks to excess
$(\exists x)(Px \ \& \ (\sim Ix))$

3. Universe = actors
R = . . . has the ability to do the part
L = . . . is seeking work
$(\exists x)(Rx \ \& \ (\sim Lx))$

Or:

Universe = people
N = . . . is an actor
R = . . . has the ability to do the part
L = . . . is seeking work
$(\exists x)((Nx \ \& \ Rx) \ \& \ (\sim Lx))$

4. Universe = people
M = . . . is a messenger
I = . . . can be trusted
$(\exists x)(Mx \ \& \ (\sim Ix))$

Or:

Universe = messengers
I = . . . can be trusted
$(\exists x)(\sim Ix)$

Or:

Universe = unidentified objects
P = . . . is a person
M = . . . is a messenger
I = . . . can be trusted
$(\exists x)((Px \ \& \ Mx) \ \& \ (\sim Ix))$

In this universe we use P to show that the claim is being made about messengers who are people rather than, say, carrier pigeons, which may be reliable or unreliable, but are not untrustworthy in quite the way people can be.

5. The answer is the same as item 4. The only difference is in the English style not the logical style.

6. Universe = people
F = . . . is a farmer
I = . . . is impressed
$(\exists x)((\sim Fx) \ \& \ (\sim Ix))$

Or (more awkwardly and unintuitively):

Universe = all objects that are not farmers
P = . . . is a person
I = . . . is impressed
$(\exists x)(Px \ \& \ (\sim Ix))$

22:3.2 Hints on translating Three things are introduced in Ex. 5 which you should always be alert to when translating any statement into a wff.

1. There is a variety of English styles and idioms that can be used to express the same logical structure. Note for example, items 4 and 5 in the exercise. We could have even added 'not all messengers are trustworthy' as still another way to say what 4 says.
2. The precise translation and especially its complexity in terms of the number of predicate letters you need depends a great deal on the universe of discourse you select. Note for example the alternatives presented in the answers to items 2, 3 4, and 6.
3. The power of the logical notation is not limited to simply representing clear cases of the four types of statements we have covered so far in Modules 21 and 22 (individual and partial exclusion). Along the way we developed tools to handle a variety of existentially quantified statements. Those that say:
   a. A specific class has at least one member, which are usually translated

   $(\exists x)Fx$

   b. At least one member of a universe is not a member of a specific class, as in

   $(\exists x)(\sim Fx)$

   c. At least one member of the universe is not a member of either of two specific classes, as in

   $(\exists x)((\sim Fx) \& (\sim Gx))$

   d. At least one member of the universe is a member of both of two classes (partial inclusion), as in

   $(\exists x)(Fx \& Gx)$

   e. At least one member of the universe is a member of one class but not of another class (partial exclusion), as in

   $(\exists x)(Fx \& (\sim Gx))$
   $(\exists x)((\sim Fx) \& Gx)$

22:3.3 Existential quantification and a finite universe Everything we said about how to rewrite statements of partial inclusion as disjunctions in 22:2.2 applies to statements of partial exclusion. Say our universe is {Brent, Mark, Donna}; then our statement is as follows.

EG. 22.11 Some messenger is not to be trusted.

Our rewrite would be the following.

EG. 22.11′ Either Brent is a messenger and he is not to be trusted, or Mark is a messenger and he is not to be trusted, or Donna is a messenger and she is not to be trusted.

Using the predicate letters as interpreted in item 4, Ex. 5, above, we can change Eg. 22.11 into the following wff.

EG. 22.11″ $(\exists w)(Mw \& (\sim Iw))$

This wff can be rewritten as a disjunction using the three-membered universe and interpreting the name letters

  b = Brent
m = Mark
  d = Donna

as follows.

EG. 22.11''' $[(Mb \ \& \ (\sim Ib)) \lor (Mm \ \& \ (\sim Im)) \lor (Md \ \& \ (\sim Id))]$

EXERCISE 6

Rewrite each of the following as disjunctions using the three-member universe {Karen, Bernard, Irma} for the English statements and {k, b, i} for the wffs.

1. Some people are loving.
2. $(\exists x)(Px \ \& \ Lx)$
3. There are people.
4. $(\exists x)Px$
5. Some things are neither people nor loving.
6. $(\exists x)((\sim Px) \ \& \ (\sim Lx))$
7. Some unloving things are imaginative.
8. $(\exists x)((\sim Lx) \ \& \ Ix)$

ANSWERS TO EXERCISE 6

1. Either Karen is a loving person, or Bernard is a loving person, or Irma is a loving person.
2. $((Pk \ \& \ Lk) \lor (Pb \ \& \ Lb) \lor (Pi \ \& \ Li))$
3. Either Karen, Bernard, or Irma is a person.
4. $(Pk \lor Pb \lor Pi)$
5. Either Karen is neither a person nor loving, or Bernard is neither a person nor loving, or Irma is neither a person nor loving.
6. $[((\sim Pk) \ \& \ (\sim Lk)) \lor ((\sim Pb) \ \& \ (\sim Lb)) \lor ((\sim Pi) \ \& \ (\sim Li))]$
7. Either Karen is unloving but imaginative, or Bernard is unloving but imaginative, or Irma is unloving but imaginative.
8. $[((\sim Lk) \ \& \ Ik) \lor ((\sim Lb) \ \& \ Ib) \lor ((\sim Li) \ \& \ Ii)]$

22:4.1 Total inclusion Consider the following example.

EG. 22.12 Everyone with the ability to do the part is looking for work.

Our first move in translation is to restate Eg. 22.12 so as to make clear its quantifier expression and its predicate expressions. Beginning with its quantifier expression, we find it necessary to speak about *all* the members of the universe of discourse using:

> For every member of the universe of discourse it is true that . . .

Asking what is true of all of them, we get the following conditional:

If they have the ability to do the part, then they are looking for work.

There are two predicate expressions in that conditional. They are

1. . . . has the ability to do the part.
2. . . . is looking for work.

The total inclusion statement tells us that every member of the first group (the class of those who have the ability to do the part) is a member of the second (those who are looking for work). But, given the contemporary interpretation, the total inclusion statement does not tell us that there actually are any members of the universe who are members of the class of those who have this ability. In other words, the total inclusion statement says that "considering *every* member of the universe, it is true that *if* they are members of the first class, *then* they are members of the second class."

To translate a statement of total inclusion perform the following steps.

1. Identify its universe of discourse and its predicate expressions.
   Universe = people
   $P = $ . . . has the ability to do the part
   $L = $ . . . is looking for work

2. Write wffs for the open predicate expressions using the same individual variable for each.
   Px
   Lx

3. Form the conditional "if the first, then the second," where the first is the open sentence derived from the subject of the original statement and the second is the open sentence derived from the predicate of the original statement.
   $(Px \supset Lx)$

4. Prefix a universal quantifier to capture the free occurrences of the individual variables in that conditional.

Applying this to Eg. 22.12, we get:

EG. 22.12″ $(x)(Px \supset Lx)$

Here are two more examples of translating total inclusion statements.

EG. 22.13 All of us will die.

EG. 22.14 Every adopted child is a wanted child.

Rewriting these two examples to make clearer their quantifier and predicate expressions we have the following.

EG. 22.13′ For every member of the universe it is true that if he or she is one of us, then he or she will die.

EG. 22.14′ For every member of the universe it is true that if he or she is adopted, then he or she is wanted.

EG. 22.13″ Universe = people
   $O = \ldots$ is one of us
   $M = \ldots$ will die
   $(x)(Ox \supset Mx)$

EG. 22.14″ Universe = children
   $F = \ldots$ is adopted
   $S = \ldots$ is wanted
   $(y)(Fy \supset Sy)$

As with our earlier translations, changes in the specified universe can alter the translation. In Eg. 22.14″ we could have changed our specifications as follows.

EG. 22.14″*a* Universe = adopted children
   $S = \ldots$ is wanted
   $(y)Sy$

This says that every member of the universe of adopted children is a member of the class of wanted adopted children. Or we could have done the following.

EG. 22.14″*b* Universe = unidentified objects
   $P = \ldots$ is a person
   $F = \ldots$ is adopted
   $S = \ldots$ is wanted
   $(y)((Py \ \& \ Fy) \supset Sy))$

which says that if anything is both adopted and a person, then it is wanted.

22:4.2 Total exclusion Statements of total exclusion are easy to translate given that they translate as universally quantified conditionals (just as statements of total inclusion did). The sole difference is that the predicate expression that occurs as the consequent of that conditional is negated. Consider the following example.

EG. 22.15 No gorillas are friendly.

Rewriting it to express its quantifier and predicate expressions we have

EG. 22.15′ For *every* member of the universe it is true that *if* it is a gorilla, then it is *not* friendly.

Using the procedure in 22:4.1 we can translate Eg. 22.15′ as follows.

EG. 22.15″ Universe = wild animals
   $G = \ldots$ is a gorilla
   $F = \ldots$ is friendly
   $(x)(Gx \supset (\sim Fx))$

Consider the following examples.

EG. 22.16 None of the spectators stayed till the end of the game.

EG. 22.16′ For every member of the universe it is true that if he or she is a spectator, then he or she did not stay till the end of the game.

EG. 22.16″ Universe = people
   $S = \ldots$ is a spectator
   $G = \ldots$ stayed till the end of the game
   $(w)(Sw \supset (\sim Gw))$

A third example is as follows.

EG. 22.17 If anyone wins the contest then he or she will not receive an honorable mention award.

Rewriting Eg. 22.17 we have the following.

EG. 22.17′ For every member of the universe of people it is true that if he or she wins the contest, then he or she will not receive an honorable mention award.

Translating, we get

EG. 22.17″ Universe = people
$R = \ldots$ wins the contest
$G = \ldots$ receives an honorable mention award
$(z)(Rz \supset (\sim Gz))$

EXERCISE 7

Here are some statements of total inclusion and statements of total exclusion; translate each.

1. All friendly things are gorillas.
2. Every person will die.
3. No advertising techniques work.
4. There are no gorillas.
5. There isn't anything but life (all members of the universe are alive).
6. Adopted children are loved.
7. Nobody wants to lose.
8. Spoiled food is dangerous.
9. The porpoise is a creature capable of thought.
10. Porpoises can think.

ANSWERS TO EXERCISE 7

1. Universe = unidentified objects
   $F = \ldots$ is friendly
   $G = \ldots$ is a gorilla
   $(y)(Fy \supset Gy)$

   Or:

   Universe = friendly things
   $(y)Gy$

2. Universe = people
   $M = \ldots$ will die
   $(y)My$

   Or:

   Universe = unidentified objects
   $P = \ldots$ is a person
   $(y)(Py \supset My)$

4. Universe = animals
   G = . . . is a gorilla
   (x)(~Gx)

5. Universe = everything
   L = . . . is life
   (x)Lx

9. Universe = animals
   P = . . . is a porpoise
   K = . . . is capable of thought
   (x)(Px ⊃ Kx)

10. This is the same as item 9; note that this change in English style does not create a change in logical structure.

22:4.3 The universal quantifier and a finite universe Suppose we know that every car will break down in less than 5 years. Given that general fact and the fact that there are only three cars in the universe, what statements of individual inclusion can we infer? We can infer a conjunction of statements of individual inclusion:

Car 1 will break down in less than 5 years, *and* car 2 will break down in less than 5 years, *and* car 3 will, too.

Or, given the fact that there are two children in the house, Karen and Mark, and given the claim "Every child in this house is intelligent," what can you infer? You can infer the conjunction

Karen is intelligent and Mark is intelligent.

If, instead, you were given a general claim, like "None of the children in this house deserve to be punished," we could infer a conjunction of individual exclusion statements.

Mark does not deserve to be punished and Karen does not deserve to be punished.

The universal quantifier is to conjunction as the existential quantifier is to disjunction. In other words. When given (∃x)Fx and the universe {a, b, c} we said that

$$((∃x)Fx \equiv (Fa \lor Fb \lor Fc))$$

So, given (x)Fx and the same universe we get

$$((x)Fx \equiv (Fa \mathbin{\&} Fb \mathbin{\&} Fc))$$

The formula (x)Fx asserts 'every member of the universe is an F.' So, if our universe is {a, b, c}, then our formula relative to that universe says "a is an F, b is an F, and c is an F." Given a universe with four members {a, b, c, d}, the formula relative to that universe says

$$(Fa \mathbin{\&} Fb \mathbin{\&} Fc \mathbin{\&} Fd)$$

In general, given any universally quantified formula and any finite universe, we can express that universally quantified formula as a conjunction. If the original formula is of the structure $(x)A$, we take the A formula (the scope formula) and simply replace its free occurrences of x with a name letter. Do this once for each member of the universe, conjoining the resulting closed wffs. Less theoretically here is a range of examples. In each case we will use the universe $\{a, b, c\}$.

1. For statements asserting that all the members of the universe are members of a given class, $(y)Gy$, write:

   $(Ga \ \& \ Gb \ \& \ Gc)$

2. For statements asserting that none of the members of the universe are members of a given class, $(y)(\sim Gy)$, write:

   $((\sim Ga) \ \& \ (\sim Gb) \ \& \ (\sim Gc))$

3. For statements of total inclusion, $(w)(Fw \supset Gw)$, write:

   $((Fa \supset Ga) \ \& \ (Fb \supset Gb) \ \& \ (Fc \supset Gc))$

4. For statements of total exclusion, $(w)(Fw \supset (\sim Gw))$, write:

   $[(Fa \supset (\sim Ga)) \ \& \ (Fb \supset (\sim Gb)) \ \& \ (Fc \supset (\sim Gc))]$

5. For statements asserting that every member of the universe which is not a member of one class is a member of a second class, $(x)((\sim Fx) \supset Gx)$, write

   $[((\sim Fa) \supset Ga) \ \& \ ((\sim Fb) \supset Gb) \ \& \ ((\sim Fc) \supset Gc)]$

   An English example of this type of statement is

   Everyone who isn't on time deserves a fine.

6. For statements asserting that every member of the universe which is not a member of one class is not a member of a second class, $(x)((\sim Fx) \supset (\sim Gx))$, write

   $[((\sim Fa) \supset (\sim Ga)) \ \& \ ((\sim Fb) \supset (\sim Gb)) \ \& \ ((\sim Fc) \supset (\sim Gc))]$

   An English example of this type of statement is

   Everyone who isn't on time deserves not to participate.

EXERCISE 8

Rewrite each of the following as conjunctions using the two-member universe $\{you, me\}$ for the English and $\{c, d\}$ for the wffs.

1. Everyone who is loving is rich.
2. $(x)(Lx \supset Rx)$
3. Nobody who is rich is hungry.
4. $(x)(Rx \supset (\sim Hx))$
5. No one is rich.
6. $(x)(\sim Rx)$
7. Every person who is not loving is poor.
8. $(y)((\sim Ly) \supset Py)$

1. If you are loving then you are rich, and if I'm loving then I'm rich.
2. $((Lc \supset Rc) \ \& \ (Ld \supset Rd))$
3. If you are rich then you are not hungry, and if I am rich then I am not hungry.
4. $[(Rc \supset (\sim Hc)) \ \& \ (Rd \supset (\sim Hd))]$
5. You and I are not rich.
6. $((\sim Rc) \ \& \ (\sim Rd))$
7. If you are not loving then you are poor, and if I am not loving then I am poor.
8. $[((\sim Lc) \supset Pc) \ \& \ ((\sim Ld) \supset Pd)]$

22:5.1 Translating to predicate logic In order to translate from English into closed wffs of predicate logic you can rely on the procedures already given in this module. These procedures can, however, be generalized into the following translation procedure.

Given an English statement:

First Reword it as necessary so as to (1) express whatever quantifier expressions it has as either the existential or the universal quantifier, and (2) isolate its predicate expressions.

Second Ascertain the truth-functional structure of the reworded statement and replace its truth-functional English words with the appropriate logical operators. Use parentheses to preserve grouping.

Third Specify a universe of discourse and then develop a "dictionary" which lists the specific interpretation for whatever name letters, predicate letters, or statement letters may be needed.

Fourth Replace quantifier expressions with the appropriate quantifier notation (where appropriate use & with the existential quantifier and $\supset$ with the universal quantifier). Replace names, predicate expressions, and statement units with the name letters, predicate letters, and statement letters needed, depending upon the interpretation given in step four. Use individual variables as needed to write open predicate wffs (of the form Fx) and to capture free occurrences of variables in those wffs by appropriate quantifiers.

Fifth Check that the resulting formula is a closed wff, that it preserves original grouping, and that it has no vacuous quantifiers [i.e., quantifiers that either capture no variables at all, as in $(y)Fx$, or which purport to capture variables that are already captured, as in $(y)(\exists y)Fy$].

22:5.2 Here are some examples of translations done using this procedure.

EG. 22.18 Every Tuesday we eat stew.

    1. For every member of the universe it is true that if it is a Tuesday then it is a day on which we eat stew.
    2. Truth-functional structure: statement unit of total inclusion
    3. Universe = days
       $F = \ldots$ is a Tuesday
       $S = \ldots$ is a day on which we eat stew
    4. $(y)(Fy \supset Sy)$

5. Check off: is a closed wff; preserves original grouping; has no vacuous quantifiers.

EG. 22.19 Either someone will give in or everyone who fights will suffer.

1. Either there is at least one member of the universe such that he or she will give in, or for every member of the universe it is true that if he or she fights then he or she will suffer.
2. $(p \lor q)$, where p is a statement that a certain class has members and q is a statement of total inclusion.
3. Universe = people
   $F = \ldots$ is one who fights
   $G = \ldots$ is one who gives in
   $S = \ldots$ is one who suffers
4. $((\exists y)Gy \lor (y)(Fy \supset Sy))$
5. Check off: is a closed wff; preserves grouping (i.e., is a disjunction); has no vacuous quantifiers.

If the wff had been written $(\exists y)(Gy \lor (y)(Fy \supset Sy))$, the structure would have been wrongly altered from a disjunction to an existential quantification.

EG. 22.20 Only hungry people eat lunch on Tuesday.

1. Of every member of the universe it is true that if they eat on Tuesday, then they are hungry.
2. Statement unit of total inclusion.
3. Universe = people
   $N = \ldots$ is one who eats on Tuesday
   $H = \ldots$ is one who is hungry
4. $(w)(Nw \supset Hw)$
5. Check off: $\checkmark \checkmark \checkmark$

When you are translating into symbolic notation remember that the meanings of statement letters, name letters, and predicate letters remain constant within any given interpretation. However, no interpretation is assigned to individual variables. They, as used in the quantifiers, can range over the entire universe, over any individual in it. Because of this it makes no difference which individual variable you choose to use in a given closed wff. For example, you can say "Every person is friendly or somebody isn't" (universe = "infinite set of unidentifiable objects," $P = "\ldots$ is a person," $F = "\ldots$ is friendly") using any of the following wffs:

$[(y)(Py \supset Fy) \lor (\exists x)(Px \& (\sim Fx))]$
$[(z)(Pz \supset Fz) \lor (\exists x)(Px \& (\sim Fx))]$
$[(v)(Pv \supset Fv) \lor (\exists v)(Pv \& (\sim Fv))]$

22:6.1 In dealing with English statements we are often faced with a wide variety of ways of expressing the quantifiers. Throughout this module we have used different examples so that the quantifiers have been expressed in a variety of ways. We wish to focus here on only two variations in style that have strong effects on logical structure.

22:6.2 Quasi-numerical expressions Besides the two quantifiers ('every' and 'at least one') which we can handle in predicate logic there are a number of other natural-language quantifier expressions. Some, like the following, specify definite limits as to the number of members of the universe being referred to:

Exactly one, exactly two, exactly three, etc.
At least one, at least two, at least three, etc.
At most one, at most two, at most three, etc.

Of these we can handle only 'at least one' with full adequacy in predicate logic. If we moved to the logic of relations we could comfortably handle all the others in the above list. Other English quantifier expressions are even more problematic. These others, called *quasi-numerical* quantifiers, set only vague limits on the amount of the universe of discourse they refer to. Here are some examples:

A few	most	nearly every
a lot	lots of	only a few
several	many	more than most
quite a few	almost all	a handful

These create special problems for formal logic since their logical force differs in universes of different sizes. For example, 'a few of us want to go' is a stronger claim if you are talking about five or six people but a weaker claim if your universe is fifty or sixty people. We are not able to adequately deal with quasi-numerical quantifiers (except 'some') in any standard system of formal logic. However, many of the arguments that these occur in are able to be evaluated in terms of their content rather than their structure.

22:6.3 Only This word is exceptionally powerful. Consider the differences between each of the following English statements.

EG. 22.21 We eat meat only on Tuesday.

EG. 22.22 We eat only meat on Tuesday.

EG. 22.23 We only eat meat on Tuesday.

EG. 22.24 Only we eat meat on Tuesday.

These can be restated as follows:

EG. 22.21' If it's a day we're eating meat, then it's Tuesday.

EG. 22.22' If we are eating something on Tuesday, then it's meat.

EG. 22.23' If there's anything we are doing to or about meat on Tuesday, then it's eating it.

EG. 22.24' If there is anyone who is eating meat on Tuesday, then it is we.

Let's compare these examples to each other. In each case the expression that follows 'only' is the sentence's predicate; the other parts of the sentence form its subject. Moreover, each of these examples is a total inclusion sentence that is best rewritten using the conditional substructure. The fact that these are total inclusion statements is only a sidelight. We can find the word 'only' in other types of statement units.

EG. 22.25 Some books are only brown.

EG. 22.26 Some who are not loved deserve only care.

EG. 22.27 Only some dogs are green.

While still others are truth-functional compounds; for example:

EG. 22.28 p only if q.

These five examples can be restated as follows.

EG. 22.25' There is at least one book and it is brown and it is no color besides brown.

EG. 22.26' There is at least one person such that he or she is not loved and he or she deserves care and that is all that he or she deserves.

EG. 22.27' Some dogs are green, and some are not.

EG. 22.28' If p, then q.

It is always important to restate an English statement into a format that makes its logical structure clear before one sets about representing that structure using symbolic notation. This little experiment with the unusually tricky word 'only' should serve to illustrate how logically diverse English is and how subtle differences in word order can cause serious differences in logical structure.

EXERCISES FOR MODULE 22
TRANSLATION AND PREDICATE LOGIC

Ex. 9 Below, on the left, are eighteen English statements. On the right are eighteen symbolizations. In the symbolizations the first predicate expression in a statement is symbolized by F, the second by G, etc.; the first-mentioned individual by a, the second by b, etc. Identify the correct translation on the right for each of the statements on the left.

1. Robert does not joke a lot.
2. Janice will come but Terri should not be invited.
3. Either Baltimore will win eighty games or Baltimore will lose the pennant.
4. If Carrie enters, she'll win the race.
5. Jack passes his courses if, and only if, he attends them.
6. Janice and Terri will come.
7. Alice and Betty like chocolate but Frances does not.
8. It is false that if George came he made a fool of himself.
9. Gilbert likes women and food.
10. If my spouse lets the issue ride, I will not be satisfied.
11. Someone is coming.
12. Everyone is here.
13. Nobody cares.
14. Some brooms drop straw.
15. All brooms drop straw.
16. No brooms drop straw.

A. $((Fa \ \& \ Fb) \ \& \ (\sim Fc))$

B. $(Fa \supset (\sim Gb))$

C. $(\sim(Fa \supset Ga))$

D. $(\sim Fa)$

E. $(Fa \equiv Ga)$

F. $(Fa \ \& \ Fb)$

G. $(Fa \ \& \ (\sim Gb))$

H. $(Fa \lor (\sim Ga))$

I. $(Fa \ \& \ Ga)$

J. $(Fa \supset Ga)$

K. $(y)Fy$

L. $(\exists x)Fx$

M. $(\exists y)(\sim Fy)$

N. $(\exists z)(Fz \ \& \ (\sim Gz))$

O. $(x)(Fx \supset (\sim Gx))$

P. $(w)(Fw \supset Gw)$

17. Some brooms do not drop straw.   Q. (∃z)(Fz & Gz)
18. Someone is not coming.   R. (x)(~Fx)

Ex. 10 Translate each of the following. Supply specific interpretations for statement letters, name letters, and predicate letters as needed.

1. Gary likes bridge.
2. Marcel likes bridge and he dances too.
3. Cheryl never plays pool.
4. Tom is not a very good cheerleader.
5. A prisoner will be punished.
6. All the prisoners will be punished.
7. The books you want are all upstairs.
8. *Proverbs* is not a book of history.
9. Some of your friends did not accept the invitation.
10. Not every eunuch is sad.
11. At least one of the kids is crying.
12. Everything I have I owe to my mother.
13. The bear is a carnivore.
14. Lawyers are never expensive.
15. There isn't even one negligent lawyer.
16. Building a house involves making many decisions.
17. Only the hardworking deserve to be rewarded.
18. None but the pure deserve the chaste.
19. There are no ministers.
20. Everything is beautiful.

Ex. 11 Here are fifteen statements. Each is followed by two alleged restatements of it. One restatement is logically equivalent to the original, the other is not. Choose the one that is equivalent. Many of the correct answers have not been taught directly. This exercise challenges you to be sharp and logical. If you are, then you will infer the correct answers.

_____ 1. Not every philosopher is wise.
    A. Every philosopher is not wise.
    B. There is at least one philosopher who is not wise.

_____ 2. No people are angels.
    A. People are not all angels.
    B. No angels are people.

_____ 3. One of the triplets, Harry, Larry, and Terry, saw me.
    A. Harry saw me or Larry saw me or Terry saw me.
    B. Harry, Larry, and Terry all saw me.

_____ 4. An apple a day keeps the doctor away.
    A. Anybody who eats an apple every day remains healthy.
    B. If some person doesn't eat apples regularly, that person will get sick.

_____ 5. All four horses have been winners.
    A. The first of the four horses has won, the second has won, the third has won, and the fourth has won.
    B. None of the horses has ever lost.

_____ 6. Not all the horses have been winners.
    A. None of the horses has been a winner.
    B. There is at least one of the horses which has not won.

_____ 7. It's false that no one has courage.
     A. Everyone has courage.
     B. Someone has courage.

_____ 8. Neither of the chemists made the test.
     A. The first chemist did not make the test and the second didn't either.
     B. Either the first chemist did not make the test or the second didn't.

_____ 9. Somewhere on this shelf is a copy of Rawl's _A Theory of Justice_.
     A. Either _A Theory of Justice_ is the first book, or it is the second, or . . . , or it is the last book on the shelf.
     B. Rawl's _A Theory of Justice_ is not on any other shelf.

_____ 10. All good things must come to an end.
     A. There is not one good thing which doesn't have to come to an end.
     B. Different people have different conceptions of a good thing.

Ex. 12 Rewrite each of the following statements so as to make more explicit its quantifier expressions, its predicate expressions, and in general its logical structure.

1. There aren't any gophers in the Tampa zoo.
2. Warm snow always packs well.
3. Computer punch cards are expensive.
4. A mosque is a place of worship.
5. Any capitalist is a reactionary.
6. You will enjoy yourself if you have the shrimp.
7. Walnut trees are deciduous.
8. Only the rich deserve the tax.
9. Certain rich people deserve to be taxed.
10. Only the rich can tolerate this tax.

Ex. 13 Translate each of the following. Supply a universe of discourse and specific interpretations of statement letters, predicate letters, and name letters as needed.

1. A person must always keep a promise.
2. George is doing the job or somebody is doing the job.
3. No lions hunt during the day.
4. Not everyone can be bought.
5. Many foreign stamps are expensive and so are some commemorative stamps.
6. Any traveler is welcome.
7. Brahms often uses augmented eighths.
8. If anybody wins, everybody will celebrate.
9. There are no people who are immortal.
10. People all die only if all people are mortal.

SELECTED ANSWERS
TO EXERCISES FOR MODULE 22

Ex. 9

1. D	2. G	3. H	4. J	5. E	6. F
7. A	8. C	9. I	10. B	11. L	12. K
13. R	14. Q	15. P	16. O	17. M	18. M

Review appropriate sections of Module 22 for each item missed.

Ex. 10

1. Hg; H = ". . . likes bridge," g = Gary
2. $(Hm \& Rm)$; H = ". . . likes bridge," R = ". . . dances," m = Marcel
4. $(\sim Gm)$; G = ". . . is a good cheerleader," m = Tom
5. $(\exists x)(Px \& Rx)$; P = ". . . is a prisoner," R = ". . . will be punished"
6. $(y)(Py \supset Ry)$; P = ". . . is a prisoner," R = ". . . will be punished"
9. $(\exists y)(Fy \& (\sim Iy))$; F = ". . . is your friend," I = ". . . accepted the invitation"
10. $(\sim(x)(Nx \supset Sx))$ or $(\exists x)(Nx \& (\sim Sx))$; N = ". . . is a eunuch," S = ". . . is sad"
12. $(x)(Hx \supset Ix)$; H = ". . . is had by me," I = ". . . is owed by me to my mother"
14. $(x)(Lx \supset (\sim Px))$; L = ". . . is a lawyer," P = ". . . is expensive"
15. Same as item 14 or $(\sim(\exists y)(Ly \& Py))$, except P = ". . . is negligent"
16. $(y)(IIy \supset Ry)$; H = ". . . is building a house," R = ". . . will make many decisions"
17. $(x)(Rx \supset Hx)$; R = ". . . deserves to be rewarded," H = ". . . is hardworking"
20. $(x)Jx$; J = ". . . is beautiful"

Review the appropriate section of Module 22 for each item missed.

Ex. 11

1. B
2. B; when one class excludes a second, the second excludes the first.
3. A
4. A; item 4 only says what happens if you eat apples regularly, not what happens if you don't.
5. A
6. B
7. B; only one person needs courage for 'no one has courage' to be false.
8. A
9. A
10. A

Be sure to review each item you missed in order to understand your mistake.

Ex. 12

1. For every member of the universe it is true that if they are gophers then they are not in the Tampa zoo.
2. For any snow it will be true that if it is warm then it packs well.
3. For any piece of paper it will be true that if it is a computer punch card it will be expensive.
4. For any building it will be true that if that building is a mosque it is a place of worship.
5. For any person it will be true that if he or she is a capitalist he or she is a reactionary.
6. For any possible action you perform, if it is an act of eating shrimp, then it is an act you will enjoy.
7. For any tree it will be true that if it is a walnut it is deciduous.
8. For any person it will be true that if she or he deserves the tax, then she or he is rich. (Alternatively, for any person it will be true that she or he deserves the tax only if she or he is rich.)
9. There are some people who are rich and who deserve to be taxed.
10. If any people can tolerate the tax, then they are rich.

If you had problems with predicate expressions, review 21:1.1 to 21:1.4; with quantifier expressions, review 21:5.3 and 21:5.4; with universe of discourses, review 22:1.2; and with logical structure, review 22:4.1 in most cases. ('Only' is discussed in 22:6.3.)

Ex. 13 In this set of answers we treat the first predicate expression as F, the second as G, the first name as a, the second as b, and so on. The universe is a set of unidentified objects.

1. $(x)(Fx \supset Gx); G =$ "... must always keep a promise"
2. $(Fa \lor (\exists x)(Gx \& Fx)); G =$ "... is a person," $F =$ "... is doing the job"
3. $(x)(Fx \supset (\sim Gx))$ or $(\sim(\exists x)(Fx \& Gx))$
4. $(\exists x)(Fx \& (\sim Gx))$ or the equivalent $(\sim(x)(Fx \supset Gx))$
5. $((\exists x)(Fx \& Gx) \& (\exists y)(Hy \& Gy))$, but not $(\exists x)((Fx \& Gx) \& Hx); F =$ "... is a foreign stamp," $G =$ "... is expensive," $H =$ "... is a commemorative stamp"
6. $(x)(Fx \supset Gx)$
7. $Fa; F =$ "... often uses augmented eighths"
8. $((\exists x)Fx \supset (y)Gy)$
9. $(\sim(\exists x)(Fx \& Gx)); F =$ "... is a person," $G =$ "... is immortal"
10. $((x)(Fx \supset Gx) \supset (y)(Fy \supset Hy))$ or $((x)(Fx \supset Gx) \supset (x)(Fx \supset Hx)); F =$ "... is a person," $G =$ "... dies," $H =$ "... is mortal"

If you missed two or more of these review the appropriate sections of this module dealing with translation into symbolic notation for each type of statement.

MODULE 23

VALIDITY IN PREDICATE LOGIC—THE DIAGRAM METHOD

In Module 23 we will develop a diagramatic test for the validity of predicate logic arguments.

● After reading Module 23 you should be able to:

1. Construct and interpret class region diagrams
2. Test predicate logic arguments for validity using class region diagrams

23:1.1 Class region diagrams In restating English assertions and in translating them into symbolic notation, we mentioned classes, individuals, and relations between them within a universe of discourse. The language of class region diagrams will need to do the same. We may begin with the fundamental idea of a class. In class region diagrams each class is represented by a circle:

If our class is the class of warriors, the circle means that every warrior is contained within it and everyone who is not a warrior is excluded from it. In this sense the circle represents the limits or boundaries of the class. Thus, you can see how we can easily diagram assertions of *individual inclusion* and *individual exclusion*. We can use our capital letters to mark what our given circle represents. For example we can label our circle F for warriors. Then since all warriors fall within the circle and all nonwarriors lie outside, you can easily understand, using g to stand for Goliath and *a* to stand for Albert Schweitzer, what the following diagram signifies:

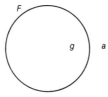

That's right, it signifies that Albert is not a warrior and that Goliath is a warrior.

23:1.2 Our next step is to represent *existentially quantified wffs*. Many of these statements, you will recall, are statements relating two classes within a universe of discourse (e.g., statements of partial inclusion and statements of partial exclusion). Clearly for two classes we will want two circles. The placement of the circles in relation to each other is important. We want to allow for every possible relationship between two classes of items in a given universe of discourse when we draw our two circles. So we need to know how many possibilities there are. Since there are two classes, there are two to the *second* power, or four, possibilities.[1] Approaching the same idea nonmathematically, suppose our two classes are tall warriors and warriors of the ancient world. Someone, like Goliath, would be both. The boy David is one, General Eisenhower is the other, and Tom Thumb is neither. Accordingly we will want to draw our circles in the class region diagrams to allow for all four of these possibilities. Here is the diagram:

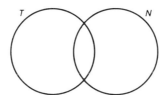

Letting T stand for tall warriors and N for warriors of the ancient world, you can easily see how to place Goliath, David, and General Eisenhower in the three regions created by the overlapping circles.

---

[1] In general, where n = the number of classes, there are 2^n possibilities. Thus, if the possibilities were mapped onto an array, and only emptiness or nonemptiness were considered possible states of each, the whole business of the decidability of class logic could be computerized. Since propositional logic is known to be ameable to mechanical decision procedures, both the levels of symbolic logic covered in this text could be treated in terms of computer-achievable symbolic systems. Here is a challenge to the reader interested in computer science to come up with a program to check symbolic arguments for validity using the machine. Remember that in predicate logic the universe is presumed to have at least one member.

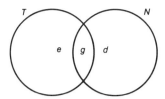

You can see that Tom Thumb falls into a region outside both the circles. He is still a man. In that sense he might have been tall and he might have been a warrior. In other words he does fit within our universe of discourse. By putting a rectangle around our circles we can symbolize the universe of discourse and have the logical place to enter our midget.

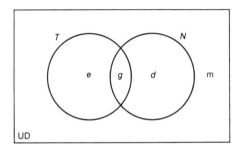

The universe of discourse is like a very large class. Every class or individual mentioned anywhere inside the rectangle is thereby an element in the universe of discourse. Once you have properly related two classes within a universe of discourse, you should not have any trouble symbolizing statements of partial inclusion and partial exclusion. Using the individual variables we used in writing wffs like $(\exists x)(Tx\ \&\ Nx)$ or $(\exists y)(Ty\ \&\ (\sim Ny))$ we can place that variable in the appropriate region as directed by the assertion. Suppose the assertion 'some tall warriors lived in ancient times' is translated $(\exists x)(Tx\ \&\ Nx)$. Then we will want to place an x in the part of the circle for tall warriors which is also a part of the circle for warriors living in ancient times. (We shall call this region the *intersection* of the two classes.)

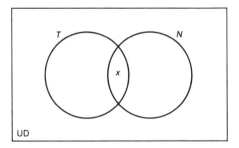

Or suppose the assertion 'some tall warriors did not live in ancient times' is translated $(\exists y)(Ty\ \&\ (\sim Ny))$. For it we will construct the diagram

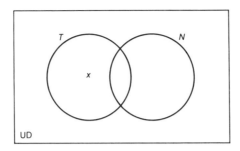

which shows that there are tall warriors who are not members of the class of warriors who lived in ancient times.

Placing an individual variable or a name letter within a region means that any class represented by that region is not empty. As a mini-exercise to test your own understanding of what the placement of an individual variable in a region means, ask yourself what would be meant by each of the following two diagrams. Provide an English translation for each.

1.

2.

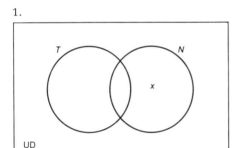

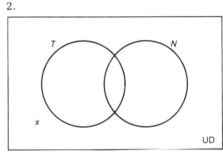

The first translated into English says "some ancient warriors were not tall," and the second says "some persons are neither tall nor warriors."

In Module 22 we encountered several different existentially quantified wffs:

1. $(\exists x)Fx$, which asserts that there is at least one member in class F
2. $(\exists x)(\sim Fx)$, which asserts that at least one member of the universe of discourse is not an F
3. $(\exists x)(Fx \& Gx)$, which is the standard translation of a partial inclusion statement
4. $(\exists x)(Fx \& (\sim Gx))$, which is the standard translation of a partial exclusion statement
5. $(\exists x)((\sim Fx) \& Gx)$, which expresses another partial exclusion
6. $(\exists x)((\sim Fx) \& (\sim Gx))$, which says that at least one member of the universe is not a member of either of two classes

Class region diagrams are powerful enough to represent all these existentially quantified wffs:

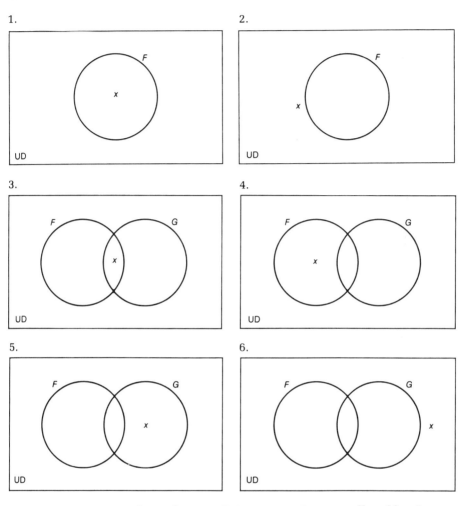

1.

2.

3.

4.

5.

6.

If we use two circles to diagram $(\exists x)Fx$ we run into a small problem because we have no information about the relationship of the F class to the G class. We have to decide between

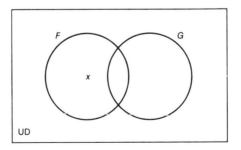

and

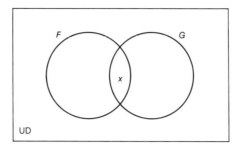

Yet neither of these is adequate since each already has a specific meaning: the first says $(\exists x)(Fx \& (\sim Gx))$ and the second says $(\exists x)(Fx \& Gx)$. No, we need another option. We can use a ⌢ to express our lack of information. We are not sure if the F we know exists is or is not a G. We can say that it is *either* one or the other this way:

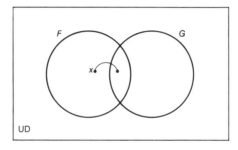

That is, $(\exists x)(Fx \& (Gx \lor (\sim Gx)))$. The x next to the ⌢ indicates that our uncertainty concerns x. If we are unsure about an individual, say Brenda, we can use

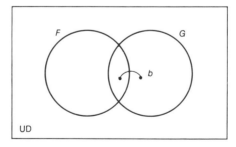

This diagram says $(Gb \& (Fb \lor (\sim Fb)))$.

23:1.3 Whereas *existentially quantified wffs indicate where individuals exist; universally quantified wffs indicate where a region is known to be empty.* A statement of total exclusion like "no gorillas are friendly" says that the intersection of the classes of gorillas and friendly animals is empty. The area that is for creatures that are both gorillas and friendly has no members. Shading in a region means that there is nothing in it; it is known to be empty.[2] To diagram 'no gorillas are friendly' we shall draw (using S for the subject's class and P for the predicate's class):

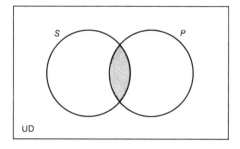

Total inclusion statements also assert that a certain region of a class is empty. Consider the statement "all gorillas are friendly." If you think about your circle for gorillas, you will notice that it has two regions, a region for gorillas that are friendly and a region for gorillas that are not friendly. Now what does the total inclusion assertion that all gorillas are friendly say about the region of the circle for any gorillas that are not friendly? It says that there are no gorillas in that region, that it is empty. Accordingly in diagraming total inclusion assertions we shall shade the region of the circle that we know to be empty.

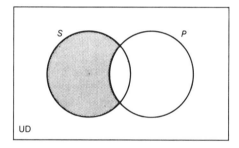

In order to test your understanding of the use of shading to represent the emptiness of an area, figure out how you would express each of the following two diagrams in English (where S = gorillas and P = friendly creatures):

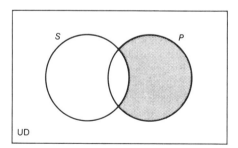

---

[2] Shading means that a region is known to be empty. Marking a variable, like x, or a name letter, like a, means that a region is known not to be empty. No marks in a region signifies that nothing is known about it.

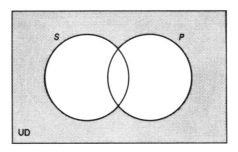

The first tells us that the shaded area, the class of friendly creatures who are not gorillas, is an empty class. In other words, "All friendly creatures are gorillas." The second shades out the whole universe of discourse except for the classes of gorillas and friendly things. In other words, "All creatures are either gorillas or friendly."

In Module 22 we encountered several different universally quantified wffs:

1. $(x)Fx$, which asserts that every member of the universe is an F
2. $(x)(\sim Fx)$, which asserts that the class F is empty
3. $(x)(Fx \supset Gx)$, which is the standard translation for total inclusion statements
4. $(x)(Fx \supset (\sim Gx))$, which is the standard translation of total exclusion statements
   Item 4 is logically equivalent to $(x)(Gx \supset (\sim Fx))$
5. $(x)((\sim Fx) \supset Gx)$, which says that every member of the universe outside of F is in G. Item 5 is logically equivalent to $(x)(Fx \lor Gx)$
6. $(x)((\sim Fx) \supset (\sim Gx))$, which says that there are no members of G outside of F
   Item 6 is logically equivalent to $(x)(Gx \supset Fx)$
7. $(x)(Fx \equiv Gx)$, which says that all the F's are G's and all the G's are F's

Class region diagrams are powerful enough to represent all these universally quantified wffs:

1.

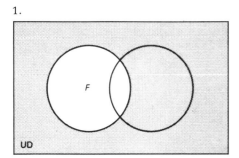

2.

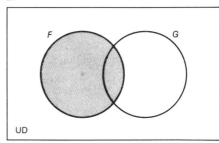

3.

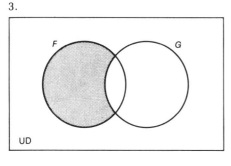

4.

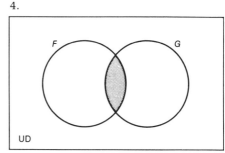

5.   6.

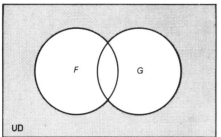   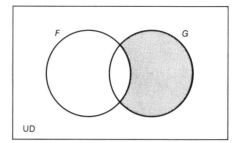

7.

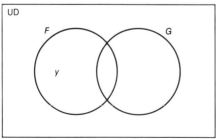

EXERCISE 1

Represent each of the following using class region diagrams that contain two circles, the left one F and the right one G.

1. $(\exists y)(Fy \ \& \ (\sim Gy))$
2. $(y)(Fy \supset (\sim Gy))$
3. $(y)(Gy \supset Fy)$
4. $(\exists w)(Fw \ \& \ Gw)$
5. $(\exists w)((\sim Fw) \ \& \ Gw)$
6. $(Fb \ \& \ (\sim Gb))$
7. Ga
8. $(x)Fx$
9. $((x)Fx \ \& \ (\exists y)Fy)$

ANSWERS TO EXERCISE 1

1.   2.

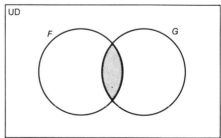   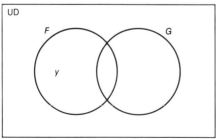

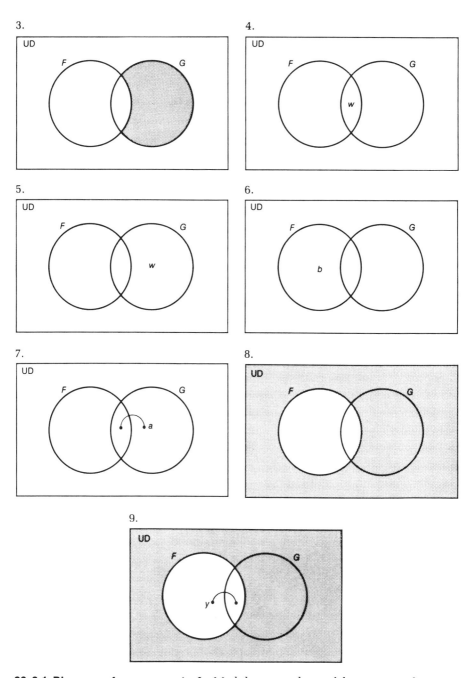

3.

4.

5.

6.

7.

8.

9.

23:2.1 Diagrams for arguments In Module 22 we learned how to translate into symbolic notation; so far in Module 23 we have learned how to represent wffs using class region diagrams. The next step is to learn how to test the validity of any argument of predicate logic that contains no more than three distinct predicate letters. Such arguments may involve relations between three classes. Accordingly we shall have to place three overlapping circles within our universe of disclosure. Again the placement of our circles will be important. With three classes, we will generate two to the third, or eight, distinct regions with which to represent all the possible kinds of relationships between the possible members of the three classes. We can achieve this arrangement as diagramed below:

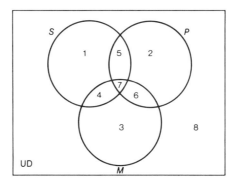

Region 1 is for the S's who are not P's and not M's, area 2 is for the P's who are not S's and not M's, and so on down to region 8, which is for the members of the universe of discourse who are not S's or P's or M's. To test your own understanding of the areas, you should describe to yourself what each represents. Start this way: "An item is in region 1 if and only if it is S, it is not P, and it is not M." You should be able to describe all eight regions saying whether any item in each is or is not S, P, and M. In other words,

An item is in region	If and only if it is
2	not S, is P, and is not M
3	not S, not P, and is M
4	S, not P, and is M
5	S, is P, and is not M
6	not S, is P, and is M
7	S, is P, and is M
8	not S, not P, and not M

Consider the argument

EG. 23.1 All horses are wild things.
All wild things run around without clothes.
So all horses run around without clothes.

The three predicate expressions in this argument generate the three classes horses, wild things, and things that run around without clothes. In order to make our diagraming follow a uniform pattern, we will adopt a traditional convention at this point. The class mentioned in the *subject* of the conclusion, in our example the class of horses, will be assigned to the upper-left-hand circle labeled S in the above diagram. The class mentioned in the *predicate* of the conclusion, in our example things that run around without clothes, will be assigned to the upper-right-hand circle labeled P in the above diagram. The third class, in our example wild things, has traditionally been called the *middle* and has been assigned to the bottom circle labeled *M* in the above diagram. The validity check you make on an argument is not influenced by which circle is assigned to represent which class, but it is easier to make validity checks if you follow a consistent pattern.

23:2.2 In order to diagram arguments you must apply what you have just learned about diagraming individual statement units.[3] Here are the few hints you will need in order to keep out of trouble. It is a good idea to diagram universally quantified statements before you diagram existentially quantified assertions or assertions about individuals. Suppose we have the premise 'some *M* is *P*,' $(\exists x)(Mx \;\&\; Px)$. You will not know whether to put your x in region 6 or region 7.

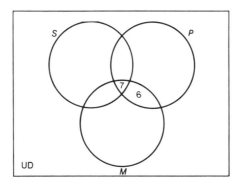

However, if some other premise of the argument were about a total class, like 'no *S* is *M*,' $(x)(Sx \supset (\sim Mx))$, then by applying the shading for it, you will be able to see that the x, denoting the existence of an individual, must go in region 6 since $(x)(Sx \supset (\sim Mx))$ implies that region 7 is empty.

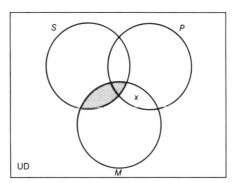

The advantage of diagraming premises about total classes first is simply that it will reduce the amount of ambiguity about how to diagram statements about individuals and existentially quantified statements. In examples like the one above, the ambiguity is eliminated. There are other examples, however, where ambiguity will remain. Suppose we have the premise 'all *S*'s are *M*'s,' $(x)(Sx \supset Mx)$. We would shade out regions 1 and 5. How then should we diagram 'some *M* is *P*'? Having shaded region 1 and 5 we still do not know whether to put our x in region 6 or 7.

---

[3] It is not possible to diagram disjunctions, conditionals, or biconditionals of quantified assertions.

Since this ambiguity is not resolved by the other premise of the argument, it should be *left* unresolved, using the ⌒ device introduced earlier.

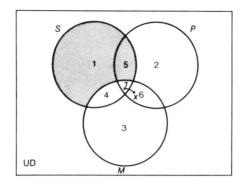

What the ⌒ₓ means here is that there exists at least one member of the class M which is also a member of P. What placing the ⌒ over the border line means is that we are not informed whether the M that is P is or is not also an S. Ambiguities like these also arise with statements about individuals. That is why they too should be diagramed after universally quantified statements. Putting a g ⌒ for (Mg & Pg) over the border of regions 6 and 7 would mean that we are not sure if Gertrude, g, is in 6 or in 7.

EXERCISE 2

Below are a number of partial statements about what is asserted in various diagrams. From the phrases provided under each select the one phrase which completes each statement making it true.

1. Diagram 1 is *incorrect* because:
   A. The circles do not overlap correctly.
   B. The convention for which circle represents which class is violated.
   C. The circles are too small.
   D. There is no shading in the universe of discourse area.

1.

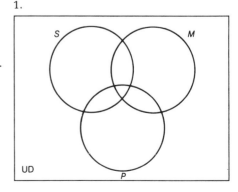

2. Diagram 2 says at least that:
   A. (x)(Mx ⊃ Px); All M is P.
   B. (∃x)Mx; There is an M.
   C. (∃x)(Sx & Px); Some S is P.
   D. (x)(Sx ⊃ Px); All S is P.

3. Diagram 2 also says:
   A. (x)(Px ⊃ (~Mx))
   B. (x)(~Mx)
   C. (x)(Sx ⊃ Mx)
   D. (~(∃x)Px)

2.

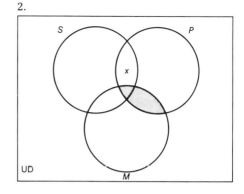

4. Diagram 3 does not say:[4]
   A. Sg
   B. The universe of discourse has at least two members.
   C. (∃x)(Sx & Px)
   D. (x)(~(Sx & Px & Mx))

5. Diagram 3 does not say:
   A. ((Sg) & (∃x)(Px))
   B. (~Pg)
   C. (∃x)(~Sx)
   D. (y)(Sy ⊃ (~My))

3.

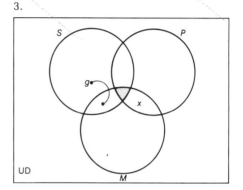

6. Diagram 4 does not say:
   A. (w)(Pw ⊃ Sw)
   B. (z)(Mz ⊃ Pz)
   C. (Ma & (~Sa))
   D. (Mb & (~Pb))

7. Diagram 4 does not say:
   A. (∃y)(Sy & (~Py))
   B. (∃y)(My ∨ Py)
   C. There are at least two individuals in the universe of discourse.
   D. No P is M.

4.

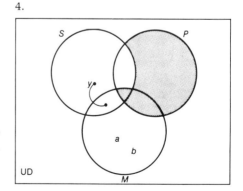

[4] In other words eliminate the three it does say.

8. Diagram 5 *says:*
   A. (x)Sx
   B. There are at least two members in the universe of discourse.
   C. (x)(~Px)
   D. (∃x)Px

5.

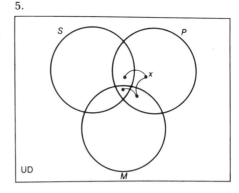

9. Diagram 6 says:
   A. (w)(Pw ⊃ Mw)
   B. (∃w)(Mw & Pw)
   C. (∃x)(Px & (~Mx))
   D. (∃x)(Mx & (~Px) & (~Sx))

10. It is true that:
    A. Diagram 6 says that "no M's are S's."
    B. Diagram 6 is wrong because region 7 is never shaded.
    C. Diagram 6 says there are no S's.
    D. Diagram 6 says there is more than one M.

6.

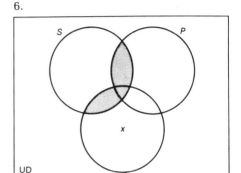

ANSWERS TO EXERCISE 2

1. B
2. C; it also says more, but that is irrelevant to the question as asked.
3. A
4. C
5. D
6. B
7. B
8. D; concerning b: the individual represented by x may lie in M outside of S, or S outside of M, or even in the overlap of S and M. But wherever it is, there is no guarantee that there is more than one.

   To diagram (∃x)Px we had to adapt the ⌢ device because there were four possibilities, not just two. The P could be in (1) both P and S, (2) both P and M, (3) just in P, or (4) all of P, S, and M.
9. D
10. A

23:2.3 Validity and class region diagrams We are now ready to use class region diagrams to determine the validity of predicate logic arguments. According to the definition of validity an argument is valid when, by virtue of the argument's structure, it is impossible for the premises to be true while the conclusion is false. If the conclusion of an argument is structurally bound to be true, given that its premises are true, then the argument is valid. We begin our application of the idea of validity to class region diagrams by noting that when we diagram a premise what we construct is a representation of what it would be like for that statement to be *true*; a certain region would be empty, would have some members in it, or would have specified individuals in it. Accordingly the question of the validity of these arguments is this: Once we have made the representations of the truth of the premises, is there any way the conclusion could be false—or, *has the representation of the conclusion's being true itself been drawn in already?*

We can restate this application of the idea of validity concentrating our attention on the conclusion. You can diagram the conclusion of an argument through the procedures you have just learned. The diagram represents what will be the case if the conclusion is true. The idea of validity guarantees us that if we have a valid argument then the conclusion must be true if the premises are all true. Consider the following valid argument.

EG. 23.2 $(x)(Mx \supset Px)$
$\underline{(y)(Sy \supset My)}$
$(x)(Sx \supset Px)$

If we diagram the conclusion of this argument we will have:

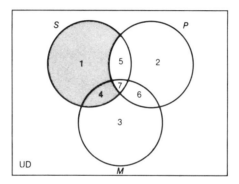

The diagram shows us that if the conclusion of the argument is true, then there will be no S's outside of the class of P's (i.e., regions 1 and 4 are empty). Suppose the argument is valid. If it is, then if the premises are true, the conclusion will also have to be true. In other words *when we diagram the premises as true we will construct a diagram that already shows the conclusion of a valid argument as true.* We can now diagram the premises. The diagram will represent the premises as true. Since the argument is valid our diagram also shows the conclusion as true. Here is the diagram of the premises:

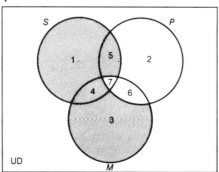

The first premise, 'all M's are P,' says regions 3 and 4 are empty, thus ruling out the existence of S's in 4. The second premise, 'all S's are M,' says that regions 1 and 5 are empty, thus ruling out the existence of S's in either one of those regions. This diagram of the premises does guarantee the truth of this conclusion, for the conclusion says that regions 1 and 4 are empty. The premise diagram shows these two regions shaded.

23:2.4 The validity checking procedure When you use class region diagrams to check validity: (1) Start by diagraming the conclusion on one diagram; (2) make a second diagram which represents all the premises. *If the argument is valid then everything marked into your representation of the conclusion must also be represented in your diagram of the premises. If the argument is invalid then something marked into your representation of the conclusion will not be diagramed into your representation of the premises. In other words, there will be a something in the* conclusion diagram not expressed in the premise diagram.

Here are six more examples.

EG. 23.3   Some M's are P.
            All S's are M.
            ∴ All S's are P.

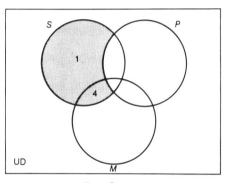

Conclusion

EG. 23.3′ (∃x)(Mx & Px)
           (x)(Sx ⊃ Mx)
           ――――――――――――
           (x)(Sx ⊃ Px)

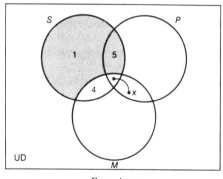

Premises

The conclusion says that regions 1 and 4 are empty. The emptiness of 4 is not marked in the premises. Since premises do not guarantee 4 to be empty, the argument is *invalid*.

EG. 23.4 No M is P.
          Some S is P.
          ∴ Some S is not M.

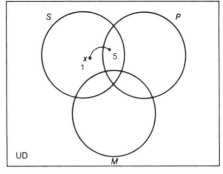

Conclusion

EG. 23.4′ $(y)(My \supset (\sim Py)$
          $(\exists x)(Sx \mathbin{\&} Px)$
          $\overline{(\exists x)(Sx \mathbin{\&} (\sim Mx))}$

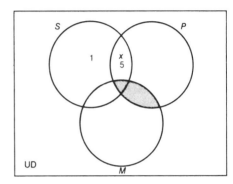

Premises

The conclusion says that *either* region 1 or region 5 has at least one member. (The conclusion does not contain information as to which of the two regions certainly has a member.) The premises, with the total exclusion premise diagramed first to resolve an ambiguity, say that region 5 has at least one member. Since the conclusion indicates a member in 1 *or* 5 and the premises together guarantee a member in 5, the argument is *valid*.

EG. 23.5 Some M is not P.
          All S is M.
          ∴ Some S is not P.

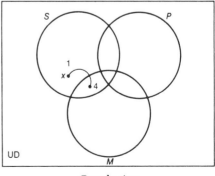

Conclusion

EG. 23.5' $(\exists x)(Mx \;\&\; (\sim Px)$
$\underline{(y)(Sy \supset My)}$
$(\exists x)(Sx \;\&\; (\sim Px))$

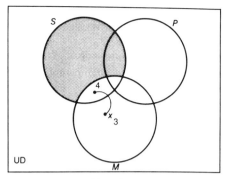

Premises

The conclusion says that *either* region 1 or 4 has a member. Diagraming 'all S is M' first leaves an unresolved ambiguity: we are not informed whether the object mentioned in premise 1 as being in M is or is not an S. The ⌢ over the border indicates that the premise is true even if the M fails to be an S. Suppose it does! Then the conclusion *may* be false. The argument is *invalid, because the conclusion can be false even if all the premises are true.*

EG. 23.6 $(\exists x)[Sx \;\&\; ((\sim Px) \;\&\; (\sim Mx))]$
$(\exists y)((\sim Sy) \;\&\; (\sim Py))$
$\underline{(x)(\sim Px)}$
$(y)(My \supset (\sim Py))$

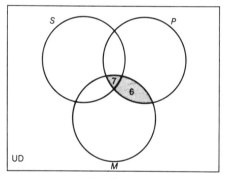

Conclusion

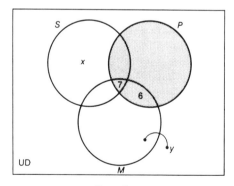

Premises

This example is valid; the conclusion is already completely drawn in the representation of the premises. The premise diagram guarantees that regions 7 and 6 are empty. Note that there are three premises in this example. We are not limited by the number of premises, only by the number of classes mentioned. Here is an example with four premises.

EG. 23.7 $(x)(Sx \lor (Mx \lor Px))$
$(x)(\sim Px)$
$(y)(Sy \equiv My)$
$(\exists x)Mx$
_____
$(\exists y)My$

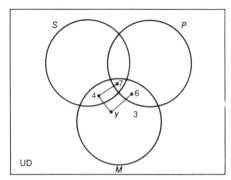

Conclusion

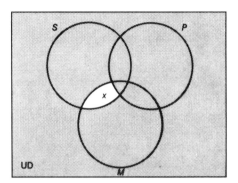

Premises

The premises guarantee that region 4 has at least one member and that it is the only region with a member. The conclusion diagram says that there is something which may be in either 7, 4, 3, or 6. Since we are guaranteed that it is in 4, the argument is *valid*. The fact that the conclusion uses *y* while the premises use *x* is irrelevant as we learned in 22:5.2. So $(\exists y)My$ in the conclusion is equivalent to $(\exists x)Mx$. Both say that there is at least one member of the universe that is an M.

EG. 23.8 $(\exists y)(Sy \mathbin{\&} (\sim My))$
$(\exists x)(Sx \mathbin{\&} (\sim Px))$
$(x)((Sx \mathbin{\&} Px) \supset Mx)$
$(y)((My \mathbin{\&} Py) \supset Sy)$
Mb
_____
$(\exists x)(Sx \mathbin{\&} Mx)$

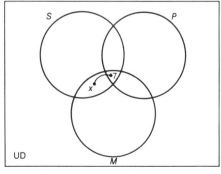

Conclusion

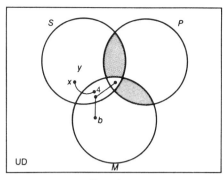

Premises

Although the premises give us a lot of information they do *not guarantee* the conclusion. The individual *b* may be totally outside of S, and the x mentioned in the premises may turn out to be only in S. In other words, regions 4 and 7 *could* turn out to be empty. If they do, then the conclusion is false. So, the argument is *invalid*.

23:3 Chain arguments It might seem that the technique of using class region diagrams to check the validity of predicate logic arguments will not allow us to check all such arguments because of the limitation to mentioning no more than three classes in any given argument. However, arguments that mention more classes can be handled in a series of steps. For example, consider:

EG. 23.9   All *G*'s are *H*.
All *F*'s are *G*.
No *H*'s are *J*.
∴ No *F*'s are *J*.

EG. 23.9′ $(x)(Gx \supset Hx)$
$(x)(Fx \supset Gx)$
$(x)(Hx \supset (\sim Jx))$
$\overline{(x)(Fx \supset (\sim Jx))}$

You can probably see that $(x)((Fx \supset Hx)$ ('all *F*'s are *H*'s') follows from this argument's first two premises. The class region diagram for this "internal" two-premised argument is exactly like the one constructed for Eg. 23.2. Once that argument is shown valid, its conclusion can become the first premise of a further internal argument, namely:

EG. 23.10   All *F*'s are *H*.
No *H*'s are *J*.
∴ No *F*'s are *J*.

EG. 23.10′ $(x)(Fx \supset Hx)$
$(x)(Hx \supset (\sim Jx))$
$\overline{(x)(Fx \supset (\sim Jx))}$

Diagraming Eg. 23.10, we get:

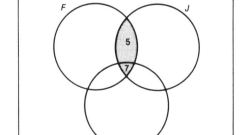

Conclusion

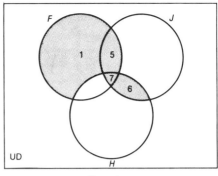

Premises

The conclusion says that 5 and 7 are empty and the premises say that 1, 5, 6, and 7 are empty. So the second subargument is valid. Since both subarguments are valid, the original argument is valid.

Thus, even though class region diagrams as presented here can handle only arguments that mention no more than three classes, longer arguments can be treated by breaking them into subarguments using the process outlined above. The result is that even long arguments of predicate logic can mechanically be checked to determine whether or not they are valid. We have achieved our goal!

EXERCISES FOR MODULE 23
VALIDITY IN PREDICATE LOGIC—THE DIAGRAM METHOD

Ex. 3 Below are a number of assertions about predicate logic and class region diagrams. Mark each 'T' for true or 'F' for false.

_____ 1. The assertion 'all S is P' says that regions 1 and 4 are empty.

_____ 2. The assertion 'all S is P' guarantees, if true, that region 1 is empty.

_____ 3. The assertion 'no M is S' says that regions 4 and 7 are empty.

_____ 4. All universally quantified assertions say that some region is empty.

_____ 5. The assertion 'some S is P' says that region 3 is empty.

_____ 6. All existentially quantified statements say that some region is empty.

_____ 7. All existentially quantified statements say that at least one individual is within the universe of discourse.

_____ 8. All existentially quantified statements say that at least one individual is in a certain region.

_____ 9. If one student drew a diagram with an x in region 2 and another student drew a diagram with a y in region 2, the diagrams would have different meanings.

_____ 10. A g in region 6 means that a definite individual, whose name is represented by g, is a P and an M, and is not an S.

_____ 11. If one student drew a diagram with an x in region 5 and another student drew a diagram with an m in region 5, the two diagrams would have the same meaning.

_____ 12. A diagram with a ⌒ g over the border of regions 1 and 4 says that g is somewhat like an S and somewhat like an M.

_____ 13. A diagram with a ⌒ x over the border of regions 2 and 6 says that the information given leaves unresolved whether some unspecified individual is in region 2 or in region 6.

_____ 14. A diagram with a z in region 7 says that region 7 has at least one individual in it and its name is 'z.'

_____ 15. The diagram for 'no S's are M's' is the same as the diagram for 'no M's are S's.'

Check your answers to Ex. 3 before you go on in the exercises.

Ex. 4 Test the following arguments for validity using class region diagrams.

1. $(x)(Sx \supset (\sim Mx))$
   $(x)((\sim Mx) \supset Px)$
   _____
   $(x)(Sx \supset Px)$

2. $(Sa \& Sb)$
   $(x)(Sx \supset Px)$
   _____
   $(Pa \& Pb)$

3. $(x)(Sx \supset Px)$
   _____
   $(\exists x)(Sx \& Px)$

4. $(x)(\sim Sx)$
   $(x)((\sim Sx) \supset Mx)$
   $(\exists x)(Mx \& Px)$
   _____
   $(\exists x)(Px \& (\sim Sx))$

5. $(y)(Sy \equiv My)$
   $(x)(Mx \equiv Px)$
   _____
   $(z)(Sx \supset Px)$

6. $(\exists x)[Sx \& ((\sim Px) \& (\sim Mx))]$
   $(Pa \lor Sa)$
   $(x)(\sim Px)$
   _____
   $(\exists x)(Mx \& (\sim Px))$

Ex. 5 Test the following arguments for validity using class region diagrams. (_Hint:_ Begin by translating each argument into predicate logic notation.)

1. Everyone is mortal. The authors are persons. So the authors are mortal.
2. No princes ride chargers. All princes eat mince meat. So whoever rides a charger eats no mince meat.
3. Some gorillas are unfriendly. Any unfriendly animal should be kept away from little babies. So some gorillas should be kept away from little babies.
4. You overfeed Rover. So he must be fat.
5. A church is a place of worship and for that reason should not be subject to excessive noise.
6. Every politician, including George Washington, has to please many constituencies. If you have to please them, then you will sometimes use very evasive language. So we can be sure that even Washington used evasive language.

SELECTED ANSWERS
TO EXERCISES FOR MODULE 23

Ex. 3

1. T
2. T
3. T

4. T (in terms of the assumptions of contemporary logic)
5. F
6. F
7. T
8. F; sometimes it is not clear which of two or more regions the individual is in.
9. F; the explanation below Eg. 23.7.
10. T
11. F; m names a specific member of the universe; x does not tell us specifically which member of the universe is in 5.
12. F; g over the border shows ambiguity and incomplete information but not vagueness of the classes.
13. T
14. F; it's true up to the part that says z names an individual. Variables are not interpreted as referring to specific members of the universe.
15. T

Ex. 4

1. Valid

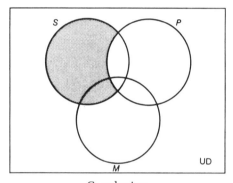
Conclusion

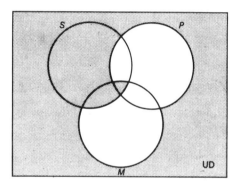
Premises

2. Valid

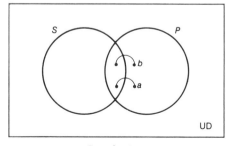
Conclusion

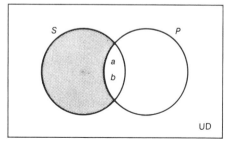
Premises

3. Invalid

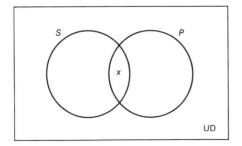

Conclusion

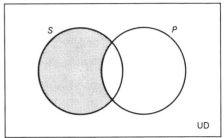

Premises

4. Valid

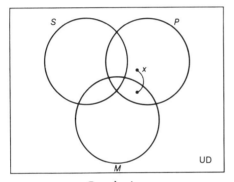

Conclusion

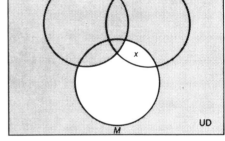

Premises

5. Valid

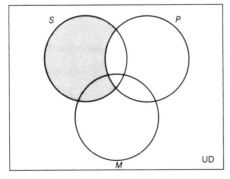

Conclusion

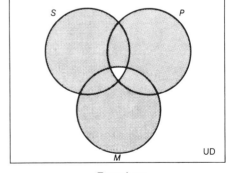

Premises

6. Invalid. We know that $(Pa \lor Sa)$ from premise 2, but we also know P is empty. So Sa is true. We do not, however, know if Ma or $(\sim Ma)$ is true.

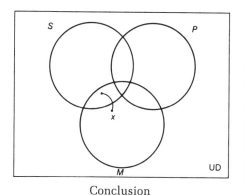

Conclusion

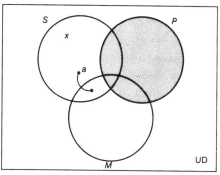

Premises

If you made errors in diagraming, review the whole module; if you made errors in interpreting the diagrams, review 23:2.4.

Ex. 5

1. UD = unidentified objects $(x)(Rx \supset Nx)$
    J = . . . is an author $(x)(Jx \supset Rx)$
    N = . . . is mortal   _____
    R = . . . is a person $(x)(Jx \supset Nx)$

    The argument is valid.

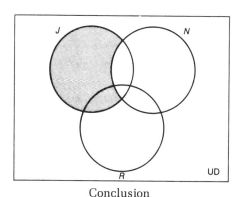

Conclusion

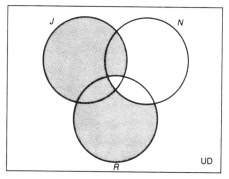

Premises

3. UD = creatures $(\exists x)(Gx \ \& \ (\sim Fx))$
    G = . . . is a gorilla $(x)((\sim Fx) \supset Kx)$
    K = . . . should be kept away from babies   _____
    F = . . . is a friendly animal $(\exists x)(Gx \ \& \ Kx)$

    The argument is valid.

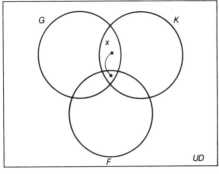

Conclusion

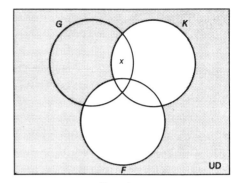

Premises

5. Enthymeme
   Conclusion = no church should be subject to excessive noise
   Premises: 1. All churches are places of worship.
            2. $(E - P)$ No place of worship should be subject to excessive noise.

UD = buildings	$(x)(Gx \supset Hx)$
G = . . . is a church	$(x)(Hx \supset (\sim Ix))$
H = . . . is a place of worship	$(x)(Gx \supset (\sim Ix))$
I = . . . should be subject to excessive noise	

The argument is valid.

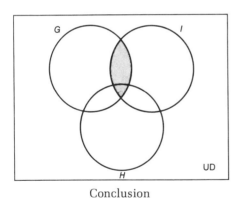

Conclusion

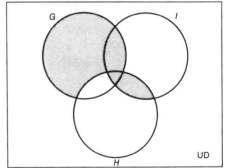

Premises

6. UD = people $(x)(Fx \supset Gx)$
   F = . . . is a politician Fa
   G = . . . must please many constituencies $(x)(Gx \supset Kx)$
   K = . . . uses elusive language Ka
   a = Washington

The argument is valid.

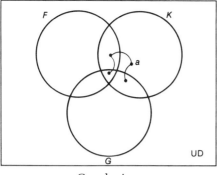

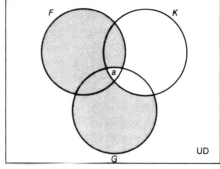

| Conclusion | Premises |

If you missed any because of translation, review Module 22; if your problem was in drawing the diagrams, review Module 23; if you were unable to interpret the diagrams once drawn, review 23:2.4.

SELF-QUIZ FOR PART TWO
USING SYMBOLS IN LOGIC

This self-quiz contains two sections; each has twenty-five questions and can be taken independently of the other. Both sections contain questions from all three chapters. Those drawn exclusively from Chapter 5 information are marked with one star. Those drawn exclusively from Chapter 6 information are marked with two stars. You can, if you wish, use the two parts as two separate self-quizzes.

Select the best answer from among those provided.

Section A:

1. The formula $[[((p \supset q) \supset p) \& (q \equiv r)] \vee (\sim p)]$:

    A. Is well formed
    B. Is a biconditional
    C. Is missing outside parentheses
    D. Contains too many grouping indicators
    E. Contains elements that are not part of our symbolic language

2. Which of the arguments below is the best translation of: "You get the children back only if you pay the ransom. You get the children back only if you do not tell the police about the kidnaping. So if you pay the ransom and do not tell the police about the kidnaping, you get the children back."?

    A. $(p \supset q)$
       $(p \supset (\sim r))$
       $\therefore [((p \& (\sim r)) \supset q]$

    B. $(q \supset p)$
       $((\sim r) \supset p)$
       $\therefore ((p \& (\sim r)) \supset q)$

    C. $(q \supset p)$
       $(r \supset p)$
       $\therefore ((q \& (\sim r)) \supset p)$

    D. $(p \supset q)$
       $(p \supset (\sim r))$
       $\therefore ((q \& (\sim r)) \supset p)$

3. The truth-table for $((p \& (q \vee p)) \supset q)$ reveals that it is:

    A. Consistent and contingent

B. Only consistent
C. A tautology and consistent
D. Inconsistent

4. The truth-table

p	q	r							
T	T	T	T	T	T	T	T	T	T
T	T	F	T	F	F	T	T	F	F
T	F	T	F	T	T	T	T	T	T
T	F	F	F	T	F	F	T	F	F
F	T	T	T	T	T	T	F	T	T
F	T	F	T	F	F	T	F	T	F
F	F	T	F	T	T	T	F	T	T
F	F	F	F	T	F	T	F	T	F

is the correct truth-table for which of the following wffs?

A. $((p \supset r) \supset (q \supset r))$ B. $((r \supset q) \equiv (q \supset p))$
C. $((q \ \& \ r) \equiv (q \lor r))$ D. $((q \supset r) \supset (p \supset r))$
E. $[((\sim p) \supset (\sim q)) \lor (p \equiv r)]$

5. "Either the senator will resign or she'll be impeached. She will receive a pension if and only if she's not impeached. Hence, if the senator doesn't resign, she'll receive no pension." Checked for validity this argument yields a truth-table with a final-value column of:

A. TTTTTTTT
B. TTTTTTFF
C. TTTFTTTF
D. TFFTTFFT

6. "I can prove it's false that nobody could bake a cake that good," insisted the little boy. "It's false because my mommy can." This argument is:

A. Invalid
B. Valid, as can be demonstrated using propositional logic
C. Valid, as can be demonstrated using predicate logic
D. Valid, but not capable of being demonstrated by either of the levels of formal logic studied in Part Two

Indicate whether each of the following is true or false.

7. A formula X logically implies another formula Y if $(Y \supset X)$ is a tautology.

8. A formula D is logically equivalent to a formula E if $(D \equiv E)$ is a tautology.

9. If the conjunction of the premises of an argument logically implies its conclusion, then the argument is sound if its premises are also all true.

*10. In which of the following are both terms distributed?
A. All S are P.   B. No S are P.
C. Some S are P.   D. Some S are not P.

**11. The diagram

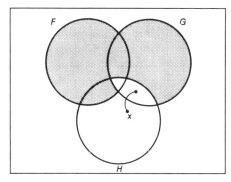

represents the statement:

A. All H's are F's.
B. All H's are G's.
C. Some non-F is either an H and a G, or is an H and not a G.
D. Something is an F and a G, or is not an F and a G.
E. There are no H's or F's other than G's.

**12. The best translation of 'Alexander the Great is brave and dead' is

A. p
B. (p & q)
C. Fa
D. (Fa & Ga)
E. (∃x)(Fx & Gx)

**13. The translation of 'Whales live in the sea and yet are not fishes' that correctly exhibits the greatest amount of logical form is:

A. (p & (~q))
B. ((x)(Wx & Fx) & (~p))
C. (x)(Wx ⊃ Sx)
D. (∃x)(p ⊃ Fx)
E. (x)[Wx ⊃ (Sx & (~Fx))]

**14. Using class region diagrams determine which of the following is true of this argument: "June is a free-lance reporter. All free-lance reporters are slaves to the press. Some slaves to the press earn good money. So Juno earns good money and is a slave to the press."

A. It is valid, and it proves that the individual marked x is not Juno.
B. The premises show that Juno is a slave to the press, but not necessarily that she earns good money.
C. It is invalid, but the premises do show that some free-lance reporters do earn good money.
D. It is valid.

**15. 'Some old men are grouchy, but not Uncle Leonard' is best translated:

A. (Ml & (~Gl))
B. ((x)(Mx ⊃ Gx) & (~Gl))
C. (~(Ml & Gl))
D. ((∃x)(Mx & Gx) & (~Gl))

16. "Some paints are not pleasant to smell. Whatever is unpleasant to smell makes it hard for me to breathe. And so some paints make it hard for me to breathe." This argument is:

A. Valid by techniques of propositional logic

B. Valid by techniques of predicate logic
C. Invalid and its three terms are 'paints,' 'unpleasant things to smell,' and 'me'
D. Invalid and its three terms are 'paints,' 'unpleasant things to smell,' and 'things that make breathing hard for me'

*17. From the fact that an O-form statement is false we can infer:

A. That an A-form statement is true
B. That an E-form statement is false
C. That an I-form statement is true
D. All of the above

18. Given any argument with premises P_1, P_2, and P_3 and conclusion C, its corresponding conditional is:

A. $(P_1 \& P_2 \& P_3 \& C)$ B. $((P_1 \& P_2 \& P_3) \equiv C)$
C. $((P_1 \lor P_2 \lor P_3) \supset C)$ D. $((P_1 \& P_2) \supset (P_3 \& C))$
E. $((P_1 \& P_2 \& P_3) \supset C)$

*19. In the syllogism

Some fathers are neglectful.
Some mothers are neglectful.
So some fathers are mothers.

The major term is:

A. Fathers   B. Mothers
C. Neglectful   D. Parents
E. None of the above

*20. The contrary of 'all parents love sleep' is:

A. Some parents love sleep.
B. Not all parents love sleep.
C. No parents love sleep.
D. Some parents are nonsleepers.
E. Only parents love sleep.

Determine whether each of the following arguments is valid or not.

21. 1. $(p \lor (\sim p))$
    2. $(p \supset q)$
    3. $(q \supset r)$
    4. $((\sim p) \supset r)$
    _____
    $\therefore r$

22. All F's are G's.
    No G's are H's.
    So some H is not an F.

23. If you want my job, then you will have to learn my work, show you are better at it than me, and persuade management that I should be let go. If you do the first two, then you will be able to do the third. But you'll not be able to demonstrate that you are better than me. So you don't want my job.

24. Albert the Great brought Greek texts into Europe. If anyone brought Greek

texts into Europe, then he or she was viewed with fear by the political leaders. So Albert was a man feared by the political leaders of Europe in those days.

25. All of those who eat lunch at the Horse and Lamb enjoy themselves. Some people who enjoy themselves complain. So none of the people who eat lunch at the Horse and Lamb complain.

Section B:

1. The best translation of $(p \supset (q \equiv r))$ is:
   A. Bats are mammals.
   B. If p, then if q then r.
   C. Either p or q, if, and only if, r.
   D. p and q, if, and only if, r.
   E. If p, then q if, and only if, r.

2. The truth-table for $(p \lor (q \lor r))$ comes out with a final value column of:
   A. TTTF   B. TTFFTTFF
   C. TTTTTTTF   D. FFFFFFFT
   E. TTTFTTTF

3. The truth-table for $(p \supset (q \supset p))$ reveals that it is:
   A. Consistent and contingent
   B. Only consistent
   C. A tautology and consistent
   D. Inconsistent

4. The argument
   $(p \supset q)$
   $(r \lor (\sim q))$
   $(\sim r)$
   ———————
   $\therefore (\sim p)$

   is:
   A. Invalid, as shown by the truth-table row where p = T, q = T, and r = F
   B. Invalid, as shown by the truth-table row where p = T, q = F, and r = F
   C. Invalid, as shown by the truth-table row where p = T, q = F, and r = T
   D. Invalid, as shown by the truth-table row where p = F, q = T, and r = T
   E. Valid

Use the accompanying diagram to answer Exs. 5 to 9.

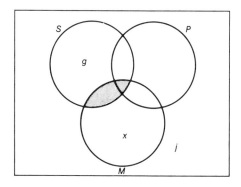

S = salty things
M = messy things
P = peppery things
g = Super Grape
j = Jam Man

**5. The diagram expresses the statement:

    A. All P are S.   B. All S are P.

    C. No S is M.   D. No P is M.

**6. The diagram expresses the statement:

    A. Some P is S.   B. Some M is S.

    C. Some M is not S and not P.   D. Some P is M but not P.

    E. Some P is not S and not M.

**7. The diagram expresses the statement:

    A. Super Grape is salty.   B. Super Grape is messy.

    C. Super Grape is peppery.   D. Super Grape is Jam Man.

    E. Super Grape is x.

**8. The diagram expresses the statement:

    A. Jam Man is salty.

    B. Jam Man is not a member of the universe.

    C. Jam Man is neither salty nor messy nor peppery.

    D. Jam Man is both messy and peppery.

**9. The diagram expresses the statement:

    A. $(x)(Sx \supset Px)$ B. $(\exists x)(Mx \,\&\, Px)$

    C. $((x)(Mx \supset Sx) \,\&\, (\sim Sg))$ D. $((\exists x)(Mx \,\&\, \sim Px) \,\&\, Sg)$

    E. $(\exists x)(Mx \,\&\, Sx)$

*10. The subcontrary of 'some S is not P' is:

    A. No S is P.

    B. All S is P.

    C. Some S is P.

    D. Some P is S.

*11. The minor term of a syllogism is:

    A. The subject of the conclusion

    B. The predicate of the conclusion

    C. The term that is in both premises

    D. All the above

*12. In a valid syllogism:

    A. The middle term is distributed at least once.

    B. If the major term is distributed in the conclusion, it is also distributed in the premise.

    C. There are not four terms.

    D. All of the above are true.

13. The falsity of 'no S are P' implies:

    A. All S are P.

    B. Some S are P.

    C. Some S are not P.

    D. No S are P.

Tell whether each of the following is true or false:

14. The negation of any contingent formula is itself a contingent formula.

15. Tautologies are never contingent.

Match the sentences in items 16 to 25 with their best translation from the list A to J below (Chapters 4 and 6 material).

A. $(p \equiv (q \lor r))$
B. $((\sim p) \lor (\sim q))$
C. $(Ga \lor (\sim Ga))$
D. $(\sim (p \lor \sim q))$
E. $(x)(Fx \supset (Gx \,\&\, Hx))$
F. $((\exists x)Fx \supset (\exists y)Gy)$
G. $(p \supset (x)Fx)$
H. $(\sim (x)(Fx \supset Gx))$
I. $((q \,\&\, r) \supset p)$
J. $[(\exists x)Kx \supset (p \equiv (\sim q))]$

16. It is not true that either Annie promised to deliver the photographs or that Gene did not promise to deliver the flowers.

17. All friendly dogs are easy to get to know and hard to avoid liking.

18. Not all pizza is gassy.

19. You can have my job only if everything is finished.

20. You can have my job if, and only if, you quit smoking either today or tomorrow.

21. Brenda is either a senior or she isn't!

22. Either you won't be able to go on Saturday or I'll not be able to get free from my job.

23. If somebody comes to this meeting, then somebody will be very happy.

24. I'll answer your questions if you and Robert both leave me alone for 5 minutes.

25. If somebody knows about the operation, then the police know if and only if you have not earned your keep.

ANSWERS TO SELF-QUIZ
FOR PART TWO

Section A:

	Answer	Reference		Answer	Reference
1.	A	14:2.1	11.	C	Module 23
2.	D	15:2.1	12.	D	21:2.1, 21:3
3.	A	17:1.1	13.	E	Module 22
4.	D	Module 17	14.	B	Module 23
5.	A	17:4	15.	D	Module 22
6.	C	Sketch prior to	16.	B	Module 19 or 23
		Chapter 5	17.	D	Module 18
7.	F	17:3	18.	E	17:4
8.	T	17:2.1	19.	B	18:3.2
9.	T	17:4; see also 11.2	20.	C	18:2.5
10.	B	19:1			

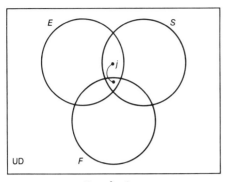

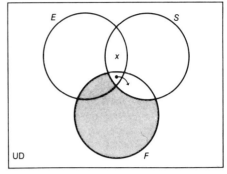

Conclusion   Premises

21. Valid. The truth-table for

$$\{[[((p \lor (\sim p)) \& (p \supset q)) \& (q \supset r)] \& ((\sim p) \supset r)] \supset r\}$$

shows the wff to be a tautology. See 17:4.

22. Using the assumption of contemporary logic discussed in the sketch after Chapter 4, this argument is not valid. Its diagrams according to Module 23 are:

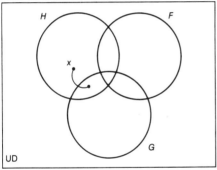

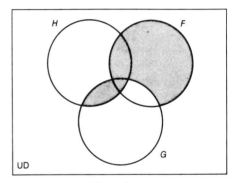

Conclusion   Premises

However, using the Aristotelian assumption discussed in the sketch it is valid. Its premises entail 'no H's are F's'; on the assumption that there are H's, it follows that 'some H is not an F.'

23. In symbolic form the argument

$(p \supset ((q \& r) \& s))$
$((q \& r) \supset s)$
$(\sim r)$
_____
$(\sim p)$ (see 15:2.1 and 17:4)

is a valid argument. The formula

$$[[((p \supset ((q \& r) \& s)) \& ((q \& r) \supset s)) \& (\sim r)] \supset (\sim p)]$$

is a tautology.

24. The argument is valid (see Modules 19 or 23). The diagrams for the argument are:

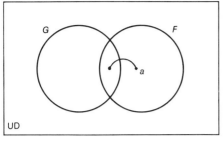 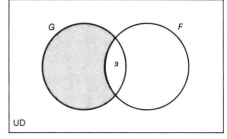

Conclusion	Premises

In syllogistic form the argument is:

All S are M.	S = all who are Albert the Great
All M are P.	M = those who brought texts to Europe
So all S are P.	P = those feared by the political leaders

25. The argument is invalid. The diagrams are

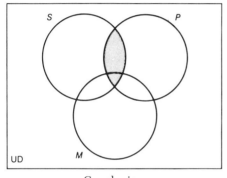 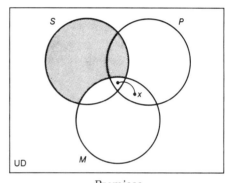

Conclusion	Premises

S = people who eat at H & L   The syllogistic form is:
P = people who complain   All S are M.
M = people who enjoy themselves   Some M are P.
                                     So no S are P.

The syllogism violates the rule if both premises are inclusions, the conclusion must also be an inclusion (see 19:3).

Section B:

	Answers	Reference		Answers	Reference
1.	E	Module 15	14.	T	based on 17:1
2.	C	Module 16	15.	T	based on 17:1
3.	C	17:1	16.	D	Module 16
4.	E	17:4	17.	E	Module 22
5.	C	Module 23	18.	H	Module 22
6.	C	Module 23	19.	G	Module 22
7.	A	Module 23	20.	A	Module 16

8.	C	Module 23	21.	C	21:2.1, 21:2.3
9.	D	Module 23	22.	B	Module 16
10.	C	18:2.5	23.	F	Module 22
11.	A	18:3.2	24.	I	Module 16
12.	D	19:3	25.	J	Module 22
13.	B	18:2.5 or Module 23			

Consider 75 percent or more correct on items taken from chapters you covered as a sign that you have mastered Part Two.

THREE
ILLOGICAL THINKING

To fully evaluate an argument you must ask three questions:

1. Is this argument logically correct?
2. Are all of its premises true?
3. Is this argument nonfallacious?

Our goal in Part Three is to learn how to make the third judgment accurately and efficiently—the judgment whether a particular argument is or is not a fallacy. In Chapter 7 we define the concept of a fallacy, in Chapter 8 we discuss fallacies of structure, and in Chapters 9 and 10 we discuss fallacies of content. Through your study of Part Three you should be able to recognize and name several species of fallacies. This ability turns out to be very practical; it helps you avoid being illogical and it helps you avoid being deceived by the fallacious arguments of others. Fallacious arguments are part of our culture; they infest the worlds of politics, business, journalism, law, advertising, and education. Logical and honest people in all these areas deplore the deliberate use of deceptively fallacious arguments; but others, perhaps believing that the end justifies the means, are less scrupulous about using fallacious arguments to prey on the gullibility of illogical people. Part Three can help you build up your defenses; it can help you avoid being deceived by fallacious arguments.

7

WHAT IS A FALLACY?

The purpose of this chapter is to characterize fallacies and to precisely define the term 'fallacy.' In so doing we present the major divisions between kinds of fallacies. The educational goal of this chapter is to learn the three basic reasons why an argument might be a fallacy.

MODULE 24
'FALLACY' DEFINED

● After reading Module 24 you should be able to:

1. Identify the central characteristics of fallacies
2. Identify the problems that make an argument fallacious
3. Identify the characteristics of acceptable arguments

24:1 Illogical thinking Illogical thinking occurs when people use arguments that are fallacious. Fallacious arguments are basically arguments that are *deceptive:* they seem to be logical and perhaps even reasonable, but on closer examination they turn out to be quite unreliable.

There are three primary reasons why an argument can be fallacious:

1. An argument can be fallacious because of structural or formal mistakes.
2. An argument can be fallacious because it is based on an assumption which, when brought to light, turns out to be false.
3. An argument can be fallacious in that it makes no logical progress toward establishing its designated conclusion.

In the next three sections we will give examples of each of these kinds of fallacies.

24:2.1 Structural fallacies Arguments that have structural flaws which make them invalid are fallacious arguments. Consider Eg. 24.1, which follows a valid inference pattern.

EG. 24.1 Either jeeps are rugged enough or tanks must be used.
Jeeps are not rugged enough.
So tanks must be used.

An argument like Eg. 24.1 can be formalized as

$$(p \lor q)$$
$$\underline{(\sim p)}$$
$$\therefore q$$

An argument that purports to follow this valid inference pattern but fails, because of a structural flaw, is the following.

EG. 24.2 Either jeeps are rugged enough or tanks must be used.
Jeeps are not rugged enough.
So tanks must not be used.

It can be translated into

$$(p \lor q)$$
$$\underline{(\sim p)}$$
$$\therefore (\sim q)$$

Notice the flaw that renders it invalid is in the different structure that its conclusion takes. This argument is flawed in its structure or form, and will be classified as a *formal fallacy*. In Chapter 8 we will discuss formal fallacies.

24:2.2 False-assumption fallacies The other two kinds of fallacies mentioned in 24:1 are both generated because of problems related to the content of arguments. The first of these two content-related types of fallacies comes about because if one or more of the assumptions upon which people base their arguments turns out to be false, a fallacious argument is generated. Here are some examples.

EG. 24.3 Most people believe that runaway inflation cannot be stopped by any type of government action.
So runaway inflation cannot be stopped by any type of government action.

Example 24.3 is based on an assumption to the effect that whatever most people believe is true. This assumption is rather obviously false. Thus, the revised argument obtained from Eg. 24.3 by adding the assumption as a new premise, Eg. 24.3', is clearly not a sound argument.

EG. 24.3' Most people believe that runaway inflation cannot be stopped by any type of government action.
Whatever most people believe is true.
So runaway inflation cannot be stopped by any type of government action.

Here are two more examples. The false assumptions are given just below each.

EG. 24.4 Harding says that we should march into battle with both guns blazing.
Well, Harding is a warmonger who is on the take from the military-industrial establishment.
He is little better than an administration lackey whose views are, no doubt, echos of those of the Joint Chiefs-of-Staff.
We should not, then, enter the battle.
False assumption: certain affiliations, economic motivations, and loyalties such as those mentioned can render everything a person says false.

EG. 24.5 I've been losing at cards all night.
This next hand must, then, be a winner.

False assumption: the hands being dealt are not independent of each other, in the sense that the postulate of insufficient reason does not apply (see 10:3.4).

We will treat fallacies of content based on false assumptions in Chapter 9.

24:2.3 No-progress fallacies The first two groups of fallacies are related to the notions of validity and soundness, respectively. The third class is composed of those arguments which make no logical progress. It contains those arguments which have conclusions that are analytically true statements, those which have inconsistent (self-contradictory) sets of premises, those which are question-begging, those which are circular, and fallacies of wrong conclusion. Each of these groups of arguments can be, or is of necessity, a group of *logically correct* arguments. And, save for the case of those with inconsistent sets of premises, none need contain arguments with false premises or false assumptions. Thus the arguments in the remaining four subgroups here can be sound arguments. Here are some examples of no-progress fallacies.

EG. 24.6 John is married and has three kids.
So John is married and has three children.

EG. 24.7 All musical instruments discovered in ancient India are made of bronze.
So all bronze musical instruments are musical instruments.

EG. 24.8 All people are mortal.
However some folks are not mortal.
Thus Bethany is alive and well.

Example 24.6 could be sound if its premise happened to be true. And since its conclusion merely restates its premise, it must be implied by that premise. (Every statement implies itself.) So we would call it logically correct and possibly sound. Yet it is not acceptable to argue for the truth of that conclusion in that way. No progress is made in moving from that premise to that conclusion. Similarly, in Eg. 24.7 the premise could be true. Since its conclusion itself is necessarily true, it cannot happen that it would be false should the premise be true. Thus Eg. 24.7 is valid and could be sound. Yet it is unreasonable to accept that premise as a reason to believe that conclusion; the premise makes no progress toward establishing that conclusion. There is no sense in which it can be taken as the grounds which establish the conclusion's truth. Likewise in Eg. 24.8 the argument is valid. The premises contradict each other, and so when one is true the other is false. Thus the premises cannot all be true at the same time. Hence the conclusion could not be false and all the premises be true, and so the argument is valid—but clearly not acceptable as an argument that progresses toward proving that its conclusion is true.

What makes these kinds of arguments fallacious is that they make no progress toward demonstrating their designated conclusion. The premises do not justify our acceptance of the conclusion as true. In such cases the informational content of the premises is not combined in ways that lead to demonstrating the alleged truth of the purported conclusion. We will deal with no-progress fallacies in Chapter 10.

24:3 Definitions Since the problems of lack of logical progress and being based on false assumptions are not structural problems which render arguments invalid, they must be regarded as *nonformal*, or, as they are usually called, *informal*, fallacies. Thus, we can set out these definitions.[1]

Def. 22 Fallacious argument = $_{df}$ an argument such that either it is structurally flawed so as to be logically incorrect, or is based on an assumption which is false or makes no logical progress

Def. 23 Formally fallacious argument = $_{df}$ an argument that is structurally flawed in such a way as to prevent it from being logically correct

Def. 24 Informally fallacious argument = $_{df}$ an argument such that it either makes no logical progress or is based upon a false assumption

24:4 Acceptable arguments Suppose that we find an argument that is logically correct, has only true premises, and is not a fallacy. If we find such an argument, and there are several, then we would be foolish not to accept it. It would be unreasonable to expect more of any argument in terms of those considerations that are raised in logic. Oh, we could say the argument is "crude," "vulgar," "offensive," "ungrammatical," "poorly organized," "easily misunderstood," "too long," etc. But these are side issues that do not affect whether or not unbiased, reasonable people should accept its conclusion as either necessarily or probably true. We can, thus, add our third and most central evaluative concept to the two we already have (*sound* and *logically correct*):

Def. 25 Acceptable argument = $_{df}$ an argument that is logically correct, with all of its premises true, and is nonfallacious.[2]

When we evaluate an argument, we are interested in finding out whether or not we should accept the argument as *proof* of its conclusion. If it is illogical, we should reject it. If it is an argument with a false premise, we should also reject it. And if it involves either a formal or an informal fallacy, we should reject it too. But if none of these is true of the argument, we would be foolish and unreasonable not to accept it.

EXERCISES FOR MODULE 24
'FALLACY' DEFINED

Ex. 1 Indicate whether each of the following is true or false.

_____ 1. All arguments that are logically incorrect because they contain structural or formal mistakes are fallacies.

---

[1] Definition 22 and those following continue the development of the conceptual system of logic started in Part One. Definition 21 was presented in Module 11.
[2] It is possible, based on Def. 22, for an argument to be classified as logically incorrect on the basis of its content but still not be called a fallacy. (These arguments are usually so logically weak as to be undeceptive.) One who wanted to include these arguments in the class of fallacies could propose a modified Def. 22, call it Def. 22'. Def. 22' could define 'fallacy' as an argument that is either logically incorrect, based on a false assumption, or makes no logical progress. Note that using Def. 22' means adjusting Def. 24 by adding "or is logically incorrect for nonstructural reasons." More importantly, however, using Def. 22' would require no changes in Def. 25.

_____ 2. All arguments that people find insulting are fallacies.

_____ 3. All arguments that are based on false assumptions are fallacies.

_____ 4. All arguments that make no logical progress in moving from the premises to the conclusion are fallacies.

_____ 5. All arguments with true premises are fallacies.

_____ 6. All logically correct arguments are fallacies.

_____ 7. All arguments that are not persuasive are fallacies.

_____ 8. All arguments that are not deductive are fallacies.

_____ 9. All fallacies are arguments.

_____ 10. A sound argument cannot be a fallacy.

_____ 11. There are both formal and informal fallacies.

_____ 12. A formal fallacy is an argument with a flaw in its structure that makes it logically incorrect.

_____ 13. An informal fallacy is a fallacy that is dressed casually.

_____ 14. A fallacy which has a mistake in its content is called an informal fallacy.

_____ 15. There are two types of informal fallacies; no progress fallacies and false assumption fallacies.

Ex. 2 Indicate whether each of the following is true or false.

_____ 1. All formally fallacious arguments are deductively valid.

_____ 2. An argument can be sound and yet not valid.

_____ 3. An argument can be logically correct if, and only if, it is valid.

_____ 4. Invalid arguments are not acceptable.

_____ 5. There are no acceptable arguments.

_____ 6. Every argument is a fallacy of one kind or another.

_____ 7. An argument that everyone accepts is what logicians call an acceptable argument.

_____ 8. No valid arguments can be fallacious.

_____ 9. Sound arguments are not necessarily acceptable arguments.

_____ 10. If at least one premise of an argument is true, it is a sound argument.

_____ 11. If all of the premises of an argument are true, it is a sound argument.

_____ 12. If at least one premise of a logically correct argument is true, it is a sound argument.

_____ 13. If all the premises of a logically correct argument are true, it is a sound argument.

_____ 14. An argument can fail to be acceptable if it is either a fallacy, has a false premise, or is not logically correct.

_____ 15. Acceptable arguments are those arguments that are worthy of being accepted by people acting reasonably.

_____ 16. The three questions to ask when fully evaluating an argument are: "Is this argument logically correct?" "Are its premises true?" and "Is it a nonfallacy?"

_____ 17. Soundness is solely a matter of logic.

_____ 18. Acceptable arguments are not formally fallacious arguments.

_____ 19. Questions of etiquette and taste are questions which bear on the acceptability of arguments from the point of view of logic.

_____ 20. Reasonable people accept only acceptable arguments.

_____ 21. Only acceptable arguments ought to be accepted if one is being reasonable.

ANSWERS TO EXERCISES
FOR MODULE 24

Ex. 1

1. T (24:3, 24:1)	2. F	3. T
4. T (24:1, 24:3)	5. F	6. F
7. F	8. F	9. T
10. F (24:2.3)	11. T	12. T
13. F	14. T	15. T

There are just three reasons why an argument might be a fallacy: it is invalid due to a structural flaw, it is based on a false assumption, or it makes no logical progress.

Ex. 2

1. F	2. F
3. T	4. T
5. F	6. F
7. F	8. F (24:2.3)
9. T (24:2.3)	10. F
11. F	12. F
13. T	14. T
15. T	16. T
17. F	18. T
19. F	20. F; unfortunately! They too make mistakes.
21. T	

If you missed two or more, review 24:4 and the relevant definitions from Chapter 3.

8

FORMAL FALLACIES

There are an uncountable number of ways that an argument can be structurally flawed so as to be invalid. In this chapter we will look at five of the most recurrent formal fallacies. In Module 25 we will examine two from propositional logic; in Module 26 we will study three from predicate logic. The educational goal of this chapter is to explain what formal fallacies are through these typical examples. You should be able to identify each of the five formal fallacies presented here by name, and be able to distinguish them from each other, from those fallacies we present in Chapters 9 and 10, and from valid arguments which may appear especially similar to them.

MODULE 25

THE FALLACIES OF AFFIRMING THE CONSEQUENT AND DENYING THE ANTECEDENT[1]

The two formal fallacies named in the title of this module occur with disturbing frequency—at times blatantly and at other times subtly.

● After reading Module 25 you should be able to:

1. Identify fallacies of affirming the consequent
2. Identify fallacies of denying the antecedent
3. Distinguish these two types of fallacies

25:1.1 Many inference patterns involve the use of conditional statements, as in these examples.

EG. 25.1 1. If it rains today the sidewalks will be wet.
2. It rained today.
3. So the sidewalks were wet.

---

[1] This module will be easier to follow if you have already covered Chapter 4. If you have not, you should focus on the English examples and exercises.

EG. 25.2 1. If it rains today the sidewalks will be wet.
2. The sidewalks were not wet.
3. So it did not rain today.

The logical structure of the two valid examples can be systematically represented by the following diagrams. Their validity can be demonstrated by truth-tables.

Valid Patterns

Pattern 1: modus ponens   Pattern 2: modus tollens

    1. $(A \supset B)$ 1. $(A \supset B)$
    2. A 2. $(\sim B)$
$\therefore$ 3. B $\therefore$ 3. $(\sim A)$

25:1.2 Modus ponens The inference pattern named *modus ponens* (which roughly means "the way of affirming the antecedent") allows as valid the inference of a wff B from two wffs A and $(A \supset B)$. That is, given any conditional statement and given the affirmation of its antecedent as true, we can validly infer that its consequent is true, as in the following.

EG. 25.3 1. If you get a grade of A on the final exam, then you will get a grade of A in the course.
2. You earned an A on the final exam.
3. So you will be given an A in the course.

EG. 25.4 1. If you drive to Toledo and to Detroit for me, I will pay you $10 plus expenses.
2. You did drive to Toledo and to Detroit for me.
3. Thus I will pay you $10 plus expenses.

The translations of Egs. 25.3 and 25.4 show that both are valid because of the modus ponens inference pattern.

EG. 25.3' $(p \supset q)$
           p
      $\therefore q$

EG. 25.4' $((p \mathbin{\&} q) \supset r)$
          $(p \mathbin{\&} q)$
      $\therefore r$

[In Eg. 25.3' $A = p$, $B = q$, and $(A \supset B) = (p \supset q)$. In Eg. 25.4' $A = (p \mathbin{\&} q)$, $B = r$, and $(A \supset B) = ((p \mathbin{\&} q) \supset r)$.]

25:1.3 Modus tollens The inference pattern named *modus tollens* (which roughly means "the way of denying the consequent") allows the inference to $(\sim A)$ from the conditional $(A \supset B)$ and the denial of the truth of B as in $(\sim B)$. Thus, given any conditional statement and the denial of its consequent, one can infer validly that its antecedent is false, as in:

EG. 25.5 1. If you get a grade of A on the final exam, then you will get a grade of A in the course.
2. I am sorry but you did not get a grade of A in the course.
3. Thus you did not earn an A on the final exam.

EG. 25.6 If Paul fixes the food and Barbara prepares the entertainment, then the party will be a success. But the party will not be a success. So it won't be the case both that Paul fixes the food and that Barbara prepares the entertainment.

The translations of Egs. 25.5 and 25.6 show that each is valid because of the modus tollens inference pattern.

EG. 25.5′ $(p \supset q)$
         $\underline{(\sim q)}$
       $\therefore (\sim p)$

EG. 25.6′ $((p \ \& \ q) \supset r)$
         $\underline{(\sim r)}$
       $\therefore (\sim (p \ \& \ q))$

25:2.1 Affirming the consequent Most people easily accept the validity of arguments which are either modus ponens or modus tollens. But at times people confuse things and forget that the valid inferences are modus ponens and modus tollens. The most confusions are the two fallacies descriptively named *affirming the consequent* and *denying the antecedent*. Here are two examples of the fallacy of affirming the consequent.

EG. 25.7   1. If it rains today the sidewalks will be wet.
           2. The sidewalks were wet.
           3. Therefore it rained today.

EG. 25.8   1. If you get a grade of A on the final exam, then you will get a grade of A in the course.
           2. You did earn a grade of A in the course.
           3. Thus you must have earned an A on your final exam.

In both cases the premises could all be true and the conclusion could still be false. There is more than one fact which could account for the wet sidewalks. There may be more than one way to earn an A in that professor's course; e.g., that professor may give an A to everyone who either writes an A term paper or gets an A on the final. These formally fallacious argument follow the demonstrably invalid inference pattern of affirming the consequent [the B in $(A \supset B)$]:

Affirming the consequent fallacy pattern

     $(A \supset B)$
       $\underline{B \hspace{3em}}$
      $\therefore A$

A	B	$[((A \supset B) \ \& \ B) \supset A]$
T	T	T T T T T T T
T	F	T F F F F T T
F	T	F T T T T (F) F
F	F	F T F F F T F

                           ↑ invalid

25:2.2 Here are two examples of the formal fallacy of denying the antecedent.

EG. 25.9 1. If it rains today the sidewalks will be wet.
2. It did not rain today.
3. So the sidewalks must not have been wet.

EG. 25.10 1. If you get a grade of A on the final exam, then you will get a grade of A in the course.
2. You did not get an A on your final exam.
3. So you cannot get an A in this course.

These two arguments are invalid; the premises do not entail their conclusions for much the same reasons as in Egs. 25.7 and 25.8. The premises could be true and the conclusion could still be false, as the following truth-table for the fallacy of denying the antecedent indicates.

Denying the antecedent fallacy pattern

$(A \supset B)$
$(\sim A)$
$\therefore (\sim B)$

A	B	$[((A \supset B)$ & $(\sim A)) \supset (\sim B)]$
T	T	T T T F F T T F T
T	F	T F F F F T T T F
F	T	F T T T T F Ⓕ F T
F	F	F T F T T F T T F

↑ invalid

EXERCISES FOR MODULE 25
THE FALLACIES OF AFFIRMING THE CONSEQUENT AND DENYING THE ANTECEDENT

Ex. 1* Several arguments are given below in symbolic form. If an argument is valid by modus ponens put 'MP' in the answer space; if it is valid by modus tollens put 'MT' in the answer space.

_____ 1. $(p \supset q)$ _____ 2. $(r \supset p)$ _____ 3. r
$\quad\quad\quad p$ $\quad\quad\quad r$ $\quad\quad\quad (r \supset s)$
$\quad\quad\therefore q$ $\quad\quad\therefore p$ $\quad\quad\therefore s$

_____ 4. $(q \supset p)$ _____ 5. $(t \supset s)$ _____ 6. $(q \supset s)$
$\quad\quad\quad (\sim p)$ $\quad\quad\quad (\sim s)$ $\quad\quad\quad (\sim s)$
$\quad\quad\therefore (\sim q)$ $\quad\quad\therefore (\sim t)$ $\quad\quad\therefore (\sim q)$

_____ 7. $((p \ \& \ s) \supset (r \ \& \ t))$ _____ 8. $[\sim(\sim(p \lor q))]$
$\quad\quad\quad (p \ \& \ s)$ $\quad\quad\quad [r \supset (\sim(p \lor q))]$
$\quad\quad\therefore (r \ \& \ t)$ $\quad\quad\therefore (\sim r)$

* If you have not worked through Chapter 4 of the text, you should not be surprised to find Exs. 1, 2, and 3 difficult to follow. You may move directly to Ex. 4.

Ex. 2* Here are several arguments in symbolic form. Identify those that are fallacies of affirming the consequent by 'AC' and those that are denying the antecedent as 'DA.'

_____ 1. $p \supset q$ _____ 2. $(p \supset q)$ _____ 3. $(r \supset (s \supset t))$
            $\dfrac{q}{\therefore p}$ $\dfrac{(\sim p)}{\therefore (\sim q)}$ $\dfrac{(\sim r)}{\therefore (\sim (s \supset t))}$

_____ 4. $(t \lor p)$ _____ 5. $(q \,\&\, r)$
            $\dfrac{(p \supset (t \lor p))}{\therefore p}$ $\dfrac{((t \equiv s) \supset (q \,\&\, r))}{\therefore (t \equiv s)}$

_____ 6. p
            $\dfrac{((\sim p) \supset (q \,\&\, s))}{\therefore (\sim (q \,\&\, s))}$

Ex. 3* Here are some arguments in symbolic notation; using the abbreviations from Exs. 1 and 2 identify each as 'MP,' 'MT,' 'DA,' or 'AC.'

_____ 1. $(q \supset p)$ _____ 2. $(p \supset q)$
            $\dfrac{q}{\therefore p}$ $\dfrac{q}{\therefore p}$

_____ 3. $(q \supset r)$ _____ 4. $(r \supset (s \supset t))$
            $\dfrac{(\sim r)}{\therefore (\sim q)}$ $\dfrac{(\sim r)}{\therefore (\sim (s \supset t))}$

_____ 5. $((p \supset q) \supset r)$ _____ 6. $((p \,\&\, r) \supset q)$
            $\dfrac{[((p \supset q) \supset r) \supset s]}{\therefore s}$ $\dfrac{q}{\therefore (p \,\&\, r)}$

_____ 7. $(q \equiv t)$ _____ 8. $(\sim p)$
            $\dfrac{(p \supset (q \equiv t))}{\therefore p}$ $\dfrac{((\sim p) \supset q)}{\therefore q}$

_____ 9. $((\sim p) \supset (\sim q))$ _____ 10. $((\sim p) \supset (\sim q))$
            $\dfrac{(\sim (\sim q))}{\therefore (\sim (\sim p))}$ $\dfrac{(\sim q)}{\therefore (\sim p)}$

Ex. 4 Here are some English arguments, as in Ex. 3; identify each as either valid by 'MP' or 'MT' or invalid by the fallacies of 'AC' or 'DA.'

_____ 1. If everyone drank cold pop, then the industry would boom. But not everybody will drink it. So the industry will not boom.

_____ 2. It is not true that she was present at the scene of the accident. Since if she were guilty then she would have been at the scene, it follows that she is not guilty!

_____ 3. If all the world looked as blah as this, then if you wanted to be original you would buy a Frurd Bluck. But the world does not look like this. So you know what you should do.

_____ 4. If a formula is well formed, it will have an even number of parentheses. This formula has an even number of parentheses. So it must be a wff.

_____ 5. The strikers want more money. If the strikers want more money we cannot meet their demands. Hence we can't meet their demands.

Ex. 1

1. MP   2. MP   3. MP   4. MT
5. MT   6. MT   7. MP   8. MT

If you missed two or more review 25:1.2 and 25:1.3.

Ex. 2

1. AC   2. DA   3. DA   4. AC   5. AC   6. DA

If you missed more than one review 25:2.1 and 25:2.2.

Ex. 3

1. MP   3. MT   5. MP   7. AC   9. MT

If you missed more than two, review Module 25.

Ex. 4

1. DA   2. MT   3. DA   4. AC   5. MP

MODULE 26

FALLACIES OF DISTRIBUTION[2]

This module is about a group of fallacies Aristotle discovered as he developed his theory of syllogisms. Of course, these fallacies infected arguments prior to Aristotle's time and are still all too common even today.

● After reading Module 26 you should be able to:

1. Identify arguments that commit a fallacy of distribution
2. Distinguish instances of those fallacies from instances of the fallacies of affirming the consequent and denying the antecedent
3. Distinguish instances of the fallacy of undistributed middle term, the fallacy of undistributed subject term, the fallacy of undistributed predicate term, and valid arguments of predicate logic.

26:1 Just as there are formal fallacies which render some propositional logic arguments invalid, there are those that render predicate logic arguments invalid. When a particular invalid inference pattern is commonly employed, it often earns a name as well as notoriety. For example, here are some arguments that commit the fallacy called the *fallacy of undistributed middle term*.

---

[2] Those who have covered Chapter 5 already will find much that is repetitive in this module; however, those who covered Chapter 6 but not 5 will see in it an entirely different approach to predicate logic. Having covered either of these two earlier chapters will make this module much easier than it would be without having learned any predicate logic.

EG. 26.1 All land animals are capable of movement.
All fishes are capable of movement.
So all land animals are fishes.

EG. 26.2 Whales are mammals.
Some mammals are land creatures.
So some whales are land creatures.

EG. 26.3 People sleep late on Saturday.
Some who sleep late on Saturday work on Saturday.
So people work on Saturday.

EG. 26.4 All humans eat vegetables.
Kozak, the flying rabbit, eats vegetables.
So Kozak is human.

26:2.1 The terms of a syllogism The formal fallacies of distribution affect arguments known as *syllogisms*. A syllogism is a three-statement argument of predicate logic. It has two premises and a conclusion. Each statement is one of the following types (discussed in Module 18):

A form: universal and individual inclusion
I form: partial inclusion
E form: universal and particular exclusion
O form: partial exclusion

Each such statement has two terms—its subject and its predicate. Now you might think that because there are three statements in a syllogism and because each statement has two terms there should be six terms altogether in a syllogism. However in a proper syllogism each term occurs twice. So there are really only *three* terms in a proper syllogism. Each of the three terms has an easily remembered name. The subject term of the conclusion is called the *subject term of the syllogism*. The conclusion's predicate term is called the *predicate term of the syllogism*.[3] The term that occurs in both premises, but not in the conclusion, is called the *middle term of the syllogism*. Here are some example syllogisms which are valid. Each of the three terms are given below each example:

EG. 26.5 All animals are mortal.
All mortal things live on or very near the surface of the earth.
Therefore all animals live on or very near the surface of the earth.

Subject term = animals
Predicate term = things living on or very near the surface of the earth
Middle term = mortal things

EG. 26.6 Some things that live in houses are cats.
All house-dwelling animals are domesticated.
Thus some cats are domesticated.

---

[3] The syllogism's predicate term is also called its *major* term and the syllogism's subject term its *minor* term.

Subject term = cats
Predicate term = domesticated animals
Middle term = house-dwelling animals[4]

If you want to check your understanding of what a syllogism is and which terms are which in a syllogism you should do Exs. 1 and 2 now.

26:2.2 Distributed terms The word 'distributed' is a technical word which has an important role to play in Aristotle's theory of syllogisms. A term is said to be *distributed in a given statement* if the statement refers to, or takes into account, each and every member of the class of objects that the term itself applies to.

Thus, consider our four types of statements.

A: All (A's) are part of the B's.
I: Some A is one of the B's.
E: None of the (A's) are any of the (B's).
O: Some A is not any of the (B's).

The following two rules of thumb identify distributed terms.

Rule 1 In the universal (and individual) statement forms (A and E) all the members of the subject terms are taken into account so *the subject terms are distributed in those A and E statements.*

Rule 2 In the exclusion statement forms (E and O) each member of the predicate class is taken into consideration and so *the predicate terms are distributed in E and O* statements. In our samples above the distributed terms are circled.

As a rule of thumb remember: The subject terms of universal (and individual) statements are distributed and the predicate terms of exclusion statements are distributed. To check your ability to distinguish distributed from undistributed terms you could do Ex. 3 now.

26:3.1 Fallacy of undistributed middle term Aristotle warned that there were many potential hazards involved in the application of his rules of syllogisms. Careless use of the rules can lead to invalid, logically unreliable arguments.[5] Certain patterns of invalidity often occur when particular rules are violated. These patterns have earned themselves names which associate them with the particular rule they violate. One such invalid inference form is the formal *fallacy of the undistributed middle term,* which violates the rule that *the middle term of a syllogism has to be distributed in at least one of the premises.*

To determine whether or not an argument commits this fallacy, use the following procedure.

1. Determine whether or not the argument is a syllogism as defined in 26:2.1.
2. Isolate the middle term.

---

[4] Example 26.6 illustrates that the syllogism's subject and predicate terms may occur in any position in the syllogism's premises. In Eg. 26.6 the syllogism's subject term happens to be the predicate of the first premise.

[5] A simplified set of rules for syllogisms is presented in Module 19. Aristotle's own set of rules is more complicated.

3. Determine if the middle term is distributed in a premise by determining (a) which of the four statement forms each premise is and (b) whether the middle term is distributed in either premise by appeal to the rules of thumb in 26:2.2. If the middle term is not distributed in either premise, the fallacy is committed.

Here are some examples of the fallacy.

EG. 26.7 1. All household appliances consume energy.
2. All human activities consume energy.
3. Thus all household appliances are human activities.

> Middle term = things that consume energy

> In premise 1 the middle term is not distributed as predicate of A-form statement. In premise 2 it is not distributed as predicate of A-form statement.

EG. 26.8 1. All who love life know what pain is.
2. Some people who know what pain is, worry.
3. Thus all who love life worry.

> Middle term = people who know what pain is

> The middle term is not distributed as predicate of A-form premise 1, or as subject of I-form premise 2.

26:3.2 Fallacies of undistributed subject term and undistributed predicate term

The idea of distributed versus undistributed terms is broad enough that there are actually three fallacies of distribution. We have looked at the fallacy of the undistributed middle term. Now let's examine the twin fallacies of undistributed subject term and undistributed predicate term.

These two fallacies are based on the same type of structural rule: a *distributed term is acceptable in the conclusion only if that term is distributed in the premise.* In other words you can't draw a conclusion about a whole class if you have only premised something about part of it. Here are two examples. See if you can pick out the syllogism's subject and predicate terms in each. Then ask yourself if either term is distributed in the conclusion while being undistributed in a premise.

EG. 26.9 Some cattle is grass-fed.
Any grass-fed animal is ecologically inexpensive.
So all cattle are ecologically inexpensive animals.

EG. 26.10 No reptiles suckle their young.
All animals that suckle their young have hair.
So no reptiles have hair.

In Eg. 26.9 the premise speaks of *some* cattle while the conclusion refers to the *whole* class; hence it illustrates the fallacy of undistributed subject term. In Eg. 26.10 the term 'things that have hair' is undistributed in the premise but distributed in the conclusion; hence it illustrates the fallacy of undistributed predicate term.

As you can see, once you can distinguish distributed from undistributed terms (using the rules in 26:2.2), you can recognize each of the three fallacies of distribution:

Fallacy of undistributed middle: middle term not distributed in either premise

Fallacy of undistributed subject term: subject term distributed in conclusion but not in premise

Fallacy of undistributed predicate term: predicate term distributed in conclusion but not in premise

EXERCISES FOR MODULE 26
FALLACIES OF DISTRIBUTION

Ex. 1 Identify the syllogisms in the following list of arguments. Use 'syl' and 'no' as your possible answers.

_____ 1. All cats fly. All flying things are in danger. So all cats are in danger.

_____ 2. Maow is a cat. If Maow is a cat, she is fat. So Maow is fat.

_____ 3. Either fish eat or they don't. If they do they survive; otherwise not. So they either do or do not survive.

_____ 4. Some fish eat. Some birds do not eat. So all birds are fish.

_____ 5. Maow is a cat. All cats eat fish. So Maow eats fish.

Ex. 2 Identify the subject term (ST), the predicate term (PT), and the middle term (MT) in the arguments indicated.

1. Example 26.1
2. Example 26.2
3. Example 26.3
4. Example 26.4
5. Example 26.9
6. Example 26.10
7. Item #1. Ex. 1
8. Item #4, Ex. 1

Ex. 3 Below each statement in the following list write each of the terms that is distributed in it.

1. All cows give milk.

2. Some little boys are not helpful people.

3. Socrates is a philosopher.

4. Not all philosophers are wise.

5. Some cold butter is nearly white in color.

6. Trees grow tall in rich soil.

7. Most business people are not unethical.

8. The President is the leader of his party.

Ex. 4 Several syllogisms are given below. Put 'fal' by any which commits a fallacy of distribution; otherwise put 'no.'

_____ 1. All people love candy. All children love candy. Thus all people are children.

_____ 2. Some children eat ice cream. Some women eat ice cream too. This entails that some children are women.

_____ 3. Plato was a teacher of Aristotle. All of Aristotle's mentors were wise. So Plato was wise.

_____ 4. Plato was threatened by the death penalty. Some, so threatened, panic. So Plato panicked.

_____ 5. All women are able to think clearly. All who can think clearly can be trained to fly jets. All women then can be trained to fly jets.

_____ 6. Most men loathe clean-up chores. But most women also loathe them. So most men are women.

_____ 7. All jet pilots have quick reactions. Big Jim has quick reactions. So he must be a jet pilot.

_____ 8. Few people read good literature. All who read good literature appreciate Faulkner. Some people appreciate Faulkner.

_____ 9. Every jet pilot lives in Los Angeles. Many Los Angeles people are not crazy about the midwest. So some jet pilots are not crazy about the midwest.

_____ 10. Socrates is mortal. If anything is a person, then it is mortal. So Socrates is a person.

_____ 11. All buttered toast tastes good. Everything that tastes good is fattening. So buttered toast is fattening.

_____ 12. Some foods are high in protein. All high-protein foods are healthy foods. So all foods are health foods.

_____ 13. Some vegetables are high in roughage content. All foods that are high in roughage content are low in calories. So vegetables are low in calories.

_____ 14. No fried foods are low in calories. Some low-calorie foods taste bland. So no fried foods taste bland.

_____ 15. This carrot is not fresh. Some of the fresh things need to be refrigerated. So this carrot does not need to be refrigerated.

Ex. 5 After you check your answers for Ex. 4, distinguish which of the three fallacies is committed by the fallacious items above. Write 'UDM,' 'FDS,' and 'FDP' for undistributed middle, fallacy of distribution in the subject, and fallacy of distribution in the predicate, respectively.

SELECTED ANSWERS TO EXERCISES
FOR MODULE 26

Ex. 1

1. Syl   2. No   3. No   4. Syl   5. Syl
If you missed one review the definition of syllogism in 26:2.1

Ex. 2

1. ST = land animals PT = fishes MT = things capable of movement	2. ST = whales PT = land creatures MT = mammals
3. ST = people PT = Saturday workers MT = Saturday late sleepers	4. ST = Kozak PT = humans MT = vegetable eaters
5. ST = cattle PT = ecologically inexpensive animals MT = grass-fed things	6. ST = creatures that suckle their young PT = thing that have hair MT = reptiles
7. ST = cats PT = things in danger MT = things that fly	8. ST = birds PT = fish MT = things that eat

Ex. 3

1. Cows   3. Socrates   4. Wise people
6. Trees   7. Unethical people
If you missed more than one, either by writing down a wrong term or by not writing down a right one, review 26:2.2.

Ex. 4

1. Fal   3. No   5. No   7. Fal
9. Fal   11. No   12. Fal   13. Fal
14. Fal   15. Fal
If you missed three or more review 26:3.1 and 26:3.2.

Ex. 5

UDM: 1, 7, 9; FDS: 12, 13; FDP: 14, 15
If you missed any of these, review 26:3.1 and 26:3.2.

OTHER FORMAL FALLACIES

We have looked at a few of the more common and, thus, more dangerous formal fallacies. Many formal fallacies of propositional logic and predicate logic go unnamed because logicians using the techniques of symbolic logic can recognize structural validity or invalidity without requiring recourse to the memorization of large numbers of valid and invalid inference patterns. The same is true of formal fallacies that occur at more advanced levels of logic. Consider, for example, the following passages which involve fallacies from the logic of relations.

EG. 26.11   Events divide into two classes in that each is either self-generating or caused to occur by some temporally earlier event. It follows, then, that all events that are not self-generating were caused to occur by some single temporally earlier event which we can name the "creation of the Universe."

EG. 26.12   The trustees were lamenting the low grade-point averages of their students when one said, "Well, I guess every student fails a course sometime." Another quipped, "Yes, let's find out which professor teaches that course and fire him or her."

At these more advanced levels the formal fallacies very often do not even have special names. Nonetheless, there are structural errors which render the arguments invalid. Learning the more advanced techniques of formal logic will enable you to recognize formal fallacies quickly and easily.

9
FALLACIES OF CONTENT: FALSE ASSUMPTIONS

The second large group of fallacies is comprised of informally fallacious arguments that are fallacious because they are based on false assumptions. Once the assumptions are discovered the argument can be reconstructed into a logically correct but unsound argument. As such, it would remain an unacceptable argument. Module 27 explains how to reconstruct arguments by pulling out their assumptions and adding these as new premises. Module 28 examines various kinds of fallacies that are species of *irrelevant appeals*. Module 29 deals with the fallacies of *playing with words* and *false dilemma*. The related fallacies of *Composition* and *Division* are explained in Module 30. Module 31 covers the *false-cause fallacy*, the *gambler's fallacy*, and *playing with numbers*. Module 32 leads us toward a discussion of strategies used to prove points as it explains the *straw-man fallacy*. Module 33 examines a type of pseudo-fallacy called *emotional appeal*, which arises when argumentation aimed at persuasion is abandoned in favor of direct efforts to bring about action by playing on a person's emotions. Module 33 also contains exercises that require an overview of all the types of fallacies covered in Chapter 9. Our educational goal is to learn how to recognize each of these fallacies by name. In order to really benefit from this chapter you should learn to identify the false assumptions which make arguments fallacious.

MODULE 27
EXHIBITING ASSUMPTIONS

Many arguments, especially those people really use when they are talking to each other, are enthymemes. They omit mention of statements that are obviously intended and assumed to be either premises or conclusions. Often these missing statements are premises; in those cases we can call them assumptions because they must be assumed to be true if the argument is to be sound. Generally, people are able to make clear their assumptions, but at times these assumptions are suppressed in the sense that they are difficult to root out and make explicit. Sometimes those assumptions are particularly slippery because we are either unaware that the argument really depends on them or inclined at first blush to regard them as plausible. In this module we will suggest how one can reconstruct an argument by taking its assumptions as additions to its set of premises.

● After reading Module 27 you should be able to:

1. Identify the assumptions of arguments
2. Distinguish good from poor reconstructions of arguments
3. Pick out the reason or reasons why a particular reconstruction is poor
4. Reconstruct arguments that are based on covert assumptions

27:1 The *assumptions* of an argument are its enthymematic (missing) premises (see 4:3). The explanations of why people might not explicitly state all their assumptions include quite a mixed bag of causes and motives: they might feel the assumptions are too obvious, boring, or time-consuming to state; they might not want to become "sidetracked" in discussing assumptions; they might know that the assumptions are false and wish to conceal them; they might not even be able to articulate their assumptions because they are deeply hidden within their own unexamined prejudices. In any case, assumptions exist and arguments are based on them. Before we get into some of the more common types of false assumptions, those which generate fallacies, we must learn how to pull out an argument's assumptions, whether they be true or false.

27:2.1 Converting to valid structure Most informal fallacies are arguments based on false assumptions. Their logical incorrectness is based on their content rather than on formal flaws. They are regarded as *informal* for that reason. Nevertheless, we do not have to abandon them with the hopeless remark, "They are informal and there is nothing we can objectively do to logically evaluate them." Informal reasoning is difficult but not impossible to evaluate. The key is to convert informal reasoning into formal reasoning. Every piece of informal reasoning can be converted into a structurally valid argument.

The first way to accomplish the conversion into a structurally valid argument is easy and surefire. One simply takes the conclusion of the original argument and makes it one of its own premises.

$$
\begin{array}{ll}
P_1 & P_1 \\
P_2 & P_2 \\
\quad\cdot & \quad\cdot \\
\quad\cdot & \quad\cdot \\
\quad\cdot & \quad\cdot \\
\underline{P_n} & P_n \\
\therefore C & \underline{P_{n+1}\,(=C)} \\
\text{Original} & \therefore C \\
& \text{New valid argument}
\end{array}
$$

Thus, for example, we can convert

EG. 27.1 1. Whenever I attend the theater there is always an oppressively large crowd.
2. Generally large crowds bother me.
3. So if I attend the theather tonight I will probably be bothered by the large crowd.

out of its current inductive condition and into the valid argument

EG. 27.2 1. Whenever I attend the theater, there is always an oppressively large crowd.

2. If I attend the theater tonight I will, in all likelihood, be bothered by the large crowd.
3. Generally large crowds bother me.
4. Thus if I attend the theater tonight I will, in all likelihood, be bothered by the large crowd.

Unfortunately this is a poor method because it automatically yields an argument that makes no logical progress. Example 27.2 does not prove or establish its conclusion as true as much as it simply offers its conclusion as a restatement of one of its premises. Such an argument, as we shall see more fully in Chapter 10, is *circular*. The premises do not come together to yield up and support their conclusion as their collective logical result. Rather one of them, by itself, implies that conclusion only because every statement implies itself. This type of argument is valid, but only in a trivial way.

27:2.2 Digging out assumptions The second way of converting arguments, digging out their assumptions, is both more difficult and more promising. This method involves adding premises to the argument until the original conclusion is structurally entailed. The premises to add are all those that are operative as its assumptions, those that contain *additional* relevant information not originally given in the argument, and those that are suppressed. For example, suppose we are originally given the following argument.

EG. 27.3   1. The people who live in this valley could have been in very bad shape because the valley floods as much as 4 feet after a hard rain.
2. But the people have built their homes on stilts.
3. So they are probably both wise and industrious.

We could convert it into a valid argument as follows.

EG. 27.4   1. The people who live in this valley could have been in very bad shape because the valley floods as much as 4 feet after a hard rain (given).
2. The people have built their homes on stilts (given).
3. If the valley floods by 4 feet of water, then the water level will be high enough so that water will flow into the village where the people have their homes (additional information).
4. If water flows into the place where people have their homes, their homes will be ruined unless precautions are taken (suppressed assumption).
5. If their homes are ruined, then the people will be in bad shape (suppressed assumption).
6. One precaution that the people can take is to put their homes on stilts (additional information).
7. Anyone who takes such a precaution must be wise because they have forethought (suppressed assumption).
8. Anyone who is able to actually put their home on stilts must be industrious, to say the least (suppressed assumption).
9. Thus these people are both wise and industrious (original conclusion).

The basic restriction on this method is that one may not add the original conclusion as a premise. Supplying the missing informational premises is, in practice, not too hard. First, it is sometimes possible to replicate situations so that the factual information becomes available once more. Second, it is often possible to puzzle the situation out so that the factual information that the original argument was probably based on becomes clear once again. Supplying the suppressed assumptions is often a bit harder because it is easy for such assumptions to go unnoticed. Sometimes you have to ask "What would the author have had to believe to say this?" or "When saying this, what did the author intend that the audience should take for granted?"

In our discussion of several of the informal fallacies we will have to uncover the false assumptions that make them fallacious. The virtue of this second method of converting informal reasoning into formal reasoning is that it lays out *all* the (suppressed) premises of the informal argument. It reconstructs the argument into one which includes all the assumptions that we have reason to believe were operative in the original argument. If any of the premises of the reconstructed argument are false, even when these premises did not appear in the original, then we have reason to find the original unacceptable. The reconstruction should reveal if the original is based on a factually false piece of assumed information, a false belief, or a prejudice.

27:3 There are some important precautions we must observe in using the method described above of reconstructing arguments. First, and most obvious, we do not want to be converting nonarguments into valid arguments. If you are not sure about how to tell arguments from nonarguments, review Module 3. Second, we must remember that there may be more than one way to "reconstruct" or "convert" an argument. It may be, for example, that one way of converting an argument makes it look like the argument was operating on one assumption which was false, but another way of converting it makes it look like it was operating on a different assumption which was true. Take, for example, the following argument.

EG. 27.5 1. My friend says that the President will probably announce a new tax system tomorrow.
2. So the President will probably announce a new tax system tomorrow.

One way to convert Eg. 27.5 is:

EG. 27.6 1. My friend says that the President will probably announce a new tax system tomorrow.
2. Whatever my friend says is true.
3. Nothing is going to happen between now and tomorrow which will cause the President to change his plans.
4. Thus the President will probably announce a new tax system tomorrow.

In Eg. 27.6, premise 2 makes explicit one important assumption, which, as it stands, is probably false. But we could have converted Eg. 27.5 this way:

EG. 27.7 1. My friend says that the President will probably announce a new tax system tomorrow.
2. Whatever my friend says about the President and about tax law is true.
3. Nothing is going to happen between now and tomorrow which will cause the President to change his plans.
4. Thus the President will probably announce a new tax system tomorrow.

The most reasonable way of avoiding the danger involved in exhibiting an assumption wrongly is to be stingy about how broadly one states the assumption. Note that premise 2 in Eg. 27.7 is much more restrictive than premise 2 in Eg. 27.6. We should not attribute to people broad and outrageous assumptions but, rather, narrow and careful assumptions. If these still turn out false, then we have better reason to regard their original arguments as fallacies than we would if we attributed the broader assumptions. We should not decide that an argument is a fallacy until we have figured out which assumption might be its narrowest base. Any other procedure would have the result of making almost everything a fallacy and also of attributing to people views that they do not hold and that they do not have to hold. It is a favorite debater's trick to attribute to people more than they believe or need to believe. But we are not trying to be sophistic debaters; rather we are trying to be reasonable and fair about the matter of evaluating each other's arguments.

27:4 Each type of informal fallacy we are going to discuss can be dangerous if not detected. In their more subtle forms, such fallacies can lead one to accept unacceptable conclusions. (The next time you buy something that you didn't really want you should ask yourself which fallacy it was that cost you money.) These kinds of fallacies turn up in all aspects of our lives, but most frequently they turn up in advertising, political speeches, editorials, and pseudointellectual discussions. Everybody seems to be deceived by such fallacies at some time or other, and everybody can be found using a fallacy now and again. This is not to say that people are deliberately out to fool each other. or that all people are foolish. It is simply to say that informal fallacies are a part of our lives and culture. We are, in many ways, an illogical people, and very often we pay for being illogical. Each day we encounter, and use, arguments. They often contain hidden assumptions that are false, and yet these assumptions are operative in our decision making. The only advice we can give ourselves is to be careful and be alert. The more serious the situation is, the more critical we should be of the arguments that people give us.

EXERCISES FOR MODULE 27
EXHIBITING ASSUMPTIONS

Ex. 1 From the list of discriptive phrases below each item, select that phrase which best describes the item.

1. All women are wise. Carol is a woman. Thus Carol is wise.
   A. Is not an argument
   B. Is based on the assumption that Carol is a happy person
   C. Is valid as it stands

2. All women are wise. So Carol is wise.
   A. Is not an argument
   B. Is based on the assumption that Carol is a woman
   C. Is valid as it stands

3. The car didn't start. So we must be out of gas.
   A. Is not an argument
   B. Is valid as it stands
   C. Is based on the assumption that if a car does not start, then it is out of gas
   D. Is based on the assumption that anything that fails is out of gas

4. People with lots of money eat in fancy restaurants.
   A. Is valid as it stands
   B. Is based on the assumption that people with lots of money are the only ones who can afford to eat in fancy restaurants
   C. Is not an argument

5. The county fair was fun. So the state fair, which will be twice as big, will be twice as much fun.
   A. Is not an argument
   B. Is valid as it stands
   C. Is based on the assumption that state fairs are always better than county fairs
   D. Is based in the assumption that what is twice as big must be twice as much fun

6. Most Americans respect the laws and try to live by them. So we can expect very little trouble in enforcing the new gun-control legislation.
   A. Is valid as it stands
   B. Is not an argument
   C. Is based on the assumption that gun-control legislation is good
   D. Is based on the assumption that people who respect the laws and try to live by them will have respect for and live by the specific gun-control legislation, and that when people live by laws then it is easier to enforce them
   E. Is based on the assumption that some people will keep their guns and that enforcement in such cases will be easy

7. I rode on the Giant Whip at the state fair. When I got off I was sicker than a dog.
   A. Is valid as it stands
   B. Is based on the assumption that the Giant Whip made me sick
   C. Is based on the assumption that the Giant Whip makes dogs sick
   D. Is not an argument

Ex. 2 In each item below, an argument is presented in an original and several reconstructed forms. Identify the best reconstruction from among the ones offered.

1. *Original:* It is not ethical to give higher grades to students you happen to like because it is not fair to the other students in the class.

Reconstructions:

A. It is not ethical to give higher grades to students you like for two reasons. First, it is unfair to the others, and second, whatever you do about grading is unethical.
B. To give higher grades to students you like is unethical because it is unfair and because it is unethical.
C. Giving higher grades to students you like is unethical. This follows from the fact that it is unfair to the other students and whatever is unfair is unethical.

2. *Original:* Many of your fellow Americans have purchased retirement land in beautiful Ohio. You should too.

Reconstructions:

A. Many Americans purchased retirement land in Ohio. So you should purchase retirement land in Ohio.
B. You should purchase some land in Ohio to retire on. Many of your fellow Americans have made such a purchase. Thus you should purchase some land there too.
C. Many of your fellow Americans have bought retirement property in Ohio. Whatever many of your fellow Americans do you should do too. So you should buy retirement land in Ohio.
D. Many of your fellow Americans have purchased retirement land in Ohio. You should do whatever any other person does. You should buy land in Ohio to retire on.

3. *Original:* Honest people tend to live longer lives since they are not shot down by the police or other criminals.

Reconstructions:

A. Honest folks are killed neither by criminals nor the police. Honest folks tend to have longer lives. So honest people tend to live longer.

B. The police and criminals shoot down dishonest people. People who are killed in this way are killed before they would naturally have died. Thus they tend not to live as long as honest people.

C. Honest people live longer lives since God blesses them with longer lives as a reward for their honesty and dishonest people are killed by the other dishonest people or the police.

D. Honest people live longer lives than dishonest people do. This follows from the fact that dishonest people are killed by the police or by other criminals.

Ex. 3 After checking the answers for Ex. 2 go back over it and explain why each poor reconstruction was poor. Select your answers from:

1. Is poor because it only puts the conclusion in as one of the premises
2. Is poor because it uses an assumption that is too broad
3. Is poor because it is only a restatement of the original argument with no added premises

1. Reconstruction A. _____; B. _____

2. Reconstruction A. _____; B. _____; D. _____

3. Reconstruction A. _____; C. _____; D. _____

Ex. 4 Reconstruct each of the following arguments by introducing their assumptions as premises of your reconstruction.

1. All children have rights. So Karen and Mark have rights.
2. At the moment of death people experience an overwhelming sense of peace. So Elizabeth knew that experience.
3. Energy is expensive, so insulate your attic if you want to save money.
4. She probably does not have pneumonia. The x-ray came back clear.
5. The holiday season is always a hectic time for you. So you should try to relax a little each day to avoid stress.
6. I see no yellow ribbons around that old oak tree. So you probably don't want me.
7. Everyone around here thinks that the reason for the crime was simple passion. So that's how we're going to treat it in the investigation.

ANSWERS TO EXERCISES
FOR MODULE 27

Ex. 1

1. C   2. B
3. C; D is too broad.   4. C
5. D; C is just a wrong choice as a possible assumption in the context of this argument.
6. D; E is a wrong choice as a possible assumption here.
7. D
8. C; not B—which is a given premise, not an assumption

If you confused argument with nonarguments, review Modules 2 to 4. If you confused assumptions with stated premises, review 27:1. If you made other mistakes, review 27:2.1., 27:2.2, and 27:3.

Ex. 2

1. C   2. C   3. B

Ex. 3

1. A, 2; B, 1   2. A, 3; B, 1; D, 2   3. A, 1; C, 2; D, 3

If you missed any of these, review 27:2.1 to 27:3.

Ex. 4 Your reconstructions should include the assumptions indicated below.

1. Karen and Mark are children.
2. Elizabeth died.
3. Insulating your attic will save energy.
4. If a person has pneumonia, a chest x-ray will not be clear.
5. Now (soon) is the holiday season. A little rest each day helps people avoid stress during a hectic time.
6. If you wanted me you would have tied a yellow ribbon around that old oak tree. If you had tied one there I would be able to see it now. I do not see any yellow ribbons around that old oak tree.
7. Whatever everyone around here thinks about the crime is true. We should conduct investigations of crimes in terms of preliminary beliefs about the motives for the crime.

As you can see in some of these items, there can often be more than one crucial assumption operating in an argument. This increases the chances that there might be a false one.

MODULE 28

SPECIES OF IRRELEVANT APPEAL

Perhaps the most common error in reasoning and argumentation is to supply an irrelevant premise on behalf of a strongly felt conclusion. When trying to support a conclusion there are many kinds of irrelevant things that a person could offer as a premise. Some of these, like the appeal to ignorance, the misuse of authority, and the abusive attack against the person (ad hominem), are used so frequently that they have earned their own names in the catalogue of fallacies. But other kinds of irrelevant appeals do not fall into one of these three species and can simply be called by the generic name *irrelevant appeals*. In this module we will examine these three species and the generic irrelevant-appeal fallacy itself.

● After reading Module 28 you should be able to:

1. Identify fallacies exemplifying each species of irrelevant appeal
2. Distinguish fallacies exemplifying each species of irrelevant appeal from those that are irrelevant appeals but cannot be classified as appeals to ignorance, abusive ad hominem, or misuse of authority
3. Construct sample irrelevant appeal fallacies

28:1 Here are some examples of the fallacy of irrelevant appeals.

EG. 28.1 (Appeal to ignorance)
Since I personally know of no evidence that proves that cigarette smoking is a contributing factor to heart attack, I can safely infer that it is not.

EG. 28.2 (Abusive ad hominem)
Who told you that I was responsible? Vincent! Don't believe that dumb Italian.

EG. 28.3 (Misuse of authority)
The distinguished medical doctor, Cliff Hanger, is here to say a few words in support of the proposition 'Mountain climbing is very safe.'

EG. 28.4 (Unclassified irrelevant appeal)
Polio vaccines have been around over 20 years now. So it's time we got a new modern way of preventing polio. We cannot tolerate old-fashioned medicine.

These arguments are, respectively, based on the following false assumptions:

1. The lack of evidence that something is true is sufficient evidence to believe it is not true.
2. Whatever an Italian (or that Italian) says is false.
3. The testimony of a medical doctor can be believed because doctors are generally knowledgeable about mountain climbing.
4. Any medical practice should be changed if it is old-fashioned, i.e., developed over 20 years ago.

The authors of these arguments believed, or purportedly believed, that the things they said were relevant to their intended conclusions. That is, the irrelevant claims were being put forth as genuine premises on behalf of these conclusions. The assumptions upon which they were advanced turn out, however, to be false. Let's look at three of the species of irrelevant appeals.

28:2.1 The fallacy of the appeal to ignorance is committed by assuming either that a conclusion is true because there is no evidence against it, or that a conclusion or policy should be accepted because none better can be thought of at the moment, both of which assumptions are false. In this fallacy the burden of proof is unfairly shifted off the author of the conclusion and onto the critic. Here are some examples.

1. We have no evidence to show that Farrylander is not a spy. Let's take him into custody.
2. If you don't like my idea, then let's hear yours. Ah! So you have nothing. Very well then, my program is best, it shall begin at once.
3. Nobody has proved that Adam existed. So, he did not exist.
4. So far nobody has been able to show that Eve never could have existed. Thus she existed.

Here is a longer example.

EG. 28.5 Many people argue that if abortion were legalized it would lead to a severe deterioration in the moral fiber of society. They suggest that the respect for human life which humanity has always managed to hold on to would be threatened. They claim that people would tend to take a casual attitude toward human life. This will, they say, lead to terrible things in the future, things beyond euthanasia which may include genetic manipulation of the species, sterilization policies, mandatory abortions, infanticide, and even the extermination of those that are socially, biologically, mentally, or politically "undesirable." But there is no evidence for their positions. They can cite no concrete cases, no hard scientific basis for their dire predictions. There is, then, absolutely no truth in them.

The false assumption in Eg. 28.5 is 'The absence of evidence to support the dire predictions is itself adequate evidence to show that they are false.'

28:2.2 Ad hominem (against the man) arguments are fallacious because they make an irrelevant claim that the conclusion of another person's argument should not be believed because of some fault alleged to be attributable to its author as a person. These fallacies attack the author of the arguments in order to get someone to reject the conclusions of arguments. Nowhere is it considered logical to reject a conclusion that has been argued for because the person who did the arguing is supposed to be, in some sense, defective. Here are some examples of ad hominem arguments.

1. Stephania is a Papist. Don't believe a thing she says.
2. You work for the government, so whatever you tell us about the war is just another administration lie.
3. Your father was an ignorant bricklayer in the back streets of Detroit. We cannot accept your proposals for urban change.
4. You're not capable of telling us what it is like to be poor. You say that "it's tough," "it's hard." What do you know? You're white!
5. You tell us that we should vote for Jackson. I say you are just another lackey who has been taken in by his smooth talk and easy money. You want us to vote for him because you want to stay on, and rake off more federal funds for yourself. We shouldn't vote for Jackson—look at your motives.
6. Ten years ago my colleague voted for raising taxes. Now she says she's against raising taxes. So she is not really for tax reform down deep. Actually she wants to have taxes go up.

The assumption operative in abusive arguments like the ad hominem arguments above is generally of this form: So-and-so is defective in some respect and so whatever he or she says is defective. The alleged defect is sometimes a matter of prejudice and bias; sometimes, however, it is simply the fact that the speaker has changed his or her mind. Example 6 above is of that kind. This kind of fallacy is another kind of irrelevant appeal. It is impossible to catalogue all the possible faults people can imagine in other people which they might use as grounds to reject statements. There are good reasons for rejecting what someone says and there are bad reasons for rejecting it. Ad hominem attacks are bad reasons.

28:2.3 In order to clarify what happens when you are confronting a genuine ad hominem argument, we should concentrate on the distinction between good reasons and bad reasons for rejecting what a person says. We must also distinguish two kinds of rejections. One way to reject what a person says is to decide that it is false, wrong, or incorrect. Another, weaker, rejection is to decide that the person has failed to *prove* what he or she says (so that we are left in the dark as to whether it is true or false).

Now let us focus on the good reasons for deciding that what a person says is false. Perhaps the easiest reason to think of is that we have independent evidence sufficient to show that what the person says is false. However, we might have other reasons, *reasons focusing on the speaker,* for deciding that what a certain person says is false. We might know that I. M. Slytongue always lies, usually lies, or lies about the subject at hand. Given these facts about Slytongue, we could legitimately argue that what Slytongue says is false, or probably false, on the grounds that Slytongue says it.

Let us now pass on to the weaker rejection of what someone says. Remember that in this rejection we do not decide that what he or she says *is* false, only that what he or she says remains questionable, that is, is not shown to be true or false. Again, the easiest good reason for rejection is that there is simply too much relevant evidence which the speaker has not discussed. The idea is that all that evidence might support (and establish) what the speaker is claiming, but that it also might support and establish the negation of the speaker's claim. Once more, though, there are good reasons *having to do with the speaker* which might reasonably lead to the weaker rejection of his or her claim. Ms. Naivite has never had an opportunity to live in the ghetto or to study ghetto life, yet she confidently offers pronouncements about ghetto life. Mr. Vested Interest asserts with confidence that Slipco is the only company to hire for the job, but we know that he is also on the board of directors at Slipco. A person's lack of opportunity to know about something, or a person's personal desire, based on something other than evidence, for us to believe certain things, make what he or she says on those topics initially suspect. In the long run we may find that what he or she says is true. But our answers to the questions, "How does she know?" (she couldn't, really) and "Why does he want us to think so?" (because of his bias, prejudice, or vested interest) make the original arguments suspect—until we receive further corroboration.

The result of this discussion is the clarification of our understanding of ad hominem arguments. We are more subtle now. We can still see that heaping abuse on the author of an argument does not make the conclusions false or unacceptable. Yet in evaluating an argument, the maker of the argument can also come in for some appropriate evaluation. What are his or her credentials as the author of the argument? The author's ignorance, attitudes, or personal involvements may render what he or she says suspect or, in an extreme case, even false. When someone's response to an argument focuses on the author of the argument, it will often be an irrelevant appeal, full of abuse. Sometimes, however, it will be a reasoned critique of the author's credentials for presenting a credible argument on the subject at hand. The former is, of course, fallacious; the latter is not fallacious and is not properly called ad hominem. Here are two examples.

EG. 28.6 Your father was an ignorant bricklayer on the back streets of Detroit. We cannot accept your proposals for urban change.

EG. 28.7 All you've done in your young life is help your father lay brick on the back-streets of Detroit. Now at the ripe old age of twenty-two you want us to accept your proposals for completely reorganizing the lumber industry in Oregon!

Example 28.6 is clearly abusive ad hominem. There is no way that the person's proposals for urban change are rendered suspect by the occupation or education of his father. Example 28.7 is very different. It says in effect that a person who has only limited experience as a bricklayer can scarcely know what would be reasonable for the lumber industry.

We need to look at three more examples.

EG. 28.8   You work for the government, so whatever you tell us about the economy is just another administration lie.

EG. 28.9   You are a top spokesman for an administration which has lied monstrously to us about the economy. So whatever you tell us about the economy is probably a hideous lie.

EG. 28.10   Everything you have told us about the economy, as the spokesperson of the administration, has turned out to be false. Most of your statements are known to be deliberate lies. What you tell us now, Ms. Spokesperson, about the economy simply cannot be trusted. It is probably a lie too.

Example 28.8 has to be counted as fallacious. Surely not all government employees are habitual liars, and so mentioning employment with the government is an abusive smear in this example. Example 28.10 is clearly not an ad hominem argument but a thorough and reasonable repudiation of the spokesperson's credentials. If the charges made in Eg. 28.10 against the spokesperson are true, then indeed there is good reason not to trust her, since the evidence warrants the claim that she is probably lying again. Example 28.9 falls between Egs. 28.8 and 28.10. But exactly where? Is Eg. 28.9 ad hominem? Is it a reputable critique of credentials? The use of emotional language and the vagueness of words like 'monstrously' make Eg. 28.9 look like an ad hominem fallacy. Yet the speaker asserting Eg. 28.9 and the spokesperson may both know very well what the lies are, why they indeed are terrible, and how many there have been. But if another person does not share this knowledge, he or she may be unable to judge whether a certain argument is ad hominem or an enthymematic but reputable critique of credentials. Therefore, supplying the correct assumptions for examples like Eg. 28.9 depends on a person's background knowledge of the situation.

28:2.4 The fallacy of the misuse of authority occurs when people cite authorities whose competence is outside of the subject matter at hand, make up fictitious authorities or facts, or confuse genuine authority with popularity, fancy titles, and ceremonial behavior.

It is not necessarily a fallacy to cite authorities. If the authorities are used, it is, logically, only to facilitate things. It is supposed to save having to reproduce the entire proof for something. Instead of the whole proof the reliable authorities give their word. They vouch for the conclusion's being true, but they could have given the proof. They should be able to supply an acceptable proof upon demand. An authority is really only as good (reliable) as what he or she can prove upon demand. What Einstein might say about physics was, accordingly, highly plausible because presumably he could have substantiated his assertions about physics.

Here are some examples of arguments that commit the fallacy of misuse of authority.

1. The distinguished professor of art and sculpture has said several times that the administration's economic policies are not serving the defense needs of our country. Believe him.
2. When Washington defeated Napoleon in Cuba he said, "Give me a horse and I'll

take you for a ride." These words of that great American should inspire you to invest in the security of your country.

3. The Queen of Ohio speaking from her home in Bowling Green said that the university there was moving ahead with vigor. She should know.
4. Joe Football says we should buy Roger Quick aftershave lotion. So, we should buy it.

The fallacy of misuse of authority is based upon the following false general assumption: Whatever anyone who is any kind of an authority or expert on anything, or who is even a fictitious authority or mere popular figure, says on any topic is true. The persuasive force of these fallacies is derived from the alleged authority of the person cited. Thus, we have specific faulty inferences such as these:

Ms. X, a popular personality, says that p, and so p is true.
Mr. X, an authority in some field or other, says that p; p is not necessarily in Mr. X's field; nevertheless, p is true.

Here are two examples; the first one is a nonfallacious use of authority and the second commits the fallacy of misuse of authority.

EG. 28.11   For four years Professor Hoodwink has studied the effects of smoking. She used the best techniques available and her studies included the broadest sampling of smoking situations. Professor Hoodwink, who is remembered from her earlier pioneering work in the study of the relationship of air pollution to lung cancer, now states that there is a clear link between smoking and cancer.

EG. 28.12   My best friend, who lived in Sante Fe and who now lives in Alberquerque, is a professional announcer. He thinks that there is a link between smoking and lung cancer. One day I heard him say at breakfast that he got his ideas from his high school math teacher and from reading a book about woodworking in a smoke-filled waiting room. There must be a link, then, since announcers are seldom wrong.

28:3 If you cannot place a particular irrelevant-appeal fallacy into one of the three subgroups mentioned already, then it should be classified under the generic title irrelevant appeal. This fallacy involves arguing for a conclusion by presenting premises that are irrelevant to the establishment of that conclusion. Since there are so many things a person could say that are irrelevant, even though the person is acting as if (or believed they were) relevant, it is not possible to give an exhaustive list.

Here are some examples of arguments that contain irrelevant appeals.

1. Because while I was in office the cost of tea in China did not affect the import quota or the winner of the Super Bowl, you should reelect me.
2. I am a great lover of small dogs. And, as such, I say that what we need today is a complete drive to end window washing on Tuesdays.
3. Most of the people in the United States believe that the emperor is a wise and just ruler. He is, thus, a wise and just ruler.
4. The old saying goes, "If you made it, you eat it." So it's your turn to cut the pork roast.
5. The National League for the Violent Defense of America is made up of well-intentioned, hardworking men and women. They say that we must rid ourselves

of the menace of Iowa. It is a state devoted to love and peace. People of good will who work hard are never wrong. So at least you should be careful not to live with anyone from Iowa.

The assumption which lies behind an irrelevant appeal is not very complex. Let p be the desired conclusion and let q be some other statement. The assumption in its generalized form is 'since q is true, p must be true.' Here are some examples: "Since many people believe such-and-such, it must be true." "Nobody who is acting with good intentions can be mistaken, so believe what they stand for." "This is true, that is true, the other thing is true, and so p, which has nothing to do with this, that, or the other, is true." Here is a longer example of an argument that makes several irrelevant appeals.

EG. 28.13 Never before have people known so much about the universe in which they live. Thus, we have grown in wisdom and are more capable than before of deciding the hard philosophical questions: "What is the meaning of life?" "Does God exist?" and "Are people free?" Today we have superb systems of communication, a higher standard of living, more leisure time, fewer children, and more money. It follows then that we worry less, have a wiser system of government, and are less prone to sins of pride than were other people. Our lives today are marked by the effects of the media, an education explosion, and burgeoning space technology. Thus at no other time has humanity's commitment to the welfare of others been stronger and more effective. Religion today is in danger though. Our space travelers did not visually experience God when they traveled into the heavens! If religion is in danger, then so is our morality. It follows then that the very concept of beauty will fall like another medieval idol before the power of human technology. We have made several changes in human life in our times. There is nothing to conclude from all this change except that we have made great progress, great progress indeed.

Here are the false assumptions operative in Eg. 28.13.

1. An increase in knowledge of the universe is an increase in the data base relevant for solving the hard philosophical questions.
2. A higher standard of living, better communications, more money, more time off, and fewer children are factors that together bring about less anxiety, better government, and less unwarranted pride.
3. Technological progress improves a person's commitment to the welfare of others.
4. God is a Being that is, or should be, visible to space travelers.
5. Beauty is a concept that is part of the study of ethics.
6. Changes in the human situation are, per se, improvements in it.

EXERCISES FOR MODULE 28
SPECIES OF IRRELEVANT APPEALS

Ex. 1 Here is a list of arguments. By each one that is any kind of irrelevent appeal put 'IA'; otherwise put 'no.'

_____ 1. I think that marijuana is perfectly safe because there has never been any evidence to prove it harmful.

_____ 2. Dr. Clearthink, a Nobel prize winner in theoretical physics, says we are not threatened by overpopulation. So we ought to stop wasting our time with population control.

_____ 3. The dean and the provost said that the tenure situation is getting very bad. They indicated that the financial problems of higher education are going to force universities and colleges to become very restrictive about granting tenure. But I don't believe them. It is too typical of administrators to cry wolf and then, while you're looking one way, to grab power and run the other way. That's the name of the game with "management"; they are all petty bureaucrats acting like Russian czars.

_____ 4. Today the unions and their bargaining agents demanded total worker control over product development and overall aspects of research funding. They also demanded membership on all corporate committees and controls, including those that were previously exclusively composed of administrative personnel. They said that these were perogatives that had been usurped by "budget administrators." Well I'm not persuaded by that hogwash. Workers always think they should be executives. They want to put their meddlesome fingers into every pie and give their "input" and "advice" at every turn. Sometimes I wonder if their lack of trust isn't a form of protoparanoia.

_____ 5. Since no one wants war, there is no reason why it shouldn't be abolished.

_____ 6. Nobody around these parts believes in socialized medicine. Most people believe it would create a bureaucratic mess within 6 months. There is, thus, no doubt that socialized medicine would fail.

_____ 7. Doctors in particular are opposed to socialized medicine. Since they are professionals in the field of medicine, it follows that whatever they oppose in their own field is as undesirable as they believe it to be.

_____ 8. When we had got to this point in the argument, and everyone saw that the definition of justice had been completely upset, Thrasymachus, instead of replying to me, said: "Tell me Socrates, have you got a nurse?" "Why do you ask such a question," I said, "when you ought rather to be answering?" "Because she leaves you to snivel, and never wipes your nose. She has not even taught you to know the shepherd from the sheep."[5]   —Plato, The Republic

_____ 9. If she would look my way, then she would be looking my way. If she were looking my way, then she would not be looking at you unless you were where I am. But either you are, or are not, where I am. So, either she is already looking at you, or she is looking my way, or she is looking at neither of us.

_____ 10. "But I observe," says Cleanthes, "with regard to you, Philo, and all speculative sceptics, that your doctrine and practice are as much at variance in the most abstruse points of theory as in the conduct of common life.[6]

_____ 11. The Senator has asserted that the United States should become friendly

---

[5] The Dialogues of Plato, Benjamin Jowett (trans.), 4th ed., vol. 2, The Clarendon Press, Oxford, 1973.

[6] David Hume, Dialogues Concerning Natural Religion, Henry D. Aiken (ed.), Hafner Press, Macmillan Publishing Company, New York, 1948.

with Cuba; the Senator is a left-wing pinko, a ruthless bureaucrat, and a notorious liar. So the United States should not become friendly with Cuba.

_____ 12. Suppose I give a student an A who does not deserve it. It would be unjust not to give all who do not deserve an A, an A as well. If I give everyone an A, whether or not they deserve it, then an A will lose its value. This is a totally undesirable consequence. It makes grading in general a waste of time, and it makes that first A I gave to the undeserving student a meaningless A. So I shall not give undeserved A's.

_____ 13. Everybody I know believes that the earth was never visited by intelligent beings from another planet. They all believe that such a visit is a physical impossibility given what we know about space travel. So it is physically impossible that this earth was ever visited by intelligent beings from another planet.

_____ 14. This work of art is bold and beautiful. Its creator was the world's greatest artist. So the world's greatest artist must be bold and beautiful.

_____ 15. The first man on the moon drank Tunky Orange Juice. It must be good for you then.

_____ 16. A gambler reasoned this way to his friend: "I say that the lion in this cage will not harm me. You, my friend, have not proved that it will harm me."

_____ 17. There is nothing wrong with my proposal to hold classes all night. Can you think of a better way to utilize the classrooms more fully?

_____ 18. The professor in class today told me that the price of real estate was inflated because of the closed market conditions. I have always enjoyed his choral music course, too. I guess that he must be right about the real estate thing; after all, he is a rather informed-looking person.

_____ 19. Why do I act this way? Well, I'll tell you, I advertise the product this way because it sells this way. And if you ask me about the morality of what I'm doing I will say, "business is business." So, friend, it is wise not to worry about the "ethics" of the matter.

_____ 20. There is no sense in going along with Cathy on this. Everybody knows that she has her own, shall we say, "problems."

Ex. 2 After reviewing the answers for Ex. 1, go through each item in Ex. 1 that is an irrelevant appeal and classify it as either an appeal to ignorance (Ig), the misuse of authority (MA), the ad hominem fallacy (AH), or simply as an irrelevant appeal but not one of the subspecies (IA).

_____ 1.	_____ 2.	_____ 3.	_____ 4.
_____ 5.	_____ 6.	_____ 7.	_____ 8.
_____ 9.	_____ 10.	_____ 11.	_____ 12.
_____ 13.	_____ 14.	_____ 15.	_____ 16.
_____ 17.	_____ 18.	_____ 19.	_____ 20.

Ex. 3 Write out eight original examples of irrelevant-appeal fallacies. Two should be appeals to ignorance, two ad hominem, two misuse of authority, and two generic irrelevant appeals. Below each write out the specific assumption that each is based on.

Ex. 1

1. IA	2. IA	3. IA
5. IA	6. IA	7. IA
9. No	10. IA	11. IA
13. IA	14. IA	15. IA
17. IA	18. IA	19. IA

If you missed two or more of these, review 28:1 and 28:3.

Ex. 2

1. Ig	2. MA	3. AH
5. IA	6. IA	7. MA
9.	10. AH	11. AH
13. IA	14. IA	15. MA
17. Ig	18. MA	19. IA

Go over each one you missed in Ex. 2 and review the section of the module related to your wrong answer as well as the section related to the right answer. You should be able to figure out why your wrong answer was wrong as well as why the right answer is right.

Ex. 3 Compare your examples to those given in the relevant sections of this module. Did you state explicitly the assumption of each of your samples?

MODULE 29

THE FALLACIES OF PLAYING WITH WORDS
AND FALSE DILEMMA

The fallacy of *playing with words* is the fallacy that trades on either the ambiguity or vagueness of words or the arbitrariness or narrowness of definitions. The *false-dilemma* fallacy arises out of circumstances that seem to indicate a real dilemma—a forced choice between options all of which are undesirable—where actually no dilemma exists. We will examine these two types of informal fallacies in this module.

● After reading Module 29 you should be able to:

1. Identify and distinguish each of the two types of fallacies
2. Distinguish these fallacies from other types of arguments
3. Construct examples of each of these types of fallacies

29:1 The fallacy of playing with words sometimes involves relying on ambiguity or vagueness to argue for a conclusion. Here are some examples of *equivocations* (which are fallacies that rely on ambiguity).

1. Pigs live in pens. Pens are the things we use for writing. So pigs live in the things we use for writing.

2. Physical objects actually have experiences! This is so because to have an experience is to react. Physical objects react. People react.

In these examples the ambiguous words were 'pen' and 'react.' Here are examples of arguments that trade fallaciously on vagueness.

3. A man with no hair is bald. A man with only five hairs is bald. A man with just one more hair would be bald. And if he had just one more he would be bald too. But this can go on indefinitely. So no matter how much hair a man has, he is bald.
4. I'm selfish. You're selfish. Everybody is selfish! So why be so harsh on a person who won't spend a penny on his or her family or on any charity.

The false assumptions operative in fallacies of these kinds are different from example to example. In general, however, those that depend on ambiguity are based on the false assumption that, at least throughout an argument, the words have one and only one meaning. Those that are based on vagueness are based on the false assumption that all meanings are precise, clear, and well defined. Our discussions of ambiguity and vagueness in Part One showed that both these assumptions fail to state the truth about our language. Here are the false assumptions that the four examples were based on.

1. The pen pigs live in is the same thing as the pen people write with.
2. The reaction between people is, in all respects, the same as the reaction between physical objects.
3. Being bald or not bald is not a matter of comparative hairiness or lack of hair, but a matter of having a precise but indeterminately large number of hairs.
4. Being selfish is just being selfish; there is no difference between being concerned about oneself and being a niggardly and stingy hoarding miser.

Another way to commit the fallacy of playing with words is to frame arguments that rely on narrow loaded definitions or on an arbitrary definition. Sometimes these kinds of arguments turn out to be circular (as we shall see when we come to the fallacy of circular reasoning). Arguments that play with words by using loaded definitions are operating on the false assumption that the words used are being used in their proper sense. Those that rely on narrow definitions are falsely assuming that the definition provided is the *only* correct definition. Here is an example that relies on a narrow definition.

EG. 29.1 We cannot know that physical objects exist. This is because to know is to have direct experience of something. The only things we directly experience are our own perceptions. We perceive bits of color and sound, but not gross physical objects.

The false assumption in Eg. 29.1 is that the *only* kind of knowledge (only meaning of 'know') is from direct (perceptual) experience. Here is an example that relies on an arbitrary (wrong) definition of 'freedom.'

EG. 29.2 One who is in bondage and drugged so as to perform all that is asked can still be really free, for freedom is the knowledge of one's situation. The more one knows about one's self the more truly free one is.

The false assumption in Eg. 29.2 is that the definition of 'being free' given in the first premise is the correct definition. It may be a definition—an arbitrary stipulative one—but it is not the correct or proper definition.

29:2 The fallacy of false dilemma   A real dilemma is a situation in which a choice is given between alternatives such that (1) these are the only alternatives, (2) a choice must be made, and (3) none of the alternatives is desirable. A false dilemma is a situation that at first appears to be a dilemma situation but where one of the three clauses is false. That is, other alternatives exist, or one need not choose, or one alternative is not bad or does not lead to the consequences alleged.

The fallacy of false dilemma occurs when one argues on the assumption that a real dilemma exists when, in fact, one (or more) of the clauses listed above is false. In the following examples, notice that in each case the author presents things as if there were a real dilemma.

1. Either we must bomb the enemy or pull out. To pull out is to surrender, which we can never do. To bomb is to overkill, which is wrong. So we are going to do wrong no matter what.
2. You will either buy a house or rent a tent. If you buy a house, you will have great expenses. If you live in a tent, you will be very inconvenienced. No matter what, there is no good way to live.
3. Either you will change your air filter or you will not. If you do, you will have to pay me $20 to do the job. If you do not, you will have to pay me $200 to fix your motor later. Pay me later or pay me now.

The false assumption in example (1) is that bombing or pulling out are the only alternatives. In (2) the false assumption is similar, but there are some other options than living in a tent or buying a house. In (3) there are no other options, but the two options do not lead to paying the speaker. You can change the air filter yourself for less than $10, you can have someone else change it, or you can not change the filter and still not have to pay the speaker $200 to fix the motor.

Here are two examples of situations wherein the author is faced with real dilemmas.

EG. 29.3   High on the face of a cliff the climber edges forward toward the top. Her ropes break and she falls a short distance onto a small ledge. She is not hurt but her gear has been lost in the short fall. She reasons: I have two choices since I cannot climb off this ledge. I can either jump to my death or stay here and starve to death—nobody will be by this way for weeks to pull me off.

EG. 29.4   The killer's trail is being uncovered by the diligent BFI detective, Getmy Mann. Mann is closing in and the desperate killer realizes her danger. The killer reasons: I can surrender and be tried for murder or I can kill the detective and escape. If I surrender I will probably be found guilty and be jailed and perhaps executed. If I kill the detective I will escape but probably only for a short while since the BFI will know that Mann was killed by me. Either way I'll eventually be jailed and maybe executed.

These dilemmas are real in the sense that a choice has to be made, either to jump or not in Eg. 29.3, either to surrender or to fight in Eg. 29.4. There are no reasonable options in either example other than those given. Each option given leads to undesirable results. Of course, you could argue that the options are not *equally* undesirable but that is not an issue in determining whether or not there is a dilemma. The fact that from certain perspectives one alternative is less or more undesirable than another may be all that the desperate people in the examples have to guide the choice they must make.

Sometimes dilemma situations like this arise.

EG. 29.5 I want to become a member of the touring chorus so that I can see Europe and have a lot of fun, and so that people will regard me as a fine singer. I know that only thirty people will be selected and of those only seven will be altos. Five altos from last year's chorus will surely be choosen. Three other girls are good altos besides myself. Two are sisters and if I lied to them about when tryouts were scheduled they would miss the tryouts and I would be assured of one of the two open positions. But what should I do? Lying is wrong, but not making the chorus is awful too.

Here the dilemma is also genuine and, all things being equal, rather more common and, in a way, more difficult than Egs. 29.3 and 29.4. The speakers in those examples will die or go to jail no matter what they choose. They know that events have closed in on them and that they cannot escape the fates that they have helped make for themselves. In Eg. 29.5 the future is open; there is both reward and pain involved in either choice. The pain of having not lived up to your own moral standards is difficult, but so is the pain of not achieving what you strive for.

There is a way out of this dilemma, and the many like it that people often find themselves in. The way is to alter or abandon certain goals or projects.

Consider another example.

EG. 29.6 If I take the test I'll surely flunk it and the course; and if I skip the test, I'll flunk the course anyway.

This looks like a real dilemma, and indeed it is for a student intent on passing the course. But if someone didn't really care about passing, the situation would be much different. We are saying, for example: "If John has certain goals (passing the course), then he has only certain options (taking the test, skipping the test), each of which has bad consequences." Here an important principle of propositional logic can come to your aid, allowing you to escape some dilemmas.

Suppose:

p = John has certain goals
q = John has undesirable option A
r = John has undesirable option B

So

$$(p \supset (q \lor r))$$

But a truth-table will show us that $(p \supset (q \lor r))$ is equivalent to $((\sim p) \lor (q \lor r))$. In other words, John will have to take one of the undersirable options unless he gives up the goals which are confining his option. What the equivalence says is that when only undesirable options are implied by having a certain goal, desire, interest, or purpose, giving up that goal, etc., provides another alternative. Maybe the goal is so precious that taking an undesirable consequence is better than abandoning the goal; logic will not make this evaluation for you. What being logical will do for you is to get you to recognize that when your goals restrict your options, abandoning or changing your goals will provide new options, which may be superior to those available if the goals are retained intact.

Here is an example of a false dilemma:

EG. 29.7   First woman: I am pregnant and I can choose either to have the child or to have the pregnancy terminated. I do not want to have the child because if I have it I'll not be able to be a good parent for it; I'm not married and I don't have a job, and besides, I'm not finished with my degree yet. But I don't feel that I can live with the idea of an abortion, I just don't think, well, that it is "right"; ah—I'm a Catholic, at least I was raised as one.

Second woman: Well, I think that you have missed some logical possibilities that would be open if you could just throw off your Catholic background. For one, you could then just go ahead with the abortion, or for that matter, you could even imitate the "Romans of old" and try infanticide.

Third woman: Don't be crude. She would not put up with anything that she feels is killing so we might as well look for other more realistic options. What about marriage, or, more reasonably, placing the child for adoption?

In Eg. 29.7 the first woman sets up the false-dilemma situation by not taking into account all the options. The second woman suggests a way or two that the first woman may not have mentioned, but, as the third points out, they lead to a more complicated dilemma. The third woman suggests two ways out that seem more promising.

To decide whether an argument is a false-dilemma fallacy first see if it is presented so as to suggest that the three conditions for a genuine dilemma, mentioned in the first paragraph of 29:2, are met. Then reexamine the situation and look for more options, for errors in judgment about whether specific options lead to undesirable ends, or for whether or not the choice is really forced. If the choice is not forced, or if there are more options than those given, or if even one option is really not undesirable, then the situation is a false dilemma. Since it is virtually impossible to tell, apart from a rather fair understanding of a person, what different people see as desirable or undesirable, we will have to restrict exercises to only those false dilemmas where there are more options than those given or where no choice is forced by the situation.

EXERCISES FOR MODULE 29
THE FALLACIES OF PLAYING WITH WORDS AND FALSE DILEMMA

Ex. 1 Several passages are given below. Identify the playing-with-words fallacies by 'PW' and the false-dilemma fallacies by 'FD.' Otherwise put 'neither.'

_____   1. Teaville U.S.A. is a dry city. Therefore it never rains there. The only thing you can get to drink there is a dry martini.

_____   2. We should either buy a car or a boat. If we buy a boat, we'll not be able to use it on land. But we can't use a new car in the water. In either case we have a problem on our hands.

_____   3. Everyone who habitually lies is not to be trusted. But everyone lies in bed each night. So no one can be trusted.

_____ 4. Two of us did not kill the bird. But one of us three did kill it. If it was not you or I, then it was John. But if it was not he or you, then it was I. I am sure that I did not do it. So if it was not you, then it was John.

_____ 5. You cannot become proficient at something unless you practice something. I practice bridge each day. This will make me proficient. Then I'll be able to play the piano well.

_____ 6. You cannot become expert at something unless you practice it. I do not practice piano at all so I will not become expert at it.

_____ 7. Judge: "You are on trial for the murder of the seventeen people killed in Krakow during the Russian invasion of Poland at the end of World War II. How do you plead?" Defendant: "Not guilty, your honor—Polaks ain't people!"

_____ 8. If we give in to the terrorists who are holed up in the hotel right now, they will return and take even more from us next time. If we fight them where they are now, then we will probably never see the hostages alive again. Therefore no matter what we do we lose.

_____ 9. Reporter: "Senator, according to the classic definition of "recession," the country has been in a severe recession for several months. Could you comment on that?" Senator: "Well, a recession may be how some would characterize our situation, but I do not believe we have or are experiencing a genuine recession. Rather, I prefer to call our situation a prolonged monetary economic hiatus.

_____ 10. Reporter: "General, can you explain to the American people why we fire-bombed German cities during World War II when we knew that many noncombatants were living in them?" General: "Yes, you see we abide by the Geneva Convention and the rules of war, but nobody in an enemy nation is really a noncombatant. Even the nurses and housewives were contributing to the total war effort of the German Reich in their own ways."

Ex. 2 Construct two original examples of the fallacy of false dilemma and two examples of the fallacy of playing with words, one through an ambiguity, the other through vagueness. State the false assumptions operative in each of your examples.

SELECTED ANSWERS
TO EXERCISES FOR MODULE 29

Ex. 1

1. PW	2. FD
5. PW; ambiguity of the reference, of "something"	6. Neither; item 5 fixed up
9. PW	10. PW

Review the appropriate sections for each one you missed to learn why your answer was wrong and why the right answer is right.

Ex. 2 Check your examples against the explanations and examples given in this module. Your false-dilemma fallacies should be presented as if they were real dilemmas. You should have stated exactly why each dilemma was false, and also exactly what ambiguity or vagueness your playing-with-words examples trade on.

MODULE 30

THE FALLACIES OF COMPOSITION AND DIVISION

These two fallacies concern the relationship between parts and wholes. Together they remind us that what is true of all the parts of a thing need not be true of the whole thing, and what is true of the whole need not be true of all of its parts.

● After reading Module 30 you should be able to:

1. Distinguish these two fallacies from each other
2. Distinguish these two fallacies from sound arguments about the relationships between parts and wholes
3. Construct examples of each of these fallacies

30:1 The *fallacy of composition* occurs in arguments that are based on this assumption: Whatever is true of each member of a given set of objects is true of the set itself. For example, the following arguments are fallacious.

1. Every senator is less than seventy years old, so the United States Senate is less than seventy years old.
2. No cell in my body has a soul of its own. Therefore, I have no soul.
3. Every part of my soap box derby car weighs less than 5 pounds, so my car weighs less than 5 pounds.

Here is a classic example adapted from social theory.

EG. 30.1   Ten ranchers have 100 head of cattle each on a range which can accommodate 1,000 healthy animals. Rancher A reasons: If I put five more head of cattle on the range, I will get 5 percent more profit. All the cattle will be less healthy, my 105 included. But most of the declining health problem will be my neighbors'. With my extra five head, I'll show a net profit. So he adds five cattle. Rancher B is as sharp and greedy as A. He reasons the same and does the same. And so with the other eight ranchers.

In Eg. 30.1 each rancher is confident that he or she will profit at the expense of the others. And, given the action of the other nine, each is better off adding the five head than not adding the five head. Shall we conclude that they are all better off? Well, no—that depends on how much the other nine are hurt every time one adds five. *What may be true of each member need not be true of the group.*

The false assumption in each of these arguments is the general claim: Whatever is true of every part is true of the whole composed of those parts. This general claim is false, but some of its particular applications are true, as in, for example: "Every piece of material that went into this house is wooden. So this house is wooden." Similarly, we can argue: "Every person in this jazz group is a woman. So this is an all-woman jazz group." But we could not conclude that the group itself was a female, only that females were its members.

30:2 The *fallacy of division* occurs in arguments that assume that any characteristic of a whole is true of each of its parts. For example, these arguments are fallacies.

1. I am going bald. So my liver is going bald.

2. The electorate is apathetic, unmoved by reason, prone to forget what happened longer ago than the past 4 months, ill-informed, and basically satisfied with the status quo. Thus, Peter is unmoved by reason, Noreen is apathetic, Don is prone to forget, Charlotte is ill-informed, and Roger is basically satisfied with the status quo since they are all voters.

Here is another example of this fallacy.

EG. 30.2   Member of the Board of Regents: Let us develop a way of funding the universities of our state on the basis of the total number of student credit hours they generate. For the sake of this procedure let us assume that the faculty member teaching an average size introductory course would deal with forty-five students. If faculty members teach two such courses, they will teach ninety students. If all students enrolled in those courses are enrolled for four credits, then they are generating 360 student credit hours. Let us call that the "full-time equivalent" for the average faculty member at the introductory level.

University official: The Board of Regents has established a guideline that says that each member of the faculty who teaches at the introductory level should teach ninety students.

The false assumption here is 'if ninety students is the teaching load for the faculty as a group (its average per faculty member) then ninety students is the appropriate teaching load for each faculty member.' The university official is the one making the false assumption. Here are two more examples of the fallacy of division.

EG. 30.3   In the long run we can see that the graph of the grades given by various professors at several universities is a bell-shaped curve swelling in the D–C–B range and diminishing in both the A and F range with about an equal number of F's and A's, an equal and greater number of D's and B's, and an even greater number of C's. So when you grade your students be sure that the graph of your assigned grades is bell-shaped.

EG. 30.4   Twenty percent more people are "conservative" at fifty than at thirty. So I must have developed many less "liberal" views in the last few years.

EXERCISES FOR MODULE 30
THE FALLACIES OF COMPOSITION AND DIVISION

Ex. 1 Several arguments are given below. If an argument is the fallacy of composition put 'comp' by it; if it is the fallacy of division put 'div' by it. If it is a correct application of reasoning about the relationships between parts and wholes put 'OK' by it.

_____ 1. The students at this college, on the average, scored in the 57th percentile on the recent nationwide exam. Bill is a student here. He must have scored in the 57th percentile.

_____ 2. About one person in six needs professional counseling at any given time. So you have probably needed counseling in the past six years.

_____ 3. We psychology professors cannot accept the amendment to the university charter that you propose. If we did accept it, it would cause enrollment cuts in the courses offered by the psychology department. This is not good for our department and would not, then, be good for our university.

_____ 4. About half the students at this college are women. So we can infer that about half the students participating in varsity football here are women.

_____ 5. About half the students in this college are women. They pay about half of the fees collected from all students and so should receive as much in support of women's physical education programs and intermural sports teams as the men receive in support of their physical education programs and intermural sports teams.

_____ 6. All physical bodies are made up of atoms. Atoms are always in motion. So all physical bodies are in constant motion.

_____ 7. America is the richest nation in the world. I am an American so I am one of the richest persons in the world.

_____ 8. The heavy storms cost the Iowa farmers $2 million this spring. Boy, if I were an Iowa farmer how could I afford to lose $2 million in one storm?

_____ 9. The smallest species of the oreodonts must have been very populous in the Nebraska area 30 million years ago since it is well established that the oreodonts generally flourished throughout Nebraska and the Dakotas at that time.

_____ 10. Prostitutes have been practicing their profession since Biblical times. It is a wonder that these folks can still keep going!

Ex. 2 Construct three original examples of the fallacy of composition and three of the fallacy of division.

SELECTED ANSWERS
TO EXERCISES FOR MODULE 30

Ex. 1

1. Div	3. Comp	4. Div	5. OK
6. Comp	7. Div	9. Div	10. Div

If you missed more than two, reread the module.

Ex. 2 Check your examples against those in the text.

MODULE 31

FALSE-CAUSE FALLACY, GAMBLER'S FALLACY, AND PLAYING-WITH-NUMBERS FALLACY

The three fallacies discussed in this module most commonly occur in the context of inductive arguments that are about either statistical probabilities or conditioning factors.

● After reading Module 31 you should be able to:

1. Identify and distinguish fallacies of each of the three types covered in the module

2. Distinguish fallacies of each of these three types from other arguments
3. Construct examples of each of these fallacies

31:1 The fallacy of *false cause* occurs when one event is mistakenly regarded as the cause of another. This can be done either (1) by thinking that what occurs at one time must be a cause of what comes later (the old *post hoc ergo propter hoc* fallacy), or (2) by taking something to be a cause which is no cause at all. Here are some examples.

1. I had a good dinner. Soon after, it rained. So it rained because I had a good dinner.
2. I was president from 1978 on. During the first two years of my administration the economy was healthy. So I can take full credit for the healthy economy of those years.
3. We changed the time of day at which we offer the death and dying course. The students seem to like the course more this term. The reason is because of the time change.
4. A dark cloud moved over my car today. So I will have bad luck all day.

In fallacies of false cause one of the following general assumptions is being made: (1) because event B occurs after event A, A must be the cause of B; (2) given any two events A and B the one is either the cause or the effect of the other. When a person commits the fallacy of false cause, he or she avoids the hard work involved in understanding what a cause is and in determining how people can know what causes what. Here is another example of the fallacy of false cause.

EG. 31.1 The history of America is a long bloody saga of human exploitation, but that is true for any country. People have always tried to exploit others. At first one family tried to exploit another, then one tribe tried to enslave a weaker one. Soon "civilization" came. Then one village or city tried to conquer and exploit another city-state. In our day this national rivalry still goes on, but in America we also reached the stage of the exploitation of one race by another and one sex by another. We know that people should be held responsible for what they do. We know that if anyone does something as evil as enslaving another person then, when justice finally returns, that individual should—no, *must*—be brought to justice. Thus it follows that you, white American male, must be brought to justice. You are responsible for the exploitation that American history knows so well.

The false assumptions that form the basis for Eg. 31.1 include: "white American males who are now alive actually caused (were responsible for) the exploitation that occurred in prior times," and "because some Americans were guilty of exploitation, all Americans of a certain group, namely white males, are now responsible." This latter false assumption is not an assumption that leads to the fallacy of false cause. It is a false assumption that suggests that one can reason that what is true of a well-defined subclass of a group is true of the entire group. (This type of false assumption obscures the crucial difference between 'some' and 'all.') This illustrates that an argument can be fallacious on more than one count.

31:2 The *gambler's fallacy* occurs when people argue on the basis of the false assumption that events that are in fact chance or random events are not independent of each other. In so doing they falsely assume that the postulate of insufficient reason (see 10:3.4) does not apply. Here are a few examples of the gambler's fallacy.

1. I flipped a fair coin once. It came up heads. Odds are that it comes up heads only half the time. It follows then that it is more likely to come up tails on the next flip.
2. Out of a deck of fifty-two playing cards I drew a king. I replaced that card. Since I already drew one king, my chances of drawing any king on my next turn are 3 in 52.
3. I am winning at dice. If we change the game to anything else, I'll start to lose.
4. Three cars have just gone by. They were all blue cars except that first one which was green. I know that 30 percent of the cars on the road these days are either blue or green. Thus not another blue or green car will go by in the next seven.
5. During tornado season one out of every four Michigan, Ohio, and Indiana counties experiences a twister each week. A tornado was sighted in Wood County, Ohio, this week—and we are in the tornado season. So we will probably not have another tornado in Wood County, Ohio, for 3 or 4 weeks.

There is a similarity between the gambler's fallacy and the false-cause fallacy in that in both cases causal connections are attributed where none exist. The difference, however, is that if all the events in question are in fact chance or random events, then attribution of some causal connection to these violates the postulate of insufficient reason, and the gambler's fallacy is committed. On the other hand if the events in question are such that the postulate of insufficient reason does not apply, but yet the events are not causally connected in the way the argument asserts, then the false-cause fallacy is being committed.

31:3 The fallacy of *playing with numbers* occurs when people misuse percentages, statistics, and averages, or, in general, misuse numbers. The sayings that "numbers lie" or that "you can do anything with percentages" are not entirely true. Rather, the truth is that people try to deceive each other and that people allow themselves to be misled. One way to fallaciously play with numbers is to make too much of percentages when the sample is small. For example, if I say that 75 percent of my students are women but do not mention that I have only four students, I could mislead you by the following argument:

1. Seventy-five percent of my students are women, so women really like my courses.

Another way to mislead people is to cite raw numbers when the sample size is very very large. For example:

2. Beware, America, the population bomb is bursting. Last year 1,018,700 children were born.

The way this argument is stated is misleading, since the figure cited may represent a net decrease of, say, 0.08 percent in the population. When the sample size is large, percentages and refined data give more useful information.

In the fallacy of playing with numbers the false assumption generally is that all of the relevant information has been presented and interpreted properly. But if the sample is small and percentages are given, then one of the relevant facts that must also be given is the size of the sample. On the other hand, if the sample is very large and only raw numbers are given, then one of the missing relevant facts is the percentage figure that the raw data translate into. Often other kinds of relevant information are omitted, like comparative information which can lend perspective to the raw data. For example, one way to put the figure which represents the number of deaths per 1,000 population in perspective is to compare that figure with the figure of deaths per 1,000 population in different years or in different countries. Statistics, averages, and percentages can be made to deceive us if we are not given all the relevant facts of the situation or if they are misleadingly interpreted or presented. A favorite trick of advertisers and other propogandists is to use accurate figures but to try to mislead the audience by restricting attention to an overly narrow reference group. For example one car is touted as having "the lowest list price of any car built in America," which sounds great until you notice the phrase 'built in' and compare the claim to that made by another ad which offers a car "with the lowest list price of any car sold in America." Both ads are equally misleading since they each tout the "list price," which is not the figure that is really relevant. They should both give the average sales price at delivery. Our perspective on raw data must be, if we are going to be reasonable, not simply a result of looking at numbers but a result of looking at numbers in the light of those relevant facts that help us adjust our evaluation of what they mean. A further discussion of the proper interpretation of statistical data is presented in Chapter 14.

Here are two examples of arguments that commit the fallacy of playing with numbers. After each one the relevant information that is missing is supplied. Each example falsely assumes that it already contains all the relevant facts.

EG. 31.2   This country spends $5 billion dollars each year on welfare. There are thousands of people on welfare who do not belong there because they are able to work. We should not spend all that money on people who could be out earning their own way. The money we spend on welfare comes out of the defense budget dollar for dollar. Thus to continue to spend $5 billion dollars a year on welfare is to support people who can work on their own and to weaken our nation's defenses.

Some of the relevant information that is missing is the total size of the federal budget, the percentage of that budget that makes up the welfare money, the percentage of those on welfare who are welfare cheaters (not everyone on welfare who can work is a cheater), the size of the defense budget, and the size of the defense budget that is sufficient to maintain national defense. Given such information we might change our conclusion considerably.

EG. 31.3   Over the past 20 years the average salary for an elementary school teacher has risen from $2,400 per year to $9,500 per year. Of course, at the same time, the average salary for a high school teacher has risen from $6,700 to $14,000 per year. It follows, then, that teachers have no basis to complain about their pay. They all have more than twice as much money coming in than they did 20 years ago.

Some of the relevant information missing here is information on changes in the cost of living over the 20-year span, information about the adequacy of the average salaries 20 years ago (if they were not adequate then, they might not be adequate now, even if they did keep pace with the cost of living), and how far some salaries deviate from the average. (Are there still some teachers earning as little as $5,000, whatever the average may be?)

FALSE-CAUSE FALLACY, GAMBLER'S FALLACY, AND PLAYING-WITH-NUMBERS FALLACY

Ex. 1 Several arguments are given below. By each that commits the gambler's fallacy put 'GF'; otherwise put 'no.'

_____ 1. The coin came up heads last time. So it will come up tails this time.

_____ 2. We have lost in the State lottery for over 200 consecutive weeks. Our luck has got to change—we'll be winners before this year is out.

_____ 3. The coin came up tails last time and the two times before that. So, it is a fifty-fifty bet that it will come up tails next time.

_____ 4. Since the chance of a coin's coming up heads is 1 in 2 and since the chance of two random events occurring in succession equals the product of their individual probabilities, the chance of tossing a coin and getting two consecutive heads is 1 in 4.

_____ 5. The chance of getting heads twice in a row is 1 in 4. The coin came up heads last time, so the chance of getting heads this time is 1 in 4.

Ex. 2 Here are several arguments. Identify those that commit the fallacy of playing with numbers by 'PN'; otherwise put 'no' in the answer space.

_____ 1. Last year 2,500 owners of the other leading luxury car switched over to our model. There is a mass exodus away from their car and toward our model.

_____ 2. The resale value of our car is a greater percentage of its sticker price than is the resale value of our competitor's car. So our car will be worth more when you trade it in.

_____ 3. Food costs are soring! The price of a can of corn went up 17.5 percent in one week.

_____ 4. "We gave our fair share to the united charities campaign. Our family gave $30 last year and $35 this year," said the vice president of the bank.

_____ 5. The birth rate and the death rate per 1,000 persons are about equal in the country today. So we have arrived at a virtual steady-state or level population size, given our restrictions on immigration, laws against resident aliens, and the insignificant emigrating population.

Ex. 3 After having reviewed the answers to Exs. 1 and 2, characterize each of the following arguments as either gambler's fallacy (GF), playing with numbers (PN), false-cause fallacy (FC), or none of these three (none).

_____ 1. The average salary for a full professor in the Arts College is more than $2,000 less than the average salary for a full professor in the Business College. This proves that the faculty of the Business College is overpaid.

_____ 2. The political atmosphere today is greatly improved over what it was a decade or so ago. There are fewer student riots, fewer problems with communist-based organizations, fewer troubles with corrupt political officials. All in all we have to say that our new president has done a fine job in his first 2 weeks in office.

_____ 3. Each day I swim fifty laps. Since I started this regime my ability as a bridge player has been quite something. This must be due to the swimming.

_____ 4. I've been playing cards all night and I've been lucky too. I'll bet all my winnings on my next hand sight unseen. It's got to be a good one.

_____ 5. Suppose we here accepted pacifism. We would not be allowed to defend ourselves even if we were being directly attacked by outsiders and our lives were in danger. But it is absurdly unreasonable to forfeit your right to self-defense in a world as vicious as ours. So, we cannot accept pacifism.

_____ 6. If both men and women are sexy, then if people are not careful, then they love children. So either people love children or they are not sexy, provided that one assumes the additional premise that they are not careful.

_____ 7. The batter is Bench. He has a .250 average and is hitless in three trips to the plate tonight. Bench is due to get a hit this time, folks.

_____ 8. From that day on little Brenda would go each evening to the woods behind her house. She climbed into her favorite apple tree and she sang until the sun went down and the sky turned red in the west. Brenda sang so well that she sang the autumn colors back into the sky.

_____ How can anyone say that our political leaders are inhumane? Why, toward the end of the war we significantly reduced American combat deaths from 500 per week to less than 50 per week by abandoning our infantry's search and destroy approach. We kept our boys on the bases and resorted to the use of high-altitude saturation bombing of areas of suspected enemy activity.

_____ 10. Our cereal is good for you. One ounce (with milk and sugar) gives 50 percent of the USDA specified minimum daily requirement of six essential vitamins and iron.

Ex. 4 Construct two original examples of the gambler's fallacy, the false-cause fallacy, and the playing-with-numbers fallacy.

SELECTED ANSWERS
TO EXERCISES FOR MODULE 31

Ex. 1

1. GF   2. GF   3. No
4. No   5. GF; the chances are 50/50—each flip is separate and the individual probability of heads is always 1 out of 2.

Ex. 2

1. PN; much relevant data are omitted, e.g., how many own the other model, what percentage is switching, and what percentage of "our" owners are switching to "their" car.
2. PN; relevant data missing here include average number of years old cars are when traded in and comparison of trade-in price to actual sales price.
3. PN; Food costs may be inflating but not necessarily at 17.5 percent per week, or 910 percent per year, as this argument suggests. Much more data are needed. The

price of one can of corn is too small to use percentages effectively; the increase could be as low as 6 cents, and the rate be exactly the "shocking high" one cited. (People often use numbers more for their shock value than as data.)

4. PN; the missing relevant facts are how much the banker earns and how much he can afford to give to this particular charity.

5. No

If you missed any, review 31:3.

Ex. 3

1. PN; relevant data missing include what the average pay is at all faculty ranks, and what the level of adequate pay at each rank should be.

2. FC   4. GF

5. None   6. None

9. PN; high-altitude saturation bombing is not likely to have been humane—unless data on how many were killed indicate that not too many enemy and civilian deaths occurred as a result of it. Of course if the deaths of enemies is taken to be irrelevant to the humanity of the war efforts, then the fallacy shifts from playing with numbers to playing with words.

10. FC and PN; no doubt the milk accounts for most of the nutritional value, but even if it did not, being "good for you" should relate to the USDA recommended daily allowance, not the starvation-level minimum daily requirement. The complexity of this example is designed to teach a lesson: if you lack background information (here about the nutritional values of milk and cereal, or about what standards are appropriate), you become unable to recognize the ways in which numbers—and you—are being played with.

If you missed any, review the sections that discuss the correct answer as well as the section that covers the mistaken answer.

Ex. 4 You should compare your examples with those in the text. Can you state the false assumption in each of your examples? Your examples of the gambler's fallacy should be applied to circumstances where the postulate of insufficient reason is known to apply correctly. On the other hand, the false-cause fallacy occurs when the principle of insufficient reason does not apply but the events involved are nevertheless not causally related to each other.

MODULE 32

THE STRAW-MAN FALLACY

This might also have been called the smoke-screen fallacy. It often occurs in the give and take of argumentation, and is committed by someone who, in reply to someone else, focuses attention on a side issue or small point and ignores the main points of the other person's presentation.

● After reading Module 32 you should be able to:

1. Identify instances of the straw-man fallacy

2. Distinguish instances of the straw-man fallacy from arguments and other passages

32:1 Often when people are arguing for something or trying to prove a point, they will present several arguments. Some will be stronger and more cogent than others. If a person were to respond by neglecting the cogent arguments and by attacking the conclusion solely because one of the secondary arguments is weak, that responder would be attacking a straw man. There are real men—good arguments—to be refuted. A similar error, also an example of a straw-man argument, occurs when people deliberately present a very weak defense of a position they are about to criticize. In so doing they make their job of criticism easier, but, of course, trivial. They have attacked a straw man instead of attacking the real supports of the position they wish to refute. In a straw-man argument, one often finds the important elements of the opposite side's views "boiled down" to distortion while trivialities are magnified.

The general false assumption upon which the fallacy of the straw man is based is: If any one of the arguments that support a given position is refuted, no matter how trivial that argument may be, then the whole position is to be rejected. The logical thing, on the other hand, is to regard independent arguments in favor of a given position as separate challenges. Each must be met if the position is to be refuted. Here are some examples of the fallacy of the straw man.

1. Some who argue for wage and price controls say that they worked before and so will work again. Well, today times are different so we should absolutely not have any wage and price controls.
2. One reason we respect our parents is because we were told to respect our parents. Where did we get this? From our parents, of course. And they probably got it from theirs. It's probably a long process of passing down mores. So there is no good reason to respect parents.
3. Some people enjoy Christmas because they open gifts, watch football, and go visit relatives. What silly reasons to have a holiday!
4. You have given me five reasons why you want a raise in pay. Well, one of them, that you need the money, I find irrelevant and a consideration that is unfair to your fellow workers. Thus, you get no raise.

EG. 32.1 Sociologist: My studies of student motivation at this university reveal that students attend college on the basis of one or more of the following reasons: to acquire the degree needed to get a good job, to learn skills needed in their lives, to achieve a measure of independence from their parents, to meet new and more interesting people, to find a spouse, to acquire a better perspective on life through pursuit of a liberal education, to participate in sports, or to acquire a deeper knowledge of a special field or discipline.

State senator: Why that information shows what an outrage it is to spend public funds on universities. We cannot support institutions which students use as a glorified dating service.

Notice the smoke screen in the senators' remarks. The information does show that some students come to college to find a spouse, but it shows also that that is not the only or the most important reason. However, the senator would have us focus on that one issue as if it were the only thing happening on campus. A lot of smoke can be generated by suggesting the impropriety of spending state funds so that young people can find wives or husbands. It is typical of this fallacy that the responder has found something that is perhaps a legitimate shortcoming or undesirable result. The fallacy involves assuming that it is the only result or that it can be viewed apart from all the others when in fact it is only a small point, a side issue, a straw man.

THE STRAW-MAN FALLACY

Ex. 1 This exercise requires identifying the various arguments that may be contained in one passage. Fill in the answer space with the best answer from the list provided.

_____ 1. *Passage:* There are two reasons why we should pay our taxes. First, we should because it is our legal responsibility. Second, we should because it is embarrassing to be caught cheating the government.

    A. This is not an argument.

    B. There are two arguments contained in the passage: (1) It is a legal obligation to pay taxes. We should fulfill our legal obligations, so we should pay taxes. (2) It is embarrassing to be caught cheating. We can avoid this embarrassment if we pay taxes. So we should pay our taxes.

    C. There is only one argument here, namely, we should pay taxes since it is our legal obligation.

    D. This passage says that we should pay taxes because our tax money is used for the public good.

_____ 2. *Passage:* There are several reasons why people refuse or fail to pay their taxes: poverty, political protest, simple failure to remember that taxes are due, personal problems like sickness, and religious convictions that taxation is wrong. But we should prosecute these people. We cannot allow absentmindedness to cost our government so much tax money each year.

    A. This is not an argument.

    B. There are two arguments given in the passage—one to the effect that we should pay our taxes and one to the effect that we should prosecute those who do not pay.

    C. The only argument in the passage above is that we should prosecute those who do not pay taxes because absentmindedness is not an excuse for costing our government money.

    D. This passage is an argument supporting the conclusion that we should not have to pay our taxes if we are poor or are making a political protest.

_____ 3. *Passage:* Agatha Christie is a better mystery writer than Sir Arthur Conan Doyle. This is so because her works have won more literary prizes than his have.

    A. This is not an argument.

    B. There are two arguments here: (1) Christie is a good writer because she wins literary prizes. (2) Doyle is a bad writer because he does not win literary prizes.

    C. There is only one argument here. Its conclusion is that we should read Christie's mysteries rather than Doyle's.

    D. There is only one argument here. Its conclusion is that Christie is superior to Doyle as a mystery writer.

_____ 4. *Passage:* Faulkner is a better writer than Steinbeck. This is so because literary critics say so. We can trust literary critics because they have good taste.

    A. There are no arguments here.

B. There are two arguments here. Their conclusions are: (1) Faulkner is a better writer than Steinbeck, and (2) literary critics can be trusted.

C. There is only one argument here and its conclusion is that Faulkner is a better writer than Steinbeck.

_____ 5. *Passage*: Shakespeare is one of the outstanding writers of all time. We know this because Shakespeare has been universally admired except by the critics of the seventeenth century, whose alleged authority we can discount because they also thought little of Homer.

A. There are no arguments here.

B. There are two arguments here. Their conclusions are (1) Shakespeare is one of the outstanding writers of all time, and (2) We can discount the alleged authority of the seventeenth-century critics who did not admire Shakespeare.

C. There is only one argument here. Its conclusion is that Shakespeare is one of the outstanding writers of all time.

D. This passage argues that Homer is no better than Shakespeare because the same critics who thought little of Shakespeare also degraded Homer.

Ex. 2 Answer the following multiple-choice questions.

_____ 1. In item 1 of Ex. 1 two reasons for paying taxes were given. Which reason given below is the more noble one?

A. Pay because it is embarrassing to be caught not paying.

B. Pay because tax money serves the public good.

C. Pay because it is your legal obligation and responsibility.

_____ 2. In item 2 above several reasons were suggested why people might refuse or fail to pay their taxes. Which of the reasons below is the least acceptable as a justification or excuse for nonpayment?

A. Poverty   D. Religious convictions
B. Political protest   E. Absentmindedness
C. Personal problems like sickness

_____ 3. Consider the passage "Christie is a better mystery writer than Doyle because she has won more literary awards, written more books, and sold more copies of her major works." The worst reason given above on behalf of the conclusion is:

A. She won more awards than he.

B. She wrote more books than he.

C. She sold more copies than he.

D. She is a better writer of mysteries than he.

_____ 4. Consider: "There are three reasons why Joe Football jumped from the NFL to the CFL: first, he gets more money; second, he gets more publicity; and third, he likes the color of the uniforms that his new team wears." The apparently least satisfactory reason given above for Joe's big move was:

A. He gets more money.

B. He gets to play more.

C. He gets more publicity.

D. He prefers the new uniforms.

E. He will be living closer to his family.

_____ 5. Consider: "If I had the money in savings or I could borrow it, then I would make a down payment on the house. I would like to buy that house because it is big enough for our family, because it's in a fine neighborhood near good schools, and because it has a cute little window above the garage door." The weakest reason for wanting to buy the house is:
A. I have the money in savings.
B. The house is in a good neighborhood.
C. The house is near good schools.
D. The house is too small for the family.
E. The house has a cute window.
F. There is no way to borrow the down payment.

Review the answers to Exs. 1 and 2 before doing Ex. 3.

Ex. 3 In each case identify the straw-man fallacies by 'SM.' If an argument given is not a straw-man fallacy, write 'no.'

_____ 1. Item 1 Ex. 1

_____ 2. Item 2 Ex. 1

_____ 3. Item 4 Ex. 1

_____ 4. Item 3 Ex. 2

_____ 5. Item 4 Ex. 2

_____ 6. Concerning item 4 in Ex. 2 I would only like to say that Joe should not have switched leagues. To do so only because he likes his new "pretty" uniforms is to have demonstrated that he never really could cut it in the "big" league.

_____ 7. Darling, I heard what you said about the house in item 5, Ex. 2. But really, we cannot buy a house only because it has a cute little window somewhere or other.

_____ 8. Item 3, Ex. 2, proves that Christie is a prolific writer and that she is also very popular. But I cannot put all my trust in literary awards because many of them are given for financial rather than artistic reasons.

_____ 9. Item 5, Ex. 1, argues that Shakespeare is one of the outstanding writers of all time. We should accept this conclusion only on better grounds than those presented in that passage.

_____ 10. My friend, you argued that continuing the war in Kentucky would be immoral, a waste of national resources, and costly in terms of human life and suffering. You also said that you found our military presence there both revolting and upsetting. Sir, I rejoice that our nation is not expected to make its crucial defense decisions on the basis of what affects your esthetic sensibilities. The war effort will continue.

SELECTED ANSWERS
TO EXERCISES FOR MODULE 32

Ex. 1

1. B   2. C   3. D   4. B   5. B

If you had problems and cannot understand all the answers, review Modules 3 and 4.

Ex. 2

1. C; B was not given
2. E, especially in a pluralistic society
3. B is the poorest. But C is not a very good reason either. (D is given as the conclusion, not one of the reasons.)
4. D seems least satisfactory.
5. E seems the weakest.

This exercise was designed to guide you in forming evaluations as much as to measure your evaluative abilities or standards. When you disagreed with an answer provided, try to see also the reasonableness of our answer.

Ex. 3

1. No   2. SM   3. No   4.   5. No
6. SM, with a bit of bitterness and ad hominem tossed in
7.   8.   9. No   10. SM

If you missed any in Ex. 3, after having done the two preparatory exercises and reviewed the answers to them, review Module 32.

MODULE 33

EMOTIONAL APPEALS

In this module we will look at emotional appeals. These are appeals to action, not argument to the effect that something should be believed. They appear to be a species of irrelevant-appeal fallacy but because they are nonarguments they cannot be called genuine fallacies, nor is it clear that an appeal to emotions or feelings is necessarily irrelevant in bringing about desired actions or behavior.

● After reading Module 33 you should be able to:

1. Identify emotional appeals
2. Construct original examples of emotional appeals

33:1 Anyone who has had trouble quitting smoking or breaking any undesirable habit knows that there is a difference between knowing what one should do and actually doing it. You can be given arguments which lead you to know what you should do. You should quit smoking because smoking is dangerous to your health and you should not do something that is dangerous to your health. But this argument may not make you quit. It may persuade or convince you about the truth of its conclusion, but it may fail to bring about action. To bring about action people often appeal to emotions. This is especially powerful and effective after the intellectual or rational aspect of our minds is satisfied. To make student drivers drive carefully and not speed, many driver training programs use movies and stories that depict the tragedy and danger of careless driving, speeding, or driving while drunk. These movies are calculated to arouse fear of careless driving, and to excite emotions of sympathy for the victims of accidents. These emotional forces are more effective in making the students be cautious than is a true abstract generalization like "the faster you drive the more likely you are to have an accident." To get someone to quit smoking you may have to appeal to emotions like fear or love, rather than to the abstract warnings printed on the sides of cigarette packages.

Emotional appeals are appeals that people make with the view of bringing about action. They often do not indicate why the person should believe that the action viewed abstractly is appropriate. Rather, they focus away from intellectual argumentation and disputation and toward getting a particular person or group of people here and now to do something or to refrain from doing something. The appeals can be made to emotions such as fear, pity, pride, love, hate, hope, anger, sorrow, joy, depression, jealousy, or envy. While such emotions do motivate action, they should not cause us to change our beliefs. Here are some examples of emotional appeals.

1. There is no telling how many people were injured on our highways last year because of faulty PCV valves. Your PCV valve may be dangerously worn right now. Buy a new Zem PCV valve today, before it's too late.
2. I'm really a very good student. I missed those lectures to study at the library because I work all night to support my sick mother and eight brothers. If I don't pass your course I'll not graduate. I'll lose my job. My life will be ruined because of you. I really know the material, even though I failed the final. I need this course badly. Please, give me a passing grade.
3. If you loved me, you would believe me when I tell you that Harold is a fool.
4. I cannot believe it. It's too horrible to be true. No, it can't be. . . . If I thought that you were really going out with someone else . . . Well, it just isn't so.
5. All college graduates are proud of their alma mater. You love the ivy halls. Contribute to the alumni fund.
6. You worked hard and you deserve the very best. Wash your clothes at Faraday laundry.

EG. 33.1 Today our land is threatened on all sides. America, the land in which our families and loved ones live and play, is now in serious danger because of the ever-present and growing pollution problem. Can we who love this land stand by and let it be slowly poisoned? Can we watch as our homes and very lives are threatened by the crush of poison gases, noise, waste, and excess population? I say 'no.' We must unite in that spirit of American self-interest that made our land great. We must join hands in the new union against pollution. Now is not the time for petty causes and personal aims. Only as one proud people can we save the land we love. If we do not do it we will have only ourselves to blame, and our children will never know the beauty of this land which we are spoiling. Think of the shame, think of the danger, think of America—join the fight against pollution!

33:2 From what we have said, you can correctly infer that emotional appeals have two main characteristics, each of which distinguishes them from arguments. First, they are exhorting that an action be done, rather than trying to present a conclusion as acceptable. Second, unlike arguments, emotional appeals, living up to their name, appeal to our emotions, endeavoring to kindle and magnify them, rather than presenting premises upon which to base beliefs. Sometimes in real life you will find one of these characteristics present while the other is absent. Sometimes bits of reasons are included along with appeals to emotions. The discerning person learns to sort out this mixture, evaluating any argument by well-established standards after separating it from any emotional appeal. With practice people can retain their rational abilities as they are themselves moved by an emotional appeal.

Given what we have said about emotional appeals, they are clearly an alternative to rational argument. But are they good or bad? How should they be evaluated? By the examples we have used we have tried to indicate that emotional appeals can support causes both base and noble. They are often more successful than reason in motivating people to action, action that may be important. So no blanket evaluation appears warranted. Moreover, detailed evaluation of emotional appeals lies beyond the scope of this book.

Still a few guides may be helpful. Emotional appeals typically attempt to engender feelings of a certain sort and also attempt to motivate people to act on the engendered feelings. Thus the evaluation of emotional appeals involves at least four broad questions:

1. Given the circumstances, is it appropriate to feel as the emotional appeal would have me feel? (If someone jars me in a crowd, is it appropriate to feel disturbed? Irritated? Is any feeling appropriate? Do the person's intentions and subsequent behavior matter?)
2. Is it appropriate to act on my feelings?
3. Even if I should act on my feelings, do I have more important plans to pursue?
4. When action based on my feelings is appropriate, is the action suggested in the emotional appeal the appropriate one?

Of course setting out four broad questions to use in evaluating emotional appeals is far from defining a fully adequate method for evaluation. Still in a time when many people believe that all evaluation is bound to be biased, the techniques of logic and the suggestions of the above paragraphs show the falsity of that assumption.

EXERCISES FOR MODULE 33
EMOTIONAL APPEALS

Ex. 1 Use 'EA' to identify the emotional appeals in the following list of passages. If a passage is not an emotional appeal, write 'no.'

_____ 1. You will sign the release. If you do not, then I cannot be held responsible for your family. There are a lot of ways that "accidents can happen," you know.

_____ 2. Judy, I've done a lot to help you out over the years through my conduct of my job as mayor of this town. Now I'll probably win reelection even without your support, but I'd sure hate to be in your shoes when I win reelection if for any reason the idea should enter my little old head that you hadn't contributed your time and efforts to my campaign. You are planning to work for me, aren't you, Judy?

_____ 3. If we get the funds we need, we will be able to devote $2 million to research. If we do that, then we will cut the development time in half. So, if we get the money we need, we can get results in half the time.

_____ 4. Give Vietnam veterans a bonus! After all, they patriotically fought an unpopular war for democratic ideals in dreadful jungles. Besides, when they come home the poor guys cannot even get jobs.

_____ 5. And when you get out on the field I want you to give 110 percent! We can win this game, we have to win this game. When the Gipper was dying he told me that some Saturday afternoon, when the team was down, when they really needed a boost, he told me to tell 'em to "win for the Gipper." So let's get out there now and do it for the Gipper!

_____ 6. Please, please find something wrong with me, doctor. If you don't, I'll be drafted. And if I am drafted I'll be sent off to war and probably killed.

_____ 7. Senator Stromwall has three beautiful kids and a handsome husband. The folks at the grass roots eat up that "family" image. We should run her for Vice-President.

_____ 8. If people have money, they can afford to contribute. If people can afford to contribute, they should be asked to give. So if people have money they should be asked to give.

_____ 9. I just want to ask you people to look into your hearts and see if there isn't a little that you can give to help these people who are less fortunate than you. Send us a dollar now.

_____ 10. It's a very simple proposition. If you don't kill the enemy, he'll kill you. The enemy knows more ways to kill than you can imagine. But he is no match for our weapons. When you get out there, they will be shooting real weapons, sniping, and booby-trapping. It's a simple matter of survival. It's kill or be killed. You will have the best training in the world and in 6 weeks you will have to use it. So pay attention—you cannot afford to make a mistake in combat.

_____ 11. Sergeant, I think we should change our approach. We work on fear too much; let's work on pride a little more.

_____ 12. Listen here, you are members of the best-trained, best-equipped, most efficient fighting force ever known. You are fighting in the service of the most powerful nation on earth—a nation dedicated to freedom and liberty for all. We have never lost a war, and we don't intend to start now. So you pay attention during the next 6 weeks and we'll make soldiers out of you—soldiers your country can be proud of.

Ex. 2 Construct three original examples of emotional appeals.

Ex. 3 Review the answers for Ex. 1 before going on to Ex. 3, which covers all of Chapter 9. Identify each passage numbered 1 to 16 below by using the answer from the following list that best characterizes it.

AI—appeal to ignorance	PN—playing with numbers	GF—gambler's fallacy
AH—ad hominem	PW—playing with words	SM—straw-man fallacy
MA—misuse of authority	FD—false dilemma	EA—emotional appeal
IA—irrelevant appeal	CF—composition fallacy	
FC—false-cause fallacy	DF—division fallacy	

_____ 1. The value of an average home in Wisconsin is $28,000. Judy owns a home in Wisconsin, so we know she is worth at least $28,000.

_____ 2. There are 2 million civil service people in our country. Each day half of them eat eggs and toast for breakfast while the other half eat cereal and milk. So the way to get a civil service job in our country is to eat either eggs and toast or cereal and milk for breakfast each day.

_____ 3. TV anouncer: Jackson has gone hitless in four trips to the plate tonight. So, he's due to get a hit.

_____ 4. Our country is run by an oligarchy of powerful and influential industrialists and academics. Thus it ought to be run by this group.

_____ 5. Jesus said he was the Promised One, but he cannot be. He is only a poor
man's son from a culturally repressed village in the Middle East.

_____ 6. Each student who wants to make good money after graduation should go
into nursing because there is a great demand for nurses in our country.
Therefore if all students went into nursing, they would all make good
money.

_____ 7. Everyone knows that the drug problem in universities is a growing
danger. There is no evidence to indicate that more state money will
change this. Thus we conclude that more money will only leave things
unchanged.

_____ 8. Long before whites came to Ohio this land belonged to the Indians. Thus
all whites should leave Ohio.

_____ 9. A man wants to feel like a man, so buy him Bucho aftershave lotion.

_____ 10. This is superstar Bruce Fernbottom here to talk about Lavender's pizza
parlors. I like their pizza. You should try one; you'll like 'em too.

_____ 11. Don't worry about the population problem. Why there is enough room in
Texas to put every United States family on their own half-acre lot. That
would leave the whole rest of the country for future growth.

_____ 12. If this cat is yours and if this cat is a father, then we can infer that this cat
is your father.

_____ 13. If American consumers cut down on how much beef they eat, farmers
will lose money on all the beef they decide to raise with low selling
prices. If American consumers keep eating beef like they did last year,
they won't be able to afford it—with the resulting high prices. Either the
consumer cuts down or keeps eating as before. So either the farmer will
lose money or the consumer will be unable to afford beef.

_____ 14. Everyone says there's a problem of traffic congestion, too much gas used,
too much time lost, too many accidents, too many hot drivers sitting
bumper to bumper in the scorching summer sun. That's nuts—almost
all cars nowadays are air-conditioned.

_____ 15. Mr. A: "100 percent of the union representatives I've known have either
been fools or thieves. Therefore they are all either thieves or idiots."
Ms. B: "But how many have you known?" Mr. A: "Two!"

_____ 16. Whoever lacks tangible means of support is a vagrant. Any vagrant is a
blight on the community. No blight on the community should be
tolerated. If any circus tightrope walker works without a net, then that
party lacks tangible means of support. Thus no such person should be
tolerated. That kind of act should not be allowed to be performed.

SELECTED ANSWERS
TO EXERCISES FOR MODULE 33

Ex. 1

1. EA   2. EA   3. No   4. EA   5. EA   6. EA   7. No
10. EA, but with clear rational elements   12. EA

If you missed more than one review 33:2.

Ex. 2 Check your examples against those in the text. Be sure you did not write an argument; emotional appeals are not arguments. Their aim is to motivate action.

Ex. 3

1. DF	4. IA	6. CF
7. AI	9. EA	11. PN
13. FD	14. SM	16. PW

Review the modules or subsections that discuss each fallacy you named as a wrong answer and the one named as the right answer so that you can see why the wrong answer is wrong and the right answer is right.

10
FALLACIES OF CONTENT: NO-PROGRESS FALLACIES

In this chapter we will learn to recognize those arguments that, while they may be logically correct and even sound, still are not acceptable because they turn out to make no logical progress toward establishing the truth of their conclusion. The educational goal of this chapter is to explain no-progress fallacies by using the five example fallacies covered here. You should learn to recognize each of the five types of no-progress fallacies by name and to be able to distinguish these fallacies from those covered in Chapters 8 and 9.

MODULE 34
THE FALLACIES OF CIRCULAR REASONING AND BEGGING THE QUESTION

These two fallacies are similar because both involve presenting a conclusion that is simply a restatement of what is already presumed. In the fallacy of circular reasoning this is explicit because the conclusion is nothing more than a restatement of one of the argument's premises. In the fallacy of begging the question the restatement is implicit, since the conclusion is actually the justification or support of one of the premises. Let us look at these in more detail.

● After reading Module 34 you should be able to:

1. Identify instances of the fallacy of circular reasoning
2. Identify instances of the fallacy of begging the question
3. Distinguish these two fallacies from each other
4. Construct examples of each of these two fallacies

34:1 Here is an example of an argument that commits the *fallacy of circular reasoning*.

EG. 34.1 1. White oak is stronger and more beautiful than pine.
2. We should not content ourselves with anything less than the best.
3. To accept less than the best is to settle for mediocrity and to take a chance that what we build will not be a superior product.

4. Our customers deserve only superior products like products made of oak, and not pine.
5. Therefore we can conclude that pine is less beautiful than, and not as strong as, white oak.

This argument cannot be invalid. Its conclusion, being only a reaffirmation of one of the premises, cannot be false if all the premises are true. But because the conclusion does not go beyond what any single premise asserts, because it is not a combination of the information of two or more of the premises, the argument is not worthy of acceptance. If we want to accept the conclusion as true we can, but doing that is simply to accept the first premise as true. The conclusion is not given any more support than what we have to support the first premise alone. The conclusion to such an argument stands as a simple unsupported statement—if it ever needed to be proved, it still needs to be proved.

An argument is circular if its conclusion is a restatement, perhaps in different words or perhaps dressed up a bit, of one of its premises. The circle is that the premise implies the conclusion and the conclusion implies the premise exactly because every statement implies itself.

EG. 34.2 To be truly free is the desire of all people. People wish to be able to pursue what they choose. Thus it is clear that liberty of choice is the wish of humanity.

EG. 34.3 All students are vegetarians during exam week. Any vegetarian is as good as any other person. Therefore, if a person is not a vegetarian during exam week, that person is not a student.

EG. 34.4 God is a Being the nonexistence of which cannot be conceived. To say "God does not exist" is to speak nonsense since, by definition, God cannot not exist. Therefore, people cannot logically think of the Being, God, truly so-called, as a being which is not.

34:2.1 To beg the question is to argue in such a way that the conclusion of the argument turns out to be a part of the support for one of the argument's premises. In other words, suppose that someone constructs a simple argument: "Since p is true, q must be true." You then begin to wonder how he or she knows that p is true. The reply comes back: "There is plenty of support for p, after all, given that q is true (!) . . ." In effect a second argument is involved. It may not be obvious, it may be implicit. The second argument has a premise of the original argument as its conclusion. Of course there is nothing wrong with supporting the premises you use in an argument. But a question-begging argument not only argues in favor of one of the original argument's premises; it uses the original argument's conclusion to support that premise. Suppose a university president says the following:

EG. 34.5 "Our university will have a strong future because its new colleges and programs will succeed. "How can you be so confident?" asked the local newspaper reporter.

"These new ventures are bound to succeed. All you have to do is look at the solid future of this university and you'll know its new ventures are bound to succeed."

The president originally argues

(Premise) = Our new colleges and programs will succeed.

(Enthymeme premise) = Any university with new programs has a strong future.

(Conclusion) = Thus the university has a strong future.

To shore up support for the stated premise, she continues with a second argument:

(Original conclusion) = The university has a solid future.

(Enthymeme premise) = Any new program in a university with a solid future will succeed.

(Original premise) = So its new ventures are bound to succeed.

But if indeed the president's reasons for believing the ventures will succeed include a belief in the solid future of the university, then the first argument is somehow out of order.

34:2.2 Can we say how the first argument misfires? Such arguments are not necessarily logically incorrect. They may be composed entirely of true premises. The rub comes elsewhere, because the arguments are used for the purpose of persuasion. Rational persuasion implies that someone, in our example the president, holds a belief of which she wants to persuade others. Persuading them rationally, through arguments, implies many things. It implies that logical arguments will be used, and that they will have true premises. It also implies that the person to whom the argument is presented is in a position to know, or at least to believe reasonably, the true premises the argument employs. After all, if someone presents you with an argument which happens to be sound, it may still be that you have no way of knowing that the premises are true. If indeed you have no way of knowing, rational persuasion fails. You have every right to reply, "What you say may very well be true, and your argument certainly is logical, but I'm in no position to figure out the truth of your premises, so I really have no adequate reason to accept your conclusion."

The assumption of rational persuasion is that questions unresolved in a person's mind can be rationally resolved by constructing arguments whose premises the hearer can recognize as true. Maybe a further argument, in support of the original, will be necessary in order for the person to be able to recognize that all the original argument's premises are true. No harm there. Rational persuasion assumes that ultimately argument will involve only premises which the person is able to recognize as true.

And here is where the president in our example upset the process with the question-begging argument. Every question-begging argument short-circuits the process of rational persuasion. This we can now see by returning to our example. The original argument concluded that the university has a strong future. Taking that conclusion as an assertion which the president wanted us to rationally come to believe, we understand the premise of the original argument, 'our new colleges and programs will succeed,' as grounds. But the reporter senses that many people may not be in a position to realize that the new colleges and programs will succeed. If they are to be rationally persuaded of the original conclusion, something more will need to be said. And here comes the short circuit. Since the original premise needs support, it ought to be supported by assertions that can be recognized as true. And one assertion that will never qualify as support is the assertion that the argument was originally trying to prove. After all, if it needed proof in the first place, it still needs proof. If it lacks proof, it remains questionable. So it cannot be used to resolve doubts about the very premise that was supposed to prove it. Clearly, a question-begging argument fails to make progress toward establishing the truth of its conclusion because eventually the conclusion is invoked as part of its own support!

Here are some more examples of question-begging arguments. In these examples see if you can see that in effect *two* arguments are being made—one on behalf of the original conclusion, the other using that conclusion as a premise from which to argue for one of the premises of the first argument.

EG. 34.6 A person is a religious person if he or she is in contact with God. I have had contact with God, who told me that this was so. I know that my contact with God was genuine, because, you see, I am a religious person.

EG. 34.7 Farmworkers put in long hours in the hot sun and earn unfairly low wages because people who are farmworkers seldom earn more than the legal minimum wage. So, in general, anyone who at best earns only the minimum wage for a long day's work is surely someone who is paid at an unfairly low rate.

In Eg. 34.6 the question that the author is avoiding is whether or not the contact with God was genuine. The situation can be reconstructed as follows. The author first gives

EG. 34.6′ 1. God told me that a religious person is one who has had contact with Him.
      2. Whatever God says is true.
      3. So a religious person is one who has had contact with Him.

    Question: How do I support premise 1 of Eg. 34.6′, i.e., how do I know that God was the one who said that to me?
    Response: I support it with the claim that I can know it was really God because I am religious and, according to the conclusion reached in Eg. 34.6′, religious people all have contact with Him.

Clearly it is not acceptable to use that assertion to support the idea that God made contact with me when His contact with me was originally used to prove that assertion. No progress is being made. The question "Was the contact genuine?" has not been resolved.

Similarly in Eg. 34.7 an issue is circumvented. The specific question at issue is "are farmworkers underpaid?" The general conclusion offered, whoever earns the legal minimum wage is unfairly paid, is not the result of examining the cost of living relative to the legal minimum wage. Rather, it is a question-begging conclusion. It is used to support the first premise of the reconstructed Eg. 34.7 given below.

EG. 34.7′ 1. Farmworkers work all day for unfair pay.
      2. Farmworkers earn the legal minimum wage.
      3. So the legal minimum wage is an unfair rate of pay.

We have no way to accept (1) unless we accept (3) [and (2) as well] because (3) is part of the support for (1). But because of this we are making no progress in turning back to agree from (1) and (2) to (3). The question of what does or does not constitute unfair wages in general or unfair wages for farmworkers in particular has been avoided.

34:3 To tell these two fallacies apart one should ask whether or not the conclusion is simply a restatement of one of its premises. If so, the argument is circular. However, if in a given passage implicitly two arguments are present such that the conclusion of the original is used as a premise in the second to support one of the premises of the original, then the original argument there is question-begging. We could picture a circular argument as

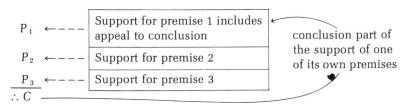

In circular arguments the conclusion *is* one of the premises.

We could picture a question-begging argument as follows:

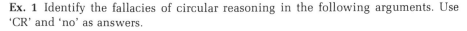

EXERCISES FOR MODULE 34
THE FALLACIES OF CIRCULAR REASONING AND BEGGING THE QUESTION

Ex. 1 Identify the fallacies of circular reasoning in the following arguments. Use 'CR' and 'no' as answers.

_____ 1. Every event ever observed and studied has been found to have a cause. Causes can be widely varied in quality, force, duration, and intensity. Thus all events ever studied and observed were caused.

_____ 2. Pete is thirty. Most thirty-year-olds survive until their thirty-first birthday. Thus the majority of those who are thirty live to be thirty-one.

_____ 3. I knocked over the first domino in a series of 100 dominoes; and I knocked it over toward the second domino in the series. The 100 dominoes were all standing up close enough to each other that if one fell over it would knock the next one over. Therefore, all the dominoes were knocked over.

_____ 4. I think we can safely say that if capital punishment deterred crime it might be justified. Capital punishment does not deter crime. Still our point is correct because one possible justification of capital punishment is its possible crime-deterrent value.

_____ 5. Whoever is drunk ought to be arrested. If anyone is arrested that person ought to be in jail. So everyone who is drunk ought to be in jail.

Ex. 2 Identify the question-begging passages (use 'QB') in the following.

_____ 1. The quality of a person's work is the only sensible basis on which to give him or her a raise in pay. This is because it is the only nonarbitrary way to distinguish the size of one person's raise from another's. And clearly making such distinctions is essential because if none is made it's preposterous to claim that the merit of a person's work is the basis for what he or she is paid.

_____ 2. Two-thirds of the last twenty coin tosses have come up heads. That is surprising, but not as surprising as it would be if two-thirds of 2,000 tosses came up heads.

_____ 3. My new customer just told me I am his favorite architect. Since people seldom lie to those they admire, I'm sure he was telling me the truth.

_____ 4. There is a limit, my friends, to the number of outrages that we can permit this administrator to visit upon us. He has hurt our careers, insulted our intelligence, undermined our solidarity, embarrassed us in public, and lied about us in private. His policies are thinly veiled efforts to rob us of our jobs and security. He is a monster to be destroyed—a danger to our profession! We must begin recall action to remove him from office at once.

_____ 5. Good students will get most of these exercises correct. For good students learn well when they study hard, and the mark of hard study is the ability to get most of these exercises right.

Ex. 3 Distinguish the passages which are circular reasoning from those that are question-begging. Use 'CR' and 'QB.'

_____ 1. The old professor eagerly pointed toward a pine tree and said, "Look at that fine specimen of a hawk." "How do you know that it's a hawk?" asked the assistant. "Why because it looks like this photograph of a hawk," came the sly reply.

_____ 2. Beyond all doubt, most legislators are good and wise. They are also rich and loyal to their parties. So several legislators are wise and good.

_____ 3. We have now returned all our prisoners to you as you can see by noting that you have the prisoner for every name on the list of prisoners. And the list was obviously complete because, with this last group returned, we have no prisoners left.

_____ 4. Anyone who had a definite set of rules of conduct by which he or she regulated their life would be a machine. No one is a machine. Still we have established that people who have a definite set of rules by which they regulate their conduct are machines.

_____ 5. Hamilton was not rich when she died. Her estate was settled quietly out of probate. Her widower took half and her lawyer took half. Then her widower married her lawyer. So Hamilton certainly was not rich at the end of her life.

Ex. 4 Construct two examples of the fallacy of circular reasoning and two examples of question-begging arguments.

SELECTED ANSWERS
TO EXERCISES FOR MODULE 34

Ex. 1

1. CR   2. CR   3. No   4. CR   5. No

If you missed any, review 34:1.

Ex. 2

1. QB   2. No   3. QB   4. No   5. QB

If you missed any, review 34:2.1.

Ex. 3

1. QB   2. CR   3. QB

If you missed any, review 34:3 and recall that sometimes an argument can beg the question by using a loaded definition, as in item 3.

Ex. 4 Check your examples against those given in the text. Do your examples meet the conditions set forth in 34:3?

MODULE 35
THE FALLACY OF WRONG CONCLUSION

In the case of the various irrelevant-appeal fallacies (see Module 28) the person committing the fallacy was mistaken about which premises to select to support a particular conclusion. This mistake led to selecting premises that were irrelevant to the truth or falsity of the conclusion. In the case of the fallacy of *wrong conclusion* a similar mistake occurs, except that here the person selects a wrong statement of the conclusion.

● After reading Module 35 you should be able to:

1. Pick out the right and the wrong conclusions of various arguments
2. Identify instances of the fallacy of wrong conclusion
3. Distinguish instances of this fallacy from other arguments

35:1 Suppose we said we wanted to argue from the premises 'all people are selfish' and 'all selfish things are mortal' to the obvious conclusion 'all people are mortal.' Further, we wanted to try to dress up the conclusion stylistically. We might supply the conclusion in any of these ways.

> People are mortal.
> If anything is a person it's mortal.
> Whatever is not mortal is not a person.

Each of these is obviously equivalent or obviously implies our desired conclusion. They are simply rewordings of the desired conclusion. No problems arise out of this unless we make a mistake in trying to supply the restatement. None of these candidates would do:

> Not all people are immortal.
> All mortal things are people.
> Some nonmortal things are nonpeople.
> Mortals are people.
> Whatever is not a person is not mortal.

These possible conclusions are *wrong conclusions* because they are not synonymous with, or obviously equivalent to, the desired conclusion, nor do they imply the desired conclusion.

35:2 The fallacy of wrong conclusion occurs when a person, knowing the proper, desired, or "right" conclusion, inadvertently or otherwise argues for a statement of the conclusion which is not synonymous with, or obviously equivalent to, or does not obviously imply the right conclusion. Such an argument, while it may turn out to be sound, is still not acceptable as a proof of the desired or right conclusion. As stated it makes no progress toward the proper intended conclusion since it does not actually draw the proper conclusion—it draws a wrong conclusion. Here are some examples of the fallacy.

EG. 35.1 Friends, as editor and director of *Star* news services and its subsidiaries, I wish to defend the view that pornography is not a danger to public morality. Our country is founded on the basis of certain rights. One of these rights is the right to a free press, a press unbridled by political interests. Without a free press there might not be any viable check on the spread of government control. Thus, it is our right and our duty to maintain the freedom of the press.

EG. 35.2 Everyone should drink three glasses of milk daily because it's nutritious. There is no more perfect food. Of course some people are allergic to milk. But if you're not allergic to milk, you should drink three glasses every day.

In Eg. 35.1 the conclusion drawn, that we should maintain a free press, does not *obviously imply* the conclusion intended, that pornography is not a public danger. In Eg. 35.2 the argument reaches a conclusion that is weaker than the one it originally set out to prove. The passage starts out as if to support a categorical conclusion, but it winds up saying only that the conclusion is true *on a certain condition*.

When trying to spot the fallacy of wrong conclusion look for an argument that contains a contrast between a conclusion that it sets out with the objective of proving and a conclusion that it actually draws. If the one drawn is not synonymous or logically equivalent to the one that it sets out to demonstrate, then the argument commits the fallacy of wrong conclusion.

EXERCISES FOR MODULE 35
THE FALLACY OF WRONG CONCLUSION

Ex. 1 In each item below you will be given a desired conclusion and the information that some person has successfully argued for an alternative conclusion. If the alternative is synonymous with, implies or is equivalent to the right conclusion put 'RC'; if not, put 'WC' for wrong conclusion.

Desired conclusion: Religious wars are the roots of current national rivalries.

_____ 1. Argued for: Current national rivalries have produced the conditions out of which religious wars arise.

_____ 2. Argued for: The grounds, or basic causes, of current nationalistic feelings can be detected in the religious wars of past years.

_____ 3. Argued for: National rivalries arise out of a variety of factors: geographical, political, and economic, but not ideological nor military.

_____ 4. Argued for: The economic history of a people explains the religious, philosophical, military, and political events that together make nations rivals.

_____ 5. Argued for: Religious wars and national rivalries arise out of ethnic and racial prejudices and differences in the degree of civilization achieved in various geographical regions.

Desired conclusion: The existence or nonexistence of a soul is not a scientifically determinable question.

_____ 6. Argued for: Science cannot prove whether or not people have souls.

_____ 7. Argued for: Whether or not people have souls, science cannot prove that God exists.

_____ 8. Argued for: There are limits to what science can determine.

_____ 9. Argued for: The soul is not a biological component of the human body viewed as a physiochemical mechanism.

_____ 10. Argued for: No scientist has, as yet, proved that people have souls.

Check the answers to Ex. 1 before going on to work Ex. 2.

Ex. 2 Identify the wrong-conclusion fallacies among the following passages. Use 'WC' for the wrong-conclusion fallacy; otherwise put 'no.'

_____ 1. In defense of the position that the newspaper did not dismiss the columnist because he took controversial points of view in his column, the editor said that she did not make it her policy to fire people because of their personal life-style.

_____ 2. The Senator, when asked whether or not the subject of anticrime legislation was discussed in the Senate last Tuesday said, "Well I was back in my home state last week, but I can tell you that several important pieces of legislation designed to curb the criminal element in our society were discussed."

_____ 3. In defense of the policy of discrimination against hiring women administrators, the superintendent of schools argued that certain jobs, like janitorial and maintenance jobs, required a degree of physical strength which was not within the range of the physical ability of most women.

_____ 4. In defense of the position that the newspaper did not dismiss the columnist because he took controversial points of view, the editor argued: "We had to cut back because of the high costs of publication these days. I put all the columnists names in a hat and drew out his as the one that we would have to cut. That's all there was to it."

_____ 5. The Senator, when asked whether or not the subject of inflation came up in a recent meeting with the President, said, "Why, no—I do not believe it came up at all."

_____ 6. The Senator, when asked whether or not the subject of inflation came up in a recent meeting with the President, replied, "I made no recommendations to the President concerning inflation."

_____ 7. In defense of the corporate policy of hiring one black and one woman for every three white males hired, the corporate executive said, "We believe in freedom and opportunity for all people and so if we have a job open it goes to the most qualified person we can find."

8. The defense lawyer walked up to the judge and said, "Your honor, my client could not have murdered Dalaney at 10:00 P.M. at his resort cottage because that morning he drove 150 miles away, to Sacramento, where he held a 2-hour conference beginning at 2:00 P.M. Witnesses will confirm all this!"

9. Those who hold that the development of technology is not a threat to our nation do so for the weakest of reasons. They argue that it is unimaginable that technological progress should lead to anything but progress in terms of our national vitality.

10. We have all heard the so-called "reasons" why we should not build the proposed dam: it costs too much, it is no better than the present facility, it will further disturb the ecology, and its proposed name is politically unfortunate. Well, I say that we cannot let the dam project be stopped just because a few citizens don't like the name we proposed. We can change the dam's name!

SELECTED ANSWERS
TO EXERCISES FOR MODULE 35

Ex. 1

1. WC; it's backwards here.
2. RC
3. WC; religious wars would be in the realm of the ideological and military factors.
4. WC; this makes economic factors, not religious wars, the root of nationalism.
5. WC; here religious wars and nationalism both grow out of the same background, but neither is said to have been grounds for or caused the other.
6. RC
7. WC; this talks about what science cannot say about God, not what it can or cannot say about human souls.
8. WC; these limits are not specified, so perhaps it is possible that science could determine whether or not people have souls and yet still be limited in other respects.
9. WC; this does not obviously rule out one of the other sciences as a tool to answer the question.
10. WC; this only says that it has not been done, not that it cannot be done.

Ex. 2

1. WC; her defense does not mean that she would not fire someone who wrote controversial columns.
2. This is a fair answer to the question.
3. The job of administrator was not covered in the superintendent's stated conclusion.
4. No; this is a proper conclusion.
5. No; this is a direct answer to the question.
6. No; the reply does not mean the subject never came up, although the Senator may hope that we draw that wrong conclusion. But since no argument has been made, no fallacy has occurred.
7. WC; this corporate executive did not defend his corporation's quota system by

arguing that an individual's qualifications were what was considered in hiring (unless he was begging the question and had used a loaded definition of 'qualifications' which would include "fitting into the sexual or racial group that the corporate quota system required").

8. WC; it is still possible for the defendant to have driven the 150 miles in time to be the killer.
9. No
10. This is a straw-man fallacy.

If you missed more than two of these, review the module and review Ex. 1 carefully.

MODULE 36

THE FALLACIES OF ANALYTICALLY TRUE CONCLUSION AND SELF-CONTRADICTORY PREMISES

In Module 36, we will treat two types of no-progress fallacies which result from an argument's being valid for either the trivial reason that its conclusion happens to be analytically true or the trivial reason that its premises happen to be self-contradictory.

● After reading Module 36 you should be able to:

1. Identify and distinguish the fallacies of analytically true conclusion and self-contradictory premises.
2. Distinguish these two fallacies from other fallacies and from nonarguments
3. Construct examples of each of these two fallacies

You might find it useful to review the concepts of analyticity (9:1.2) and inconsistency (17:1.1).

36:1 One kind of trivially valid argument is one with an *analytically true conclusion*. As such, the conclusion can never be false even in the event that all the premises are false. Indeed, the truth or falsity of the premises, or even their meaning or logical structure, are entirely irrelevant to the truth of the conclusion. The conclusion will be true in any case, since it is analytically true. Thus the argument will never have a set of true premises and a false conclusion. Thus, it is valid! But it is valid in a trivial way. Such an argument makes no logical progress. It does not combine the premises to draw out the logical consequences they contain. Indeed, in these kinds of cases the conclusion need not have anything to do with the premises. These arguments are valid; if their premises were true they would be sound. They are not, however, worthy of acceptance.

EG. 36.1 All people who own cars have an interest in the problem of pollution. So all people who own cars are people who own cars.

EG. 36.2 Never has the world known a person who has offered the country so much but also asked so much in return. This person's hunger for power and fame is surpassed only by a personal greed and lust for wealth that is unequalled in recent history. None of us would want to have this person for a personal friend. But yet we all owe the person so very much. And, so, this person is a person.

36:2.1 Another type of trivially valid argument is one that has an inconsistent or *self-contradictory* set of premises. The set of premises can be inconsistent if either a single premise is analytically false, as in

EG. 36.3 1. $(p \& (\sim p))$
2. $(q \supset r)$
$\therefore s$

or if taken together they contradict each other, as in

EG. 36.4 1. $(p \supset q)$
2. p
3. $(\sim q)$
$\therefore r$

Truth-tables for these examples will show that they are valid; but since the premises never mention the content of the conclusions, s and r, the validity is suspect. In Eg. 36.3 the first premise is analytically false. Because of this the premises cannot all be true, and, as a further result, they cannot all be true when the conclusion is false. Thus, Eg. 36.3 is valid in a trivial way. Similarly, by modus ponens (see 25:1.2) from premise 1 and premise 2 of Eg. 36.4 we can validly infer q. But q and $(\sim q)$ are contradictory. Because of this fact, the formula

$$[[((p \supset q) \& p) \& (\sim q)] \supset r]$$

will be a tautology, and Eg. 36.4 will be valid, also in a trivial way.

In examples such as Egs. 36.3 and 36.4 the premises offer no support or proof of the truth of the conclusion. (Actually they could be entirely irrelevant to the conclusion.) Yet the arguments are valid because of the mere fact that the premise set is inconsistent. (Such an argument could never be sound because there is no way to make every statement in an inconsistent set of statements come out simultaneously true.) In arguments that commit the fallacy of self-contradictory premises there is no progress made toward establishing the conclusion as true. No matter whether the conclusion is true or false, even if it is analytically false, this kind of argument would be valid. In effect an argument with inconsistent premises says that its conclusion must be true if what could never possibly be true were true. Precious little assurance! Because of this such arguments are not reliable and not acceptable. Here are some examples of this fallacy.

EG. 36.5 Either today is the day that the repairman will come or today is not the day that he will come. He cannot possibly come today. He cannot possibly not come today. He is not, therefore, today, a good repairman.

EG. 36.6 Whatever I say you will not become afraid. (Nobody who becomes afraid can live with their thoughts.) My saying something to you makes you think of it and you will fear whatever you think of. But anyone, even one who fears, can live with what I say. So, you may not fear to think what I fear to say.

36:2.2 Arguments like the examples above offer no special problems because their self-contradictory premises make them unsound. The only possible concern they offer is that it is hard to see what the "proper" conclusions might be. This, however, is only a passing problem. The fact is that there is no "proper" or "right" conclusion for such an argument. They are just unacceptable, unfortunate, arguments. The thing to do with them is to start over from the beginning, rooting out any analytically false or self-contradictory premises and determining which of the pair of inconsistent premises is true.

EXERCISES FOR MODULE 36
THE FALLACIES OF ANALYTICALLY TRUE CONCLUSION AND SELF-CONTRADICTORY PREMISES

Ex. 1 Here are several statements or sets of statements. If an item is analytically true put 'AT,' if it is self-contradictory put 'SC,' and otherwise put 'neither.'

_____ 1. All horses are horses.

_____ 2. What you see is what you get.

_____ 3. All unmarried women are under the age of twenty-nine.

_____ 4. Sometimes people swim but human beings are not capable of swimming.

_____ 5. What is one person's meat is another's poison.

_____ 6. I want to ask you to leave the room at once.

_____ 7. All brown books are easy to read. No books are easy to read unless they are green.

_____ 8. Students who are late for the final exam will be automatically given a grade of zero on that exam. Nobody with a zero on the final will pass the course.

_____ 9. The workers united and now they pay their dues to the unions instead of the industrialists. Someone should free the workers from the workers.

_____ 10. There are no workers who can claim that the unions have not improved their lives.

_____ 11. This true sentence is false.

_____ 12. A true statement is one that is not not true.

Ex. 2 Identify the arguments in the following list that have analytically true conclusions by 'ATC'; otherwise put 'no.'

_____ 1. Political figures are people who have lots of money, lots of personality, and lots of nerve. With nerve comes the ability to get things done. But this takes money. Yet, money does not come to those who have no personality. So whoever has money, nerve, and a lot of personality is someone with wealth, guts, and personality.

_____ 2. Klapietes was a more personable philosopher than it might appear from reading her major works. This is so because she was known to have been especially fond of the company of men and because she had enough pride to have made her want to be well thought of as a person.

_____ 3. Bruhinian threats are no news. It is their long-standing national policy to provoke antagonism and present a hostile front.

_____ 4. Religious freedom is merely a promise, not a reality in the United States today. We are not able to worship snakes, nor would many communities accept women ministers yet. Thus that good old-time religion is good old-time religion.

Ex. 3 Identify the arguments which commit the fallacy of self-contradictory premises from among the following. Use 'SCP' and 'no' for your answers.

_____ 1. Toy boxes are for toys not cats! If you put your cat into the toy box it will become very upset. If it becomes upset, I will be upset. If I am upset, you will get a spank. So if you put your cat into the toy box, you will get a spank. Do you understand me?

_____ 2. Many people detest living in wet, cold climates. If people like cold weather they should move to Alaska. The people in Alaska find the weather more attractive than it may seem to be to those who have never visited there. Nobody minds living in wet, cold areas anyway. So why not move to Alaska?

_____ 3. London, England, is an interesting and beautiful place to visit. But there is no city in Great Britain that is worth your time at least in terms of a visit, because most are ugly and the rest are totally uninteresting. So visit Rome.

_____ 4. I always notice class merchandise. This is my line of work you see. So if the things you want to show me are good, I'll notice them.

Ex. 4 Distinguish the fallacies of analytically true conclusion and self-contradictory premises from among the following passages; use 'ATC,' 'SCP,' and 'neither' for your answers.

_____ 1. She is a worthless incompetent. I wouldn't trust her to tell me whether or not it's sunny outside even if she and I were both standing outside together. You should be careful about accepting her opinion on anything if you know what's good for you.

_____ 2. Loan sharks are not kinds of fishes. They are people who feed on the needs of people and create more problems for those people than they solve. They lend at high interest rates and collect at higher ones. The only thing to conclude is that those who live dangerously are flirting with trouble.

_____ 3. Porter knew everything about it because she helped set it up. Anyone who knew even a little about the deal would have necessarily been suspicious about it. Porter was not suspicious in the least, no question about that. We must infer that Porter is not very ethical.

_____ 4. I have nothing to say except that I was not there at the time of the shooting.

_____ 5. The prosecuting attorney faced the defendant coldly and matter-of-factly. You say that you were not there at the time of the shooting. But you knew that it was a shooting. Only the killer could have known that. You must, then, be the killer.

Ex. 5 Construct three examples of the fallacy of self-contradictory premises and two examples of the fallacy of analytically true conclusion.

Ex. 6 Indicate whether the following are true or false.

_____ 1. All no-progress fallacies are necessarily valid.

_____ 2. Fallacies of wrong conclusion come about by arguing for a conclusion that doesn't entail, nor is synonymous with, nor is equivalent to the proper conclusion.

_____ 3. All arguments that are circular are valid.

_____ 4. All question-begging arguments are species of the wrong-conclusion fallacy.

_____ 5. Arguments with analytically true conclusions are valid but make no logical progress because their validity is trivial, since they do not ensure that the information in the premises have been combined to yield the conclusion.

_____ 6. Arguments with self-contradictory premises can be sound arguments.

_____ 7. Some arguments make "no progress" because they reason in a circle, others because they avoid or circumvent the central issue, others because they offer the wrong conclusion, and still others cannot guarantee that progress was made toward proving their conclusions inasmuch as they are trivially valid.

SELECTED ANSWERS
TO EXERCISES FOR MODULE 36

Ex. 1

1. AT	2. Neither	3. Neither	4. SC
5. Neither	6. Neither	7. SC	8. Neither
9. Neither	10. Neither	11. SC	12. AT

If you missed one or more review Module 9.

Ex. 2

1. ATC   2. No   3. No; playing with words, yes   4. ATC

If you missed one or more review 36:1.

Ex. 3

1. No   2. SCP   3. SCP   4. No

If you missed any review 36:2.1.

Ex. 5 Check your answers by demonstrating, if possible, using the methods learned in Part Two, that the premises are self-contradictory or that the conclusions are analytically (logically) true.

Ex. 6

1. F   2. T   3. T   4. F   5. T   6. F   7. T

Review the appropriate module for each item missed if you do not see why the answer given here is right.

SELF-QUIZ FOR PART THREE
ILLOGICAL THINKING

Answer the following multiple-choice questions by selecting the best answer from among those provided.

1. Arguments are acceptable if, and only if, they are:

   A. Logically correct and sound
   B. Sound and fallacious
   C. Nonfallacious and logically correct
   D. Sound and nonfallacious
   E. Logically correct and fallacious

2. Informal fallacies:

   A. All have false assumptions
   B. Are all no-progress arguments
   C. Are logically correct
   D. Are either no-progress arguments or can be converted into logically correct arguments by adding their false presuppositions as premises
   E. Are never used in trying to persuade people

3. A fallacy is, by definition, essentially:

   A. A kind of statement   B. A mistaken argument
   C. A false assumption   D. A means of contraception
   E. A tool intentionally used by
      honest people

4. "The corporation is very unreceptive to change. Therefore, Vice President Halferson is unlikely to consider your proposal seriously." The fallacy involved in this passage is:

   A. Misuse of authority   B. Composition
   C. Division   D. Irrelevant appeal
   E. False dilema

5. "You can't prove that she was to blame for the misfortune, so it must actually have been someone else who was responsible." The fallacy involved here is:

   A. All for one and one for all   B. Appeal to ignorance
   C. Playing with words   D. Irrelevant appeal
   E. Self-contradictory premises

6. "No-fault auto insurance ought to be universally adopted. Virtually no accidents are deliberate. Whatever is nondeliberate happens by chance, and nobody is responsible for what happens by chance." The fallacy involved is:

   A. Composition   B. Playing with numbers
   C. Playing with words   D. Undistributed middle term
   E. Straw-man fallacy

7. "Why do I love you? Well, I love you because I love you. You cannot argue with the validity of that!" This passage:

   A. Begs the question   B. Is circular reasoning
   C. Is an appeal to emotions   D. Is the fallacy of affirming the
   E. Is the fallacy of affirming the obvious   consequent

8. "If we refuse to bargain, the administration will reject all our demands. But if we don't make our demands known, then too they'll be ignored. Since there aren't any other choices, we're bound to lose any way you look at it." This passage is:

A. Nonfallacious argument   B. Denying the antecedent
C. Playing with words   D. Affirming the consequent
E. False dilemma

9. "All the officers of this company are ready to consider seriously any new proposal they hear. So it stands to reason that this company is receptive to change." The fallacy involved is:

A. Division   B. Playing with numbers
C. False cause   D. Composition
E. Appeal to ignorance

10. "You can't expect a box elder tree to provide much shade for you. It's really a very poor tree. You can see how poor it is by sawing off a branch and observing what poor lumber its soft fibers make." The fallacy is:

A. Appeal to ignorance   B. Appeal to emotion
C. False cause   D. Misuse of authority
E. Playing with words

11. "There were people 75 years ago predicting we'd soon run out of many things we still have in abundance. So you know perfectly well we're not really going to run out of natural resources in the next seventy-five years now any more than we did a generation ago." The fallacy is:

A. Straw-man argument   B. Begging the question
C. Gambler's fallacy   D. False cause
E. Irrelevant appeal

12. "If you want to grasp how degenerate this neighborhood is, just consider: It's a very old neighborhood. Lots of neighborhoods degenerate as they age. Many houses in the neighborhood are being sold. You really can't hope for a neighborhood to maintain itself forever." The fallacy is:

A. Irrelevant appeal   B. False dilemma
C. Circular reasoning   D. Denying the antecedent
E. Division

13. "The General has become a paid consultant for Rockhead Multinational. So even though he does know a lot about military material his endorsement of Rockhead for the contract should not be the only thing that leads us to accept their bid." This argument is:

A. Logically correct   B. A fallacy of ad hominem appeal
C. A straw-man fallacy   D. Composition fallacy
E. No-progress fallacy

14. "Softwood trees grow much more quickly than hardwoods. You can scarcely notice a year's growth looking, say, at a walnut tree. Softwoods are more profitable to grow—whole forest areas are often cut these days and turned over to pine-monoculture. So you see hardwoods simply don't grow as fast as your softwoods." This argument is:

A. Appeal to emotion   B. Circular reasoning
C. Denying the antecedent   D. Fallacy of wrong conclusion
E. Fallacy of analytically true conclusion

15. "We should avoid the strike! Here's why: First of all it will cost us too much

money. Second we know it will be ineffective. We should certainly avoid anything that is both costly and useless." This passage is:

A. Logically correct as it stands   B. An emotional appeal
C. The fallacy of playing with words   D. The fallacy of false dilemma
E. The fallacy of self-contradictory premises

16. "Whenever I golf in the morning I score about 49 or 50 for nine holes. So I would do better if I played golf at some other time of the day." The argument is:

A. Logically correct   B. Playing-with-numbers fallacy
C. Fallacy of false cause   D. Misuse of authority
E. Fallacy of composition

17. "Some Octavian premiers have had strong leftist political support. Few, however, have ruled without a broad political base. So some who have been supported by leftists have ruled without broad political base." The above argument is:

A. Valid by class logic   B. Fallacy of affirming the consequent
C. Fallacy of denying the antecedent   D. Fallacy of undistributed middle term

18. "The evidence shows that Mr. AA, Mr. BB, and Mr. CC are the only persons who had reasons to murder Mr. DD. However, BB has an alibi: he was out of the country at the time. CC also has an alibi: he was in jail at the time of the murder of DD. AA was seen near DD's home shortly after the murder wielding a bloody knife. A knife was used in the murder. So it seems that AA murdered DD." The argument is:

A. Justified   B. A fallacy of undistributed middle
C. An emotional appeal   term
E. A fallacy of denying the antecedent   D. A fallacy of false cause

19. "If we set limits on free choice, then we destroy what is of greatest value to mankind. But we do not set limits on free choice. So we do not destroy what is of greatest value." This argument can be identified as a:

A. Fallacy of affirming the con-   B. Fallacy of undistributed middle
   sequent   term
C. Valid argument   D. Fallacy of denying the antecedent
E. Fallacy of all for one and one for all

20. "French cuisine is the best in this world. It is far superior to German or Italian. Although Chinese cuisine is in truth unsurpassed. When I get talking about all this good food I just have to conclude you should never pass up a Greek meal." This passage:

A. Is not an argument   B. Makes no logical progress
C. Commits the fallacy of undistributed   D. Is a playing-with-words fallacy
   middle term   E. Is circular

21. "There must have been an intelligent designer of the universe. This conclusion is certain because it is analytically true that whatever is designed was designed by some intelligent being, and from the fact that the universe seems to have been harmoniously designed." This passage:

A. Is a deductive argument   B. Is a fallacy of circular reasoning

C. Is the fallacy of false cause   D. Is the fallacy of wrong conclusion
E. Is the fallacy of undistributed
   middle term

22. "The sentence X is true if, and only if, the sentence Y is false. But Y is not false. So X is not true." This passage is:

A. A justified argument   B. A valid argument
C. A fallacy of denying the antecedent   D. Not an argument
E. A fallacy of affirming the consequent

23. "A person of integrity will honor commitments. A wise person will honor commitments also. Thus a person of integrity is wise." This passage is:

A. The fallacy of undistributed middle term B. The fallacy of division
C. The fallacy of the straw man   D. The fallacy of undistributed
E. An acceptable argument   predicate term

24. "If any member of the director's staff is involved in the scandal, then her or his immediate superior is also involved. The lowest-level aide was definitely proved to be involved. Thus, every member of the director's staff is involved." This passage is:

A. A formal fallacy   B. The fallacy of false cause
C. An emotional appeal   D. Not an argument
E. A deductive argument

25. "Everyone knows that the drug problem in universities is a growing danger. There is no evidence to indicate that less State money will change this. Thus we conclude that less money will only make things worse." This argument is:

A. A playing-with-numbers fallacy   B. Logically correct
C. An emotional appeal   D. The fallacy of false cause
E. The fallacy of appeal to ignorance

26. There is an old Black Swamp legend about an extraordinarily successful old trapper named Bull who used to live on raw meat, fish, and garlic. Bull would often be asked how it was that he was such a success at trapping animals. His reply was always the same: "I breath on 'em and they just gives up." This story portrays Bull:

A. Using the false-cause fallacy   B. Using the gambler's fallacy
C. Appealing to ignorance   D. Committing a fallacy of division
E. Using a straw-man argument

27. "The world is full of people who treat others rudely, and John is just one of those kind of people." This passage is:

A. Not an argument   B. A fallacy of composition
C. A fallacy of division   D. Correct reasoning about parts and wholes
E. None of the above

28. "All people are evil. It is also true that all gods are evil. So all people are gods and all gods are people." This passage is:

A. The fallacy of affirming the   B. The fallacy of undistributed middle
   consequent   term
C. The fallacy of undistributed   D. An appeal to emotion
   subject term   E. The fallacy of playing with words

29. "Long before the European settlers came to Ohio this land belonged to the Native Americans. Most Native Americans and Native American culture, though, have vanished from the land. There has been a program of cultural and racial genocide carried out in Ohio. The Native American culture was one of the most beautiful ever to have developed in North America." This passage is:
    A. The fallacy of false cause   B. A straw-man fallacy
    C. An irrelevant appeal   D. The fallacy of false dilemma
    E. Not an argument

30. All formal fallacies:
    A. Contain mistakes in content   B. Are errors of perception
    C. Are false assumptions   D. Are invalid arguments
    E. Make no logical progress

31. "People who have dogs are people with children. No Indians have dogs. So no Indians have children." This argument is:
    A. Valid   B. Question-begging
    C. A fallacy of undistributed   D. A fallacy of affirming the consequent
       predicate term   E. A fallacy of false dilemma

32. "Not only are the Russian people being told by their leaders that the Soviet Union is pursuing a policy of peaceful coexistence but the nuclear weapons possessed by both the United States and the U.S.S.R. are such a deterrent that large-scale war in the future seems unlikely." This passage is:
    A. Analytically true   B. An illogical argument
    C. An ad hominem fallacy   D. Not an argument
    E. An emotional appeal

33. "The president of the college has said that the best automobile to buy is a Gord. Since she is president it would seem that the Gord must be a fine car to buy." This passage is:
    A. A wrong-conclusion fallacy   B. A logically correct argument
    C. The fallacy of misuse of authority   D. The fallacy of straw man
    E. A playing-with-words fallacy

34. "All people are fast. All fasts are for religious reasons or political consciousness-raising. So all people are interested in political consciousness-raising." This passage is:
    A. The fallacy of self-contradictory premises   B. The fallacy of false dilemma
    C. The fallacy of composition   D. The fallacy of playing-with-
    E. Not a fallacy at all   words

35. Original: "Soft-nose bullets are better as police ammunition. This is so because they are less likely to ricochet." Which of the following reconstructions is the best?
    A. Soft-nose bullets are better ammunition for police. This follows from the fact that they are superior to other types of ammunition.
    B. Bullets are less likely to ricochet if they are soft and do not bounce off hard objects like cars or buildings. So soft-nose bullets are better as police ammunition.
    C. Bullets that are less likely to ricochet are less likely to harm possible by-

standers. Soft-nose bullets are less likely to ricochet. Since police always risk harming bystanders, soft-nose bullets are better ammunition for police.

D. Bullets that are less likely to ricochet are not able to harm bystanders. Police always risk harming bystanders except if they use soft-nose bullets. So soft-nose bullets are better ammunition for police.

36. "All our citizens have the right to vote. But blacks are not citizens. So the blacks in our country do not have the right to vote," explained the grandmother to the child.

"But, grandma, I don't get it. Aren't the blacks citizens, too?"

"No, honey. They can't be, only people who have the right to vote can be citizens."

In the above exchange the grandmother commits the fallacy of:

A. Wrong conclusion   B. Undistributed middle term
C. Denying the obvious   D. Begging the question
E. False dilemma

ANSWERS TO SELF-QUIZ
FOR PART THREE

	Answer	Reference		Answer	Reference
1.	D	24:4	19.	D	25:2.2
2.	D	24:3	20.	B	36:2
3.	B	24:1	21.	A	Module 10
4.	C	30:2	22.	B	Chapter 4
5.	B	28:2.1	23.	A	26:3.1
6.	C	29:1	24.	E	Module 10
7.	B	34:1	25.	E	28:2.1
8.	E	29:2	26.	A	31:1
9.	D	30:1	27.	A	Modules 3 and 4
10.	E	29:1	28.	B	26:3.1
11.	E	28:3	29.	E	Modules 3 and 4
12.	A	28:3	30.	D	24:2.1
13.	A	28:2.3	31.	C	26:3.2
14.	B	34:1	32.	D	Modules 3 and 4
15.	A	Chapters 5 or 6	33.	C	28:2.4
16.	C	31:1	34.	D	29:1
17.	D	26:3.1	35.	C	27:3
18.	A		36.	D	34:2

If you missed ten or less you have achieved adequate understanding of the material. We suggest that no matter how many you missed you review each of them to be sure you understand the answer.

FOUR

LOGICAL THINKING

We have already learned to make a number of evaluations of arguments. We learned how to recognize a large variety of fallacies, and we learned how to determine the validity of propositional logic and predicate logic arguments. But we did not examine the *strategies* that can be employed to argue logically. In this part we will examine three varieties of proof strategies: the *direct*, *indirect*, and *conditional* strategies. We will examine the relationship between arguments and proofs. We will learn how to recognize and use proof strategies to build logical arguments of both the deductive and inductive varieties. Chapter 13 applies what we learn about strategies to symbolic propositional logic by developing a system with which we can naturally deduce the conclusions of arguments in symbolic notation. Chapter 14 applies logical strategies to contemporary research design, thereby developing the important realm of inductive logic.

11

ARGUMENTS AND PROOFS

So far we have been looking at arguments primarily as sets of statements. As such they can be evaluated as logically correct, as sound, and as acceptable. As such they also exhibit various logical strategies. Part Four will focus on these strategies. Part of the educational goal of this chapter is to acquire a preliminary understanding of the two basic kinds of arguments: those that exhibit the direct strategy and those that exhibit the indirect strategy. However, there is another way to look at arguments. Some arguments are put to use as proofs. The other part of the educational goal of this chapter is to examine those arguments that are proofs so as to determine what a logical proof is.

MODULE 37

DIRECT AND INDIRECT ARGUMENTS

There are two ways to state an argument's conclusion. You can assert that it is true or you can assert that it cannot be false. The difference between these two is not just a matter of style. The difference determines the choice of strategies you can use in assembling the premises of the argument. In this module we look at some preliminary examples of each of these two types of arguments; later we will devote a module to each.

● After reading Module 37 you should be able to:

1. Identify and distinguish some simple examples of direct and indirect arguments
2. State the definitions of 'direct argument' and 'indirect argument'

37:1.1 An argument is a set of statements such that one is presented as the logical consequence of the others. There are two ways to express this relationship. We can say 'given the premises the conclusion must be true' or 'given the premises the conclusion cannot fail to be true.' Here are four pairs of example arguments. In each pair the first simply presents its conclusion as true; the second denies that the conclusion can fail to be true.

EG. 37.1 If the dogs fight then children flee. The dogs are fighting. So the kids are running away.

EG. 37.1' Suppose the children are not running away. The dogs are fighting. And if the dogs are fighting, then the children are fleeing. So it cannot be that the children aren't running away.

EG. 37.2 Look, almost everyone can do dishes. Plato was a person. So this shows that he probably could do dishes.

EG. 37.2' Suppose Plato couldn't do dishes. He was a person. But this means that someone couldn't do dishes. We know that virtually everyone can do dishes. So we should conclude that it is probably false that Plato couldn't do dishes.

EG. 37.3 The headlights don't go on. One very plausible reason for this could be that the battery is dead. So it probably is dead.

EG. 37.3' Suppose the battery were not dead. If it were not, then the headlights would work. That is, they would work if other things were in good working order. But they don't go on. So it is not reasonable to believe that the battery is not dead.

EG. 37.4 Either statement A is true or statement B is. But B is false. So A must be true.

EG. 37.4' Suppose A is false. We know that either A or B is true. And we also know B is false. But then A must be true. Now A cannot be both true and false. So it is not the case that A is false.

37:1.2 Note the differences in the way the two arguments in each pair present their conclusions. If we let p stand for the conclusion's positive statement unit in each case, we can focus more clearly on the difference. In Eg. 37.1 and 37.1' we have

$$\therefore p$$

as contrasted with

So it cannot be that not p.

In Eg. 37.2 we concluded

So this shows that probably p

as opposed to the conclusion of Eg. 37.2',

So we should conclude that it is probably false that not p.

Example 37.3 concludes

So probably p

whereas Eg. 37.3' concludes

So it is not reasonable to believe not p.

In Egs. 37.4 and 37.4' we have this contrast clearly stated already.

This difference in the way the conclusion is stated is the difference between direct arguments and indirect arguments. Building on the conceptual system started earlier, we can state the definitions of these two basic kinds of arguments.

Def. 26 Direct argument = $_{df}$ an argument such that its conclusion statement is presented as simply true

Def. 27 Indirect argument = $_{df}$ an argument such that its conclusion is presented as the assertion that the negation of a particular statement is false

Check to see that Egs. 37.1′, 37.2′, 37.3′, and 37.4′ fit Def. 27, whereas the other four fit Def. 26.

37:2 If you look at Egs. 37.1′ to 37.4′ you will note that they also differ from direct arguments in the way that their premises are assembled. All the indirect arguments *explicitly* make an assumption. They all assume that some statement is false. Ultimately each one repudiates this assumption to conclude that the statement actually cannot be false. This way of proceeding constitutes a general proof strategy—one that involves making an assumption only to later reject it and conclude the opposite of that assumption. This strategy is called the *strategy of indirect proof.* We will discuss it in detail in Chapter 12. You might review the four examples of indirect arguments to verify that the indirect proof strategy is being used in each of them.

Direct arguments are much more forthright. Direct arguments require no assumptions and do not present their conclusions in as roundabout a way as indirect arguments do. Just as there is a general strategy of indirect proof followed by indirect arguments, so there is a general strategy of *direct proof* followed by direct arguments. In Chapter 12 we will also examine the direct proof strategy.

EXERCISES FOR MODULE 37
DIRECT AND INDIRECT ARGUMENTS

Ex. 1 For the passages below, if an item is an argument identify it as either a direct argument (DA) or an indirect argument (IA). If it is not an argument at all put 'no.'

_____ 1. Listen to what I say.

_____ 2. Slavery is legal in our state. You can keep any people as indentured servants provided you treat them humanely. Thus the fact that they may object is legally irrelevant within our jurisdiction.

_____ 3. Draft animals are beasts of burden. People are sometimes made to be like draft animals for other people. But this does not mean that they are beasts of burden, since to say that something is like something else is to say, in the same breath, that it is nevertheless different.

_____ 4. Blacks, Chicanos, and Native Americans are all victims of psychological violence. Here is why: They are discriminated against in the job market; their cultures are called "subcultures" and are virtually ignored in our schools. They are stereotyped in our literature and called "violent," "lazy," "stupid," and "illiterate" in our classrooms. They are being forced, not physically but subtly, to conform to the white Protestant middle-class culture. This is a kind of psychological violence.

_____ 5. We hope that greater advances in science, especially genetics and bio-chemistry, will lead to eventual control over physical characteristics and psychological traits.

_____ 6. Suppose we do not take the van east for the holidays. If we don't, we will have to buy snow tires and get the brakes fixed for the other car. That will be expensive work. It is unreasonable for us to incur large expenses to fix the other car up at that time of the year. So, it is not the case that we won't take the van east for the holiday.

Ex. 2 State the definition of direct argument and indirect argument.

ANSWERS TO
EXERCISES FOR MODULE 37

Ex. 1

1. No   2. DA   3. DA   4. DA   5. No   6. IA

If you missed items 1 or 5 review Modules 3 and 4. If you missed any of the others review 37:2.

Ex. 2 Your definitions should be exactly like Def. 26 and Def. 27 given in 37:1.2.

MODULE 38
PROOFS

In this module we will examine proofs. We will learn that only some arguments are proofs. We will also examine the concerns that can be raised with regard to the purposes to which proofs can be put.

● After reading Module 38 you should be able to:

1. Distinguish the basic characteristics of proofs, especially as they relate to arguments
2. State the definition of 'proof'

38:1.1 Persuasion An argument is a set of statements such that one is presented as the logical consequence of the others. Nothing in the definition of 'argument' tells us what arguments are actually used to do. Arguments can be used for a variety of purposes. One chief purpose is as a tool for persuasion. To persuade is to convince someone of the truth of some statement. If the person you are trying to persuade is reasonable, then he or she will probably be susceptible to persuasion by means of acceptable arguments. The effort to persuade even a reasonable person can still fail for a number of reasons. The person may not believe the premises are true. The person may not be able to see the logical correctness of the argument you use. The person may mistakenly think your argument is a fallacy. Or the person may have knowledge that the conclusion of your argument is false (such could be the case if your argument, though acceptable, were not valid but only justified).

The list of possible reasons why an acceptable argument may fail to persuade grows even longer if the person you are trying to persuade is unreasonable, grossly illogical, or massively uninformed. In order to improve your persuasive powers you can study a number of skills, only some of which relate directly to logic and logical thinking. Many others concern the style or manner in which you present yourself and your arguments. Learning to convince people is not the same as learning to demonstrate that a statement is true, although for some audiences and in some cases the same methods can be used for both purposes.

38:1.2 Proof Our concern here is not primarily persuasion but rather *demonstration,* i.e., showing that a statement is true. Thus we will be looking at arguments as tools for demonstration or proof. Here, then, is a definition of proof.

> **Def. 28** Proof = $_{df}$ an argument presented as an acceptable argument with a view toward establishing the truth of its conclusion by relying on sufficiently obvious premises

To try to prove something is to argue intending to show that your conclusion is true. The adequacy of a proof is a matter of (1) logic and (2) the obviousness of its premises. If your proof is nonfallacious and logically correct, and if its premises are sufficiently obvious to remove reasonable doubts about the conclusion, then you have proved (shown, demonstrated, established) your conclusion to be true.

38:2 Having said that a proof is an argument we have committed ourselves to a variety of claims about proofs.

First Since a proof is *an argument,* it will have premises and a conclusion. It may be an enthymeme. The methods of evaluating arguments that we have discussed will apply. We can ask if a proof is logically correct, sound, and acceptable. It can be assembled using any available strategy for constructing direct or indirect arguments.

Second Given that a proof is presented *as an acceptable* argument with a view toward establishing its conclusion as true we can expect that it will be presented *as if:*

1. Its premises are all more or less obviously true (at least more obvious than its conclusion is).
2. It is not a fallacy.
3. Its premises taken together nontrivially entail or strongly support its conclusion.

But, since a proof is merely presented *as if* these three things were so, we must be alert to the possibility that one or more of them may fail to be true. If one or more fails to be true, this will make the proof *inadequate,* that is, unsuccessful as a demonstration. However, the unsuccessful proof is still, by definition, a proof. In other words, an argument is a proof not because of its being an acceptable argument, but because of *the way it is presented.*

Third To say that a proof's premises are presented as *more or less obviously true* is to say that in presenting a proof an author argues from what is relatively well known to what is relatively unknown.

Suppose you were to try to prove to someone in tenth-century Europe that the world is round. The following acceptable (sound, nonfallacious) argument would be inadequate: "If motion pictures were taken from the moon they would reveal both the curvature and the rotation of the earth. So the earth can scarcely be any other shape besides spherical." This acceptable argument is unacceptable as a proof to those Europeans because, although the premise is true, they cannot know it to be true. Since they cannot be sure that it is true, they cannot use it as a basis for clearing up their doubts or eliminating their disbelief of the conclusion.

What makes premises *sufficiently* obvious is relative. It is relative to what a person knows and to what knowledge is available to that person and others about him or her. Given two people and the *differences* in the background knowledge they bring to a question, what would be a reasonable doubt for one could be unreasonable for the other. A person who did not know that it is possible to take photographs could reasonably doubt alleged evidence that photographs show the earth to be spherical. A second person who thought the earth flat but understood photography would not have that ground for rationally doubting the evidence of photographs.

Fourth A proof is presented *as if it were nonfallacious.* People do not present their proofs with anything less than the belief that they are not fallacies. If someone were to try to prove (establish the truth of) something by deliberately using a fallacy, we would have to question his or her rationality or integrity or both! (If someone were to try to prove something, not realizing that the proof was a fallacy, that would simply be a mistake.)

Fifth A proof is presented *as if its premises entailed or strongly supported its conclusion in a nontrivial way.* Normally people deny that trivially valid arguments are genuine proofs at all.

Sixth As a tool for advancing knowledge, a proof is a means of working with known information so as to draw out the logical consequences of that information. In proving something we move from firm ground to new ground. The author of the proof takes his or her own premises as rather obviously true. If the author is unsure about a premise then she or he should indicate this doubt by claiming the premise to be only an *assumption* or *supposition*. However, we cannot blindly rely on the proof's author. The author of a proof may err both with regard to how obvious something really is and with regard to whether it is actually true at all.

EXERCISES FOR MODULE 38
PROOFS

Ex. 1 Indicate whether each of the following is true or false.

_____ 1. Proofs are nonarguments.

_____ 2. Proofs are arguments presented as if they were acceptable arguments.

_____ 3. Proofs can be fallacious.

_____ 4. Proofs can be logically incorrect.

_____ 5. Proofs can be sound.

_____ 6. When an argument is not presented with a view toward establishing its conclusion as true, it is not a proof.

_____ 7. To establish the truth of a conclusion for someone (to persuade) is not necessarily the same as to demonstrate objectively the truth of a statement.

_____ 8. Arguments can be used to filibuster as well as to try to persuade.

        9. Proofs are presented as if they were trivially valid arguments.

      10. If an argument is not acceptable it cannot be an adequate proof.

      11. A proof is an argument presented as if its premises were all more or less obviously true.

      12. A proof is an argument that is nonfallacious.

      13. A proof is a logically correct argument.

      14. A direct proof tries to establish the truth of its conclusion.

      15. An indirect proof tries to establish that its conclusion cannot avoid being true.

Ex. 2 State the definition of proof.

SELECTED ANSWERS
TO EXERCISES FOR MODULE 38

Ex. 1

2. T	4. T	6. T
7. T	8. T	10. T
12. F; "as if"	14. T; see Module 37, Def. 26.	15. T; see Module 37, Def. 27.

If you missed two or more of items 1 to 13, review this module.

Ex. 2 (See Def. 28 in 38:1.2.)

12

PROOF STRATEGIES

In Module 37 we said that two basic kinds of arguments are direct arguments and indirect arguments. We also suggested that direct arguments use the direct proof strategy and indirect arguments use the indirect proof strategy. In this chapter we will learn about those two strategies and then about the conditional proof strategy. The educational goal of this chapter is to learn to distinguish arguments employing these different proof strategies.

MODULE 39

THE DIRECT PROOF STRATEGY

Module 39 presents the direct proof strategy. We will learn its chief characteristics and look at some example arguments constructed using the direct proof strategy.

● After reading Module 39 you should be able to:

1. Identify arguments that employ the direct proof strategy
2. Identify the chief characteristics of the direct proof strategy

39:1.1 Three generic proof strategies In Chapter 11 we said that there were *two fundamental kinds* of arguments: direct arguments and indirect arguments.[1] This basic distinction readily yields two broad general strategies for developing logical arguments to be used as proofs: the direct proof strategy and the indirect proof strategy. We discuss the conditional proof strategy, which is used in conjunction with one of the other strategies, in Module 42.

39:1.2 Strategy What is a strategy? It is a tactic or way of doing something within a given set of rules in order to accomplish most efficiently and effectively a certain goal. There are strategies for all sorts of things. For example, the games of bridge or

---

[1] This is not to deny that arguments can also be classified using other categories. We can also distinguish them as inductive or deductive, as logically correct or incorrect, as fallacious or nonfallacious, as sound or unsound. But our aim here is to focus on how they are put together, how their assumptions, premises, and conclusions are presented when they are used as proofs.

Monopoly have rules, but quite apart from the rules there are more or less effective ways of playing those games as one tries to win. These various ways are strategies. Each of these strategies is calculated, more or less accurately, to lead to success. One human activity involving strategy is offering proofs. There are, within the rules of offering acceptable arguments, a wide variety of ways that a person can assemble premises and present assumptions and conclusions so as to generate arguments that are proofs. These various ways of generating proofs are proof strategies. Some ways lead to direct arguments, others to indirect arguments. Let us begin with the most straightforward strategy—the general strategy of direct proof.

39:2.1 Direct proof strategy defined The direct proof strategy yields what were called in Module 37 *direct arguments*. Recall that in such an argument the conclusion is simply drawn as true. The general strategy of direct proof then (i.e., the strategy used to build logical direct arguments to be used as proofs) is simply:

(D) Direct proof strategy: Assemble a nonfallacious argument such that its premises are more or less obviously true, and such that together they, nontrivially, either entail or strongly support the truth of the desired conclusion.

39:2.2 Here are some examples of arguments that could easily be direct proofs if they were put into a context in which their author would be using them as demonstrations.

EG. 39.1 A ruler is effective if he or she is able to respond to crisis situations calmly and objectively. Zoron responds to crises very emotionally. Brondopa responds calmly but with an obvious bias in favor of strong military action. Only Brokazoo responds both objectively and unemotionally. So only Brokazoo will make an effective ruler.

EG. 39.2 It does not seem possible to both conduct the war and settle our problems on the home front. Therefore, we probably should either pull out of the war or put aside our domestic problems while we pursue the war.

EG. 39.3 Either there will be a playoff game on TV today or the children's hour will be on. If a game is on, Mom will want to watch it. If the children's hour is on, then the kids will want to watch that. In either case, then, the TV set will be used today.

EG. 39.4 Virtually all the people in the sample indicated a preference for making Martin Luther King day a national holiday. The sample was composed of both whites and blacks drawn from both urban and rural backgrounds. The demographic proportions in the sample were approximately the same as those of the general population at large. So we can infer that most people would probably favor establishing Martin Luther King day as a national holiday.

EXERCISES FOR MODULE 39
THE DIRECT PROOF STRATEGY

Ex. 1 Identify arguments employing the direct proof strategy from among the following passages. Use 'DPS' and 'no.'

_____ 1. A man with hereditary blindness many generations ago propagated a family that now has 180 living blind members in it. Since each blind person costs the government $5,000 per year, the government is paying $900,000 per year to support the people who have inherited the blindness of that man.

_____ 2. Hereditary diseases are costly in terms of human feelings as well as in terms of dollars. We should avoid costly diseases if we can. We can avoid hereditary diseases by sterilization and selective breeding. We should, thus, begin programs of sterilization and selective breeding to curb hereditary diseases.

_____ 3. It is tragic to think that some people will not let themselves be put out, even a little, on behalf of another person.

_____ 4. A larger-than-average percentage of men in prison on death row have an extra Y chromosome. Thus having an extra Y chromosome should be grounds for acquittal. Its presence indicates a biological factor that makes criminal behavior unavoidable.

_____ 5. A larger-than-average percentage of men on death row have an extra Y chromosome. Since this is a biological factor which may contribute to criminal behavior, such people if found guilty of a crime should be given indefinite sentences, which, in fact, are life sentences.

_____ 6. Suppose that we abandon the project now. All our hard work will have been wasted—2 years down the drain for nothing. No, that's an unacceptable waste. We should not abandon the project.

_____ 7. Apply to one or both surfaces; join. If cement thickens, add a small portion of thinner and stir.

Ex. 2 The following exercises involve the direct proof strategy.

_____ 1. The conclusion 'china dishes are easy to clean' follows from which set of statements:

A. China dishes are easy to clean.
B. China is easy to clean.
C. Suppose china dishes were not easy to clean. Then they would be very unpopular. But they are far from unpopular.

_____ 2. The conclusion 'TV pictures are hard on your eyes' follows from which set of statements?

A. All TV pictures are hard on your eyes.
B. Looking at brightly lit surfaces is hard on your eyes. TV pictures are brightly lit surfaces.
C. Suppose TV pictures were not hard on your eyes. If they were not, then TV sets would not be so expensive. But they are terribly expensive.

_____ 3. The conclusion 'mobile homes are fire hazards' follows from which set of statements?

A. Brick homes are fire hazards.
B. Enclosed compartments with poor ventilation and few exits that are

constructed out of highly flammable materials are fire hazards. This describes mobile homes perfectly.

    C. Suppose mobile homes were not fire hazards. If this were so, then it would not be the case that a greater percentage of people die in mobile-home fires than in other type of home fires.

Ex. 3 Indicate whether each of the following is true or false.

_____ 1. The direct proof strategy is a procedure that tells how to do something.

_____ 2. Inductive arguments cannot be direct proofs.

_____ 3. Acceptable proofs built using the direct proof strategy can be trivially valid.

_____ 4. Proofs built using the direct proof strategy are nonarguments.

_____ 5. The direct proof strategy involves making an explicit assumption or supposition.

_____ 6. Every direct proof contains an explicit assumption.

_____ 7. The conclusion of a direct proof is necessarily a true statement.

_____ 8. There is only one generic strategy of proof.

SELECTED ANSWERS
TO EXERCISES FOR MODULE 39

Ex. 1

1. DPS   3. No; this is a nonargument.
5. DPS   6. No; this is an indirect proof (see Module 37).
7. No; this is a nonargument.

Ex. 2

1. B; (A) would make it trivially valid; this violates the strategy. (C) would be used if we were building indirect proofs (see Module 37).
2. B; neither (A) nor (C) for the same reasons as in item 1.
3. B; (A) is irrelevant; (C) would make an indirect proof.

Ex. 3

1. T
2. F; note 'strongly support' in D.
3. F; note 'nontrivially' in D.
4. F; all proofs are arguments by Def. 28.
5. F; indirect proofs do, however, involve making an explicit assumption or supposition (see Module 37).
6. F; notice that the strategy does not call for making an explicit assumption (other strategies like those covered in the next modules will).
7. F; a strategy holds the promise of success but it cannot guarantee it.
8. F; there are three generic strategies; direct proof strategy, indirect proof strategy, and conditional proof strategy.

MODULE 40

THE INDIRECT PROOF STRATEGY

The strategy of indirect proof involves making an assumption which one ultimately wishes to show to be false. The assumption made is the negation of what one desires to prove true. By showing that this assumption is false, one is showing that the negation of the assumption must consequently be true. In this module we will exhibit this basic proof of strategy in more detail.

● After reading Module 40 you should be able to:

1. Recognize and identify indirect proofs
2. Distinguish indirect proofs from direct proofs

40:1 Consider the following examples of indirect arguments, each of which was built using the general strategy of indirect proof. You will probably find some of these example arguments to be more logically cogent than the others; nevertheless, they are all indirect proofs of one species or another.

EG. 40.1 Suppose that statement A is true. We know that A implies B. We also know that B is false. But because A implies B, B must be true given our assumption. That makes B both true and false. But that is impossible. So our assumption must be wrongheaded; A cannot be true.

EG. 40.2 Suppose we were to switch to daylight saving time. If we do then we will have to milk the cows 1 hour before they are ready because we always milk them at 6:00 A.M. But it's ridiculous to milk cows before they're ready. So we should not switch to daylight time.

EG. 40.3 Suppose that Jesus was entirely God and not a man. If this were so, then certain events depicted in the New Testament would not make sense. How could God undergo temptation? What point is there in a God's being baptized in the Jordan River? Why should a God fear a human death as Jesus did his crucifixion? One possible answer to these and similar events is that Jesus was only playing at being human. But this explanation is both psychologically and theologically unacceptable for other reasons. Thus it seems probable that Jesus was not entirely God but was also a human.

EG. 40.4 Suppose that Jesus was entirely a human and not God. If this were so, then the event of his resurrection, as recorded in the New Testament, would be impossible. Thus Jesus was not entirely a human but must have been God also.

40:2 Indirect proof strategy defined The general strategy of indirect proof always involves assuming that the negation of the desired conclusion is true. This assumption, together with other premises, is then portrayed as leading to absurd, unacceptable consequences, the chief specimen of which is a manifest contradiction, as in Eg. 40.1. Once it is clear that the assumption together with the other premises leads to absurd results, the author then backs away from those absurd consequences by rejecting the assumption. To reject the assumption is to assert as the conclusion of the argument that the assumption (the negation of the desired conclusion) cannot be true. See if you can detect this pattern of inference in the four examples given in 40:1.

We can state the indirect proof strategy as follows:

(I) Indirect proof strategy:
   1. Assume explicitly that the desired conclusion is not true.
   2. Assemble other more or less obviously true premises such that these, together with the previous assumption, lead logically and nonfallaciously to some absurd consequence.
   3. Then, because of the inadmissability or unpalatability of the inferred absurdity, infer that the assumption made in step 1 is false, and so the conclusion cannot fail to be true.

40:3 All indirect proofs involve making an assumption more or less explicitly. Moreover, the assumption made is the negation of the eventual conclusion. These two facts make it possible to easily recognize indirect proofs and distinguish them from other proofs.

40:4 The inference process of the indirect proof strategy runs something like this:

1. I wish to prove that p.
2. I shall see what happens if I assume $(\sim p)$.
3. This assumption, together with other premises that I have more confidence are true, yields *absurd* consequences.
4. Because my assumption of $(\sim p)$ resulted in absurd consequences, [such as the manifest contradiction $(q \& (\sim q))$], and because I am more certain that the other premises are true than I am about my assumption that $(\sim p)$, I shall reject $(\sim p)$.
5. Having rejected $(\sim p)$ as yielding an absurdity, I infer that p is true.

You might ask: Why reject the assumption and not one of the other premises? Well, don't forget, this is a strategy or tactic that can be used to develop proofs. We are, logically speaking, free to reject either the explicit assumption or any of the other premises. But our goal of proving the desired conclusion true leads us to reject the assumption rather than any of the other premises. Further, we have selected statements as premises that are, at least to us, more or less obviously true. We would, then, not be inclined to reject one of them.

40:5 There is one class of indirect proofs in which the assumption of the negation of the desired conclusion is not so obvious. That case is the critique of somebody else's view. Here's an example.

EG. 40.5 Dr. Surefire says the University should teach classes around the clock. If those classes are held, few students will enroll. The professors will have to be paid and the University will wind up losing money. Surely there should be no 3:00 A.M. classes. So it is ridiculous and self-defeating to hold classes around the clock.

In this argument the consequences of Dr. Surefire's policy are drawn out and alleged to be absurd. The desired conclusion, that classes should not be held in late night hours, say between 11:00 P.M. and 7:00 A.M., is drawn in a literary way at the end of the passage. Dr. Surefire's idea is clearly contrary to the conclusion. In fact the argument assumes the negation of the conclusion when Dr. Surefire's suggestion is examined. But this example is typical of critique because it is not clear until the end of the argument that Dr. Surefire's suggestion is the negation of the conclusion.

40:6 The indirect proof strategy is often called the *reductio ad absurdum* strategy. An argument that employs it is called a *reductio* argument. *Reductio* is Latin for "reduction." Thus, as the name indicates, these arguments *reduce an assumption to absurdity* by pointing out its absurd consequences. We used reductio methods of reasoning several times in our examples; recall our discussion of the puzzles in Module 1. Also, there was the partial truth-table technique in Chapter 4. At that point we urged that you reason this way about certain invalid arguments:

EG. 40.6 Suppose that a given argument of propositional logic were valid. If it were its corresponding conditional would be T on every row of its truth-table. However, using a certain distribution of truth-values we can get an F on at least one row of its (partial) truth-table. It is contradictory to maintain that its table's final value column is all T's and that it contains at least one F. So the assumption must be wrong; the argument must be invalid.

EXERCISES FOR MODULE 40
THE INDIRECT PROOF STRATEGY

Ex. 1 Answer the following multiple-choice questions.

_____ 1. If 'the Governor is a wise and capable leader' is false, which of the following is true?

A. The Governor is neither wise nor capable.
B. The Governor is not a wise and capable leader.
C. The Governor is really not the governor.
D. The state legislature is more powerful than the Governor.

_____ 2. The indirect proof strategy always involves:

A. Gathering data
B. Developing an ordering of objects in a class
C. Searching for relevant theories
D. Assuming the opposite of what one wishes to prove
E. Framing an hypothesis which one wishes to confirm

_____ 3. If we prove that $(\sim p)$ is false, which of the following have we shown to be true?

A. $(\sim(\sim p))$
B. $(\sim p)$
C. p
D. q
E. $(\sim q)$

_____ 4. The inference pattern of double negation allows that $(\sim(\sim A))$ is logically equivalent to A. [Or, from $(\sim(\sim A))$ one can infer A, and from A one can infer $(\sim(\sim A))$.] The truth-table for this equivalence is:

A.

A	$(A \equiv A$
T	T T T̸
F	F̸ T F̸

B.

A	$((\sim A) \equiv (\sim A))$
T	F̸ T̸ T F̸ T̸
F	T̸ F̸ T T̸ F̸

C.

A	$((\sim(\sim A)) \equiv (\sim A))$		
T	T FT	F	FT
F	F TF	F	TF

D.

A	$(A \equiv (\sim A))$
T	T F FT
F	F F TF

E.

A	$[A \equiv (\sim(\sim A))]$
T	T T T FT
F	F T F TF

Ex. 2 Distinguish the indirect proofs from the direct proofs in the following. Use 'IP' and 'DP' as your answers.

_____ 1. Professor Black is an outstanding teacher. We have a great deal of evidence to support this conclusion. He is well liked by his students, both undergraduate and graduate. He receives high scores on student course evaluations. His classes are always full. His students do very well when compared to other students who have studied the same subject with other professors.

_____ 2. Euthanasia is not a legal means to take care of the problems of overpopulation. This is so because the president of the AMA has said so.

_____ 3. Suppose that we did build a dam across the Detroit River. This would help us with our problem of the falling water levels of the Great Lakes. But this would also cause flooding in the Detroit metropolitan area. The results of this would be humanly and financially disastrous. This means that we should not build such a dam.

_____ 4. The average professor in an Ohio college or university teaches about sixty junior-level students per term if assigned to teach only junior-level courses. If all these students are taking a four-credit course, then his or her courses are generating about 240 student credit hours. Let us say that 240 student credit hours is about one person's work load for a given term. Thus if this is a person's work load, then any faculty member who is producing more than 240 student credit hours in junior-level courses is overworked.

_____ 5. Contemporary philosophy is making great strides in the realm of symbolic logic. We are now able to work with systems of symbolic logic which go far beyond the elementary syllogistic methods of Aristotle, which managed to remain as the only symbolic techniques of moment until the late nineteenth century. The impact of the advances in symbolic logic are now being felt in all other scientific and precise disciplines. Thus symbolic logic has moved into a significantly more important place among the methodological tools of human beings as we pursue knowledge.

_____ 6. Surely there is no Paynesville barber who both is a male citizen of Paynesville with a growing beard and shaves all and only those men who do not shave themselves. For suppose there is such a barber. Then if he shaved himself, he would not shave himself; and if he did not shave himself, then he would shave himself. In other words, he would shave himself if, and only if, he did not shave himself. But this is contradictory. Thus there must be no such barber.

Ex. 3 Indicate whether each of the following is true or false.

_____ 1. Indirect proofs are not arguments.

_____ 2. The indirect proof strategy involves making an assumption.

_____ 3. Assumptions, premises, and conclusions in actual passages can be written down in almost any order depending on the literary style of the argument's author.

_____ 4. In an indirect proof one tries to show that an assumption is absurd.

_____ 5. In an indirect proof one tries to show that a particular statement cannot fail to be, or cannot avoid being, true.

SELECTED ANSWERS
TO EXERCISES FOR MODULE 40

Ex. 1

1. B; not A because $(\sim(p \& q))$ is not logically equivalent to $((\sim p) \& (\sim q))$.
2. D
3. A and C, which are logically equivalent
4. E

Ex. 2

1. DP   3. IP   5. DP

If you missed any of these review this module.

Ex. 3

1. F   2. T   3. T   4. T   5. T

If you missed any of these review the basic definition of proof in Module 38 and also review the indirect proof strategy discussed in this module.

MODULE 41

PROOFS BY REDUCTION TO CONTRADICTIONS, VICIOUS REGRESSION, AND INTUITIVE ABSURDITIES

There are three species of the indirect proof strategy. They all reduce the undesirable assumption to one or another kind of absurdity—either a logical absurdity, like a manifest contradiction, a quasi-logical absurdity, or an intuitive personal kind of subjective absurdity. In Module 41 we will look at each of these three substrategies of indirect proof.

● After reading Module 41 you should be able to:

1. Identify examples of each of these three indirect proof substrategies
2. Distinguish between examples of direct proofs and each species of indirect proof

41:1 The three species of reductio arguments There are three species of the indirect proof strategy; they can be distinguished by the differences in the kind of absurdity that they appeal to as grounds for the rejection of the assumption. The chief, indeed paradigmatic, type of indirect proof is *reduction to contradiction*. An example is:

EG. 41.1 Suppose that I did buy stock in Trippoka, Inc. All the Trippoka stock-holders are corporate officers. This makes me a corporate officer. But I am not a corporate officer. So it cannot be the case that I bought stock in Trippoka Inc.

The strategy of reduction to contradiction endeavors to show that the assumption in conjunction with the other premises logically implies an explicit contradiction. In Eg. 41.1 the contradiction was that the author both was and was not a corporate officer. Since a contradiction is never true, and thus totally inadmissible, the strategy calls for the rejection of the assumption. We will discuss this species in 41:2.1.

The second species is *reduction to vicious regression*. In this strategy the author endeavors to show that the assumption together with the other premises leads to a regression that is in some way vicious. Here is an example.

EG. 41.2 Suppose we were to insist that in a conceptual system all terms must be defined and that each term must be defined solely by appeal to the meanings of previously defined terms. If we did this we would be able to define term 10 only by appeal to some earlier defined terms, say 9 and 8. These two terms must be defined, too. They, according to our assumption, must be defined by appeal to previously defined terms 7, 6, 5, and 4. We cannot stop the process because all terms must be defined. So we would have had to create definitions for terms 7, 6, 5, and 4 using the definitions of previously defined terms 3, 2, 1, and 0. But these too must be defined using previously defined terms. Either we will have to violate our assumed restrictions or we will be committed to trying to create conceptual systems that have no circularity and no appeal to primitive terms in their definitions. This latter task is, as indicated above, infinite in scope. So the principle we originally assumed, that all terms in a conceptual system should be defined and each should be defined by appeal to the meanings of previously defined terms, must be rejected as unfeasible.

In 41:3.1 we will discuss the strategy of reduction to vicious regression by explaining what a regression is and why some regressions are vicious. Vicious regressions, as we shall see in a moment, are not always associated with contradictions, yet they do form at least a quasi-logical barrier making it seem absurd to continue further with an assumption.

The third variety of indirect proof is the *reduction to intuitive absurdity* strategy. An author using this strategy tries to show that a particular assumption must be rejected because it is in irreconcilable conflict with his or her set of fundamental beliefs, attitudes, and values. That is, given that the author will not (or psychologically cannot) make an adjustment in his or her fundamental mind-set, the assumption which conflicts with that mind-set is viewed, from that perspective, as absurd and worthy of rejection.[2] This can occur even though the conflict is not a contradiction.

EG. 41.3 We are starving to death and our income can only support four people. But there are seven of us. Now suppose that we were to select three of us to kill. If we killed three then the other four could live. But no, killing

---

[2] Some philosophers maintain that there are only two species of indirect proof, namely, reduction to contradiction and reduction to vicious regression. They argue that a fuller exposition of the author's mind-set in terms of the values, principles, beliefs and attitudes it contains would show any reduction to intuitive absurdity proof to be really an underdeveloped reduction to contradiction.

people is immoral and completely out of the question. We cannot solve our problem that way!

This example, which clearly follows the general indirect proof strategy, reduces its assumption to an irreconcilable conflict with a chief principle in the author's value system. It would not be illogical to solve the author's problem by killing, but, as indicated in the example, it would be absurdly immoral. In this case that fact alone is enough grounds for the author to reject the proposed solution to the problem as unthinkable. We will give more examples in 41:4.1. Now you may, if you wish, check your ability to recognize reductio arguments by doing Ex. 1.

41:2.1 Reduction to contradiction This is the prime species of the indirect proof strategy. The absurdity derived has the most force in unseating the undesirable assumption because one is faced with a dilemma of either admitting the contradiction or retracting the assumption. Of course, the dilemma is only momentary at best, in that the assumption was undesirable in the first place. Yet it is clearly a matter of *strategy* that one chooses to reject the assumption that the desired conclusion is false rather than, say, one of the other premises of the proof, although these are placed in equal logical jeopardy by the resulting contradiction, as was the assumption which is thought to have generated it. From a strictly logical point of view (discounting strategy), unless the assumption was inconsistent in the first place, it could not have generated the contradiction alone and, so, is no more fit a candidate for rejection than would be its fellow premises.

41:2.2 The logical structure behind the reduction to contradiction strategy of proof can be mapped out in two ways.

1. The contradiction can be a direct contradiction of the undesirable assumption.
   Desired conclusion $= C$

   1. $(\sim C)$ (assumption)
   2.   Premise$_2$
   3.   Premise$_3$
   .
   .
   .

   n.   Inference of C (from lines 1, 2, and 3 as premises)
   $n + 1$. C and $(\sim C)$ (from the facts in lines 1 and n)
   $n + 2$. $(\sim(\sim C))$ (rejection of the assumption in line 1 because of the contradiction that resulted in line $n + 1$)
   $n + 3$. C (by double negation; see Ex. 1, item 4, Module 40)

2. The contradiction can occur between various consequences of the assumption and the other premises.
   Desired conclusion $= C$

   1. $(\sim C)$ (assumption)
   2.   Premise$_2$
   3.   Premise$_3$
   .
   .
   .

   k.   Inference to q (from premises and/or assumption)
   .
   .
   .

n.   Inference to (~q) (from premises and/or assumption)

n + 1. (q & (~q)) (manifest contradiction from lines k and n)

n + 2. (~(~C) (rejection of assumption because it led to the contradiction on line n + 1)

n + 3. C (by double negation from line n + 2)

41:2.3 Here are more examples of proofs that use the reduction to contradiction strategy.

EG. 41.4   Suppose that Plato is not a free agent. If Plato is not a free agent he is under contract. If he is under contract he is a professional football player. But Plato is not a professional football player. So it must not be the case that Plato is not a free agent.

EG. 41.5   The usual way of treating necessary and sufficient conditions in symbolic logic is by regarding them as simple truth-functional relationships. But, as such, they lead to paradox. It turns out that every event is either a necessary or a sufficient condition for every other event. In most theories of the world this is not true. Thus the usual way of treating necessary and sufficient conditions in symbolic logic is absurd and mistaken for it contradicts most theories of the world.

41:2.4 The practice of describing counterexamples in order to *disconfirm* theories is another instance of reduction to contradiction. Suppose, for example, that someone proposes for consideration the hypothesis that shadows have weight. To confirm this he or she develops an argument based on the observable facts that water evaporates slower when it is in a shadow than when it is in direct sunlight. This, the person contends, is due to the weight of the shadow holding down the molecules of water. We might begin to attack this hypothesis by the following counterargument.

EG. 41.6   1. Suppose that shadows have weight.
2. Then the weight of the shadow must be measurable.
3. When we place a balancing scale on the ground so that half is in the sunlight and half is in a shadow, the scale does not tip toward the shadow.
4. Thus the weight of the shadow is not measurable.
5. Item 2 contradicts item 4.
6. Thus the hypothesis assumed in item 1 must not be true.

There is much more that could be said about the procedure of giving counterexamples. As a preliminary we must understand that alleged counterexamples, and purported disconfirmations in general, are sometimes inconclusive. This is so because of several factors. At the lowest level we have factors of a very straightforward kind; for example, the counterarguments attempting to show that an hypothesis is not true may be problematic because the alleged counterexample it is based on misses the point, or the description of it is not factually possible, or the argument itself contains a false assumption. The latter might be a problem with Eg. 41.6. The shadow weight may be measurable, but not on an instrument like the one used in step 3. A second level of debate is reached when the author of the original hypothesis seeing the counterevidence quickly revises the hypothesis by the addition of ad hoc restrictions. A third level of debate comes when the purported counterexamples themselves become the objects of dispute, when whether or not they are genuine is debated. This level frequently revolves around terminological disputes, i.e., disputes over definitions and intuitions. Here simply describing a counterexample fails to persuade because, apart from more theoretical considerations, all attempts to state counterexamples at this stage are challenged. Fortunately, most disputes do not get beyond the first or second level. Thus, the procedure of refutation by appeal to counterexamples is basically a useful and reliable method of disconfirmation.[3]

41:3.1 Reduction to vicious regression The second kind of absurdity is that which occurs when an explanation or a theory results in a *regression*. A regression is simply a long series of similar events, or a long series of similar steps in a process, or similar items in a sequence. The regression may be infinite or indefinite; it may be vicious or not vicious. Here are two examples of arguments using the strategy of reduction to vicious regression:

EG. 41.7
1. Let us assume Plato's theory that something is a man only because it participates in the form *manness*. Plato's theory also says that all forms of *manness* are men.
2. If the theory is true, then *manness* can be a man only because *manness* participates in something, call it *manness₂*, which is also a man.
3. Nothing can participate in itself or in any earlier form, so *manness* is not the same as $manness_2$.
4. But how is $manness_2$ a man except that it participates in $manness_3$?
5. Clearly, the same can be said of $manness_3$, generating a need for $manness_4$.
6. This process can go on without stop, generating an indefinite number of forms of *manness*.
7. Plato's theory was supposed to explain how it was that something became and is probably called "a man."
8. Because of the regression discovered in (6), his theory does not explain anything; it only puts off the question.
9. Thus we must reject Plato's theory.

EG. 41.8 An ornithologist explained to her younger colleague, "This thing is called a bird because it looks like a bird." The younger friend asked, "Well, I don't mean to be difficult, but how do you know if something looks like a bird?" "Well, you simply compare it to another bird," was the ornithologist's reply. "But how can we be sure that the other thing is a bird?" asked the young one. "By comparing it to still another bird," came the confident reply. "Ah, now I see, you really don't know, do you! Or, at least, if you know, you are not willing to give me a good explanation," responded the younger person.

41:3.2 Some regressions are not vicious. For example, moving from the assertion of p to 'it is true that p' to 'it is true that it is true that p' and so on is harmless because each statement, albeit different from the others, is logically equivalent to each of the others. Thus all are true or all are false together. Other regressions manifest distinctions in their first stages but in subsequent stages seem to be little more than grammatical manipulations. Such is the case with the difference between $(\sim p)$ and

---

[3] We used the method as early as Module 1 because of its commonly accepted logical and persuasive force. If you wish to examine the use of counterexample in more detail see Facione, "Counterexamples and Where They Lead," *Philosophy and Phenomenological Review*, vol. 36, no. 4, June 1976, pp. 523–530.

$(\sim(\sim p))$. The logical difference between these first two cases apparently loses importance as one moves to $[\sim(\sim(\sim p))]$ and $[\sim[\sim(\sim(\sim p))]]$ and so on. Each beyond the first two is simply equivalent to one of the first two. Similarly, there seems to be a difference between 'A knows that p' and 'A knows that he knows that p' which seems not to be operable as one moves to 'A knows that he knows that he knows that p', and so on.

41:3.3 Some regressions are vicious. While we look at some examples here, you should notice the different reasons why different regressions are vicious.

First Regressions may overcomplicate matters. Suppose, for example, that we had a theory we wished to defend. Suppose too that each time we defend it our adversary points out a counterexample. In response we make an amendment to our theory. But in response the adversary offers still another counterexample. We amend, she objects, and so it goes. So long as we can amend, we have successfully defended our theory, but we have made it so complicated that it might now have to be rejected as being too complicated to be practical or too complicated to be put into use.

Second On the other hand, a regression that makes something incompletable is also vicious. If, for example, each amendment of our theory carried with it the seeds of another counterexample, we could never completely articulate our theory. Each amendment would lead to a further objection no matter how many amendments we make.

Third A third way that a regression can be vicious is if its presence robs the theory of explanatory force. In Egs. 41.7 and 41.8 theories are rejected for just this reason. The regressions there discovered show that the proffered explanations do not really clarify or explain anything; rather, they just put off the issue.

Because the reasons why regressions can be vicious are varied and because not all regressions are vicious it seems wise to regard that absurdity as distinct from the blatant logical absurdity of manifest contradiction and yet as more forceful that the nonlogical absurdity appealed to in the third species of indirect proof.

When trying to distinguish between reduction to contradiction and reduction to vicious regression you should first ask yourself if any explicit contradiction is derived. If so, then the strategy employed is best classified as reduction to contradiction even if it is a vicious regression that leads the author to that contradiction. Consider this example.

EG. 41.9
1. Suppose we accept the theory that all reality is generated out of a previously existing reality of matter and energy.
2. If this is true, then whatever now exists must have come from what existed at some earlier time t.
3. What existed at t must have come from what existed at an earlier time t'.
4. This movement backward in time is infinite. Whatever exists at a given time must have been generated out of what existed previously.
5. But, then, nothing would now exist for there would be no beginning to the sequence.
6. We would have to say of any potential first reality that it could not exist unless the general principle accepted in (1) were false.
7. But something does exist now. So what could not exist must have existed, and this is a contradiction.
8. So we must reject the theory given in (1) as false and say that there

must have been a first reality which was not generated out of a previously existing reality of matter and energy.

In Eg. 41.9 the regression is vicious just because it does lead to a contradiction. This represents a fourth way that regression can be vicious. But the reason for classifying Eg. 41.9 as a reduction to contradiction rather than a reduction to vicious regression is that in making our classification we are trying to determine the specific strategy the argument, as presented to us, is most explicitly following. If an author rejects an assumption because it leads to a contradiction, then the *overall strategy* is reduction to contradiction no matter what internal substrategies the author may have relied on in order to make that contradiction clear. If you wish, you may check your ability to recognize reduction to vicious regression by doing Ex. 2 now.

41:4.1 Reduction to intuitive absurdity People often use the indirect proof strategy with more concern for their overall goal of persuasion than concern for the requirements of logic. Thus, they may not attempt to reduce the undesired assumption to one of the logical or quasi-logical absurdities, contradiction, or vicious regression. More often they will try to reduce things to an intuitive absurdity.[4] People do this by arguing that a given assumption is in conflict with common and important beliefs or values, leads to impractical results, or seems unreasonable or "unrealistic" to them in some way or other. Many times such arguments turn out to be informally fallacious, but at times they are fine tools for showing where wisdom lies. Here are some examples of arguments that use the strategy of reduction to intuitive absurdity.

EG. 41.10 Suppose we give in to the terrorists now. If we do this time, then we will encourage terrorism and establish undesirable precedents of surrender. It is absurd and undesirable for us to do these things. So we should not give in.

EG. 41.10 Karen, I can't give Snoopy another kiss now. I have kissed all your animals goodnight, and you too. You agree that everyone has been kissed since Snoopy. But if I kiss Snoopy again then everyone will have to be kissed once again. (Karen laughs.) So if I do all that kissing, I'll be here for another hour! So I should not kiss Snoopy again.

EG. 41.12 Suppose we all accepted pacifism. We would not be allowed to defend ourselves even if we were being directly attacked and our lives were in danger. But it is absurdly unreasonable to forfeit your right to self-defense in a world as vicious as ours. So we cannot accept pacifism.

41:4.2 The basic strategy evident in these examples is clearly the indirect proof strategy; but obviously these arguments lack the logical force of the earlier two kinds of reductio arguments. The authors of the arguments do not present the absurdity they see as either an explicit contradiction or a vicious regression. Yet it is clear that they make an attempt at appealing to some kind of absurdity in order to discredit the assumption, even though the absurdity is more subjective than logical. It is dislike of a dangerous precedent in Eg. 41.10 that causes the author to say it is absurd to give in to the terrorists, and it is the undesirability of overly long bedtime routines

---

[4] Because the statement the argument's author finds to be intuitively absurd may, in reality, be neither false nor contradictory, this form of the indirect proof strategy can *not* be reduced to either reduction to contradiction nor to modus tollens.

in Eg. 41.11 and a concern over self-preservation in Eg. 41.12 that prompts the author there to view surrender of the right of self-defense absurd.

41:4.3 To understand and appraise reductions to intuitive absurdities, you will want to focus on the kind of absurdity involved. Many parents would find any practice which made saying goodnight overly long a most undesirable practice. Some children would not. Many people would find giving up the right to self-defense a ridiculous idea; most pacifists would not. If people set out to offer you a reduction to intuitive absurdity proof, they will probably suggest that a certain position leads to consequences they regard as absurd. (If they accept their own argument, that is exactly what they will do.) Your mind-set or intuitions may be quite different however. Their alleged intuitive absurdity may seem to you to be an acceptable consequence of the original position. "Of course," the pacifist might say, "I give up my right to self-defense. True peace can only exist in a society where all persons give up both practices of aggression and the right to self-defense. When I give up my right, I simply take a small step in a wonderful direction." No matter whether we agree with the pacifist, the alleged absurdity adduced in the argument is not a logical absurdity. It has simply been shown that pacifism involves something that is, for unspecified reasons, unacceptable to the argument's author but acceptable to the pacifist.

What this means is that reductions to intuitive absurdity are effective tools of persuasion only among people who share a given set of fundamental beliefs, values, principles, and attitudes. They will thus see the consequence inferred from the original assumption as indeed absurd. People who do not share their perspectives or world views may accept the logical correctness of the argument, if it is correct, but they will disagree with the truth of the premise which alleges the absurdity of the inferred consequence. And, so, reject the argument as unsound.

41:5 Distinguishing species of indirect proofs We have examined the three species of indirect proofs. To tell one from the other one should ask: What kind of absurdity is being appealed to? If it is a manifest contradiction, then the strategy is reduction to contradiction. If it is a subjective incompatibility resulting from conflicts with one's fundamental beliefs and values which allegedly make a given statement unacceptable, then the strategy is reduction to intuitive absurdity. If it is a vicious regression (except one that leads to a manifest contradiction), then it is the strategy of reduction to vicious regression.

EXERCISES FOR MODULE 41
PROOFS BY REDUCTIONS TO CONTRADICTION, TO VICIOUS REGRESSION, AND TO INTUITIVE ABSURDITIES

Ex. 1 Identify the reduction to contradiction arguments among the following. Use 'RC' or 'no' for your answers.

_____ 1. I love Bethany and Carol. I love Christopher and Jerome. These are my only children. So I love all my children.

_____ 2. Suppose the earth were flat. If it were flat then it would be impossible for any person to circumnavigate the earth. But several sea captains have done it. So it cannot be true that the earth is flat.

_____ 3. The president decided to decree that there should be a committee which would be charged with the task of reviewing the work of all and only those committees that do not review their own work. But there could not be such a committee! For suppose there were. Then either it should review its own work or it should not. But if it does not, then it should. Yet if it does, then it should not. So it should review its own work if, and only if, it should not review its own work. And this is clearly contradictory.

_____ 4. Suppose we define a set as an individual which is the collection of individuals. If we so this, then sets can have other sets as their members.

Ex. 2 Identify the reductions to vicious regression among the following passages. Use 'VR' and 'no' for your answers.

_____ 1. The Greek sophist Zeno once argued that an arrow shot at a target would never reach its mark. He reasoned that before it could reach the target it would have to travel half way to its target. This would take some time. But once at that point it would have to travel half way from where it was to the target. Again more time would be needed. But the process of transversing these distances would involve the arrow in an infinite number of moves from wherever it was to half way from its target. Thus an infinite number of moments of time would be needed for the arrow to reach the target. Because an infinite number of moments of time could never be passed, the arrow would never reach the target.

_____ 2. The teacher says, "There will be an exam this week. It will be a surprise in the sense that you will not know on the morning of the exam that the exam will be that day." A student says, "But then there can be no exam as you describe it. It cannot be on Friday since we would know Friday morning that it had not been on any earlier day. Thus Friday is ruled out. But then it cannot be on Thursday since we would know it had not occurred on Monday, Tuesday, or Wednesday and could not be on Friday. Similarly we can rule out Wednesday, Tuesday, and Monday."

_____ 3. The exam was held on Tuesday. So there must have been something wrong with the student's argument since the exam was a surprise in the requisite sense.

_____ 4. Each day that I work I earn $5. Thus if I work for a week I will earn $35. If I work for a month I'll earn $150. If I work every day in a year I'll earn 365 times $5 or $1,825. I also conclude that if I worked every day of a leap year I would earn $1,830. Well, these inferences can go on and on.

Ex. 3 Identify the reduction to intuitive absurdity arguments from among the following. Use 'RIA' and 'no' as your answers.

_____ 1. Suppose we changed the tax law regarding capital gains and abolished the 50 percent exclusion on earnings on property held for more than 6 months. If we did this there might be an immediate stock market crash because investors would face paying tax on twice as much money as they now would pay taxes on. This new tax burden would cause them to sell out and sell out low. Thus prices would dive. It would be ridiculous to bring down the stock market, especially when we are trying to improve the economy. So we should not change this aspect of the tax law.

_____ 2. If Brenda loved John, she would buy him a new car today. But she will not buy him a new car today. So she does not love him.

_____ 3. Suppose we tried to curb inflation by restricting spending and curbing government work projects. This would cause soaring unemployment. But that would force us into a severe economic depression. The depression would be worse for us than the inflation is. So we should not try to curb inflation by restricting spending and curbing government work projects.

_____ 4. Sure, we can let an eight-year-old babysit for a six-year-old. But if we did that then they would probably wreck the house and they might even get into some very dangerous situations. It's just silly to risk that. We shouldn't let the eight-year-old sit for our six-year-old.

Ex. 4 Review the answers to each of the first three exercises. Be sure you understand those answers. Then distinguish the three types of reductio arguments in the list of arguments below. Use 'RC,' 'VR,' and 'RIA' for your answers.

_____ 1. The cruel judge passed sentence, saying, "You will be executed before the end of the month, but the execution will be a surprise to you in that you shall not be informed of the exact day of the execution." The guilty criminal said, "Well it cannot be the last day of the month because if it hasn't been till then, I would certainly not be surprised by its occurrence. But if the last day is ruled out, the execution cannot be on the second to last day. For if it had not occurred till then, and it could not be on the last day, then it would not be a surprise coming on the second to last day. Similarly I could not be executed on the third to last day. But I can eliminate each day in turn. So there will be no surprise execution!"

_____ 2. The angry fan wrote a letter to the president of the league complaining that her favorite team, which finished the season with five wins, five losses, and no ties, should be ranked ahead of another team which had finished the season with no wins, no losses, and ten ties. The president responded, "Suppose the two teams had the records that you claim they have. Our league has eleven teams in it. Each team plays each other once during the season. So it would be logically impossible for one team to finish with no ties and another to finish having tied every other team. Thus the teams do not have the season records you attribute to them."

_____ 3. Suppose people were truly free. If they were truly free, then they would find fulfillment in their labor activity. People today find their labor activity boring and dehumanizing. They find no fulfillment in it. Thus people today are not truly free. So we cannot assume that they are.

_____ 4. Let us assume that men sometimes knowingly and willingly choose to perform an evil action. Everyone knows that any evil action will ultimately bring misery upon its agent. This means that people sometimes knowingly and willingly choose to bring misery upon themselves. This is absurd—everyone tries to avoid misery. We must conclude, therefore, that men do not knowingly and willingly choose to perform evil actions.

_____ 5. Things cannot go on this way. If they did we would soon be broke. We have to make a change right now.

_____ 6. Suppose we adopted a policy of reverse discrimination as a means to achieve social justice. Since any person is a member of some minority group or other, reverse discrimination would go on and on. Once one minority was on top some other one would be on the bottom. Since the process would never stop, social justice would never be achieved. So we should not adopt a policy of reverse discrimination as a means to achieve social justice.

_____ 7. Let us assume that, as you claim, Ms. Woodhead did not mean it when she said that her lover should be pushed over a cliff. But if she did not mean it, she would not have pushed him over the cliff. However, she did push him over the cliff. So contrary to what you claim, she did mean what she said.

_____ 8. Suppose God exists. If a God as we think of Him exists, then there should be no such thing as evil in the world. God is defined as that Being which is all-good and all-powerful. If God allows or created evil, then He is not all-good. If He neither allows it nor created it, then He is not all-powerful. Thus the existence of evil shows that no God as we think of Him exists.

_____ 9. Suppose we give in to the kids now. If we do so, then we will be encouraging bad character and disrespect. But it is absurd and undesirable for us to do these things. Thus we should not give in.

_____ 10. You Italians say that no man can be wiser than his father. But that is ridiculous. If a man cannot be wiser than his father, then how wise could his father be? You would have to answer, "No wiser than the first man's grandfather." And he could not be wiser than his father, and so on and so forth. Well, this means that no man could be wiser than the first man was. But he, having no father, could know nothing for he had nobody to learn from. So all men know as much as he does, namely, nothing. But you claim to know that you are right, so you cannot be right for you would then know something which is more than nothing.

SELECTED ANSWERS
TO EXERCISES FOR MODULE 41

Ex. 1

1. No   2. RC   3. RC   4. No

If you missed any of these review 41:2.1 to 41:2.4.

Ex. 2

1. VR   2. VR   3. No   4. No

If you missed any of these review 41:3.1 to 41:3.3.

Ex. 3

1. RIA
2. No; this is a modus tollens argument (see 25:1.3)—it is a direct proof.
3. RIA
4. RIA

If you missed any, review 41:4.1 to 41:4.3.

Ex. 4

2. RC
5. The enthymematic premise is: It is ridiculous to go broke willingly.
6. VR
7. RC
9. RIA
10. RC; "You know something and you know nothing."

If you missed more than two, review 41:5 and the sections of this module that deal with each item for which you did not supply the correct answer: Reduction to Contradiction, 41:2.1 to 41:2.4; reduction to vicious regressions, 41:3.1 to 41:3.3; reduction to intuitive absurdity, 41:4.1 to 41:4.3.

MODULE 42

THE CONDITIONAL PROOF STRATEGY

At times proofs aimed at establishing the truth of a particular conclusion must be supplemented by proofs that the premises of the original proof are also true. In this way the original proof can be shown to be sound as well as logically correct. At other times, questions about premises can be handled by developing a new argument using the conditional proof strategy.

● After reading Module 42 you should be able to:

1. Identify arguments employing the conditional proof strategy
2. Pick out the characteristics and chief uses of the conditional proof strategy

42:1.1 The *chief use* of the conditional proof strategy is to establish the truth of conditional statements. If we wished to prove that a conditional $(A \supset B)$ were true we could use direct proof or indirect proof, but both these strategies could be facilitated by explicitly assuming as an additional premise that A is true. Since we ultimately want to establish 'if A then B,' we might as well assume that A is true and then work to prove B. With the assumption of A we can procede to use direct proof to try to derive B:

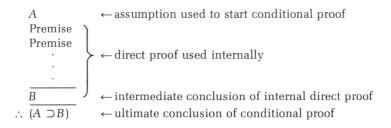

$$A \qquad \leftarrow \text{assumption used to start conditional proof}$$

Premise ⎫
Premise ⎬ ← direct proof used internally
   · ⎭

$$\underline{\quad B \quad} \qquad \leftarrow \text{intermediate conclusion of internal direct proof}$$
$$\therefore (A \supset B) \qquad \leftarrow \text{ultimate conclusion of conditional proof}$$

Or we could try to establish that on the assumption that A is true B could not fail to be true by using an internal indirect proof:

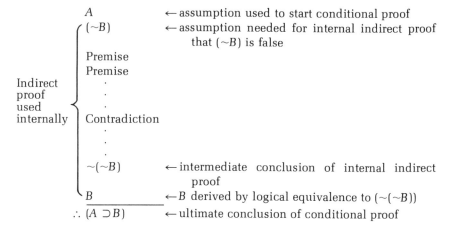

Although the logical structure of the conditional proof strategy looks more complicated when it is fully written out, in actual practice it is easier to demonstrate B from more premises and assumptions (the original premise plus A), than from fewer (just the original premises).[5]

42:1.2 The strategy of *conditional proof* is to:

1. Begin by assuming explicitly the truth of the antecedent of the desired conditional conclusion.
2. Work to develop an internal proof of the consequent of the originally desired conclusion.
3. When the consequent has been proved (using any proof strategy), then infer that this results from the assumption that the antecedent was true. The inference is made explicit by stating the desired conditional statement as the argument's conclusion.

Here are two examples of the conditional proof strategy. Each proves the same conditional conclusion: If a person does not enjoy life at all, he or she cannot appreciate sex. The first uses an internal direct proof; the second does it using an internal indirect proof.

EG. 42.1 Suppose someone does not enjoy life at all. If that person does not enjoy life at all, then he cannot appreciate the things that affirm life and human existence. Sex is one of the main things that affirms life and human ex-

---

[5] In Chapter 4 we tested propositional logic arguments for validity by seeing if their corresponding conditionals were tautologies. There is a corresponding conditional for every argument, not just for propositional logic arguments. That corresponding conditional is $((P_1 \& P_2 \& \ldots \& P_n) \supset C)$, where $(P_1 \& P_2 \& \ldots \& P_n)$ is the conjunction of the argument's premises and C is its conclusion. If $C = (A \supset B)$, then the corresponding conditional for an argument with two premises P_1 and P_2 would be $((P_1 \& P_2) \supset (A \supset B))$, which is logically equivalent to $((P_1 \& P_2 \& A) \supset B)$. So if we establish that the latter is logically correct, we will have established that the original argument is logically correct.

istence. Therefore if someone does not enjoy life at all, then he cannot appreciate sex.

EG. 42.2 Suppose that someone does not enjoy life at all. Now suppose further that such a person does appreciate sex. If she does appreciate sex, then she appreciates something which affirms life and human existence because that is what sex does. Yet if the person appreciates something that affirms life and human existence, then she must enjoy life, at least to some extent. But it is contradictory to hold that someone can both enjoy life to some extent and also not enjoy it at all. So if someone does not enjoy life at all, then she cannot appreciate sex.

42:1.3 Distinguishing proof strategies We can use the following decision procedure to determine in particular cases which proof strategy is being used. Ask: Does the proof make a more or less explicit assumption A such that its conclusion is either 'A cannot be true' or 'if A is true then B is true'? If not, then the proof is a direct proof. If so, then it is an indirect proof in the first case or a conditional proof in the second case. To tell what kind of indirect proof one is dealing with, use the procedure in 41:5.

42:2 Questionable premises When we were describing proofs in general (in Chapter 11), we said that the premises of a proof were presented as if they were more or less obvious (at least to the author of the proof). If the author wanted to indicate that a given premise was, in his or her opinion, less than obvious, then he or she was to do so by calling it an *assumption* or *supposition*. We, however, are not obligated to grant that the premises of a proof are true just because the author of the proof acts as if they are. We have to evaluate them and decide for ourselves if they are true. When we do this evaluation, we will probably not have much to go on besides our background knowledge. Our evaluation of a given premise as true or false is an important part of our total evaluation of the proof. If a given premise is obviously true, then we should admit that it is and move on. But if we cannot determine whether a given premise is true, then we must say that it is *questionable*. And there are several reasons why a given premise may be questionable to a given person. It simply might concern a field that the person knows little or nothing about. Or the person may question the honesty or sincerity of the author of the proof on whose authority he or she is being expected to accept the premise. A person can find a premise questionable if it contains unfamiliar or ill-defined terms, or if the person who is supposed to accept the premise simply does not understand the terms it uses.

42:3.1 Dealing with questionable premises We said that the chief use of the conditional proof strategy is to establish the truth of conditional statements. One important case when this comes in handy is in dealing with proofs that have questionable premises. If one or more of the premises of a proof were questionable or debatable, you might wish to accept the proof *provisionally*. The condition under which the conclusion is accepted as true is that the questionable premise is true. *If* it is true, the conclusion is true. Should it turn out to be false, then the conclusion could be rejected. Suppose, for example, we find someone arguing:

EG. 42.3 God loves all men. John is a man. So God loves John.

Here the second premise is more or less obviously true given that we know who John is. But the first premise is not obvious. It is a matter of some theological debate and speculation. Thus if we accept the conclusion of this proof as true it can only be on the provision that we are also willing to take the first premise as true as well. Since the burden of proof is on the author of the proof to show, if challenged, that the premises are true, let us examine the two ways that the author might reasonably try to meet the challenge.

First the author might try to remove the questionable or debatable aspects of the less than obvious premise by offering independent proof to establish it, perhaps by using an argument like this:

EG. 42.4 God loves whatever is finite. God loves whatever he created. Whatever God created is finite. God created men. So all men are finite and God loves them all.

Now if we accept the proof expressed in Eg. 42.4, then we have to accept the conclusion of the earlier proof, Eg. 42.3, as true without provisions. This is so because accepting Eg. 42.2 involves agreeing that it is true that God loves all men. On the other hand, we might reasonably reject the proof expressed in this example because it contains premises we find questionable. The more questionable premises a proof contains, the more difficult it is to accept it, even provisionally. You should remember, though, that it is sometimes possible to resolve doubts about a suspicious premise *by providing an independent proof for the truth of the questionable premises.* Sometimes this works, especially when all that one has to do is to make a few points clearer. Sometimes this fails, especially when in trying to prove that a given premise is true one uncovers deeper, more questionable, and more difficult issues.

If the author of Eg. 42.3 fails in the first reasonable way of responding to our challenge, he or she can try the second way. The author could weaken the original proof by converting it into a proof of a conditional statement rather than insisting on its establishing an absolute statement. Example 42.3 could be reworked into:

EG. 42.5 John is a man. So if God loves all men, then God loves John.

Now we have a new proof. The new proof is a simple reworking of the old one. The new proof makes it explicit that one of the premises of the old proof was obvious and that the other premise was questionable. *The questionable premise now appears as the antecedent of the conditional statement which is the new proof's conclusion.*[6]

42:3.2 This second way to finish a proof with a questionable premise is to *convert the proof into a weaker argument.* Here is where conditional proof strategy comes in. One can convert a proof with a questionable premise into a weaker argument by making the questionable premise the antecedent of a new conditional conclusion, the consequence of which is the conclusion of the original argument. Symbolizing this, we can begin by taking our original argument to be:

EG. 42.6 P_1
P_2
P_3
.
.
.
———
$\therefore C$

---

[6] Recall that $((P_1 \ \& \ P_2) \supset C)$ is equivalent to $(P_1 \supset (P_2 \supset C))$.

If our questionable premise were P_3, then we would convert the original argument into:

EG. 42.7 P_1
             P_2
     ─────────────
     $\therefore (P_3 \supset C)$

This method always works because it does not go beyond the scope of the original argument to bring in new premises or new information. The only thing that this does, besides weaken the original conclusion, is make explicit the premise which was regarded as questionable. The new conclusion now asserts that if the questionable premise were true, then the original conclusion would be true. The conditional proof strategy comes into play here because it can be used to establish the weaker argument even if it was not used in the original argument. To arrive at the weaker conclusion by means of the conditional proof strategy in our symbolized example we could do the following.

EG. 42.8   Assume P_3.
            Assert P_1.
            Assert P_2.
            Infer C.
            Conclude $(P_3 \supset C)$ by the conditional proof strategy.

Applying this to Eg. 42.3 we can construct the following argument.

EG. 42.9   Assume that God loves all men. John is a man. So if God loves all men, then God loves John.

42:3.3 We can apply the conditional proof strategy in other cases too. If what is questionable to us is which course of action to pursue, then, using conditional proof strategy, we could construct several arguments each of which shows what would happen if a different alternative were selected. The conclusions would be of the form "should I choose to do x, then the result would be y." For example, suppose you had $2,500 and were debating what to do with it. You might form arguments like the following:

EG. 42.10   Suppose I decide to buy a new car. A new car costs, on the average, $6,300. Since I have only $2,500, I would have to borrow $3,800. So if I decided to buy a car, I will have to borrow $3,800.

EG. 42.11   Suppose I put my money into a savings account. A savings account earns interest which at current rates is 3 to 6 percent behind the rate of inflation. Thus my money would lose about 3 to 6 percent of its buying power per year in a savings account.

EXERCISES FOR MODULE 42
THE CONDITIONAL PROOF STRATEGY

Ex. 1 Identify the conditional proofs among the following. Use 'Cd' and 'no' as your answers.

_____ 1. Suppose that we define the term 'God' to mean "that Being the nonexistence of which cannot be thought." Thus for there to be a God there

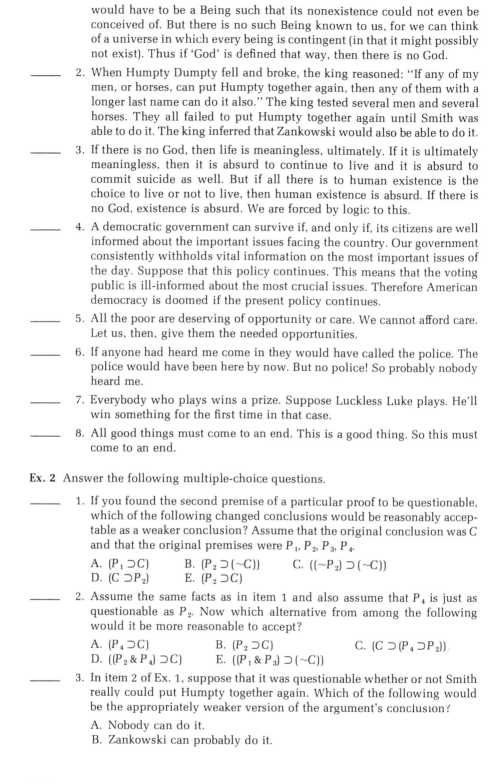

would have to be a Being such that its nonexistence could not even be conceived of. But there is no such Being known to us, for we can think of a universe in which every being is contingent (in that it might possibly not exist). Thus if 'God' is defined that way, then there is no God.

_____ 2. When Humpty Dumpty fell and broke, the king reasoned: "If any of my men, or horses, can put Humpty together again, then any of them with a longer last name can do it also." The king tested several men and several horses. They all failed to put Humpty together again until Smith was able to do it. The king inferred that Zankowski would also be able to do it.

_____ 3. If there is no God, then life is meaningless, ultimately. If it is ultimately meaningless, then it is absurd to continue to live and it is absurd to commit suicide as well. But if all there is to human existence is the choice to live or not to live, then human existence is absurd. If there is no God, existence is absurd. We are forced by logic to this.

_____ 4. A democratic government can survive if, and only if, its citizens are well informed about the important issues facing the country. Our government consistently withholds vital information on the most important issues of the day. Suppose that this policy continues. This means that the voting public is ill-informed about the most crucial issues. Therefore American democracy is doomed if the present policy continues.

_____ 5. All the poor are deserving of opportunity or care. We cannot afford care. Let us, then, give them the needed opportunities.

_____ 6. If anyone had heard me come in they would have called the police. The police would have been here by now. But no police! So probably nobody heard me.

_____ 7. Everybody who plays wins a prize. Suppose Luckless Luke plays. He'll win something for the first time in that case.

_____ 8. All good things must come to an end. This is a good thing. So this must come to an end.

Ex. 2 Answer the following multiple-choice questions.

_____ 1. If you found the second premise of a particular proof to be questionable, which of the following changed conclusions would be reasonably accep-table as a weaker conclusion? Assume that the original conclusion was C and that the original premises were P_1, P_2, P_3, P_4.

    A. $(P_1 \supset C)$ B. $(P_2 \supset (\sim C))$ C. $((\sim P_2) \supset (\sim C))$
    D. $(C \supset P_2)$ E. $(P_2 \supset C)$

_____ 2. Assume the same facts as in item 1 and also assume that P_4 is just as questionable as P_2. Now which alternative from among the following would it be more reasonable to accept?

    A. $(P_4 \supset C)$ B. $(P_2 \supset C)$ C. $(C \supset (P_4 \supset P_2))$
    D. $((P_2 \& P_4) \supset C)$ E. $((P_1 \& P_3) \supset (\sim C))$

_____ 3. In item 2 of Ex. 1, suppose that it was questionable whether or not Smith really could put Humpty together again. Which of the following would be the appropriately weaker version of the argument's conclusion?

    A. Nobody can do it.
    B. Zankowski can probably do it.

C. If Smith can't do it, then nobody can.

D. If Smith can do it, then Zankowski can do it.

E. If Zankowski could do it, Smith could have done it too.

_____ 4. One reasonable way to complete a proof with a questionable premise is:

A. To appeal to emotions

B. To find independent proofs of the unquestionable premises

C. To find an independent proof of the questionable premise

D. To beg the question

E. To start over from the beginning

_____ 5. Which of the following is not a reasonable use of the conditional proof strategy?

A. To prove conditional statements true

B. To finish proofs with questionable premises

C. To help indicate the possible results of taking various courses of action

D. To help indicate the possible results of making various decisions

E. None of the above

Ex. 3 Indicate whether each of the following is true or false.

_____ 1. The conditional proof strategy does not require that subproofs be used.

_____ 2. Only the indirect proof strategy requires making an assumption.

_____ 3. It is never the case that people should provisionally accept proofs with doubtful or questionable premises.

_____ 4. The conditional proof strategy can use any proof strategy, even another instance of the conditional proof strategy, as a subproof within itself.

_____ 5. The chief use of the conditional proof strategy is to prove that conditional statements are true.

SELECTED ANSWERS
TO EXERCISES FOR MODULE 42

Ex. 1

1. Cd

3. No. 'There is no God' is never set forth as an *assumption*. It is the antecedent of a conditional *assertion*.

5. No

7. Cd

If you missed any of these review 43:1.1 to 43:1.3.

Ex. 2

1. E   2. D   3. D   4. C   5. E

If you missed items 1, 2, or 3 review 43:3.2. If you missed item 4 review 43:3.1. If you missed item 5, review 43:3.3 and 43:3.1.

Ex. 3

1. F   2. F   3. F   4. T   5. T

13

DEDUCTIVE ARGUMENTS: A SYSTEM OF NATURAL DEDUCTION FOR PROPOSITIONAL LOGIC

In Chapter 4 we developed a system of propositional logic so that we could symbolically represent the structure of certain arguments. The structure that we were able to represent is that which logicians assume to be relevant in determining the validity of those arguments. We also developed a testing procedure, the method of truth-tables, which we could apply to a given argument to decide whether or not it was valid. The method of truth-tables is a perfectly reliable method, but it has some obvious shortcomings. It is easy to make a simple mistake using that method when one is filling in columns and crossing out T's and F's. Second, the method is uneconomical; it takes more time and more paper than is really necessary to determine the validity or invalidity of easy arguments. Third, the method can become both tedious and cumbersome if the number of variables in a given argument gets much beyond three or four. Fourth, the method seems artificial and unnatural. It works, but it is not like really *deducing* or *deriving* the conclusion from the premises. A more natural procedure than constructing a complicated table for an argument's corresponding conditional would simply be to set forth the premises of the argument and then manipulate them structurally, drawing out their intermediate conclusions, until the desired conclusion emerges. This is what a *natural deduction* system is all about. The educational goal here is to learn to demonstrate the validity of propositional logic arguments using a natural deduction system.

MODULE 43

THE MECHANICS OF NATURAL DEDUCTION— PROPOSITIONAL LOGIC I

In using a system of natural deduction you will typically begin with the given premises of an argument. You will then begin drawing inferences and making strategic assumptions—all in accordance with specific rules—in an attempt to deduce the desired conclusion of the argument.

In Module 43 we will describe in greater detail what a natural deduction system is and we will introduce some of the rules we will use in our system. In Module 44 we will complete the job of introducing the rules of our system.

● After reading Module 43 you should be able to:

1. Identify wffs of our system of natural deduction
2. Explain why each of the steps of sample deductions is justified by appeal to the rules of the system presented in this module
3. Identify the type of inference allowed by each rule presented in this module

43:1.1 Let us name our system of propositional logic P. The syntax of P explains and defines how to write wffs of P.

The syntax (grammar) of P:

P shall use the following symbols:

1. An infinite number of statement letters: $p,q,r,s,t,u,p_1, q_1, r_1, \ldots$
2. Grouping indicators:) and (
3. Logical operators: $\sim$, &, $\supset$, $\vee$, $\equiv$

The formation rules for P shall be: Any finite sequence of symbols of P will be a formula of P (but only certain formulas of P shall be considered *well formed*).

A well-formed formula of P, abbreviated wff, is defined as follows.

1. Any statement letter of P is considered a wff.
2. If we have any wff, call it A, then $\sim A$ is to be considered a wff too.
3. If we have any two wffs, call them A and B, then the following constructions will also be considered wffs: $(A \ \& \ B)$, $(A \vee B)$, $(A \supset B)$, and $(A \equiv B)$.
4. No other construction is considered a wff of P.

The semantics of P explain and define how to interpret or read P's wffs.

The semantics (meaning) of P:

The statement variables of P will be taken to stand for specific statement units of a natural language, like English, or they will be understood to be referring to the truth-value *true* or the truth-value *false*.

A wff of P shall be considered to be *true* if, and only if:

1. It is a statement letter of P and either it refers to the truth value *true* or the natural-language statement unit for which it stands is true; or
2. It is a wff of the structure $\sim A$, and A is *false*; or
3. It is a wff of the structure $(A \ \& \ B)$ and both A and B are *true*; or
4. It is a wff of the structure $(A \vee B)$ and either A or B is *true*; or
5. It is a wff of the structure $(A \supset B)$ and it is not the case that A is *true* and B is *false*; or
6. It is a wff of the structure $(A \equiv B)$ and either both A and B are *true* or both A and B are *false*.

43:1.2 As you can probably grasp upon inspection, what is here called the syntax and the semantics of P is little more than a formal way of presenting ideas you learned in Chapter 4. You should notice, though, that a rule of Chapter 4—one set of parentheses for each logical operator—has been modified: it no longer applies to the tilde, although it remains intact for the other four operators. This change is acceptable because it is a simplification which introduces no ambiguities. For example, in $\sim (p \supset q)$ the parentheses tell you that the entire conditional is negated. The formula says something like "loving someone does not guarantee the consequence that one marries that person." In $(\sim p \supset q)$, p, but not the whole conditional, is negated.

The semantics of P also accord with Chapter 4. If a statement letter has been arbitrarily assigned T it shall be regarded as true; also we shall regard it as true if it represents a true statement. Definitions 2 to 6 are completely in accord with the definitions of the logical operators given in Chapter 4.

Once these similarities to Chpater 4 are apparent, you should have little trouble identifying wffs in P. Here are a few formulas for you to consider.

1. $((p \supset q) \supset \sim r)$ (wff)
2. $[(p \supset \sim(r \vee s)) \, \& \, t$ (missing a])
3. $\sim(\sim\sim p \equiv \sim p)$ (wff)
4. $[((r \, \& \, s) \vee (t \, \& \, u_1)) \supset \sim[p \vee (q \vee (q \vee s_2))]]$ (wff)

43:2.1 A *system of natural deduction* is a system which tells you how to manipulate the symbolically represented premises of an argument so that the symbolic representation of the desired conclusion is achieved. The rules of a system of natural deduction are like the rules of a card game. They tell that this or that move or "play" is permitted. The players are allowed to use any strategy they wish provided only that they do not violate the rules of the game. To use a system of natural deduction one needs a measure of ingenuity; one has to decide upon a strategy in accordance with the rules of the system. This makes proving that an argument is valid by using natural deduction a more interesting, challenging, and enjoyable way of proving validity.

Natural deduction has a shortcoming too. We can use natural deduction to prove that arguments are valid, but we cannot use it to prove that they are invalid. A truth-table, for all its problems, was *theoretically complete*. In other words, it would tell if an argument was valid and it would tell if it was not. Our system of natural deduction will only be able to tell us that an argument is valid. If we are able to derive the desired conclusion from the argument's premises, then the argument is valid. But if we cannot derive the desired conclusion from those premises then we will not know whether the argument is valid or not. It may be that the argument is indeed invalid and that was why we are unable to derive its conclusion. Or it may be that we are simply not skilled enough with our system to see how to get the conclusion.

43:2.2 Proofs in P The system of natural deduction for P will be a system of *rules of inference* which tell us how to create acceptable sequences or lists of wffs of P. Each wff in a sequence will be considered a *line* in a *proof*. The lines will be written downward in a list. To the left of each line we will have its *line number*, and we may have a number of *stars*. The stars will be explained later. To the right of each line we will put its *annotation*, that is, the explanation of how that line qualifies as a line of the proof in accordance with the rules of our system of natural deduction.

The rules of our system tell us how to set down lines of a proof. One rule will allow us to introduce new lines as *premises* of a proof. One rule will allow us to introduce new lines as *assumptions*.[1] Several rules will indicate how we might manipulate existing lines to have them interact with each other so that *consequences* of our premises and assumptions can be derived. Two rules are for *dispatching* our assump-

---

[1] This rule will be especially useful to us should we wish to use either the reduction-to-contradiction strategy or the conditional-proof strategy.

tions.² These two rules allow us to make explicit certain relationships that we have deduced as existing between an assumption and its consequences.

The stars that we mentioned earlier are going to be used to indicate the assumptions a line of a proof are based on. Each assumption of a given line will be represented by a star to the left of that line. If a line is based on no assumptions, then it will have no stars to its left.

Our system can be used to prove two kinds of things. It can be used to prove that certain wff's of P are tautologies. *Any wff that is an unstarred line of a proof which contains no premises and is constructed using our system of natural deduction will be a tautology.* Our system can also be used to prove that a certain conclusion is logically implied by a given set of premises. To prove this we will introduce the given premises and derive the desired conclusion. If we derive the desired conclusion using our system, and if our proof contains no undispatched assumptions, then it is logically implied by those premises. In this way *we will be able to prove that arguments are valid.* We will show that their conclusions are logically implied by their premises. This, of course, is the major purpose of our system.

We will be able to use all three proof strategies discussed in Chapter 12 in our system: the strategies of direct proof, conditional proof, and reduction to contradiction.

We will use thirteen different rules of inference in our system of natural deduction. After the presentation of each rule two examples will be given of its use. Note that all the rules are about how one might manipulate *whole lines* of proofs. Manipulating parts of lines is nowhere permitted. Most of the rules indicate how two or more lines can be made to interact. We will present these in Module 44. Here in Module 43 we present only those rules that involve no more than one line of a proof.

Rule 1 Rule of assumption:

Any wff of P whatsoever can be put down as a line of proof. Annotate using 'RA' (which abbreviates 'rule of assumption'). Number the line appropriately, and introduce a star with a subscript which is the same number as the line number itself.

EG. 43.1 $*_1$ 1. p RA
$*_2$ 2. $(p \supset q)$ RA
$*_3$ 3. $\sim p$ RA

EG. 43.2 .
.
.
$*_{78}$ 78. $(p \lor (q \equiv r))$ RA

The rule of assumption may seem odd to you. You may sense quite rightly that if you can introduce any assumption you can deduce any conclusion. Indeed you can. But you may feel that surely you haven't proved a conclusion if you had to introduce outrageously false—or even dubious—assumptions in order to reach your conclusion. Again this judgment is correct. But beware the false dilemma! When people introduce an outrageously false or suspect assertion from which they logically deduce a conclusion all they have really proved is an implication, a conditional assertion: If the assumption were true, the conclusion would be. Thus the rule of assumption says, in effect: "Well, let's catalogue this assumption of yours and see what fol-

---

² As we shall see in Module 44, one is used with reductio arguments the other with conditional proofs.

lows from it." In P any conclusion derived from an assumption will have at its left a star referring back to that assumption, and so we always retain the basic ideal that a conclusion is *proved* only as well as the starred assumptions are *known true*. To show that an argument is valid we will have to derive its conclusion and do so having dispatched all the strategic assumptions we may have made along the way. Proving validity involves showing that a conclusion follows from its given premises, not from its premises and further assumptions. Example 43.2 shows that additional assumptions can be introduced at any point in a proof in P. The chief use of the rule of assumption is to introduce lines that begin the strategy of reduction to contradiction or the strategy of conditional proof.[3] So in practice the wff's we choose to introduce by the rule of assumption will not be selected randomly but will be selected with one or another of these strategies in mind.

Rule 2 Rule of premise:

When trying to demonstrate that a given argument is valid, any wff presented as a premise in that argument may be set down as a line of a proof. Annotate 'RP' (which abbreviates 'rule of premise'). Number the line appropriately.

EG. 43.3 Suppose you wish to try to derive the conclusion $(q \lor r)$ from the premises p, $(r \supset s)$, $\sim s$, and $(\sim r \supset q)$. You may begin a proof by:

    1. p   RP
    2. (r ⊃ s)   RP
    3. ~s   RP
    4. (~r ⊃ q)   RP

EG. 43.4 Suppose you are given

$(q \lor p)$
$\sim q$
$\therefore p$

and asked to prove it valid using natural deduction. You may introduce the premises into your proof at any point, such as in

    *₁ 1. ~p   RA
       2. (q ∨ p)   RP
       3. ~q   RP

The purpose of the rule of premise is to get into play the stated premises of an argument. This is what the rule allows. Using this rule you are restricted, however, to introducing only premises actually given in the original argument. Any other statement or wff you wish to introduce must be brought in as an explicit assumption using the rule of assumption.

43:2.3 Rules that apply to one line We are now ready to look at some rules of inference that apply to single, previously entered lines.

Rule 3 Simplification:

If (A & B) is line j, then one may set down A or B as line n. Annotation: 'Sj'. Carry down all the stars of line j to line n.

---

[3] See Chapter 12 for discussions of these strategies.

EG. 43.5

    ·

    ·

    ·

      3. $(p \mathbin{\&} q)$ ANN[4]

      4. p S_3

      5. q S_3

EG. 43.6 $*_1$ 17. $(((p \mathbin{\&} q) \supset r) \mathbin{\&} (s \mathbin{\&} p))$ ANN

         $*_1$ 18. $((p \mathbin{\&} q) \supset r)$ S_{17}

           ·

           ·

           ·

         $*_1$ 37. $(s \mathbin{\&} p)$ S_{17}

           ·

           ·

           ·

         $*_1$ 41. p S_{37}

Rule 4 Addition:

If A is line j, then one may set down $(A \lor B)$ or $(B \lor A)$ as line n. Annotation: '$A\,j$'.
Carry down to line n all the stars of line j.

EG. 43.7   ·

          ·

          ·

    $*_2$ 4. $(p \equiv q)$ ANN

          ·

          ·

          ·

    $*_2$ 10. $((p \equiv q) \lor (r \supset s))$ A_4

EG. 43.8   ·

          ·

          ·

      7. p ANN

          ·

          ·

          ·

      12. $[((q \lor r) \supset p) \lor p]$ A_7

These two rules are written in a logician's technical way, but with a few explanations you will be able to see what is going on. First, there is the mention of 'line j' and 'line n.' Given that earlier alphabet letters are used for earlier lines, the letters simply represent any line numbers. The vertical dots : represent lines that have not been written out because they are irrelevant to the example.

You may also wonder about the justifications for these rules. Formally, we can see that the inferences authorized by these rules will always be valid. That is $((A \mathbin{\&} B) \supset A)$, $((A \mathbin{\&} B) \supset B)$, $(A \supset (A \lor B))$, and $(A \supset (B \lor A))$ are all tautological structures, as you can confirm by truth-tables.

---

[4] 'ANN' stands for whatever annotation that line may have.

Informally we often construct an argument which proves a stronger conclusion than we desired. For example, to the question "where's Lyle?" you might answer, "He told me he and Sandy were going to the movie this evening. So they're there now." From this conjunctive conclusion, "Lyle is at the movie and Sandy is at the movie," it obviously follows, in accord with our rule of simplification, that Lyle is at the movie.

Similarly, someone may ask, "Is Joan or Emily going to do the job?" One might reply, "Yes, I'm sure Joan will—she promised and she's very dependable." Unexpressed but yet relied on is the rule of addition. You are sure that either Joan or Emily will do the job because you know, and argued, that Joan will.

The third and final rule that applies to only one line is based on the idea of logical equivalence. It allows us to substitute certain formulas for others that are logically equivalent to them.

Rule 5 Substitution:

If A is line j, then one may set down A' as line n provided that A' is logically equivalent to A. Annotation: 'Sub$_j$'. Carry down to n all the stars of j.

EG. 43.9

    4. $(p \ \& \ q)$ ANN

    8. $\sim(\sim p \lor \sim q)$ Sub$_4$

EG. 43.10

$*_3$ 5. $((\sim\sim p \supset q) \lor (p \supset q))$ ANN

$*_3$ 8. $((p \supset q) \lor (\sim p \lor q))$ Sub$_5$

Here is a list of some helpful equivalences which may be used in association with the rule of substitution. You may wish to know their traditional names, which are written beside them. There are, of course, several other equivalencies which are not mentioned here. We can always check to see if two wffs are equivalent by using the method of truth-tables.

1. A is logically equivalent to $\sim\sim A$ (double negation).
2. A is logically equivalent to $(A \lor A)$ (tautology).
3. A is logically equivalent to $(A \ \& \ A)$ (tautology).
4. $(A \ \& \ B)$ is logically equivalent to $(B \ \& \ A)$ (commutation).
5. $(A \lor B)$ is logically equivalent to $(B \lor A)$ (commutation).
6. $(A \lor B)$ is logically equivalent to $\sim(\sim A \ \& \ \sim B)$.
7. $(A \ \& \ B)$ is logically equivalent to $\sim(\sim A \lor \sim B)$.
8. $\sim(A \lor B)$ is logically equivalent to $(\sim A \ \& \ \sim B)$ (DeMorgan's theorem).
9. $\sim(A \ \& \ B)$ is logically equivalent to $(\sim A \lor \sim B)$ (DeMorgan's theorem).
10. $(A \supset B)$ is logically equivalent to $(\sim A \lor B)$ (material implication).

11. $\sim(A \supset B)$ is logically equivalent to $(A \;\&\; \sim B)$ (material implication).
12. $(A \supset B)$ is logically equivalent to $(\sim B \supset \sim A)$ (transposition).
13. $(A \equiv B)$ is logically equivalent to $((A \supset B) \;\&\; (B \supset A))$ (equivalence).
14. $(A \equiv B)$ is logically equivalent to $((A \;\&\; B) \lor (\sim A \;\&\; \sim B))$.
15. $(A \;\&\; (B \;\&\; C))$ is logically equivalent to $((A \;\&\; B) \;\&\; C)$ (association).
16. $(A \lor (B \lor C))$ is logically equivalent to $((A \lor B) \lor C)$ (association).
17. $(A \;\&\; (B \lor C))$ is logically equivalent to $((A \;\&\; B) \lor (A \;\&\; C))$ (distribution).
18. $(A \lor (B \;\&\; C))$ is logically equivalent to $((A \lor B) \;\&\; (A \lor C))$ (distribution).
19. $((A \;\&\; B) \supset C)$ is logically equivalent to $(A \supset (B \supset C))$ (exportation).
20. A tautology is logically equivalent to any tautology.
21. An inconsistent wff is logically equivalent to any inconsistent wff.[5]

EXERCISES FOR MODULE 43

THE MECHANICS OF NATURAL DEDUCTION— PROPOSITIONAL LOGIC I

Ex. 1 Below are ten formulas of P. Determine for each whether it is well formed. If it is, mark it 'wff.' If not, cite the reason why it is not from this list: (A) a logical operator is missing; (B) a statement letter is missing; (C) parenthesis or parentheses are missing. Some formulas may fail to be well formed in more than one way.

_____ 1. p

_____ 2. $p \lor \sim q$

_____ 3. $[(p \equiv r) \equiv [(q \equiv p) \;\&\; ((q \supset r) \;\&\; (r \supset q))]]$

_____ 4. $[((p \lor q) \;\&\; r) \equiv ((p \;\&\; r) \lor (p \;\&\; q))]$

_____ 5. $(\sim(\sim\sim p \lor q) \equiv \sim(\sim p \lor q))$

_____ 6. $q \supset (\sim r \supset s)$

_____ 7. $[((q \;\&\; p)r) \supset s]$

_____ 8. $(\sim(p \supset r) \equiv p \;\&\; \sim)$

_____ 9. $(\sim(p \lor r) \equiv (\sim p \;\&\; \sim r))$

_____ 10. $\sim(p \supset r) \lor (s \;\&\; t)$

Ex. 2. Below are two proofs. Each uses only rules presented in this module. There are, however, errors in the annotations of some of the lines. Where necessary correct the annotation by crossing out the faulty annotation and writing in the proper annotation.

$*_1$ 1. q RP
     2. p RA
     3. $(q \lor s)$ Sub_1

---

[5] Our rule of substitution actually allows the inference from one tautology to another tautology regardless of the statement letters actually mentioned. Thus, from $(p \supset p)$ one could infer $(q \lor \sim q)$. Some find this valid inference unpalatable and unnatural on the grounds that there is nothing concerning q in our tautology about p. Of course, this possibility could easily be ruled out if one wished. One could impose a restriction on one's own use of the rule of substitution. The restriction to impose would be: The wff inferred by substitution in line n must contain occurrences of all and only those statement letters which occurred in the original wff on line j.

1. $(q \supset s)$		$*_2$ 5. $(\sim r \ \& \ (q \supset s))$	Sub
2. $(s \supset p)$		$*_1$ 6. $(q \supset s)$	Sub
3. $((q \supset s) \ \& \sim r)$	RA	7. $(\sim s \supset \sim q)$	Sub_1
4. $(\sim s \lor p)$	2	8. $\sim r$	Sub_5

Ex. 3 Answer the following multiple-choice questions.

_____ 1. The rule of assumption is useful because:
   A. Some proof strategies call for making explicit assumptions
   B. A conclusion can be shown valid only if it is assumed
   C. The premises alone may not imply the conclusion
   D. Some wffs are logically equivalent to others

_____ 2. The rule of premise allows one to introduce:
   A. Any wff one wants to use as a premise for the sake of strategy
   B. Any wff one wishes to incorporate into the argument
   C. Only those wffs that are the given premises of the argument under investigation
   D. Any wff that is logically equivalent to a given premise of the argument under investigation

_____ 3. The rule of addition allows:
   A. From $(A \lor B)$ infer B
   B. From A infer $(B \lor C)$
   C. From A infer $(A \supset B)$
   D. From A infer $(A \lor B)$

_____ 4. The rule of simplification allows:
   A. From $(A \lor B)$ infer A
   B. From $(A \ \& \ B)$ infer B
   C. From $(A \supset B)$ infer $(\sim B \supset \sim A)$
   D. From B infer $(A \lor B)$

_____ 5. The rule of substitution allows one to:
   A. Put down any two equivalent wffs
   B. Put down any wff that is equivalent to any wff already introduced as an earlier line
   C. Put down any wff that is implied by, but not necessarily equivalent to, any earlier wff
   D. Put down any wff that implies some earlier wffs

The ability to remember the variety of formulas to which a given formula is equivalent is for many students the hardest part of constructing proofs of desired conclusions. Accordingly before going to Module 44 you should study the equivalences under Rule 5 and try the following exercise.

Ex. 4 Below are ten formulas. Opposite each are two formulas. In each case only one is equivalent to the original. Can you tell which?

1. $((p \ \& \ q) \supset r)$ i. $((p \supset q) \supset r)$
                                 ii. $(p \supset (q \supset r))$

2. $(\sim p \lor \sim q)$ i. $(\sim p \ \& \sim q)$
                                 ii. $\sim (p \ \& \ q)$

3. $\sim (p \lor q)$ i. $(\sim p \ \& \sim q)$
                                 ii. $\sim (p \ \& \sim q)$

4. $(p \lor (q \lor r))$ i. $(p \ \& \ (q \lor r))$
                                ii. $((p \lor q) \lor r)$

5. $((p \lor q) \ \& \ r)$ i. $(p \lor (q \ \& \ r))$
                                ii. $((p \ \& \ r) \lor (q \ \& \ r))$

6. $((p \ \& \ q) \lor r)$ i. $((p \lor r) \ \& \ (q \lor r))$
                                ii. $((p \ \& \ r) \lor (q \ \& \ r))$

7. p i. $(p \lor q)$
                                ii. $(p \lor p)$

8. $((p \lor q) \supset (r \supset s))$ i. $[((p \lor q) \ \& \ r) \supset s]$
                                ii. $[((p \lor r) \ \& \ q) \supset s]$

9. $((\sim p \lor s) \ \& \ \sim q)$ i. $\sim((p \supset s) \supset q)$
                                ii. $(\sim (p \supset s) \supset q)$

10. $((p \supset q) \supset (r \supset s))$ i. $(\sim (r \supset s) \supset \sim (p \supset q))$
                                ii. $(\sim (r \supset s) \supset \sim (p \ \& \ \sim q))$

SELECTED ANSWERS
TO EXERCISES FOR MODULE 43

Ex. 1

1. wff   3. wff   5. wff   7. A   9. wff

If you missed any, review 43:1.1 and 43:1.2.

Ex. 2 Correctly written, these proofs are:

	1. q	RP		1. $(q \supset s)$	RP
$*_2$	2. p	RA		2. $(s \supset p)$	RP
	3. $(q \lor s)$	A_1	$*_3$	3. $((q \supset s) \ \& \ \sim r)$	RA
				4. $(\sim s \lor p)$	Sub_2
			$*_3$	5. $(\sim r \ \& \ (q \supset s))$	Sub_3
			$*_3$	6. $(q \supset s)$	S_5
				7. $(\sim s \supset \sim q)$	Sub_1
			$*_3$	8. $\sim r$	S_5

Ex. 3

1. A   2. C   3. D   4. B   5. B

Ex. 4

1. ii; by (19)   2. ii; by DeMorgan's (9)   3. i; by (8)
4. ii; by (16)   5. ii; by (18) and (4)   6. ii; by (18) and (5)
7. ii; by (2)   8. i; by exportation (19)   9. i; by (10) and (11)
10. i; by transposition, (12)

MODULE 44

THE MECHANICS OF NATURAL DEDUCTION—
PROPOSITIONAL LOGIC II

Having begun to develop our system of natural deduction by explaining rules for introducing wffs as lines of proofs and for discussing inferences from single lines of proofs, let us now complete the development of the system by explaining rules for drawing inferences from more than one line and for dispatching any assumptions we have introduced into our proofs.

● After reading Module 44 you should be able to:

1. Explain why each of the steps of sample deductions is justified by appeal to the the rules of the system as presented in Modules 43 and 44
2. Identify the theoretical reasons justifying each rule of the system
3. Identify the type of inference allowed by each rule of the system

44:1.1 Rules that apply to two lines Most of the rules of inference in P allow inferences from two preceding lines to a third, conclusion, line. One of them is disjunctive syllogism.

Rule 6 Disjunctive syllogism:
If $(A \lor B)$ is line j and either $\sim A$ or $\sim B$ is line k, then one may set down either B or A as line n. (Set down B as n if k is $\sim A$; set down A as n if k is $\sim B$.) Annotation: '$DS_{j,k}$'. Carry down all the stars of both j and k.

EG. 44.1		1. $(p \lor q)$	RP
		2. $\sim p$	RP
		3. q	$DS_{1,2}$

EG. 44.2

.
.
.

$*_6$ 7. $((r \ \& \ s) \lor (t \equiv p))$ ANN

.
.
.

$*_3$ 11. $\sim(t \equiv p)$ ANN

.
.
.

$*_3*_6$ 15. $(r \ \& \ s)$ $DS_{7,11}$

Rule 6 indicates that there are two forms of disjunctive syllogism: (1) From $(A \lor B)$ and $\sim A$, one may set down B, and (2) from $(A \lor B)$ and $\sim B$ infer A. Truth-tables show that the two forms given below are equally valid.

$(A \lor B)$ $(A \lor B)$
$\dfrac{\sim A}{\therefore B}$ $\dfrac{\sim B}{\therefore A}$

In both cases one premise asserts a disjunction, which requires at least one true disjunct for it to be true. The second premise says one of the disjuncts is false. So in both cases, if both the premises are true, the other disjunct must be true, which is exactly what the conclusion asserts. Since the interaction of at least two lines is required for an inference like disjunction syllogism, both the premise lines are mentioned in the annotation at the right.

Here are four more rules involving two lines. Note that both of the needed lines must occur in the proof before a rule can be applied; however the order in which the needed lines occur (i.e., which is before which) does not matter so long as they are both there before the rule is applied.

Rule 7 Modus ponens:

If A is line number j and $(A \supset B)$ is line number k, then one may set down B as line n. Annotate: '$MP_{j,k}$'. Carry down to line n any stars (and their subscripts, of course) of lines j and k.

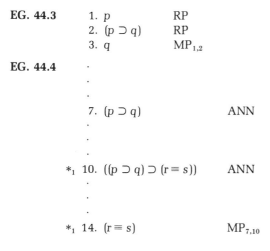

EG. 44.3   1. p RP
        2. $(p \supset q)$ RP
        3. q $MP_{1,2}$

EG. 44.4   ·
       ·
       ·
       7. $(p \supset q)$ ANN
       ·
       ·
       ·
    $*_1$ 10. $((p \supset q) \supset (r \equiv s))$ ANN
       ·
       ·
       ·
    $*_1$ 14. $(r \equiv s)$ $MP_{7,10}$

Rule 8 Modus tollens:

If $(A \supset B)$ is line j and $\sim B$ is line k, then one may set down $\sim A$ as line n. Annotation: '$MT_{j,k}$'. Carry down any stars of lines j and k.

EG. 44.5   1. p RP
        2. $(p \supset q)$ RP
    $*_3$ 3. $\sim q$ RA
    $*_3$ 4. $\sim p$ $MT_{2,3}$

EG. 44.6   ·
       ·
       ·
       9. $((q \equiv s) \supset \sim p)$ ANN
       ·
       ·
       12. $\sim\sim p$ ANN
       ·
       ·
       34. $\sim (q \equiv s)$ $MT_{9,12}$

Rule 9 Conjunction:

If A is line j and B is line k, then one may set down $(A \& B)$ or $(B \& A)$ as line n. Annotation: '$C_{j,k}$'. Carry down to line n all the stars of both j and k.

EG. 44.7

          .
          .
          .

$*_1$ 4. $(p \supset q)$ ANN

          .
          .
          .

$*_5$ 8. $(r \equiv (s \lor p))$ ANN

          .
          .
          .

$*_1*_5$ 15. $[(p \supset q) \,\&\, (r \equiv (s \lor p))]$ $C_{4,8}$

EG. 44.8

          .
          .
          .

        7. q ANN

          .
          .
          .

       11. $(p \,\&\, r)$ ANN

          .
          .
          .

       19. $((p \,\&\, r) \,\&\, q)$ $C_{7,11}$

Rule 10 Hypothetical syllogism:

If $(A \supset B)$ is line j and $(B \supset C)$ is line k, then one may set down $(A \supset C)$ as line n.
Annotation: '$HS_{j,k}$'. Carry down all the stars of both j and k to n.

EG. 44.9   1. $(t \,\&\, r)$ RP
                   2. $(p \supset q)$ RP
                   3. $(q \supset (p \lor r))$ RP
                   .
                   .
                   .

                 17. $(p \supset (p \lor r))$ $HS_{2,3}$

EG. 44.10 .
                  .
                  .

$*_1*_4$ 11. $(q \supset (r \equiv s))$ ANN

          .
          .
          .

$*_6*_7$ 17. $((r \equiv s) \supset (t \lor p))$ ANN

          .
          .
          .

$*_1*_4*_6*_7$ 27. $(q \supset (t \lor p))$ $HS_{11,17}$

We now turn to an inference pattern having three premise lines and a conclusion. As before, the order in which the premise lines occur does not matter as long as they are all there.

Rule 11 Constructive dilemma:

If $(A \supset B)$ is line j and $(C \supset D)$ is line k and $(A \vee C)$ is line m, then one may set down $(B \vee D)$ as line n. Annotation: '$CD_{j,k,m}$'. Carry down to line n all the stars of j, k, and m.

EG. 44.11

	1.	$(p \supset (q \ \& \ r))$	RP
	2.	$(s \supset (q \ \& \ s))$	RP
$*_3$	3.	$(p \vee s)$	RA

.
.
.

| $*_3$ | 7. | $((q \ \& \ r) \vee (q \ \& \ s))$ | $CD_{1,2,3}$ |

EG. 44.12

.
.
.

| $*_4$ | 5. | $((p \vee q) \supset r)$ | ANN |

.
.
.

| $*_4$ | 8. | $((s \equiv p) \supset (q \supset r))$ | ANN |

.
.
.

| $*_{10}$ | 11. | $((p \vee q) \vee (s \equiv p))$ | ANN |

.
.
.

| $*_4*_{10}$ | 15. | $(r \vee (q \supset r))$ | $CD_{5,8,11}$ |

You might note in Eg. 44.12 that both lines 5 and 8, involved here in applying constructive dilemma, have $*_4$ as a premise. Thus $*_4$ is carried down to line 15, but it need not be mentioned twice because the function of the stars is to show the *original* premises on which a subsequent line depends. How many times does not matter.

The five inference rules you have just learned (modus ponens, modus tollens, conjunction, hypothetical syllogism, and constructive dilemma) are fairly easy to use alone.[6] It is only a bit tougher to use them together with an equivalence. Often, however, these rules can be applied only after an equivalence has been cited.

[6] If our goal were to streamline the system we could do so by eliminating rules which yield inferences that can be gained without those rules. For example, using disjunctive syllogism we can get B from $(A \vee B)$ and $\sim A$. But we could also get B from the same two lines as follows. First get $(\sim A \supset B)$ from $(A \vee B)$ by substitution. Then use $\sim A$ and $(\sim A \supset B)$ to get B by modus ponens. Or, if you don't want to use modus ponens, then do this. Get $(\sim B \supset A)$ from $(A \vee B)$ by substitution, now use $\sim A$ to derive $\sim\sim B$ by modus tollens. Use substitution again to get B from $\sim\sim B$. Rules that contribute no inferences that could not be duplicated by combinations of other rules are called *dependent* rules in a system. A system with very few or no dependent rules is perhaps quite elegant, yet is very hard to work with. A system like P, with many dependent rules, gives you a greater chance to see alternative ways to accomplish your goals.

Below are ten sets of premises and their conclusions. In each case the conclusion follows through the use of substitution and *one* of the rules explained in 44:1.1. See how well you can do in writing down the next two lines of each proof by appealing to an equivalence and to one of the rules of 44:1.1.

	Premises		Conclusion
A.	1. $(p \supset q)$	RP	A. q
	2. $\sim\sim p$	RP	
B.	1. $((p \ \& \ q) \supset r)$	RP	B. $(q \supset r)$
	2. p	RP	
C.	1. $\sim(p \supset q)$	RP	C. r
	2. $((p \ \& \sim q) \supset r)$	RP	
D.	1. $(p \supset q)$	RP	D. $(p \supset r)$
	2. $(\sim r \supset \sim q)$	RP	
E.	1. $(\sim p \vee \sim p)$	RP	E. $\sim q$
	2. $(q \supset p)$	RP	
F.	1. $(q \supset p)$	RP	F. $\sim\sim p$
	2. q	RP	
G.	1. $(\sim p \vee \sim q)$	RP	G. $\sim r$
	2. $(r \supset (p \ \& \ q))$	RP	
H.	1. $(\sim p \vee \sim q)$	RP	H. $\sim r$
	2. $((p \supset \sim q) \supset \sim r)$	RP	
I.	1. $(p \vee (q \vee r))$	RP	I. r
	2. $\sim(p \vee q)$	RP	
J.	1. $\sim\sim q$	RP	J. $(q \ \& \ (r \supset q)$
	2. $(r \supset q)$	RP	

ANSWER TO EXERCISE 1

A. 3. p Sub$_3$ (using equiv. 1)   or   3. $(\sim p \vee q)$ Sub$_1$ (using equiv. 10)
    4. q MP$_{1,3}$ 4. q DS$_{2,3}$

B. 3. $(p \supset (q \supset r))$ Sub$_1$ (using equiv. 19)
    4. $(q \supset r)$ MP$_{2,3}$

C. 3. $(p \ \& \sim q)$ Sub$_1$ (using equiv. 11)
    4. r MP$_{2,3}$

D. 3. $(q \supset r)$ Sub$_2$ (using equiv. 1)
    4. $(p \supset r)$ HS$_{1,3}$

E. 3. $\sim p$ Sub$_1$ (using equiv. 2)
    4. $\sim q$ MT$_{2,3}$

F. 3. p MP$_{1,2}$
    4. $\sim\sim p$ Sub$_3$ (using equiv. 1)

G. 3. $\sim(p \ \& \ q)$ Sub$_1$ (using equiv. 9)
    4. $\sim r$ MT$_{2,3}$

H. 3. $(p \supset \sim q)$ Sub$_1$ (using equiv. 10)
    4. $\sim r$ MP$_{2,3}$

I. 3. $((p \vee q) \vee r)$ Sub$_1$ (using equiv. 16)
    4. r DS$_{2,3}$

J. 3. q   Sub₁ (using equiv. 1)
    4. (q & (r ⊃ q))   C₂,₃

If you had trouble with these proofs, you should probably review the substitution listed in 43:2.3 and in the final appendix of this book.

44:1.2 Rules to dispatch assumptions The final two rules of inference formalize procedures you learned in Chapter 12. The two complex strategies for which formal rules are given are reduction to contradiction and conditional proof. As in the proof strategies from which they derive, these next two rules make explicit the force of the assumptions introduced earlier into our proofs using the rule of assumption.

Rule 12 Rule of reductio:

*If A is line j and C and ~C are lines k and m, where *j is a star of either line k or line m, then one may set down ~A as line n. Annotation: 'Red$_{*_j,k,m}$'.* Carry down to n all the stars of lines k and m but do not carry down *j. (The assumption indicated by *j is now dispatched. This is indicated by its being written into the annotation of line n.)

EG. 44.13

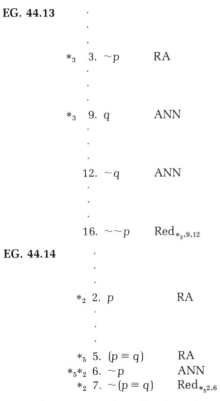

EG. 44.14

Example 44.13 is a formalized version of the heart of a typical reduction to contradiction argument. The rule of assumption is used to justify line 3, where ~p will be the negation of the desired conclusion. The deduction of q and ~q then justifies the inference drawn in line 16 of ~~p.

You will notice that the rule of reductio is broad enough to entitle you to negate any assumption line used in deriving either of the two contradicting lines. Thus in

Eg. 44.14 the rule would justify your writing the negation of line 2, rather than the negation of line 5, as line 7. In this kind of situation, a person constructing a proof is called upon to make a strategic judgment. The presence of lines 2 and 6 is sufficient to show that at least one of the assumptions of one of those lines is false. The judgment you exercise in choosing what to write for line 7 will be of this form:

The assumptions lead to a contradiction and, so, are incompatible with each other. At least one of them must then be rejected. I have provisionally accepted the original assumption (line 2) as true, but I am in doubt about the truth of the other assumption (line 5). So I will negate that assumption, rather than the other, by the rule of reduction.[7]

  Example 44.14 introduces one further possible complexity. Sometimes a line, like 2, will be involved in the deduction of its own negation (line 6) as indicated by the presence of both $*_2$ and $*_5$ to the left of line 6. Although this may seem like a strange case, it is a real possibility when using the indirect proof of strategy. (See 41:2.2.)

Rule 13 Conditionalization:

If A is line j and B is line k then one may set down $(A \supset B)$ as line n provided that $*j$ is one of line k's stars. Annotation: 'Cd$_{*j,k}$'. Carry down all the stars of line k but do not carry down $*j$. (The premise indicated by $*j$, namely the wff A, is now dispatched. This fact is indicated by $*j$'s being mentioned in the annotation of line n.)

EG. 44.15 $*_1$ 1. p RA
.
.
.

     $*_1$ 38. $(q \equiv (p \vee r))$ ANN
       39. $[p \supset (q \equiv (p \vee r))]$ Cd$_{*_1,38}$

EG. 44.16 $*_1$ 1. p RA
      $*_2$ 2. q RA
      $*_3$ 3. r RA
      $*_3$ 4. $(r \vee s)$ A$_3$
        5. $(r \supset (r \vee s))$ Cd$_{*_3,4}$
    $*_1*_2$ 6. $(p \& q)$ C$_{1,2}$
      $*_2$ 7. $(p \supset (p \& q))$ Cd$_{*_1,6}$
        8. $[q \supset (p \supset (p \& q))]$ Cd$_{*_2,7}$

The rule of conditionalization formalizes the useful strategy of conditional proof. Suppose the conclusion you want to prove is a conditional, $(p \supset q)$. It is usually easier to construct a deduction which employs the rule of assumption to introduce p, derives q, and then uses conditionalization to reach $(p \supset q)$ rather than trying to construct a direct proof of $(p \supset q)$.[8]

---

[7] Our main concern is to show the logical consequences of a given set of premises. But given that the conjunction of the premises and an assumption $(P_1 \& P_2 \& P_3 \& A)$ leads to a contradiction, say $(r \& \sim r)$, we have no strictly logical reason why we could not reject any one of the conjuncts. Only the strategic considerations of how indirect proofs work lead us to reject A and retain $(P_1 \& P_2 \& P_3)$, which are, hopefully, the exact premises of the original argument given us to test.

[8] In some less complete systems of natural deduction the rule of conditionalization is made to do the job of dispatching assumptions for both the reduction to contradiction

44:2.1 A first step to becoming familiar with the twelve rules of inference is to recognize which rules sample inferences employ. Here are some sample proofs using system P. Cover the annotation column with a piece of paper. See if you can determine the proper annotation for each line before looking.

EG. 44.17 Prove that the wffs $(\sim p \vee q)$ and $(q \supset r)$ logically imply $(p \supset r)$.

1.	$(\sim p \vee q)$	RP
2.	$(q \supset r)$	RP
3.	$(p \supset q)$	Sub_1
4.	$(p \supset r)$	$HS_{3,2}$

EG. 44.18 Prove that the wffs $(p \supset q)$, $\sim r$, and $(\sim r \supset \sim q)$ logically imply $\sim p$.

1.	$(p \supset q)$	RP
2.	$\sim r$	RP
3.	$(\sim r \supset \sim q)$	RP
4.	$\sim q$	$MP_{2,3}$
5.	$\sim p$	$MT_{1,4}$

EG. 44.19 Prove that the wffs $(\sim p \vee (q \supset r))$, $((q \supset r) \supset t)$, and $(\sim p \supset s)$ logically imply $(t \vee s)$.

1.	$(\sim p \vee (q \supset r))$	RP
2.	$((q \supset r) \supset t)$	RP
3.	$(\sim p \supset s)$	RP
4.	$(t \vee s)$	$CD_{1,2,3}$

Here are three more examples. The first is a direct proof, the second a conditional proof, and the third a reduction to contradiction. All three involve a number of intermediate inferences before the desired conclusion emerges.

EG. 44.20 Prove that the wffs $(p \vee \sim q)$, $(\sim p \& (r \supset s))$, and $(q \vee r)$ logically imply s.

1.	$(p \vee \sim q)$	RP
2.	$(\sim p \& (r \supset s))$	RP
3.	$(q \vee r)$	RP
4.	$\sim p$	S_2
5.	$\sim q$	$DS_{1,4}$
6.	r	$DS_{5,3}$
7.	$(r \supset s)$	S_2
8.	s	$MP_{6,7}$

EG. 44.21 Prove that the wffs $((p \vee q) \supset (r \& s))$ and $((s \vee t) \supset u)$ logically imply $(p \supset u)$.

	1.	$((p \vee q) \supset (r \& s))$	RP
	2.	$((s \vee t) \supset u)$	RP
$*_3$	3.	p	RA

---

strategy and the conditional proof strategy. We could have developed our system that way if we wished to conflate these two distinct strategies. Had we done so you would have been able to do an indirect proof as follows: Assume $\sim C$ (the negation of the conclusion) by the rule of assumption. Derive the contradiction $(r \& \sim r)$. Using conditionalization write: $(\sim C \supset (r \& \sim r))$. Using substitution then write C.

$*_3$ 4. $(p \lor q)$ A_3
$*_3$ 5. $(r \& s)$ $MP_{4,1}$
$*_3$ 6. s S_5
$*_3$ 7. $(s \lor t)$ A_6
$*_3$ 8. u $MP_{7,2}$
     9. $(p \supset u)$ $CD_{*_3,8}$

EG. 44.22 Prove that the wffs $((p \& q) \supset r)$ and $(q \& \sim r)$ logically imply $\sim p$.

     1. $((p \& q) \supset r)$ RP
     2. $(q \& \sim r)$ RP
$*_3$ 3. p RA
     4. q S_2
$*_3$ 5. $(p \& q)$ $C_{3,4}$
$*_3$ 6. r $MP_{1,5}$
     7. $\sim r$ S_2
     8. $\sim p$ $Red_{*_3,6,7}$

These sample proofs all indicate that the given premises taken together logically imply the desired conclusions. In Eg. 44.20 the last line indicates that the wff s is logically implied by the wffs in lines 1, 2, and 3 together. This is how to interpret any proof that employs the rule of premise. Similarly, the wff in the last line of Eg. 44.21 is logically implied by the first two lines of that sample. And the wff p in the last line of Eg. 44.22 is logically implied by the wffs in the first two lines of that sample proof. In both cases intermediate assumptions were used to aid in the derivation and then were ultimately dispatched.

EXERCISES FOR MODULE 44
THE MECHANICS OF NATURAL DEDUCTION—
PROPOSITIONAL LOGIC II

Ex. 2 Below are five proofs. Each contains errors of annotation. (The wffs are not wrong, but the reasons that justify them are not well stated and/or the proper stars are not given.) Identify the errors and correct them by putting a circle around the faulty annotation and writing the proper annotation in the margins.

1. To prove: that the wffs $(q \supset r)$, p, and $(p \supset q)$ logically imply r.

     1. $(q \supset r)$ RP
     2. p RP
$*_3$ 3. $(p \supset q)$ S
$*_2$ 4. q $MP_{1,2}$
     5. r $MP_{1,4}$

2. To prove: that the wffs $(s \supset p)$, $\sim p$, and $((t \lor \sim s) \supset q)$ logically imply q.

     1. $(s \supset p)$ RP
     2. $\sim p$ RP
     3. $((t \lor \sim s) \supset q)$ RP
     4. $\sim s$ $MP_{1,2}$
     5. $(t \lor \sim s)$ Λ_4
     6. q $MP_{3,5}$

3. To prove: that q, $((\sim p \supset \sim q) \lor r)$, and $\sim r$ logically imply p.

```
      1. q                          RP
      2. ((~p ⊃ ~q) ∨ r)           RP
      3. ~r                         RP
      4. (~p ⊃ ~q)                 DS₂,₃
      5. ~~q                        RP₁
      6. ~~p                        MT₄,₅
      7. p                          Sub₆
```

4. To prove: that $(\sim p \vee q)$ and $(\sim r \supset \sim q)$ logically imply $(p \supset r)$.

```
       1. (~p ∨ q)                 RP
       2. (~r ⊃ ~q)                RP
  *₃   3. p                        RP
  *₃   4. ~~p                      Sub₃
  *₃   5. q                        HS₁,₄
  *₃   6. ~~q                      Sub₅
  *₃   7. ~~r                      MT₂,₆
  *₃   8. r                        Sub₇
       9. (p ⊃ r)                  Cd*₃,₉
```

5. To prove: that $\sim(p \ \& \ \sim q)$, $(\sim q \vee r)$, and p logically imply r.

```
       1. ~(p & ~q)               RP
  *₂   2. (~q ∨ r)                RP
       3. p                        RP
  *₄   4. ~r                       Red
  *₄   5. ~q                       DS₂,₄
  *₂*₄ 6. (p & ~q)                HS₃,₅
       7. ~~r                      Red*₄,1,6
       8. r                        S₇
```

Ex. 3 Complete phrases 1 to 8 below, selecting your responses from the following list.

A. From A and $(A \supset B)$, infer B.

B. From A and $(A \supset B)$, infer A.

C. From $\sim B$ and $(A \supset B)$, infer $\sim A$.

D. From $\sim A$ and $(A \supset B)$, infer $\sim B$.

E. From $(A \vee B)$ and $\sim A$, infer B.

F. From A, infer $(A \vee B)$.

G. From $(A \ \& \ B)$, infer B.

H. From A and from B, infer $(B \ \& \ A)$.

I. From $(B \supset C)$ and $(C \supset D)$, infer $(B \supset D)$.

J. From $(B \supset C)$ and $(B \vee C)$, infer $(C \vee D)$.

K. From $(A \vee C)$, $(A \supset D)$ and $(C \supset B)$ infer $(D \vee B)$.

L. From a contradiction infer the negation of one of its assumptions.

M. From a wff A on a line with an assumption infer the conditional 'If the assumption, then A.'

N. Introduce any wff of P as an explicit assumption.

_____ 1. The rule of hypothetical syllogism allows . . .

_____ 2. Disjunctive syllogism allows . . .

_____ 3. The rule of conditionalization allows . . .

_____ 4. The rule of reduction allows . . .

_____ 5. Modus ponens allows . . .

_____ 6. The rule of conjunction allows . . .

_____ 7. Modus tollens allows . . .

_____ 8. The rule of constructive dilemma allows . . .

Ex. 4 Check your answers for Ex. 2 before going on. Provide a correct annotation for each of the following proofs.

1. To prove: that $(p \supset (q \supset r))$, $((\sim r \lor s) \& p)$, and $\sim s$ logically imply $\sim q$.

    1. $(p \supset (q \supset r))$
    2. $((\sim r \lor s) \& p)$
    3. $\sim s$
    4. $(\sim r \lor s)$
    5. $\sim r$
    6. p
    7. $(q \supset r)$
    8. $\sim q$

2. To prove: that the wffs $((p \& q) \supset r)$, $(s \supset (p \& t))$, and s logically imply $(q \supset r)$.

    1. $((p \& q) \supset r)$
    2. $(s \supset (p \& t))$
    3. s
    4. $(p \& t)$
    5. p
    6. $(p \supset (q \supset r))$
    7. $(q \supset r)$

3. To prove: that the wffs $(p \equiv q)$, $(\sim q \lor r)$, and $((s \lor t) \& \sim (r \& \sim q))$ logically imply $(p \equiv r)$.

    1. $(p \equiv q)$
    2. $(\sim q \lor r)$
    3. $((s \lor t) \& \sim (r \& \sim q))$
    4. $\sim (r \& \sim q)$
    5. $(r \supset q)$
    6. $((p \supset q) \& (q \supset p))$
    7. $(q \supset p)$
    8. $(r \supset p)$
    9. $(q \supset r)$
    10. $(p \supset q)$
    11. $(p \supset r)$
    12. $((p \supset r) \& (r \supset p))$
    13. $(p \equiv r)$

4. To prove: that $(r \supset p)$, $(s \supset q)$, and $((p \& q) \supset t)$ logically imply $((r \& s) \supset t)$.

    1. $(r \supset p)$
    2. $(s \supset q)$
    3. $((p \& q) \supset t)$
    4. $(r \& s)$
    5. r
    6. p
    7. s
    8. q

9. $(p \ \& \ q)$
10. t
11. $((r \ \& \ s) \supset t)$

5. To prove: that the wffs $\sim s$, $(\sim (r \ \& \ q) \vee s)$, $(\sim r \supset r)$, and $(\sim p \supset (q \ \& \ t))$ logically imply p.

1. $\sim s$
2. $(\sim (r \ \& \ q) \vee s)$
3. $(\sim r \supset r)$
4. $(\sim p \supset (q \ \& \ t))$
5. $(\sim\sim r \vee r)$
6. $(\sim\sim r \vee \sim\sim r)$
7. $\sim\sim r$
8. $\sim (r \ \& \ q)$
9. $(\sim r \vee \sim q)$
10. $\sim q$
11. $(\sim q \vee \sim t)$
12. $\sim (q \ \& \ t)$
13. $\sim\sim p$
14. p

Ex. 5 Below are some reasons—some good, some bad, and some inappropriate—why a rule of inference is justifiable. The annotation of a proof lists the rules of inference which apply to the lines of the proof. Take the *corrected* annotations for Ex. 4, items 4 and 5, and select the reason from the following list by virtue of which each line is justified. For example, for item 3 of Ex. 2, the lines are justified by: (1) J; (2) J; (3) M; (4) M; (5) M.

J. In a natural deduction what is proved is not that the conclusion is true but that the conclusion is a valid consequence of its premises or assumptions.
K. Any statement logically implies a tautology.
L. This rule is a formalized statement of a valid proof strategy.
M. The conclusion of this inference is such that if it were made the consequent of a conditional whose antecedents were the premises of this inference, the conditional proposition formed would be tautological.
N. Every statement follows logically from some statement.

SELECTED ANSWERS
TO EXERCISES FOR MODULE 44

Ex. 2

1.	3.	$(p \supset q)$	RP
	4.	q	$MP_{2,3}$
2.	4.	s	$MT_{1,2}$
3.	5.	$\sim\sim q$	Sub_1
4.	$*_3$ 3.	p	RA
	$*_3$ 5.	q	$DS_{1,4}$
	9.	$(p \supset r)$	$Cd_{*_3,8}$
5.	2.	$(\sim q \vee r)$	RP
	$*_4$ 4.	$\sim r$	RA
	$*_4$ 6.	$(p \ \& \ \sim q)$	$C_{3,5}$

If you missed any, review the appropriate section or sections from **43:2.1** to **44:1.2**.

Ex. 3

1. I   2. E   3. M   4. L
5. A   6. H   7. C   8. K

If you missed any review the statement of that rule.

Ex. 4

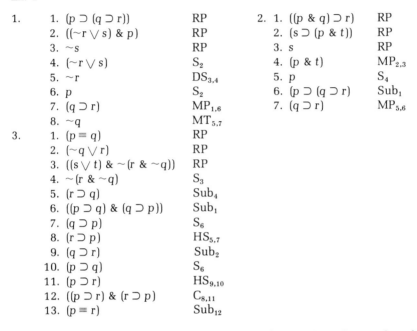

1. 1. $(p \supset (q \supset r))$ RP
    2. $((\sim r \lor s)\ \&\ p)$ RP
    3. $\sim s$ RP
    4. $(\sim r \lor s)$ S_2
    5. $\sim r$ $DS_{3,4}$
    6. p S_2
    7. $(q \supset r)$ $MP_{1,6}$
    8. $\sim q$ $MT_{5,7}$

2. 1. $((p\ \&\ q) \supset r)$ RP
    2. $(s \supset (p\ \&\ t))$ RP
    3. s RP
    4. $(p\ \&\ t)$ $MP_{2,3}$
    5. p S_4
    6. $(p \supset (q \supset r))$ Sub_1
    7. $(q \supset r)$ $MP_{5,6}$

3. 1. $(p \equiv q)$ RP
    2. $(\sim q \lor r)$ RP
    3. $((s \lor t)\ \&\ \sim(r\ \&\ \sim q))$ RP
    4. $\sim(r\ \&\ \sim q)$ S_3
    5. $(r \supset q)$ Sub_4
    6. $((p \supset q)\ \&\ (q \supset p))$ Sub_1
    7. $(q \supset p)$ S_6
    8. $(r \supset p)$ $HS_{5,7}$
    9. $(q \supset r)$ Sub_2
   10. $(p \supset q)$ S_6
   11. $(p \supset r)$ $HS_{9,10}$
   12. $((p \supset r)\ \&\ (r \supset p))$ $C_{8,11}$
   13. $(p \equiv r)$ Sub_{12}

In a larger proof like this, it helps to see your goal. Once the inference from line 12 to line 13 is clear, you can see that your object is to prove lines 8 and 11.

4. 1. $(r \supset p)$ RP
    2. $(s \supset q)$ RP
    3. $((p\ \&\ q) \supset t)$ RP
    $*_4$ 4. $(r\ \&\ s)$ RA
    $*_4$ 5. r S_4
    $*_4$ 6. p $MP_{1,5}$
    $*_4$ 7. s S_4
    $*_4$ 8. q $MP_{2,7}$
    $*_4$ 9. $(p\ \&\ q)$ $C_{8,6}$
    $*_4$ 10. t $MP_{3,9}$
   11. $((r\ \&\ s) \supset t)$ $Cd_{*_4,10}$

5. 1. $\sim s$ RP
    2. $(\sim(r\ \&\ q) \lor s)$ RP
    3. $(\sim r \supset r)$ RP
    4. $(\sim p \supset (q\ \&\ t))$ RP
    5. $(\sim\sim r \lor r)$ Sub_3

6. $(\sim\sim r \lor \sim\sim r)$		Sub$_5$†
7. $\sim\sim r$		Sub$_6$† (or Sub$_3$)
8. $\sim(r \,\&\, q)$		DS$_{1,2}$
9. $(\sim r \lor \sim q)$		Sub$_8$
10. $\sim q$		DS$_{7,9}$
11. $(\sim q \lor \sim t)$		A$_{10}$
12. $\sim(q \,\&\, t)$		Sub$_{11}$
13. $\sim\sim p$		MT$_{4,12}$
14. p		Sub$_{13}$

If you missed more than five lines of the above annotations, make a careful review of 43:2.1 to 44:2.1.

Ex. 5

4.	1. J	5.	1. J
	3. J		3. J
	5. M		5. M
	7. M		7. L
	9. L		

MODULE 45

THE TECHNIQUES OF NATURAL DEDUCTION— PROPOSITIONAL LOGIC

You have learned the rules of inference in our system and how to annotate a proof showing the deriviation and the justification of each line. Now it's time to learn the techniques and study the strategies you can use to demonstrate that certain arguments are valid.

● After reading Module 45 you should be able to:

1. Construct natural deduction proofs
2. Demonstrate the validity of propositional logic arguments using the natural deduction system P

45:1.1 Clues Whenever you are constructing a natural deduction, you are, in effect, puzzling out a mystery. You need to be sharp and discerning. Accordingly it is good strategy to collect as many clues as you can. The first step in your strategy will be to look at the conclusion you are trying to deduce. You should notice both its form and its relation to the premises. By its form we mean whether it is a negated or unnegated formula and whether it is a conjunction, a disjunction, a conditional, a biconditional, or a simple statement unit. The strategies most likely to allow you to deduce a particular conclusion are determined partially by the form of the conclusion.

After establishing the form of the conclusion, you will want to notice the relation of the conclusion to the premises. There are only a few possibilities.

---

† Steps 5 and 6 are superfluous, but perhaps intuitively helpful.

1. The conclusion or its equivalent occurs, asserted or negated, as a part of one of the premises.
2. At least one of the statement letters of the conclusion does not occur, either asserted or negated, in any premise, and at least one does occur.
3. All the conclusion's statement letters do occur in the premises, asserted or negated, but they occur spread out over at least two premise lines.
4. All the conclusion's statement letters are in one of the premises but not in a form equivalent to the conclusion.
5. The conclusion occurs, asserted or negated, as one of the premises.
6. None of the conclusion's statement letters occurs, asserted or negated, in the premises.

The strategies and rules of inference that will be most helpful to you are determined not only by the form of the conclusion but also by which of these six relations holds between premises and conclusion.

We will start to show the usefulness of these clues by examining fourteen examples. Eventually we will construct natural deductions for each of them. As your first step toward constructing the deductions determine the form of each of the conclusions and the relation of each to its premises.

EG. 45.1 $(p \supset q) \qquad /\therefore r$
$(t \ \& \ p)$
$(q \supset r)$

EG. 45.2 $(p \lor r) \qquad /\therefore \sim(q \supset s)$
$\sim r$
$(p \supset (q \ \& \ \sim s)$

EG. 45.3 $(q \supset r) \qquad /\therefore r$
$(\sim r \supset \sim p)$
$(p \lor q)$

EG. 45.4 $(p \ \& \ q) \qquad /\therefore (r \ \& \ s)$
$(p \supset r)$
$(\sim s \supset \sim q)$

EG. 45.5 $(\sim p \supset (r \ \& \ \sim s)) \qquad /\therefore \sim(t \lor s)$
$(q \lor \sim t)$
$\sim q$
$(t \equiv p)$

EG. 45.6 $(p \supset r) \qquad /\therefore (r \lor q)$
$(\sim s \supset q)$
$\sim q$
$(\sim s \lor p)$

EG. 45.7 $(\sim q \equiv p) \qquad /\therefore (\sim r \lor s)$
$((q \lor \sim r) \lor s)$
p

EG. 45.8 $[((p \ \& \ q) \supset r) \ \& \ \sim s] /\therefore \sim p$
$((q \supset r) \supset (s \lor t))$
$\sim t$

EG. 45.9 $(p \equiv q) \qquad /\therefore (p \ \& \ q)$
$(p \lor q)$

EG. 45.10 $(q \lor \sim s) \qquad /\therefore (s \supset (r \supset p))$
$(t \equiv q)$
$((t \ \& \ r) \supset p)$

EG. 45.11 $(p \supset q) \qquad /\therefore (r \equiv s)$
$(\sim r \supset \sim q)$
$(\sim s \lor p)$
s

EG. 45.12 $((p \supset q) \supset r) \qquad /\therefore \sim(p \equiv q)$
$(\sim r \lor s)$
$(s \supset (q \ \& \ \sim p))$

EG. 45.13 No premises $\qquad /\therefore (p \supset (q \supset p))$

EG. 45.14 $(p \supset r) \qquad /\therefore \sim p$
$(p \supset q)$
$(\sim q \lor \sim r)$

Partial answers are as follows.

Eg. 45.1. The conclusion is a simple asserted statement unit. It occurs as the consequent of the third premise.

Eg. 45.2: The conclusion is a negated conditional. It is equivalent to the consequent of the third premise.

Eg. 45.3: The conclusion is a simple asserted statement unit, the consequent of the first premise.

Eg. 45.4: The conclusion is a conjunction, the first conjunct being the consequent of the second premise and the second conjunct being the statement letter which is negated in the antecedent of the third premise.

Eg. 45.5: The conclusion is a negated disjunction, the first disjunct occurring negated as the second disjunct in the second premise and asserted in the biconditional fourth premise, and the second disjunct occurring negated as the second conjunct forming the consequent of the conditional first premise.

Eg. 45.13: The conclusion is a conditional, the consequent of which is itself a conditional such that its consequent is also the antecedent of the main conditional. Since the deduction has no premises provided, the statement letters do not occur in any premises provided in the material given in this example.

45:1.2 Deriving statement units The information you have just gathered concerning the form of the conclusion and its relation to the premises will aid you in deducing the conclusions of these problems. But you need to put the information together with what you know about the rules of inference. Since different rules work on different forms of premises and conclusions, let's look at several examples. The conclusions of Egs. 45.1, 45.3, 45.8, and 45.14 are all simple statement units, negated or asserted. None of these conclusions occurs, asserted or negated, as a premise. This means that you must ask: What rules allow me to infer a single statement letter? Reviewing the rules you can see that there is modus ponens, modus tollens, disjunctive syllogism, simplification, substitution (from the double negation of the conclusion or from the alternation of the conclusion with itself), and rule of reductio. No other rules allow you to conclude either a single statement unit or its negation unless the conclusion is already one of the premise lines.

48:2.1 Let us now look at Eg. 45.1.

EG. 45.1 $(p \supset q)$ $/ \therefore r$
     $(t \ \& \ p)$
     $(q \supset r)$

We have already observed that the conclusion r is the consequent of the conditional third premise. We have now noted the rules that can possibly shake a single letter loose. Since r is the consequent of a conditional, you should think of modus ponens as a likely rule to employ. Using it requires getting q alone as a line of proof. Since the only other occurrence of q is as the consequent of the first premise, another use of modus ponens is indicated, this one requiring having p alone as a line of proof. The second premise being a conjunction of t and p, the rule of simplification can be used to infer p. Thus, thinking about how you can deduce r has led you to be able to construct the following proof.

EG. 45.1′ 1. $(p \supset q)$ RP
       2. $(t \ \& \ p)$ RP
       3. $(q \supset r)$ RP
       4. p S_2
       5. q $MP_{1,4}$
       6. r $MP_{3,5}$

Let us now focus on Eg. 45.3, recalling our strategy in Eg. 45.1 as a model to be both used and modified.

EG. 45.3 $(q \supset r)$ $/\therefore r$
          $(\sim r \supset \sim p)$
          $(p \lor q)$

The occurrence of the conclusion as the consequent of the first premise again suggests the use of modus ponens. Similarly the occurrence of the negation of the conclusion as the antecedent of premise 2 suggests the use of modus tollens and double negation. Accordingly you look for a premise from which you can derive either q or $\sim p$. Unfortunately there is no such premise, and so an alternative strategy must be developed. Here it is important for you to have in mind the entire list of rules that might allow r to be deduced. With modus ponens and modus tollens ruled out, and disjunctive syllogism being inapplicable, only simplification, substitution, and rule of reductio are left. Simplification would require deducing from a conjunction in which r was one conjunct, but since r is not part of any conjunction in the premises, simplification is not a promising rule to use here. Fortunately both the remaining rules can form the basis of a proof of the conclusion. If we introduce $\sim r$ as an assumption we will be able to deduce $\sim q$ by modus tollens and $\sim p$ by modus ponens. The conjunction of these two results can then be shown to contradict the third premise by substitution.

EG. 45.3′   1. $(q \supset r)$ RP
              2. $(\sim r \supset \sim p)$ RP
              3. $(p \lor q)$ RP
    $*_4$ 4. $\sim r$ RA
    $*_4$ 5. $\sim p$ MP$_{2,4}$
    $*_4$ 6. $\sim q$ MT$_{1,4}$
    $*_4$ 7. $(\sim p \,\&\, \sim q)$ C$_{5,6}$
          8. $\sim(\sim p \,\&\, \sim q)$ Sub$_3$†
          9. r Red$_{*_4,7,8}$

In its own way, this proof, using the rule of reductio, works out the idea that if either p or q is true then r will be true. You can see it by saying 'if p is true r is,' and 'if q is true r is.' This suggests that you could develop a constructive dilemma with $(p \lor q)$ as the disjunction. To work the constructive dilemma you would need the two premises $(p \supset r)$ and $(q \supset r)$. The latter is premise 1. How is the former related to premise 2, which mentions p and r? Actually, they are equivalent—being technically called *contrapositives*. And so you can write:

EG. 45.3″   1. $(q \supset r)$ RP
            2. $(\sim r \supset \sim p)$ RP
            3. $(p \lor q)$ RP
            4. $(p \supset r)$ Sub$_2$
            5. $(r \lor r)$ CD$_{1,3,4}$
            6. r Sub$_5$

Both these deductions are correct, thereby illustrating that the rules are permissive enough to allow you sometimes to reach the same conclusion by more than one strategy or sequence of lines. As long as each line of a proof is justified by one of the rules, each deduction of the conclusion is equally correct. You are free to develop whichever is more intuitive to you.

---

† See equivalence 6 in the list given in 43:2.3 under the explanation of the rule of substitution. The one we use in Eg. 45.3′ is $((A \lor B) \equiv \sim(\sim A \,\&\, \sim B))$.

Let us now consider Eg. 45.8, which demands the proof of a single negated statement letter. What makes Eg. 45.8 more complex is that a larger number of transformations must be made in order to establish the conclusion. Moreover, typically, some of the crucial transitions, as in Eg. 45.3", depend on recognizing equivalent forms of a given line.

EG. 45.8 $[((p \ \& \ q) \supset r) \ \& \sim s]$ $/ \therefore \sim p$
           $((q \supset r) \supset (s \lor t))$
           $\sim t$

The statement letter in the conclusion is found unnegated in the antecedent of a conditional in premise 1. If it could be there alone—without the conjunct q—the conclusion might be obtained first by simplifying premise 1 down to its first conjunct (the conditional) and then by applying modus tollens. This leaves us with two crucial questions—how to remove q from the antecedent and where to find the negation of the consequent. The rule of substitution comes to your aid to answer each of these questions: $((p \ \& \ q) \supset r)$ is equivalent to $(p \supset (q \supset r))$. So now you can get $\sim p$ if you can get $\sim (q \supset r)$. Since $(q \supset r)$ is the antecedent of premise 2, you begin to look for another application of modus tollens. What you need is $\sim (s \lor t)$. What you clearly have in premises 1 and 3, respectively, is $\sim s$ and $\sim t$. Here again substitution is crucial: $\sim (s \lor t)$ is equivalent to $(\sim s \ \& \sim t)$. You are now ready to write your deduction, which should go as follows.

EG. 45.8′
   1. $[((p \ \& \ q) \supset r) \ \& \sim s]$ RP
   2. $((q \supset r) \supset (s \lor t))$ RP
   3. $\sim t$ RP
   4. $((p \ \& \ q) \supset r)$ S_1
   5. $(p \supset (q \supset r))$ Sub_4
   6. $\sim s$ S_1
   7. $(\sim s \ \& \sim t)$ $C_{3,6}$
   8. $\sim (s \lor t)$ Sub_7
   9. $\sim (q \supset r)$ $MT_{8,2}$
  10. $\sim p$ $MT_{5,9}$

You should not be disturbed that in both uses of modus tollens it is not a simple statement unit which is negated. Remember that in the statement of the rule "From $(A \supset B)$ and $\sim B$ infer $\sim A$," A and B can stand for any wffs, however complex. Many of the more complex deductions require applying the rules to complex wffs.

Here are two more examples of arguments whose conclusions are statement units.

EG. 45.15 $(p \supset (r \ \& \ s))$ $/ \therefore s$
           $\sim q$
           $(q \lor p)$

EG. 45.16 $(r \lor s)$ $/ \therefore r$
           $(s \supset t)$
           $(\sim t \lor r)$

See if you can construct a proof of each. Since you know the form of the conclusion, you should gather your clues by determining where the conclusion occurs in the premises and by recalling the rules for deriving single statement units. After working your own deduction you may examine those below. Remember that you may have a correct alternative deduction.

EG. 45.15' 1. $(p \supset (r \ \& \ s))$ RP
        2. $\sim q$ RP
        3. $(q \lor p)$ RP
        4. p $DS_{2,3}$
        5. $(r \ \& \ s)$ $MP_{1,4}$
        6. s S_5

EG. 45.16' 1. $(r \lor s)$ RP
        2. $(s \supset t)$ RP
        3. $(\sim t \lor r)$ RP
        4. $(t \supset r)$ Sub_3
        5. $(s \supset r)$ $HS_{3,4}$
  $*_6$ 6. $\sim r$ RA
  $*_6$ 7. $\sim s$ $MT_{5,6}$
  $*_6$ 8. r $DS_{7,1}$
      9. $\sim\sim r$ $Red_{*_6,6,8}$
    10. r Sub_9

45:2.2 Deriving conjunctions Having in mind the strategies for deducing a statement letter or a negated statement letter, we may pass on to strategies for deducing conjunctions. Clearly if the whole conjunct exists as a unit, the strategies for deducing it are the same as those for deducing a single statement letter for the simple reason that you can treat the conjunction as a simple unit. Usually, however, you will find part of the conjunction in one premise line and part in another. In this case your strategy will be to develop intermediate proofs of each conjunct and then use the rule of conjunction to bring them together to form the overall conclusion. When each unit of the conjunction is a simple statement letter, your strategy will become one of the strategies for deriving a single statement letter discussed in 45:2.1. If one or both of the conjuncts is complex, then you will need to turn to the strategies we will be developing for whatever logical operations are involved. Let's look at Eg. 45.4.

EG. 45.4 $(p \ \& \ q)$ $/\therefore (r \ \& \ s)$
        $(p \supset r)$
        $(\sim s \supset \sim q)$

Since r and s occur separately in the premises, systematic proofs of each are in order.

EG. 45.4' 1. $(p \ \& \ q)$ RP
        2. $(p \supset r)$ RP
        3. $(\sim s \supset \sim q)$ RP
        4. p S_1
        5. r $MP_{2,4}$
        6. $(q \supset s)$ Sub_3 6. q S_1
        7. q S_1 7. $\sim\sim q$ Sub_6
        8. s $MP_{1,6}$ or   8. $\sim\sim s$ $MT_{3,7}$
        9. $(r \ \& \ s)$ $C_{6,8}$ 9. s Sub_8
                                      10. $(r \ \& \ s)$ $C_{6,9}$

As indicated earlier, the strategies for proving simple statement-letter conclusions are the same whether those units are negated or unnegated. Once one gets into conclusions which are complex units this rule does not hold. For example, suppose the conclusion you are to derive is $\sim(p \ \& \ q)$. This conclusion is not a *conjunction* at all, appearances to the contrary. It is a *negation* which truth-table analysis reveals to be equivalent to the *disjunction* $(\sim p \lor \sim q)$. Accordingly the procedures appropriate for proving this conclusion are those, not yet indicated, for deriving disjunctions. However, if indeed the negation of a conjunction is a disjunction, as we have just seen, the negation of a disjunction and the negation of a conditional are both equivalent to conjunctions: $\sim(A \lor B)$ is equivalent to $(\sim A \,\&\, \sim B)$; and $\sim(A \supset B)$ is equivalent to $(A \,\&\, \sim B)$. The upshot of these latter two equivalences is that if you are to prove something having one of the left-hand forms, you can profitably proceed by aiming to prove something of the right-hand form by the strategies outlined above and then rely on one of the above equivalences to allow the final move to the statement of your conclusion. Example 45.5 provides us with an example of this procedure. See if you can work out a deduction before consulting ours.

EG. 45.5′

1.	$(\sim p \supset (r \,\&\, \sim s))$	RP	$/ \therefore \sim (t \lor s)$
2.	$(q \lor \sim t)$	RP	
3.	$\sim q$	RP	
4.	$(t \equiv p)$	RP	
5.	$\sim t$	$DS_{2,3}$	
6.	$((t \supset p) \,\&\, (p \supset t))$	Sub_4	
7.	$(p \supset t)$	S_6	
8.	$\sim p$	$MT_{5,7}$	
9.	$(r \,\&\, \sim s)$	$MP_{1,8}$	
10.	$\sim s$	S_9	
11.	$(\sim t \,\&\, \sim s)$	$C_{5,10}$	
12.	$\sim (t \lor s)$	Sub_{11}	

Here are two more examples of arguments whose conclusions are conjunctions.

EG. 45.17 $((p \,\&\, r) \lor (p \,\&\, s))$ $/ \therefore (p \,\&\, t)$
$\ (\sim t \supset q)$
$\ \sim q$

EG. 45.18 $((p \,\&\, r) \lor (p \,\&\, s))$ $/ \therefore (p \,\&\, r)$
$\ (p \supset q)$
$\ (q \lor \sim s)$

See if you can construct a proof for each. Remember to figure out the form in which the conclusion letters are found in the premises. In Eg. 45.17 the proof of t is easy enough. Scrutinizing shows that the proof of p can come only from the first premise. So what rules are relevant to use? In Eg. 45.18 $(p \,\&\, r)$ can be obtained if $\sim(p \,\&\, s)$ can be found and disjunctive syllogism can be used. So how can you manipulate premises 2 and 3 to obtain $\sim(p \,\&\, s)$?

EG. 45.17′

1.	$((p \,\&\, r) \lor (p \,\&\, s))$	RP
2.	$(\sim t \supset q)$	RP
3.	$\sim q$	RP
4.	$\sim \sim t$	$MT_{2,3}$
5.	t	Sub_4
6.	$(p \,\&\, (r \lor s))$	Sub_1
7.	p	S_6
8.	$(p \,\&\, t)$	$C_{5,7}$

EG. 45.18′

1.	$((p \,\&\, r) \lor (p \,\&\, s))$	RP
2.	$(p \supset q)$	RP
3.	$(q \supset \sim s)$	RP

4. $(p \supset \sim s)$		$HS_{2,3}$
5. $\sim(p \& s)$		Sub_4
6. $(p \& r)$		$DS_{1,5}$

48:2.3 Suppose you are trying to *prove a conditional statement*. What rules of inference might you use? Of course if your conditional occurs intact in the premises, you can go after it as though it were a simple unit. Probably, though, the antecedent and consequent of the conditional will be in different lines. Then hypothetical syllogism may be in order, as in:

EG. 45.19 $(p \supset q)$ $/\therefore (p \supset r)$
                  $(q \supset r)$

Or you may need to use substitutions before employing hypothetical syllogism, as in:

EG. 45.20 $(\sim p \lor q)$ $/\therefore (p \supset r)$
                  $(\sim r \supset \sim q)$

The premises in Eg. 45.20 are equivalent to those in Eg. 45.19, and so after appropriate substitutions, hypothetical syllogism can again be employed.

Now consider Eg. 45.10.

EG. 45.10 $(q \lor \sim s)$ $/\therefore (s \supset (r \supset p))$
                $(t \equiv q)$
                $((t \& r) \supset p)$

This example is only a bit tougher. Just remember that the conditional $(r \supset p)$ is the consequent of the larger conditional you want to prove. Now you can set up two uses of hypothetical syllogism by the proper transformations of each premise. Try to work out your own deduction before looking at the one that follows.

EG. 45.10′
1. $(q \lor \sim s)$		RP
2. $(t \equiv q)$		RP
3. $((t \& r) \supset p)$		RP
4. $(s \supset q)$		Sub_1
5. $((t \supset q) \& (q \supset t))$		Sub_2
6. $(t \supset (r \supset p))$		Sub_3
7. $(q \supset t)$		S_5
8. $(s \supset t)$		$HS_{4,7}$
9. $(s \supset (r \supset p))$		$HS_{6,8}$

When you want to prove a conditional assertion, you can also make effective use of the strategy of conditional proof. Begin by assuming the antecedent by the rule of assumption, and then deduce the consequent. Then you can reach the desired conclusion by conditionalization. Start again from the three premises above and see what deduction will be possible if we assume s. You can now get along with less reliance on the rule of substitution.

EG. 45.10″
	1. $(q \lor \sim s)$		RP
	2. $(t \equiv q)$		RP
	3. $((t \& r) \supset p)$		RP
$\Vert_4$	1. ε		RA
$*_4$	5. $\sim\sim s$		Sub_4
$*_4$	6. q		$DS_{1,5}$
	7. $((t \supset q) \& (q \supset t))$		Sub_2

8. $(q \supset t)$	S_7
*₄ 9. t	$MP_{6,8}$
10. $(t \supset (r \supset p))$	$Sub_3.$
*₄ 11. $(r \supset p)$	$MP_{9,10}$
12. $(s \supset (r \supset p))$	$Cd_{*_4,11}$

As this deduction illustrates, the usual effect of assuming the antecedent of a conditional conclusion is that you will then rely more on the rules of disjunctive syllogism, modus ponens, and modus tollens.

When your conclusion is of the conditional form $(A \supset B)$, the possibility of using conditional proof should be clear to you. The usefulness of conditional proof, however, is much broader, partly because of formulas that are equivalent to conditionals. (Our point here is parallel to the point about extending strategies for proving conjunctions to formulas equivalent to them.) Here you should bear in mind that $(A \supset B)$ is equivalent to $\sim(A \,\&\, \sim B)$ and similarly $(A \supset B)$ is equivalent to $(\sim A \lor B)$. Consider Eg. 45.7.

EG. 45.7 $(\sim q \equiv p)$ $/\therefore (\sim r \lor s)$
        $((q \lor \sim r) \lor s)$
        p

Since $(\sim r \lor s)$ is equivalent to $(r \supset s)$, you can construct a proof of EG. 45.7 by assuming r, the negation of the first disjunct, and then deducing s, the second disjunct. Conditionalization will then give you $(r \supset s)$, and substitution will get you the desired conclusion. Try to construct the proof before looking at our deduction.

EG. 45.7′

	1. $(\sim q \equiv p)$	RP
	2. $((q \lor \sim r) \lor s)$	RP
	3. p	RP
	4. $((\sim q \supset p) \,\&\, (p \supset \sim q))$	Sub_1
	5. $(p \supset \sim q)$	S_4
	6. $\sim q$	$MP_{4,5}$
*₇	7. r	RA
*₇	8. $(\sim q \,\&\, r)$	$C_{6,7}$
*₇	9. $\sim(q \lor \sim r)$	Sub_8
*₇	10. s	$DS_{2,9}$
	11. $(r \supset s)$	$Cd_{*_7,10}$
	12. $(\sim r \lor s)$	Sub_{11}

The negation of a biconditional may look forbidding, but if you notice that it too is equivalent to a conditional, then you can recognize the strategies you may use to deduce such a conclusion. Consider Eg. 45.12.

EG. 45.12 $((p \supset q) \supset r)$ $/\therefore \sim(p \equiv q)$
                $(\sim r \lor s)$
                $(s \supset (q \,\&\, \sim p))$

One way of understanding the negation of a biconditional is as asserting that if the conditional works one way, then it fails to work the other way. That is, $\sim(A \equiv B)$ is equivalent to $(A \supset B) \supset \sim(B \supset A)$. Looking at the right-hand side of this equivalence you can see that the consequent $\sim(B \supset A)$ can be rewritten as the conjunction $(B \,\&\, \sim A)$. So to prove $\sim(A \equiv B)$ you can assume $(A \supset B)$ and deduce $(B \,\&\, \sim A)$. See if you can do this for Eg. 45.12.

EG. 45.12'

	1.	$((p \supset q) \supset r)$	RP
	2.	$(\sim r \lor s)$	RP
	3.	$(s \supset (q \ \& \sim p))$	RP
$*_4$	4.	$(p \supset q)$	RA
$*_4$	5.	r	$MP_{1,4}$
$*_4$	6.	$\sim\sim r$	Sub_5
$*_4$	7.	s	$DS_{2,6}$
$*_4$	8.	$(q \ \& \sim p)$	$MP_{3,7}$
	9.	$((p \supset q) \supset (q \ \& \sim p))$	$Cd_{*_4,8}$
	10.	$\sim(p \equiv q)$	Sub_9

45:2.4 Deriving disjunctions and biconditional statements Strictly speaking, you don't really need any further strategies to handle disjunctions or biconditional conclusions. Whether negated or affirmed they are always equivalent to some other formula for which strategies have been provided.

$(A \lor B)$	is equivalent to	$(\sim A \supset B)$
$\sim(A \lor B)$	is equivalent to	$(\sim A \ \& \sim B)$
$(A \equiv B)$	is equivalent to	$((A \supset B) \ \& \ (B \supset A))$
$\sim(A \equiv B)$	is equivalent to	$((A \supset B) \supset (B \ \& \sim A))$

Still there will be times, especially for disjunctions, when some alternative strategies will be assets. In particular you should notice two rules, the rule of addition and the rule of constructive dilemma, which will help you to prove disjunctive conclusions. Consider Eg. 45.6.

EG. 45.6 $(p \supset r)$ $/\therefore (r \lor q)$
             $(\sim s \supset q)$
             $\sim q$
             $(\sim s \lor p)$

Can the rule of addition be used to deduce the conclusion? Since $\sim q$ is a premise you should try to deduce r and then use addition to get $(r \lor q)$.[9] Try it. Now what about constructive dilemma? r and q are consequents of two conditionals, so if you could find a third premise which was a disjunct of the antecedents you would be in business. Here are the two deductions.

EG. 45.6'

1.	$(p \supset r)$	RP
2.	$(\sim s \supset q)$	RP
3.	$\sim q$	RP
4.	$(\sim s \lor p)$	RP
5.	$\sim\sim s$	$MT_{2,3}$
6.	p	$DS_{4,5}$
7.	r	$MP_{1,6}$
8.	$(r \lor q)$	A_7

EG. 45.6''

1.	$(p \supset r)$	RP
2.	$(\sim s \supset q)$	RP
3.	$\sim q$	RP

[9] Recall that A logically implies $(A \lor B)$. If you know that the Olympics are held every 4 years, then you can answer 'Yes' to the question: The Olympics are held every three or four years, aren't they? Or, to give another example, if you bought a house it logically follows that you bought either a car or a house.

4. $(\sim s \lor p)$ RP
5. $(q \lor r)$ $\text{CD}_{1,2,4}$
6. $(r \lor q)$ Sub_5

Notice that Eg. 45.6″ actually ignores premise 3, so it shows that lines 1, 2, and 4 logically imply line 6. Obviously if lines 1, 2, and 4 imply line 6, then lines 1, 2, 3, and 4 imply it also.

45:2.5 The strategies suggested up to now will suffice for most conclusions without too much trouble especially if you keep in mind not only what the conclusion is but also what it is equivalent to. Still there will be some deductions that present peculiarities, as exemplified by Egs. 45.13 and 45.14.

Example 45.13 is odd because it has no premises. It reads simply:

No premises: $/\therefore (p \supset (q \supset p))$

Now you may remember that a conclusion can be deduced when no premises are given if, and only if, it is a tautology, which $(p \supset (q \supset p))$ is. Still, how should the proof go? If you are to apply any rule of inference, you must have at least one premise line to apply it to. So you will need to supply premise lines in these cases, and then get rid of them. Since only the rule of assumption allows you to introduce wffs that are not originally given as premises, you must use it to make some assumptions. These, in turn, allow you to get your proof going. Similarly, since only conditionalization and the rule of reductio allow you to dispatch assumptions, you must use one of these two rules. Try conditionalization on Eg. 45.13 and reductio on Eg. 45.14.

EG. 45.13′ $*_1$ 1. p RA
        $*_1$ 2. $(\sim q \lor p)$ A_1

Right here at premise 2 is the crucial move of the deduction. Having introduced the antecedent of the conditional p, you use p for something else it also is, namely, the consequent of the consequent of the conclusion!

        $*_1$ 3. $(q \supset p)$ Sub_2
           4. $(p \supset (q \supset p))$ $\text{Cd}_{*_1,3}$

EG. 45.14′   1. $(p \supset r)$ RP
            2. $(p \supset q)$ RP
            3. $(\sim q \lor \sim r)$ RP
        $*_4$ 4. $\sim\sim p$ RA
        $*_4$ 5. p Sub_4
        $*_4$ 6. r $\text{MP}_{1,5}$
        $*_4$ 7. q $\text{MP}_{2,5}$
        $*_4$ 8. $(r \,\&\, q)$ $\text{C}_{6,7}$
            9. $(\sim r \lor \sim q)$ Sub_3
           10. $\sim (r \,\&\, q)$ Sub_9
           11. $\sim\sim\sim p$ $\text{Red}_{*_4,8,10}$
           12. $\sim p$ Sub_{11}

45:2.6 The strategies that we have now considered will allow you to deduce any conclusion derivable in our system. The only remaining factor is the complexity of the deduction. Some deductions are long. Many intermediate conclusions must be deduced before the desired conclusion can be inferred. Here you should remember that any strategy you have learned for deducing a conclusion works equally well whether that conclusion is the desired ultimate conclusion of the whole argument or only an intermediate conclusion. For example, the strategies for deducing a conditional proposition remain unchanged whether the conditional is an intermediate or the final conclusion. Here is a rather long deduction for you to work with. You should approach it through a number of substrategies for deducing intermediate conclusions.

EG. 45.21 $(p \supset q)$ $/ \therefore (t \& q)$
      $[\sim r \lor (\sim s \supset (t \& p))]$
      $(\sim r \supset \sim q)$
      $\sim (p \supset s)$

Your conclusion is a conjunction. You will need to deduce each conjunct separately. q occurs most promisingly as the consequent of premise 1. If p can be written as a line, q will follow by modus ponens. t occurs only in premise 2. You will need to figure out first how to eliminate $\sim r$ as an alternative, and then how you can deduce $\sim s$, from which $(t \& p)$ will follow. Try it before you look at one possible correct deduction.

EG. 45.21'   1. $(p \supset q)$ RP
        2. $[\sim r \lor (\sim s \supset (t \& p))]$ RP
        3. $(\sim r \supset \sim q)$ RP
        4. $\sim (p \supset s)$ RP
        5. $(p \& \sim s)$ Sub_4
        6. p S_5
        7. q $\text{MP}_{1,6}$
        8. $\sim\sim q$ Sub_7
        9. $\sim\sim r$ $\text{MT}_{3,8}$
       10. $(\sim s \supset (t \& p))$ $\text{DS}_{2,9}$
       11. $\sim s$ S_5
       12. $(t \& p)$ $\text{MP}_{10,11}$
       13. t S_{12}
       14. $(t \& q)$ $C_{13,7}$

45:3 Chart of rules of thumb   Here is a chart which pulls together all the hints, rules of thumb, and strategies that we have been discussing.

   Note: All these procedures depend on the assumption that the argument is valid. If the argument is valid, you can demonstrate its validity if you follow these steps.

Step 1   Identify the form of the conclusion as one of: A, $\sim A$, $(A \& B)$ $\sim (A \& B)$, $(A \lor B)$, $\sim (A \lor B)$, $(A \supset B)$, $\sim (A \supset B)$, $(A \equiv B)$, $\sim (A \equiv B)$.

Step 2   Note the relationship of the conclusion to the premises. The possibilities are:

  (i) The conclusion or its equivalent occurs intact asserted or negated as a part of one of the premises.
 (ii) At least one of the statement letters of the conclusion does not occur in any premise, and at least one does occur.
(iii) All the statement letters of the conclusion occur in the premises but not all occur in the same premise.
(iv) All the conclusion's statement letters occur in one premise but not in a form equivalent to the conclusion.

(v) The conclusion occurs asserted or negated as one of the premises.

(vi) None of the statement letters of the conclusion occurs in any of the premises.

Step 3a Follow these suggestions if (i), (ii), (iii), or (iv) of Step 2 is true.

Working for	Use
1. A statement letter or the negation of a statement letter	Use modus ponens, modus tollens, disjunctive syllogism, simplification, or substitution, with direct proof; or substitution especially after indirect proof and reduction.
2. $(A \ \& \ B)$	Work for A and work for B; then use conjunction.
3. $\sim(A \ \& \ B)$	Work for the equivalent disjunction, $(\sim A \lor \sim B)$.
4. $(A \lor B)$	Work for A and infer $(A \lor B)$ by addition or use constructive dilemma, or assume $\sim A$, work for B, conditionalize to $(\sim A \supset B)$, and infer $(A \lor B)$ by substitution.
5. $\sim(A \lor B)$	Work for the equivalent conjunction, $(\sim A \ \& \ \sim B)$
6. $(A \supset B)$	Assume A by using RA, then work for B and use conditionalization to infer $(A \supset B)$. Sometimes hypothetical syllogism is useful here too.
7. $\sim(A \supset B)$	Work for the equivalent conjunction $(A \ \& \ \sim B)$.
8. $(A \equiv B)$	Assume A by using RA, then infer B, and use conditionalization to get $(A \supset B)$; then assume B by using RA, then infer A, and use conditionalization to get $(B \supset A)$. Finally use conjunction to get $((A \supset B) \ \& \ (B \supset A))$, then substitution for $(A \equiv B)$.
9. $\sim(A \equiv B)$	Work for $((A \supset B) \supset (B \ \& \ \sim A))$ using the strategies outlined above for conditionals and conjunctions.
10. $(A \supset A)$	To derive $(A \supset A)$, or any other tautology, the best strategies are conditionalization and reduction.

11. Note: The only rule that can be used to break apart $(A \equiv B)$ is substitution. In other words if a biconditional occurs as a premise required in a deduction, then the first step you will always need to take with that biconditional is to translate it into an equivalent form, usually as follows: $(A \equiv B)$ is equivalent to $((A \supset B) \ \& \ (B \supset A))$, and to $((\sim A \lor B) \ \& \ (\sim B \lor A))$, and to $(\sim(A \ \& \ \sim B) \ \& \ \sim(B \ \& \ \sim A))$, and to $((A \ \& \ B) \lor (\sim A \ \& \ \sim B))$.

Step 3b If either (v) or (vi) of Step 2 is true, then follow these strategies:

(v) The conclusion occurs asserted as a premise. Infer the conclusion from that premise by substitution on the basis of the tautology $(A \equiv A)$. Suppose the conclusion occurs negated as a premise. With a conclusion A and a premise of the form $\sim A$, the only way the argument is going to be valid is if the rest of the premises $(B \ \& \ C)$ contradict $\sim A$. In other words in a case of this sort you are, in effect, proving that the premises are inconsistent by deriving $\sim((B \ \& \ C) \ \& \ \sim A)$. Begin by assuming that $\sim A$ is true; use the rule of assumption as, say, line 1. When you reach $\sim((B \ \& \ C) \& \ \sim A)$, you have actually constructed a reduction-to-contradiction argument. You can finish your deduction with:

$*_i$ (n)	$\sim((B \ \& \ C) \ \& \ \sim A)$	ANN
$*_i$ (n + 1)	$(p \ \& \ \sim p)$	Sub_n
$*_i$ (n + 2)	p	S_{n+1}
$*_i$ (n + 3)	$\sim p$	S_{n+2}
(n + 4)	$\sim\sim A$	$\text{Red}_{n+2,n+3,*_i}$
(n + 5)	A	Sub_{n+4}

(vi) None of the statement letters of the conclusion occurs in the premises. An argument of this sort will be valid only if the conclusion is a tautology. Technically one might construct an adequate deduction by deriving any tautology and inferring the conclusion by substitution since all tautologies are logically equivalent. If you are aiming for a more intuitive deduction or if you attend to the restriction suggested in footnote 5 in 43:2.3 then your best procedure for deriving tautologies will be reduction and conditionalization.

The following three deductions were derived using the rules of thumb charted above.

EG. 45.2 $(p \lor r)$ $/\therefore \sim(q \supset s)$
$\sim r$
$(p \supset (q \ \& \sim s))$

EG. 45.2' Step 1. The conclusion is of the form $\sim(A \supset B)$.
Step 2. The conclusion is equivalent to the $(q \ \& \sim s)$ which occurs in premise 3.
Step 3a. Seek to use modus ponens to break off $(q \ \& \sim s)$. Work for p to use with premise 3 and modus ponens. Use $\sim r$, premise 1, and disjunctive syllogism to get p.

1. $(p \lor r)$ RP
2. $\sim r$ RP
3. $(p \supset (q \ \& \sim s))$ RP
4. p $DS_{1,2}$
5. $(q \ \& \sim s)$ $MP_{3,4}$
6. $\sim(q \supset s)$ Sub_5

EG. 45.9 $(p \equiv q)$ $/\therefore (p \ \& \ q)$
$(p \lor q)$

EG. 45.9' Step 1. Work for a conclusion that is a conjunction.
Step 2. Possibility (iv) applies.
Step 3a. First thoughts are to try to pull p and q out of the two premises. Note 11 suggests that we must try to reformulate premise 1.

1. $(p \equiv q)$ RP $/\therefore (p \ \& \ q)$
2. $(p \lor q)$ RP
3. $(p \ \& \ q) \lor (\sim p \ \& \sim q)$ Sub_1

Having used the equivalence in line 3 it now becomes clear that $(p \ \& \ q)$, the conclusion, occurs intact as a part of one line. We can now try to break it out using disjunctive syllogism.
4. $\sim(\sim p \ \& \sim q)$ Sub_2
5. $(p \ \& \ q)$ $DS_{4,3}$

EG. 45.11 $(p \supset q)$ $/\therefore (r \equiv s)$
$(\sim r \supset \sim q)$
$(\sim s \lor p)$
s

EG. 45.11' Step. 1. Work for a biconditional.
Step 2. Option (iii) applies.

Step 3a. Try to pull r out; s is already available as premise 4. Follow strategy 8.

	1. $(p \supset q)$	RP	$/\therefore (r \equiv s)$
	2. $(\sim r \supset \sim q)$	RP	
	3. $(\sim s \lor p)$	RP	
	4. s	RP	
$*_5$	5. r	RA (work for s)	
$*_5$	6. $(r \& s)$	$C_{4,5}$	
$*_5$	7. s	S_6	
	8. $(r \supset s)$	$Cd_{*_5,7}$	

Lines 6 and 7 are necessary since the rule of conditionalization cannot be applied unless the wff in the antecedent of the conditional to be inferred is an assumption of the line where the consequent is written.

We have s in line 4, but we have to reintroduce it as a starred assumption in order to use conditionalization to get $(s \supset r)$. We will pull r out of 2 if we get $\sim\sim q$. That can be derived from q, which we can get out of line 1 and p; p is available from line 3 and $\sim\sim s$ by disjunctive syllogism.

$*_9$	9. s	RA
$*_9$	10. $\sim\sim s$	Sub_4
$*_9$	11. p	$DS_{10,3}$
$*_9$	12. q	$MP_{11,1}$
$*_9$	13. $\sim\sim q$	Sub_{12}
$*_9$	14. $\sim\sim r$	$MT_{13,2}$
$*_9$	15. r	Sub_{14}
	16. $(s \supset r)$	$Cd_{*_9,15}$

Now we put lines 15 and 8 together to get the desired biconditional, as our original strategy indicated.

	17. $((r \supset s) \& (s \supset r))$	$C_{16,8}$
	18. $(r \equiv s)$	Sub_{16}

EXERCISES FOR MODULE 45
THE TECHNIQUES OF NATURAL DEDUCTION—PROPOSITIONAL LOGIC

Ex. 1 In the light of the form of the conclusion and its relation to the premises, determine the likely rule or rules for deducing the desired conclusion. (Don't worry about intermediate conclusions and strategies.)

From premises	To prove	From premises	To prove
1. $(p \supset q)$ $(\sim r \supset \sim q)$	$(p \supset r)$	2. $(p \supset (q \lor r))$ $(\sim q \& \sim r)$ $(s \supset p)$	$\sim s$
3. $(p \equiv \sim q)$ r $(\sim r \lor p)$	$(\sim q \lor s)$	4. $((p \& q) \& r)$ $(s \supset \sim(q \& r))$	$\sim(p \supset s)$
5. $((t \lor r) \supset s)$ p $(\sim p \lor \sim s)$	$(\sim t \& \sim r)$	6. $((p \& q) \supset r)$ $\sim(p \supset r)$	$\sim q$

From premises	To prove	From premise	To prove
7. $(p_1 \supset (\sim q \vee r))$	$(s \vee r)$	8. $((p \,\&\, q) \supset r)$	$\sim p$
$\quad (p_2 \supset (s \vee t))$		$\quad (p \supset \sim r)$	
$\quad (p_1 \,\&\, p_2)$		$\quad q$	
$\quad (\sim q \,\&\, \sim t)$			
9. $(p \supset r)$	$\sim p$	10. $(r \supset q)$	$((r \vee s) \supset p)$
$\quad ((p \,\&\, q) \supset \sim r)$		$\quad (\sim p \supset \sim q)$	
$\quad (\sim p \vee q)$		$\quad (\sim s \vee t)$	
		$\quad \sim(t \,\&\, \sim p)$	

Ex. 2 Check the answers to Ex. 1. In the light of those answers, work out a strategy for deducing intermediate conclusions for each of the items.

Ex. 3 Check the answers to Ex. 2. In the light of those answers, write a correct deduction of the desired conclusion for each of the ten items.

Ex. 4 For each of the following items, show, using natural deduction, that the given premises logically imply the stated conclusion.

Premises	Conclusion
1. $((p \vee q) \supset r),\ \sim(\sim p \,\&\, \sim q)$	$\therefore r$
2. $(p \supset q),\sim(q \vee r)$	$\therefore \sim p$
3. $p, \sim p$	$\therefore q$
4. $((p \supset q) \supset s),\sim(r \vee s)$	$\therefore p$
5. $((p \,\&\, q) \vee (r \,\&\, s)),(p \supset \sim p)$	$\therefore r$
6. $(p \equiv q),(p \vee q)$	$\therefore p$
7. $((p \supset q) \supset r),((s \vee t) \supset (p \,\&\, q)),s$	$\therefore r$
8. $(p \equiv q),(q \supset (r \,\&\, s)),\sim r$	$\therefore \sim p$
9. $((p \vee q) \supset (r \,\&\, s)),(r \supset t),(\sim t \,\&\, s)$	$\therefore \sim p$
10. $[((p \vee q) \,\&\, r) \supset (q \,\&\, r)],((p \vee q) \,\&\, r)$	$\therefore (q \,\&\, r)$
11. $((p \,\&\, q) \supset r),p,((p \,\&\, \sim q) \supset \sim r)$	$\therefore (q \equiv r)$
12. $(p \supset q),\sim(q \,\&\, \sim r)$	$\therefore (p \supset r)$
13. $(p \supset q)$	$\therefore (\sim(q \,\&\, r) \supset \sim(r \,\&\, p))$
14. $((\sim p \,\&\, q) \supset r),\sim(q \supset p),((r \supset s) \,\&\, (r \supset q))$	$\therefore (s \vee q)$
15. $((p \,\&\, q) \equiv r),(\sim r \supset (\sim p \vee s)),p$	$\therefore (\sim s \supset (p \,\&\, q))$

SELECTED ANSWERS
TO EXERCISES FOR MODULE 45

Ex. 1

1. A. Conditionalization could perhaps be used if p were assumed as an additional premise. It is *always promising* to assume the antecedent wff A if you are working for a conditional wff $(A \supset B)$ and then use conditionalization.
   B. Hypothetical syllogism could perhaps be used if a conditional with r as consequent could be generated. (Using hypothetical syllogism is usually harder than using conditionalization.)
2. Modus tollens could be used with premise 3 if $\sim p$ could be derived.
3. Addition could be employed if $\sim q$ were derived. (Deriving $(\sim q \vee s)$ immediately seems unlikely, as does deriving s and then adding $\sim q$, since s does not occur in any of the premises.)

4. A. Since the conclusion is equivalent to a conjunction, $(p$ & $\sim s)$, using the rule of conjunction is promising.
   B. Using indirect proof strategy would give you a powerful conditional premise for an ultimate use of reduction.
5. A. If $\sim t$ and $\sim r$ were deduced separately, conjunction would be used.
   B. The conclusion would follow by substitution if $\sim(t \vee r)$ were derived.
6. A. Modus tollens could perhaps be used with $\sim r$ if q could become the antecedent of a conditional like $(q \supset r)$.
   B. Disjunctive syllogism could perhaps be used if $\sim q$ could become one disjunct of a disjunction like $(\sim p \vee \sim q)$.
   C. Reduction could be perhaps used if q were introduced as a premise. (Hereafter reduction will only be mentioned if it is especially promising. *It is always possible* to use indirect proof to derive a valid conclusion.)
7. A. Addition would yield the conclusion from either r or s.
   B. At first sight it also seems that the conclusion might follow constructive dilemma.
   C. $\sim s$ could be assumed, s derived; then reduction and addition would give the conclusion.
8. A. Reduction could yield the conclusion by indirect proof.
   B. From $(p \supset \sim p)$ the conclusion follows by substitution if one chose to try a more roundabout strategy and assume p to derive $\sim p$ and then use conditionalization.
9. Same as item 8.
10. A. Use conditionalization after p is derived with the added premise $(r \vee s)$.
    B. Use substitution after deriving conjunction $((s \supset p)$ & $(r \supset p))$.

Ex. 2

1. A. Once you have p and your other premises are conditional you should expect to use modus ponens and modus tollens.
   B. The only premise containing r is the second. You must find a conditional equivalent to $(\sim r \supset \sim q)$ with r as consequent.
2. To derive $\sim p$ you will need to use premise 1. Since it is conditional, modus tollens is suggested. Since the only premise involving q or r is 2, look there for something equivalent to or implying $\sim (q \vee r)$. You can begin alternatively by applying hypothetical syllogism to premises 1 and 3.
3. $\sim q$ can be derived if p can be derived, p can be derived if disjunctive syllogism can be applied to premise 3.
4. A. To use conjunction you must get each conjunct separately. p can be obtained by simplification. Since s is the antecedent of a conditional, modus tollens is promising for deriving $\sim s$.
   B. With the premise $(p \supset s)$, and with p available from premise 1, s can be derived; another application of modus ponens will give $\sim (q$ & $r)$. Then you need to figure out whether $\sim (q$ & $r)$ is equivalent to or implies the negation of anything asserted about q or r in premise 1.
5. A. Upon examination this strategy is not very promising because t and r only occur in the antecedent of premise 1, where they are together in a disjunction.
   B. Modus tollens with $\sim s$ could be used to derive $\sim (t \vee r)$ from premise 1. To derive $\sim s$ you should turn to premise 3, a disjunction, which suggests looking to obtain $\sim \sim p$ and then applying disjunctive syllogism.
6. A. To get q as an antecedent of a conditional, you will have to transform

premise 1, most easily to $(p \supset (q \supset r))$, so that through modus ponens, most likely, $(q \supset r)$ can be obtained. The goal would then be to get $\sim r$ so as to be able to apply modus tollens.

B. The most likely way to get $\sim q$ in a disjunction is to get $\sim (p \ \& \ q)$, which is equivalent to $(\sim p \lor \sim q)$. Since $(p \ \& \ q)$ is the antecedent of a conditional, the most likely means of negating it would be to get $\sim r$ and apply modus tollens.

C. Once q were assumed, it would be plausible to look for p, apply modus ponens, get r and look for $\sim r$.

7. A. The most promising processes for deriving r or s are identical and are applied to premises 1 and 2, respectively. You should look to get the consequent of those premises by applying modus ponens if you can find p_2 or p_1. Then disjunctive syllogism seems promising, since both consequents are disjunctions. $\sim q$ and $\sim t$ are available from premise 4.

B. Unfortunately neither r nor s occurs alone in the consequent of a conditional, nor can they easily be derived.

C. Once $\sim s$ is assumed, it seems promising to concentrate on premise 2; $(s \lor t)$ can be derived by modus ponens. Then disjunctive syllogism with $\sim t$ will give you s for the contradiction needed to apply reduction.

8. A. After p is assumed, conjunction with q and applications of modus ponens will yield a contradiction.

B. Assume p; use it to get $\sim r$ by modus ponens. $\sim r$ with premise 1 gives $\sim (p \ \& \ q)$, which is equivalent to $(\sim p \lor \sim q)$. Use an equivalence of premise 3 to get $\sim p$ by disjunctive syllogism.

9. A. After p is assumed, you are again aiming to derive $(r \ \& \ \sim r)$. r simply requires an application of modus ponens. $\sim r$ requires first getting q, to be conjoined with p. Disjunctive syllogism applied to premise 3 yields q.

B. Assume p; derive r by modus ponens. Use $\sim\sim r$ and modus tollens to get $\sim (p \ \& \ q)$, which is equivalent to $(\sim p \lor \sim q)$. Use $\sim\sim p$ to get $\sim q$ by disjunctive syllogism. Then $\sim p$ is available from premise 3 and disjunctive syllogism. Use conditionalization to get $(p \supset \sim p)$.

10. A. An added premise like $(r \lor s)$—a disjunction—is likely to be helpful either for constructive dilemma or, by substitution to $(\sim r \supset s)$, for hypothetical syllogism. To be successful with either strategy, premises 3 and 4 must be converted by substitution to conditionals.

B. To derive $(s \supset p)$ assume s and derive p; then use conditionalization. To derive $(r \supset p)$ use the same strategy.

Ex. 3

1. A.		1. $(p \supset q)$	RP
		2. $(\sim r \supset \sim q)$	RP
	$*_3$	3. p	RP
	$*_3$	4. q	$MP_{1,3}$
	$*_3$	5. $\sim\sim q$	Sub_4
	$*_3$	6. $\sim\sim r$	$MT_{2,5}$
	$*_3$	7. r	Sub_6
		8. $(p \supset r)$	$Cd_{*_3,7}$
B.		1. $(p \supset r)$	RP
		2. $(\sim r \supset \sim q)$	RP
		3. $(q \supset r)$	Sub_2
		4. $(p \supset r)$	$HS_{1,3}$
2.		1. $(p \supset (q \lor r))$	RP

2. $(\sim q \ \& \sim r)$	RP
3. $(s \supset p)$	RP
4. $\sim(q \lor r)$	Sub$_2$
5. $\sim p$	MT$_{1,4}$
6. $\sim s$	MT$_{3,5}$
Or, after line 3, proceed:	
4. $(s \supset (q \lor r))$	HS$_{1,3}$
5. $\sim(q \lor r)$	Sub$_2$
6. $\sim s$	MT$_{5,4}$

3.
1. $(p \equiv \sim q)$	RP
2. r	RP
3. $(\sim r \lor p)$	RP
4. $\sim\sim r$	Sub$_2$
5. p	DS$_{2,3}$
6. $((p \supset \sim q) \ \& \ (\sim q \supset p))$	Sub$_1$
7. $(p \supset \sim q)$	S$_6$
8. $\sim q$	MP$_{5,7}$
9. $(\sim q \lor s)$	A$_8$

4. A.
1. $((p \ \& \ q) \ \& \ r)$	RP
2. $(s \supset \sim(q \ \& \ r))$	RP
3. $(p \ \& \ q)$	S$_1$
4. p	S$_3$
5. r	S$_1$
6. q	S$_3$
7. $(q \ \& \ r)$	C$_{5,6}$
8. $\sim\sim(q \ \& \ r)$	Sub$_6$
9. $\sim s$	MT$_{2,8}$
10. $(p \ \& \sim s)$	C$_{4,9}$
11. $\sim(p \supset s)$	Sub$_{10}$

B.
	1. $((p \ \& \ q) \ \& \ r)$	RP
	2. $(s \supset \sim(q \ \& \ t)$	RP
*$_3$	3. $(p \supset s)$	RA
	4. $(p \ \& \ q)$	S$_1$
	5. p	S$_4$
*$_3$	6. s	MP$_{3,5}$
*$_3$	7. $\sim(q \ \& \ t)$	MP$_{2,6}$
	8. q	S$_4$
	9. r	S$_1$
	10. $(q \ \& \ r)$	C$_{8,9}$
	11. $\sim(p \supset s)$	Red$_{*_3,7,10}$

5. A. The answer to Ex. 2, item 5(A), indicates that no deduction using this strategy is promising.

B.
1. $((t \lor r) \supset s)$	RP
2. p	RP
3. $(\sim p \lor \sim s)$	RP
4. $\sim\sim p$	Sub$_2$
5. $\sim s$	DS$_{2,3}$
6. $\sim(t \lor r)$	MT$_{1,5}$
7. $(\sim t \ \& \sim r)$	Sub$_6$

6. A.
1. $((p \ \& \ q) \supset r)$	RP
2. $\sim(p \supset r)$	RP

	3.	$(p \supset (q \supset r))$	Sub_1
	4.	$(p \ \& \sim r)$	Sub_2
	5.	p	S_4
	6.	$(q \supset r)$	$\text{MP}_{3,5}$
	7.	$\sim r$	S_4
	8.	$\sim q$	$\text{MT}_{6,7}$
B.	1.	$((p \ \& \ q) \supset r)$	RP
	2.	$\sim (p \supset r)$	RP
	3.	$(p \ \& \sim r)$	Sub_2
	4.	$\sim r$	S_3
	5.	$\sim (p \ \& \ q)$	$\text{MT}_{1,4}$
	6.	$(\sim p \lor \sim q)$	Sub_5
	7.	p	S_3
	8.	$\sim\sim p$	Sub_7
	9.	$\sim q$	$\text{DS}_{6,8}$
C.	1.	$((p \ \& \ q) \supset r)$	RP
	2.	$\sim (p \supset r)$	RP
$*_3$	3.	q	RA
	4.	$(p \ \& \sim r)$	Sub_2
	5.	p	S_4
$*_3$	6.	$(p \ \& \ q)$	$C_{3,5}$
$*_3$	7.	r	$\text{MP}_{1,6}$
	8.	$\sim r$	S_4
	9.	$\sim q$	$\text{Red}_{*_3,7,8}$
7. A.	1.	$(p_1 \supset (\sim q \supset r))$	RP
	2.	$(p_2 \supset (s \lor t))$	RP
	3.	$(p_1 \ \& \ p_2)$	RP
	4.	$(\sim q \ \& \sim t)$	RP
	5.	p_2	S_3
	6.	$(s \lor t)$	$\text{MP}_{2,6}$
	7.	$\sim t$	S_4
	8.	s	$\text{DS}_{6,7}$
	9.	$(s \lor r)$	A_8

B. The answer to Ex. 2, item 5(A), indicates that no deduction using this strategy is promising.

C.	1.	$(p_1 \supset (\sim q \lor r))$	RP
	2.	$(p_2 \supset (s \lor t))$	RP
	3.	$(p_1 \ \& \ p_2)$	RP
	4.	$(\sim q \ \& \sim t)$	RP
$*_5$	5.	$\sim s$	RA
	6.	p_2	S_3
	7.	$(s \lor t)$	$\text{MP}_{2,6}$
$*_5$	8.	t	$\text{DS}_{5,7}$
	9.	$\sim t$	S_4
	10.	$\sim\sim s$	$\text{Red}_{*_5,8,9}$
	11.	s	Sub_{10}
	12.	$(s \lor r)$	A_{11}
8. A.	1.	$((p \ \& \ q) \supset r)$	RP
	2.	$(p \supset \sim r)$	RP
	3.	q	RP
$*_4$	4.	p	RA

	*₄	5.	$(p \,\&\, q)$	$C_{3,4}$
	*₄	6.	r	$MP_{1,5}$
	*₄	7.	$\sim r$	$MP_{2,4}$
		8.	$\sim p$	$Red_{*_4,6,7}$
B.		1.	$((p \,\&\, q) \supset r)$	RP
		2.	$(p \supset \sim r)$	RP
		3.	q	RP
	*₄	4.	p	RA
	*₄	5.	$\sim r$	$MP_{4,2}$
	*₄	6.	$\sim(p \,\&\, q)$	$MT_{5,1}$
	*₄	7.	$(\sim p \lor \sim q)$	Sub_6
		8.	$\sim\sim q$	Sub_3
	*₄	9.	$\sim p$	$DS_{8,7}$
		10.	$(p \supset \sim p)$	$Cd_{*_4,9}$
		11.	$\sim p$	Sub_{10}
9. A.		1.	$(p \supset r)$	RP
		2.	$((p \,\&\, q) \supset \sim r)$	RP
		3.	$(\sim p \lor q)$	RP
	*₄	4.	p	RA
	*₄	5.	r	$MP_{1,4}$
	*₄	6.	$\sim\sim p$	Sub_4
	*₄	7.	q	$DS_{3,6}$
	*₄	8.	$(p \,\&\, q)$	$C_{4,7}$
	*₄	9.	$\sim r$	$MP_{2,8}$
		10.	$\sim p$	$Red_{*_4,5,9}$
B.		1.	$(p \supset r)$	RP
		2.	$((p \,\&\, q) \supset \sim r)$	RP
		3.	$(\sim p \lor q)$	RP
	*₄	4.	p	RA
	*₄	5.	r	$MP_{1,4}$
	*₄	6.	$\sim\sim r$	Sub_5
	*₄	7.	$\sim(p \,\&\, q)$	$MT_{6,2}$
	*₄	8.	$(\sim p \lor \sim q)$	Sub_7
	*₄	9.	$\sim\sim p$	Sub_4
	*₄	10.	$\sim q$	$DS_{9,8}$
	*₄	11.	$\sim p$	$DS_{10,3}$
		12.	$(p \supset \sim p)$;	$Cd_{*_4,11}$
		13.	$\sim p$	Sub_{12}
10. A.		1.	$(r \supset q)$	RP
		2.	$(\sim p \supset \sim q)$	RP
		3.	$(\sim s \lor t)$	RP
		4.	$\sim(t \,\&\, \sim p)$	RP
	*₅	5.	$(r \lor s)$	RA
		6.	$(s \supset t)$	Sub_3
		7.	$(t \supset p)$	Sub_4
		8.	$(s \supset p)$	$HS_{6,7}$
		9.	$(q \supset p)$	Sub_2
		10.	$(r \supset p)$	$IIS_{1,9}$
	*₅	11.	$(p \lor p)$	$CD_{5,\,8,\,10}$
	*₅	12.	p	Sub_{11}
		13.	$((r \lor s) \supset p)$	$Cd_{*_5,12}$

B.
	1. $(r \supset q)$	RP
	2. $(\sim p \supset \sim q)$	RP
	3. $(\sim s \lor t)$	RP
	4. $\sim(t \ \& \sim p)$	RP
$*_5$	5. s	RA
$*_5$	6. $\sim\sim s$	Sub_5
$*_5$	7. t	$\text{DS}_{3,6}$
	8. $(t \supset p)$	Sub_4
$*_5$	9. p	$\text{MP}_{8,7}$
	10. $(s \supset p)$	$\text{Cd}_{*_5,9}$
$*_{11}$	11. r	RA
$*_{11}$	12. q	$\text{MP}_{11,1}$
$*_{11}$	13. $\sim\sim q$	Sub_{12}
$*_{11}$	14. $\sim\sim p$	$\text{MT}_{2,13}$
$*_{11}$	15. p	Sub_{14}
	16. $(r \supset p)$	$\text{Cd}_{*_{11},15}$
	17. $((r \supset p) \ \& \ (s \supset p))$	$\text{C}_{10,16}$
	18. $((r \lor s) \supset p)$	Sub_{17}

Ex. 4

5.
	1. $((p \ \& \ q) \lor (r \ \& \ s))$	RP	$/\therefore r$
	2. $(p \supset \sim p)$	RP	
	3. $(\sim p \lor \sim p)$	Sub_2	
	4. $\sim p$	Sub_3	
	5. $(\sim p \lor \sim q)$	A_4	
	6. $\sim(p \ \& \ q)$	Sub_5	
	7. $(r \ \& \ s)$	$\text{DS}_{6,1}$	
	8. r	S_7	

10.
	1. $[((p \lor q) \ \& \ r) \supset (q \ \& \ r)]$	RP	$/\therefore (q \ \& \ r)$
	2. $((p \lor q) \ \& \ r)$	RP	
	3. $(q \ \& \ r)$	$\text{MP}_{1,2}$	

15.
	1. $((p \ \& \ q) \equiv r)$	RP	$/\therefore (\sim s \supset (p \ \& \ q))$
	2. $(\sim r \supset (\sim p \lor s))$	RP	
	3. p	RP	
$*_4$	4. $\sim s$	RA	
$*_4$	5. $(p \ \& \sim s)$	$\text{C}_{3,4}$	
$*_4$	6. $\sim(\sim p \lor s)$	Sub_5	
$*_4$	7. $\sim\sim r$	$\text{MT}_{6,2}$	
$*_4$	8. r	Sub_7	
	9. $[((p \ \& \ q) \supset r) \ \& \ (r \supset (p \ \& \ q))]$	Sub_1	
	10. $(r \supset (p \ \& \ q))$	S_9	
$*_4$	11. $(p \ \& \ q)$	$\text{MP}_{8,10}$	
	12. $(\sim s \supset (p \ \& \ q))$	$\text{Cd}_{*_4,11}$	

14

INDUCTIVE ARGUMENTS: ELEMENTARY RESEARCH DESIGN

The educational goal of this chapter is to provide you with some useful skills to help you deal with the complex area of inductive logic. By studying this chapter you can learn the basic skills involved in framing and testing clear hypotheses.

Logicians have been well rewarded in assuming that validity is a matter of the form or structure of an argument. Whether or not an argument is justified, on the other hand, is quite impossible to determine on a purely formal basis. In fact, justified arguments may use forms which are structurally invalid. Thus logicians approach the problem of how to show whether or not arguments are justified by regarding justification not as a matter of form but as a matter of content.

Our first concern when trying to show a deductive argument to be logically correct is to try to prove that it is structurally valid. Because of this the whole range of techniques for determining validity is often called *deductive logic*. On the other hand, our first effort when trying to show inductive arguments to be logically correct is to try to show that they are justified in terms of their content. The range of techniques for determining justification is known as *inductive logic*.

Inductive logic also differs from deductive logic in the degree and the extent to which it is understood. The understanding of some areas of deductive logic, like the propositional and predicate logic developed in Chapters 4 to 6, is virtually complete and unchanging. On the other hand, the incompleteness of human understanding of all areas of inductive logic has the consequence that no set views or systematic approaches are established beyond controversy. Some ideas and basic skills, however, are relatively clear and rather well established, and our presentation will concentrate on these.

MODULE 46

FRAMING CLEAR HYPOTHESES

Back in Module 10 we presented examples of three kinds of inductive arguments: inductions dealing with mathematical probabilities, inductions involving causal connections, and inductions involving statistical connections. The first competency of this module involves distinguishing cases in which inductions involving mathematical probabilities are appropriate from cases in which the appropriate inductions involve either causal or statistical connections. In order to develop this competency the appropriate uses of inductions involving mathematical probabilities will be discussed first. You will come to see that when the appropriate induction is not based on mathematical probabilities, then it involves either a causal or statistical connection. Once you are able to distinguish inductions involving one of the connections, you will be ready to develop the competencies necessary for constructing clear hypotheses.

● After reading Module 46 you should be able to:

1. Calculate mathematical probabilities
2. Distinguish cases in which mathematical probability applies from those in which it does not apply
3. Distinguish observational terms from nonobservational terms
4. Quantify hypotheses
5. Distinguish hypotheses asserting causal connections from those asserting statistical connections
6. Distinguish hypotheses with high degrees of initial plausibility from those with lower degrees of initial plausibility relative to given sets of data

46:1.1 You can begin to grasp the distinguishing character of inductions based on *mathematical probabilities* by considering the following examples.

EG. 46.1 I need a total of at least nine on my next two rolls of the die to win the game. I probably will not win.

EG. 46.2 Drawing one card to complete an inside straight requires that of the forty-seven cards not in my hand, the one I draw will be one of the four in the deck which completes the straight, not any of the forty-three which fail to complete it. I will have to be very lucky to complete the straight.

How do inductions like these work? Clearly, Egs. 46.1 and 46.2 are justified inductive arguments, but what principles justify them? Well, you might say, thinking about Eg. 46.1, a die has six sides, numbered one to six. In order to roll a total of at least nine in two rolls, a person must roll a three and a six, or a four and a five, or some combination of fives and sixes. But there are also the possibilities that he or she will roll one of the many other combinations. Indeed there are more possible combinations that will yield less than nine than there are combinations that will yield a total of nine or more. So it is more probable that he or she will roll less than nine than nine or more.

This thinking is certainly logical. It is right to presume that the events in question are, in this case, random or equiprobable. Logicians have wanted to understand more deeply what is involved in such thinking. They have noticed that it involves the following steps.

1. All the possibilities are laid out (in Eg. 46.1, the possible combinations of two rolls of a die).
2. The number of favorable possibilities is counted (in Eg. 46.1, the combinations adding to nine or more).
3. The number of unfavorable possibilities is counted. [Alternatively you subtract the number obtained in (2) from the number in (1).]
4. The probability of the favorable outcome is computed as the percentage of possibilities which are favorable.

The percentage is expressed either numerically or by relatively imprecise English terms like 'probable,' 'usual,' 'often,' 'seldom,' 'unlikely,' and 'infrequent.' See if you can take Eg. 46.2 and explain its thinking, going through each of these steps.

46:1.2 Random possibilities Logicians have been especially interested in step 4, which is really a rule of interpretation. It tells you how to compute the probability on the basis of how the favorable possibilities relate to total possibilities. According to step 4, the probability is equal to the result of dividing the favorable possibilities by the total number of possibilities. What this equation assumes is that *all the possibilities are equally likely.* Logicians call this assumption the principle of insufficient reason. This means that they have insufficient reason (no substantial reason) to believe that one possibility is more likely than any other. If they did have such grounds or reasons to think that some alternatives were more likely to occur, then they could not use the procedure specified in step 4. For instance, suppose a certain coin were weighted so that the one possibility (of tails) occurred three times as often as the other possibility (of heads). This weighting of the coin would provide what is lacking with normal coins, namely, a reason why each of the alternative outcomes is not equally possible. The same reasoning applies to a loaded die or a stacked deck of cards.

The distinguishing characteristic of inductions based on mathematical probabilities is that these inductions all rely on the principle of insufficient reason. In other words, in working from the assumption that each of the outcomes is equally possible, it is assumed that the actual occurrence of any one possibility can be looked at as a "random" event whose probability is $1/n$, where n is the total number of possibilities.

EXERCISE 1

This preliminary exercise relates to calculating mathematical probabilities where the principle of insufficient reason is presumed to apply. Construct the mathematical probability of each of the following. Remember that the mathematical probability is favorable possibilities divided by total possibilities. Check your answers as you go along.

1. The probability that a flipped coin will land tails
2. The probability that a flipped coin will land tails on two successive flips
3. The probability that a flipped coin will land heads on two successive flips
4. The probability that a flipped coin will land tails on exactly one of two successive flips
5. The probability that a flipped coin will land tails on at least one of two successive flips
6. The probability of rolling a six on a roll of a normal die
7. The probability of rolling either a six or a five on a roll of a die
8. The probability of rolling either a four or a five or a six on a roll of a die
9. The probability of rolling a six on a die and then rolling a six on the next roll
10. The probability of rolling two sixes on two dice at the same time
11. The probability of rolling a six on one die while at the same time rolling either a four or a five or a six on a second die

12. The probability of picking one of the four kings out of a deck of fifty-two cards on one pick
13. The probability of picking one of the remaining three kings out of the remaining fifty-one cards.

For the next group of exercises assume that there are 100,000,000 cars on the roads of the United States. Assume 20 percent are white. Assume that the white cars are randomly distributed throughout the United States.

14. The probability that the first car past a randomly chosen intersection will be white
15. The probability that the second car past the intersection will be white, on the assumption that the first car does not return

ANSWERS

TO EXERCISE 1

1. $1/2$
2. $1/4$. Notice that on each flip, the odds of tails are $1/2$. On two successive flips, the odds can be computed as $1/2 \times 1/2$, that is $1/4$.
3. $1/4$
4. $1/2$ [$1 - (1/4)$, from item 2, and $-(1/4)$, from item 3]
5. $3/4$; from items 4 and 2. ($1 =$ the total of all four possibilities, each $1/4$. That is, $1/4 + 1/4 + 1/4 + 1/4 = 1$.)
6. $1/6$
7. $1/6 + 1/6 = 1/3$. The probability of a five or a six equals the probability of a five ($1/6$) plus the probability of a six ($1/6$).
8. $1/2$; same procedure as for item 7
9. $1/6 \times 1/6 = 1/36$
10. $1/36$; same procedure as for item 9
11. $1/6 \times 1/2 = 1/12$
12. $4/52 = 1/13$
13. $3/51 = 1/17$
14. $20,000,000/100,000,000 = .20000000$
15. $19,999,999/99,999,999 = .19999999$

The closeness of these two answers—especially compared to the differences in the answers to items 12 and 13—shows you why statisticians distinguish sampling procedures for small groups like decks of cards or rabbits in a woodlot, etc., from sampling procedures for large groups like cars in the United States or television viewers. Whether the king is put back in the deck greatly affects the odds of drawing another king. Whether a car may come back around the block or not affects the odds of the next car's being white by approximately .0000001, not very much.

If you missed more than four items, review the background material in 46:1.1 and 46:1.2. Notice that to compute the probability of *both* of two things happening you *multiply* their probabilities, but to compute the chances of *either* of two things happening you *add* their individual probabilities.

46:2.1 The principle of insufficient reason Inductions based on mathematical probabilities form a very small part of the inductions which interest human beings.

For instance, if you let go of your briefcase, it will fall. It is scarcely "equally possible" that it will rise, or remain suspended in the air.

Probably no one has seriously thought that the different possibilities concerning the briefcase are equally possible. But consider other examples. The sex of a newborn baby has been regarded as subject to mathematical probabilities. Many persons have thought that there is no more reason why a baby should be male than female. Careful observations, however, have falsified this idea. It has been observed that (1) the ratio of male to female babies is not 1:1, but more like 104:100, (2) the ratio of male to female babies climbs in direct relationship to the quality of the prenatal care of the mother, and (3) the sex of the newborn can be positively connected with such factors as the time of conception within the menstrual cycle and the intercourse practices of the parents in the weeks immediately prior to conception. Each of these observations conflicts, in some way, with the application of the principle of insufficient reason to the sex of newborns.

Actually, (2) and (3) conflict in one way with application of the principle of insufficient reason, and (1) conflicts in a different way. Later on in the module (46:7.2 and 46:7.3), the difference between how (2) and (3) conflict and how (1) conflicts will prove important, so let's define the difference carefully right here. Both (2) and (3) suggest reasons that might be given to explain the higher probability of a male. But (1) does not provide any such suggestions. It simply shows that the birth of a male is more frequent without any hint of why this might be so.

We shall regard the principle of insufficient reason as inoperative relative to a given set of possibilities when empirical evidence suggests, as does (1), that in the long run the possibilities do not occur with equal frequency or that there is a reason *why* one set of possibilities is more likely to occur than another set, as is suggested by (2) and (3). In cases like the movements of the briefcase, the relevant observations are so many and so gross that we scarcely recognize our reliance on observations. In cases like the sex of newborns, the relevant observations are fewer and so much more subtle that people can fail to recognize the importance of such observations.

EXERCISE 2

Given the knowledge cited in each item below, distinguish those cases in which mathematical probabilities seem applicable from those in which they don't. (Remember that adding further information, e.g., the deck is stacked, can always upset the judgment you are asked to make here. Therefore stick simply to the information provided.)

1. Many 1973 Plymouths are found to have defective trunk locks. The defective locks do not seem to be associated with any particular supplier, date of supply, or assembly plant. Apparently one-twentieth of the cars have the defects. Is the distribution throughout the market area of the cars having the defects subject to mathematical probabilities?
2. Sixty-five percent of all 1973 Plymouths were manufactured with air conditioning. Is the distribution of the cars with air conditioning subject to mathematical probabilities?
3. Sixty-five percent of 1973 Plymouths were manufactured with air conditioning. Seventy percent of those manufactured with air conditioning were sent to dealers

in the southern half of the country. Is the distribution of air-conditioned cars subject to mathematical probabilities?

4. Sixty-five percent of 1973 Plymouths were manufactured with air conditioning. Ninety-five percent of the new cars sold in Minnesota during the 1973 model year did not have air conditioning. Is the distribution of the 1973 Plymouths with air conditioning subject to mathematical probabilities?

5. Strangely enough, 80 percent of the 1973 Plymouths with defective trunk locks also have air conditioning, which is found more often in warmer climates. Is the distribution of the cars having the defects subject to mathematical probabilities?

6. Contrary to item 5, 65 percent of the Plymouths with defective locks have air conditioning, just as do 65 percent of all 1973 Plymouths. Is the distribution of the cars having the defect subject to mathematical probabilities?

7. Sixty-five percent of all 1973 Plymouths were manufactured with air conditioning. It is warmer in the south than in the north. People are more concerned with staying cool while driving if they typically drive in warmer climates. Is the distribution of the 1973 Plymouths with air conditioning subject to mathematical probabilities?

EXERCISE 3

Check the answers for Ex. 2 and be sure you understand them before you proceed. Then, consulting the following list, cite the reason why mathematical probabilities are or are not applicable to each of the items of Ex. 2.

A. All the information supplied is compatible with the assumption that the possible distributions of the cars throughout the market area are all equally likely.

B. The information supplied involves observations that these distributions do not occur with equal frequency.

C. The information supplied cites a general reason, understanding, or theory from which it is rational to infer that these distributions do not occur with equal frequency.

ANSWERS TO EXERCISES 2 AND 3

Ex. 2

1. Yes, given this knowledge, even though on the basis of general background knowledge you may reasonably suspect that some localizable cause must bring about the defects.

2. Yes, given this knowledge.

3. No; there is reason to believe that more of them are in the south than in the north.

4. No; there is reason to believe that the percentage of air air-conditioned 1973 Plymouths in Minnesota is lower than elsewhere.

5. No; there is reason to believe that more air-conditioned cars are in the warmer climates.

6. Yes; 65 percent is the percentage in this example for both air-conditioned Plymouths and Plymouths which, if they have defective locks, are also air-conditioned. If, as in item 5, it were more probable that a car would have the defect if

it were air-conditioned than if it were not, then mathematical probabilities would no longer be applicable.

7. No

If you missed more than two review 46:2.1.

Ex. 3

1. A   2. A   3. B   4. B
5. B   6. A   7. C

If you missed any review 46:2.1.

46:2.2 When an inductive assertion cannot be based on mathematical probabilities, one or another of the two other kinds of induction come into play. Maybe the inductive assertion expresses a causal connection, and maybe it expresses a statistical connection. In either case we can call the statement under investigation a *hypothesis*.

A very important preliminary step is *the framing of a clear statement of the causal or statistical hypothesis which is to be supported*. You may regard that hypothesis as the *conclusion of an inductive argument*. If you take proper care in the way in which you state that hypothesis, then the hypothesis itself will suggest the kinds of evidence you should supply to support it. In Module 47 you will learn the procedures for determining whether the hypothesis can be supported in the way it needs to be. The statements of support become the premises of the inductive argument on behalf of the hypothesis. After the argument is constructed you can evaluate its strength.

46:3.1 Ruling out equiprobability The first step in framing a clear causal hypothesis involves working with the observations which lead you to believe that the subject under discussion cannot be adequately handled on the basis of mathematical probabilities. Those observations suggest somehow that the occurrences in question are not random. They will also suggest something about what the deviation from random occurrence appears to be. For example, suppose that you are about to eat one of eight portions of a chicken dinner. Background knowledge of food strongly suggests that whether the dinner is toxic is not a question amenable to mathematical probabilities. We would operate by assuming that either all the portions will be toxic or none of the portions will be toxic. But why is this so?

The basis for our believing this "all or nothing" proposition is twofold, just as in the case of the newborn. In part we would be relying upon our *past experiences* (observations) that when a prepared recipe of food is separated into individual portions it is seldom or never the case that some portions are poisonous while others are not. But in part, too, we would be relying on more general knowledge about the preparation of food. We might assume that any poison would have been introduced in the cooking or the handling of the entire batch of food. We might then infer accordingly that anything that was true of one portion of the food would likely be true of other portions as well. These observations and reasonings would then lend initial support to the idea that induction based on mathematical probabilities would not be appropriate here.

46:3.2 Initial plausibility The next question you must face is why we should frame one hypothesis about the chicken dinner rather than the other. Should we assert that the entire dinner is toxic or that none of it is? You might reason, "This meal has been prepared from nontoxic food substances, and preparation processes have avoided spoilage problems. So the entire dinner is not toxic." In other circumstances you might reason, "This food after being prepared was left uncooked in a warm place for many hours or days so the food is probably toxic." There are two important features of these lines of reasonings.

1. You can probably see very clearly that these reasonings begin from different premises recording diverging observations about the preparation of the food.
2. They also depend upon a general understanding of what causes food to be toxic. Implicit in the reasoning is the general causal understanding that food poisoning develops from long exposure of food to relatively warm temperatures.

The reasoning so far presented amounts to what we shall call the *initial plausibility* of an assertion diverging in one direction or another from mathematical probabilities. This initial plausibility is not a proof that the assertion is correct. It is *simply a basis for choosing one possibility, one divergence from random occurrences, as more likely and therefore as more worthy of being tested* than the other possibilities. Each of these reasonings gives support to the idea that its conclusion is more probable than the conclusions of the other argument. Neither, however, really attempts to show that its conclusion is justified.

In order to show that one of the conclusions is justified, a number of tests and further observations will be important. When these tests are conducted or the observations are made, the record of those observations will form premises supporting or failing to support its conclusion.

EXERCISE 4

Items 1 to 5 below cite certain background knowledge and a record of certain observations. Below is given a set of initially plausible hypotheses. For each "data" statement pick the hypothesis which is initially most plausible, given only that data statement as background.

Data statements:
1. The DL-7 has crashed three times during electrical storms. No other DL-7 crashes have occurred.
2. The DL-7 has crashed three times during storms, but only once is there any record of electrical disturbances during the storm. No other DL-7 crashes have occurred.
3. The DL-7 has crashed three times: once during an electrical storm, once in a (non-electrical) snowstorm, and once in clear weather. The DL-5 has flown the same flights as many times without mishap.
4. The DL-7 has never crashed. Since the building of the DL-7, the DL-5, which has a similar tail design, has crashed twice. Each time the tail design was cited by the Federal Aviation Commission as the problem causing the crash.
5. The DL-5 and the DL-7, which have similar tail designs, have each suffered severe tail vibrations during takeoff.

Hypotheses:
A. DL-7 crashes are more likely during hot weather than during cold weather.
B. DL-7 crashes are more likely than DL-5 crashes.
C. DL-7 crashes are more likely during electrical disturbances than otherwise.

D. If the DL-7 does crash it is more probable that it has had tail problems than that it has had some other kind of problem.

E. The DL-7 tail probably vibrates because of the way it is designed.

F. DL-7 crashes are more likely during stormy weather than during clear weather.

G. In stormy weather the strong winds tend to accentuate the tail vibrations of the DL-5 and the DL-7.

ANSWERS TO EXERCISE 4

1. C   2. F   3. B   4. D   5. E

If you missed any review 46:3.1 and 46:3.2.

46:4.1 Observability In order to test and observe what is relevant to the truth of the proposed conclusion, it will be necessary for you to state the conclusion with a considerable degree of *precision*. It is important for you to use clear and unambiguous language. To support the conclusion (hypothesis), we must be able to make pertinent *observations*. Sometimes the language of the conclusion will leave some question about exactly what to observe. Suppose, for example, that someone says his or her paper boy is dependable. What should you try to observe to determine whether the assertion is true? Is it sufficient if the boy delivers a paper every day? Or is it important that he put it on the porch? Does he need to put it between the storm door and the inner door? Does he need to arrive between 4:45 and 5:00 A.M.? Without answers to questions like these you do not know what to observe and you do not know the relevance of what the paper boy does to whether he is appropriately called "dependable."

46:4.2 Qualifying specifications There is a process, which is largely linguistic, which we can use to make clear what observations are relevant to establishing the truth of a hypothesis.

With talk these days about radiation in milk and cholesterol in egg yolks, we have become accustomed to the thought that many substances may be toxic in a variety of ways. Yet it may still seem extreme to say that water—pure water—is toxic. Still, it is in fact true that a person who drinks 3 gallons of water at once will die. In the same sense, salt is toxic. A famous method of suicide in ancient China was the ingestion of one cup of salt.

Normally, of course, we think of both water and salt as nontoxic. And in the quantities in which people regularly consume them, far from being toxic, they are usually beneficial to one's health. Yet almost any substance is harmful in some quantity and lethal in some (usually greater) quantity. Quite clearly, then, a term like 'toxic' requires *qualifying specifications* if it is to have a satisfactorily precise meaning. The ambiguity of 'toxic' in its general use is sufficient to prevent the formulation of precise statements of probabilities. To eliminate this ambiguity, it is first necessary to specify, say, a level of behavioral impairment and a lethal level. Second, it will not be adequate to speak of substances as toxic or nontoxic at either level. Substances toxic in one quantity will be nontoxic in another, lesser quantity. So again we will need to revise our way of speaking; we must speak of a given amount of a substance as constituting or failing to constitute a toxic dose. Third, our second refinement will itself need to be refined. A lethally toxic dose of aspirin for a 25-pound child may not even impair the behavior of a 250-pound adult. So again we will need to refine our vocabulary to account for differences in persons who ingest a substance. We will need to say, for example, that water containing seven parts per million of mercury will impair the behavior of an average adult drinking a normal amount of that water per day for 60 or more days.

46:5.1 We are now ready to generalize about the way in which we went about refining and redefining the meaning of 'toxicity.' We wanted to clarify the *observations pertinent* to determining whether a substance is toxic. But since observation is so central, it is necessary to know *what* should be observed. Every clarification we made in the meaning of 'toxic' has been designed to clarify which observations are pertinent and which are not. Ambiguity must be eliminated, often by distinguishing and defining different senses. Vagueness must be substantially reduced, often by introducing quantitative measurement.

Let us consider some other assertions.

EG. 46.3 The students at Tuscon University are bright.

EG. 46.4 The water of Lake Erie is dirty.

EG. 46.5 Ghetto children are culturally disadvantaged.

EG. 46.6 Religion is a compensatory device.

EG. 46.7 Employment law is sexist.

In all five assertions there is some unclarity, given the way in which the assertions are written, about what observations are solicited by the predicate terms 'sexist,' 'bright,' 'dirty,' 'culturally disadvantaged,' and 'compensatory device.' 'Sexist' clearly means "having an unfair bias against the members of one sex," but beyond that further clarity would be desirable. Should we mean "against the members of either sex" or, because most complaints are about antifeminist bias, should we mean "against women"? The interests of the investigator will determine this, but an explicit clarification should be made so that both the investigator and the audience hearing the assertion know what is really meant. More covertly, standards of "fairness" will also require clarification so that the unfairness of a bias can be seen by any trained observer. Otherwise the investigator may simply impose his or her own bias in a hidden way, by observing unfairness according to some individualized, unannounced meaning of 'unfair.'

What problems do you perceive now in the term 'bright' found in Eg. 46.3? Can you follow the hints suggested above in order to provide a clarification of the pertinent observations?

Once we get down to Eg. 46.4 our problem is compounded—not only does the predicate term 'dirty' require clarification, but, perhaps more subtly, so does the subject term 'water of Lake Erie.' 'Water of Lake Erie' raises different questions. What are the boundaries of the lake? Where do tributaries end and where does the lake begin? Moreover, is all the water asserted to be polluted, or is it simply asserted that there are significant subareas of the lake that are substantially polluted by some pollutant or other? These questions must be settled.

Now consider Egs. 46.5 and 46.6. Each has a subject term and a predicate term requiring redefinition so that the pertinent observations will be clarified. The reference class of 'ghetto children' will require clarification. Observable manifestations of the advantages of culture will need to be spelled out, etc. What steps would you take toward making each of these terms observational?

46:5.2 Reliability and validity When you set out to define a term so as to make it observational, there are various pitfalls you will need to avoid. Researchers are aware and concerned about two in particular. On the one hand, it is important that the terms in the definition should have the same meaning to everybody. More exactly, what is important is that everybody who might test a hypothesis in which the term occurs must be inclined to make the same observations. For example, if a sloppy definition of toxicity did not distinguish between behavioral impairment and death, then two observers might make very different observations about whether a teaspoon of nutmeg taken by an average adult is toxic. It will certainly impair behavior but it will probably not cause death. Similarly, if a 'sexist law' is defined as "a law having an unfair bias," then different observers, with different standards of fairness, may make different observations about whether something is sexist. An *observational definition* is good if on the basis of that definition you *can rely on different observers to make the same observations in the same circumstances*, at least most of the time. This is what they mean when they say that an observational definition has *reliability*.

Sometimes in an attempt to overcome problems of unreliability, you may fall prey to the other serious danger. You find something that certainly can be observed and that everyone will observe in the same way. But it is not really what you wanted to observe. Suppose you wanted to be able to define 'motivation' so that everyone could observe whether the students in a given class were motivated to learn. It would be difficult to come up with a reliable definition of 'motivation.' So in frustration you might say to yourself, "Well let's just say that a motivated student waves his or her hand in the air whenever the teacher asks a question." Then of course every observer could see how frequently each student waved a hand in response to questions. But is hand waving an acceptable definition of learning motivation? Clearly it is rather arbitrary! If you really want to study learning motivation, you are changing the subject if you actually study hand waving. The students might wave their hands only out of a motivation to please their teachers, not out of a desire to learn. Also they might be highly motivated to learn, but too shy, too modest, or too uncertain of themselves to raise their hands. Observing hand waving can be equated with observing learning motivation only by gross, arbitrary stipulation, as we have just suggested. Yet without reflection, this definitional equation may seem plausible, and it will certainly seem attractive because of its reliability. Nevertheless, we have determined that when you observe constant hand waving you are not necessarily observing high learning motivation. Although you have a reliable observational definition, it is arbitrary and off the point; thus it cannot be accepted.

Such arbitrary observational definitions have a name which is well established in inductive logic and research: they are called *invalid. Notice that given this definition and the definition of 'valid' which logicians apply to* arguments, *the terms 'valid' and 'invalid' are ambiguous.* Two technical, stipulative definitions of 'valid' are operative. In the logician's use, what is valid or invalid is an argument, and validity is a matter of logical structure. In the researcher's use what is valid or invalid is a definition which purports to specify an observational equivalent, and its validity is a matter of nonarbitrariness (of whether what it tells one to observe is really what one has set out to study).

EXERCISE 5

Below you will find a series of terms, each of which is defined twice. One of the definitions successfully defines the term making it observational. The other fails in some way or another. Mark the successful observational definition 'obs' and the unsuccessful definition 'no.'

1a. A *dependable* paper boy is a reliable paper boy.
 b. A *dependable* paper boy delivers a paper each day to each customer.
2a. A *short* account is a set of no more than three assertions.
 b. A *short* account is an account whose total length is at least one standard deviation shorter than the length of the average account.
3a. By 'Lake Erie' is meant the Great Lake bounded on the northwest by the Detroit River and on the northeast by Niagara Falls.
 b. By 'Lake Erie' is meant the southwesternmost of the five Great Lakes.
4a. By 'Lake Erie' is meant the Great Lake with the purest greenish-blue cast.
 b. By 'Lake Erie' is meant the shallowest of the Great Lakes.
5a. The *average* line to which saltwater comes in along a coast is that line to which it usually comes in.
 b. The *average* line to which saltwater comes in along a coast is that line determined by recording the line to which the water comes in over a period of one lunar year and mathematically computing the average.
6a. By 'national shoreline' is meant that strip of land extending from the line which is the average line to which the water comes in to a line 3 miles inland from the average water line.
 b. By 'national shoreline' is meant that strip of land extending in from the line which is the average line to which the water comes in, to a line 200 miles inland from the average water line.
7a. To say that a person has a *higher* standard of living is to say that her or his disposable income, after inflation has been accounted for, has risen.
 b. To say that a person has a *higher* standard of living is to say that she or he feels better about what she or he can buy.
8a. To say that a person has a *higher* standard of living is to say that her or his ability to meet stated nutritional, medical, educational, and cultural needs has increased.
 b. To say that a person has a *higher* standard of living is to say that her or his ability to meet needs has increased.
9a. An *industrious* worker is one who enjoys his or her work.
 b. An *industrious* worker is one who works longer hours than the average and has a greater than average output.

EXERCISE 6

Check the answers for Ex. 5. Be sure you understand the explanations of why the wrong answers are wrong. Now notice that there are three broad ways in which a definition may fail in making a term observational:

A. It may be that anybody would be as unable to observe the property in question after the definition, as they had been before.
B. It may be that different people would be inclined to make different observations on the basis of the provided definition.
C. It may be that everyone would be inclined to make the same observations, but the definition would be arbitrary and so the observations would really be observations of the wrong property.

For each unsuccessful definition in Ex. 5, determine why it fails, using reason (A), (B), or (C) above. In some cases there is some plausibility to more than one reason.

ANSWERS TO EXERCISES 5 AND 6

Ex. 5

1. b; 'reliable' is a rough synonym of 'dependable,' but neither term clarifies just what observations are appropriate.
2. a; b is a step in the direction of observability, but without a statement about the length of the average account and the size of the standard deviations, the information provided by the definition is incomplete.
3. a; b is observational, too, but what it tells you to observe clearly isn't Lake Erie but Lake Michigan.
4. b; what might seem pure greenish blue to you might not seem pure greenish blue to another person, and what might seem pure greenish blue when the sun is shining might not seem pure greenish blue when it is overcast.
5. b; 'average' and 'usual' are rough synonyms, but neither term provides a procedure for determining the average water line.
6. a; b is observational, too, but there is no way that land up to 200 miles from an ocean can properly be called shoreline.
7. a; it is notoriously difficult to observe how someone feels: b does not overcome this difficulty.
8. a; a clarifies which needs are to be considered and that the person's statement of the needs is to define them; b does neither of these.
9. b; a leaves it unclear how one is to observe a person's enjoyment of his or her work.

If you missed any review 46:4.1 to 46:5.2 (see also 6:3, 7:2.1, and 7:2.4).

Ex. 6

1. A
2. A
3. C
4. B
5. A
6. C
7. A or B; people would look for different things to see whether someone feels better.
8. A or B; the reasons are similar to those given for item 7.
9. A or B; people who think they can observe enjoyment will probably look for different things (same as items 7 and 8).

If you missed any review 46:4.1 to 46:5.2.

46:6 Inductive conclusions Now that you are able to recognize and distinguish clarified observational terms from ambiguous or vague nonobservational terms, you are ready to shift your focus to another aspect of the conclusions of inductive arguments. These conclusions will be assertions of individual or class inclusion or exclusion. In this way they are exactly like the conclusions of arguments considered in Chapter 5 and 6. The inclusion and exclusion statements in predicate logic are either about a total class (like 'all F's are G's' or 'no F's are G's'), or they are about an indefinite part of a class ('at least one F is G' or 'at least one F is not G'). Inductive arguments, on the other hand, can easily be about any percentage of a class from 0 to 100 percent. Here are some examples:

EG. 46.8   Twenty-one percent of all men die in the first year after their retirement.

EG. 46.9   Seventy-five percent of all Caucasians have dark hair.

EG. 46.10   Forty-eight percent of all high school graduates attend college.

EG. 46.11   Whenever a base and an acid are combined, a salt is formed (100 percent of the time).

When you are attempting to state the conclusion of an inductive argument, it is not enough to clarify the terms of your conclusion so as to make them observational. You *must also indicate how frequently the classes mentioned in the conclusion are related to each other in the manner specified* by the conclusion. In other words, your conclusion should take the form 'N percent of all F's are G's.'

46:7.1 Background knowledge   One final feature of inductive conclusions needs to be clarified before we can say that we have framed good hypotheses. Consider two examples.

EG. 46.12   Twenty-five percent of all college students cohabit with a member of the opposite sex sometime during their college career.

EG. 46.13   Twenty-five percent of all Caucasians have blue eyes.

In terms of all of the distinctions we have made so far, these two examples are identical. You may, however, feel that there *is* a difference between these examples. And if you have some background knowledge concerning these statistics, you will be able to see that indeed there is a difference between them. While both assertions are true, at least approximately, Eg. 46.12 is at best true of *present-day* students. It was not true even in the 1960s, for then dorm policies and regulations inhibited cohabitation. On the other hand, Eg. 46.13 is not true only of the present-day population. If certain very plausible assumptions are made, we can say not only that the truth of Eg. 46.13 holds for present-day Caucasians, but that it will also hold 100 years from now—as it held 100 years ago. Of course, in order to assert this, we will have to assume that the reproductive habits of blue-eyed Caucasians will not be significantly different from the reproductive habits of non-blue-eyed Caucasians in any generation. But, having made this assumption, we can make use of a *general understanding* supplied to us by modern genetic theory. Our understanding of dominant and recessive genes and how they interact assures us that what is being asserted is not merely true for an isolated year, but is an inductive assertion equally acceptable through time.

46:7.2   The difference between these two examples of inductive conclusions is a rather significant one, both in the names that we will give to distinguish them, and, as we shall see in Module 47, in the methods appropriate to testing them. The background provided to us by genetic theory provides a model of the causal mechanism by virtue of which we can expect that as long as the reproductive habits of persons with these recessive genes are substantially the same as those with dominant genes, the proportion of persons within the population with traits reflecting recessive genes will remain substantially constant. On the other hand, there is no theory explaining or providing any clear causal explanation which would allow us to make similar comments about Eg. 46.12. Given our knowledge and the causal connections of which we are aware, the connection asserted in Eg. 46.12 is certainly a *statistical correlation, but without any theoretical framework in terms of which to understand it, it cannot be viewed as a causal connection.*

46:7.3 Distinguishing causal from statistical connections We will distinguish between inductive arguments which conclude causal connections and inductive arguments concluding statistical connections on the basis of the state of human knowledge at a given time. If the connection is presented in the argument on the basis of a general theory, which has been confirmed and is creditable in the light of established findings, then, because of that theory, we can understand the assertion made in the conclusion of that inductive argument as expressing a causal regularity (one not confined to present times and circumstances). Without such a confirmed theoretical understanding, observations may make it very clear that the conclusion is true, but observations alone do not suffice to show that a *causal* connection is involved. Thus, the distinction between causal connections and statistical connections is made on the basis of whether there is a *general confirmed theoretical framework through which observations can be explained* and understood.[1]

There is an important corollary to making the distinction between causal and statistical connections in this fashion. The corollary is already implicit in Egs. 46.12 and 46.13. Both these examples, it should be noted, are about a fraction of a total population; neither is about 100 percent of the population. Thus, in accordance with these examples, you should see now that inductive arguments concluding with causal connections need not have conclusions about 100 percent of their subject class. Moreover, statistical connections *can* have conclusions about 100 percent of their classes. *The percentage of the classes is not the distinguishing factor* between inductions expressing causal connections and those expressing statistical connections.

46:8 You have now gone through the steps of framing a hypothesis. The hypothesis will express either a causal or a statistical connection. It will specify two classes or an individual and a class. When two classes are involved, it will specify a percentage of the members of the one class. It will say that the one class, or a percentage of it, is either included or excluded in the other. And the classes mentioned will have been defined in such a way that it will be possible to make observations pertinent to determining whether members of those classes exist and are related in the way hypothesized.

EXERCISES FOR MODULE 46
FRAMING CLEAR HYPOTHESES

Ex. 7 In the light of each of the following data statements, choose the initially plausible hypothesis.

1. In 77 of the last 90 years it has snowed during September in Yellowstone National Park.

[1] In other words we are defining our terms so that three items are synonymous: a hypothesis is statistical at a given time $=_{df}$ it is one that is not causal at that time $=_{df}$ it is one that lacks explanation on the basis of a confirmed, creditable theoretical framework which is part of the common knowledge of the group examining the hypothesis at that given time.

A. There is always snow in Yellowstone in September.

B. There is always snow in Yellowstone sometime during the winter.

C. Sometimes there is snow in Yellowstone in September.

D. There is seldom snow in Yellowstone during September.

E. Usually it will snow in Yellowstone during September.

2. No one filling out a United States census form in 1970 was born in 1850.

A. Few people were born in 1850.

B. Most people born in 1850 falsified their reports.

C. No one born in 1850 was living in the United States in 1970.

D. Less than 50 percent of those born in 1850 were alive in 1970.

E. Of those born in 1850, 80 percent were dead by 1970.

3. In 1973 737 murders were committed in Detroit. There were 720 in Chicago in the same year.

A. Since the population of Detroit is approximately 150 times 737, if you live in Detroit 50 years, the chances are 1 in 30 that you will be murdered.

B. In Detroit the number of murders on any given day is most likely two.

C. Few people are murdered.

D. Living in Detroit is more dangerous than living in Chicago.

E. Detroit had more murders than Chicago in 1970.

4. Below is a chart. On the left is the number of hours that weather in the Pittsburgh area has been dominated by a stagnant high-pressure system. On the right is the mean, or average, level of air pollution after such a number of hours. The Environmental Protection Agency standard of 100 for satisfactory air quality is employed.

Hours	Average air-pollution index
120	230
108	210
96	180
84	155
72	130
60	110
48	90
36	75
24	60

A. Air quality in Pittsburgh is usually satisfactory.

B. The average of all highs stagnant for 60 or more hours over Pittsburgh will be associated with unsatisfactory air quality.

C. Pittsburgh almost always has unsatisfactory air quality after 84 hours of domination by a stagnant high.

D. Pittsburgh rarely has unsatisfactory air quality after only 24 hours of domination by a stagnant high.

E. The average of all highs stagnant for 48 or more hours over Pittsburgh will be associated with unsatisfactory air quality.

5. On the graph below the vertical axis represents the number of hours that a high-pressure system has been stagnant over Buffalo, New York. The horizontal axis represents a level of air quality maintained. The numbers on the graph are percentages: the percentage of times that a certain air quality has been maintained after so many hours during the last 3 years in Buffalo. (Thus the percentage of

40 in the bottom left-hand corner of the graph means that an air quality of "excellent" or better has been maintained, after 24 hours of constant domination by a stagnant high, on 40 percent of the occasions in Buffalo during the last 3 years.) (*Note:* There is more than one correct answer.)*

Hours	Excellent	Good	Satisfactory	Unsatisfactory	Air-pollution alert
120	0	0	0	2	40
108	0	0	0	10	60
96	0	0	0	35	70
84	0	0	2	60	85
72	0	4	15	78	96
60	0	10	20	88	99
48	2	25	60	99	100
36	15	35	80	100	100
24	40	80	98	100	100

A. It is very improbable that satisfactory air quality will be maintained in Buffalo after 84 hours of constant domination by a stagnant high.
B. For 72 hours of domination by a stagnant high in Buffalo satisfactory air quality is not maintained 85 percent of the time.
C. Once an air-pollution alert goes into effect in the Buffalo area it always stays in effect until the high-pressure system moves out.
D. Excellent quality air is found in Buffalo less than half the time.
E. Good-quality air can usually be maintained in Buffalo during a stagnant high only if the high remains stagnant for less than 36 hours.

Ex. 8 Check the answers for Ex. 7. Be sure you understand why each correct answer is correct. Now consider each correct answer. In the light of *your* background knowledge, is each hypothesis causal or statistical? To answer reasonably, *list* the items of your knowledge in virtue of which you conclude that each hypothesis is causal or statistical.

ANSWERS TO EXERCISES
FOR MODULE 46

Ex. 7

1. E; (A) is too strong, (C) and (D) are too weak, and (B) goes beyond the data to the different, although related, subject of snow during the entire winter.
2. C; (D) and (E) both draw inferences about what happened to those born in 1850 and additionally they each understand their case quantitatively. A and B also draw inferences—and less reasonable ones at that—to account for the data concerning 1850 births.
3. B; (A) treats mathematically the probability that any resident of Detroit will be killed—subject to the principle of insufficient reason—which seems unwarranted. The ambiguity of the term 'few' and the vagueness of the term 'dangerous'

* The "40" at the top of the right-hand column means that there is an "air-pollution alert" 60 percent of the time if a high has been stagnant for 120 hours. The "100" at the bottom of the column means there is never an alert after only 24 hours.

disqualify (C) and (D). The inference in E is on a different, if related topic—
murders in 1970.

4. B; (A) is not made plausible because no data are supplied about how often stagnant highs dominate Pittsburgh weather. (C) and (D) involve the same mistake.
Consider (C): true, after 84 hours the average air quality is 155, but the data
supplied do not tell you how frequently the average is under 100 (standard of
satisfactory) after 84 hours. Perhaps 25 percent of the time it is under 100. Since
(C) says it is *almost always* over 100, (C) has not been directly supported by the
data presented.

5. A, B, C, E; (D) makes the same mistake as is made in 4(A).

If you missed any review 46:6.1.

EX. 8

1. With sufficient knowledge about air currents over the Pacific, weather in moun-
tainous regions, and the northerly location of Yellowstone, the hypothesis is
causal, but otherwise statistical.

2. With sufficient background about the causes of human mortality, the hypothesis
is causal.

3. There is no adequate background knowledge now available by virtue of which
murders in Detroit, Chicago, or large cities, or the relations between murders in
Detroit and murders in Chicago, could be regarded as causal.

4. The hypothesis is causal given sufficient background knowledge about pressure
systems, air currents in pressure systems, and the behavior of pollutants in those
air currents.

If you missed any review 46:7.1 to 46:8.

MODULE 47

CONFIRMING AND DISCONFIRMING HYPOTHESES

When you have followed the procedures given in Module 46 you will have framed
an hypothesis clearly expressing either a causal or a statistical connection. In an
inductive argument that hypothesis will form the conclusion. One kind of premise
in support of that conclusion will state those factors, theoretical and observational,
which led you in the first place to choose this hypothesis rather than some other
deviation from mathematical probabilities. The other premises in the inductive argument will state the results of observations and tests used to determine whether the
hypothesis is true. The construction and carrying out of these tests will be discussed
here. The objectives for this module concern the tests which are pertinent to verifying
(proving true) hypotheses which have been clarified following the procedures of
Module 46.

● After reading Module 47 you should be able to:

1. Identify the kinds of tests which are pertinent to the confirmation of causal and
statistical hypotheses

2. Distinguish good from bad reasons why particular hypotheses are unsupported
by given sets of data

3. Determine what further information would be required to provide adequate support for a given hypotheses relative to a given but possibly inadequate data set
4. Frame competing hypotheses relative to a given data set, which hypotheses must be ruled out in the process of confirming a given hypothesis
5. State the general strategy for attempting to confirm an hypothesis

47:1.1 Other possibilities Consider for a moment an obviously weak argument.

EG. 47.1 Professor Snorin Borin always has many students asleep in his lectures. They probably take sleeping pills before they come to class.

Granting that the argument is weak, what can you say about why it is weak? Suppose you start with the basic idea of *justification,* that is, if the premise is true the conclusion is at least very likely to be true. Working from that idea you could say that there are many ways in which the premise of Eg. 47.1 might be true while the conclusion was false. Perhaps the students are bored. Perhaps the dingy atmosphere of his particular classroom puts students to sleep. Perhaps the students are under the influence of some other kind of drug. In other words, there are many plausible ways in which the premise of Eg. 47.1 can be true while its conclusion is false. So the argument can't reasonably be counted as logically correct.

47:1.2 Let us fill out our account of Eg. 47.1 a bit without substantially affecting the weakness of this argument. Suppose that you know that this professor has more sleepers in class than there are in other classes, and suppose that you also know that many of these students take sleeping pills. If observations have been made to support these two facts, then there will be an initial plausibility to the hypothesis that the students are asleep because of taking sleeping pills. But initial plausibility is not the same as justification! An initially plausible hypothesis is simply a hypothesis which explains, or fits well with, observed deviations from random patterns. Our "perhaps" list shows that even though the conclusion has an initial plausibility —it does explain the observed deviations from random patterns—there are many plausible ways in which it could turn out to be false. Other contrary but initially plausible hypotheses might be true instead. The argument therefore is not logically correct even though the hypothesis has initial plausibility. There are *alternative accounts* of the observed facts. If any of these other possibilities is true, the conclusion of Eg. 47.1 may be false.

You are now ready to grasp the central idea of justification. Every one of the "perhaps" we listed above represents a way—a *plausible* way—in which the premise of Eg. 47.1 may be true while its conclusion is false. Accordingly the argument is not justified. The plausible possibilities that the conclusion will be false while the premise is true have not even been considered in the argument of Eg. 47.1, much less ruled out. In other words we can say that a justified argument is one in which the premises not only confirm the conclusion but *consider* and somehow *rule out* the various ways in which the conclusion might turn out false. It will rule out alternative hypotheses even though they are initially plausible.

This insight about justification can be transformed into a procedure for the testing of arguments involving causal or statistical hypotheses as conclusions.

1. You should look at such a hypothesis and find out what initial plausibility it has.
2. Then you should ask yourself: In what other plausible ways might I be able to account for the deviations from random patterns sighted in the observations?

A justified argument will both provide further positive support for the truth of its stated conclusion and also provide a kind of negative support: it will have premises supporting the assertion that the alternative initially plausible hypotheses are false.

47:2 Alternative conclusions It is clear now that in every justified inductive argument concluding either a causal or statistical connection, there will be premises providing an initial plausibility for the conclusion. However, very often alternative, contrary conclusions will also fit with these premises. Subsequent premises will then be necessary both to support the stated conclusion and to rule out the alternative (initially plausible) conclusions. There are three questions to consider:

1. What operational definition of 'initially plausible hypothesis' will allow us to determine the range of conclusions which should be considered and either supported or ruled out?
2. What kinds of tests are relevant to supporting and ruling out initially plausible hypotheses?
3. Since by definition justified arguments have premises which *strongly support* their conclusion, how can the appropriate strength of the support be determined? Similarly, how can one determine when an alternative hypotheses has been sufficiently ruled out or falsified?

47:3.1 Let's try to clarify the idea of initial plausibility through a fairly simple, concrete example.

EG. 47.2 It was a cold night (−10°C) when John went out to his car. He hoped it would start. He remembered only too well that this car often failed to start once the temperature dropped below 0°C. He got into the car, turned on the lights for exactly 1 minute to warm up the battery, turned them off, pumped the gas carefully, and tried to start the car. It didn't start. Unfortunately, the wind was howling strongly enough that John could not hear whether the engine had even turned over. Then John noticed the gas gauge. It registered low enough that the tank was surely within a gallon of being empty. Perhaps he was out of gas, he thought.

Why did John's car fail to start? Of course, as you approach this question, your freedom is limited: either you work simply from the information provided in the example, or you speculate, perhaps on the basis of your own greater information about the usual problems involved in a car's failure to start. If your speculation is to be reasonable, it will ultimately rest on experience and on your understanding of cars. Since the basic elements of experience and an understanding of cars is already built into the example, we can come to understand initial plausibility simply working from the information provided.

What hypotheses about the car's failing to start are initially plausible in this situation? Because of John's experience with his car it is plausible (not only to John but to anyone else who is aware of his experience) that the car will not start simply because it is too cold. Because of the simple understanding that the gas gauge reflects the level of gas in the gas tank and the understanding that the car will not start unless the engine receives sufficient gas, it is also plausible that the car will not start because it is out of gas.

On the other hand, it is rather implausible that the battery is run down: John turned on the lights, we know that the lights work, and again we know from our understanding of cars that the lights would not work if the battery were down. Some persons, however, might not know that turning lights on for a minute tends to warm the battery up. They might believe that the battery would be run down by this operation, and that different background belief would make it more plausible to them that the battery was run down! This does not mean that it is plausible relative to the total body of information available to people in our culture. But what it does show is that initial plausibility can only be assessed relative to background knowledge, either the individual's or the culture's! Therefore, whenever careful research is to be done to determine justifiability of an inductive argument, *it is imperative that the research include a clear statement of the background knowledge that is taken for granted in the course of the research.* Without a clear statement of the assumed background knowledge there is no authoritatively rational way of deciding whether a hypothesis is initially plausible or initially implausible. In formal research a review of the relevant literature on the previous research concerning a subject is used to define the assumed background knowledge.

47:3.2 Degrees of initial plausibility Certain factors complicate deciding whether an hypothesis is initially plausible. Initial plausibility is a matter of more and less, not a matter of yes or no. Suppose, in our example, that the temperature were 0°C, not −10°C. Since in the past John's troubles have been at the freezing point and colder, a temperature of 0°C is borderline. He might have troubles and might not. On the other hand, if the temperature had plunged to −20°C and the car had been out in that frigid temperature for many hours, then the hypothesis of the car's not starting because of the cold would be even more plausible than we originally imagined. Sharp border lines between initially plausible hypotheses and initially implausible hypotheses will not always be possible. When these borderlines are not sharp, honest research requires open acknowledgement of this situation combined with explicit statements about the practical interests or limitations by virtue of which a somewhat arbitrary boundary line is drawn.

47:3.3 Initial plausibility and background knowledge Not only is initial plausibility to some extent a matter of degree, it is also subject to change in the light of further observations and understanding. Before John observed the gas gauge he had no information to support the hypothesis that he might be out of gas. Similarly, as we described the example, he has no information to support the hypothesis that the engine has been stolen from his car. On the basis of John's information it is not initially plausible that the car has no engine. Yet if he looked under the hood and found no engine, that hypothesis would immediately become very plausible. Similarly, a changed understanding of the way cars work can also change the initial plausibility of a hypothesis. Perhaps John should not have been surprised when he found no engine under his hood. Perhaps his car is an electric car which runs directly on large batteries. Thus understanding of how a car works greatly modifies the initial plausibility of various hypotheses.

The fact that the initial plausibility of a hypothesis is relative to background knowledge—experience and understanding—is not hard to comprehend. It is harder, however, to act appropriately in the light of this fact when one is conducting research. Part of conducting research is the process of gathering further information about the subject. That information is gathered for the purpose of supporting one of the hypotheses and disconfirming others. Sometimes, however, the information does something else: it shows that a further hypothesis, not originally considered plausible, should, in the light of the new information, be considered plausible. When

John looks at his gas gauge he has little difficulty in realizing that another hypothesis has gained initial plausibility. But when a researcher has carefully read the literature on previous research, it is very easy for the researcher to assume that the previous research *guarantees* that only certain hypotheses can be considered initially plausible. Overcoming this kind of prejudice has often been hard—a fact to which the history of science adequately attests.

47:3.4 We have now outlined the reasons why determining the initially plausible hypotheses in researching a subject is not a completely cut-and-dried thing. Still the procedures for making this determination can and should be set out with whatever degree of rigor is possible.

1. The background information and understanding of the subject should be stated clearly.
2. The relative plausibility of various hypotheses should be determined on the basis of this background.
3. In borderline cases, the reasons for calling a hypothesis initially plausible or initially implausible should be expressed.
4. When further information is collected, it should be examined to determine whether any other hypotheses, not originally thought of as initially plausible, should be added to the list of initially plausible hypotheses in the light of this further information. You may check your understanding of initial plausibility by doing Ex. 1 now.

47:4.1 The question raised in Eg. 47.2 was why John's car did not start one night. That is a question about a particular single incident. The questions raised in research projects differ from that of Eg. 47.2 in that they are general, not particular. For instance,

EG. 47.3 When John got the tow truck out to help him later in the evening, he asked the driver, "How often does a car's failure to start occur in cold weather?" To this the driver responded, "55 percent of our calls for non-starting cars in the last 6 months have come when the temperature was below freezing. We've been keeping track at the station."

This information from station records makes it initially plausible that 55 percent of all car-starting failures occur in weather 0°C or below. Clearly this is a statistical assertion, not a causal assertion. Many factors could make the statistic true this year and false at another time. Cars might, for instance, have stronger or more insulated batteries at another time. No theoretical explanation for the connection is offered by either person.

Since the connection here is statistical, you can begin to discern what, in general, is involved in the support of a statistical connection. You might begin by trying to define each of the ways in which the asserted connection can be false, even if the tow-truck's response is true, that is, reflects accurate station records. You should notice that each way in which the asserted connection can be false while the driver's response is true will constitute a way in which the argument concluding the alleged connection from the premise of the driver's response will be invalid. In other words our question is the question of the *justification of arguments having conclusions that assert statistical connections.* If the driver's response can be true while contrary statistical connections remain plausible, then the following argument is unjustified.

Premise: 55 percent of our calls for nonstarting cars in the last 6 months have come when the temperature was 0°C or less.

Conclusion: 55 percent of all car-starting failures occur in weather 0°C or less.

Accordingly, in order *for the argument to be viewed as justified, premises will need to be added ruling out each of the alternative initially plausible hypotheses.* Let's see what this means in our example.

The premise talks about one gas station. Maybe it is an atypical gas station. Maybe it specializes in foreign cars, like John's, and maybe foreign cars respond to cold weather differently from domestic cars. Maybe it is located in a town, and its calls are much different from those received by gas stations along super-highways. Probably you have thought of other ways in which the station may be atypical. Certainly *a justified argument concluding a statistical connection requires premises to the effect that the collected data is representative,* not atypical, of the classes mentioned in the conclusion!

The premise of the original argument reports data concerning a sample of car-starting failures. We have not seen that the argument will be unjustified unless it also contains the premise that the sample is typical. We concentrated on the possibility that the station might be an atypical station. If you have learned this lesson well, you will be able to pick out several further ways in which the sample cited in the original premise might not be typical of the classes mentioned in the conclusion. An inductive argument for a statistical conclusion will be unjustified as long as it remains plausible that the sample mentioned in the original premise is atypical in *any* way that might plausibly influence the capacity of the sample to represent the entire group accurately.

What ways have you now noticed in which the original sample in Eg. 47.3 may be atypical? Here are a few. Is the climate where this gas station is located representative of climates throughout the nation? With respect to this question, are elements other than temperature (say, humidity or altitude, for example) relevant to whether the climate of the sample station is representative? Are the calls accurately recorded? Are the car-starting failures which are called into gas stations representative of the wider class of all the car-starting failures? Might it be true that when cars fail to start because of lack of gas, people are frequently too far from a phone to telephone a station, whereas when they tend to leave their cars out in the cold they also have gone somewhere where a phone is more readily available?

The possibility that *reported* cases will be unrepresentative of total cases is very often sufficiently real and important that it deserves special notice. Suppose we want to know whether some crime, say rape, is more frequent, per 1,000 persons, today than it was 25 years ago. After the term has been appropriately clarified by reference to legal definitions and after it has been determined that the definitions have not changed in the course of those years, one might be tempted to use police records of reported rapes as a record of the frequency of rape at each of these times. Yet problems arise here concerning whether reported cases are typical of all cases. Assuming that all the reports describe genuine rapes, at least two distinct questions arise concerning whether the reports are representative.

1. How accurate are the police records? Perhaps different procedures in various police departments led officers to record fewer of the reported rapes at one of the times in question and more at another.
2. What percentage of the rape victims called the police at each of these times?

Perhaps attitudes about the shame of rape or the cooperativeness and effectiveness of the police were sufficiently different at these two times that the percentage of reported rapes was much higher at the one time than at the other.

47:4.2 Representative data When you are dealing with statistical connections, the initially plausible hypothesis will typically state or assume that the sample statistics originally available are representative not only of the sample itself but also of the entire population. The alternative initially plausible hypothesis will state for some rather definite reason the statistics, while true of the sample, are not true of the entire population. Speaking rather generally, there are four reasons why the statistics true of the sample would not be true of the entire population.

1. The sample population has certain characteristics not true of all or even most of the rest of the population (e.g., the records kept at a gas station at a minor intersection in a small town of rural Montana might not be representative of the problems handled by all or even most other gas stations). As we did in Part Two, let us use capital letters to stand for characteristics of objects. Here we can say that the sample population (the observed F's) has a certain characteristic H which most or all of the rest of the population (the unobserved F's) lacks. Maybe, in other words, the connection does not hold generally between F's and G's (between car-starting failures and low temperatures). Maybe the connection holds only for car-starting failures reported in rural locations (F's that are H's).
2. The sample population lacks certain characteristics which all or most of the rest of the population have. (The gas station is not a service station, it just pumps gas, and as a favor the owner provides road service to a few of his close friends.) Again using symbols, the car-starting failures reported to gas stations (the F's) when those gas stations are *not* service stations (the non-J's) may be G's (car-starting failures in low temperatures), while F's that are J's are not G's in this quantity at all.
3. The data about the sample population have not been accurately recorded. (The gas station owner really wanted to know what calls the station got, but the workers who recorded the calls took it as a joke.) In our symbolism, 55 percent of the recorded calls of F's (car-starting failures) were recorded as G's (during times of low temperature), but it is false that 55 percent of all F's were G's.
4. The reported data about the sample population are not typical of the entire population even in the area of the sample. (Some kind of data go unreported because phones are unavailable to report the incidents, because people are embarrassed to report them, etc.) Fifty-five percent of the reported F's are G's, but a far different percentage of the unreported F's in the sample area are G's.

Whenever the sample data suggest one statistical hypothesis about an entire population, you should think about the items in the list above to help in deciding what alternative hypotheses should be considered.

Here is another case where data are collected about a sample.

EG. 47.4 The births at Hitchcock County Hospital increased from one every third day to one every other day between 1965 and 1975. Form this it was suggested that the national birth rate went up 50 percent during these years.

Here are some alternative hypotheses concerning this example. They are presented in pairs. For each pair you should make a judgment about which one is an alternative

initially plausible hypothesis and which is not. Of course you will need to rely somewhat on background knowledge.

EG. 47.4′ A. The birth rate at the similarly expensive private hospital in the county
   is likely to have changed during the decade relative to that at the
   county hospital.
   B. The birth rate is likely to be related to the overall population growth
   of the county during the decade.

EG. 47.4″ A. Hitchcock County is very large and has poor roads. Consequently a
   large percentage of births take place on the way to the hospital. In
   1965 the hospital recorded only births taking place in the hospital.
   In 1975 all newborns placed in the nursery were counted no matter
   where they were born. On the basis of this additional information it
   is hypothesized that the birth rate in the county is largely unchanged.
   B. In 1965 only live births were recorded at the hospital. In 1975 birth
   records also included babies born dead.

EG. 47.4‴ A. Because of the unusually high percentage of women of childbearing
   age coming into the county population it is hypothesized that the
   national norm will not show so great an increase (if there is any
   increase at all).
   B. Because of the unusually high percentage of white Protestants in the
   population it is hypothesized that the national norm will not show
   so great an increase (if there is any increase at all).

In the first set of alternatives, Eg. 47.4′, alternative A has not been made plausible
at all. No clear difference between the private hospital and the county hospital has
been suggested. Alternative B is much more plausible especially if you take into
account the background fact that some counties are growing much faster than others,
so that births per day are likely to rise in those counties that are gaining residents.
In the second set of alternatives, Eg. 47.4″, alternative A is much more plausible.
The extra information provided in A suggests that records of births actually taking
place in the hospital may show no significant change in the decade. The difference
in record keeping stated in B could account for a small increase, but your background knowledge should be sufficient to assure you that it is not likely that there
is a hospital where one-third of the babies are born dead. In the third set of alternatives, Eg. 47.4‴, alternative A is again more plausible. According to A an unusually high percentage of women of childbearing age have come into the county.
You should expect then that the birth rate would be higher than the national average
—unless of course it were also true that throughout the nation this same change in
the female population was occurring. Alternative B is implausible because there is
no reason to believe that white Protestant women have more children than other
women. It is also implausible because even if Hitchcock County also was pre-
dominately white and Protestant 10 years earlier, there is no reason to believe that
white Protestants began having more children in those 10 years.

47:4.3 Constructing arguments Once you have assembled a list of the original
initially plausible statistical hypothesis and the alternative initially plausible statistical hypotheses, that list of hypotheses clarifies what you must do in order to construct a justified argument in favor of any one of the initially plausible hypotheses.
When that information has been found, premises stating it can be written. Your in-

ductive argument will then be built on the following schema or pattern of development.

Preliminary outline of justified statistical argument:

Premise: Information gathered from a certain sample shows that n percent of all F's are G's.

Initially plausible hypothesis and tentative conclusion of the inductive argument: n percent of all F's are G's.

On the basis of background knowledge available as a matter of common knowledge or as a result of previous research, it is alternatively initially plausible that:

1. Since most F's in the sample were H's, n percent of all F's are G's only if those F's are H's.
2. Since most F's in the sample were not J's, n percent of all F's are G's only if those F's are not J's.
3. Since the sample data were not accurately recorded, it is unreliable to infer anything about all F's from the data.
4. Since there is reason to believe that whether people will report about their F's may be related to whether their F's are G's, it is likely that reported F's are more, or less, likely to be G's than nonreported F's.

Further premise: Further information confirms one of the initially plausible hypotheses and further information also rules out the competing initially plausible hypotheses.

Conclusion: Therefore, the confirmed initially plausible hypothesis is true (and its competitors are false).

We have now examined the entire schema for inductive arguments with conclusions expressing statistical connections. Subject to further refinement on one subject, namely, how strong the confirmation and disconfirmation should be, we can now say that any such inductive argument is justified if it follows this schema. In other words, every such argument that is unjustified fails to include part of the above schema.

47:4.4 Justification versus validity The difference between justification and validity amounts to this: A valid argument is one in which the truth of the premises rules out every way—every *conceivable* way—in which the conclusion might be false. A justified argument whose conclusion expresses either a statistical or a causal connection is one in which the truth of the premises rules out every *plausible* way in which the conclusion might be false. The list of initially plausible hypotheses does not include all the possible hypotheses. But in a justified argument it does include all the plausible hypotheses. The additional premises in a justified argument confirm one of those hypotheses and disconfirm all its competitors. Still leaving aside the strength of the confirmation and disconfirmation, we may say that the justified argument rules out alternatives to its conclusion, as does the valid argument. The difference is that the valid argument rules out all *possible* competing alternatives whereas the justified argument rules out all *plausible* competing alternatives.

Thus it is important to list all the alternative initially plausible hypotheses. If any one of them is ignored, when additional information is collected the information may do nothing to disconfirm the ignored hypothesis. In fact the information might actually tend to confirm it!

47:5.1 Testing causal hypotheses is more complex than testing statistical hypotheses because causal hypotheses claim more than do statistical hypotheses. Statistical hypotheses assert that at a certain time and under the circumstances prevailing at that time a certain percentage of a specified class has certain characteristics. This is the description of Eg. 46.12.

EG. 46.12   Twenty-five percent of all college students cohabit with a member of the opposite sex some time during their college career.

A causal hypothesis, like Eg. 46.13, also claims at least that much.

EG. 46.13   Twenty-five percent of all Caucasians have blue eyes.

Causal hypotheses make all the claims of statistical hypotheses, and they must be tested for sampling errors (see 47:4.2). However, even if you can overcome all the problems about the representativeness of your sample, there are further claims made by a causal hypothesis which require support. Whereas statistical hypotheses make claims only about the present time and prevailing circumstances, causal hypotheses make claims both about present time and prevailing circumstances and *about other times and changed circumstances*. A statistical hypothesis asserts that *at the present time under prevailing circumstances n* percent of all *F*'s are *G*'s. Suppose that up until now most *F*'s are *H*'s. Also suppose that from now on no *F*'s are *H*'s. A statistical hypothesis is not about those changed circumstances, but if a causal hypothesis is true, then *F*'s will be *G*'s when they are no longer *H*'s just as frequently as they have been *G*'s under circumstances when most *F*'s were *H*'s. Accordingly the tests pertinent to statistical hypotheses apply to causal hypotheses, but further tests are required to confirm causal hypotheses because they claim so much more.

47:5.2 Principles of causality   If we learn to identify the extra kinds of claims made by causal hypotheses, we will be able to see what information is relevant to confirm or disconfirm those claims. There are several ideas involved in our modern understanding of causation which imply the relevance of further kinds of information.

First   *If the cause occurs, then its effect will follow.* In other words the occurrence of the cause is sufficient to bring about its effect; nothing else is necessary—nothing else is required for the effect to occur.

A statistical connection says no more than that when some thing is *F* then in *n* percent of the cases it is *G under the variety of presently prevailing circumstances*. In other words the truth of the statistical connection is not undermined if the relationship between the *F*'s and the *G*'s does not remain the same when presently prevailing circumstances change. In clear contrast, a causal connection says that no matter how other circumstances might change, if something is *F* (the cause), then *n* percent of the time that something will have its *G* (the effect).

Once this difference between statistical and causal connections is clarified, you should see that causal hypotheses are subject to a further test because they alone claim that changing the prevailing circumstances will not affect the proposed connection. For example, eye color might be hypothesized to be a genetic trait. Statistical correlations done with mice might be used to help to confirm this connection. But probably the mice studied to make the statistical correlations would be fed a rather standard normal diet. Here in our example this diet represents presently prevailing circumstances. The causal claim that eye color is a genetic trait could be challenged by suggesting that genetic factors are not sufficient to determine eye color. It would be suggested that the correlations between genetic factors and eye color need no longer hold if the presently prevailing circumstances of normal diet were changed. Here a test needs to be set up. Diet needs to be varied from the norm.

Of course some diets would kill the mice or render them sterile. But according to the original causal hypothesis that eye color is a genetic trait, any variation in diet that still allows the mice to reproduce should have no effect on the eye color of the offspring. Whenever a causal hypothesis is true, then changing presently prevailing circumstances will have no impact on the hypothesized connection.

Second *If something necessary to the effect fails to occur, the effect will not occur.* When we say that A causes B, it does not have to be true that without A, B is not. B may have two different causes, so that without A, B occurs whenever the other cause, C, exists. Even so, people often know that in certain circumstances no other cause of B, except maybe A, exists. If no other cause of B exists in those circumstances, then B should occur only if A does.

This idea also makes a useful test of causal hypotheses. Suppose we want to confirm the causal hypothesis that mercury poisoning is killing the fish in a certain stream. Our hypothesis will be more difficult to confirm if it happens that an unusual type of algae has been growing in the stream in recent years, those years when the fish have been dying. One way to gain this confirmation would be to remove the algae. Then we could employ our first idea: If mercury is the cause, then after circumstances are changed—the algae is removed—the effect will still follow. But suppose it is technically difficult or impossible to remove the algae. Then another way to gain the required confirmation would be to invoke our second idea. According to the hypothesis, mercury is necessary to the effect, i.e., the death of the fish in the stream, so if the mercury were removed from the stream, then the fish should stop dying, or, more exactly, they should stop dying at the accelerated rate of the past few years. The hypothesis then will be confirmed if it happens that when the industry discharging its waste mercury into the stream stops the discharge so that the amount of mercury in the stream declines, the fish stop dying at the accelerated rate of recent years.

When the cause and effect mentioned in a hypothesis can occur in varied quantities, a third idea about causes provides a further test relevant to the confirmation of causal hypotheses.

Third *The quantity of the effect will change in proportion to changes in the quantity of the cause.* Indeed, it would be relevant to test the hypothesis that the mercury is killing the fish by reference to this idea. If the death rate among the fish has increased by 20 percent in water with 7 parts per million of mercury, then we might expect that the increase will be greater if the concentration rises and the increase will be less if the concentration falls. At the extremes we might expect, say, that no fish will live at all in water with 90 parts per million of mercury and that fish will die only at normal rates in water free of mercury.

In our example of the fish kill we are dealing with a direct proportion: when mercury pollution *increases,* death rate *increases.* You should notice that our third idea is stated generally enough that it includes the possibility of inverse proportions. For example, researchers have shown that as the number of persons quitting smoking *increases* in a group, the number of deaths due to lung cancer *decreases* in the group.

47:5.3 These three principles present a fairly clear picture of why causal claims are more complex and difficult to verify than statistical claims. Carrying out the tests suggested by these principles requires judgements about plausibility, as do the judgments about alternative initially plausible statistical hypotheses. A causal hypothesis is like a statistical hypothesis in this respect: when we are verifying it we try to rule out the other *plausible* alternatives. When Galileo wanted to test hypotheses about the factors influencing the fall of different objects, he reasonably thought of weight and size and gravitational attraction as plausible factors to consider. Even if he had always dropped the objects from the tops of leaning buildings, however, he could have reasonably believed that the architecture of those buildings did not affect the fall of the objects. There is simply no plausible connection, even though there are conceivable connections, between the architecture of the buildings and the fall of objects dropped from them. Accordingly, Galileo's hypotheses require the confirmation of studies on objects of different sizes and weights, but no one could complain that the hypotheses were inadequately confirmed because all the objects were dropped from the tops of Gothic buildings!

47:5.4 Justified causal arguments We may conclude our discussion of causal connections by noting that justification means the same thing whether we are talking about an inductive argument whose conclusion states a statistical hypothesis or about an inductive argument whose conclusion states a causal hypothesis. In either case a justified argument is one which strongly supports its conclusion by defining the class of initially plausible hypotheses in the light of some data and by appeal to further information which confirms one hypothesis and rules out all its plausible competitors. The difference between arguments with these two different conclusions is that since the conclusions asserting causal connections assert more, more is required in order to confirm them and to rule out the larger number of competing alternatives which they have.

47:6.1 Justification and degrees of support Throughout our discussion of justification we have said that the conclusion of a justified argument is *strongly supported* by its premises. Similarly we have said that when justified arguments conclude statistical or causal connections, one hypothesis must be *highly confirmed* and all plausible competing hypotheses must be *ruled out*. We must now face the final question of *how strongly* the conclusion should be supported, how highly the accepted hypothesis should be confirmed, and how thoroughly the alternatives should be ruled out. The answers to these questions are complicated, but they can be outlined in an understandable way. Recall our discussion of mathematical probabilities (46:1.1 and 46:1.2).

Suppose you were throwing a die and it came up three, four times in a row. That would be rather surprising. As a matter of chance that sequence will happen only once in 1,296 rolls. But now suppose you role three, four more times in a row. The odds against that sequence are geometrically greater; it should occur once in 6^8 rolls. Such a phenomenal sequence suggests that the die is loaded. The eight successive rolls of a three make it plausible that mathematical probabilities do not apply to this die. Other principles besides the principle of insufficient reason must explain its behavior.

The general point suggested by this examples is that the principle of insufficient reason represents the regularity which is known to exist with normal dice. The imagined sequence of eight successive threes represents a significant departure from that regularity. The idea of *significant departure* can be made rather precise and used to answer our question about how strong the support should be in an inductive argument. An intuitive idea of significant departure would be vague and probably no two people would use it in exactly the same way. Consequently it seems wise to provide a mathematical or quantitative definition of the idea.

To form this definition we begin with what we know. In our example we would begin with two pieces of knowledge: we know how to compute probabilities on the basis of the principle of insufficient reason and we know that the principle applies to normal dice. Three successive threes will be improbable, but, in accordance with the principle of insufficient reason, four successive threes will be six times as improbable as three. Once the probability of certain events is computed—relative to what we know—a decision must be made about whether that computed, quantitative probability represents a *significant* departure from what our knowledge leads us to expect. Here there is room for a degree, albeit a rather small degree, of vagueness. Some research is conducted on the stipulation that if the particular events which occur would be expected to occur only once in 100 times in the light of what we know, then the occurrence of those events constitutes a significant departure from that regularity. Other research is conducted on the alternative stipulation that if the occurring events would be expected only 5 times in 100, then their occurrence constitutes a significant departure from the norm. Which assumption should be made is determined by the kind of research being done. In either case the general idea is that if the occurring events are instances of known regularities, then there are only certain ways in which they will happen. When events occur as they never—or almost never —would (in the light of known regularities), it becomes clear that in these cases some other factors must be involved, or else they would not happen as they do. There is a small degree of stipulation involved here: What numbers should be used to define 'never—or almost never' in a precise way? It is in answering this question that researchers vary between the answers "only once in 100 times" and "only 5 times in 100." This is the kind of procedure through which the term *statistically significant deviation* is defined.

47:6.2 Defining highly confirmed hypotheses Suppose that we have framed a number of clear alternative initially plausible hypotheses for explaining some occurrences not adequately accounted for by known regularities. We will then want to gather further data to support one of the hypotheses and rule out its competitors. The rough idea of ruling out a competing hypothesis is: With what we know, the data we have now collected in studies would never—or almost never—turn out as they have if the competing hypothesis were true; therefore, it must be false. We can define the ruling out (disconfirmation) of a competing hypothesis as follows.

> **Def. 29** A hypothesis is *disconfirmed* = $_{df}$ in the light of what we know, all the collected data would have turned out as it has only once, or only 5 times, in 100

Similarly, we can define the high confirmation of a hypothesis as follows.

> **Def. 30** A hypothesis is *high confirmed* = $_{df}$ in the light of what we know, all the collected data would have turned out as they have at least 95, or at least 99, times in 100

In fields like the natural sciences where our knowledge is more integrated and more exact, the higher standard is used both for ruling out and for highly confirming hypotheses. In fields like education and social psychology where our knowledge is less thorough, less integrated, and less exact, the weaker standard is preferred.

Note that these definitions establish a range from 0 to 100. We can think of 0 as impossibility, 100 as absolute certainty, and 50 as random. If the data would have turned out as they have, 75 or 80 times out of 100, then we have weak, or perhaps moderate, support for the hypothesis. But we would not have strongly supported it or highly confirmed it. Similarly we cannot be confident about disconfirmation until we reach the 5 or the 1 mark on our scale.

47:6.3 We may now complete our definition of the justification of arguments concluding statistical or causal connections. Most of the concept was presented in 47:4.3. But there we left the concept incomplete by confining it to statistical conclusions and by leaving 'strong support' vague and intuitive. In the light of 47:5.1 to 47:6.2 and our definitions of when a hypothesis is disconfirmed or highly confirmed we can complete the schema to which *all justified arguments concluding statistical or causal connections* conform.

Final outline of justified arguments, statistical and causal:

Premise: Information gathered from a certain sample shows that n percent of F's are G's.

Initially plausible hypothesis and tentative conclusion of the inductive argument: n percent of all F's are G's.

On the basis of background knowledge available as a matter of common knowledge or as a result of previous research, it is alternatively plausible that:
  1. Since most F's in the sample were H's, n percent of all F's are G's if those F's are H's.
  2. Since most F's in the sample were not J's, n percent of all F's are G's if those F's are not J's.
  3. Since the sample data were not accurately recorded, it is unreliable to infer anything about all F's from the data.
  4. Since there is reason to believe that whether people will report about their F's may be related to whether their F's are G's, it is likely that reported F's are more, or less, likely to be G's than nonreported F's.

Further premise: Further information highly confirms one of the initially plausible hypotheses and further information also disconfirms the competing initially plausible hypotheses.

Conclusion: Therefore, the highly confirmed initially plausible hypothesis is true (and its competitors are false).

47:7 General strategy Combining what we learned in Module 46 with what we learned in this module we can outline a general strategy to be used in attempting to confirm or disconfirm a causal or statistical hypothesis. You begin with information (or a preliminary study) which suggests a number of initially plausible hypotheses. Using the techniques of Module 46, the outline in 47:6.3, and relevant other research or background knowledge, you then identify the full list of plausible alternative hypotheses and carefully frame them. Finally you conduct the research necessary to supply the premises used in confirming one of the alternatives and ruling out the others.

EXERCISES FOR MODULE 47
CONFIRMING AND DISCONFIRMING HYPOTHESES

Ex. 1 Below you are provided with packages of information and an initially plausible hypothesis. Following each such set is a list of alternative hypotheses. In the light of the information provided, identify those which are plausible from those which are not.

A. Mr. Worthy Developer has built 300 houses, half of which have fireplaces, in Fairview in the last year. Thirty new home owners have registered complaints that the chimney on their fireplaces does not draw the smoke up properly. It is generally known that chimneys do not draw well unless they are built high enough above the level of the roof. Mr. Developer is known to have subcontracted with masons to build the chimneys and those masons have a reputation for cutting corners in their work, so it is initially plausible that the fireplace chimneys in the development do not draw properly because they are not high enough.

Alternatively it is also plausible that:

A1. Excess smoke in the houses resulted from burning green wood which is known to have been sold to some home owners in the development.

A2. Excess smoke in the houses resulted from burning dry wood which is known to have been sold to some home owners in the development.

A3. The chimneys of the noncomplaining owners are high enough because the prevailing winds in the area strike them at a different angle and generally take the smoke away, whereas the different position of the fireplaces of the complaining owners means that the prevailing winds strike them differently.

A4. The noncomplaining owners do not have fireplaces.

A5. The noncomplaining owners do not have fireplaces or do not use them so often as the complaining homes.

A6. Two of the owners did not open their fireplace flues sufficiently to allow the smoke to go up the chimney.

B. Three hundred fish of many unrelated species have just died in the Pomolo River. Such a large number of fish would not die normally in such a small area of the river at a given time. The Driveman Company, located on the Pomolo, is known to generate a waste product that would kill the fish if dumped into the river. It is initially plausible that the Driveman Company has polluted the river, causing the fish to die.

Alternatively it is plausible that:

B1. A disease has attacked the fish.

B2. The plants on which the fish feed have begun to secrete a poison.

B3. The river, which flows rapidly, has cut its way into poisonous chemicals which geologists know underlie the river bed.

B4. An unusual number of old fish happened to be swimming in the one area of the Pomolo.

B5. The new Advancement Company which generates sulphur dioxide as a waste product is polluting the river.

Ex. 2 Below you are provided with a hypothesis which is purportedly supported by data from a sample, which data are also summarized for you. This material is followed by ten assertions that the inference from sample to hypothesis is faulty for a certain reason. Identify these assertions as good or bad reasons why the hypothesis is poorly supported.

All students in the College of Education at Nowhere University student teach. Before student teaching some never get into public school as a part of their university work. The rest volunteer for a program where they are in public schools 3 days a week during one term as a part of learning teaching methods prior to student teaching. A researcher wanted to know whether student teachers' concerns about teaching would be more mature at the end of student teaching if the student teacher had classroom experience before entering student teaching. The researcher defined 'mature concerns about teaching' as concerns about the *effects* of the classroom situation upon the *student*, and 'immature concerns about teaching' as concerns about the *teacher* and the *process* of teaching in the classroom. One term the researcher asked all the student teachers, at the close of their student teaching, to pick their ten greatest concerns about teaching from a list of fifty randomly ordered mature and immature concerns about teaching. The concerns chosen by student teachers with prior classroom experience were no more mature nor more immature than those chosen by student teachers with no prior classroom experience besides student teaching. So the researcher inferred the correctness of the hypothesis that classroom experience prior to student teaching does not help student teachers to develop more mature concerns about teaching.

The inference from the sample to the hypothesis is faulty because:

1. Other classroom experiences prior to student teaching might do more to help student teachers develop more mature concerns. For instance, individual tutoring might make them more aware of the needs of their pupils.
2. Classroom experiences prior to student teaching might help student teachers to teach more effective lessons, even though their concerns are no more mature.
3. The definition of 'mature' is stipulative.
4. The same classroom experiences prior to student teaching might help student teachers develop more mature concerns if they were accompanied by different experiences outside the classroom. (Perhaps the college professors could interpret the significance of the classroom activities differently.)
5. The students at Nowhere University are less secure than the average student and therefore they might tend more strongly toward immature concerns about teaching.
6. It is plausible that the amount and intensity of destructive criticism suffered by student teachers at Nowhere University is significantly higher than that suffered by student teachers, thereby overcoming any maturing effects of the pre-student teaching program.
7. It is plausible that the amount and intensity of destructive criticism suffered by the students at Nowhere University in their prestudent teaching classroom experience is sufficiently high to overcome any maturing effects of the experience.
8. It is plausible that differences in the attitudes of professors at Nowhere as compared to professors elsewhere allow similar classroom experiences to have maturing effects elsewhere.
9. Student teachers might deliberately have reported concerns that were not important to them: information from researcher's hypothesis in disconfirmation of this assertion has not been provided.
10. Most of the students at Nowhere University come from a rural background and from German ancestry.

Ex. 3 Check the answers for Ex. 2. Be sure you understand why each assertion is or is not a reason why the inference from sample to hypothesis is faulty. Now reconsider each assertion which expresses a good reason. In each case some further observations would be required in order for the mentioned defect in the inference to be overcome. Define the kind of test or observations that would be required to confirm or disconfirm the alternative hypotheses suggested.

Ex. 1

A1. Plausible

A2. Implausible; dry wood burns with much less smoke than green or wet wood.

A3. Plausible, but winds from other directions will probably give some of the other people problems on some—less frequent—occasions

A4. Implausible; since 150 homes with fireplaces were built it is plausible that many noncomplaining owners do have fireplaces

A5. Plausible

A6. Plausible, although it does not account for the problems of the other twenty-eight

B1. Implausible; possible, but no presented information positively supports this possibility

B2. Implausible; again possible, but still no presented information positively supports this possibility

B3. Plausible in the light of facts about the geology and geography of the area

B4. Implausible; possible, but all the information presented leads one to suppose a random distribution of fish of different ages along the length of the river

B5. Plausible

If you missed three or more review 47:1.1 to 47:3.4.

Ex. 2

1. Good reason
2. Bad reason; (2) is true, but it is not contrary to what the researcher inferred.
3. Bad reason; the definition is not terribly arbitrary—it's rather appropriate. Moreover, even if it were arbitrary, the quality of the research's inference is not affected because 'mature' is used in the same sense—however arbitrary—throughout the argument.
4. Good reason
5. Good reason
6. Good reason
7. Good reason
8. Good reason
9. Good reason
10. Bad reason; it has not been made plausible that students from rural background or German ancestry are on these counts any different from any other students in their concerns about teaching.

If you missed more than three, review 47:4.1 to 47:7.

Ex. 3

1. Similar students would have to go through alternative in-classroom prestudent teaching experiences. Then they would be asked to list their concerns about teaching. Their lists would then be compared to similar students who had no classroom experience before student teaching.

4. A definite program of "different" experiences outside the classroom would need to be defined. Similar students would have to go through both the classroom experiences and the alternative out-of-classroom experiences. Then they would be

asked to list their concerns about teaching. Their lists would again be compared, as in (1).

5. 'Secure' would have to be defined so as to become an observational term. Then a representative sample of non-Nowhere-University students and a representative sample of Nowhere University students would have to be observed. Comparison would then be required to decide whether Nowhere University students were less secure than other students.

6. 'Destructive criticism' would have to be defined so as to become an observational term, and so that amounts and intensitities of destructive criticism can be observed. Then sampling and comparison, as in (5), can proceed. Destructive criticism suffered during student teaching would be watched for.

9. Two kinds of checks against such dishonesty can be set up: checks within the testing process and checks of the process. Within the process, the students can be asked to choose among prestated concerns. The concerns can be subtly restated elsewhere on the survey so that the dishonesty of any unwary dishonest student can be exposed. Outside of the process, the concerns expressed in words and in behavior can be matched against the survey result. Discrepancies will again suggest that the survey form has not been taken seriously.

If you did not understand the answers given review 47:4.1 to 47:6.3 once more.

SELF-QUIZ FOR PART FOUR
LOGICAL THINKING

Below are fifteen passages. Mark by each the letter for the phrase best describing the passage.
A. Conditional Proof
B. Fallacious argument
C. Direct proof
D. Nonargument
E. Reduction to contradiction
F. Reduction to vicious regress
G. Reduction to intuitive absurdity

1. If you hold a bond issued by a state or any political subdivision of a state, then the interest that bond earns for you is not subject to federal income tax.

2. Suppose you own federal savings bonds. Interest earned by federal savings bonds is subject to federal income tax. So if you hold such bonds, the interest they earn for you is taxable.

3. People who are degree candidates may exclude scholarships from their taxable income. Lynn Harris is enrolled in an accredited degree program. She has received a $2000 scholarship because of her high grades. This scholarship is not something that she will have to pay tax on then.

4. The income tax law of the federal government provides people who are married and who file a "joint" return with a lower tax rate. People who are single generally do not qualify for this lower rate. Any tax system which discriminates between people as to their rate of taxation is defective. So the federal income tax system is defective.

5. Many people are upset with the fact that the federal income tax regulations are so complicated and also that these regulations provide for many distinctions and

exceptions. However, our economy is very complicated. There are many different ways to earn a living and many different ways to spend income. Any tax
system which did not provide for as many of these variations in individual
living patterns and social and personal needs as possible would surely be defective. The federal tax system is a good system because it tries to cope with
these variations.

6. Suppose we agree to use the new edition in our next course. If we do that, then
we will have to revise our whole course and rework all the example exercises.
There are only 3 weeks left before the course begins. I don't see us being able to
do all that work in the time remaining. I don't think we should use the new
edition.

7. We have surrendered our right to free speech. We have surrendered our right to
privacy. We have surrendered our rights to liberty and to the pursuit of happiness. What is left if we continue this policy of nonresistence? Do you want to
turn over and die too!? Well, so far as I am concerned, that's ridiculous.

8. I'm sorry honey, but Daddy can't buy gifts for "all the friends in the world." If I
bought you a gift it would cost some money. Right? Now if I buy gifts for all your
friends it would cost more money, right? Yes, now you can see that before I
bought gifts for all of their friends, and for all the friends of those friends, I
would run out of money! I could not finish the project.

9. Most systems of evaluation allow one to score on a scale with the categories
excellent, good, average, poor, unacceptable. Let us correlate these value words
with the numbers 5, 4, 3, 2, 1. Reliable surveys show that no matter what the
topic being evaluated, the average score is 4.25 on the 5–1 scale. These strongly
suggest either that "good" work is now the norm, or that people evaluate too
generously, which was our original hypothesis.

10. All arguments are proofs and all proofs are arguments. Some arguments are
fallacies. So some proofs are fallacies.

11. Noreen, Roger, and Betsy are all married. Suppose that they are not all married to
each other. Assume, too, that Noreen is not married to Betsy. If two of the three
are married to each other, it follows that if your previous suppositions are true,
either Noreen is married to Roger or Betsy is married to Roger.

12. $*_1$ 1. p RA
     2. $(\sim q \supset \sim p)$ RP
     3. $(\sim q \lor r)$ RP
     4. $(q \supset r)$ Sub_3
     5. $(p \supset q)$ Sub_2
     6. $(p \supset r)$ $\text{HS}_{4,5}$
  $*_1$ 7. r $\text{MP}_{1,6}$
     8. $(p \supset r)$ $\text{Cd}_{*_1,7}$

13.   1. r RP
     2. $(r \supset p)$ RP
  $*_3$ 3. $(\sim p \lor \sim p)$ RA
  $*_3$ 4. $\sim p$ Sub_3
     5. p $\text{MP}_{1,3}$
     6. $\sim(\sim p \lor \sim p)$ $\text{Red}_{*_3,4,5}$
     7. $(p \,\&\, p)$ Sub_6
     8. p Sub_7

14. Suppose that we accepted the principle that the end does not justify the means.
This would put an end to successful human action because human suffering is a
precondition to any successful venture. Since human suffering is to be avoided,

in avoiding it we would not be able to perform successful ventures. So if we accepted the principle, then we would put an end to successful human actions.

15. Suppose human suffering is a concomitant precondition to any successful human venture. If it is, we will not be able to end human suffering. For if we are successful in ending it, then we will have performed a successful human venture, but by so doing we will be causing human suffering. This means we will be both ending it and bringing it about; but that is a contradiction.

16. Either there is a Santa Claus or there is not. If not, then thousands of people are both liars and participants in a conspiracy to deceive small children. If there is, then thousands are wrong not to believe in him. Since disbelief and deception are both wrong, it follows that in either case thousands are wrong.
   A. Conditional proof
   B. False dilemma fallacy
   C. Indirect proof
   D. False cause fallacy

17. Suppose that for a word to have meaning it must refer to something. If that were so, then we could not tell whether or not 'Santa' had meaning until we found its purported referent—Santa. Since no one ever saw Santa, no one can confirm that 'Santa' is meaningful. But it is! So words need not refer to anything in order to be meaningful.
   A. Generic direct proof
   B. Nonargument
   C. Indirect proof
   D. Conditional proof

18. Statistics show that half of all serious or fatal accidents involve drunk drivers. So if you drink don't drive.
   A. Fallacy of irrelevant appeal
   B. Nonargument—emotional appeal
   C. Enthymematic direct proof
   D. Enthymematic conditional proof

19. Exoprin has been found more effective in the relief of pain other than backache. So if you have a backache take Exoprin.
   A. Irrelevant appeal fallacy
   B. Conditional proof
   C. Nonargument
   D. Indirect proof with suppressed assumption: Suppose you do have a backache.

20. $((p \supset q)\ \&\ {\sim}r) \lor p)$
   A. Is not a wff of P because a logical operator is missing
   B. Is not a wff of P because a statement letter is missing
   C. Is not a wff of P because a parenthesis or parentheses are missing
   D. Logically implies ${\sim}p$
   E. Logically implies ${\sim}r$

21. $[((pq) \lor r) \supset s]$
   A. Is not a wff of P because a logical operator is missing
   B. Is not a wff of P because a statement letter is missing
   C. Is not a wff of P because a parenthesis or parentheses are missing
   D. Logically implies ${\sim}p$
   E. Logically implies ${\sim}r$

22. $((p \supset {\sim}p)\ \&\ {\sim}r)$
   A. Is not a wff of P because a logical operator is missing
   B. Is not a wff of P because a statement letter is missing
   C. Is not a wff of P because a parenthesis or parentheses are missing
   D. Logically implies ${\sim}p$
   E. Logically implies ${\sim}r$

23. $({\sim}r \lor ({\sim}r\ \&\ p))$
   A. Is not a wff of P because a logical operator is missing
   B. Is not a wff of P because a statement letter is missing

C. Is not a wff of P because a parenthesis or parentheses are missing
D. Logically implies $\sim p$
E. Logically implies $\sim r$

Choose the errors of annotation in the following proofs from the list which follows:

24.
1. $(q \supset p)$ — RP
2. $(\sim r \vee q)$ — RP
3. $(q \mathbin{\&} s)$ — RP
4. $(s \equiv t)$ — RP
5. s — Sub_3
6. $((s \supset t) \mathbin{\&} (t \supset s))$ — Sub_4
7. $(s \supset t)$ — S_6
8. t — $MT_{3,7}$
9. $(r \supset q)$ — Sub_2
10. $(r \supset p)$ — $Cd_{1,9}$
11. $((r \supset p) \mathbin{\&} t)$ — $Cd_{8,10}$
A. Line 5 should be S_3.
B. Line 8 should be $MP_{5,7}$
C. Line 9 should be $(\sim r \supset q)$.
D. Line 10 should be $HS_{1,9}$.
E. Line 11 should be $C_{8,10}$.

25.
1. $(q \supset p)$ — RP
2. $(\sim r \vee p)$ — RP
3. $(q \mathbin{\&} s)$ — RP
4. $(s \equiv t)$ — RP
5. s — S_3
6. $(s \supset t) \mathbin{\&} (t \supset s)$ — Sub_4
7. $(t \supset s)$ — S_6
8. $(\sim p \supset \sim q)$ — Sub_1
9. q — S_3
10. $\sim\sim q$ — Sub_9
11. $\sim\sim p$ — $MP_{8,10}$
12. $(\sim\sim p \mathbin{\&} (t \supset s))$ — $Cd_{7,11}$
A. Line 5 should be Sub_3.
B. Line 10 should be Sub_8.
C. Line 11 should be $MT_{8,10}$.
D. Line 12 should be $C_{7,11}$.
E. Line 12 is an invalid inference.

Construct annotation for the following proofs.

26. From $((s \vee t) \mathbin{\&} r)$ and $(p \supset (\sim q \mathbin{\&} \sim r))$, prove $\sim p$:
1. $((s \vee t) \mathbin{\&} r)$
2. $(p \supset (\sim q \mathbin{\&} \sim r))$
3. r
4. $((p \supset \sim q) \mathbin{\&} (p \supset \sim r))$
5. $(p \supset \sim r)$
6. $\sim\sim r$
7. $\sim p$

27. From $(p \vee q)$ and $(p \supset q)$ prove q:
1. $(p \vee q)$
2. $(p \supset q)$

3. $(\sim p \supset q)$
4. $(\sim q \supset \sim p)$
5. $(\sim q \supset q)$
6. $(\sim \sim q \vee q)$
7. q

28. Prove that $((p \supset q) \supset (\sim q \supset \sim p))$ is a tautology.
 1. $\sim((p \supset q) \supset (\sim q \supset \sim p))$
 2. $((p \supset q) \& \sim(\sim q \supset \sim p)$
 3. $\sim(\sim q \supset \sim p)$
 4. $\sim q \& \sim \sim p$
 5. $(p \supset q)$
 6. $\sim q$
 7. $\sim p$
 8. $\sim \sim p$
 9. $\sim \sim((p \supset q) \supset (\sim q \supset \sim p))$
 10. $((p \supset q) \supset (\sim q \supset \sim p))$

29. Construct a proof that $\sim p$ and $(q \supset (r \supset s))$ logically imply $(p \supset (r \supset s))$.

30. Construct a proof that $(s \equiv (t \& r))$ and $((q \vee p) \supset s)$ logically imply $(p \supset r)$.

From the following data construct the probable population specified in items 31 to 33.

Data: In September there are thirty eleventh-grade boys and twenty eleventh-grade girls in Timberfalls High School. Nationwide the number of eleventh-grade boys is equal to the number of eleventh-grade girls. It is probable that four students will transfer into the eleventh-grade class. It is probable that five students will transfer out of the eleventh-grade class.

31. If five students transfer out, then there will probably be _____ boys and _____ girls.

32. If four students transfer in, then there will probably be _____ boys and _____ girls.

33. If five students transfer out and then four students transfer in, there will probably be _____ boys and _____ girls.

Let us examine the basis upon which it was determined to be probable that five students would transfer out of Timberfalls High School. Below are certain possible discoveries one might make. In each case the question is: If this discovery were made, what *kind* of reason, *if any*, would this discovery give for doubting the hypothesis that five students (10 percent) of the eleventh-grade class will transfer out?

34. Of the current eleventh-grade class 75 percent comes from rural homes, whereas 60 percent of the sample students, the students of the past two eleventh-grade classes, came from homes in town.
 A. Original hypothesis is suspicious because characteristics of sample are relevantly different from characteristics of present population.
 B. Original hypothesis is still acceptable because differences between characteristics of sample and characteristics of present population do not seem relevant.
 C. Original hypothesis is suspicious because data on which hypothesis was based were inaccurately reported.
 D. Original hypothesis is suspicious because of inadequate or changed definitions of terms.

35. The hypothesis is based on records for the past 10 years. Two years ago a new

company employing 50 people in their forties and fifties moved into town. Movin-On, Inc., transfers its employees to plants in other towns an average of once every 3 years.

    A. Original hypothesis is suspicious because characteristics of sample are relevantly different from characteristics of present population.

    B. Original hypothesis is still acceptable because differences between characteristics of sample and characteristics of present population do not seem relevant.

    C. Original hypothesis is suspicious because data on which hypothesis was based were inaccurately reported.

    D. Original hypothesis is suspicious because of inadequate or changed definitions of terms.

36. The information about this year's class is desired so that the number of students going on the junior trip in April can be estimated. Employment is seasonal in Timberfalls, and much of the population leaves in late November and returns in May. Students have been understood to have transferred out of school in past years if, and only if, school records show them attending the school in the fall and attending some other school at the close of the school year.

    A. Original hypothesis is suspicious because characteristics of sample are relevantly different from characteristics of present population.

    B. Original hypothesis is still acceptable because differences between characteristics of sample and characteristics of present population do not seem relevant.

    C. Original hypothesis is suspicious because data on which hypothesis was based were inaccurately reported.

    D. Original hypothesis is suspicious because of inadequate or changed definitions of terms.

37. Of the members of sampled junior classes 15 percent have been left-handed, but 32 percent of the present class is left-handed.

    A. Original hypothesis is suspicious because characteristics of sample are relevantly different from characteristics of present population.

    B. Original hypothesis is still acceptable because differences between characteristics of sample and characteristics of present population do not seem relevant.

    C. Original hypothesis is suspicious because data on which hypothesis was based were inaccurately reported.

    D. Original hypothesis is suspicious because of inadequate or changed definitions of terms.

38. 'Painting by Dali' means a painting signed by Dali:

    A. Is not a valid definition

    B. Is not a reliable definition

    C. Is not valid and is not reliable as a definition

    D. Is an acceptable observational definition

39. 'Painting by Dali' means a painting in the surrealist style (Note: Dali does paint in the surrealist style):

    A. Is not a valid definition

    B. Is not a reliable definition

    C. Is not valid and is not reliable as a definition

    D. Is an acceptable observational definition

40. A lake shall be said to be polluted if, and only if, significant amounts of any

pollutant are detected in a contiguous area equal to more than 3 percent of the lake's surface:

A. Is not a valid definition
B. Is not a reliable definition
C. Is not valid and is not reliable as a definition
D. Is an acceptable observational definition

41. A lake shall be said to be *polluted* if, and only if, significant amounts of mercury, phosphorus, or any other elements not natural to the lake are detected in a contiguous area equal to more than 3 percent of the lake's surface.

42. The hotshot promoter Sal Newstuff has introduced another fancy frozen vegetable dish into his successful line of fancy frozen vegetable dishes. The cost of the new line is comparable to the cost of other items in the line, but the new item has not sold as well as other items did when they were introduced. Because a smaller advertising budget was alloted, it is initially plausible that the item has not sold so well because it has been advertised less. Which of the following are also plausible?

A. People are not much attracted to stuffed parsnips.
B. Grocery stores have refused to stock the new line.
C. Showing rather sick people saying, "I'm stuffed with stuffed parsnips," is an unattractive advertising campaign.
D. Given a sharp recent upswing in inflation, customers are less inclined to try expensive new lines of groceries.
E. Food spoilage problems have adversely affected customer reaction to the new line.

ANSWERS TO SELF-QUIZ
FOR PART FOUR

1. D	2. A	3. C
4. C	5. C	6. G
7. G	8. F	9. C
10. C	11. A	12. A
13. E	14. A	15. E

16. B; first, there are other options, e.g., Santa may exist but several may not know that. Second, the consequences may not all be bad.

17. C

18. C; suppressed premises: if you drink and drive your chances of being involved in a serious accident are greater than normal.

19. A; the product, according to the premise, works on pain *other than* backache.

20. C	21. A	22. D and E
23. E	24. A, B, D, and E	25. C and D

26.
1. $((s \lor t) \,\&\, r)$		RP
2. $(p \supset (\sim q \,\&\, \sim r))$		RP
3. r		S_1
4. $((p \supset \sim q) \,\&\, (p \supset \sim r))$		Sub_2
5. $(p \supset \sim r)$		S_4
6. $\sim\sim r$		Sub_3
7. $\sim p$		$MT_{5,6}$

27.
  1. $(p \vee q)$ RP
  2. $(p \supset q)$ RP
  3. $(\sim p \supset q)$ Sub$_1$
  4. $(\sim q \supset \sim p)$ Sub$_2$
  5. $(\sim q \supset q)$ HS$_{3,4}$
  6. $(\sim\sim q \vee q)$ Sub$_5$
  7. q Sub$_6$

28.
  *$_1$ 1. $\sim((p \supset q) \supset (\sim q \supset \sim p))$ RA
  *$_1$ 2. $((p \supset q) \mathbin{\&} \sim(\sim q \supset \sim p))$ Sub$_1$
  *$_1$ 3. $\sim(\sim q \supset \sim p)$ S$_2$
  *$_1$ 4. $(\sim q \mathbin{\&} \sim\sim p)$ Sub$_3$
  *$_1$ 5. $(p \supset q)$ S$_2$
  *$_1$ 6. $\sim q$ S$_4$
  *$_1$ 7. $\sim p$ MT$_{5,6}$
  *$_1$ 8. $\sim\sim p$ S$_4$
  9. $\sim\sim((p \supset q) \supset (\sim q \supset \sim p))$ Red$_{*_1,7,8}$
  10. $((p \supset q) \supset (\sim q \supset \sim p))$ Sub$_9$

29.
  1. $\sim p$ RP
  2. $(q \supset (r \supset s))$ RP
  3. $(\sim p \vee (r \supset s))$ A$_1$
  4. $(p \supset (r \supset s))$ Sub$_3$

As you probably discovered, the second premise given here is unnecessary.

30.
  1. $(s \equiv (t \mathbin{\&} r))$ RP
  2. $((q \vee p) \supset s)$ RP
  *$_3$ 3. p RA
  *$_3$ 4. $(q \vee p)$ A$_3$
  *$_3$ 5. s MP$_{2,4}$
  6. $((s \supset (t \mathbin{\&} r)) \mathbin{\&} ((t \mathbin{\&} r) \supset s))$ Sub$_1$
  7. $(s \supset (t \mathbin{\&} r))$ S$_6$
  *$_3$ 8. $t \mathbin{\&} r$ MP$_{5,7}$
  *$_3$ 9. r S$_8$
  10. $(p \supset r)$ Cd$_{*_3,9}$

31. 27 boys and 18 girls
32. 32 boys and 22 girls
33. 29 boys and 20 girls
34. A
35. A
36. D
37. B
38. D, unless (1) Dali left some paintings unsigned or signed them differently, or (2) somebody else signs "Dali." In these cases the answer is A.
39. C; others paint in this style and not all observers can observe the style unless it is less technically characterized.
40. D
41. B; 'significant amount' is not precise enough to be observable.
42. A, C, D; B and E might be true but there is no reason provided for thinking so.

Questions 1 to 19 relate to Chapters 11 and 12. Questions 20 to 30 relate to Chapter 13. Questions 31 to 42 relate to Chapter 14.

If you answered about 80 percent of the questions covering chapters you studied you have satisfactorily achieved the objectives of those chapters.

APPENDIX

DEFINITIONS OF KEY CONCEPTS

Argument = $_{df}$ a set of statements one of which is purportedly implied, entailed, strongly supported, or strongly warranted by the others

Conclusion = $_{df}$ the statement in an argument that is purported to be implied, entailed, strongly supported, or strongly warranted by the other statements in the argument

Premises = $_{df}$ those statements which purportedly strongly support or warrant, imply, or entail an argument's conclusion

Logic = $_{df}$ the study of the relationships between the premises and the conclusions of arguments

Logically correct argument = $_{df}$ an argument such that its premises either entail, imply, strongly support, or strongly warrant its conclusion

Truth-value = $_{df}$ that characteristic of a sentence that it is alleged to have when it is described as being true or being false

Deductive argument = $_{df}$ an argument such that it is purportedly not possible for its conclusion to be false and all its premises to be true

Inductive argument = $_{df}$ an argument such that it is purportedly improbable, although possible, that its conclusion be false given that all its premises are true

Valid argument = $_{df}$ an argument such that its premises entail or imply its conclusion on the basis of the logical form or structure of the argument

Justified argument = $_{df}$ an argument such that its premises, on the basis of their content, give strong support or a strong warrant to the truth of its conclusion

Sound argument = $_{df}$ a logically correct argument such that all of its premises are true

Fallacious argument = $_{df}$ an argument such that either it is structurally flawed so as to be invalid, or is based on an assumption which is false or makes no logical progress

Acceptable argument = $_{df}$ an argument that is logically correct, with all of its premises true, and is nonfallacious

Proof = $_{df}$ an argument presented as an acceptable argument with a view toward establishing the truth of its conclusion by relying on sufficiently obvious premises

RULES OF INFERENCE

NATURAL DEDUCTION SYSTEM P

Rule 1 Assumption: Any wff can be assumed.

Rule 2 Premise: Any premise wff may be stated.

Rule 3 Simplification: From (A & B) infer A.

Rule 4 Addition: From A infer (A ∨ B).

Rule 5 Substitution: Replace formula 1 with formula 2, if they are equivalent.

Here are sample equivalences:

A	~~A	Double negation
A	(A ∨ A)	Tautology
A	(A & A)	Tautology
(A & B)	(B & A)	Commutation
(A ∨ B)	(B ∨ A)	Commutation
(A ∨ B)	~(~A & ~B)	
(A & B)	~(~A ∨ ~B)	
~(A ∨ B)	(~A & ~B)	DeMorgan's theorem
~(A & B)	(~A ∨ ~B)	DeMorgan's theorem
(A ⊃ B)	(~A ∨ B)	Material implication
~(A ⊃ B)	(A & ~B)	Material implication
(A ⊃ B)	(~B ⊃ ~A)	Transposition
(A ≡ B)	((A ⊃ B) & (B ⊃ A))	Equivalence
(A ≡ B)	((A & B) ∨ (~A & ~B))	
(A & (B & C))	((A & B) & C)	Association
(A ∨ (B ∨ C))	((A ∨ B) ∨ C)	Association
(A & (B ∨ C))	((A & B) ∨ (A & C))	Distribution
(A ∨ (B & C))	((A ∨ B) & (A ∨ C))	Distribution
((A & B) ⊃ C)	(A ⊃ (B ⊃ C))	Exportation
Any tautology	Any tautology	
Any inconsistent wff	Any inconsistent wff	

Rule 6 Disjunctive syllogism: From (A ∨ B) and ~A infer B.

Rule 7 Modus ponens: From (A ⊃ B) and A infer B.

Rule 8 Modus tollens: From (A ⊃ B) and ~B infer ~A.

Rule 9 Conjunction: From A and B infer (A & B).

Rule 10 Hypothetical syllogism: From (A ⊃ B) and (B ⊃ C) infer (A ⊃ C).

Rule 11 Constructive dilemma: From (A ⊃ B) and (C ⊃ D) and (A ∨ C) infer (B ∨ D).

Rule 12 Reductio: If A is an assumption of either C or ~C, then from C and ~C infer ~A.

Rule 13 Conditionalization: If A is an assumption of C, then from C infer (A ⊃ C).

INDEX

Family resemblance, 49
Finite universe, 226–227, 232, 237
Form/content distinction, 80, 81
Formal fallacies, 291–303
Formal system, 85
Formalization, 99
Formally fallacious argument, (definition 23) 288
Framing hypotheses, 447–464
Free variable, 216

G

Generalization arguments, 80
Grouping indicators, 116

H

Highly confirmed hypothesis, (definition 30) 476
Hypothesis, 447–481
Hypothetical syllogism, rule of, 414–415

I

I form statements, 175
Implication, 61
   logical, 149–151, 153–156
   (*See also* Entailment, principle of)
Inadequate proof, 373
Inclusion:
   individual, 200–201
   partial, 198–199, 223–227
   total, 196–198, 233–235
Inconsistent premises, 356–357
Inconsistent wff, 146–147
Indirect argument, 369–372, (definition 27) 371
Indirect proof strategy, 380–384, 397
Individual variable, 212–213
Inductive argument, 71–73, (definition 17) 73, 76–81, 447–481
Inductive logic, 76–81
Inference patterns, 405–420
Informally fallacious argument, (definition 24) 288
Initial plausibility, 453–455
Inscription, 18

Insufficient reason, postulate or principle of, 78, 79, 449–453
Intension, 48
Intensional definitions, 48–50, 52–54
Interpretation:
   predicate logic, 209, 211
   propositional logic, 122
Irrelevant sentences, 17, 23, 24

J

Joint implication, 151–153
Justified argument, (definition 19) 84–88, 465–481
Justified causal argument, 475–477
Justified statistical argument, 472, 475–477

L

Language, logical elements in, 15, 16
Loaded definitions, 73
Logic, (definition 7) 60
Logical, being, 4–9
Logical connectives, 116
Logical equivalence, 148–149, 153
Logical implication, 149–151, 153–156
Logical operators, 116
   (*See also* Truth-functional operators)
Logically correct, 14, 19, 20, (definition 8) 61, 62, 83, (definition 20) 84
Logically true/false, 66

M

Main logical operator, 139
Major premise, 180–181
Major term of a syllogism, 180–181
Material implication, 408–409
Mathematical probabilities, 78, 79, 448–453
Meaning, 30–39
Mention of a word, 32
Middle term of a syllogism, 180–181
Minor premise, 180–181
Minor term of a syllogism, 180–181
Missing assertions, 24–26
Modus ponens, 292, 413
Modus tollens, 292, 413

N

Name letter, 208
Narrow definitions, 42, 43
Necessitate, 61
Negation, 15, 109, 115
Negative statement, 172–173
No progress fallacies, 287, 345–365

O

O form statement, 175
Observational definitions, 455–459
'Only,' 241–242
Open predicate expression, 218
Open sentence, 213–214
Open texture, 49, 50
Open wff of predicate logic, 218
Operational definitions, 51–54

P

Paradigm tables, 135–136
Partial truth-table technique, 153–158
Particular statements, 174
Persuasion, 372–373
Persuasive, being, 7–9
Peter of Spain, 185
Positive statement, 172–173
Predicate class, 192
Predicate expression, 205–207
Predicate letter, 208
Predicate logic, 164–169, 192–282
Predicate term of syllogism, 180–181
Premise, 12, 13, 17–20, 23–26,
    (definition 5) 60, 404–406
  rule of, 406
Primitive term, 59
Probability:
  mathematical, 78, 79, 448–453
  principle of (P), 85
Proof, 372–375, (definition 28) 373
  adequate, 373
  inadequate, 373
Proof strategies, 376–401
Proofs in system *P*, 404–405
Propositional logic, 99–169
Provisional acceptance, 397–399
Purport, 14, 17, 60, 85

Q

Quality:
  rules of, 189
  of a statement, 172–173
Quantifier expressions, 214
Quantifiers, 215
Quantity of statement, 175
Quasi-numerical expressions, 240
Questionable premises, 397–399

R

Reasonable, being, 4–9
Recursive definitions, 51–54
Reductio, rule of, 417–418
Reductio ad absurdum, 382
Reduction:
  to contradiction, strategy, 384–388,
    391
  to intuitive absurdity, strategy,
    384–386, 390–391
  of syllogisms, 172
  to vicious regression, strategy,
    384–386, 388–391
Reference class, 40–44, 48
Reliable definition, 457–459
Representative data, 468–472

S

Schema for justified arguments, 477
Scope of quantifiers, 218
Self-contradictory statements, 146–147
Self-contradictory wff, 146–147
Semantics of *P*, 403–404
Set (*see* Class)
Sets of assertions, 17
Sharp, being, 4–9
Shortcut truth-table technique, 153–158
Simplification, rule of, 406–407
Sound argument, (definition 21) 87, 88
Square of opposition, 176–180
Statement, (definition 2) 59, 60
  (*See also* Assertive sentence;
    Utterance)
Statement compounds, 100–101
Statement letters, 116
Statement unit, 99–103, 113, 427–430,
    437

Statistical hypothesis, 460–461, 468–473
Statistical inference, 79
Statistically significant deviation, 475–477
Stipulative definitions, 32–34, 42, 52–54
Subalternant statement, 179
Subalternate statement, 179
Subalterns, 179
Subcontrary statements, 179–180
Subject class, 192
Subject-predicate analysis, 172
Subject term of syllogism, 180–181
Substitution, rule of, 408–409
Support, 61
Supposition (see Assumption)
Syllogism, 170–191
Syllogisms, rule of, 188–190
Syllogistic analysis, 187–188
Syntax of P, 403–404
Synthetic statement, (definitions 14 and 15) 68–69
System P, rule of, 490

Tolerable ambiguity, 40
Translation procedures:
    predicate logic, 221–242
    propositional logic, 119–129
Transposition, law of, 409
Truth-functional compound, 105–109
Truth-functional operators, 105–111, 115, 133–136
Truth-tables, 133–144, 153–158
Truth-value, (definitions 9 and 10) 65, 101, 133

U

Universal quantifiers, 214, 237, 251–255
Universal statement, 174
Universe of discourse, 222–223
Use/mention convention, 32
Utterance, 18

V

Vagueness, 40–42, 210, 456–457
Valid argument, (definition 18) 84–88, 472
Valid definitions, 457–459
Validity:
    and class region diagrams, 260–267
    in propositional logic, 151–153, 157–158
    by syllogism, 185–190
Venn, John, 294
Venn diagrams (see Class region diagrams)
Vicious regressions, 389–390

T

Tautology, 146–147
    law of, 408
Temporal connections, 100
Temporal statement compounds, 100–101
Term, 171, 297
Theoretically complete, 404
Tip off words:
    for biconditionals, 109
    for causal connections, 101
    for classes, 41, 195–196
    for conclusions, 23, 24
    for conditionals, 107–108
    for conjunctions, 106
    for deductive arguments, 73–74
    for disjunctions, 106
    for inductive arguments, 77
    for negation, 110
    for premises, 23, 24
    for quantifier expressions, 214–215
    for temporal connections, 100

W

Warrant, 61
Weak support, 61
Well-formed formula:
    of P, 403
    of predicate logic, 216–217
    of propositional logic, 115–117